Applied Behavior Analysis for Teachers

Seventh Edition

Paul A. Alberto
Georgia State University

Anne C. Troutman
University of Memphis

Upper Saddle River, New Jersey
Columbus, Ohio

Library of Congress Cataloging-in-Publication Data

Alberto, Paul.
Applied behavior analysis for teachers / Paul A. Alberto, Anne C. Troutman—7th ed.
p. cm.
Includes bibliographical references and index.
ISBN 0-13-117994-2
1. Behavior modification. 2. Students—Psychology. 3. Human behavior. I. Troutman, Anne C. II. Title.

LB1060.2.A43 2006
371.102'4—dc22

2005041462

Vice President and Executive Publisher: Jeffery W. Johnston
Acquisitions Editor: Allyson P. Sharp
Development Editor: Heather Doyle Fraser
Editorial Assistant: Kathleen S. Burk
Production Editor: Sheryl Glicker Langner
Production Coordination: Norine Strang, Carlisle Publishers Services
Design Coordinator: Diane C. Lorenzo
Cover Designer: Ali Mohrman
Cover Photo: Superstock
Production Manager: Laura Messerly
Director of Marketing: Ann Castel Davis
Marketing Manager: Autumn Purdy
Marketing Coordinator: Brian Mounts

This book was set in Garamond by Carlisle Publishers Services. It was printed and bound by Courier/Kendallville, Inc. The cover was printed by Coral Graphic Services, Inc.

Pearson Education Ltd.
Pearson Education Singapore Pte. Ltd.
Pearson Education Canada, Ltd.
Pearson Education—Japan
Pearson Education Australia Pty. Limited
Pearson Education North Asia Ltd.
Pearson Educación de Mexico, S.A. de C.V.
Pearson Education Malaysia Pte. Ltd.

10 9 8 7 6 5 4 3 2
ISBN: 0-13-117994-2

Preface

We prepared the first edition of *Applied Behavior Analysis for Teachers* over 20 years ago because we needed a technically sound, systematically organized, and readable text for our own students. We want students to understand concepts of applied behavior analysis and also to know how to apply those concepts in classrooms and other settings. Applied behavior analysis can make a difference; its principles can be used to teach academic skills, functional skills, and appropriate social behavior. Applied behavior analysis is an overall management system, not a collection of gimmicks for keeping students under control.

This is not a cookbook providing simple step-by-step directions for solving every possible problem an educator might encounter. That would be impossible in any event: What makes working with children and young adults so much fun is that every one is different and no one procedure will be effective for all of them. We want students to be able to use the principles to create their own recipes for success. Successful application of the principles requires the full and active participation of a creative educator. Because we believe so strongly that applied behavior analysis is the most powerful teaching tool available, we stress learning to use it appropriately and ethically.

Instructors will be interested in knowing that the text is as technically accurate and as well documented as we could make it. At the same time, we've tried to enliven it with examples students will enjoy reading. Our examples describe students from preschool through young adulthood functioning at various levels of ability. We describe poor teachers as well as excellent ones. Many of our examples describe the kind of teachers we think we are and hope your students will be—good teachers who learn from their inevitable mistakes.

Text Organization

The text is organized in a manner that allows instructors to assign students a behavior-change project concurrently with lectures and readings. The text progresses from identifying a target behavior to collecting and graphing data, selecting an experimental design, to conducting a functional analysis, arranging consequences, arranging antecedents, and generalizing behavior change. We've tried to provide students with the basics of a teaching technology that will serve as a solid foundation for other methods courses.

Updated and Expanded Coverage

In preparing this seventh edition, we took to heart suggestions from colleagues and thoughtful letters from students using the book. We did, however, consider the mousetrap example in Chapter 10 sufficiently illustrative to retain in spite of a letter from an irate animal rights activist who believed that we advocate violating the civil rights of poor defenseless mice.

We have expanded and, we believe, improved, the chapter on functional assessment and functional analysis. We believe these tools, along with the development of Behavior Support Plans (also described in Chapter 10), promise to provide teachers with powerful ways of dealing with some of the most challenging behaviors students display, often without resorting to traditional, aversive, or punitive methods.

We have, as always, searched the professional literature so that we can share with you the latest developments in the field. After rigorous consultation with various experts, including nieces, nephews, and grandchildren, we have updated our examples and tried to use current slang expressions and to address contemporary interests of children and young adults. We also found ourselves, once again, updating the prices of items whenever money was mentioned.

Features of the Text

We have provided a series of classroom "snapshots" showing teachers implementing the principles of applied behavior analysis in a variety of settings. We hope these anecdotes will give you a sense of what it's like to be a teacher using these principles and of the powerful effects they can produce. We also hope that you will sense the joy, pride, and just sheer fun that teachers using the principles experience. The snapshots are in Chapter 13, but you might enjoy reading them earlier to see if you recognize some of the principles you're learning about.

Throughout the book you will find marginal notes that refer readers to the book's Companion Website (CW). These notes integrate technology with the text and cue readers to look for more information or resources on the website, invite them to gauge their understanding of chapter content by taking interactive self-quizzes, and direct them to Web-based activities for reflection and problem solving.

Supplements

The seventh edition has an enhanced supplement support package including a Companion Website, a supplementary online book entitled *Graphing in Excel: A Step-by-Step Approach,* an Instructor's Manual with Test Items, a computerized test bank, and assessment software (Test Gen).

Companion Website: Located at *http://www.prenhall.com/alberto* the Companion Website for this text includes a wealth of resources for both professors and students. The Syllabus Manager™ enables professors to create and maintain the class syllabus online while also allowing the student access to the syllabus at any time from any computer on the Internet. The student portion of the website helps students gauge their understanding of chapter content through the use of online chapter reviews, resources, data sheets, activities related to the *Graphing in Excel* book, discussion questions on a national message board, and interactive self-assessments.

Graphing in Excel: A Step-by-Step Approach: Written by David Gihak, Paul Alberto, Anne Troutman, and Margaret Flores. This supplemental book is available online for download at *http://www.prenhall.com/alberto* and connects to Chapters 4 and 5 in the text.

IM with Test Items and TestGen Software: The Instructor's Manual (also available online at the Instructor's Resource Center, described on the next page, is organized by chapter and contains chapter objectives, summaries, and outlines key terms and definitions, in-class activities, homework assignments, video resources, additional text resources, and test items (including multiple choice, true/false, short answer, and essay questions). The computerized version of these test items (TestGen) is available in both Windows and Macintosh format, along with assessment software allowing professors to create and customize exams and track student progress.

Overhead Transparencies/PowerPoints: The transparencies—available in PowerPoint slide format by going to the Instructor's Resource Center, described below—highlight key concepts, summarize content, and illustrate figures and charts from the text.

Instructor Resource Center: The Instructor Resource Center at *www.prenhall.com* has a variety of print and media resources available in downloadable, digital format—all in one location. As a registered faculty member, you can access and download pass-code protected resource files, course management content, and other premium online content directly to your computer.

Digital resources available for *Applied Behavior Analysis for Teachers,* Seventh Edition by Paul A. Alberto and Anne C. Troutman include:

- Text-specific PowerPoint Lectures
- An online version of the Instructor's Manual

To access these items online, go to *www.prenhall.com* and click on the Instructor Support button and then go to the Download Supplements section. Here you will be able to log in or complete a one-time registration for a user name and password. If you have any questions regarding this process or the materials available online, please contact your local Prentice Hall sales representative.

Acknowledgments

We would like to thank all the people who helped us in the process of producing the seventh edition of *Applied Behavior Analysis for Teachers,* including all the professionals at Merrill/Prentice Hall with whom we worked. Thanks to Heather Doyle Fraser and Kathy Burk. We appreciate the suggestions provided by those who reviewed the text: Jennifer Austin, University of South Florida; E. Paula Crowley, Illinois State University; Philip L. Gunter, Valdosta State University; Therese C. Johnston, Kent State University; Paul R. Malanga, University of South Dakota; Benjamin Smith, University of Texas at Austin;

Once again, we thank Nancy Wilder for moral support, positive reinforcement, and a huge push at the end of the project. Thanks for the help, Nancy.

Educator Learning Center: An Invaluable Online Resource

Merrill Education and the Association for Supervision and Curriculum Development (ASCD) invite you to take advantage of a new online resource, one that provides access to the top research and proven strategies associated with ASCD and Merrill—the Educator Learning Center. At **www.educatorlearningcenter.com,** you will find resources that will enhance your students' understanding of course topics and of current educational issues, in addition to being invaluable for further research.

How the Educator Learning Center Will Help Your Students Become Better Teachers

With the combined resources of Merrill Education and ASCD, you and your students will find a wealth of tools and materials to better prepare them for the classroom.

Research

- More than 600 articles from the ASCD journal *Educational Leadership* discuss everyday issues faced by practicing teachers.
- A direct link on the site to Research Navigator™ gives students access to many of the leading education journals, as well as extensive content detailing the research process.
- Excerpts from Merrill Education texts give your students insights on important topics of instructional methods, diverse populations, assessment, classroom management, technology, and refining classroom practice.

Classroom Practice

- Hundreds of lesson plans and teaching strategies are categorized by content area and age range.
- Case studies and classroom video footage provide virtual field experience for student reflection.
- Computer simulations and other electronic tools keep your students abreast of today's classrooms and current technologies.

Look into the Value of Educator Learning Center Yourself

A four-month subscription to Educator Learning Center is $25 but is **FREE** when packaged with any Merrill Education text. In order for your students to have access to this site, you must use this special value-pack ISBN number **WHEN** placing your textbook order with the bookstore: 0-13-155985-0. Your students will then receive a copy of the text packaged with a free ASCD pincode. To preview the value of this website to you and your students, please go to **www.educatorlearningcenter.com** and click on "Demo."

Brief Contents

Contents

5

Single-Subject Designs 117

PROVIDING FOR GENERALIZATION OF BEHAVIOR CHANGE 337

TEACHING STUDENTS TO MANAGE THEIR OWN BEHAVIOR 361

12

Responsible Use of Applied Behavior Analysis Procedures 381

13

Putting It All Together 399

Note: Every effort has been made to provide accurate and current Internet information in this book. However, the Internet and information posted on it are constantly changing, so it is inevitable that some of the Internet addresses listed in this textbook will change.

Chapter 1

Roots of Applied Behavior Analysis

Did you know that . . .

- There may be some validity in your mother's claim that "You're just like your father"?
- Chemicals in your brain may affect your behavior?
- Pretzels preceded M&Ms as rewards for good behavior?
- Benjamin Franklin used applied behavior analysis?

Chapter Outline

Why do people behave as they do? Why do some people behave in socially approved ways and others in a manner condemned or despised by society? Is it possible to predict what people are likely to do? What can be done to change behavior that is harmful to an individual or destructive to society?

In an effort to answer questions like these, human beings have offered explanations ranging from possession by demons to abnormal quantities of chemicals in the brain. Suggested answers have been debated, written about, attacked, and defended for centuries and continue to be offered today. There are good reasons for continuing to investigate human behavior. Information about the development of certain behaviors in human beings may help parents and teachers find the best way of child-rearing or teaching. If we know how people are likely to behave under certain conditions, we can decide whether to provide or avoid such conditions. Those of us who are teachers are particularly concerned with changing behavior; that is, in fact, our job. We want to teach our students to do some things and to stop doing others.

To understand, predict, and change human behavior, we must first understand how human behavior works. We must answer as completely as possible the "why" questions asked above. Therefore, Alexander Pope's dictum that "the proper study of mankind is man" (perhaps rephrased to "the proper study of humanity is people") needs no other revision; it is as true in the 21st century as it was in the 18th.

This chapter discusses the requirements for meaningful and useful explanations of human behavior. It then describes several interpretations of human behavior that have influenced large numbers of practitioners, including teachers. The discussion traces the historical development of a way to understand and predict human behavior called **applied behavior analysis.***

THE USEFULNESS OF EXPLANATIONS

A useful theory has inclusiveness, verifiability, predictive utility, and parsimony.

If a way of explaining behavior is to be useful for the practitioner, it must meet four requirements. First, it should be *inclusive*. It must account for a substantial quantity of behavior. An explanation has limited usefulness if it fails to account for the bulk of human behavior and thus makes prediction and systematic change of behavior impossible. Second, an explanation must be *verifiable;* that is, we should be able to test in some way that it does account for behavior. Third, the explanation should have *predictive utility.* It should provide reliable answers about what people are likely to do under certain circumstances, thereby giving the practitioner the opportunity to change behavior by changing conditions. Fourth, it should be *parsimonious.* A parsimonious explanation is the simplest one that will account for observed phenomena. Parsimony does not guar-

*Words printed in **boldface** in the text are defined in the glossary at the end of the book.

antee correctness (Mahoney, 1974) because the simplest explanation may not always be the correct one, but it prevents our being so imaginative as to lose touch with the reality of observed data. When the bathroom light fails to operate at 3 a.m., one should check the bulb before calling the electric company to report a blackout. There may be a blackout, but the parsimonious explanation is a burned-out bulb. In examining some of the theories developed to explain human behavior, we shall evaluate each explanation for its inclusiveness, verifiability, predictive utility, and parsimony.

To access PowerPoint lecture notes on this topic, go to the "Lecture Notes" module in Chapter 1 of the Companion Website.

Biophysical Explanations

Some theorists contend that human behavior is controlled by physical influences.

Since physicians of ancient Greece first proposed that human behavior was the result of interactions among four bodily fluids or "humors"—blood, phlegm, yellow bile (choler), and black bile (melancholy)—theorists have searched for explanations for human behavior within the physical structure of the body. Such theories have included those based on genetic or hereditary factors, those that emphasize biochemical influences, and those that suggest aberrant behavior is caused by some damage to the brain. The following anecdote indicates a belief in hereditary influences on behavior.

Professor Grundy Traces the Cause

Having observed an undergraduate student's behavior for some time, Professor Grundy noticed that the student was consistently late for class (when he came at all), invariably unprepared, and frequently inattentive. Because Grundy was certain his dynamic, meaningful lectures were not related to this behavior, he decided to investigate the matter. He paid a visit to the high school attended by the student and located his 10th-grade English teacher, Ms. Marner. "Yes, DeWayne was just like that in high school," said Ms. Marner. "He just didn't get a good background in middle school."

Professor Grundy then went to visit the middle school. "You know," said the guidance counselor, "a lot of our kids are like that. They just don't get the foundation in elementary school." At the elementary school, Professor Grundy talked to the principal. "DeWayne was like that from day one. His home situation was far from ideal. If we don't have support from the home, it's hard to make much progress."

Professor Grundy, sure that he would at last find the answer, went to talk to DeWayne's mother. "I'll tell you," said DeWayne's mother, "he takes after his father's side of the family. They're all just like that."

Genetic and Hereditary Effects

DeWayne's mother explained his inappropriate behavior by referring to hereditary influences. Could she have been right? The effects of heredity on human behavior, both normal and atypical, have been investigated extensively. There is little question that mental retardation, which results in significant deficits in a wide range of behaviors, is sometimes associated with chromosomal abnormalities or with the inheritance of recessive genes (Patton, Payne, & Beirne-Smith, 1990). Evidence indicates that other behavioral characteristics have some hereditary basis as well. Serious behavior disorders, such as that labeled *schizophrenia,* as well as less dramatic conditions as those labeled *depression* (Klein & Last, 1989), and *reading disabilities* (Olson, Wise, Conners, Rack, & Fulker, 1989), and *aggression* (Thomas & Birch, 1984) apparently also have some hereditary component.

In addition, inheritance appears to affect some behavioral characteristics that are not necessarily labeled *deviant* or *atypical.* Thomas and Chess (1977) conducted a study of 136 children whose development has been closely monitored for a number of years. The authors identified nine categories of behavior that they labeled *temperament.* The categories included activity level, rhythmicity (regularity), approach or withdrawal, adaptability, intensity of reaction, threshold of responsiveness (sensitivity to stimuli), quality of mood (disposition), distractibility, and attention span and persistence. That these aspects of temperament are observable shortly after birth and remain consistent throughout childhood indicates that they have some constitutional, if not genetic, basis. There is evidence that some clusters of temperamental characteristics may predispose children to be "difficult" (Thomas & Birch, 1984) but that environmental factors such as child-rearing practices have an equal or greater influence on development.

When DeWayne's mother explained her son's behavior to Professor Grundy, her claim that DeWayne takes after his father's family may have involved a degree of truth. It is possible that certain genetic characteristics may increase the probability of certain behavioral characteristics.

Biochemical Explanations

Some children with disabilities show biochemical abnormalities.

Some researchers have suggested that certain behaviors may result from excesses or deficiencies of various substances found in the body. These chemical substances are labeled differently from those hypothesized by the ancient Greeks but are often held responsible for similar disturbances of behavior.

Biochemical abnormalities have been found in some children with serious disturbances of behavior labeled *autism* or *childhood psychosis* (Boullin, Coleman, O'Brien, & Rimland, 1971). Investigation of such factors, however, has established only that biochemical abnormalities exist, not that they cause the disorder.

Other behavior disturbances characterized as hyperactivity, learning disability, or mental retardation have been linked to biophysical factors such as hypoglycemia (Wunderlich, 1977), malnutrition (Cravioto & Delicardie, 1975), and allergic reactions (Feingold, 1975). It is often suggested that biochemical or other physiological factors may, along with other influences, result in damage to the brain or central nervous system.

Professor Grundy Learns to Think in Circles

Professor Grundy, as part of his instructional duties, visited student teachers. On his first trip to evaluate Ms. Harper in a primary resource room, he observed that one student, Ralph, wandered continuously about the room. Curious about such behavior, because the other students remained seated, Professor Grundy inquired, "Why is Ralph wandering around the room? Why doesn't he sit down like the others?" Ms. Harper was aghast at such ignorance on the part of a professor.

"Why, Ralph is hyperactive, Professor Grundy. That's why he never stays in his seat."

"Ah," replied the professor. "That's very interesting. How do you know he's hyperactive?"

With barely concealed disdain, Ms. Harper hissed, "Professor, I know he's hyperactive because he won't stay in his seat."

After observing the class for a few more minutes, he noticed Ms. Harper and the supervising teacher whispering and casting glances in his direction. Professor Grundy once again attracted Ms. Harper's attention. "What," he inquired politely, "causes Ralph's hyperactivity?"

The disdain was no longer concealed. "Professor," answered Ms. Harper, "hyperactivity is caused by brain damage."

"Indeed," responded the professor, "and you know he's brain damaged because . . . "

"Of course I know he's brain damaged, Professor. He's hyperactive, isn't he?"

Brain Damage

Hyperactivity is not necessarily caused by brain dysfunction.

The circular reasoning illustrated by Ms. Harper is, unfortunately, not uncommon. Many professionals explain a great deal of students' inappropriate behavior similarly. The notion that certain kinds of behavior result from brain damage has its roots in the work of Goldstein (1939), who studied soldiers returning from World War I having suffered head injuries. He identified certain behavioral characteristics, including distractibility, perceptual confusion, and hyperactivity. Observing similar characteristics in some children with retardation, some professionals concluded that the children must also be brain injured (Strauss & Werner, 1942; Werner & Strauss, 1940) and that the brain injury was the cause of the behavior. This led to the identification of a hyperkinetic behavior syndrome (Strauss & Lehtinen, 1947), assumed to be the result of brain injury. This syndrome included such characteristics as hyperactivity, distractibility, impulsivity, short attention span, emotional lability (changeability), perceptual problems, and clumsiness. Subsequently, the term *minimal brain dysfunction* was used to describe a disorder assumed to exist in children who, although they had no history of brain injury, behaved similarly to those who did. There is, however, little empirical support for using the possibility of brain injury to account for problem behavior in all children who show such behavioral characteristics. Even when brain damage can be unequivocally shown to exist, there is no proof that it causes any particular behavior or that hyperactivity is a result of that damage for any particular individual (Werry, 1986).

Large numbers of children are presently being defined as "at risk" for the development of academic and social problems because of the effects of both influences before birth (such as parental malnutrition or substance abuse) and environmental factors (Davis & McCaul, 1991). In recent years fetal alcohol syndrome (Batshaw & Conlon, 1997), smoking by expectant mothers (Hetherington & Parke, 1986), illegal drug use by expectant mothers (Shriver & Piersal, 1994), and pediatric AIDS (Diamond & Cohen, 1987) have resulted in increased learning and behavioral problems in children. Although there are clear indications that these factors result in biochemical, central nervous system, and other physiological abnormalities, no specific behavioral deficit or excess is directly attributed to any specific factor (Gelfand, Jenson, & Drew, 1988).

The Usefulness of Biophysical and Biochemical Explanations

The search for explanations of human behavior based on physiological factors has important implications. As a result of such research, the technology for preventing or lessening some serious problems has been developed. Perhaps the best known example of such technology is the routine testing of all infants for phenylketonuria (PKU), a hereditary disorder of metabolism. Placing infants with PKU on special diets can prevent the mental retardation formerly associated with this disorder (Berry, 1969). It is possible that future research may explain a good deal more human behavior on a biological or hereditary basis. Currently, however, only a small part of the vast quantity of human behavior can be explained in this way.

Some biophysical explanations are testable, meeting the second of our four requirements for usefulness. For example, scientists can definitely establish the existence of Down syndrome by observing chromosomes. Some metabolic or biochemical disorders can also be scientifically verified. Verification of such presumed causes of behavior as minimal brain dysfunction, however, is not dependable (Werry, 1986).

Even with evidence of the existence of some physiological disorder, it does not follow that any specific behavior is automatically a result of the disorder. For the teacher, explanations based on presumed physiological disorders have little predictive utility. To say that Rachel cannot walk, talk, or feed herself because she is developmentally delayed as a result of a chromosomal disorder tells us nothing about the conditions under which Rachel might learn to perform these behaviors. Ms. Harper's explanation of Ralph's failure to sit down on the basis of hyperactivity caused by brain damage does not provide any useful information about what might help Ralph learn to stay in his seat. To say that Harold cannot read because he is a child at risk is to put Harold at the greater risk of not learning because we have low expectations for him. Even apparently constitutional differences in temperament are so vulnerable to environmental influences (Thomas & Birch, 1984) that they provide only limited information about how a child is apt to behave under given conditions.

The final criterion, parsimony, is also frequently violated when physical causes are postulated for student behaviors. Searching for such causes often distracts teachers from simpler, more immediate factors that may be controlling behaviors in the classroom. Perhaps the greatest danger of such explanations is that some teachers may use them as excuses not to teach: Rachel cannot feed herself because she is developmentally delayed, not because I have not taught her. Ralph will not sit down because he is brain damaged, not because I have poor classroom management skills. Irving cannot read because he has dyslexia, not because I have not figured out a way to teach him. Biophysical explanations may also cause teachers to have low expectations for some students. When this happens, teachers might not even try to teach things students are capable of learning. The chart summarizes the usefulness of biophysical theory.

The Usefulness of Biophysical Theory

	Good	Fair	Poor
Inclusiveness			✓
Verifiability		✓	
Predictive Utility			✓
Parsimony			✓

Developmental Explanations

Observation of human beings confirms that many predictable patterns of development occur. Physical growth proceeds in a fairly consistent manner. Most children start walking, talking, and performing some social behaviors such as smiling in fairly predictable sequences and at generally predictable chronological ages (Gesell & Ilg, 1943). Some theorists have attempted to explain many aspects of human behavior—cognitive, social, emotional, and moral—based on fixed, innate developmental sequences. Their proposed explanations are meant to account for normal as well as "deviant" (other than the accepted or usual) human behavior. The following sections review two of the numerous developmental theories and examine their usefulness in terms of inclusiveness, verifiability, predictive utility, and parsimony.

A Freudian by the Garbage Can

Upon returning to the university after observing student teachers, Professor Grundy prepared to return to work on his textbook manuscript, now at least 7 months behind schedule. To his horror, his carefully organized sources, notes, drafts, and revisions were no longer "arranged" on the floor of his office. Worse, his carefully organized sticky notes had been removed from the walls, door, windows, and his computer. Professor Grundy ran frantically down the hall, loudly berating the custodial worker who had taken advantage of his absence to remove what he considered "that trash" from the room so that he could vacuum and dust.

As Grundy pawed through the outside garbage can, a colleague offered sympathy. "That's what happens when an anal-expulsive personality conflicts with an anal-retentive." Grundy's regrettably loud and obscene response to this observation drew the additional comment, "Definite signs of regression to the oral-aggressive stage there, Grundy."

"Well, well, Professor Grundy, did you lose something or are you just doing 'research' on the things you professors throw away?"

Psychoanalytic Theory

Although many different explanations of human behavior have been described as psychoanalytic, all have their roots in theories of Sigmund Freud (Fine, 1973), who described human behavior in an essentially developmental manner (Kessler, 1966). Freud's assertion that normal and aberrant human behavior may be understood and explained on the basis of progression through certain crucial stages (Hall, 1954) is perhaps the most commonly accepted and most widely disseminated of his theories. The hypothetical stages include oral (dependent and aggressive), anal (expulsive and retentive), and phallic (when gender awareness occurs). These stages are believed to occur before the age of six and if mastered, result in emergence into the latency stage, which represents a sort of rest stop until puberty, when the last stage, the genital stage, emerges.

This theory suggests that people who progress through the stages successfully become relatively normal adults. In Freud's view, problems arise when a person fixates (or becomes stuck) at a certain stage or when anxiety causes a regression to a previous stage. People who fixate at or regress to the oral-dependent stage may merely be extremely dependent, or they may seek to solve problems by oral means such as overeating, smoking, or alcohol or drug abuse. A person fixated at the oral-aggressive stage may be sarcastic or verbally abusive. Fixation at the anal-expulsive stage results in messiness and disorganization; at the anal-retentive stage, in compulsive orderliness.

A Stage Theory of Cognitive Development

Jean Piaget was a biologist and psychologist who proposed a stage theory of human development. Piaget's descriptions of the cognitive and moral development of children have had extensive impact among educators. Like Freud, Piaget theorized that certain forces, biologically determined, contribute to development (Piaget & Inhelder, 1969). The forces suggested by Piaget, however, are those enabling the organism to adapt to the environment—specifically, assimilation, the tendency to adapt the environment to enhance personal functioning, and accommodation, the tendency to change behavior to adapt to the environment. The process of maintaining a balance between these two

To access more information on Piaget, go to the "Web Links" module for Chapter 1 of the Companion Website.

forces is called equilibration. Equilibration facilitates growth; other factors that also do so are organic maturation, experience, and social interaction. Piaget's stages include sensory-motor (birth to 1½; years), preoperational (1½; to 7 years), concrete operations (7 to 11 years), and formal operations (12 years to adulthood). (December & Jenkins, 1970).

The Usefulness of Developmental Explanations

Both developmental theories we have discussed are inclusive; they apparently explain a great deal of human behavior, cognitive and affective, normal and deviant. Verifiability, however, is another matter. Although Piagetian theorists have repeatedly demonstrated the existence of academic and preacademic behaviors that appear to be age related in many children (Piaget & Inhelder, 1969), attempts to verify psychoanalytic explanations have not been successful (Achenbach & Lewis, 1971). Considerable resistance to verifying theoretical constructs exists among those who accept the psychoanalytic explanation of human behavior (Schultz, 1969). Although it can be verified that many people act in certain ways at certain ages, this does not prove that the cause of such behavior is an underlying developmental stage or that failure to reach or pass such a stage causes inappropriate or maladaptive behavior. There is little evidence to verify that the order of such stages is invariant or that reaching or passing through earlier stages is necessary for functioning at higher levels. (Phillips & Kelly, 1975). The chart summarizes the usefulness of developmental theory.

The Usefulness of Developmental Theory

	Good	Fair	Poor
Inclusiveness	✓		
Verifiability			✓
Predictive Utility		✓	
Parsimony			✓

To enhance your understanding of these theories, go to the "Activities" module for Chapter 1 of the Companion Website.

Some developmental theories can predict what some human beings will do at certain ages. By their nature these theories offer general information about average persons. However, "a prediction about what the average individual will do is of no value in dealing with a particular individual" (Skinner, 1953, p. 19). Developmental theories do not provide information about what conditions predict an individual's behavior in specific circumstances. The practitioner who wishes to change behavior by changing conditions can expect little help from developmental theories.

Developmental explanations of behavior are equally inadequate when judged by the criterion of parsimony. To say that a child has temper tantrums because he is fixated at the oral stage of development is seldom the simplest explanation available. Because of their lack of parsimony, developmental explanations may lead the teacher to excuses as unproductive as those prompted by biophysical explanations. Teachers, particularly teachers of students with disabilities, may wait forever for a student to become developmentally ready for each learning task. An explanation that encourages teachers to take students from their current levels to subsequent levels is clearly more useful than a developmental explanation—at least from a practical point of view. We might expect Professor Grundy's developmental colleagues, for example, to explain Grundy's difficulty with the concept of hyperactivity on the basis of his failure to reach the level of formal operational thinking required to deal with hypothetical constructs. Might there be a more parsimonious, more useful explanation of his behavior? Professor Grundy continues to collect theories of behavior in the following episode.

Professor Grundy Gains Insight

Having been thoroughly demoralized by his interaction with his student teacher, Professor Grundy decided to pay another surprise visit that afternoon. He was determined to avoid subjecting himself to further ridicule. He did not mention Ralph's hyperactivity but instead concentrated on observing Ms. Harper's teaching. Her lesson plan indicated that she was teaching math, but Professor Grundy was confused by the fact that her group was playing with small wooden blocks of various sizes. Ms. Harper sat at the table with the group but did not interact with the students.

At the conclusion of the lesson, Professor Grundy approached Ms. Harper and asked her why she was not teaching basic addition and subtraction facts as she had planned.

"Professor," stated Ms. Harper, "I conducted my lesson exactly as I had planned. The students were using the blocks to gain insight into the relationship among numbers. Perhaps you are not familiar with the constructivist approach, but everyone knows that true insight is vital to the learning process and that it is impossible to teach children; we can only facilitate their own inner construction of knowledge."

Professor Grundy, knowing better but unable to help himself, asked, "Have they constructed 2 + 2 = 4 yet?"

"Professor," hissed Ms. Harper, "that's not the point. Rote learning is meaningless. I don't care if the children know that 2 + 2 = 4. It is the process that is important, not the outcome. I want them to construct a cognitive map of the meaning of the numerical system and its application to authentic problems."

COGNITIVE EXPLANATIONS

The educational theory espoused (in a somewhat exaggerated form, to be sure) by Ms. Harper is based on an explanation of human behavior and learning that combines elements of developmental theory, especially Piagetian, with a theory first described in Germany in the early part of the 20th century. The first major proponent of this explanation was Max Wertheimer (Hill, 1963), who was interested in people's perception of reality.

Wertheimer suggested it was the relationship among things perceived that was important rather than the things themselves. People, he said, tend to perceive things in an organized fashion, so that what is seen or heard is different from merely the parts that compose it. He labeled an organized perception of this type a *gestalt,* using a German word for which there is no exact English equivalent but which may be translated as "form," "pattern," or "configuration." The word *gestalt* has been retained by English-speaking advocates of this view, and we call this explanation Gestalt psychology. Koffka (1935) applied Wertheimer's theories to learning as well as perception. He concluded that learning in human beings is also a process of imposing structure on perceived information. Wertheimer also applied gestalt theory to human problem-solving. He studied children's and adults' insights into geometric problems and concluded that meaningful solutions depended on insight and that rote learning—even if it led to correct solutions to problems—was less useful.

To further your understanding of Gestalt Psychology, go to the "Web Links" module for Chapter 1 of the Companion Website.

Gestalt psychology has had considerable influence on education. The best known educator to espouse this approach to understanding behavior is Jerome Bruner (1960). What has come to be called the cognitive theory of education places an emphasis on rearranging thought patterns and gaining insight as a basis for learning new academic and social behaviors. The resulting teaching practices are called discovery learning. Learning is explained on the basis of insight, pattern rearrangement, and intuitive leaps. Teachers do not impart knowledge; they merely arrange the environment to facilitate discovery. Motivation is presumed to occur as a result of innate needs that are met when organization is imposed on objects or events in the arrangement. Motivation is thus intrinsic and need not be provided by the teacher. In its latest manifestation, cognitive

Educators who espouse gestalt theory encourage "discovery learning."

theory applied to education has been termed constructivism. This approach holds that teachers cannot provide knowledge to students; students must construct their own knowledge in their own minds (Brooks, 1990). "Rather than behaviours or skills as the goal of instruction, concept development and deep understanding are the foci" (Fosnot, 1996, p. 10).

Principles derived from Gestalt psychology have also been applied to social behavior, notably in the work of Lewin (1951). His approach has been called *field theory* or *cognitive field theory*. Lewin described human social behavior as based on factors within the person's "life space," the environment as it is perceived by the person and as it affects the person's behavior. He asserted that different people perceive and value environmental objects and events in different ways and that forces exist within people to move them toward or away from these objects or events. Based on a complex procedure for "mapping" or drawing diagrams of people's life spaces, Lewin stated that predictions could be made about what people would do based on the value of the events and the strength of the force. Changing behavior thus depends on changing people's perceptions of their life space and the relationships among the various events and objects in it.

The Usefulness of Cognitive Explanations

Cognitive theory explains a great deal of human behavior. Theorists can account for both intellectual and social behavior. Virtually all behavior can be explained as the result of imposing structure on unstructured environmental events or of perceiving the relative importance of such events. Thus, cognitive theory meets the criterion of inclusiveness.

The theory lacks verifiability, however. Because all the processes that are supposed to take place occur internally, there is no way to confirm their existence. Only the outcome is verifiable—the process is assumed.

The predictive utility of cognitive theory is also extremely limited. In academic areas, the teacher who uses a discovery or constructivist approach has very little control over what students will discover or construct. Most advocates of this approach would insist that they do not want to predict outcomes of learning. Unfortunately, this unwillingness to control the outcome of the teaching-learning process has led to rather poor results. Educational practices based on a cognitive approach have been less successful than those emphasizing direct instruction (Engelmann & Carnine, 1982).

The predictive utility of cognitive field theory is somewhat greater than that of cognitive theory. If we know enough about the objects and events in a person's life space, the value that she assigns them, and her motivation to approach or avoid them, we may be able to predict behavior. Given all this information, of course, we could almost certainly predict behavior without recourse to theory.

Addressing our final criterion, we must conclude that cognitive theory is not parsimonious. In neither intellectual nor social areas are the explanations necessary to understanding or predicting behavior.

The Usefulness of Cognitive Theory

	Good	Fair	Poor
Inclusiveness	✓		
Verifiability			✓
Predictive Utility			✓
Parsimony			✓

Although all the theories described so far provide information about human behavior, none of them meets all four of our criteria. The explanations we have provided are very general, and our conclusions about their usefulness should not be taken as an indication that they have no value. We simply believe they provide insufficient practical guidance for classroom teachers. After the following vignette, we shall describe a behavioral explanation of human behavior that we believe most nearly reaches the criteria of inclusiveness, verifiability, predictive utility, and parsimony.

Professor Grundy Takes Action

Professor Grundy had an absolutely rotten day. A number of the students in his 8 a.m. class—including, of course, DeWayne—had come in late, disrupting his lecture. He had been ridiculed by a student teacher; his precious manuscript had been retrieved from the dumpster in a sadly wrinkled and malodorous condition; his colleague had made repeated references to "anal-expulsive" and "oral-aggressive" tendencies during the day in spite of Grundy's protests.

After arriving at home and pouring himself a large drink for medicinal purposes, Grundy decided something must be done. He made several detailed plans and retired for the evening, confident he was on the right track. The next morning he arose, enthusiastically determined, in spite of a slight headache, to put his plans into action.

His first step was to arrive at his 8 a.m. class 5 minutes early—somewhat of a novelty because he usually arrived several minutes late. He spent the extra 5 minutes chatting affably with students and clarifying points from the previous day's lecture when asked to do so. At 8:00 sharp, he presented each of the five students present with an "on-time slip" worth 2 points on the next exam.

After the morning lecture, Professor Grundy proceeded to his office, where he affixed to the door a large sign reading "PLEASE DO NOT CLEAN THIS OFFICE TODAY." He then opened the window, wondering just what the biology department had deposited in the dumpster to cause so strong a smell. He spent an hour reorganizing his notes.

Next, Grundy once again visited Ms. Harper, this time suggesting that she would receive an unsatisfactory grade for student teaching unless she learned to control Ralph's behavior and to teach basic math facts. Her habitual expression of disdain changed to one of rapt attention. Professor Grundy had observed that Ralph, because he was too "hyperactive" to remain in his seat, spent the time while other students worked wandering from toy to toy in the free-time area of the classroom. He suggested that Ms. Harper allow Ralph to play with the toys only after remaining in his seat for a specified length of time: very short periods at first, gradually increasing in length. Grundy further suggested the student teacher make flash cards of basic addition and subtraction facts, allowing the students to play with the colored blocks after they had learned several combinations.

"The librarian sent me over to pick up one of your 48 overdue books . . . if you're . . . uh . . . done with it."

Returning happily to his office, the professor encountered his psychoanalytically oriented colleague, who once again jocularly repeated his insights into Grundy's character. Ignoring the comments, the professor began an animated conversation with his secretary, praising the rapidity with which she was helping him reorganize his manuscript. She assured him it had first priority, because she couldn't wait to be rid of the stinking pages.

Within a short time, Professor Grundy felt that he had things under control. Most of the students enrolled in his 8 a.m. class were present and on time every morning, even though Grundy had begun to give "on-time slips" only occasionally. Ms. Harper had stopped sneering and started teaching. Ralph's wandering had decreased dramatically, and the math group had learned to add and subtract. Grundy continued to ignore his colleague's comments, which gradually ceased when no response was forthcoming, and his notes and drafts were rapidly being transformed into freshly processed manuscript. The only negative outcome was a sharp note from campus security stating that the condition of his office constituted a fire hazard and that it must be cleaned immediately.

Behavioral Explanations

In the preceding vignette, Professor Grundy emerged as the behaviorist that he is. To solve some of his problems, he used techniques derived from yet another explanation of human behavior. The behavioral explanation states that human behavior, both adaptive and maladaptive, is learned. Learning occurs as a result of the consequences of behavior. To put it very simply, behavior that is followed by pleasant consequences tends to be repeated and thus learned. Behavior that is followed by unpleasant consequences tends not to be repeated and thus not learned. By assuming that his students, including DeWayne, came to class late, that the custodian cleaned, that the student teacher ridiculed, that Ralph wandered, and that his psychoanalytic colleague teased because they had learned to do so, Professor Grundy was able to teach them to do other things instead. In doing so, he applied several learning principles underlying the behaviorists' view of human behavior. The following sections introduce these principles, each of which will be discussed in detail in later chapters.

Positive Reinforcement

Chapter 7 describes reinforcement in detail.

Positive reinforcement describes a functional relationship between two environmental events: a **behavior** (any observable action) and a **consequence** (a result of that action). Positive reinforcement is demonstrated when a behavior is followed by a consequence that increases the behavior's rate of occurrence.

Many human behaviors are learned as a result of positive reinforcement. Parents who praise their children for putting away toys may teach the children to be neat; parents who give their children candy to make them stop screaming in the grocery store may teach the children to scream. The cleaning behavior of Professor Grundy's custodian undoubtedly was learned and maintained through positive reinforcement, as was the wit of Grundy's psychoanalytic colleague. Grundy used positive reinforcement (on-time tickets, conversation, and time with toys) to increase his students' rate of coming to class on time and the amount of time Ralph stayed in his seat.

Negative Reinforcement

Negative reinforcement describes a relationship among events in which the rate of a behavior's occurrence increases when some (usually aversive or unpleasant) environmental condition is removed or reduced in intensity. Human beings learn many behaviors when acting in a certain way results in the termination of unpleasantness.

Professor Grundy, for example, learned that opening windows results in the reduction of unpleasant odors in closed rooms. Similarly, his secretary reorganized his manuscript rapidly because when she finished, she could throw away the smelly papers.

PUNISHMENT

Chapter 8 describes punishment and extinction in detail.

Punishment also describes a relationship: a behavior is followed by a consequence that decreases the behavior's future rate of occurrence. An event is described as a **punisher** only if the rate of occurrence of the preceding behavior decreases. Behaviorists use the word **punishment** as a technical term to describe a specific relationship; confusion may arise because the same word is used in a nontechnical sense to describe unpleasant things done to people in an effort to change their behavior. To the behaviorist, punishment occurs only when the preceding behavior decreases. In the technical sense of the term, something is not necessarily punishment merely because someone perceives the consequent event as unpleasant. A behaviorist can never say, "I punished him, but it didn't change his behavior," as do many parents and teachers. It is punishment only if the functional relationship can be established. People could say that Professor Grundy's verbal threat to Ms. Harper, for example, was apparently a punisher: her ridiculing comments to him stopped. Of course, we wish he had used a more positive approach.

EXTINCTION

When a previously reinforced behavior is no longer reinforced, its rate of occurrence decreases. This relationship is described as **extinction.** Recall from our vignette that when Grundy no longer reacted to his colleague's ridicule, the behavior stopped. For a behaviorist, all learning principles are defined on the basis of what actually happens, not what we think is happening. Grundy may have thought he was punishing his colleague by yelling or otherwise expressing his annoyance. In reality, the rate of the behavior increased when Grundy reacted in this way; the real relationship was that of positive reinforcement. The behavior stopped when the positive reinforcer was withdrawn.

ANTECEDENT CONTROL

Requirements that a functional assessment or analysis be performed for students with disabilities before changes in placement can be made (See Chapter 6 for a detailed discussion.) have greatly increased interest in antecedent control. Teachers and researchers have come to rely much more frequently on examination of antecedent events and conditions, those occurring before the behavior, to determine what might be setting the stage for appropriate or challenging behaviors. There is also increased emphasis on manipulating antecedent conditions or events to manage behavior.

Stimulus control is the focus of Chapter 9.

An antecedent that occurs immediately before a behavior is called a discriminative stimulus and is said to "occasion" (to set the occasion for) a behavior. There is a functional relationship, called **stimulus control,** between behavior and an **antecedent stimulus** rather than behavior and its consequences. Consequences must have been present during the development of the relationship, but the antecedent condition or event now serves as a signal or cue for the behavior. In our vignette, the custodian's adherence to posted notices had apparently been reinforced in the past, so Professor Grundy's sign was effective even in the absence of a reinforcer or a punisher.

Recently, researchers have been investigating more distant varieties of antecedent events and conditions (Smith & Iwata, 1997). Often referred to as **setting events,*** these conditions or events may occur simultaneously with a discriminative stimulus or hours or even days before (Horner, Vaughn, Day, & Ard, 1996). They may occur in the same setting or in a completely different one. They influence behavior by temporarily changing the value or effectiveness of reinforcers. The simplest kinds of setting events to describe are deprivation and satiation. A student, sweating buckets, who has just come in from the playground after playing a hard game of kickball is likely to be more responsive to a soft drink as a potential reinforcer than one who has just consumed a soda in the air-conditioned cafeteria. Setting events, however, can be much more complex. Kazdin (2000) described three types of setting events: social, physiological, and environmental. Bailey, Wolery, & Sugai (1988) subdivided environmental setting events into instructional dimensions, physical dimensions, social dimensions, and environmental changes. These varieties of conditions and events may include variables as diverse as a noisy or uncomfortably warm classroom (environmental), the presence of a disliked staff member or peer (social), or a headache (physiological). Bailey et al. (1988) included considerations about instructional materials that may not be age appropriate or gender appropriate. It may be that no reinforcer will (or indeed should) induce a teenage boy to touch, much less read, a colorfully illustrated book about the little mermaid. We believe that issues of students' ethnic or cultural heritage can also serve as setting events. Students are much more motivated to interact with materials that portray people like themselves (Gay, 2002). Attention to cultural diversity may enable teachers to provide reinforcers that are more meaningful and powerful and to avoid strategies that are ineffective or offensive. Strategies such as Personalized Contextual Instruction (Voltz, 2003) that embed instruction into contexts of interest to students in a given setting (Voltz, 1999) may enhance the value of reinforcers. The following anecdote describes a classroom using this approach.

*Some authors (Michael, 2000) use the term *establishing operations* to describe what we call setting events; others use the terms interchangeably; others differentiate between the terms. Until the confusion about terminology (sometimes within a single edited text) is cleared up (Horner & Harvey, 2000), we prefer to use the term *setting events*.

Music Hath Charms

Ms. Garcia, a general education teacher, Mr. Walden, a special education teacher, and Ms. Nguyen, a paraprofessional, share the responsibility for an inclusive primary class of 25 students that they privately agree "gives new meaning to the term diversity." Their students range in age from 7 to 9. They have 14 boys and 11 girls; 12 African-American students, 8 Hispanic students, and 4 Asian students. They have 7 children with learning disabilities, 4 children with behavior disorders, and 2 children who are intellectually gifted. And they have Yuri, a boy from Russia who has autism. What the children have in common is eligibility for free or reduced-price lunch and the fact that all of their teachers believe every one of them is capable of great things.

Things had been going well; the teachers used the standard curriculum and a combination of group and individual teaching. They used a simple point system with the class as a whole (the students could earn tangibles and activities for completing work and behaving appropriately) and implemented more complex Behavioral Intervention Plans with some children with more challenging behaviors. The students were making good academic progress but, as Mr. Walden stated at a meeting one afternoon, "Nobody seems real excited about school except us." The three teachers decided to implement an integrated unit approach that Ms. Garcia had learned about in a class she was taking at the local university and researched on the internet and at the university library. The next morning Ms. Garcia explained the plan to the students, asking them to think about what they would like to study. The students seemed to think the teachers must be kidding and made several suggestions ranging from sports to dinosaurs, but most of the interest appeared to center around music.

"Rap!" shouted several students. "Salsa!" suggested others. "All right," agreed Ms. Garcia, as Ms. Nguyen and Mr. Walden moved around praising students who were attending, "Let's make a list of what we already know about music and then a list of things we would like to know. Ms. Nguyen, would you help Yuri put the sticky notes with our ideas on the board?"

After almost an hour they had a good list to start out with and the teachers were startled to see that it was almost lunchtime. They were even more startled to realize that no one had given the students points all morning and that verbal praise and pats on the back had been enough.

Other Learning Principles

In addition to these major learning principles, Professor Grundy illustrated the use of several other influences on human behavior described by behaviorists. These influences include **modeling** and **shaping.** Modeling is the demonstration of behavior. The professor had been modeling inappropriate behavior—coming to class late—and his students had apparently been imitating that behavior. Many behaviors, both appropriate and inappropriate, are learned by imitating a model. Infants learn to talk by imitating their parents; adults can learn to operate complex machinery by watching a demonstration.

Shaping uses the reinforcement of successive approximations to a desired behavior to teach new behavior. Grundy suggested that Ms. Harper use shaping to teach Ralph to stay in his seat. She was initially to reinforce sitting behavior when it occurred for short periods of time and gradually increase the sitting time required for Ralph to earn the reinforcer. Many behaviors are taught by shaping. Parents may praise a young child effusively the first time she dresses herself, even if her blouse is on inside out and her shorts are on backward. Later she may earn a compliment only if her outfit is perfectly coordinated.

The Task of the Behaviorist

If you can see it, hear it, feel it, or smell it, it's observable. If you can count it or measure it, it's quantifiable.

Behaviorists explain the development of both typical and atypical human behavior in terms of the principles just described. An important aspect of this approach is its emphasis on behavior. To qualify as a behavior, something must be *observable* and *quantifiable* (Baer, Wolf, & Risley, 1968). We must be able to see (or sometimes hear, feel, or even smell) the behavior. To make such direct observation meaningful, some way of measuring the behavior in quantitative terms (How much? How long? How often?) must be established. Behaviorists cannot reliably state that any of the relationships described as learning principles exist unless these criteria are met.

Skinner (1953) suggested that behaviorists are less concerned with explaining behavior than with describing it. The emphasis, he states, is on which environmental factors increase, decrease, or maintain the rate of occurrence of specific behaviors. It is important to note that behaviorists do not deny the existence of physiological problems that may contribute to some behavioral problems. Nor do most behaviorists deny the effects of heredity (Mahoney, 1974) or even developmental stages (Ferster, Culbertson, & Boren, 1975). Their primary emphasis, however, is on present environmental conditions maintaining behavior and on establishing and verifying functional relationships between such conditions and behavior.

The Usefulness of Behavioral Explanations

One of the most common criticisms of the behavioral approach is that it leaves much of human behavior unexplained. Emphasis on observable behavior has led many to assume that behavioral principles cannot account for any but simple motor responses. However, Skinner (1953, 1957, 1971) applied basic learning principles to explain a wide variety of complex human behavior, including verbal behavior and sociological, economic, political, and religious beliefs.

The fact that behavioral principles have not accounted for all aspects of human behavior should not lead to the assumption that they cannot. In the years since Skinner first identified the principles of behavior that developed into the discipline of Applied Behavior Analysis, many aspects have been accounted for. Many phenomena have yet to be explained. "In the meantime—which may last forever—the best strategy is to isolate variables that influence important behavior and manipulate those variables to make life better" (Poling & Byrne, 1996, p. 79). Because behaviorists refuse to theorize about what they have not observed, explanation must await verification. Behaviorists are ready temporarily to sacrifice some degree of inclusiveness for verifiability.

Verifiability is the essence of the behavioral explanation. Other theorists posit a theory and attempt to verify it through experimental investigation. Behaviorists, on the other hand, investigate before formulating what may be described as generalizations rather than theories. That adult attention serves as a positive reinforcer for most children (Baer & Wolf, 1968; Harris, Johnston, Kelley, & Wolf, 1964) is an example of such a generalization. This statement was made only after repeated observations established a functional relationship between children's behavior and adult attention. The chart summarizes the usefulness of behavioral theory.

The Usefulness of Behavioral Theory

	Good	Fair	Poor
Inclusiveness		✓	
Verifiability	✓		
Predictive Utility	✓		
Parsimony	✓		

The focus of the behavioral approach is changing behavior. Predictive utility is an essential part of any behavioral explanation. Functional relationships are established and generalizations are made precisely so that they can be used to change maladaptive or inappropriate behavior and increase appropriate behavior. Behaviorists are reinforced by changing behavior, not by discussing it. Unless it is possible to use generalizations to predict what people will do under certain conditions, behaviorists see little point in making the statements. An enormous body of evidence exists, representing the application of learning principles to human behavior. Such data make possible the prediction of behavior under a wide variety of conditions.

"Explanatory fictions" explain nothing. Behaviorists explain behavior on the basis of observation, not imagination.

Behavioral explanations are parsimonious, satisfying our fourth criterion for usefulness. Describing behavior solely in terms of observable, verifiable, functional relationships avoids the use of "explanatory fictions." Such fictions are defined only in terms of their effects, resulting in the circular reasoning we discussed earlier. Rather than invoking "hyperactivity"—an example of an explanatory fiction—to explain Ralph's out-of-seat behavior, Professor Grundy chose a behavioral approach to look at what happened before and after Ralph left his seat. In this way, behaviorism avoids explanations distant from observed behavior and its relationship to the environment. It is unacceptable to explain out-of-seat behavior by labeling the cause as hyperactivity or to explain messiness as fixation at or regression to the anal-expulsive stage of behavior. Neither explanation adds anything useful to our information about the problem.

Haughton and Ayllon (1965) offered one example of the fluency with which many professionals are willing to invoke unparsimonious explanations of behavior. The authors were working with a hospitalized mental patient whose behavior for many years had been limited to sitting and smoking cigarettes. After a period during which smoking was limited, the patient was given cigarettes only when standing up and holding a broom. The patient began carrying the broom most of the time. Two psychiatrists were asked to observe and evaluate the patient's behavior. Both offered lengthy and complex explanations, suggesting that the broom served a function similar to that of a young child's "blankie" or that it represented an infant she wished she had, or the scepter of an omnipotent queen. When staff members stopped giving cigarettes to the woman while she was carrying the broom, she stopped carrying the broom. Although we stated earlier that the parsimonious explanation may not always be correct, in this case it was. Even when the development of unusual behavior is not as easy to trace as in this example, the assumption that such behaviors are being maintained by current environmental conditions and that the behavior may be changed by changing the environment is not merely parsimonious, it is supremely optimistic. The teacher who concentrates on discovering and changing the environmental conditions maintaining students' inappropriate or maladaptive behavior does not give up on them because they are culturally different, retarded, brain damaged, emotionally disturbed, hyperactive, at risk, or developmentally unready to learn; she teaches them. If students' behavior is described in terms of behavioral excesses (too much moving around) or deficits (too little reading), as suggested by Gelfand and Hartmann (1975) and Hersen and Bellack (1977), rather than in terms of explanatory fictions, the teacher can go about the business of teaching—decreasing behavioral excesses and overcoming behavioral deficits.

Historical Development of Behaviorism

Behaviorism as a science has roots in philosophical and psychological traditions originating several centuries ago. The learning principles described earlier certainly existed before being formally defined. People's behavior has been influenced since the beginning of civilization. In the following section, we will examine several historical descriptions of how people have used the relationship between behavior and its consequences. Then we will trace the development of behaviorism as a formal way of explaining, predicting, and changing human behavior.

Historical Precedents

The arrangement of environmental conditions in order to influence behavior is by no means a recent invention. It is said that the ancient Romans put eels in the bottom of wine cups to decrease excessive drinking.

Crossman (1975) provided an historical example of the use of positive reinforcement.

> There is a fascinating history behind the pretzel. About 610 A.D. an imaginative Alpine monk formed the ends of dough, left over from the baking of bread, into baked strips folded into a looped twist so as to represent the folded arms of children in prayer. The tasty treat was offered to the children as they learned their prayers and thereby came to be called "pretiola"—Latin for "little reward." [From the back of a Country Club Foods pretzel bag, Salt Lake City.] (p. 348).

Several innovative educators developed elaborate programs of reward and punishment to manage their students' behavior. In the early 19th century, Lancaster (Kaestle, 1973) instituted a system in Great Britain that was later also used in the United States. Students earned tickets that could be exchanged for prizes or money. They lost tickets when they misbehaved.

Educators used behavioral principles long before the principles were formally identified.

Benjamin Franklin demonstrated that adults' behavior could also be changed, using a rather different positive reinforcer.

> We had for our chaplain a zealous Presbyterian minister, Mr. Beatty, who complained to me that the men did not generally attend his prayers and exhortations. When they enlisted, they were promised, besides pay and provisions, a gill of rum a day, which was punctually serv'd out to them, half in the morning, and the other half in the evening; and I observ'd they were as punctual in attending to receive it; upon which I said to Mr. Beatty: 'It is, perhaps, below the dignity of your profession to act as steward of the rum, but if you were to deal it out and only just after prayers, you would have them all about you.' He liked the tho't, undertook the office, and, with the help of a few hands to measure out the liquor, executed it to satisfaction, and never were prayers more generally and more punctually attended; so that I thought this method preferable to the punishment inflicted by some military laws for non-attendance on divine service. [From: Franklin, Benjamin, American Philosophical Society.] (Reprinted in Skinner, 1969, p. 247.)

Behavioral principles operate whether anyone is consciously using them.

Parents and teachers have likewise applied the principles of learning in their efforts to teach children. "Clean up your plate and then you can have dessert," says the parent hoping for positive reinforcement. "When you finish your arithmetic, you may play a game," promises the teacher. Parents and teachers, whether they are aware of it or not, also use punishment: the child who runs into the street is spanked; the student who finishes his assignment quickly is given more work to do. All of us have heard "Just ignore him and he'll stop. He's only doing it for attention." If he does stop, we have an example of extinction. Of course, many parents and teachers extinguish appropriate behavior as well, paying no attention to children who are behaving nicely. Negative reinforcement is demonstrated in many homes every day: "You don't play outside until that room is clean." Teachers also use negative reinforcement when they require students, for example, to finish assignments before going to lunch or to recess. Kindergarten teachers who ask their charges to use their "inside voices" are trying to establish stimulus control. Whenever teachers show their students how to do something, they are modeling.

It becomes apparent that a person does not need to know the names of the relationships involved to use them. Indeed, applying behavioral learning principles sounds a lot like common sense. If it is so simple, why must students take courses and read books? Why have such quantities of material been written and so much research conducted?

The answer is that it is inefficient to fail to arrange environmental conditions so that functional relationships are established, or to allow such relationships to be randomly established, or to assume that such relationships have been established based only on common sense. This inefficiency has resulted in high levels of maladaptive behavior in schools and sometimes frighteningly low levels of academic and preacademic learning. It is our aim in writing this book to help teachers become applied behavior analysts. The derivation and definition of the term applied behavior analysis will be discussed in the remaining sections of this chapter.

Philosophical and Psychological Antecedents

The roots of the behavioral viewpoint are firmly planted in a 19th-century philosophical movement known as *positivism*, which in its turn evolved from the 17th-century writings of Francis Bacon (Smith, 1992). Positivism's earliest proponent, Auguste Comte, emphasized that the only valid knowledge was that which was objectively observable. Comte apparently arrived at such a standard as a result of his attempt to make a systematic survey of all knowledge. To limit his task, he decided to accept only knowledge that resulted from direct observation.

A second important contribution came from animal psychology, influenced by the work of Charles Darwin (Boring, 1950), which emphasized the continuity between animal and human behavior and thus suggested that something about human beings could be learned through the careful observation of lower animals. Animal psychology focused on the adaptation of physical structures in the body to the environment. This focus led to consideration of mental processes in the same light and to a psychological movement known as *functionalism*.

Functionalism was a third important influence on the development of a behavioral approach to explaining human behavior. William James, whose work was a precursor of behaviorism (Boring, 1950), emphasized that Dewey and James Angell were also influential in turning the emphasis in American psychology from an introspective, theorizing model to one emphasizing a practical, observational approach.

Respondent Conditioning

Most people are aware of the work of Ivan Pavlov, who observed that when a tone was sounded as dogs were fed, the dogs began to salivate when they heard the tone even when food was not present. (Anyone who feeds dogs can observe a similar phenomenon when the dogs arrive drooling when they hear the food pans being taken from the dishwasher.) Pavlov's work has been extremely influential in the development of contemporary psychology and education. His precise observation and measurement have served as a model for experimental research to this day. His classic experiment involved pairing food powder (which elicits salivation, an automatic reflex) with a tone that would normally have no effect on dogs' salivation. The presentation of the tone preceded the presentation of the food powder; after repeated pairings, salivation occurred when only the tone was presented (Hill, 1970). The food powder was labeled the *unconditioned stimulus* (UCS); the tone, the *conditioned stimulus* (CS). Salivation is an unconditioned response to food powder and a conditioned response to the tone. The relationship may be represented as shown in the accompanying diagram.

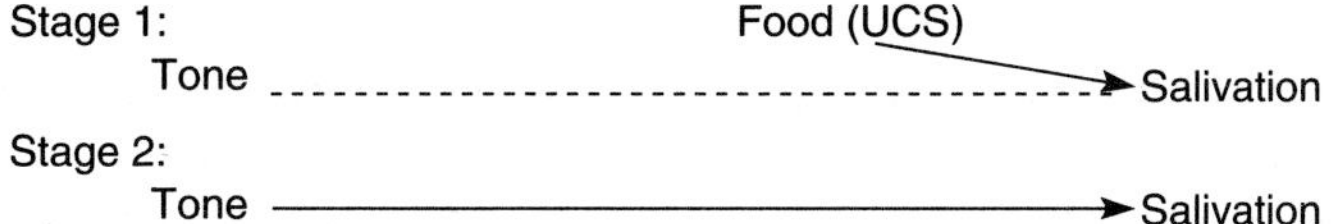

The process of pairing stimuli so that an unconditioned stimulus elicits a response is known as *Pavlovian, classical,* or *respondent conditioning*. Such conditioning is the basis of a method of behavior change known as behavior therapy. Behavior therapists concentrate on breaking up maladaptive, conditioned reflexes and building more adaptive responses. These therapists often work with people who have problems such as irrational fears or phobias. They also help those who want to change habits such as smoking, overeating, or excessive alcohol consumption. A detailed discussion of behavior therapy is beyond the scope of this text.

Associationism

Another influential experimenter whose research paralleled that of Pavlov was Edward Thorndike. Thorndike studied cats rather than dogs, and his primary interest was discovering associations between situations and responses (Thorndike, 1931). He formulated two laws that profoundly influenced the subsequent development of behavioral science. The Law of Effect (Thorndike, 1905) states that "any act which in a given situation produces satisfaction becomes associated with that situation, so that when the situation recurs the act is more likely than before to recur also" (p. 203). Second is the Law of Exercise, which states that a response made in a particular situation becomes associated with the situation. The relationship of the Law of Effect with the principle of positive reinforcement is obvious. The Law of Exercise is similarly related to the stimulus control principle discussed earlier.

Behaviorism

If we were all Watsonians, we couldn't say, "She hurt my feelings," "My mind wandered," or "Use your imagination."

The use of the term *behaviorism* was originated by John Watson (1914, 1919, 1925). Watson advocated the complete abolition of any datum in psychology that did not result from direct observation. He considered such concepts as mind, instinct, thought, and emotion both useless and superfluous. He denied the existence of instinct in human beings and reduced thought to subvocal speech, emotion to bodily responses. A Watsonian behaviorist of our acquaintance once responded to a question by saying, "I've changed my mind (you should excuse the expression)." The true Watsonian does not acknowledge the existence of any such entity as "mind."

Watson and Raynor (1920) conditioned a startle response in a baby, Albert, by pairing a white rat (CS) with a loud noise (UCS). Watson contended that all "emotional" responses such as fear were conditioned in similar ways. In an interestingly related procedure, Jones (1924) desensitized a 3-year-old child who showed a fear response to white rabbits and other white furry objects by pairing the child's favorite foods with the rabbit. This procedure was unfortunately not carried out with Albert, who moved away before his conditioned fear could be eliminated. Albert may still be scared of white rats, which may have created a number of problems in his life, including preventing his employment as a behavioral psychologist. Watson later suggested that Albert might eventually seek Freudian therapy to overcome his strange fears and that his problems might be attributed to an unresolved Oedipal complex (Pierce & Eppling, 1999).

Operant Conditioning

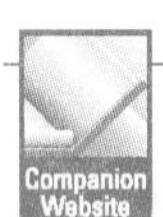

For more information on B. F. Skinner, go to the "Web Links" module for Chapter 1 of the Companion Website.

The learning principles described at the beginning of this section are those suggested by proponents of an *operant conditioning* model for explaining, predicting, and changing human behavior. The best known operant conditioner was B. F. Skinner (1904–1988), who first distinguished operant from respondent conditioning.

Operant behaviors are emitted voluntarily; respondent behaviors are elicited by stimuli.

Respondent conditioning, you will recall, deals with behaviors elicited by stimuli that precede them. Most such behaviors are reflexive; that is, they are not under voluntary control. Operant conditioning (sometimes called *instrumental conditioning*), on the other hand, deals with behaviors usually thought of as voluntary rather than reflexive. Operant conditioners are concerned primarily with the consequences of behavior and the establishment of functional relationships between behavior and consequences. The behavioral view described earlier is that of operant conditioning, which will be the emphasis of the entire text.

Skinner's early work was with animals, primarily white rats. In this, he followed in the tradition of earlier behaviorists, to whom this particular animal was so important that one researcher (Tolman, 1932) dedicated a major book to *Mus norvegious albinius,* a strain of white rats. Bertrand Russell, the philosopher, is said to have suggested facetiously that the different emphases in European (primarily gestalt, introspective, and theorizing) and American (primarily behavioral, active, observational) studies may have resulted from differences in the breeds of rats available. Whereas European rats sat around quietly waiting for insight, American rats were active go-getters, scurrying around their cages and providing lots of behaviors for psychologists to observe.

Skinner also worked with pigeons. He explained (1963) that, while in the military during World War II, he was assigned to a building whose windowsills were frequented by these birds. Because there was very little to do, he and his colleagues began to train the pigeons to perform various behaviors. This subsequently developed into a rather elaborate, successful, although ultimately abandoned before fully operational, project to train pigeons to deliver guided missiles to enemy vessels. Although "Project Pigeon" was a source of personal and professional frustration to Skinner, it is credited with moving his interest firmly and finally from the laboratory into applied settings (Capshew, 1993).

Early application of operant conditioning techniques to human beings was directed toward establishing that the principles governing animal behavior also govern human behavior. The use of these principles to change human behavior—usually called *behavior modification*—did not really emerge in nonlaboratory settings until the 1960s. One of the authors remembers being told in an experimental psychology course in 1961 that there was some indication operant conditioning could be applied to simple human behavior. As an example, the instructor laughingly described college students' conditioning their professor to lecture from one side of the room simply by looking interested only when he stood on that side. The instructor insisted that it would not be possible to modify his behavior in this way, because he was aware of the technique. He was wrong; he was backed into one corner of the room by the end of the next lecture.

To access a list of journals that publish research using applied behavior analysis, click on the module for other resources in Chapter 1 of the Companion Website.

At that time, however—in spite of Skinner's (1953) theoretical application of operant conditioning techniques to complex human behavior and pioneer studies such as those of Ayllon and Michael (1959) and Birnbrauer, Bijou, Wolf, and Kidder (1965)—few people anticipated the enormous impact that the use of such principles would have on American psychology and education and on other disciplines, including economics (Kagel & Winkler, 1972). The application of behavior modification in real-life settings had become so prevalent by 1968 that a new journal, the *Journal of Applied Behavior Analysis,* was founded to publish the results of research. In Volume 1, Number 1, of the journal, Baer, Wolf, and Risley (1968) defined applied behavior analysis as the "process of applying sometimes tentative principles of behavior to the improvement of specific behaviors, and simultaneously evaluating whether or not any changes noted are indeed attributed to the process of application" (p. 91).

Applied behavior analysis must deal with socially important, observable behaviors. Relationships between behaviors and interventions must be verified.

Baer and his colleagues (1968) suggested that for research to qualify as applied behavior analysis, it must change socially important behavior, chosen because it needs change, not because its study is convenient to the researcher. It must deal with observable and quantifiable behavior, objectively defined or defined in terms of examples, and clear evidence of a functional relationship between the behavior to be changed and the experimenter's intervention must exist. In a more recent retrospective analysis of the progress of applied behavior analysis since 1968, the same authors (Baer, Wolf, & Risley, 1987) suggested that in spite of considerable opposition and in light of many failures of the procedures in real settings, applied behavior analysts should persevere. They stated, "current theory has worked far too well to be abandoned in the face of what are more parsimoniously seen as technological rather than theoretical failures" (p. 325). In other words, we still cannot always make what we know ought to work actually work, but that is a problem of implementation not an indication of the inadequacy of applied behavior analysis as a discipline. Johnston (1996) recently suggested that a greater separation of applied research from service delivery might provide more controlled conditions for research and thus enable more progress.

To enhance your understanding of applied behavior analysis, go to the "Activities" module for Chapter 1 of the Companion Website.

Applied behavior analysis is more rigorously defined than behavior modification. In our earlier vignette, Professor Grundy apparently succeeded in modifying behavior, but he failed to meet the criterion of analysis—he had no way of knowing for sure whether his techniques changed behavior or whether the change was mere coincidence. This book is designed to help teachers become applied behavior analysts, effective modifiers of behavior, and efficient analyzers of the principles of learning involved in all aspects of their students' performance.

Teachers who learn and practice the principles of applied behavior analysis can help their students master functional and academic skills in a systematic and efficient manner and can document their students' progress for parents and other professionals. They can manage behavior positively so that their focus remains on learning. They can teach students to get along with peers and adults and to make good choices. By providing learning environments that are safe, joyful, and successful, they can make enormous differences in students' lives.

Summary

We described a number of approaches to explaining human behavior. We evaluated these approaches in terms of their inclusiveness, verifiability, predictive utility, and parsimony. We also described an explanation of human behavior that appears to us to be the most useful—the behavioral explanation.

In tracing the history of the behavioral approach to human behavior, we emphasized the development of a science of applied behavior analysis. We discussed the necessity for concentrating on socially useful studies of human behavior and on careful observation of the establishment of functional relationships. We also provided a rationale for learning and using the principles of applied behavior analysis and some examples of their use in various educational settings.

Key Terms

applied behavior analysis
positive reinforcement
behavior
consequence
negative reinforcement
punisher
punishment
extinction
stimulus control
antecedent stimulus
setting events
modeling
shaping

Discussion Questions

1. Why do applied behavior analysts consider biophysical, developmental, and cognitive explanations of behavior less useful than a behavioral explanation?
2. What useful information might teachers gain from biophysical, developmental, or cognitive information about their students?
3. What differentiates the historical examples of the use of consequences to change behavior from applied behavior analysis?
4. What is the difference between operant and respondent conditioning? Why, in a text for teachers, have we chosen to emphasize operant conditioning?

Chapter 2

Preparing Behavioral Objectives

Did you know that . . .

- If a composer orchestrates without the melody in mind, the Dixie Chicks could sound like Santana?
- There are reasons for writing behavioral objectives besides satisfying legal or administrative requirements?
- Aggression is in the eye of the beholder?
- Even professors write behavioral objectives?
- Ninety percent may not be a passing grade?
- Accuracy is not always enough?

Chapter Outline

Definition: A behavioral objective is a statement that communicates a proposed change in behavior. It describes a level of performance and serves as a basis for evaluation.

In this chapter we will discuss the first step in carrying out a program for behavior change: defining the target behavior—the behavior to be changed. A target behavior may be selected because it addresses a behavioral deficit (such as too few math skills) or a behavioral excess (such as too much screaming). After the behavior to be changed has been identified, a written **behavioral objective** is prepared. A behavioral objective describes the behavior that should result from the instruction or intervention that is planned. It describes the intended outcomes of instruction, not the procedures for accomplishing those outcomes (Mager, 1997).

A behavioral objective for a student who demonstrates a deficit in math skills would describe the level of math performance the student should reach. A behavioral objective for a student who screams excessively would describe an acceptable level of screaming. Anyone reading a behavioral objective should be able to understand exactly what a student is working to accomplish. Because behavioral objectives are such an integral part of planning for student behavior change, they are required as part of the IEP for students with disabilities. We will also talk about the relationship between objectives and the IEP.

You will meet some teachers who are learning to use a behavioral approach in their teaching. Through them, you will encounter some of the difficulties of putting behavioral programs into effect. Consider the plight of Ms. Samuels, the resource teacher, in the following vignette.

Are We Both Talking About the Same Thing?

Ms. Wilberforce, the third-grade teacher, was in a snit.

"That special ed consulting teacher," she complained to her friend, Ms. Folden, "is absolutely useless. I asked her 2 months ago to work on vowels with Martin and he still doesn't know the short sounds."

"You're absolutely right," agreed Ms. Folden, "I told her last September that Melissa Sue had a bad attitude. The longer the special ed teacher sees Melissa Sue, the worse it gets. All Melissa Sue does now is giggle when I correct her. It seems to me that we were better off without special ed teachers."

Meanwhile, Ms. Samuels, the special ed teacher, was complaining bitterly to her supervisor.

"Those general education teachers are so ungrateful. Just look at what I've done with Martin. He can name all the vowels when I ask him, and he even knows a little song about them. And Melissa Sue, who used to pout all the time, smiles and laughs so much now. I've done exactly what the teachers asked—why don't they appreciate it?"

Definition and Purpose

Behavioral objectives improve communication.

The preceding vignette illustrates one of the most important reasons for writing behavioral objectives: to clarify the goals of a student's behavior-change program and thus to facilitate communication among people involved in the program. Because it is a written statement targeting a specific change in behavior, the objective serves as an agreement among school personnel, parents, and students about the academic or social learning for which school personnel are taking responsibility.

An objective may also serve to inform students of what is expected. It is a statement of proposed student achievement and tells students what they will be learning or in what manner and to what degree their behavior is to change. Providing students with a statement of proposed learning outcomes enables them to match their performance with a standard of correct or expected performance. This allows for ongoing evaluation and provides informative feedback and reinforcement (Gagne, 1985, p. 309).

A second reason for writing behavioral objectives is that a clearly stated target for instruction facilitates effective programming by the teacher and ancillary personnel. A clearly stated instructional target provides a basis for selecting appropriate materials and instructional strategies. Mager (1997) pointed out that "machinists and surgeons do not select tools until they know what they're intending to accomplish. Composers don't orchestrate scores until they know what effects they are trying to create" (p. 14). Clearly written behavioral objectives should prevent the classroom teacher from using materials simply because they are available or strategies simply because they are familiar. The selection of materials and teaching strategies is more likely to be appropriate if objectives are clearly defined.

There is yet another excellent reason for writing behavioral objectives. Consider the following account.

A Matter of Opinion

Mr. Henderson, the teacher of a preschool class for students with developmental delays, hurried to the principal's office in a state of complete panic. The parents of Alvin, one of his students, had just threatened to remove the boy from school. They insisted Mr. Henderson was not teaching Alvin anything and was not making it possible for Alvin to spend more time with his general education kindergarten class. Mr. Henderson had agreed in August to work on toilet training with Alvin and felt the boy had made excellent progress. Alvin's parents, however, were upset because Alvin still had several accidents every week. They and the kindergarten teacher insisted that Mr. Henderson had not reached his stated goal.

"I have toilet trained Alvin," howled Mr. Henderson. "Wouldn't you consider only two or three accidents a week all right?"

Behavioral objectives help evaluate progress.

Mr. Henderson's panic could have been prevented if a clearly written objective statement had come out of the August meeting. If a definition of *toilet trained* had been established at the beginning of the year, there would have been no question as to whether that objective had been achieved. Behavioral objectives provide for precise evaluation of instruction. When a teacher identifies a deficit or an excess in a student's behavioral repertoire, he has identified a discrepancy between current and expected levels of functioning. If the teacher states a performance criterion (the ultimate goal) and records ongoing progress toward this goal, both formative (ongoing) and summative (final) evaluation of intervention procedures become possible so that programs can be changed as necessary and plans made for the future. Ongoing evaluation and measurement enable the teacher, the student, or a third party to monitor progress continuously and to determine when goals have been reached. Continuous monitoring minimizes individual interpretations or prejudices in judgment when instructional procedures or a student's performances are evaluated.

Pinpointing Behavior

Before an objective can be written or a behavior change program initiated, the target behavior must be described clearly. Referral information may often be vague and imprecise. To write effective objectives, the applied behavior analyst must refine broad generalizations into specific, observable, measurable behaviors. This process is frequently referred to as **pinpointing** behavior.

Pinpointing may be accomplished by asking a series of questions, usually including "Could you please tell me what he *does?*" or "What exactly do you want her to *do?*" For example, teachers often refer students to a behavior analyst because of "hyperactivity." The referring teacher and the applied behavior analyst must define this hyperactive behavior by describing exactly what is occurring. Is it that the student, like Ralph in Ms. Harper's class, wanders around the room? Does he tap his pencil on the desk? Does he weave back and forth in his chair?

Many categories of behavior may result in referrals and require pinpointing. Here are a few examples, with some questions that may help to refine the definition:

- *Sebastian can't do math:* Is the problem that he does not have basic arithmetic computation skills, or that he cannot finish his problems within the time limit set, or that he refuses to attempt the problems?
- *Stella is always off task:* Is the problem that she stares out the window, or that she talks to her neighbor, or that she scribbles in her book instead of looking at the chalkboard?
- *Chance is always disturbing others:* Is he grabbing objects from someone, or talking to others during lessons, or hitting his neighbor, or knocking neighbors' books off the desk, or pulling someone's hair?
- *Maggie's lab projects are a mess:* Is it that she cannot read the instructions in the lab manual, or that her handwriting is sloppy, or that she does not do the prescribed steps in the right order, or that she can do the experiments but cannot write the results coherently?
- *Laura throws tantrums:* Is she crying and sobbing, or is she throwing herself on the floor, or is she throwing objects around the room?

A teacher may ask a similar series of questions in describing more complex or abstract categories of behaviors. If the referring teacher said, "Carol doesn't use critical thinking skills," the applied behavior analyst would want to know if Carol

1. distinguishes between facts and opinions;
2. distinguishes between facts and inferences;
3. identifies cause–effect relationships;
4. identifies errors in reasoning;
5. distinguishes between relevant and irrelevant arguments;
6. distinguishes between warranted and unwarranted generalizations;
7. formulates valid conclusions from written material;
8. specifies assumptions needed to make conclusions true. (Gronlund, 1985, p. 14)

Other issues may need to be addressed. If, for example, a student is out of his chair at inappropriate times, the teacher's concern may be either the number of times he gets out or the length of time he stays out. The student who gets up only once, but stays up all morning, is doing something quite different from the student who hops in and out of his seat every few minutes. Different intervention strategies and data collection techniques are needed. For complex behaviors such as temper tantrums, during which many discrete behaviors may occur simultaneously, it may be helpful to list the behaviors in some order of priority. They might be listed, for example, in order from least to most interference to the child or to the environment. After referral information has been refined so that target behaviors can be clearly described, **educational goals** and eventually behavioral objectives can be written.

Educational Goals

Goals precede objectives.

Objectives should be derived from a set of educational goals that provide the framework for the academic year. These goals should evolve from an accumulation of evaluation information and should be correlated with curriculum planning. Goals define the anticipated academic and social development for which the school will take responsibility. During goal selection, educators estimate what proportion of the student's educational potential is to be developed within the next academic year. Thus, educational goals (long-term objectives) are statements of annual program intent, whereas behavior objectives (short-term or instructional objectives) are statements of actual instructional intent, usually for a 3- to 4-month period (quarterly) for individuals with more severe disabilities and for the length of time of the school's grading period for students with mild disabilities.

Establishing Goals

A multidisciplinary team, including the student's parents or guardian and often the student herself, is responsible for setting goals for students who need special services and have been formally referred. When gathering data on which to base a student's educational program, the team will review the results of various evaluations. These evaluations include information that has been gathered by educational specialists and related service professionals to determine the student's current level of functioning. These data may include reports from:

Formal sources of information for goal setting.

1. *School psychology:* scores, for example, on the Wechsler Intelligence Scale for Children - IV (Wechsler, 2003), Bayley Scales of Infant Development - II (Bayley, 1993), or the Childhood Autism Rating Scale (Schopler, Reichler, & Renner, 1986).
2. *Education:* scores from the Wide Range Achievement Test - Revision 3 (Wilkinson, 1993), Key Math Diagnostic Arithmetic Test, Revised-NU (Connolly, 1998), Woodcock Reading Mastery Tests, Revised (Woodcock, 1998), Brigance Diagnostic Inventory of Basic Skills, Revised (Brigance, 1999).
3. *Adaptive behavior:* AAMR (American Association on Mental Retardation) Adaptive Behavior Scale-School Edition, 2nd Ed. (Lambert, Nihira, & Leland, 1993), or the Vineland Adaptive Behavior Scale-Classroom Edition (Sparrow, Balla, & Ciccetti, 1998).
4. *Therapeutic services:* results of physical therapy, occupational therapy, speech-language pathology evaluations.
5. *Physical health:* neurological, pediatric, vision, hearing screenings.

Informal sources of information for goal setting.

In addition to these more formal sources, the goal-setting group should also consider parental desires and concerns. Recommendations from previous teachers are considered as well. The social and academic environmental demands of the present classroom, the home, the projected educational placement, or a projected work site should be examined. Based on this accumulated information, the committee proposes a set of educational goals for the student. An estimate of progress is then included in the long-term objectives prepared for the student's IEP.

For students who have not been identified as having special needs, formulating educational goals does not involve such an extensive accumulation of information. Assessment may be limited to group achievement tests supplemented by informal teacher-made assessments. Goal setting also is constrained by the adopted curriculum. For example, each class of fourth graders in a given school district is usually expected to learn the same things. Under a standard curriculum, all students at a certain grade level are to be instructed in the natural resources of Peru, the excretory system of the earthworm, multiplication of fractions, and reading comprehension. The teacher's task is to translate these goals into reasonable objectives for each member of a particular class, some of whom may already know these things and some of whom lack the basic skills necessary to learn them. The teacher may write behavioral objectives for the class as a whole, giving consideration to the general characteristics of the group. In addition, if the teacher is to help a particular student who is having problems or to teach a reading group that is progressing slowly, that teacher may write additional behavioral objectives to prescribe a course of instruction that will facilitate learning.

Educational goals for individual students must be developed on the basis of evaluation data but should also consider other factors:

1. the student's past and projected rate of development compared with long-range plans for the future
2. the student's presenting physical and communicative capabilities
3. inappropriate behaviors that must be brought under control because they interfere with learning
4. skills the student lacks for appropriate functioning in the home, school, and social environments
5. the amount of instructional time available to the student within the school day and within the total school experience
6. prerequisites necessary for acquiring new skills
7. the functional utility of the skills (what additional skills may be built on these?)
8. the availability of specialized materials, equipment, or resource personnel (such as a speech and language pathologist or occupational therapist)

Write goals in observable and quantifiable terms.

Because educational goals are projected over long periods of time, they are written in broad terms. For practical application, however, they need to be written in terms that are observable and quantifiable. As you learned in Chapter 1, applied behavior analysts deal only with observable behaviors.

For students who are not disabled or who have mild disabilities, goals are needed only for each curriculum area. For very young students or those with severe disabilities, goals should be written in a number of domains of learning:

1. cognitive
2. communication
3. motor
4. social

5. self-help
6. vocational
7. maladaptive behavior

Hypothetical long-term goals for Jason, a student with learning problems in math, and for Tanika, a student with severe disabilities, are listed below.

Long-term educational goals for a student with mild disabilities.

Jason will

Arithmetic: Master basic computation facts at the first-grade level.

Social studies: Demonstrate knowledge of the functions of the three branches of the federal government.

Reading: Be able to identify relevant parts of a story he has read.

Science: Demonstrate knowledge of the structure of the solar system.

Language arts: Increase the creative expression of his oral language.

Physical education: Increase his skills in team sports.

Jason's general education teacher will be responsible for setting all goals except the one in arithmetic. Jason will probably go to a part-time special education class (resource room) for arithmetic. Compare Jason's goals with Tanika's.

Long-term educational goals for a student with severe disabilities.

Tanika will

Cognitive: Categorize objects according to their function.

Communication: Demonstrate increased receptive understanding of functional labels.

Motor: Develop gross motor capability of her upper extremities.

Social: Learn to participate appropriately in group activities.

Vocational: Complete assembly tasks for a period of at least 1 hour.

Maladaptive behavior: Decrease out-of-seat behavior.

Self-help: Demonstrate the ability to dress independently.

Teachers convert these broad goals into statements of instructional intent (behavioral objectives).

Behavioral objectives are not simply restatements of goals; they break goals into teachable components. Complex goals may generate many objectives. A goal that states a student will learn to play cooperatively with other children, for example, may require individual objectives identifying the need to share, to take turns, and to follow the rules of a game.

Components of a Behavioral Objective

In order to communicate all the necessary information and provide a basis for evaluation, a complete behavioral objective should

1. identify the learner.
2. identify the target behavior.
3. identify the conditions of intervention.
4. identify criteria for acceptable performance.

Identify the Learner

Use the student's name.

Behavioral objectives were initially designed to promote individualization of instruction (Gagne, 1985). To promote individualization, the teacher must reidentify the specific student or students for whom each objective is developed. Restatement reinforces the teacher's focus on the individual learner and communicates this focus to others. Thus, we include in a behavioral objective statements such as

- John will . . .
- The fourth graders will . . .
- The participants in the training program will . . .
- The members of the Rappers cooperative learning team will . . .

Identify the Target Behavior

State what the student will do.

After the team selects and defines deficient or excessive target behaviors, the teacher identifies exactly what the student will be doing when the desired change has been achieved. This statement spells out a precise response that is representative of the target behavior.

There are three basic purposes for including this component in the behavioral objective:

1. It ensures that the teacher is consistently observing the same behavior. The observation and recording of the occurrence or nonoccurrence of exactly the same behavior allows for an accurate and consistent reflection of the behavior in the data to be collected.
2. The statement of the target behavior allows for confirmation by a third party that the change observed by the teacher has actually occurred.
3. The precise definition of the target behavior facilitates continuity of instruction when people other than the teacher are involved.

To achieve these three purposes, the target behavior must be described so that its occurrence is verifiable. Precise description minimizes differing interpretations of the same behavior. A student's performance of a given behavior can best be verified when the teacher can see or hear the behavior or see or hear a direct product of the behavior. To attain this precision and clarity in an objective, the verb used to delineate the behavioral response should describe a behavior that is directly *observable, measurable,* and *repeatable.*

Though teachers of the gifted would like students to "discover" and art teachers would like students to "appreciate," objectives described in this manner are open to numerous interpretations. For example, it would be difficult for a third party to decide whether a student had performed the following behaviors:

- *recognize* the difference between big and little
- *understand* the value of coins
- *develop* an appreciation of Melville
- *remain* on task during group work
- *refrain* from aggression

The use of such vague terms leads to confusion and to disagreement about whether a behavior is occurring. Because any behavior can be described in a number of ways, everyone involved in a behavior-change project must agree upon a common description of the behavior. This description is the **operational definition** of the behavior. It

TABLE 2–1
Operational definitions of on-task behavior.

Umbreit, Lane, & Dejud (2004)	Looking at the materials or teacher as requested, writing numbers or words related to the assigned task, and complying with instruction.
Wood, Murdock, Cronin, Dawson, & Kirby (1998)	(1) Being in one's seat unless addressing the class or otherwise appropriately out of seat; (2) using materials appropriately (e.g., pen or pencil, books, paper); (3) working on the assigned task; (4) following teacher directions or asking the teacher questions about the task; and (5) accepting teacher feedback appropriately (e.g., did not yell, throw objects, curse, slam books or doors, kept hands and feet to self).
Firman, Beare, & Lloyd (2002)	Writing relevant to the lesson; reading/making eye contact with assigned material during the appropriate time; raising a hand to get the teacher's attention; talking to the teacher; following the teacher's commands; walking to the pencil sharpener or areas where materials are located and immediately returning to seat; or making the self-monitoring form.
Callahan & Rademacher (1999)	Attending appropriately to the instructional task scored when Seth was observed looking at the teacher or relevant task materials (e.g., textbook worksheet, paper) and/or participating as required during instructional time. The definition was summarized on a piece of paper for Seth. The paper included an age-appropriate graphic and the words "ON TASK MEANS: (1) I'm in my seat, (2) I'm working quietly, and (3) I'm looking at the teacher or my materials."
Boyle & Hughes (1994)	Manual, purposeful involvement with the task, with delays of no longer than 3 seconds between task steps.
Brooks, Todd, Tofflemoyer, & Horner (2003)	For individual seat work: "keeping eyes on work, keeping pencil in hand, and working on the assignment quietly." During group instruction: "keeping eyes on speaker, keeping hands free of materials, and following group directions."

is the definition under which everyone will operate when discussing, observing, counting, reporting, or consulting about this student's performance of this behavior. As much ambiguity as possible is eliminated. The operational definition contains an agreed-upon description of observable and measurable characteristics of the motor performance of the behavior. These characteristics are clearly stated so that everyone can agree that it has been or has not been performed.

A variety of approaches can be taken to operationally define a behavior. Examples of several ways to define on-task behavior are presented in Table 2–1. An operational definition may contain a list of specific behaviors considered to represent the broader behavior in question. Umbreit, Lane, & Dejud (2004) used a short list of representative behaviors. Wood, Murdock, Cronin, Dawson & Kirby (1998) and Firman, Beare, & Loyd (2002) used more extensive lists. Within their definition, Wood et al. further defined a behavior with negative examples. Callahan and Rademacher (1999) prepared a list for the observer and a list specifically for the student. In some cases, an element of time is included. Boyle and Hughes (1994), for example, imply a rate of behavior. For Brooks, Todd, Tofflemoyer, & Horner (2003) on-task behavior was a concern during individual seatwork and during group instruction. Therefore, an operational definition was written for both instructional formats. Operational definitions with multiple indicators may make it harder to count accurately the number of times a behavior occurs, making it difficult to know when the student has reached the criterion. One way to avoid this potential problem is to operationally define the outcome of a complex behavior. To measure on-task behavior, for example, the objective may indicate the number of math problems to be completed within a time limit. The student can accomplish this outcome only by remaining on task. (This difficulty is discussed further in Chapter 3.)

Aggression is an example of a general description of behavior that may be operationally defined both functionally—in terms of its consequences or outcomes—or topographically—in terms of the movements comprising the behavior (Barlow & Hersen, 1984). The authors define aggression functionally as "an act whose goal response is injury to an organism." Finkel, Derby, Weber, & McLaughlin (2003) used this approach by defining aggressive behavior as "any aberrant behavior that involved making physical contact with others in an attempt to injure." (p. 113). Aggression has been defined topographically as hitting, kicking, or biting the teacher (Lerman, Iwata, Shore, & Kahng, 1996); hitting, pushing, kicking, scratching, or hair pulling (Vollmer, Borrero, Lalli, & Daniel, 1999); hair pulling (grasping or pulling hair with fingers) or forceful hitting, kicking, or pinching others (Marcus & Vollmer, 1996); or forceful hitting or throwing objects at others (Lalli, Casey, & Kates, 1995). Providing specific examples of the target behavior increases clarity.

The need for an operational definition is reduced when more precise verbs are used in the objective. Increased precision also promotes more accurate recording of data. A precise behavioral description such as "will sort" rather than "will discriminate," "will circle" rather than "will identify," or "will state orally" rather than "will know" is less likely to be interpreted differently by different observers and reduces the need for repeated verbal or written clarification. Here are some more examples of precise behavioral descriptions:

- will point to the largest item in an array
- will verbally count the equivalent in dimes
- will write a translation of the prologue to *The Canterbury Tales*
- will look at his book or the speaker

One guide for selecting appropriate verbs has been offered by Deno and Jenkins (1967). Their classification of verbs is based on agreement of occurrence between independent classroom observers. They arrived at the three sets of verbs shown in Table 2–2, categorized as *directly observable action verbs, ambiguous action verbs,* and *not directly observable action verbs.*

In order to evaluate a description of a target behavior, Morris (1976) suggests using his IBSO (Is the Behavior Specific and Objective?) Test questions:

1. Can you count the number of times the behavior occurs in, for example, a 15-minute period, a 1-hour period, or 1 day? Or, can you count the number of minutes it takes for the child to perform the behavior? That is, can you tell someone the behavior occurred X number of times or X number of minutes today? (Your answer should be yes.)

2. Will a stranger know exactly what to look for when you tell him/her the target behavior you are planning to modify? That is, can you actually see the child performing the behavior when it occurs? (Your answer should be yes.)

TABLE 2–2
Observability classification of verbs.

Action Verbs That Are Directly Observable		
to cover with a card	to draw	to place
to mark	to lever press	to cross out
to underline	to point to	to circle
to repeat orally	to walk	to say
to write	to count orally	to read orally
to shade	to put on	to name
to fill in	to number	to state
to remove	to label	to tell what
Ambiguous Action Verbs		
to identify in writing	to check	to construct
to match	to take away	to make
to arrange	to finish	to read
to play	to locate	to connect
to give	to reject	to select
to choose	to subtract	to change
to use	to divide	to perform
to total	to add	to order
to measure	to regroup	to supply
to demonstrate	to group	to multiply
to round off	to average	to complete
to inquire	to utilize	to summarize
to acknowledge	to find	to borrow
to see	to convert	to identify
Action Verbs That Are Not Directly Observable		
to distinguish	to be curious	to solve
to conclude	to apply	to deduce
to develop	to feel	to test
to concentrate	to determine	to perceive
to generate	to think	to create
to think critically	to discriminate	to learn
to recognize	to appreciate	to discover
to be aware	to become competent	to know
to infer	to wonder	to like
to realize fully	to analyze	to understand

Note: From "Evaluating preplanned curriculum objectives" by S. Deno and J. Jenkins (Philadelphia: Research for Better Schools, 1967.) Reprinted by permission.

3. Can you break down the target behavior into smaller components, each of which is more specific and observable than the original target behavior? (Your answer should be no.) (p. 19)

Identify the Conditions of Intervention

Conditions are antecedent stimuli related to the target behavior.

The third component of a behavioral objective is the statement of conditions. The statement of conditions lists antecedent stimuli, including instructions, materials, and setting.

It may also include the types of assistance available to the students. These elements may be part of the natural environment in which the behavior is to be performed or they may be provided by the teacher as part of a specific learning task. The statement of conditions helps assure that all aspects of the learning experience will be consistently reproduced.

The teacher may set the occasion for an appropriate response using any or all of several categories of antecedent stimuli:

1. Verbal requests or instructions:
   Sam, point to the little car.
   Debbie, add these numbers.
   Jody, go back to your desk.
2. Written instructions or format:
   Diagram these sentences.
   Find the products.
   Draw a line from each word to its definition.
3. Demonstration:
   This is how you use litmus paper.
   This is how to operate . . .
4. Materials to be used:
   A worksheet with 20 single-digit addition problems
   A tape recorder with the "play" button colored green and the "stop" button colored red
5. Environmental setting or timing:
   In the vocational workshop
   In the cafeteria
   On the playground
   During independent study period
   During transition between classes
6. Manner of assistance:
   Independently
   With the aid of a number line
   With partial physical assistance from the teacher
   Receiving only verbal prompts

Providing appropriate antecedent stimuli will be discussed in Chapter 9.

The teacher must be sure that the verbal or visual cue planned does in fact provide an opportunity for the desired response by the student. That is, a teacher should deliver an unambiguous request or instruction to the student. The teacher who holds a flash card with the word get and says, "Give me a sentence for get," is likely to hear, "I for get my milk money" or "I for get my homework."

The materials described in the objective should ensure stimulus consistency for the learner and reduce the chance for inadvertent, subtle changes in the learning performance being requested. For example, presenting a red, a blue, and a green sock and asking the student to "point to red" is a less complex task than presenting a red car, a blue sock, and a green cup and making the same request. Giving the student a page with written instructions to fill in the blanks in sentences is less complex when a list of words that includes the answers is provided. Asking the student to write a story based on a stimulus picture is different from asking the student to write a story without visual stimulus.

The following are examples of condition statement formats:

- Given an array of materials containing . . .
- Given a textbook containing 25 division problems with single-digit divisors . . .

- Given the manual sign for toilet . . .
- Given the use of a thesaurus and written instructions . . .
- Given a pullover sweater with the label cued red and the verbal cue . . .
- Given a ditto sheet with 20 problems containing improper fractions having unlike denominators and the written instruction to "Find the products" . . .
- Without the aid of . . .

Careful statement of the conditions under which the behavior is to be performed may prevent problems like the one encountered by Ms. Samuels in the vignette that follows.

Ms. Samuels Teaches Long Division

Ms. Samuels was once again in trouble with a general education teacher. She and Mr. Watson, the sixth-grade math teacher, had agreed she would work on long division with Harvey. Ms. Samuels had carefully checked to be sure the method she taught Harvey to use in the resource room was the same as Mr. Watson's. She made dozens of practice worksheets, and Harvey worked long-division problems until he could do them in his sleep.

Ms. Samuels was predictably horrified then when Mr. Watson asked her if she ever planned to start working on division with Harvey. Investigation revealed that in the general education classroom, Harvey was expected to copy the problems from the math book to notebook paper; he made so many copying errors, he seldom got the correct answer. The conditions under which the task was to be performed were thus significantly different.

As part of a plan of instruction for students with learning problems, teachers may need to include extra support in the form of supplementary cues, such as a model of a completed long-division problem for the student to keep at his desk. It is important to include a description of such supplementary cues in the condition component of the behavioral objective to avoid misunderstandings. When the cue is no longer needed, the objective may be rewritten.

Identify Criteria for Acceptable Performance

Criterion statements set minimum performance standards.

In the criterion statement included in a behavioral objective, the teacher sets the standard for minimally acceptable performance. This statement indicates the level of performance the student will be able to achieve as a result of the intervention. The performance itself has been defined; the criterion sets the standard for evaluation. Throughout the intervention process, this criterion is used to measure the effectiveness of the intervention strategy selected to meet the behavioral objective.

The basic criterion statement for initial learning or **acquisition** indicates the *accuracy* of a response or the response's *frequency of occurrence.* Such statements are written in terms of the number of correct responses, the student's accuracy on trial presentations, the percentage of accurate responses, or some performance within an error of limitation. Here are some sample criterion statements:

17 out of 20 correct responses

label all 10 objects correctly

with 80% accuracy

on 80% of opportunities

20 problems must be answered correctly (100% accuracy)

4 out of 5 trials correct

on 5 consecutive trials

complete all steps in the toilet-training program independently list all four of the main characters in a book report of no less than 250 words

with no more than 5 errors in spelling

on each occasion

See Chapter 3 for an extended discussion of duration and latency.

Two additional types of criteria may be included when time is a critical dimension of the behavior. *Duration* is a statement of the length of time the student performs the behavior. *Latency* is a statement of the length of time that elapses before the student begins performing the behavior.

- Criterion statements addressing duration:

will complete within 1 hour

for at least 20 minutes

for no more than 1/2 hour

will return within 10 minutes

within 2 weeks

- Statements addressing latency:

within 10 seconds after the flash card is presented

within 1 minute after a verbal request

Certain types of content require particular criterion levels. When a student is acquiring basic skills on which other skills will be built, a criterion of 80% may not be high enough. For example, learning "almost all" of the multiplication facts may result in a student's going through life never knowing what 8 × 7 is. There are other skills as well that require 100% accuracy. Remembering to look both ways before crossing the street only 90% of the time may result in premature termination of the opportunity for future learning!

For certain students, a disability may influence the force, direction, or duration of the criterion set by the teacher. For example, a student may not be able to hammer a nail all the way into a piece of wood; range-of-motion limitations may influence motor capability for reaching; hypotonic muscles (those with less-than-normal tone) may limit the duration of walking or sitting; or a muscular condition may limit the perfection of cursive handwriting.

Writing criterion statements in terms of percentage requires care. How many problems, for example, would a student have to solve correctly to satisfy a 90% criterion on a 5-item math quiz?

When setting criteria for acceptable performance, teachers must be careful to set goals that are sufficiently ambitious, yet reasonable. Selection should be based on the nature of the content, the abilities of the students, and the learning opportunities to be provided. Criteria should provide for the development of a functional skill. There is no sense in teaching a student to play a game only so well that he gets beaten every time he plays or in teaching a student to do math problems only well enough to earn a high F in the general education classroom. There is evidence (Fuchs, Fuchs, & Deno, 1988) that setting ambitious goals results in more learning, but teachers should not set unobtainable goals that will result in frustration for students.

In addition to considering the number or percentage correct and the accuracy of response, writers of behavioral objectives must also determine the number of times a student must meet a criterion to demonstrate mastery. For example, how often must Jane perform a behavior successfully on 8 out of 10 trials before the teacher will be convinced of mastery and allow her to move on to the next level of learning or to the next behavioral objective?

It may be inferred from an open-ended criterion statement that the first time a student reaches 85% accuracy, the skill will be considered "learned" or that from now until the end of the school year, the teacher will continually test and retest to substantiate the 85% accuracy. Either inference could be false. Therefore, a statement such as one of the following should be included in the behavioral objective to provide a point of closure and terminal review:

85% accuracy *for 4 consecutive sessions*

85% accuracy *for 3 out of 4 days*

on 8 out of 10 trials *for 3 consecutive teaching sessions*

will return within 10 minutes on *3 consecutive trips to the bathroom*

FORMAT FOR A BEHAVIORAL OBJECTIVE

A management aid for the teacher in writing behavioral objectives is the adoption of a standard format. A consistent format helps the teacher include all the components necessary for communicating all intended information. No single format is necessarily superior to others; teachers should simply find one that is compatible with his or her writing style or with administrative policy. Here are two such formats.

Format 1

Conditions: Given 20 flash cards with preprimer sight words and the instruction "Read these words."

Student: Sam

Behavior: will read the words orally

Criterion: within 2 seconds for each word with 90% accuracy on 3 consecutive trials.

To increase your skills in writing objectives, go to the "Activities" module for Chapter 2 of the Companion Website.

Format 2

Student: Marvin

Behavior: will write in cursive handwriting 20 fourth-grade spelling words

Conditions: from dictation by the resource teacher

Criterion: with no more than 2 errors for 3 consecutive weeks.

The following behavioral objectives may be derived from the educational goals previously set for students Jason and Tanika.

Arithmetic

Goal: Jason will master basic computation facts at the first-grade level.

Objective: Given a worksheet of 20 single-digit addition problems in the form 6 + 2 and the written instruction "Find the sums," Jason will complete all problems with 90% accuracy for 3 consecutive math sessions.

Social Studies

Goal: Jason will demonstrate knowledge of the functions of the 3 branches of the federal government.

Objective: After reading pages 23–26 in the text *Our American Heritage,* Jason will list the 10-step sequential process by which a bill becomes a law. This list will have no more than one error of sequence and one error of omission. This will be successfully accomplished on an in-class exercise and on the unit-end test.

Reading

Goal: Jason will be able to identify relevant parts of a story he has read.

Objective: Given the short story "The Necklace," Jason will write a minimum 200-word paper that (1) lists all the main characters and (2) lists the sequence of main actions, with no more than 2 errors.

Science

Goal: Jason will demonstrate knowledge of the structure of the solar system.

Objective: Given a map of the solar system, Jason will label each planet in its proper position from the sun with 100% accuracy on 2 consecutive sessions.

Language Arts

Goal: Jason will increase the creative expression of his oral language.

Objective: Given an array of photos of people, objects, and locations, Jason will tell a 5-minute story to the class that makes use of a minimum of 7 items, on 3 out of 5 days.

Physical Education

Goal: Jason will increase his skills in team sports.

Objective: Given a basketball, Jason will throw the ball into the hoop from a distance of 10 feet, 8 out of 10 trials for 4 consecutive gym classes.

Recall from our earlier discussion that although Jason has mild learning problems, Tanika has much more severe disabilities. Here are some objectives and corresponding goals for Tanika.

Cognitive

Goal: Tanika will be able to categorize objects according to their function.

Objective: Given 12 Peabody cards (4 foods, 4 clothing, 4 grooming aids), a sample stimulus card of each category, and the verbal cue "Where does this one go?", Tanika will place the cards on the appropriate category pile with 100% accuracy, for 17 out of 20 trials.

Communication

Goal: Tanika will demonstrate increased receptive understanding of functional labels.

Objective: Given an array of 3 objects found in her snack-time environment (cup, spoon, fork) and the verbal cue "Pick up the . . . ," Tanika will hand the teacher the named object 9 out of 10 times for four consecutive snack times.

For more information on writing behavioral objectives, go to the "Web Links" module for Chapter 2 of the Companion Website.

Motor

Goal: Tanika will develop gross motor capability of her upper extremities.

Objective: Given a soft rubber ball suspended from the ceiling and the verbal cue "Hit the ball," Tanika will hit the ball causing movement 10 out of 10 times for 5 consecutive days.

Social

Goal: Tanika will learn to participate appropriately in group activities.

Objective: When sitting with the teacher and two other students during story time, Tanika will make an appropriate motor or verbal response to each of the teacher's questions when called upon a minimum of 3 times in a 10-minute period for 5 consecutive days.

Self-Help

Goal: Tanika will demonstrate the ability to dress herself independently.

Objective: Given a pullover sweater with the back label color-cued red and the verbal cue "Put on your sweater," Tanika will successfully complete all steps of the task without physical assistance 2 out of 3 trials for 4 consecutive days.

Vocational

Goal: Tanika will complete assembly tasks for a period of at least 1 hour.

Objective: Given the four parts of a plumbing "U" in sequential order, Tanika will assemble at a rate of one per 3 minutes without error during 3 vocational periods for 4 weeks.

Maladaptive Behavior

Goal: Tanika will decrease out-of-seat behavior.

Objective: In the period from 9:00 to 9:20 a.m. (functional academics), Tanika will remain in her seat, unless given permission by the teacher to leave, for 5 consecutive days.

Professor Grundy's Class Writes Behavioral Objectives

It was the time of the semester for Professor Grundy's 8 o'clock class to learn about behavioral objectives. After presenting a carefully planned lecture (remarkably similar to the first part of this chapter), Grundy asked if there were any questions. Dawn Tompkins stopped filing her nails long enough to ask, with a deep sigh, "Yes, Professor, would you please tell me what a behavioral objective is, exactly?"

"I was under the impression, young lady, that I had done just that," replied Grundy. "Is anyone else confused?"

A chorus of muttering and rumbling ensued from which Grundy was able to extract clearly only two questions: "Is this covered in the book?" and "Will it be on the test?"

After once more presenting a drastically abbreviated description of the components of a behavioral objective, Grundy announced that each member of the class was to write a behavioral objective for the curriculum area of science and present it to him for checking before leaving class. This announcement, followed by a chorus of groans and considerable paper shuffling, also brought forth a flurry of hands:

"You mean list the components?"

"No," said Grundy. "Write an objective."

"You mean define a behavioral objective?"

"No," said Grundy. "Write one."

"But you never said anything about writing them."

"What," Grundy retorted, "did you think was the purpose of the lecture?"

After everyone who lacked these tools had been provided with paper and pencil, silence descended upon the class. DeWayne was the first one finished and proudly presented his objective to the professor:

To understand the importance of the digestive system.

"Well, DeWayne," said the professor, "that's a start, but do you not remember that a behavioral objective must talk about behavior? Remember the list of verbs I gave you . . ." When DeWayne continued to look blank, Grundy rifled through his briefcase and found a copy (see Table 2–2).

"Look here," the professor said, "use one of these directly observable verbs."

DeWayne returned some time later with his rewritten objective:

To label the parts of the digestive system.

"Good, DeWayne," sighed the professor, "that's a behavior, all right. Now, do you recall the components of a behavioral objective?" Once again, DeWayne looked blank. Grundy carefully wrote:

Conditions Student Behavior Criteria

across the long side of the automatic teller receipt DeWayne had evidently found in his wallet. (Grundy was not surprised to note that the receipt indicated a negative balance.) DeWayne returned to his desk.

An hour and a half later, as Grundy was regretting ever having made this assignment, DeWayne returned again:

Given an unlabeled diagram of the human digestive system, fourth-grade students will label the major parts of the digestive system (mouth, esophagus, stomach, small intestine, large intestine) with no errors.

Grundy read DeWayne's objective with interest, because his own digestive system was beginning to be the major focus of his attention. "Excellent, DeWayne," said the professor. "I suppose it's too late to get lunch in the cafeteria. Why didn't you do this in the first place?"

"Well, Professor," answered DeWayne, "I didn't really understand what you wanted. I'm still not sure I could do another one."

After getting some crackers from a vending machine, Grundy returned meditatively to his office. He found a piece of paper and began to write as he munched:

Given a worksheet listing appropriate verbs and the components of a behavioral objective, students enrolled in Education 411 will write five behavioral objectives including all components.

After musing for a few minutes, he added:

. . . in less than half an hour.

"Perhaps," Grundy muttered to himself, "if I had been sure what I wanted and told the students at the front end, they would have had less trouble figuring it out."

Expanding the Scope of the Basic Behavioral Objective

Once a student or group of students has acquired the behavior described in an objective, teachers may simply note that the objective has been mastered and move on to the next one in the sequence. This may be inappropriate unless the student can perform the behavior in circumstances different from the initial teaching environment. In order for the students to have functional behaviors, those that can be performed under different conditions, to different criteria, or in the absence of reinforcement contingencies, provision must be made to expand students' ability to use the behavior. Two possible perspectives on expanded use are

1. programming according to a hierarchy of response competence.
2. programming according to a hierarchy of levels of learning.

Hierarchy of Response Competence

A measure of response accuracy (8 out of 10 correct, for example) is only one dimension for evaluating performance. It represents the acquisition level of response competence. At this level, we merely verify the presence of the ability to do something the student was not previously able to do and the ability to do it with some degree of accuracy. Moving to measures of competence in performance beyond accuracy, beyond this acquisition level, requires alterations or additions to the statements of criteria and conditions. Such alterations reflect a hierarchy of response competence. Once a child can perform the behavior, we are then concerned with fluency, or rate, of performance, as well as performance under conditions other than those imposed during the initial teaching process.

A response hierarchy should contain the minimum levels of acquisition, fluency, maintenance, and generalization.

As an example of the use of this hierarchy, let us assume John has reached the acquisition level on the following objective:

> ***Given two quarters, two dimes, two nickels, and one penny and the verbal cue "John, give me your bus fare," he will hand the teacher coins equaling 75 cents 8 out of 10 trials for three consecutive sessions.***

To enhance your skills in writing objectives, go to the "Activities" module for Chapter 2 of the Companion Website.

Lauren has reached acquisition on this objective:

> ***Given a worksheet with 20 division problems with two-digit dividends and single-digit divisors, Lauren will write the correct answer in the appropriate place on the radical with 90% accuracy for 4 consecutive days.***

After John and Lauren have met these stated criteria for their performances, the teaching concern should turn to their **fluency** of performance, or the rate at which they perform the behavior. Fluency refers to the appropriateness of the rate at which the student is accurately performing this newly acquired response. In John's case, we know that he can select the appropriate coins to make 75 cents, but this does him little good if when we take him to the bus, it takes him 5 minutes to do it. The bus driver cannot wait this long. In Lauren's case, we know she can now solve division problems, but it takes her so long that either we interrupt her when her reading group is scheduled or she misses part of her reading lesson so she can finish her problems.

In both instances, the students are demonstrating accurate performance at an inappropriate rate. Recognizing the necessity for an appropriate rate of performance, a teacher can indicate an acceptable fluency when the behavioral objective is written. This is accomplished by adding a time limit to the statement of criteria, as found in parentheses in the following objectives:

> ***Given two quarters, two dimes, two nickels, and one penny and the verbal cue "John, give me your bus fare," he will hand the teacher coins equaling 75 cents (within 30 seconds) 8 out of 10 trials for three consecutive sessions.***

> ***Given a worksheet with 20 division problems with two-digit dividends and single-digit divisors, Lauren will write the correct answer in the appropriate place on the radical (within 20 minutes) with 90% accuracy for 4 consecutive days.***

For typical learners and those with mild disabilities, the rate is often included in the initial objective, thus combining acquisition and fluency in a single instructional procedure. Instructional attention is given to fluency because when a student's performance becomes fluent, the behavior is retained longer, persists during long periods on the task, is less affected by distractions, and is more likely to be available in new learning situations (Pierce & Cheney, 2004).

It is not necessary to adjust the original behavioral objective to include the level of competence labeled **maintenance.** Maintenance is the ability to perform a response over time without reteaching. Maintenance-level competence is confirmed by using postchecks or probes, during which the teacher rechecks the skill to be sure the student can still do it. Maintenance may be promoted through building in the opportunity for overlearning trials and distributed practice. *Overlearning* refers to repeated practice after an objective has been initially accomplished. An optimum number of overlearning opportunities is approximately 50% of the number of trials required for acquisition of the behavior. If it takes John 10 teaching sessions to learn to tie his shoes, we should ideally provide 5 additional sessions for overlearning. *Distributed practice* is practice that is spread out over time (as opposed to *massed practice,* which is compressed in time). An example of massed practice familiar to college students is cramming for an exam. The material may be learned between 10 p.m. and 6 a.m. the night before the test, but most of it will be rapidly forgotten. If maintenance is desired, the preferable approach is studying for short periods every evening for several weeks before the exam, using distributed practice. Another means of providing for maintenance, alteration of schedules of reinforcement (Skinner, 1968), will be discussed in Chapter 7.

Programming for maintenance will be discussed in Chapter 10.

Distributed practice is a more efficient way of learning for long-term maintenance.

The level of response competence labeled **generalization** is of great importance in assuring that a behavior is functional. A student has a generalized response if she can perform—and adapt, if necessary—the behavior under conditions different from those in place during acquisition. A generalized response is one that also continues to occur after instruction has been terminated. A response may be generalized across at least four basic dimensions. The condition statement may be written to reflect the student's ability to perform the behavior in response to various verbal or written instructions, with various materials, for or with various persons, and in various environments (settings). The following examples illustrate this point.

Various Instructions

Given an array of coins and the verbal instruction, "Give me bus fare" ("Give me 75 cents," "Give me what you need for the bus") . . .

Given a worksheet with 30 one-digit subtraction problems and the verbal (or written) instruction, "Find the difference" ("Solve these problems," "Write the answers to these problems") . . .

Various Materials

Will write his name, address, phone number, and birth date in the appropriate blanks on at least three different job application forms . . .

Will demonstrate the multiplicative principle of math using counting chips (a number line, paper and pencil) . . .

Various Persons

Will use the sign for "toilet" as a signal of need to her teacher (parent) . . .

Will comply with instructions from his math (English, social studies, science) teacher (mother, father, coach, piano teacher) . . .

Various Settings

Will pull up his pants after toileting in the restroom in the special education class (in the restroom near the class he joins for art) . . .

Will remain in his seat and complete assignments in math (English, social studies, science) class . . .

Hierarchy of Levels of Learning

For more information on this topic, go to the "Web Links" module for Chapter 2 of the Companion Website.

It may seem that writing behavioral objectives inevitably focuses teacher attention on concrete, simple forms of learning. Indeed, this has been one of the most frequent criticisms of a behavioral approach. It is not necessary, however, to confine behavioral objectives to lower levels of learning. Bloom (1956) has proposed hierarchies of learning in cognitive, affective, and psychomotor areas. These hierarchies classify possible learning outcomes in terms of increasingly abstract levels. They are helpful in writing objectives in behavioral terms because they suggest observable, measurable behaviors that may occur as the result of both simple and complex learning. The cognitive hierarchy, which will serve as our example, contains six levels of learning, as shown in the diagram (Bloom, 1956).

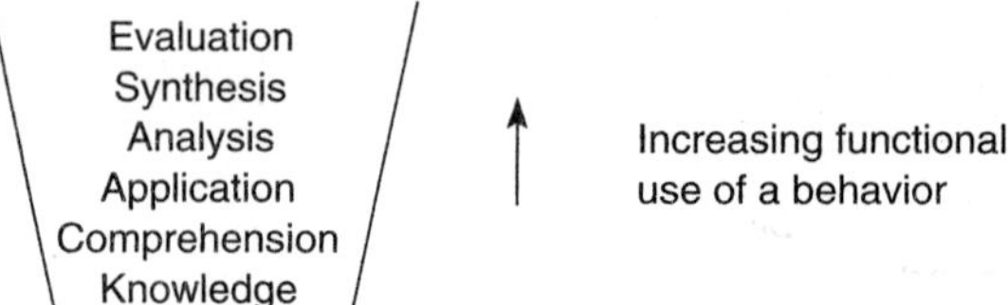

Many behavioral objectives are written in terms of the knowledge level of the hierarchy—we simply want students to demonstrate they know or remember something we have taught them. Once the student has achieved mastery on the lowest of the six levels, the teacher can shift programming toward higher levels of learning by preparing subsequent objectives that alter the target behavior and criterion statements. As an aid in this process, Gronlund (1985) prepared a table (Table 2–3) that illustrates behavioral terms appropriate to describe target behaviors at each level of learning.

Knowledge

Bloom (1956) defines learning at the *knowledge level* as the recall or recognition of information ranging from specific facts to complete theories. These memory functions are the only behavior to be demonstrated at this basic level of cognitive learning. The following acquisition objectives are examples written for students at this level:

> ***After reading*** **Biology for Your Understanding** ***and completing the exercise in Chapter 2, Virginia will list the biological categories of the Linnaean system in their order of evolutional complexity without error during two class sessions and on a unit-end exam.***
>
> ***Given the symbols for the arithmetic processes of addition, subtraction, multiplication, and division, Danny will respond with 90% accuracy on a multiple-choice test of their labels and basic functions.***
>
> ***Given a list of Shakespearean plays, Deborah will underline the names of the tragedies with no more than one error.***

Comprehension

Once the student has reached the performance criterion at the knowledge level, the teacher moves to the *comprehension level,* the understanding of meaning. The student may demonstrate comprehension by paraphrasing and providing examples.

Here are some sample objectives at this level:

> ***Given the Linnaean system of biological classification, Virginia will provide a written description of an organism in each category. The description will include at least one factor that distinguishes the category from others.***

TABLE 2–3
Examples of general instructional objectives and behavioral terms for the cognitive domain of the taxonomy.

Illustrative General Instructional Objectives	Illustrative Behavioral Terms for Stating Specific Learning Outcomes
Knows common terms Knows specific facts Knows methods and procedures Knows basic concepts Knows principles	Defines, describes, identifies, labels, lists, matches, names, outlines, reproduces, selects, states
Understands facts and principles Interprets verbal material Interprets charts and graphs Translates verbal material to mathematical formulas Estimates future consequences implied in data Justifies methods and procedures	Converts, defends, distinguishes, estimates, explains, extends, generalizes, gives examples, infers, paraphrases, predicts, rewrites, summarizes
Applies concepts and principles to new situations Applies laws and theories to practical situations Solves mathematical problems Constructs charts and graphs Demonstrates correct usage of a method or procedure	Changes, computes, demonstrates, discovers, manipulates, modifies, operates, predicts, prepares, produces, relates, shows, solves, uses
Recognizes unstated assumptions Recognizes logical fallacies in reasoning Distinguishes between facts and inferences	Breaks down, diagrams, differentiates, discriminates, distinguishes, identifies, illustrates, infers, outlines, points out, relates, selects, separates, subdivides
Evaluates the relevancy of data Analyzes the organizational structure of a work (art, music, writing)	
Writes a well-organized theme Gives a well-organized speech Writes a creative short story (or poem, or music) Proposes a plan for an experiment Integrates learning from different areas into a plan for solving a problem Formulates a new scheme for classifying objects (or events, or ideas)	Categories, combines, compiles, composes, creates, devises, designs, explains, generates, modifies, organizes, plans, rearranges, reconstructs, relates, reorganizes, revises, rewrites, summarizes, tells, writes
Judges the logical consistency of written material Judges the adequacy with which conclusions are supported by data Judges the value of a work (art, music, writing) by use of internal criteria Judges the value of a work (art, music, writing) by use of external standards of excellence	Appraises, compares, concludes, contrasts, criticizes, describes, discriminates, explains, justifies, interprets, relates, summarizes, supports

Note: Reprinted by permission of Prentice-Hall, Inc., Upper Saddle River, NJ, from *How to Write and Use Instructional Objectives,* 5/e by Norman E. Gronlund. Copyright © 1991.

Given a worksheet of 40 basic arithmetic examples requiring addition, subtraction, multiplication, and division, Danny will complete the sheet with 90% accuracy.

Given the metaphoric passage, "Oh that this too, too solid flesh would melt . . ." from Hamlet, *Deborah will write an essay describing the literal intent of the passage. The essay will be a minimum of 300 words.*

Application

Programming at Bloom's *application level* requires the student to use the method, concept, or theory in various concrete situations. Consider these objectives:

Given the names of five organisms and the Linnaean system, Virginia will place each in its proper category and write a list of rationales for placement. Each rationale will contain a minimum of two reasons for placement.

Given a set of 10 paragraphs that present problems requiring an arithmetic computation for solution, Danny will write the correct answer, showing all computations with 100% accuracy.

After reading Hamlet, *Deborah will be able to explain the parallels between Hamlet's ethical dilemma and the problem of abortion and to cite an additional current parallel example of her own choosing.*

Analysis

Analysis is the ability to break down material into its constituent parts in order to identify these parts, discuss their interrelationship, and understand their organization as a whole. The following objectives are analytically oriented:

Given a list of five organisms, Virginia will use appropriate references in the library to investigate and report to the class the role of the organisms in either the food chain or in the ecological stability of their habitat.

Given a written statement of the associative property, Danny will be able to explain accurately to the class, using examples at the chalkboard, the property's relation to the basic additive and multiplicative functions.

After having read Hamlet *or* Macbeth, *Deborah will guide the class in a discussion of the play's plot development. This discussion will be based upon a schematic representation of each scene that she will provide in written form.*

Synthesis

At the cognitive level of *synthesis,* the student should demonstrate the ability to bring parts together resulting in a different, original, or creative whole:

Given a list of reference texts, Virginia will write a 1,000-word summary explaining the biological classifications in Darwin's theory of evolution. The paper will be evaluated on the basis of accuracy, completeness, organization, and clarity.

Given the numerical systems of base 10 and base 2, Danny will orally demonstrate the use of the functions of addition, subtraction, multiplication, and division within each system.

Given the study of the Shakespearean tragedy Macbeth, *Deborah will rewrite the end of the play in iambic pentameter, assuming that the murder of the king was unsuccessful.*

Evaluation

The highest level of learning demonstrated in this hierarchy is *evaluation*. The student is asked to make a judgment of value:

Based on the principles of mutual exclusion, Virginia will devise a taxonomy for the classification of means of transportation and provide a justification for the categories created and their constituent parts.

Given a set of unknown values and a given arithmetic computational function, Danny will explain the probability of differing answers that may be correct.

Given plays by Shakespeare and Bacon, Deborah will state a preference for one and justify her preference in a 500-word essay based on some element(s) of style.

LEARNING LEVELS FOR THE LEARNER WITH LIMITATIONS

In most instances of planning for expanded instructional intent, we tend to focus on a hierarchy-of-response competence for learners with significant disabilities and a hierarchy of levels of learning for the typical or above-average learner. This dichotomy is not necessarily warranted simply by the level of the student's functioning. Consider the following examples of how we may write behavioral objectives for the limited learner in conjunction with levels of learning:

Knowledge:	Given a common coin and the verbal cue, "What is the name of this," George will state the appropriate label on 18 out of 20 trials for five consecutive sessions.
Comprehension:	Given a common coin and the verbal cue "What is this worth?" George will count out the coin's equivalent in pennies and state something to the effect that "A dime is worth 10 pennies" on 8 out of 10 trials for each coin.
Application:	When presented with 10 pictures of food items, each with its cost written on it, George will count out coins equal to the amount written upon the verbal cue "Show me the amount" on 18 out of 20 trials.
Analysis:	When presented with pictures of items, each with its cost printed on it, a $1 bill, and a verbal cue such as "Can you buy a pencil and a newspaper?" George will respond correctly on 18 out of 20 trials.
Synthesis:	Given a $1 bill and the instruction to buy various priced items, George will simulate the buying exchange and decide whether he was given correct change without error on 10 trials.
Evaluation:	Given a $1 bill and a 5-mile ride from the workplace to his home, George will use the $1 for the bus ride rather than a candy bar.

Even learners with limitations can acquire higher-level cognitive skills.

BEHAVIORAL OBJECTIVES AND THE IEP

IDEA requires an IEP for every student with a disability.

The development of educational goals (long-term objectives) and behavioral objectives (short-term objectives) for students in need of special education services was included as one of the mandates of the original Education for All Handicapped Children Act of 1975 (P.L. 94-142), and its current successor, the Individuals with Disabilities Education Act of 1997 (P.L. 105-17, IDEA). Among the results of this legislation have been the formalization of the planning aspects inherent in the writing of goals and objectives and the provision for active parental participation in the educational planning process. This planning process ultimately results in the development of an **Individualized Education Program (IEP).** The IEP has at its core the listing of the goals and objectives for the student's educational program for the year. In addition to this core element an IEP contains components or statements regarding transition planning and services, positive behavioral interventions and supports, participation in state and district assessments, extended school year services, participation in the general education

To enhance your understanding of IEPs, go to the "Web Links" module for Chapter 2 of the Companion Website.

curriculum (including necessary modifications), and interaction with students not identified as disabled. The federal rules and regulations include six elements as part of the core IEP:

1. a statement of the student's present levels of educational performance
2. a statement of annual goals, including short-term instructional objectives
3. appropriate objective criteria and evaluation procedures and schedules for determining, on at least an annual basis, whether the short-term instructional objectives are being achieved
4. a statement of the specific special education and related services to be provided to the student
5. projected dates for initiation of services and the anticipated duration of the services
6. the extent to which the student will be able to participate in general education programs, and any modifications or accommodations necessary to enable that participation

These elements demonstrate a parallel in procedural format between the development of behavioral objectives and the development of the IEP. Both processes include the accumulation of data to determine the student's current levels of performance, the statement of appropriate goals, the development of behavioral objectives (short-term) for attaining the goals, and a review of objective mastery. Neither a behavioral objective nor an IEP short-term objective contains a statement of the instructional methodology to be used for achieving the objective (Bateman & Linden, 1998; Mager, 1997).

On the sample form (see Figure 2–1), the components that describe the target behavior and the conditions under which it is to be performed are placed in the column labeled "Short-Term Instructional Objectives." The component that states the criteria for mastery is placed in the correspondingly labeled column.

The following behavioral objective has been transferred onto the sample form in Figure 2–1:

Given a worksheet of 20 single-digit addition problems in the form 6 + 2 and the written instruction, "Find the sums," Leon will complete all problems with 90% accuracy for three consecutive math sessions.

To manage an IEP and monitor its constituent objectives, teachers should observe the following recommendations:

1. Short-term objectives should be sequentially related to goal statements (long-term objectives).

Student: Leon

Short-Term Instructional Objectives	Person Responsible	Criteria for Mastery	Date Reviewed	Mastery Yes No
1. Complete 20 single-digit addition problems in the form 6 + 2, given written instructions to "find the sum"		90% accuracy for 3 consecutive math sessions		

FIGURE 2–1 ***Sample IEP.***

2. In the case of students with mild disabilities, the goals and short-term objectives should deal directly with the reason for their referral for special education services. "They need be written only for the special services necessary to meet the child's needs arising from the disability, not for the child's total program, unless all areas are so affected" (Bateman & Linden, 1998, p. 43).
3. For students with moderate, severe, and profound disabilities, two or three short-term objectives per curriculum domain should be included in the IEP because in most cases all areas of the student's educational performance are affected by the disability.
4. New short-term objectives should not be added until maintenance has been achieved on current objectives and generalization instruction has begun.
5. Management of the IEP should be a continuous process. Teachers and administrators should not overlook the regulations stating that a review should be conducted "on at least an annual basis," not "only on an annual basis."
   (a) The objectives for students with mild disabilities should be reviewed as soon as achievement has been verified to assess whether the original need for special education services still exists.
   (b) Reasonable review dates should be set for objectives of students with moderate and severe disabilities. As objectives are met, the teacher should add new short-term objectives and notify the committee members, including the parents, in writing, with full justification provided at the annual review. Such a procedure will foster the student's progress and prevent stagnation of instruction until the full committee can be gathered.
6. Review dates should be set considering the need for instruction at higher levels of learning to promote full functional use of a skill.

When Jason's math skills are at grade level, he no longer has a disability.

Tanika's objectives should be reviewed frequently so that she will make the maximum possible progress.

In addition to the basic core, two additional planning components are contained in the IEP. These are the Individual Transition Plan and the Behavioral Intervention Plan.

The Individual Transition Plan

The **Individual Transition Plan (ITP)** is that component of the IEP that attempts to link long-term planning for a student's postsecondary life with the annual school year planning of the core IEP. When a student reaches the age of 14, the IEP team must begin to determine what instructional and educational experiences will assist the student to prepare for transition from secondary education to postsecondary life. By the time a student reaches the age of 16, his IEP must also address necessary transition services to be provided by the school or some other agency. The ITP is written to address these issues.

To increase your understanding of ITPs, go to the "Web Links" module for Chapter 2 of the Companion Website.

The purpose of the ITP is to help the student, family members, educators, and adult service providers focus on the student's future after completing secondary school. Tentative decisions are made about the student's living arrangements, community involvement, employment, and postsecondary education. These decisions are examined annually to determine the need for revision in light of the student's skill mastery and evolving preferences. The IEP team must determine what, if any, instruction, related services, community experiences, employment, and other adult living objectives are necessary to meet the postsecondary goals. After transition outcomes are identified, more specific IEP goals and objectives are developed annually to ensure that students will be ready for the transition.

The relationship between transition outcome recommendations of the ITP and IEP goals and objectives can be illustrated as follows:

ITP Outcome Recommendation: Obtain a supported employment position in the food-services industry.

IEP Annual Goal: Lana will participate in three community-based vocational instruction sites during the 2000–2001 school year.

IEP Objectives:

1. Given a set of models, Lana will separate glasses, dishes, and silverware with at least 90% accuracy in three work sites on six occasions.
2. Lana will train in three food-service work sites on a task analysis of dishwashing, independently completing 100% of the task steps, at the indirect level of supervision, for a range of 6 to 8 hours a week, for no more than 215 hours.

Transition Outcome Recommendation: Live semi-independently in an apartment with a roommate with supervision provided by Peachtree Residential Supports, Inc.

IEP Annual Goal: Sally will learn to prepare simple meals in a variety of settings.

IEP Objectives:

1. Sally will independently operate a microwave oven to prepare a prepackaged meal at home, at school, and in the breakroom on the vocational training site, 2 days per week for 12 weeks.
2. Given a list (picture/word) of five breakfast items, Sally will locate and purchase at least four of the items in the local grocery once per week during September, November, and January.

Transition Outcome Recommendation: Enrollment in the Fannin County Technical College program in Nursery and Landscape Management.

IEP Annual Goal: Jacob will enroll in the Earth Science course.

IEP Objective: Given the unit on rock formations, Jacob will identify at least 5 of the 8 rock formations, on four of five opportunities by the end of the grading period.

The Behavioral Intervention Plan

To enhance your understanding of BIPs, go to the "Web Links" module for Chapter 2 of the Companion Website.

The **Behavioral Intervention Plan (BIP)** is the component of the IEP that attempts to link the management of behaviors that impede instruction with positive intervention strategies to reduce the occurrence of inappropriate behaviors and increase socially and contextually appropriate behavior. In order to make this connection, a BIP includes the following elements:

1. the operational definition of the target behavior impeding instruction
2. the results of a Functional Behavior Assessment. A Functional Behavior Assessment is conducted to determine the purpose (function) the inappropriate behavior serves for the student. It requires analysis of data collected on the events that precede (antecedents) and follow (consequences) the target behavior (see Chapter 6).
3. the intervention strategies to be used. These are selected based on the function of the inappropriate behavior. When selecting an intervention strategy, the IEP team is required to consider, if appropriate, strategies including positive behavioral interventions and supports to address behaviors that interfere with learning. Such

strategies and supports are reinforcement based and may also include curriculum and instructional modifications and changes in the classroom environment.

4. the behavioral objectives that state the agreed-upon change in the form or rate of the inappropriate behavior, or alternative behaviors that serve the function of the inappropriate behavior for the student

The following is an example of these elements of a BIP (an example of a full BIP appears in Chapter 6).

Operational definition of the impeding behavior: Leon has tantrums during individual math work times. His tantrums consist of banging his hands and arms on the desk, tearing his papers, and yelling "no, no, no."

Perceived function of the inappropriate behavior resulting from a Functional Behavior Assessment: An analysis of the data indicates that Leon engages in tantrums in order to escape from the academic demand placed on him during math work group.

Positive Behavior Intervention: (a) Differential reinforcement schedule of hand raising. Begin with redirection of the flailing hands and the teacher's asking: "Leon, do you need help with your work or do you need a break (break defined as 2 minutes with assignment removed from desk); (b) initially reduce the number of math problems he must complete during the 20-minute period; and (c) provide three problems to do first with an assigned classmate at beginning of math work group.

Behavioral Objective(s): Given a 20-minute period of individual math work (division problems with two-digit divisors), Leon will raise his hand when (a) needing assistance or (b) wanting a break from work, 100% of instances for four weeks.

According to IDEA there are two circumstances that require the preparation of a BIP (Turnbull, Wilcox, Stowe, & Turnbull, 2001):

1. If at the time of the development, review, or revision of an IEP the team is aware of a pattern of behavior that impedes the learning of the student or of another student, a BIP should be developed as part of the IEP.
2. At the time that an occurrence of behavior subjects a student to disciplinary action (that results in a suspension of up to 10 days, or that results in a change of placement, e.g., suspension, expulsion, or removal to an Interim Alternative Educational Setting): (a) if a BIP does not exist, the team must develop one, and (b) if the IEP contains a BIP, it must be reviewed for necessary modifications.

SUMMARY

We described the process of writing behavioral objectives and the relationship between such objectives and the IEP required for students with disabilities. This process is an integral part of any program for behavior change, whether the program is directed toward academic or social behavior. A program for changing behavior is unlikely to be successful unless we are sure what constitutes success. Behavioral objectives facilitate communication, so that everyone knows the goal of instruction. They also provide for evaluation, so that everyone knows whether the goal has been reached.

As part of an overall behavior change project, go to the "Activities" module for Chapter 2 of the Companion Website.

Key Terms

behavioral objective
pinpointing
educational goals
operational definition
acquisition
fluency
maintenance
generalization
Individualized Education Program (IEP)
Individual Transition Plan (ITP)
Behavioral Intervention Plan (BIP)

Discussion Questions

1. Most teachers are required to write objectives as a part of lesson planning or in IEPs. Many teachers consider writing objectives as unnecessary paperwork. Does the time taken to write objectives improve instruction or are those teachers right?
2. What is the significance of a criterion statement? For what kinds of objectives are criterion statements more or less important?
3. Replace each of the following vague verbs with one that is more specific:

   Mario will be able to discriminate between a few and a lot.

   Mario will be able to recall the major rivers of the United States.

   Mario will be able to identify the parts of a flower.

   Mario will be able to understand the results of global warming.

   Mario will know the 6 and 8 multiplication tables.

   Nikki will recognize the main characters of a story.

   Nikki will appreciate the differences among various cultures.

   Nikki will be competent in telling time.

   Nikki will appreciate the works of Monet.

   Nikki will learn to operate a calculator.

Chapter 3

Procedures for Collecting Data

Did you know that . . .

Teachers react strongly to suggestions that they collect data in their classrooms:

- "I don't have time to write down everything anyone does."
- "I just don't think I can manage shuffling all those sheets of paper, handling stopwatches and wrist counters, and giving proper cues. When am I supposed to concentrate on teaching?"
- "This data collection adds an extra hour a day, at least, in summarizing the data, putting the data on graphs, and so on. Where's that time supposed to come from?"
- "Give me a break."

Chapter Outline

Most teachers regard the kind of data collection procedures that we shall discuss in this chapter with the same enthusiasm they reserve for statistics. In some cases, their comments are thoroughly justified. Some of the systems we will review are not practical for everyday classroom use. Classroom teachers may never use some of the more complex systems. Understanding how these systems work, however, helps in understanding published research about applied behavior analysis. This chapter describes the most common data collection systems and shows how many of them can be adapted for classroom use.

A Rationale

Companion Website *To enhance your knowledge about data collection, go to the "Supplementary Lecture Notes" module for Chapter 3 of the Companion Website.*

Even after accepting the feasibility of data collection in the classroom, many teachers see little value in it. Beyond recording grades on tests, most teachers have traditionally kept very few records of their students' academic and social behaviors. There are, nevertheless, excellent reasons for teachers to collect classroom data.

First, observation and measurement make it possible to determine very accurately the effects of a particular instructional strategy or intervention. Precise observation and measurement of behavior enable teachers to determine the success or failure of their strategies. Second, the types of data collection procedures discussed in this chapter allow for ongoing (formative) as well as terminal (summative) evaluation of instruction or intervention. The data collected enable teachers to make decisions and alterations during the course of a program rather than waiting, perhaps for weeks or months, to see if it was ultimately successful. Such use of systematic formative evaluation significantly increases students' achievement, both statistically and practically (Fuchs & Fuchs, 1986). Finally, collecting and reporting effect-based data is the ultimate tool of accountability.

By writing behavioral objectives, teachers communicate their intent to change particular behaviors. They also state the criteria they will use to judge whether change procedures have been successful. In many classroom situations, the intervention's effect on the students' original level of performance would be evaluated by administering a pretest and posttest. However, the precision desired within a behavioral approach to instruction and in program evaluation necessitates additional data.

Behavioral evaluation requires observation of students' current functioning and ongoing progress.

Behavioral evaluation has two requirements. The first is a detailed observation of a student's current functioning. This observation should reflect the conditions and description of the behavior stated in the objective. For example, a behavioral objective stating that students should solve 25 long-division problems in 30 minutes requires that the teacher determine how many long-division problems the students can already solve in 30 minutes. Secondly, evaluation of an instructional program must facilitate ongoing monitoring of the teaching and learning process and provide a system for terminal evaluation. Evaluation must be continuous so that programs can be adjusted as instruction progresses. As the students in our example receive instruction in long division, the teacher might record daily how many problems they solve in 30 minutes, thus providing continuous evaluation. The monitoring process can provide guidelines for continuing or changing instructional techniques and help avoid false assumptions about student progress. Such false assumptions are unfortunately very common, as illustrated by the following vignette.

Ms. Waller Goes Electronic

Ms. Waller was ecstatic. After months of complaining that she had no materials to use to teach reading to her most challenging reading group, she had received several computers and a program to teach reading. The salesman proudly demonstrated the machine and pointed out the features that justified the hundreds of dollars invested.

"All you have to do," he assured her, "is hook the little, er, students up to these here headphones, drop in a CD-ROM, and turn this baby on. Everything else is taken care of . . . you don't do a thing."

Ms. Waller briskly administered the pretest included in the materials, scheduled each student for 15 minutes a day on the computer, and assumed that her worries were over.

At the end of the school year, Ms. Waller administered the posttest. Imagine her distress when, although several members of the group had made remarkable progress, some students had made none at all.

"I don't understand," she wailed. "The computer was supposed to do everything. How was I supposed to know it wasn't working?"

"Perhaps," suggested her principal, kindly, as he wished her success in her new career as an encyclopedia salesperson, "you should have checked before now."

CHOOSING A SYSTEM

Dimensions for observation of behavior.

The first step in the evaluation of ongoing measurement of behavior is the selection of a system of data collection. The characteristics of the system selected must be appropriate to the behavior being observed and to the kind of behavior change desired.

Behavior may be measured and changed on a number of dimensions (White & Haring, 1980).

1. *Frequency:* The frequency of behavior is simply the number of times a student engages in it.

   Brett got out of his seat 6 times in 30 minutes.
   Yao did 6 of 10 *math problems during a timed trial.*
   Marvin had 8 *tantrums Wednesday.*
   Lois' hand was in her mouth 5 times *during storytelling.*

   When determining frequency of occurrence of a behavior, we count the number of times the behavior occurs within an observation period (for example, 10 seconds or a 40-minute science class). If we want to make comparisons of the frequency of a behavior across observation periods (from one lunch period to another), the observation periods should be of the same length.

   If a behavior can occur only a limited number of times, that information should be provided as part of the frequency data. Knowing that Yao solved 6 math problems correctly, for example, has little meaning unless we also know that there were 10 math problems in all. For some behaviors there is no maximum or *ceiling* number. For example, there is no maximum number of times a student may call out or leave her seat during class.

2. *Rate:* The rate of behavior is frequency expressed in a ratio with time.

   Brett got out of his seat 0.2 times per minute.
   Yao did 0.6 math problems per minute *during a 2-minute time trial.*

Marvin had 1.3 tantrums per hour *in a 6-hour school day.*
Lois put her hand in her mouth 0.5 times per minute *during a 10-minute story time.*

If all the observation periods are the same length, one simply reports the number of occurrences and the length of the observation periods. Rate, however, is most often used to compare the occurrence of behavior among observation periods of different lengths. Converting frequency data to rate data enables us to compare data if we are unable to standardize observation periods or opportunities to respond. It makes it possible to compare data, for example, if observation periods are interrupted or if worksheets have different numbers of problems. Rate is calculated by dividing the number of times a behavior occurred by the length of the observation period. For example, if Brett got out of his seat 6 times during the 30-minute math lesson on Monday morning, his rate is 0.2 per minute (6 occurrences divided by 30 minutes). If he left his seat 8 times during a 40-minute social studies class with the fourth grade, his rate is still 0.2 per minute (8/40). The rate is the same across observation periods and, in this example, across settings.

3. *Duration:* The duration of a behavior is a measurement of how long a student engages in it.
   Brett was out of his seat for a total of 14 minutes.
   Brett was out of his seat an average of 3 minutes *per instance.*
   Yao worked on her math for 20 minutes.
   Marvin's tantrum lasted for 65 minutes.
   Lois had her hand in her mouth for 6 minutes.

   Duration is important when the concern is not the number of times Brett gets out of his seat, but how long he is out of his seat each time he gets up or how long he stays up during a given observation period. He may leave his seat only twice during a 40-minute lesson, but if he stays up for several minutes each time, that is a different problem from popping up and going right back down again. If we record the duration of Brett's out-of-seat behavior, we can state that he was out of his seat for a total of 8 minutes during the 30-minute class, or we can report the length of each instance, or we can compute the average amount of time he spent out of his seat during each instance.

4. *Latency:* A behavior's latency is the length of time between instructions to perform it and the occurrence of the behavior.
   After I told Brett to sit in his chair, it took him 50 seconds to sit down.
   After the teacher said, "Get to work," Yao stared into space for 5 minutes before she started her math.
   It took 20 minutes for Marvin to become quiet *after I put him in time-out.*
   I told Lois to take he hand out of her mouth; it was 2 minutes *before she did so.*

   Latency is relevant when the concern is not how long it takes a student to do something, but how long it takes to begin to do it. For example, Yao may solve 60% of her math problems correctly within an acceptable amount of time *once she starts,* but it takes her 7 minutes to get started.

5. *Topography:* The topography of behavior is the "shape" of the behavior—what it looks like.
   Yao writes all the 4s backwards *on her math paper.*
   Marvin screams, kicks his heels on the floor, and pulls his hair *during a tantrum.*
   Lois's hand sucking involves her putting her fingers in her mouth up to the knuckles.

Topography describes a behavior's complexity or its motor components. A tantrum, for example, may involve many behaviors performed simultaneously. Some behaviors consist of a chain, or sequence, of individual responses that usually occur together.

6. *Force:* The force of behavior is its intensity.
   Yao writes so heavily that she makes holes in her paper.
   Marvin screams so loudly that the teacher three doors down the hall can hear him.
   Lois's hand sucking is so intense that she has broken the skin on her thumb.

   Describing the intensity or force of a behavior often results in a qualitative measure that is hard to standardize. We are attempting to communicate how loud a scream is (usually without the use of an audiometer), how hard a child is banging a table, or how forcefully he is hitting himself or another child.

7. *Locus:* The locus of a behavior describes where it occurs, either in the environment or, for example, on the child or victim's body.
   Brett walks to the window *and stares outside.*
   Yao writes the answers to her math problems in the wrong spaces.
   Marvin hits his ears *during a tantrum.*
   Lois sucks the fingers of her left hand.

Locus describes either the target of the behavior or where in the environment the behavior is taking place.

The Professor Effects a Rescue

As Professor Grundy was walking to his car, he observed a congregation of students, including DeWayne, gathered around something that was not visible to him. His curiosity aroused, he strolled over to the group. As he got closer, he observed the object of the students' interest, which was an extremely large white dog. The animal was panting, its head was drooping, and it appeared emaciated. Its coat was matted and filthy, and it was dragging about 3 feet of chain from a metal choke collar drawn tightly around its neck.

"Look, Professor," said DeWayne, "I think it's a white St. Bernard. Do you think it bites?"

"See here," said the professor firmly, "it is dangerous to approach strange dogs. Someone should call the campus police and tell them to alert the city animal control officers." The dog, apparently determining that the professor was the highest authority present, staggered over to him, rested his huge head against Grundy's leg, and gazed at him soulfully with large, brown eyes.

"On the other hand," said the professor, taking the end of the chain and gently tugging, "perhaps I'll just make a call myself." The professor returned to his department with the dog. As he passed the departmental secretary, she gasped with alarm and began, "Professor, you can't . . . "

Grundy took his stopwatch from his pocket, activated it, and handed it to her. "This won't take 5 minutes," he said. "Time the duration and see for yourself." The professor placed a call to a colleague at the veterinary school who, upon hearing Grundy's description of the animal and its condition, stated, "What you've got there is a Great Pyrenees. What's he doing? I can hardly hear you."

"What he is doing," answered the professor, "is scratching. The topography of the behavior is that he is using his left hind foot to scratch behind his left ear. His foot is moving at a rate of 75 movements per minute according to the second hand on my watch. The force is sufficient to scatter dog hair and various other debris over a 3-foot radius, and his foot is hitting the floor between every third to fourth scratch with sufficient force to be heard in the lobby. He has been scratching for 3 minutes now, and he began scratching within 15 seconds of entering my office."

"Oh," said the veterinarian a little blankly, "probably fleas." (The professor looked furtively down the hall hoping the secretary couldn't hear.) "Why don't you bring him by the clinic and we'll check him out. It sounds like he's been on the road for a while. If he's healthy, we can see about getting in touch with a rescue society. They have a lot of trouble placing those big guys, though."

As Grundy returned through the lobby, retrieving his stopwatch from the secretary and confirming the duration of his stay as 4 minutes, 34 seconds, the secretary said, "He's really a sweet bunny of a boy, isn't he?" The dog wagged his long, plumy tail weakly. "Look, Professor, I think the sweetie likes me."

"His name," stated the Professor firmly, "is Burrhus."

The decision to use a particular system of data collection is based partly on the dimension of behavior that is of concern and partly on convenience. Systems for collecting data can be classified into three general categories. The first is recording and analyzing written reports that ideally include a full record of behaviors emitted during an observation period. The second is the observation of tangible products resulting from a behavior. The third is recording a sample of the behavior as it occurs. These systems may be categorized as follows:

Analyzing written records:	Anecdotal reports
Observing tangible products:	Permanent product recording
Observing a sample of behavior:	Event recording
	Interval recording
	Time sampling
	Duration recording
	Latency recording

Anecdotal Reports

Anecdotal reports are written to provide as complete a description as possible of a student's behavior in a particular setting or during an instructional period. Anecdotal reports do not identify a predefined or operationalized target behavior. After recording and analyzing data, the observer expects to identify a specific behavior that needs changing. Anecdotal reports are useful primarily for analysis, not for evaluation.

Teachers, parents, and therapists frequently use an anecdotal system of data collection to describe some general disturbance that is taking place or a lack of academic progress. For example, it might be reported that "Sheila constantly disrupts the class and does not complete her own work" or "During therapy sessions, I cannot seem to get Sheila under control to do the needed speech remediation."

Reports such as these are common and should prompt the applied behavior analyst to pinpoint the behavior (see Chapter 2). Should the specific behavior continue to elude identification, the analyst must further isolate and identify a target behavior that may be the source of the complaint in the natural setting of the behaviors—such as at the dinner table or in the classroom during reading period—and attempt to write down everything that occurs.

This system of data collection produces a written description of nearly everything that occurred in a specific time period or setting. It results in a report written in everyday language, describing individuals and interactions rather than isolated marks on a data sheet. Wright (1960) provided some guidelines for writing anecdotal reports:

Guide to writing anecdotal records.

1. Before beginning to record anecdotal data, write down the setting as you initially see it, the individuals in the setting and their relationships, and the activity occurring as you are about to begin recording (for example, lunch, free play).
2. Include in your description everything the target student(s) says and does and to whom or to what.
3. Include in your description everything said and done to the target student(s) and by whom.
4. As you write, clearly differentiate fact (what is actually occurring) from your impressions or interpretations of cause or reaction.
5. Provide some temporal indications so you can judge the duration of particular responses or interactions.

Structuring an Anecdotal Report

After observations have been made, an anecdotal report must be analyzed to determine the behavior(s), if any, that should be the subject of a behavior-change program. The observations in this initial anecdotal format are difficult to separate into individual

9:40 a.m.: Brian is walking around the room, touching various things such as plants on the windowsill. Teacher says, "It's now time for reading group. Everybody bring your books to the round table. You too, Brian." Teacher goes to table. Brian continues to wander. Teacher, in louder voice, "I'm still waiting." She goes and puts her hand on his shoulder. Brian pulls his shoulder out from under her hand. She takes him by the hand to the group of four other students. Brian sits. Teacher says, "Open your books. Where is your book, Brian?" Brian says, "Back there." "Back where, Brian?" "In my desk." "Go get it." "I will read from her book." "No, Brian, please go get your own book" (about 15 seconds pass). "Now, Brian, we are all waiting for you." Brian says, "So wait, we have plenty of time." Teacher stands. Brian gets up, goes to his desk (where he sits). When first student, Larry, is finished reading, teacher says, "Brian, come back here. It's almost your turn to read." Brian comes back to the table. Carl is reading. Brian makes a noise with his nose. Karen, sitting to his left, giggles and says, "Yuk." Teacher tells Karen to stop talking. Brian makes nose noise again. Karen, "Oh, yuk, yuk." Teacher says, "Brian, I see you. Stop it. Do we all see Brian? That is no way to behave when we are learning." Brian drops his book, bends down to get it, his chair falls. Teacher tells him to "come sit next to me." Brian moves his chair and begins to hum quietly. Teacher stands, moves three feet away from table, and tells Brian to move his chair "over here away from the group." Back at table she says, "Do we all see Brian and what happens when you disturb the group?" Larry raises his hand. "Yes, Larry." Larry says, "They don't get to read." Teacher says, "Yes, very good, Larry. Now let's read again: your turn, Mary." Mary starts reading. Brian is rocking in his chair, Karen looks and giggles. Brian continues to rock: his chair falls backward. Teacher reprimands him, takes him to front of room, and puts him in chair facing blackboard. Brian is singing. Larry yells, "Stop singing. You're disturbing me." Brian quiets down, begins drawing on blackboard (teacher is seated with her back to him). Brian intermittently sings loud enough to be heard. Twice teacher says, "Quiet down, Brian." Reading group ends (17 minutes later). Students are told to line up at the door. On the way out teacher tells Brian how good he was while separated from the group. "But tomorrow you will have to read first in group." 10:35 a.m.: Brian is sent to P.E. with classmates.

FIGURE 3–1 ***Excerpt from an anecdotal report.***

behaviors and relationships, so it is helpful to present the anecdotal data in a more schematic manner for review. Bijou, Peterson, and Ault (1968) employed a system for sequence analysis in which they redrafted an anecdotal report into a form that reflects a behavioral view of environmental interactions. By this system, the contents of the report are arranged into columns divided to indicate antecedent stimuli, specific responses, and consequent stimuli. This table format clearly represents the temporal relationship among individual behaviors, the antecedents that stimulate them, and the consequences that maintain them.

The anecdotal report in Figure 3–1 was taken in an elementary classroom. It records a period of interaction between a student named Brian, his teacher, and the members of his reading group.

Using the approach suggested by Bijou and his colleagues, the beginning of this report could be transposed into columns as begun in Figure 3–2. The antecedents, behaviors, and consequences are numbered to indicate the time sequence. Note that transposing the report makes it apparent that, in several instances, consequences of a given response can become the antecedents for a succeeding response.

When the content of an anecdotal report has been arranged in a format that clearly presents the sequence of and the relationships among behavioral events, the source of the problem behavior may be determined. The following questions help in analysis:

Questions for analyzing anecdotal information.

1. What are the behaviors that can be described as *inappropriate?* The behavior analyst should be able to justify labeling the behaviors as inappropriate, given the setting and the activity taking place.
2. Is this behavior occurring frequently, or has a unique occurrence been identified?

Time	Antecedent	Behavior	Consequence
9:40 a.m.		1. Brian is walking around room.	
	2. Teacher: Time for group. . . . You too, Brian." T moves to table.		
		3. B continues to walk.	
			4. T: "I'm still waiting."
	5. T puts hand on B's shoulder.		
		6. B pulls shoulder.	
			7. T takes B's hand and leads him to table.
		8. B sits.	
	9. T: "Where is your book, B?"		
		10. B: "Back there."	
			11. T: "Back where?"
		12. B: "In my desk."	
			13. T: "Go get it."
		14. B: "I will read from her book."	

FIGURE 3–2 ***Structure of an anecdotal report.***

3. Can reinforcement or punishment of the behavior be identified? Teachers, parents, other children, or some naturally occurring environment event may deliver consequences, intentionally or otherwise.
4. Is there a pattern to these consequences?
5. Can antecedents to the behavior(s) be identified?
6. Is there a pattern that can be identified for certain events or stimuli (antecedents) that consistently precede the behavior's occurrence?
7. Are there recurrent chains of certain antecedents, behaviors, and consequences?
8. Given the identified inappropriate behavior(s) of the student and the patterns of antecedents and consequences, what behavior really needs to be modified, and who is engaging in the behavior (for example, the referred student, the teacher, or the parent)?

The use of anecdotal reports is not always practical for general education teachers. Special education teachers may be called upon to observe students who are having behavioral or academic difficulty or who are in the process of being referred for special education services. For such observation, skill in recording and analyzing anecdotal data in extremely valuable. Anecdotal reports can enable these teachers to determine what factors in the classroom are occasioning or maintaining appropriate and inappropriate behaviors. This information will serve as the basis for making decisions about possible changes in the classroom environment or in behavior-management strategies. Anecdotal observation may also be used as a first step in a longer process for dealing with persistent, highly disruptive, or seriously harmful behaviors. This process, known as functional assessment (see Chapter 6), requires detailed observation, analysis, and manipulation of objects and events in a student's environment to determine what is occasioning and maintaining the behaviors.

PERMANENT PRODUCT RECORDING

Permanent product recording is the easiest to use, but not all behaviors leave a permanent product.

Teachers have been using **permanent product recording** since the first time a teacher walked into a classroom. A teacher uses permanent product recording to grade a spelling test, verify the creation of a chemical emulsion, or count the number of cans a student has placed on a shelf. *Permanent products* are tangible items or environmental effects that result from a behavior. Permanent products are outcomes of behavior; thus, this method is sometimes called *outcome recording*. This type of recording is an ex post facto method of data collection.

To collect permanent product data, the teacher reviews the statement of the behavior as written in the behavioral objective and determines what constitutes an acceptable outcome of the behavior. For example, if the behavior is building a tower of blocks, the objective states whether the student is required to place one block on top of another or whether the blocks should be arranged in a certain color sequence. If the behavior is academic, conditions also are specified. For example, the objective may specify the number of spelling errors permitted in a written paragraph or the number of references required in a term paper. If the behavior is vocational, quality may be specified as well as the number of widgets to be assembled. In each case, the teacher reviews the operational definition of the behavior. After evaluating the products of the required behavior, the teacher simply notes how many of the products were produced and how many were acceptable according to the definition.

Because the concrete results of a behavior are being evaluated and recorded, the teacher does not have to observe the student directly engaged in the behavior. Convenience is the explanation for the frequent use of permanent product recording in the classroom: It causes minimal interference with a classroom schedule.

Applications of permanent product recording.

The versatility of permanent product recording makes it useful in a variety of instructional programs and settings. In the home, permanent product recording has been used to record data on incontinence (Adkins & Matthews, 1997), encopresis (O'Brien, Ross, & Christophersen, 1986), and room cleaning (Dyer, Schwartz, & Luce, 1984). In vocational settings, this method has been used to record outcomes of tasks ranging from pot scrubbing (Grossi & Heward, 1998) to computer typing (Wacker et al., 1988). In educational settings, it has been used to record data on basics such as cup stacking (Zarcone, Fisher, & Piazza, 1996) and diverse academic tasks such as spelling accuracy (Grskovic & Belfiore, 1996; McNaughton, Hughes, & Ofiesh, 1997), completion and accuracy of arithmetic problems (Freeland & Noell, 1999; Jolivette, Wehby, Canale, & Massey, 2001; Neef, Nelles, Iwata, & Page, 2003; Wood, Frank, & Wacker, 1998), and performance on science and foreign language quizzes (Cavanaugh, Heward, & Donelson, 1996; Lloyd, Eberhardt, & Drake, 1996). It has also been used to record the length of essays (De La Paz, 1999), the quantity of bathroom graffiti (Mueller, Moore, Doggett, & Tingstrom, 2000), the complexity of sentence writing (heward & Eachus, 1979), and the development of fine motor control in cursive writing (Trap, Milner-Davis, Joseph, & Cooper, 1978). Permanent product recording is also the method used to monitor completion and accuracy of homework assignments (Hinton & Kern, 1999; Olympia, Sheridan, Jenson, & Andrews, 1994).

The main advantage of permanent product recording is the durability of the sample of behavior obtained. The permanent product is not apt to disappear before its occurrence can be recorded. In light of this, the teacher may keep an accurate file of the actual products of certain target behaviors (such as test papers) or a report of the products for further review or verification later.

Permanent product recording may include the use of audiotape, videotape, and digital recording systems. With recording equipment, teachers can make samples of specific transitory behaviors that would not ordinarily produce a permanent product. Samples of behavior in hectic settings such as play groups can be recorded and analyzed at leisure. Samples of behaviors from nonschool settings such as a student's home can be made by parents and brought to professionals for analysis. Individual and group samples of expressive language, for example, have been audiotaped (Matson, Sevin, Fridley, & Love, 1990; Orsborn, Patrick, Dixon, & Moore, 1995) and videotaped (Watkins, Sprafkin, & Krolokowski, 1990). Samples of student performance in general and special education settings have been videotaped to allow collaboration among interdisciplinary team members to determine educational goals and intervention techniques (Anderson, Hawkins, Hamilton, & Hampton, 1999). Audiotaping and videotaping allow for data collection after the fact, just as grading a student's exam or composition after school does.

What permanent products or outcomes might be observed for each of the behavioral dimensions discussed in the section on choosing a system of data collection?

Behavioral dimensions for which permanent product recording may be used.

Rate: number of written products of any academic behavior per unit of time

Duration or **latency:** unfortunately do not lend themselves to permanent product recording unless recording equipment is available

Topography: the correct formation of letters or numerals; following a pattern in such activities as pegboard designs block building, or vocational assemblies

Force: too light, too heavy, or uneven pressure when writing or typing; holes kicked in a classroom wall by a student having a tantrum

This list of examples is by no means exhaustive. Because permanent product recording is relatively simple and convenient, teachers can be imaginative in defining behaviors in terms of their outcomes. We have known teachers who operationally defined

- *test anxiety* as the number of visible erasures on a test paper
- *sloppiness* as the number of pieces of scrap paper on the floor within 2 feet of a student's desk
- *hyperactivity* as the number of table tennis balls still balanced in the pencil tray of a student's desk

The following vignette examines one use of permanent product recording.

Mr. Martin Observes Room Cleaning

Mr. Martin, while majoring in special education, was a night-shift assistant at a residential institution for students with severe emotional and behavioral problems. One of his duties was to see that each bedroom was cleaned before bedtime. He decided to establish some system for reinforcing room cleaning but was uncertain about what he should measure. When he tried measuring and reinforcing the time students spent cleaning their rooms, he found that, although there was a great deal of scurrying around, the rooms were still very messy. Because the major problem appeared to be clothes, toys, and trash scattered on the floors, beds, and other furniture, he decided to use the number of such objects as his measure. Each evening before lights-out, he stood at the door of each bedroom with a clipboard containing a sheet of paper with each resident's name and a space for each day of the week. He rapidly counted the number of separate objects scattered in inappropriate places and entered the total in the space on his data sheet.

Observational Recording Systems

Whereas the permanent product method of data collection records the outcome of a behavior, **observational recording systems** are used to record behavior samples as the behavior is actually occurring. A data collector may choose from several basic observational recording systems. Teachers who are interested in recording the number of times a behavior is occurring may select **event recording.** Those who want to find the proportion of a specified time period during which the behavior occurs may select **interval recording** or **time sampling. Duration recording** allows the teacher to determine the length of time the student spends performing some behavior. **Latency recording** measures the length of time it takes a student to start doing something. An illustration of the relationship between observational recording procedures and the components of a behavioral, stimulus-response sequence is shown in Figure 3–3. Copies of data sheets appearing in this chapter and in Chapter 9 are provided on the website (*www.prenhall.com/alberto*).

Event Recording

Event recording provides an exact count of how many times a behavior occurs.

Event recording is a frequently used observational recording procedure because it most directly and accurately reflects the number of times a behavior occurs. When using event recording, the observer makes a notation every time the student engages in the target behavior. Tallying these notations gives an exact record of how often the behavior occurred. A count of the target behavior is made during a specified observation period—for example, during a reading period or during lunch. Recording how often the behavior occurs within a given time period documents its frequency. If the lengths of the observation periods are constant, the observer may simply report the number of times the behavior occurred, its frequency, or its rate, the number of times it occurred per minute or hour during that period. Rate may also be reported if the observation periods vary in length. Another strategy is arbitrarily to standardize the length of the observation period, for example, by taking data for just the first 20 minutes of the period each day.

Event recording is usually the method of choice when the objective is to increase or decrease the number of times a student engages in a certain behavior. Event recording may be used to record an increase in an appropriate social behavior, such as counting the number of times a student shares a toy with a classmate. It may be used to record an increase in an academic response (counting the number of correctly defined science

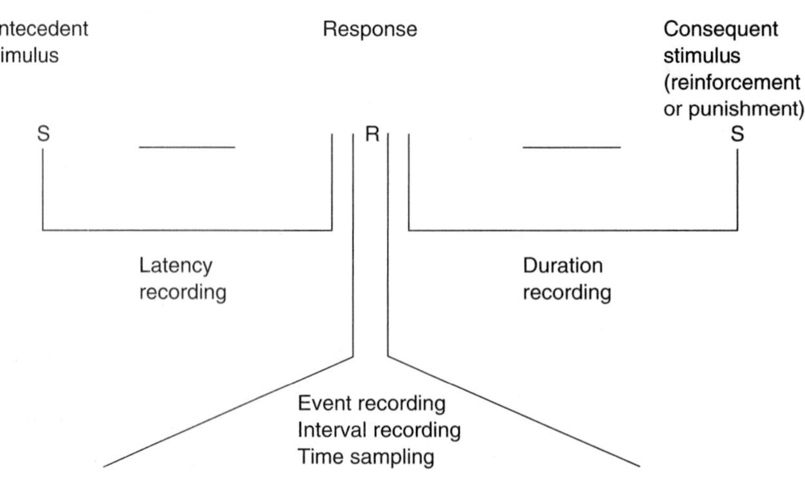

FIGURE 3–3
Observational data collection systems as related to the basic behavioral paradigm.

vocabulary words) or a decrease in an inappropriate behavior (counting the number of times a student curses during physical education class). Because the teacher attempts to record the exact number of times the behavior occurs, event recording must be used behaviors that are discrete. **Discrete behaviors** have an obvious, or agreed upon, beginning and end. The observer can make an accurate frequency count because she can clearly judge when one occurrence ends and the next begins. Event recording has been used for counting and recording behaviors in a range of content areas, including academics: picture naming (Stromer, MacKay, McVay, & Fowler, 1998), words spelled with a voice output communication device (Schlosser, Blischak, Belfiore, Bartley, & Barnett, 1998), mouse clicking on correctly spelled words (Birnie-Selwyn & Guerin, 1997), word recognition and oral reading (Browder & Minarovic, 2000; Didden, Prinsen, & Sigafoos, 2000; Eckert, Ardoin, Daly, & Martens, 2002; Skinner, Cooper, & Cole, 1997), money selection and counting (Denny & Test, 1995; Schloss, Kobza, & Alper, 1997), and reading and science vocabulary words (Johnson, Schuster, & Bell, 1996; Schuster, Morse, Griffen, & Wolery, 1996;); number of words in an essay (Wolfe, Heron, & Goddard, 2000); communication: yes/no responses (Neef, Walters, & Engel, 1984), question asking (Taylor & Harris, 1995; Williams, Donley, & Keller, 2000) and question answering (Secan, Engel, & Tilley, 1989), conversation skills (Dattilo & Camarata, 1991), and manual signs (Partington, Sundberg, Newhouse, & Newhouse, & Spengler, 1994); self-help: accepting bites of food (Piazza, Patel, Gulotta, Seven, & Layer, 2003), drinking from a cup (Hagopian, Farrell, & Amari, 1996), and toileting initiations (Bainbridge & Myles, 1999); social skills: waiting one's turn, looking at the person who is speaking (Laushey & Heflin, 2000), and saying "please" (Drasgow, Halle, & Ostrosky, 1998); sports skills: soccer (Ziegler, 1994) and basketaball (Vollmer & Bourret, 2000). Event recording has also been used to count instances of inappropriate behavior, such as eye poking (Smith, Russo, & Le, 1999), having tantrums (Dunlap & Fox, 1999), hand mouthing (Lerman & Iwata, 1996), face slapping, head banging (Sigafoos, Penned, & Versluis, 1996), and eating cigarette butts (Piazza, Hanley, & Fisher, 1996), throwing, hitting, spitting, and cursing (Kamps, Kravits, Stolze, & Swaart, 1999; Kee, Hill, & Weist, 1999), and dropping to the floor (Smith & Churchill, 2002).

Event recording can be used only for discrete behaviors.

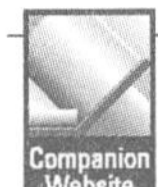

For more information on data collection and interpretation, go to the "Web Links" module for Chapter 3 of the Companion Website.

Event recording may also be used when teaching from a task analysis. A task analysis is a list of the individual steps that when chained together form a complex behavior such as hand washing or solving addition problems. During instruction the teacher records the performance of the steps listed in the task analysis. The steps of a task analysis are a series of discrete behaviors. The teacher can thus record a student's performance on each step as an individual, discrete behavior. A task analysis for teaching a secondary-age student with moderate disabilities to clean tables, for example, might consist of 12 steps; the first five of which could be: (1) place bucket on table, (2) pick up cloth, (3) place cloth in soap and water, (4) wring out cloth, and (5) rub section one of table (Smith, Collins, Schuster, & Kleinert, 1999). Each of these steps is a discrete behavior with a clear, or clearly definable, beginning and ending. Progress toward acquiring individual steps or the entire task of table cleaning can be recorded through event recording (see Figure 3–9 for a data sheet used to record a student's performance of this behavior).

Examples of event recording with task analysis include skills in the school such as using a calculator, operating an audio tape recorder, accessing a computer program, or sharpening pencils (Werts, Caldwell, & Wolery, 1996); in the home for self-help skills such as dressing (Sewell, Collins, Hemmeter, & Schuster, 1998), self-catheterization (McComas, Lalli, & Benavides, 1999), and self-administration of insulin and home care such as making coffee, washing dishes, or washing windows (Steed & Lutzker, 1999); in the community for skills such as cashing a check, crossing a street, mailing a letter

(Branham, Collins, Schuster, & Kleinert, 1999), using an ATM and making a purchase with a cash card (Cihak, Alberto, Kessler, & Taber, 2004), and counting money using the one-more-than method (Denny & Test, 1995). A complete discussion of task analysis appears in Chapter 9.

Some labels for behavior may be used to describe what are actually a number of different responses, each of which may or may not occur each time the so-called behavior occurs. Examples that many teachers try to target for change are on-task or off-task behavior, appropriate or inappropriate verbalizations, in-seat or out-of-seat behavior, or disturbing one's neighbor. For accurate event recording, a standard definition, with an agreed-upon beginning and end, is necessary. In other words, such behaviors can be made discrete by defining them operationally (see Chatper 2).

Certain behaviors, however, may not be adequately measured using event recording, This data collection procedure is not appropriate in the following instances:

1. Behavior occurring at such a high **frequency** that the number recorded may not reflect an accurate count. Certain behaviors, such as the number of steps taken while running, some stereotypic behaviors (such as hand flapping or rocking by students with severe disabilities), and eye blinking may occur at such high frequencies that it is impossible to count them accurately.
2. Cases in which one behavior or response can occur for extended time periods. Examples of such behaviors might be thumb sucking or attention to task. If out-of-seat behavior were being recorded, for instance, a record showing that the student was out of her seat only one time during a morning would give an inaccurate indication of what the student was actually doing if this one instance of the behavior lasted from roll call to lunchtime.

An advantage of event recording, in addition to accuracy, is the relative ease of the data collection itself. The teacher does not need to interrupt the lesson to take data. The teacher may simply make a notation on an index card or paper on a clipboard, make slash marks on a piece of tape around his wrist, or transfer paper clips from one pocket to another. This information may be tallied and transferred to a data sheet similar to the one presented in Figure 3–4.

FIGURE 3–4 ***Basic data sheet for event recording.***

Event Recording Data Sheet

Student: PATRICIA
Observer: MRS. COHEN

Behavior: INAPPROPRIATE TALK-OUTS (NO HAND RAISED)

	Time Start Stop	Notations of occurrences	Total occurrences
5/1/95	10:00 10:20	~~////~~ ~~////~~ //	12
5/2/95	10:00 10:20	~~////~~ ////	9

Student: JEREMY
Observer: MS GARWOOD

Behavior: Errors in oral reading

	CAROL	5/1/95	EXERC. #2	READER PG. 7.	
SUBSTITUTIONS					
MISPRONOUNCIATIONS					
INSERTIONS					
REPETITIONS					

***FIGURE 3–5* Data sheet for event recording.**

Event recording is also easily used for many academic behaviors. Figure 3–5 is a data sheet used for recording the errors made during an oral reading exercise. The teacher simply places a mark in the appropriate row as a particular error is made. The column heads may record the day of week, the child who is reading, dates, page number from the reader where the mistake was made, and so on.

Using the data sheet in Figure 3–6, a teacher can record the correct verbal reading of sight words. The sight words chosen for the student are listed in the left column.

The succeeding columns provide space to indicate whether the student's reading of the word was correct or incorrect. The total number (or percent) correct is recorded at the bottom of the column (On April 12th, for example, Deepa read 5 words correctly—though not the same five as on April 10th). Data on the number of words identified correctly may be taken during instruction as the teacher records Deepa's response as correct or incorrect each time she is asked to read a word. This is referred to as trial-by-trial data collection. Data may be taken instead at the conclusion of the instructional session by giving Deepa the opportunity to read each word one more time and recording only those responses. This is one form of probe data collection. A simple method for recording correct and incorrect answers when using flash cards is to mark directly on the back of the card on which the word (or other cue) is printed. These marks can be transferred later to a summary data sheet.

For the more mechanically inclined, counting devices are commercially available. Although these make data collection easier and more accurate, they entail some expense and may break. An inexpensive counter sold for tallying purchases in a grocery store or golf strokes may be useful. Stitch counters designed to fit on the end of a knitting needle come in sizes large enough to fit on a pen. Drash, Ray, and Tudor (1989, p. 453) describe the following four-step procedure for using most simple, inexpensive pocket calculators to record event data:

1. Press number 1
2. Press 1 key
3. Press 5 key
4. Press 5 key to record each subsequent event

Student: **Inclusive Dates:**

OBJECTIVE: Given the following list of 12 sight words found in general merchandise stores (e.g., Wal-Mart), Deepa will verbally state each.

Criterion: with 100% accuracy for 4 consecutive sessions.

Dates/Trials

Items	4/10	4/12								Comments
restrooms	+	+								
exit	+	–								
girls	–	+								
housewares	–	–								
pet	+	–								
supplies	–	+								
checkout	–	–								
express	–	+								
shoes	+	–								
linens	–	+								
videos	+	–								
electronics	–	–								
Total Correct	5/12	5/12								

FIGURE 3–6 ***Data sheet for event recording.***

These steps set up the calculator so that each time the 5 key is pressed, it will cumulatively add each occurrence of the behavior. At the end of the observation period, the observer subtracts 1 from the cumulative total (because 1 was recorded during the initial setup), and the exact total of occurrences for the observation period will appear on the calculator. With practice, and perhaps a small piece of tape on the 5 key as a prompt, an observer can do this with calculator in her pocket. (Anyone who attempts to teach wearing garments without pockets needs a carpenter's apron.)

Recording Controlled Presentations

One variation on the event-recording technique is the use of **controlled presentations** (Allyon & Milan, 1979). In this method, the teacher structures or controls the number of opportunities the student will have to perform the behavior. Most often this method consists of presenting a predetermined number of opportunities, or trials, in each instructional session. A **trial** may be viewed as a discrete occurrence because it has an identifiable beginning and ending. A trial is defined by its three behavioral components: an antecedent stimulus, a response, and a consequent stimulus (S-R-S). The delivery of the antecedent stimulus (usually a verbal cue) marks the beginning of the trial, and the delivery of the consequent stimulus (reinforcement, correction, or punishment) signifies the termination of the trial. For example, in a given session the teacher may decide that a student will be given 10 opportunities, or trials, to respond by pointing to specified objects upon request. Each trial is then recorded as correct or incorrect. Controlled presentation allows the teacher to monitor progress simply by looking at the number of correct responses for each session.

Figures 3–7 and 3–8 present variations of data sheets used for the collection of discrete trial or controlled presentation data. The data sheet in Figure 3–7 (variation of Saunders & Koplik, 1975) is arranged from left to right for 15 sessions. Within each session, or column, there are numbers representing up to 20 trials. The teacher records dichotomous data (whether the response was correct or incorrect) using the following simple procedure:

After each trial

1. Circle the trial number that corresponds to a correct response.
2. Slash (/) through the trial number that corresponds to an incorrect response.

After each session

1. Total the number of correct trials (those circled).
2. Place a square around the corresponding number in the session column that corresponds to the number of correct trials.
3. To graph directly on the data sheet, connect the squared numbers across the sessions to yield a learning curve.
4. The column on the far right allows the number of correct trials per session (the number with the square around it) to be converted to the percentage of trials correct. If the number of correct trials in a 20-trial session was 8, looking at the last column, we see that the percentage correct is 40.

Figure 3–8 is a modification of the previous data sheet that allows the observer to use it for up to six students working on the same task or for up to six tasks for the same student. Controlled presentations and specifically constructed data sheets are also used for two additional instructional needs. Data sheets may be constructed to use when teaching chained tasks through the use of a task analysis, and for use when the teacher wants to record prompts (e.g., verbal or physical assistance) used to assist student performance during instruction. These instructional and data-recording strategies are discussed in Chapter 9.

Classroom teachers can improve instruction by using controlled presentations. For example, a teacher might want to be sure to ask each member of a seminar group five questions during a discussion on early Cold War events and the Berlin Wall. A very

	2-18	2-20	2-21	2-25	2-27	2-28	3-4	3-6	3-7	3-11	3-13	3-14	3-18	3-20	3-21	
	20	20	20	20	20	20	20	20	20	20	20	20	20	20	20	100
	19	19	19	19	19	19	19	19	19	19	19	19	19	19	19	95
	18	18	18	18	18	18	18	18	18	18	18	18	18	18	18	90
	17	17	17	17	17	17	17	17	17	17	17	17	17	17	17	85
	16	16	16	16	16	16	16	16	16	16	16	16	16	16	16	80
	15	15	15	15	15	15	15	15	15	15	15	15	15	15	15	75
	14	14	14	14	14	14	14	14	14	14	14	14	14	14	14	70
	13	13	13	13	13	13	13	13	13	13	13	13	13	13	13	65
	12	12	12	12	12	12	12	12	12	12	12	12	12	12	12	60
	11	11	11	11	11	11	11	11	11	11	11	11	11	11	11	55
	10	10	10	10	10	10	10	10	10	10	10	10	10	10	10	50
	9	9	9	9	9	9	9	9	9	9	9	9	9	9	9	45
	8	8	8	8	8	8	8	8	8	8	8	8	8	8	8	40
	7	7	7	7	7	7	7	7	7	7	7	7	7	7	7	35
	6	6	6	6	6	6	6	6	6	6	6	6	6	6	6	30
	5	5	5	5	5	5	5	5	5	5	5	5	5	5	5	25
	4	4	4	4	4	4	4	4	4	4	4	4	4	4	4	20
	3	3	3	3	3	3	3	3	3	3	3	3	3	3	3	15
	2	2	2	2	2	2	2	2	2	2	2	2	2	2	2	10
	1	1	1	1	1	1	1	1	1	1	1	1	1	1	1	5
Session	1	2	3	4	5	6	7	8	9	10	11	12	13	14	15	%

Target behavior/skill Sorting Full vs Not Full

Criterion 90% correct trials for 3 consecutive sessions

Materials restaurant containers for salt, pepper, sugar, ketcup, mustard, napkins

Student Carmen

FIGURE 3–7 **Data collection sheet for use with controlled presentations.**
Note: Adapted from "A multi-purpose data sheet for recording and grapbing in the classroom," by R. Saunders and K. Koplik. *AAESPH Review,* 1975. Copyright 1975 by the Association for the Severely Handicapped. Reprinted with permission.

Name: Peter
Task: Functional Counting to 10
Date:

10	10	10	10	10
9	9	9	9	9
8	8	8	8	8
7	7	7	7	7
6	6	6	6	6
5	5	5	5	5
4	4	4	4	4
3	3	3	3	3
2	2	2	2	2
1	1	1	1	1

Comments:

Calvic
Functional Counting to 10

10	10	10	10	10
9	9	9	9	9
8	8	8	8	8
7	7	7	7	7
6	6	6	6	6
5	5	5	5	5
4	4	4	4	4
3	3	3	3	3
2	2	2	2	2
1	1	1	1	1

Comments:

Tonya
Functional Counting to 10

10	10	10	10	10
9	9	9	9	9
8	8	8	8	8
7	7	7	7	7
6	6	6	6	6
5	5	5	5	5
4	4	4	4	4
3	3	3	3	3
2	2	2	2	2
1	1	1	1	1

Comments:

Name: Rita
Task: Functional Counting to 10
Date:

10	10	10	10	10
9	9	9	9	9
8	8	8	8	8
7	7	7	7	7
6	6	6	6	6
5	5	5	5	5
4	4	4	4	4
3	3	3	3	3
2	2	2	2	2
1	1	1	1	1

Comments:

Dylana
Functional Counting to 10

10	10	10	10	10
9	9	9	9	9
8	8	8	8	8
7	7	7	7	7
6	6	6	6	6
5	5	5	5	5
4	4	4	4	4
3	3	3	3	3
2	2	2	2	2
1	1	1	1	1

Comments:

Roy
Functional Counting to 10

10	10	10	10	10
9	9	9	9	9
8	8	8	8	8
7	7	7	7	7
6	6	6	6	6
5	5	5	5	5
4	4	4	4	4
3	3	3	3	3
2	2	2	2	2
1	1	1	1	1

Comments:

FIGURE 3–8 **Data collection sheet for use with controlled presentations.**

Note: From *Vocational Habilitation of Severely Retarded Adults: A Direct Service Technology,* by G. Bellamy, R. Horner, & D. Inman (Baltimore: University Park Press, 1979). Copyright © 1979 University Park Press, Bultimore. Reprinted by permission.

Behavioral dimensions appropriate to event recording.

simple data sheet with the names of the students and a space to mark whether answers were correct or incorrect would provide valuable information for analysis and evaluation.

Event recording (including controlled presentation) lends itself to the observation of the rate of frequency of behavior, for example:

Companion Website *For additional data sheet examples, go to the "Web Links" module for Chapter 3 of the Companion Website.*

- number of times Mel talks out in an hour
- number of times Charlie hits another student in a 20-minute recess
- number of questions Melissa answers correctly during a 15-minute world geography review
- number of times Sam answers questions in a whisper
- number of times Mary throws trash on the floor
- number of stairs Eliot climbs putting only one foot on each step

Ms. Stallings Counts Tattling

Four of the students in Ms. Stallings's third-grade class seemed to spend most of their time telling her what other students were doing wrong. Ms. Stallings was worried about this for two reasons: the students were not working efficiently and they were driving her up the wall. When she asked her colleague Ms. Barbe for advice, Ms. Barbe suggested that the first thing to do was to find out how often each of the students was tattling.

"Otherwise," she said, "you won't know for sure whether whatever you do to stop them is working."

Ms. Stallings decided to count an instance of tattling each time a student mentioned another student's name to her and described any number of inappropriate behaviors. Thus, "Johnny's not doing his work and he's bothering me," was counted as one instance, but "Harold and Manolo are talking," was counted as two instances. She then went back to Ms. Barbe.

"How can I write it down every time they do it?" she asked. "I move around my room all the time, and I don't want to carry paper and pencil."

Ms. Barbe laughed. "No problem," she answered, "I'm sure that's why dry beans come in so many sizes and shapes. I just pick a different bean for each student, put a handful of each in my right pocket, and transfer by feel to my left pocket when I observe the behavior. Just be sure you get them out before your clothes go into the washer."

Interval Recording and Time Sampling

The observer counts intervals, not discrete behaviors.

Interval recording and time sampling data collection systems are ways of recording an approximation of the actual number of times behavior occurs. Instead of counting each occurrence of the behavior, the teacher counts the number of intervals of time within observation periods during which the behavior occurs. With these methods it is possible to record continuous behaviors (behaviors of longer duration) and high-frequency behaviors that may be incompatible with event recording. Interval recording and time sampling have been used with behaviors such as task engagement (Bryan & Gast, 2000; Massey & Wheeler, 2000; Todd, Horner, & Sugai, 1999), cooperative toy play (Van Camp et al., 2000), and sharing (Reinecke, Newman, & Meinberg, 1999); tantrums and aggressive behaviors such as hitting, kicking, biting scratching, and throwing objects (Charlop-Christy & Haymes, 1998; Lalli, Kates, & Casey, 1999); yelling and bizarre vocalizations (Magee & Ellis, 2000; Wilder, Masuda, O'Connor, & Baham, 2001); stereotypy (Kennedy, Meyer, Knowles, & Shukla, 2000) and self-injury (Irvin et al., 1996; Wacker et al., 1996); and drooling (Lancioni, Brouwer, & Coninx, 1992), hand mouthing (Irvin, Thompson, Turner, & Williams, 1998), and thumb sucking (Friman, 2000).

In terms of making the closest representation of the actual occurrence of the behavior, event recording is the most accurate, interval recording is next, and time sampling is the least exact (Repp, Roberts, Slack, Repp, & Berkler, 1976). Each system, however, has its advantages and disadvantages.

Interval Recording

When using interval recording, the teacher defines a specific time period (usually between 10 minutes and an hour) during which the target behavior will be observed. This observation period is then divided into equal intervals. These intervals are typically 5, 10, or 15 seconds long, occasionally up to 30 seconds. The shorter the interval is, the more accurate the data. The teacher draws a series of boxes representing the time intervals. In each box or interval the teacher simply notes whether the behavior occurred (+) or did not occur (−) *at any time during the inverval.* Therefore, each interval has only one notation. The data sheet for a 5-minute observation period shown in Figure 3–9 has been divided into 10-second intervals. During the first minute of the observation period, the target behavior occurred during two of the intervals, the second and third. Over the total 5-minute period, the target behavior occurred during 12, or 40%, of the intervals.

Interval recording does not provide an exact count of behaviors but is especially appropriate for continuous behaviors.

Because of the way these interval data are recorded, only limited conclusions can be drawn from the record of the behavior's occurrence. Regardless of whether the behavior occurred once or five times during the interval, a single notation is made. Therefore, the actual number of occurrences is not included in the record. If, in the preceding example, cursing was being recorded, all the teacher could say was that, during two of the intervals, the student cursed. There were at least two instances of this behavior, but there may have been more. Even if the student cursed 11 times during the second interval, only one notation would have been made. Recording occurrences of discrete behaviors, such as cursing or hitting, is known as *partial-interval recording* (the behavior does not consume the entire interval).

Student: Darius
Date: 8-29
Time Start: 9:10
Observer: Mrs. Heflin
Behavior: On-task (eyes on paper or writing on paper)
Setting: 4th period math
Time End: 9:15

Length of Intervals in Seconds

Length of Observation Period in Minutes	10"	20"	30"	40"	50"	60"
1'	−	+	+	−	−	−
2'	+	+	−	−	−	+
3'	+	−	−	+	+	+
4'	−	+	+	+	−	−
5'	−	−	−	−	−	−

Number (Percent) of Intervals of Occurrence: 12 intervals, 40% of intervals
Number (Percent) of Intervals of Nonoccurrence: 18 intervals, 60% of intervals

FIGURE 3–9 Interval recording data sheet.

Behaviors such as walking around the room or being off task may begin in one interval and continue unbroken into the next interval. Such timing would appear as two instances, because it would be recorded in two intervals in this instance, but the same duration of behavior would appear as only one instance if it fell within a single interval. Recording ongoing behaviors that may continue for several intervals is known as *whole-interval recording* (the behavior consumes the entire interval).

An additional problem encountered with interval data collection is created by the shortness of each interval in which the notation is to take place. It is very difficult to teach and collect interval data simultaneously. The teacher must keep an eye on a student or students, observe a stopwatch or second hand on a watch, and note the occurrence or nonoccurrence of the target behavior all within a matter of seconds; a third-party observer is often required.

The necessity of looking down at the data sheet to make a recording might cause even an observer to miss an occurrence of the behavior, resulting in inaccurate data. The need to look at one's watch to check the passage of the interval is eliminated by videotaping the observation period and using the time on the VCR to note intervals (Miltenberger, Rapp, & Long, 1999). Observers can also time intervals using an audiotape with beeps at the end of each interval, or set a timer with a seconds indicator and an audible signal, or use commercial products such as the WatchMinder or Invisible Clock that will Chime or vibrate at selected intervals. Another way of simplifying the task is to build in opportunities for recording as part of the schedule. The observer alternates intervals for observing and scoring, as shown in the sample row from a data collection sheet in Figure 3–10.

Figures 3–11 and 3–12 are examples of interval recording sheets for a 15-minute period divided into 10-second intervals. Looking at the notations of occurrence and nonoccurrence, the data collector can infer certain information:

1. approximate number of occurrences of the behavior
2. approximate duration of the behavior within the observation period
3. distribution of the behavior across the observation period

Assuming that off-task behavior during a written arithmetic assignment is recorded in both examples, the behavior appears to have occurred in 38 of the 90 intervals (see Figure 3–11). The successive intervals in which the behavior occurred indicate that the off-task behavior occurred over long durations (3 minutes each), but it appears to have been confined primarily to two periods. When reviewing such data, teachers should analyze the situation for some indication of what seem to be the immediate precipitating factors. In this example, off-task behavior may have been due to the two sets of written instructions on the worksheet, which prompted the student to ask a neighbor what to do.

In Figure 3–12, the off-task behavior is distributed throughout the time period. The teacher might find that the off-task behavior coincided with times when another student asked a question. Therefore, this student's problem may be distractibility rather than inability or unwillingness to read instructions.

FIGURE 3–10
Interval recording with 5-second scoring interludes.

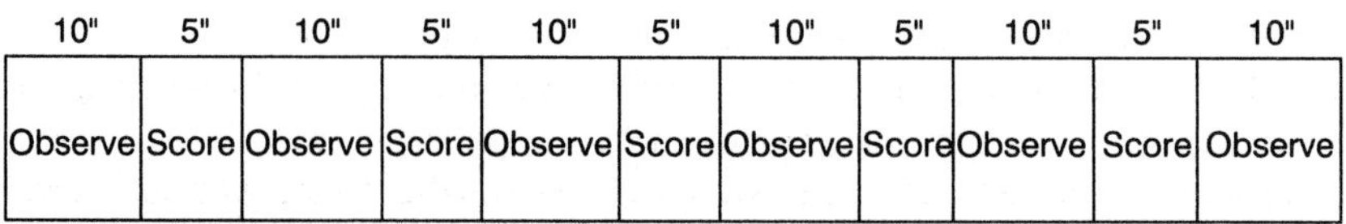

10"	5"	10"	5"	10"	5"	10"	5"	10"	5"	10"
Observe	Score	Observe	Score	Observe	Score	Observe	Score	Observe	Score	Observe

Minutes	10-second intervals 1	2	3	4	5	6
1	O	O	O	X	X	X
2	X	X	X	X	X	X
3	X	X	X	X	X	X
4	X	X	O	O	O	O
5	O	O	O	O	X	O
6	O	O	X	O	O	O
7	O	O	O	O	X	O
8	X	X	X	X	X	X
9	X	X	X	O	X	X
10	X	X	X	X	X	O
11	O	O	O	O	O	O
12	O	O	O	O	O	O
13	O	O	O	X	O	O
14	O	O	O	O	O	X
15	O	O	O	O	O	O

Student MALCOLM
Date 2/24
Observer MR. RILEY
Time Start 9:15
Time End 9:30
Behavior OFF-TASK

Note occurrence within the 10-second interval.

X = occurrence
O = nonoccurrence

Data summary

Number of intervals of occurrence: 38
Percent of intervals of occurrence: 42%
Number of intervals of nonoccurrence: 52
Percent of intervals of nonoccurrence: 58%

FIGURE 3–11 ***Interval recording of off-task behavior.***

Time Sampling

Time sampling allows for only one observation per interval.

In order to use time sampling, the data collector selects a time period in which to observe the behavior and divides this period into equal intervals. This process is similar to that employed with interval recording, but the intervals for time sampling are usually minutes rather than seconds. Such a format allows for observing the behavior over longer periods of time (Ayllon & Michael, 1959). To record these data, the observer draws a series of boxes representing the intervals. The observer simply notes in each box (interval) whether the behavior was occurring (X) or not (O) when the student was observed at the end of the interval. Each interval therefore has only one notation. Note that the time sampling procedure differs from interval recording in that the student is observed only *at the end of the interval* rather than throughout it.

Figure 3–13 shows a data sheet for a 1-hour observation period occurring between 9:05 a.m. and 10:05 a.m. 3 days a week. The hour is divided into six 10-minute intervals. On Monday the target behavior (walking around the room without permission)

10-second intervals

12 3 456

Minutes						
1	X	X	X	X	O	X
2	O	X	X	O	O	O
3	O	O	O	O	X	O
4	O	O	X	X	X	O
5	O	X	O	O	O	O
6	X	X	O	X	X	O
7	O	O	X	O	O	O
8	O	O	O	X	X	X
9	X	O	O	O	O	X
10	O	O	X	O	O	X
11	O	O	O	X	X	O
12	X	X	X	X	O	O
13	O	O	O	O	O	X
14	X	O	X	O	O	O
15	O	X	X	X	X	X

Student LEROY
Date 9/18
Observer MS HEILBRUNER
Time Start 11:00
Time End 11:15
Behavior OFF-TASK

Note occurrence within the 10-second interval.

X = occurrence
O = nonoccurrence

Data summary

Number of intervals of occurrence: 38
Percent of intervals of occurrence: 42%
Number of intervals of nonoccurrence: 52
Percent of intervals of nonoccurrence: 58%

FIGURE 3–12 ***Interval recording of off-task behavior.***

was occurring at the end of four of the intervals: the first, second, fourth, and fifth. On Wednesday it was occurring at the end of three intervals: the first, fifth, and sixth. On Friday it was occurring at the end of four intervals: the first, fourth, fifth, and sixth. The teacher may summarize the number of intervals at the end of which the behavior was occurring for each day or each week or record the daily average for the week. As time sampling allows for longer periods of observation, the teacher could take data on the student's target behavior for the entire morning. The data sheet in Figure 3–14 allows for a morning's observation period of three hours, with each hour divided into four 15-minute intervals.

Two fairly simple ways of recording time sampling data are to set a timer to ring at the end of the interval and to observe the behavior when the timer rings or to use a tape with prerecorded sounds at chosen intervals that can be heard using an earpiece. To prevent students' figuring out the schedule and performing (or not performing) some behavior only at the end of the interval, the intervals may be of varying lengths. For example, a 10-minute time sampling recording system might have intervals of 8, 12,

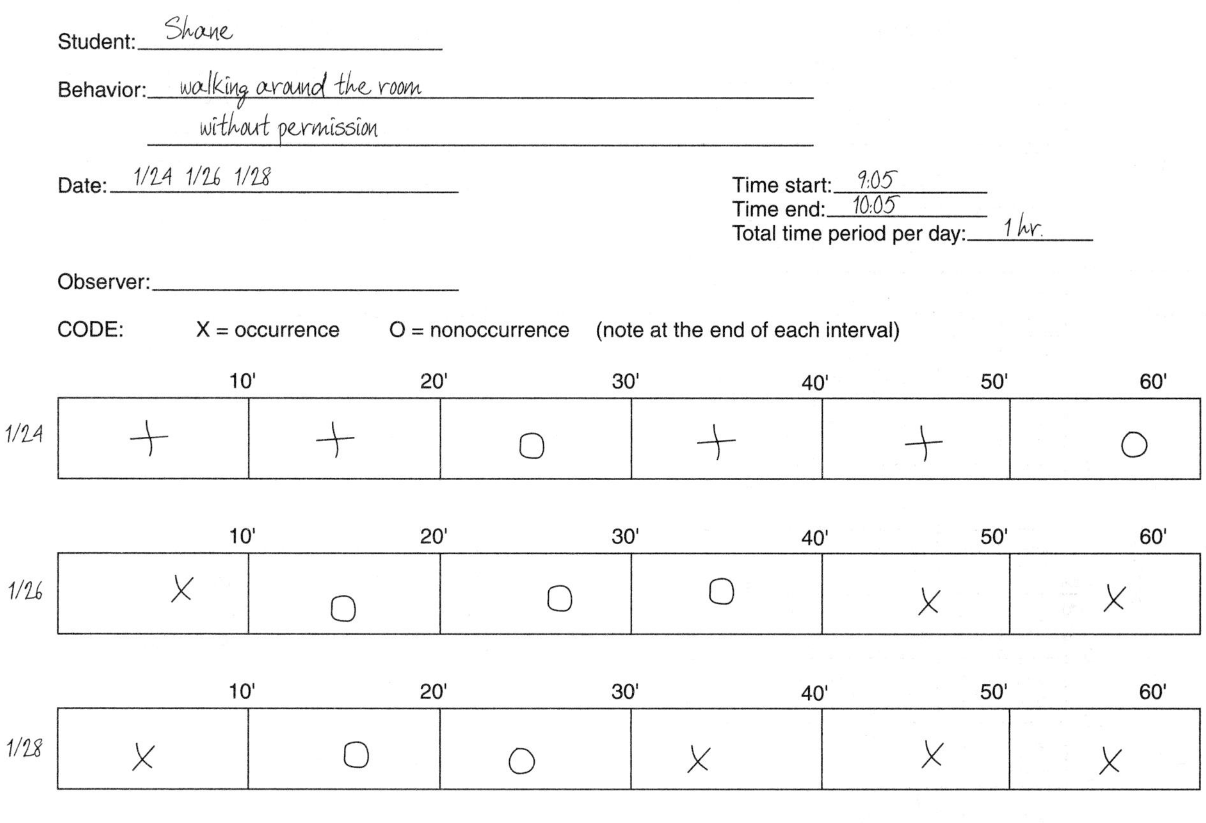
Student: Shane

Behavior: walking around the room without permission

Date: 1/24 1/26 1/28

Time start: 9:05
Time end: 10:05
Total time period per day: 1 hr.

Observer:

CODE: X = occurrence O = nonoccurrence (note at the end of each interval)

	10'	20'	30'	40'	50'	60'
1/24	+	+	O	+	+	O
1/26	X	O	O	O	X	X
1/28	X	O	O	X	X	X

Data Summary
Daily: Mon. number of intervals of occurrence:
percent of intervals of occurrence:
number of intervals of nonoccurrence:
percent of intervals of nonoccurrence:

Weekly: number of intervals of occurrence:
percent of intervals of occurrence:
number of intervals of nonoccurrence:
percent of intervals of nonoccurrence:

Average daily: number of intervals of occurrence:
percent of intervals of occurrence:
number of intervals of nonoccurrence:
percent of intervals of nonoccurrence:

FIGURE 3–13 ***Time sampling data sheet for a 1-hour observation period, with 10-minute intervals, 3 days during a week.***

6, 14, 9, and 11 minutes. The average interval duration would be 10 minutes, but the students would not know when they were about to be observed. Common sense indicates the need to hide the face of the timer.

An observer may miss a lot of behavior when using time sampling.

Because of the method of recording time sampling data, only limited conclusions can be drawn about the behavior recorded. As with interval recording, the behavior may have occurred more than once within the 10-minute observation interval. A particularly serious drawback with time sampling occurs when a single instance of a behavior occurs just before of just after the observer looks up to record the occurrence, resulting in a record of nonoccurrence.

The longer the time sampling interval, the less accurate the data will be.

When time sampling intervals are divided into segments by minutes as opposed to seconds, the procedure allows for longer periods between observations. It is, therefore, more practical for simultaneous teaching and data collection. Indeed, the interval may be set at 15, 30, 45 minutes, or more, allowing for observation throughout an entire day or class

Student:____________________

Behavior:____

Date:____________________

Time start:__________
Time end:__________
Total time period:__________

Observer:____________________

CODE: X = occurrence O = nonoccurrence (note at the end of each interval)

15	30	45	00
15	30	45	00
15	30	45	00

Data Summary

Number of intervals of occurrence:
Percent of intervals of occurrence:
Number of intervals of nonoccurrence:
Percent of intervals of nonoccurrence:

FIGURE 3–14 ***Time sampling data sheet for a 3-hour observation period, with 15-minute intervals.***

period. As the interval gets longer, however, the similarity between the data recorded and the actual occurrence of the behavior probably decreases (Saudargas & Zanolli, 1990).

Time sampling is suitable primarily for recording behaviors that are frequent or of long duration, such as attention to task, out-of-seat behavior, or thumb sucking.

Although time sampling is practical for classroom use, its usefulness may diminish as a behavior-change program progresses successfully. For example, if Barry's teacher decides to use time sampling to record his out-of-seat behavior, she may observe that during baseline almost all of her observations indicate that Barry is out of his seat when she records at 15-minute intervals during the first 90 minutes of school. However, when a contingency is applied—Barry, you will receive one token for each 15 minutes that you stay in your seat—the procedure will become less useful; for example, if the teacher holds to her recording procedure, records out-of-seat behavior only at the end of the interval, and provides the reinforcer if Barry beats the clock to his seat. If the procedure is successful in spite of this assumption, the data may reflect a complete absence of the behavior long before it has really been eliminated. Barry may be out of his seat for a short while a number of times that do not happen to coincide with the end of intervals. At this point, because the behavior is occurring less frequently and for shorter durations, event or duration recording may be as practical and much more accurate.

Behavioral dimensions appropriate to interval and time sampling recording.

Data collected using interval recording or time sampling can be used to measure behavior along the frequency dimension by reporting the number of intervals during which the behavior occurred. These data, however, cannot be converted to rate. One cannot say that a certain behavior occurred at the rate of two per minute when what was recorded was the behavior occurring during two 10-second intervals in a 60-second period. Interval and time sampling data are most often expressed in terms of the percentage of intervals during which the behavior occurred. The procedure for converting raw data into percentages will be discussed in the next chapter.

Measurement of duration can be approximated using interval recording, but this procedure does not lend itself to measures of latency. Force, locus, and topography may be measured, as with event recording, if they are included in the operational definition.

To recapitulate some of the important points and differences concerning interval recording and time sampling:

1. Both interval recording and time sampling provide an approximation of how often a behavior occurred. Neither is as accurate as event recording, which provides an exact count of occurrences.
2. Because interval recording divides an observation period into smaller intervals (usually seconds in length rather than minutes) than does time sampling, it provides the closer approximation to actual occurrence
3. Interval recording is usually used for a short observation period (perhaps 15 minutes), whereas time sampling is used for longer periods of time (an entire morning).
4. Because time sampling divides an observation period into longer intervals, it is easier to manage while teaching.
5. The occurrence of a behavior is noted and recorded at any time during an interval when using interval recording. The occurrence of a behavior is noted and recorded only at the end of an interval when using time sampling.
6. For both interval recording and time sampling, the observer reports the number of intervals in which a behavior occurred (or did not occur), not the number of times it occurred. That information is not recoverable from data collected using these methods.

Ms. Simmons Observes Pencil Tapping

Ms. Simmons is an elementary-school consultant teacher for students with learning disabilities. One of her students, Arnold, tapped his pencil on the desk as he worked. He completed a surprising number of academic tasks but tapped whenever he was not actually writing. This behavior was very annoying to his general education teacher.

Ms. Simmons had tried counting pencil taps but found that Arnold tapped so rapidly that the pencil was a blur.

She was working with another student, Shane, on paying attention and concentrating. She decided that recording interval data would be an excellent task for Shane. She carefully defined the behavior, provided Shane with a recording sheet on a clipboard, gave him a stopwatch, and told him to mark a + in the box if Arnold tapped during a 10-second interval and – if he didn't. She left Shane to observe and went to teach a small group. Very soon, she heard the sound of the clipboard hitting the floor and an expression of annoyance totally unacceptable in the classroom.

"I'm sorry, Ms. Simmons," said Shane, "but how the [explective deleted] am I 'posed to watch the kid, the watch, and the sheet at the same time?"

Realizing that she had asked too much of a student who had difficulty concentrating, Ms. Simmons revised her procedure. She took her cassette recorder home and prepared to make a tape that would "bleep" every 10 seconds. She set up the recorder next to her electronically controlled microwave oven and touched the "clear" button every 10 seconds as she watched the stopwatch. She had to start over only once when her teenage son, who had learned to expect dinner after a small number of "bleeps" (see Chapter 9 for a discussion of stimulus control), came in to ask when and what he was going to be fed.

The next day Ms. Simmons provided Shane with earphones and a 15-minute tape divided into 10-second intervals. Shane was able to record pencil tapping this way very efficiently, even though he couldn't hear it.

Variations on the Data Collection Sheet

These data collection procedures are very flexible. They can be used to record data on several students simultaneously.

On the interval recording and time sampling data collection sheets presented so far, the teacher records the occurrence or nonoccurrence of a behavior for a single student. These basic data collection formats are, however, flexible tools that can be adapted easily to meet a variety of instructional situations. The most common adaptations are for: (1) a data sheet that is more descriptive of a target behavior whose operational definition may include several topographies (for example, stereotypic behavior defined as hand flapping, body rocking, and finger flicking); (2) a data sheet to accommodate taking data on more than one behavior at a time (for example, out of seat and talking); and (3) a data sheet to accommodate data for more than one student at a time.

Each of these data collection needs may be met by using coded data. Data collected simply to record the occurrence or nonoccurrence of a single behavior are called dichotomous data. The teacher is recording that the behavior either occurred or did not occur. For a fuller description of a behavior's various topographies or to record multiple behaviors, each behavior or variation is assigned a letter code to be used during data collection. If the observer wants to record data for multiple students, each student is assigned a letter code to be used on the data sheet.

There are at least three basic formats for coded data sheets: a legend coded data sheet, a prepared code data sheet, and a track coded data sheet. Each format can be used with either interval recording or time sampling.

Coded date sheet with a simple legend. A coded data collection sheet may have a legend like the one on a road map listing the behaviors being observed and a code for each. The example at the top of Figure 3–15 shows a few rows of data from an observation period during which interval recording was used to record occurrences of "disturbing one's neighbor." The legend includes codes for hitting (H), talking (T), and pinching (P). In this example, during the first minute of observation, Hector hit his neighbor during the first interval, talked during the third and fourth intervals, and talked and hit his neighbor during the fifth interval.

If the teacher wants to collect data on the same behavior being performed by more than one student, she may use this same format by providing a code for each student. For example, on the bottom of Figure 3–15, the teacher has made an adapted interval recording data sheet on which he will record occurrences of talking during the change of class by Jan (J), Ruth (R), and Veena (V). In this example, during the first minute of observation, Jan and Ruth were talking during the first interval and Ruth was talking during the second and fourth intervals. Veena was not recorded as having talked until the second interval of the second minute.

Coded data sheet with a prepared format. A second type of coding, represented in Figure 3–16, uses letter codes for multiple behaviors or multiple students that are preentered in each cell (the space representing an interval) of the data sheet (Alberto, Sharpton, & Goldstein, 1979). With this prepared format the observer simply places a slash through the appropriate letter(s) indicating the behavior(s) that occurred or the student(s) who engaged in the behavior. The example at the top of Figure 3–16 shows rows of data from a 3-hour observation period during which the teacher used time sampling to record Sylvia's social interaction. The operational definition of social interaction included six potential elements, each with a Code: I: student initiated the interaction, R: student responded to an initiation by someone else, S: the interaction was with another student, A: the interaction was with an adult, V: the interaction was verbal, and P: the interaction was physical. In this example, during the first hour, Sylvia's first recorded social interaction was verbal in response to an adult, occurring at the end of the third interval.

Student: Hector

Date: 9-18

Observer: Ms. Hughes

Time Start: 9:10

Time End: 9:15

Behavior Codes

H = hitting T = talking P = pinching

Minutes	10"	20"	30"	40"	50"	60"
1	H	—	T	T	T H	—
2	—	P	P	—	—	—
3	—	—	—	T	T	—
4	H	—	—	—	—	—
5	—	H	—	T H	T H	—

Student: Jan, Ruth, Veena

Date: 9-14

Observer: Mr. Nelson

Behavior: Talking during change of class

Time Start: 11:05

Time End: 11:10

Student Codes

J = Jan R = Ruth V = Veena

Minutes	10"	20"	30"	40"	50"	60"
1	JR	R	—	R	—	—
2	—	RV	—	RV		R
3	JR	—	RV	RV	—	—
4		—	—		—	—
5	—	—	—	RV	R	—

FIGURE 3–15 ***Legend coded data sheets for an interval recording observation.***

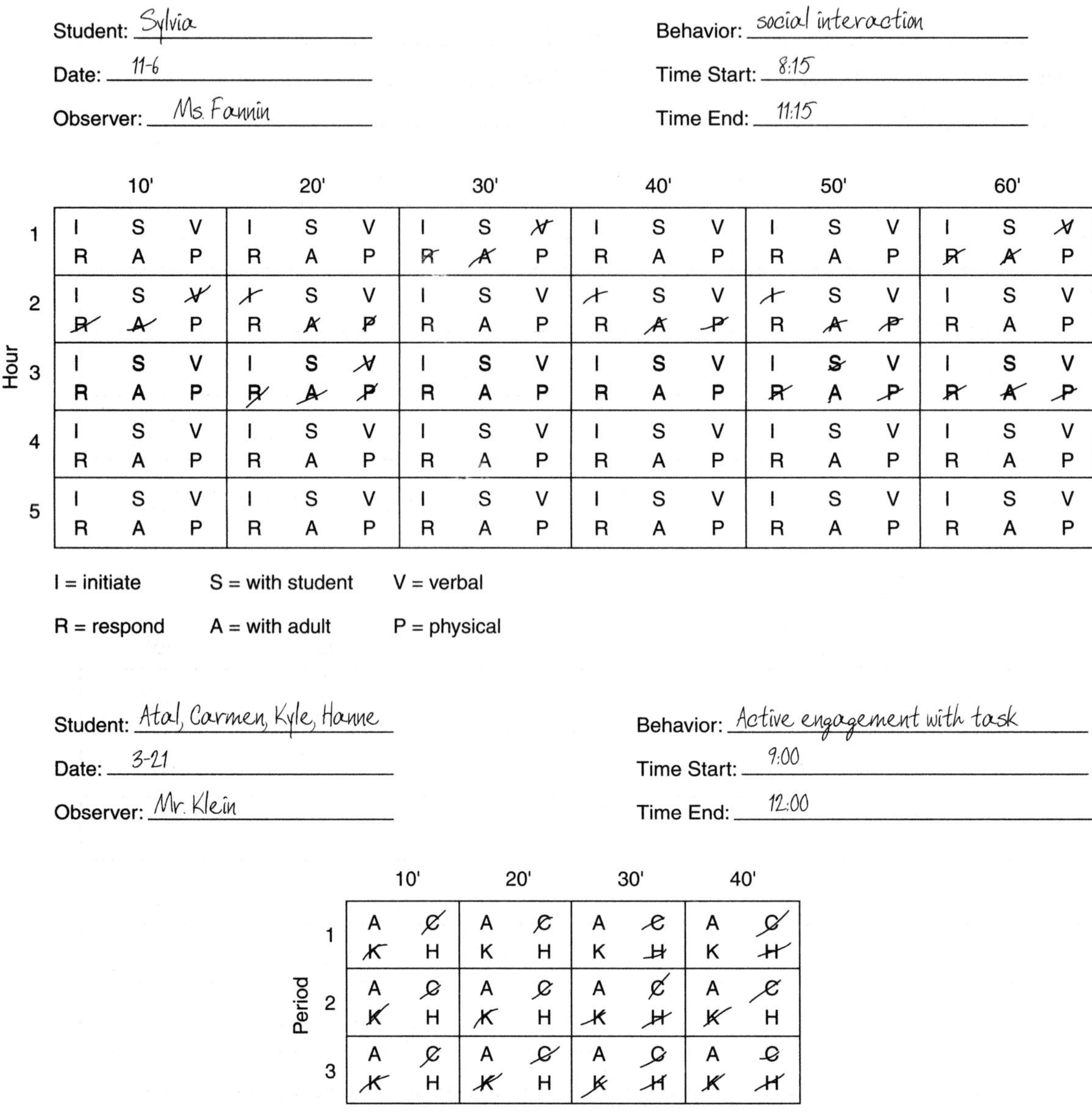

Student: Sylvia
Date: 11-6
Observer: Ms. Fannin
Behavior: social interaction
Time Start: 8:15
Time End: 11:15

Hour	10'	20'	30'	40'	50'	60'
1	I S V R A P	I S V R A P	I S V R A P	I S V R A P	I S V R A P	I S V R A P
2	I S V R A P	I S V R A P	I S V R A P	I S V R A P	I S V R A P	I S V R A P
3	I S V R A P	I S V R A P	I S V R A P	I S V R A P	I S V R A P	I S V R A P
4	I S V R A P	I S V R A P	I S V R A P	I S V R A P	I S V R A P	I S V R A P
5	I S V R A P	I S V R A P	I S V R A P	I S V R A P	I S V R A P	I S V R A P

I = initiate S = with student V = verbal
R = respond A = with adult P = physical

Student: Atal, Carmen, Kyle, Hanne
Date: 3-21
Observer: Mr. Klein
Behavior: Active engagement with task
Time Start: 9:00
Time End: 12:00

Period	10'	20'	30'	40'
1	A C K H	A C K H	A C K H	A C K H
2	A C K H	A C K H	A C K H	A C K H
3	A C K H	A C K H	A C K H	A C K H

A = Atal K = Kyle C = Carmen H = Hanne

FIGURE 3–16 ***Prepared coded data sheets for a time sampling observation.***

If the observer wants to record the occurrence of a single behavior across several students, each student's code is placed in one cell. At the bottom of Figure 3–16, there is an adapted time sampling data sheet on which "active engagement with their task" was recorded for four students across three morning class periods. In this example, during the first period, Carmen and Kyle were actively engaged at the end of the first interval, Carmen at the end of the second, and Carmen and Hanne at the end of the third and fourth.

Coded data sheet using tracks. A third format for coding more than one behavior or for coding more than one student is the use of a tracking format (Bijou et al., 1968). The top of Figure 3–17 shows on-task behavior being recorded, but the teacher also

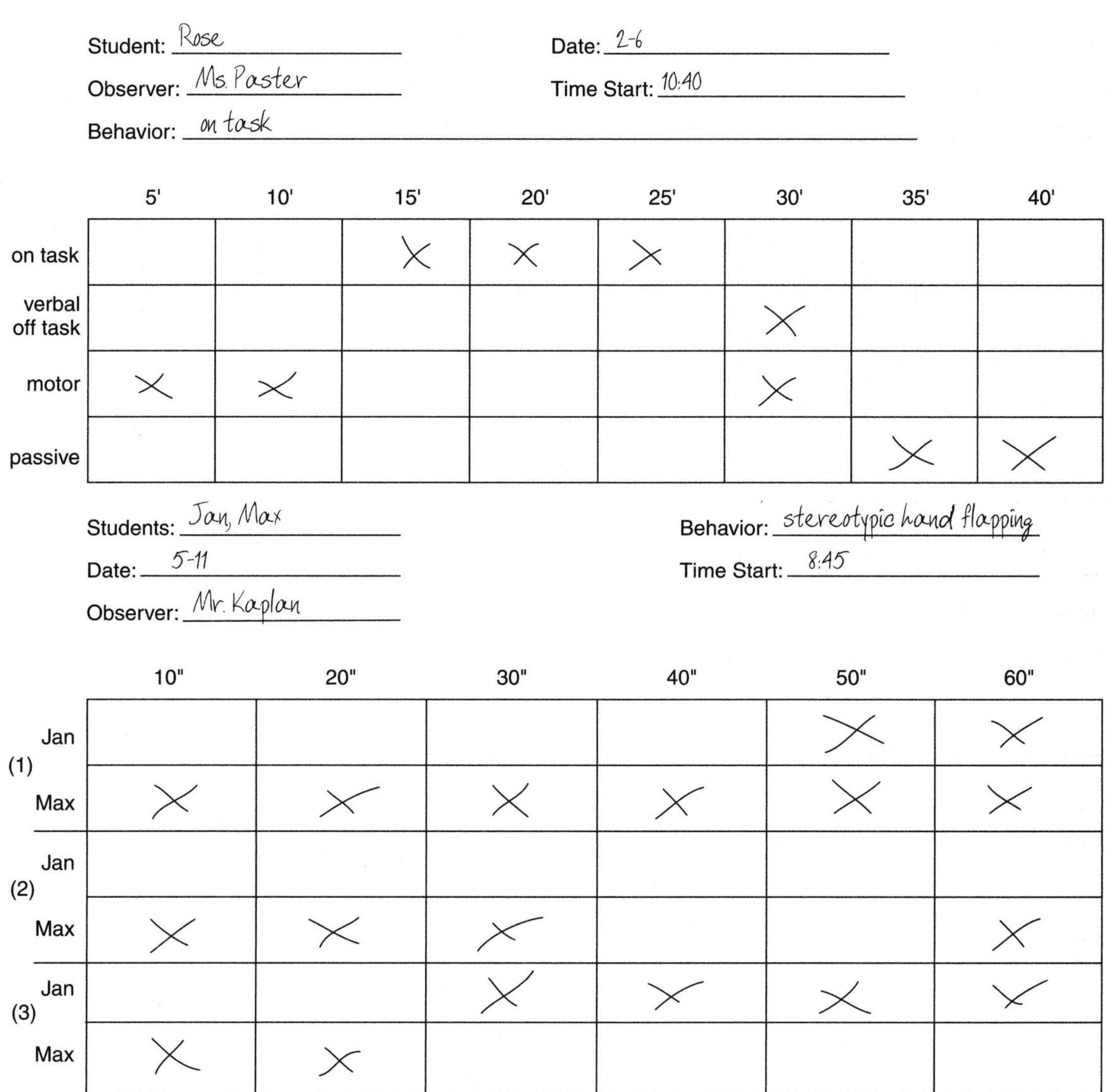
Student: Rose
Date: 2-6
Observer: Ms. Paster
Time Start: 10:40
Behavior: on task

	5'	10'	15'	20'	25'	30'	35'	40'
on task			X	X	X			
verbal off task						X		
motor	X	X				X		
passive							X	X

Students: Jan, Max
Behavior: stereotypic hand flapping
Date: 5-11
Time Start: 8:45
Observer: Mr. Kaplan

Minute		10"	20"	30"	40"	50"	60"
(1)	Jan					X	X
	Max	X	X	X	X	X	X
(2)	Jan						
	Max	X	X	X			X
(3)	Jan			X	X	X	X
	Max	X	X				

FIGURE 3–17 ***Track coded data sheets (top for time sampling, bottom for interval recording).***

Use codes to record data on several behaviors simultaneously.

wanted to know the general nature of any off-task behavior. Therefore, in addition to providing space to note the occurrence or nonoccurrence of on-task behavior, she provided track rows to indicate the general nature of any off-task behavior that occurred. The teacher would simply put a check mark in the appropriate cell(s) to indicate which behavior(s) occurred. This time sample data sheet indicates that at the end of the first and second 5-minute intervals, Rose was engaged in a motor off-task behavior; at the end of the third, fourth, and fifth intervals, she was on task; she was verbally and motorically off task at the end of the sixth; and she was passively off task at the end of the last two intervals.

In many instances, a teacher's concern is with several students in the same class who exhibit the same behavior. In such cases, data may be collected on several students at the same time. The basic data collection sheet can be adapted for this purpose by adding additional rows or tracks for each student's data. For example, at the bottom of

Figure 3–17 are a few rows of such an adaptation to an interval recording sheet to allow for collecting data on stereotypic hand flapping engaged in buy Jan and Max during the same observation period. In this example, during the first minute, Jan engaged in the behavior during the fifth and sixth intervals, and Max engaged in the behavior during each of the six intervals.

Variations for collecting data on students as a group. One way of adapting interval recording or time sampling for use with a group is the *round-robin* format (Cooper, 1981; Lloyd, Bateman, Landrum, & Hallahan, 1989). With this format the observer obtains an estimate of the group's behavior by observing and recording the behavior of a single group member during each interval. When conducting a language lesson, for example, the teacher might choose to monitor the group's attending behavior. As presented in Figure 3–18 the language period is divided into equal 15-second intervals to accommodate a group of four students, with the name of each group member assigned to each interval.

In this example, Kate is observed for occurrence or nonoccurrence of attending during the first 15-second interval of each minute; Michael's attending is observed and recorded during the second interval of each minute; Harry's during the third, and Jody's during the fourth. Because each student is observed during only one of the intervals per minute, on a round-robin basis, the resulting data provide a representation of the whole group's attending behavior, but not an accurate representation of the attending behavior of any single member of the group. Another data collection method must be used to focus on individual students. The round-robin format may also be used when collecting data on a whole class. In order to measure on-task behavior, Sutherland, Wehby, & Copeland (2000) observed each of four rows of students in rotation. Using time sampling, the teacher noted at the end of each interval whether all the students in the selected row were oriented toward the appropriate task or person and thus, as operationally defined, on task. Using random order, the teacher observed each row of students several times during the observation period.

A method of data collection similar to time sampling and useful for recording group behavior is **PLACHECK** (Planned Activity Check). Doke and Risley (1972) used the PLACHECK procedure to record participation of children in required-versus-optional activities in a day-care center. At 3-minute intervals, observers recorded the number of children participating in an appropriate manner in each available activity. Dyer et al.

	1st 15-second interval	2nd 15-second interval	3rd 15-second interval	4th 15-second interval
	Kate	Michael	Harry	Jody
1				
2				
3				
4				

FIGURE 3–18 ***Round-robin format of interval recording.***

(1984) used an adapted form of PLACHECK to record participation in age-appropriate and functional activities by students with severe behavior disorders. At the end of each interval, the number of students engaged in each of various activities was recorded. The PLACHECK procedure allows the observer to compare the number of students engaged in various activities across a period of time and also to compare the number of students engaged in each activity (or any activity at all) with the total number of students present.

DURATION AND LATENCY RECORDING

Duration and latency recording emphasize measures of time rather than instances of behavior.

Event recording, interval recording, and time sampling collection techniques focus primarily on exact or approximate counts of the occurrence of a behavior. Duration and latency recording differ from these systems in that the focus is on a temporal rather than a numerical dimension of the behavior.

DURATION RECORDING

You could measure average duration of tantrums, of time spent on task, of recreational reading.

Duration recording is used when the primary concern is the length of time a student engages in a particular behavior. For example, if a teacher wants to know about a student's out-of-seat behavior, either event recording or duration recording might be appropriate. Event recording would provide information about the number of times a student left her seat. If, however, the teacher's concern is *how long* she stays out of her seat, the most appropriate data collection method would be duration recording. In this example, event recording would mask the temporal nature of the target behavior. Although event data might indicate that the number of times the student left her seat had decreased substantially, it would not reveal that the length of time spent out of seat might actually have increased.

Duration recording, like event recording, is suitable for behaviors that have an easily identifiable beginning and end. It is important to define clearly the onset of the behavior and its completion. Using clearly stated operational definitions, researchers have measured the duration of academic engagement (Kamps, et al., 1999; Koegel, Koegel, Frea, & Fredeen, 2001; Lane et al., 2003); in-seat behavior (Roane, Fisher, & McDonough, 2003); appropriate social interactions (Chin & Bernard-Opitz, 2000; Kamps, Dugan, Potucek, & Collins, 1999; Shukla, Kennedy, & Cushing, 1999); vocational skills such as sweeping floors, bussing tables, stuffing enevelopes, and filing (Grossi & Heward, 1998; Worsdell, Iwata, & Wallace, 2002); leisure activity (Stewart & Bengier, 2001; Zhang, Gast, Horvat, & Dattilo, 2000); inappropriate behaviors such as finger or thumb sucking (Ellingson et al., 2000; Stricker, Miltenberger, Garlinghouse, Deaver, & Anderson, 2001); and aggressive behaviors such as biting, kicking, scratching, pushing, hitting, and spitting (Oliver, Oxener, Hearn, & Hall, 2001; Romaniuk et al., 2002).

The observer may time the duration of the behavior using the second hand of a watch or wall clock, but a stopwatch makes the process much simpler. For certain behaviors such as seizures or tantrums, an observer may use an audio or video recorder. The duration of the episode may be determined later using the resulting permanent product and a stopwatch or the automatic timer on the VCR.

Total duration could be used to record the time spent talking, reading, or playing with toys.

There are two basic ways to record duration data: average duration and total duration. The average duration approach is used when the student performs the target behavior routinely or with some regularity. In a given day, the teacher measures the length of time consumed in each occurrence (its duration) and then finds the *average duration* for that day. If the behavior occurs at regular but widely spaced intervals (for example, only once per day or once per class period), the data may be averaged for the week.

One behavior that can be measured by duration data is time spent in the bathroom. Perhaps his teacher feels that each time John goes to the bathroom, he stays for an unreasonable length of time. To gather data on this behavior, she decides to measure the amount of time he takes for each trip. On Monday, John went to the bathroom three times. The first trip took him 7 minutes, the second 11 minutes, and the third 9 minutes. If she continued to collect data in this manner during the rest of the week, the teacher would be able to calculate John's average duration of bathroom use for the week.

Total duration recording measures how long a student engages in a behavior in a limited time period. This activity may or may not be continuous. As an example, the target behavior "appropriate play" might be observed over a 15-minute period. The observer would record the number of minutes the student was engaging in appropriate play during this period. The child might have been playing appropriately from 10:00–10:04 a.m. (4 minutes), from 10:07–10:08 a.m. (1 minute), and from 10:10–10:15 a.m. (5 minutes). Although such a behavior record is clearly noncontinuous, these notations would yield a total duration of 10 minutes of appropriate play during the 15-minute observation period.

Latency Recording

Latency recording measures how long a student takes to begin performing a behavior once its performance has been requested. This procedure measures the length of time between the presentation of an antecedent stimulus and the initiation of the behavior. For example, if a teacher says, "Michael, sit down" (antecedent stimulus) and Michael does, but so slowly that 5 minutes elapse before he is seated, the teacher would be concerned with the latency of the student's response. Latency recording has been used to measure the time between an antecedent instruction and students' beginning to put away toys (Shriver & Allen, 1997), beginning academic assignments (Belfiore, Lee, Vargas, & Skinner, 1997; Hutchinson, Murdock, Williamson, & Cronin, 2000; Wehby & Hollahan, 2000), beginning the steps of self-catheterization (McComas et al., 1999), initiating transitions (Ardoin, Martens, & Wolfe, 1999), between incidents of Pica (Pace & Toyer, 2000), and latency to the onset of destructive behavior as a means of escaping academic and self-care tasks (Zarcone, Crosland, Fisher, Worsdell, & Herman, 1999).

As seen in Figure 3–19, a basic collection sheet for duration or latency data should provide information on the temporal boundaries that define the procedures. A duration recording data collection sheet should note the time the student began the response and the time the response was completed. A latency recording data collection sheet should note the time the student was given the cue to begin a response (antecedent stimulus) and the time he actually began to respond.

Duration and latency recording are closely matched to the behavioral dimensions of duration and latency. Consideration of topography, locus, and force may also apply here. For example, a teacher might want to measure

- how long Calvin can perfectly maintain a position in gymnastics
- how long Rosa talks to each of a number of other students
- how long after being given a nonverbal signal to lower her voice Ellen actually does so
- how long David maintains sufficient pressure to activate a microswitch

How Can All This Be Done?

Thinking about all that goes on in a classroom can make the tasks in this chapter seem overwhelming. In fact, they may be headed for the pile of advice that is "just not practical in my class" of 34 students in freshman English with 6 "inclusion students" of varying disabilities, or of 14 students with behavioral disorders and hyperactivity, or of

Latency Recording Data Sheet	Duration Recording Data Sheet
Student: EDITH Observer MR HALL	Student: SAM Observer MS. JAMES
Behavior: TIME ELAPSED BEFORE TAKING SEAT	Behavior: TIME SPENT IN BATHROOM
Operationalization of behavior initiation:	Behavior initiation:
	Behavior termination:

Date	Time		Latency
	Delivery of S^D	Response initiation	

Date	Time		Duration
	Response initiation	Response termination	

FIGURE 3–19 ***Basic formats for latency and duration recording data sheets.***

6 students with severe mental retardation or autism. Before tossing this chapter aside, remember that we acknowledged in the first paragraph that some of this may not be practical on a daily basis. Knowing this content, however, will enable you to design an appropriate data-based accountability system and will enable you to read educational research with more authority and be better prepared to apply it in your classroom. Data collection should be a tool that contributes instructional logic to classroom management. Data collection provides the basis for selecting appropriate objectives, arranging instructional groupings, and meeting the requirements of accountability. Well, then, how *can* all this be done? Here are some suggestions about how much data to collect, who should collect it, and what kind of help technology can provide.

One question to ask about how much data to collect is: How much data should I collect within an instructional session? One can either collect trial-by-trial data (recording *all* occurrences of the behavior) or collect probe data (recording only a *sample* of the occurrences). Trial-by-trial data collection during *instruction* records whether every response during the session is correct or incorrect. Probe data (data on some, but not all, responses) can be collected in two ways. It may be collected just before or just after an instructional session. If the teacher is about to conduct a 20-minute lesson on multiplying by 6, she may probe or sample student knowledge before beginning the lesson (measuring what the student has maintained since the last lesson), or she may probe just after the lesson (measuring what the student just learned) by asking the student to multiply a sample of numbers by 6. The term probe is also used to mean recording correct or incorrect use of a target behavior in an untrained setting (multiplying by 6 in the grocery store when shopping for a group) or within an untrained variation of the response (in a word problem).

During *behavior-change programs,* trial-by-trial data collection means continuous data recording for the entire period the contingency is in place; for example, recording instances or intervals of verbal aggression during all of PE or recording intervals of attending during the whole general education science class. There are several ways to use probe data with behavior change programs: (a) a contingency may be in effect all day, but student behavior is sampled by collecting data only during specific time periods: the first 10 minutes of each class period, the first five times the student has the opportunity to greet someone verbally, or (b) students' behavior may be probed or sampled during time periods when the contingency was not initially taught, or (c) students' behavior may be probed or sampled in environments where the contingency was not initially taught.

Another question to ask is: How often should I collect data during a week? Some advice is provided in the professional literature. Data collected once every two or three days closely approximates data collected daily (Bijou, Peterson, Harris, Allen, & Johnston, 1969). Fuchs and Fuchs (1986) reviewed studies in general education and special education in which formative evaluation was used for academic learning with preschool, elementary, and secondary students. They concluded that systematic formative evaluation was effective whether data were recorded daily or twice per week. Farlow and Snell (1994) suggested when implementing a new behavior program or teaching a new skill, data should be collected every day or every teaching session until the student shows steady progress over six data points or 2 weeks. At that point accurate and reliable judgments of ongoing progress can be made with data collected twice a week. When a learning problem is suspected, data should be recorded daily while programmatic adjustments are made. Once progress is seen over approximately 2 weeks, then data collection twice a week is sufficient.

The teacher is not the only one who can or should collect data. You can get someone to help collect data. Counting by ones is not a higher order skill. Appropriate training and practice, however, is essential to reliable data collection.

In a cotaught class, the special and general educator can collaborate on data collection to monitor progress of all the students in the class. In classrooms and community settings the teacher and paraeducators can all collect data. A speech-language pathologist can collect data on communication objectives, and a physical or occupational therapist can collect data on a student's learning to self-catheterize or climb stairs. In special and general education classes, especially classes in which students with disabilities are included, peers can be trained as data collectors in dyads and small groups (Marchand-Martella, Martella, Bettis, & Blakely, in press; Simmons, Fuchs, Fuchs, Hodges, & Mathes, 1994). Students should record data on themselves whenever possible. The ability to self-assess through recording one's own behavior is a component of independence. This is explored in detail in Chapter 11.

There is low-tech and high-tech assistance available for data collection. We have already described a variety of low-tech options that range from paper clips and golf counters for event recording, kitchen timers and stopwatches for duration recording, audiotapes with prerecorded chimes, and watches that chime and vibrate at specific intervals. Whenever possible we suggest making a permanent product with videotape. It is always easier and more accurate to record data on a high-frequency or disruptive behavior later while watching it on videotape rather than when trying to manage the behavior at the same time.

High-tech computerized systems have greatly advanced the ease and accuracy of data collection. Kahng and Iwata (1998) described and reviewed key characteristics of 15 computerized data collection systems that use primarily laptop computers. They suggested these systems can improve reliability and accuracy of behavioral recording compared to paper-and-pencil methods. Most of the systems reviewed use IBM-compatible software; five use MacOS. The systems have a range of capabilities from those that can collect frequency, interval, time sampling, duration, and latency data (e.g., Behavioral Evaluation Strategy & Taxonomy, The Behavior Observer System, or The Direct Observation Data System) to those with a limited range, such as the Ecobehavioral Assessment System Software, which can collect interval data, or the Social Interaction Continuous Observation Program for Experimental Studies, which can collect frequency and duration data. Most of the systems include data analysis programs, and about a third include a program to compute interobserver agreement.

A potential concern when using a computerized recording system in the classroom and other applied settings is the introduction of obtrusive materials that are likely to add confounding variables to a natural environment. Such materials increase the likelihood of students' reactivity to novel materials and may change students' behavior. Research procedures that are obtrusive produce rival explanations and conclusions (Krathwohl, 1998).

A possible method of collecting observational data while remaining unobtrusive is to use a Personal Digital Assistant (PDA), commonly referred to as a handheld computer, such as the "Palm." PDAs provide the teacher and researcher with portability, ease and versatility of data recording, and immediate data analysis. The data can be exported form the PDA to a desktop computer. With software such as Microsoft Excel or Lotus 123, the data can be converted into spreadsheets, graphs, or tables for further analysis.

An example of a software program that can be used in the classroom is *Count It* (Molgaard, 2001), a shareware database that can be downloaded easily to a PDA. *Count It* can file individual behaviors and offers functions for customized data recording. The online manual provides detailed explanations, and the author is accessible through electronic mail. Figure 3–20 provides instructions for the use of *Count It* for event recording that were developed for use in general and special education classes in a local school system (Cihak & Alaimo, 2003).

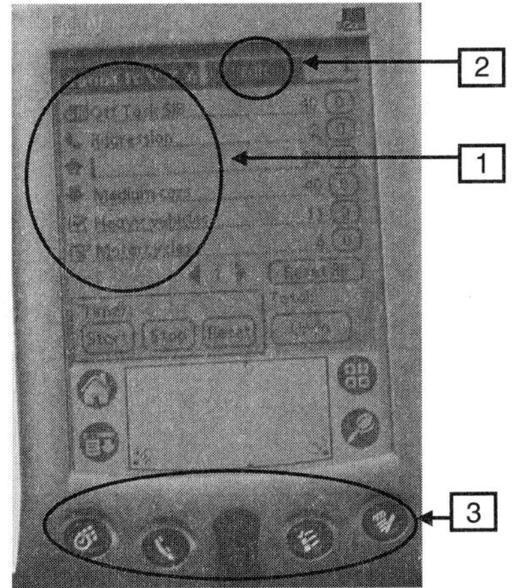

1 = counters, 2 = edit, and 3 = hardware

Instructions for Event Recording

There is an option of recording one target behavior or dependent variable at a time, or multiple dependent variables. First, label *Counters* with a specific target behavior by selecting *Edit*. Next, delete the existing labels, type in the new labels, select *Done*, and then *Edit*. The hardware buttons on the PDA correspond to the specified label. Repeat the step until all target responses or dependent variables are cataloged. During the observation, press the hardware button that denotes the specific response. The counter will automatically increase the dependent variable by one. At the end of the observation the total frequency for each response is displayed.

***FIGURE 3–20* Using the Count It shareware to collect event data.**

Adapted by Cihak & Alaimo, 2003. Used by permission.

Summary of Data Collection Systems

Questions for the data collector. How to choose a recording system.

To increase your understanding of data collection, go to the "Activities" module for Chapter 3 of the Companion Website.

The five observational systems available to the data collector are event recording, interval recording, time sampling, duration recording, and latency recording. Figure 3–21 summarizes the decision making involved in selecting the system appropriate for a particular target behavior. This process is based on a series of questions to be answered by the data collector:

1. Is the target behavior numerical or temporal?
2. If it is numerical:
   (a) Is the behavior discrete or continuous?
   (b) Is the behavior expected to occur at a high, moderate, or low frequency?
   (c) Will I be able to collect data during intervention or instruction, or will I need a third party to collect the data so as not to interrupt instruction?
3. If it is temporal, do I want to measure the time before initiation of the response or time elapsed during performance of the response?

Reliability

When data collection depends on human beings, there is always the possibility or error. Even in the case of permanent product data, which are easiest to record, mistakes may happen. Teachers occasionally count math problems as incorrect even when they are

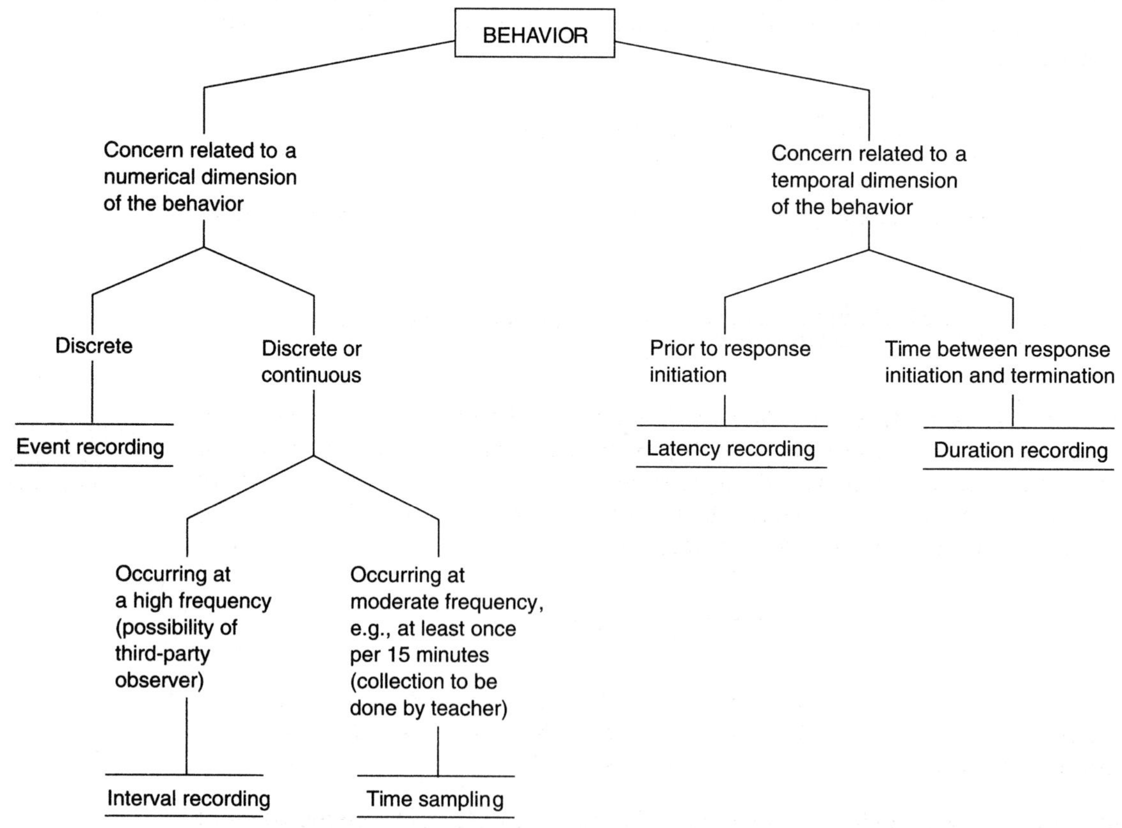

FIGURE 3–21 ***Selected observational recording procedures.***

correctly done or overlook a misspelled word in a paragraph. Because there is something tangible, however, the teacher can easily recheck the accuracy of **reliability** of her observations of the behavior. In using an observational recording system, however, the teacher does not have this advantage. The behavior occurs and then disappears, so she cannot go back and check her accuracy. To be sure the data are correct, or reliable, it is wise to have a second observer simultaneously and independently record the same behavior periodically. When this is done, the two observations can be compared and a coefficient or percent of *interobserver reliability,* or *interobserver agreement,* may be computed (Baer, 1977; Johnston & Pennypacker, 1993; Sidman, 1960).

Computing reliability for permanent product data.

To check event recording, the teacher and a second observer, a paraprofessional or another student, simultaneously watch the student and record each instance of the target behavior. After the observation period, the teacher calculates the coefficient of agreement or reliability by dividing the smaller number of recorded instances by the larger number of recorded instances. For example, if the teacher observed 20 instances of talking out in a 40-minute session, and the second observer recorded only 19, the calculation would be 19/20 = 0.95. Therefore, the coefficient of interobserver agreement would be 0.95, or 95%.

Computing reliability for event recording.

This method of calculating reliability for research purposes lacks a certain amount of precision and has therefore been referred to as a gross method of calculation. "The problem is that this method does not permit the researcher to state that both observers saw the same thing or that the events they agreed on were all the same events" (Tawney & Gast, 1984, p. 138). In other words, there is no absolute certainty that the 19 occurrences noted by the paraprofessional were the same ones noted by the teacher.

The reliability of duration and latency data is determined by a procedure similar to that of event recording, except that the longer time is divided into the shorter, as in the following equation:

$$\frac{\text{Shorter number of minutes}}{\text{Longer number of minutes}} \times 100 = \text{percent of agreement}$$

When using interval recording or time sampling, the basic formula for calculating reliability is:

$$\frac{\text{Agreements}}{\text{Agreements + Disagreements}} \times 100 = \text{percent of agreement}$$

If the data shown represent 10 intervals during which the teacher and the paraprofessional were recording whether or not Lauren was talking to her neighbor, we see that their data agree in 7 intervals (that is, intervals 1, 2, 3, 4, 6, 7, and 8); their data are not in agreement in 3 intervals (that is 5, 9, and 10). Therefore, using the basic formula, the calculation for reliability would be as follows:

Computing reliability for duration and latency recording.

$$\frac{7}{7+3} \times 100 = 70\%$$

	1	2	3	4	5	6	7	8	9	10
Teacher	X	X	-	-	X	X	-	-	X	-
Paraprofessional	X	X	-	-	-	X	-	-	-	X

Under certain research circumstances an additional, more rigorous determination of reliability should be considered. This should be a calculation of *occurrence reliability* or *nonoccurrence reliability.* When the target behavior is recorded to have occurred in less than 75% of the intervals, occurrence reliability should be calculated. When the target behavior is recorded to have occurred in more than 75% of the intervals, nonoccurrence agreement should be computed (Tawney & Gast, 1984). These coefficients are determined with the same basic formula (agreements/[agreements + disagreements] × 100), except only those intervals in which the behavior occurred (or did not occur) are used in the computation.

FACTORS THAT MAY AFFECT DATA COLLECTION AND INTEROBSERVER AGREEMENT

To increase your understanding of interobserver agreement, go to the "Activities" module for Chapter 3 of the Companion Website.

In general, applied behavior analysts aim for a reliability coefficient of around 0.90. Anything less than 0.80 is a signal that something is seriously wrong. A low coefficient of reliability can often be explained by examining the operational definition of the behavior; sloppy definitions, those that do not expressly state a behavior's topography or when it begins and ends, result in low reliability. The observers may not have been told exactly what they are to observe. Insufficient agreement may also be due to a lack of sufficient training in the data collection system. Either the primary or secondary observer may not be employing the mechanics of the data collection system correctly, resulting in differing records of the occurrence of the behavior. The environment in which data is collected may also be a factor. In natural settings such as classrooms, homes, communities, and workplaces, many variables may affect behavior and many behaviors may be occurring simultaneously. Given all that may be going on in natural settings, an observer who is unfamiliar with the setting and collects data only occasionally for reliability purposes will be less at ease and possibly more distracted during data collection, and her data may be less accurate than that of an observer who is regularly in that setting (Fradenburg, Harrison, & Baer, 1995; Repp, Nieminen, Olinger, & Brusca, 1988).

Kazdin (1977) suggested four sources of bias that can also affect interobserver agreement: reactivity, observer drift, complexity, and expectancy.

Reactivity: As teachers are well aware, the presence of an observer can affect the behavior of both the students being observed and of the teacher. This effect is known as reactivity (Repp et al., 1988). A student who knows that he is being observed may react by being very "good" or may put on an unruly show, either of which will give a false view of a target behavior. Some teachers give more prompts to a target student when an observer is present (Hay, Nelson, & Hay, 1977), and some increase their rate of instruction and positive feedback, both of which may affect the typical occurrence of the behavior (Hay, Nelson, & Hay, 1980). Simply knowing another person is present collecting reliability data can influence the accuracy of the primary observer. Such knowledge has influenced reliability data by as much as 20 to 25%. It is suggested that reliability checks should be unobtrusive or covert, if possible, or that the second observer collect data on several students including the target student, or that the second observer be someone familiar to the student, such as a classroom paraprofessional. Some of these suggestions may not be practical in every instance, but just limiting communication between the first and second observer during the observation period can reduce their influence on one another's observations.

Observer Drift: Observer drift is the tendency of observers to change the stringency with which they apply operational definitions. Over time an observer may reoperationalize the definition as it becomes less fresh in his mind. The observer may begin to record as "instances" behaviors that do not exactly conform to the operational definition. If the operational definition appears on every copy of the data sheet, the observer can easily consult it. Observers should periodically review definitions together and conduct practice sessions during the course of the program.

Complexity: A third influence on the reliability of data concerns the complexity of the observational coding system. The more complex the system, the more the reliability is in jeopardy. Complexity refers to the number of different types of a response category being recorded (for example, the number of types of disruptive behavior being observed simultaneously), the number of different students being observed, or the number of different behaviors being scored on a given occasion. In a classroom, the teacher may mitigate the effects of complexity by limiting the number of behaviors or students observed at any given time.

Kazdin (1977) provides suggestions for limiting complexity bias in research studies.

Expectancy: The fourth bias is that of expectancy. Observers' preconceived notions about students based on their past experiences with them or on information from parents or previous teachers have the potential to bias their interpretation of what they are seeing. In addition, when observers are teachers who expect behavior change (because of the terrific job they did with their intervention), they are likely to find it. The reverse is also true; a teacher who has decided that nothing can be done with a student is not likely to see a change in behavior accurately.

Observers may be biased because of the student's sex, race, appearance, or previous history. In addition, a bias may result from the purpose of the observation (Repp et al., 1988). Teachers may be biased data collectors if the failure of a behavior-change strategy will result in a problem student's being moved to a different environment.

The procedures described in this section are adequate to determine reliability for most teachers, especially if efforts are made to control bias. More stringent standards are sometimes applied in research studies. The student who is interested in learning more about interobserver reliability should consult Hawkins and Dotson (1975) and the series of invited articles on this topic in Volume 10 (1977) of the *Journal of Applied Behavior Analysis*.

SUMMARY

We described the various dimensions of behavior (i.e., frequency, rate, duration, latency, topography, focus, and locus) and their relationship to data collection. Data collection procedures discussed included anecdotal reports, permanent product recording, and various observational recording systems (event recording, interval recording, time sampling, duration recording, and latency recording). To assist teachers to increase the accuracy of their data, procedures for determining interobserver agreement were outlined. As professionals responsible for student learning, teachers collect data to make determinations about the success or need for change in their instruction or behavioral intervention.

KEY TERMS

permanent product recording
observational recording systems
event recording
interval recording
time sampling
duration recording
latency recording
discrete behaviors
frequency
controlled presentations
trial
PLACHECK
reliability

DISCUSSION QUESTIONS

1. Jerry's behavior in his fifth-grade class was reported as "disruptive." The consulting teacher visited his classroom to collect some initial referral data. (a) She went into his class for 30 minutes on 3 days to count instances of "disruptive" behavior. (b) On 3 days she checked every 20 minutes between 9 a.m. and noon to see if he was being disruptive. (c) For 1 hour on Tuesday morning and a Thursday afternoon, she sat in Jerry's class and wrote down everything he did, his teacher did, and significant actions of other students. What observational recording system did she use in each instance?
2. Susan never gets her math problems done before the end of class. To help determine the nature of her problems, the teacher could (a) give her a set of problems and record how long it was before she began to work, or (b) record how long it took her to complete the set of problems once she had begun. What recording system is being used in each instance?
3. Four student data collectors were observing John, a fourth-grade student. John was doing poorly in spelling. Observer 1 divided his observational time into 15-second intervals and noted whether John was working in his spelling workbook during each interval. Observer 2 went to John's desk at the end of the spelling period and counted the number of answers John had written in his spelling workbook. Observer 3 counted each time John put his pencil on the workbook and wrote something. Observer 4 divided the period into 5-minute intervals and recorded whether John was working in his spelling workbook at the end of each interval. What recording procedure is each observer employing?
4. Mrs. Carrington wanted the students to help her check their knowledge of multiplication facts. The students were divided into pairs in order to ask each other the 7, 8, and 9 multiplication table facts and record their accuracy. Each student was given a packet of flash cards that had the problem statement on one side and the answer on the back of the card. Also, on the back was a place to mark whether the answer given by his or her partner was correct or incorrect. What recording procedure is being used by the students?
5. Describe the various dimensions of the following behaviors.

   (a) mutual toy play
   (b) writing in a daily journal
   (c) kicking furniture
   (d) cleaning the glass doors in the frozen-food section of the grocery
   (e) writing the letters of the alphabet
   (f) riding a tricycle
   (g) using a mouse to select the correct answer on a computer screen
   (h) completing a sheet of long-division problems
   (i) inititiating social greetings
   (j) flicking fingers in front of one's eyes

6. The following is an anecdotal report of one session of community-based vocational instruction. Todd, his classmate Lucy, and their teacher were at Pets-Are-Us. The session's task was to move 4-pound bags of birdseed from the storeroom to the shelves at the front of the store. Transpose the information in the anecdotal report into the A-B-C column format.

May 3, 9:20 a.m.: Teacher, Todd, and Lucy are in the storeroom. Teacher explains the task. She tells both students to pick up a bag and follow her. They do, and place bag on proper shelf. She leads them back to storeroom. Teacher tells Todd to pick up a bag of seed; he walks away. She tells him a second time. Teacher picks up a bag and takes Todd by the hand and walks out to the shelf. She hands him the bag and points to where it belongs; he puts the bag on the shelf. She tells him to go back to storeroom for another. In the storeroom she tells him to pick up a bag from the pile. The third time he is told, he picks one up and goes out front and puts a bag on shelf. On the way out to the floor with the next bag, Todd stops at a birdcage, drops bag, and begins to talk to birds. Several minutes later teacher comes for him. He ignores her. She puts his hands on bag then leads him to shelf. She then takes him to storeroom. He refuses to lift a bag. She hands him one. He drops it on floor. This is repeated twice. She takes a bag and leads him back out to the shelf. She tells him to go back to the storeroom. She goes to check on Lucy. Ten minutes later she finds Todd sitting on floor eating candy from his fanny pack. She takes the candy, tells him it is for later. She tells him again to go to the storeroom. When she looks for him again, he is at the rabbit cage. She leads him back to storeroom. Tells him to pick up bag. After third delivery of instruction teacher holds bag in front of him; he doesn't move his arms. She places his arms around the bag. He lets it drop through his hands and it splits open. She scolds. She goes to get broom. She returns, and he is sitting on the floor eating the birdseed. Teacher tells Todd, "Your behavior is not acceptable. Therefore, you will no longer be allowed to work today. Sit over there and time yourself out until we leave. I am very disappointed in your work behavior today."

Chapter 4

Graphing Data

Did you know that . . .

- A picture is worth a thousand data points?
- Connecting the dots is not just child's play?
- Graphs can be used as a communication tool?
- The same set of data can be graphed in more than one way?
- Graphing hasn't changed much since you learned to do it in elementary school?

Chapter Outline

The Simple Line Graph
- Basic Elements of the Line Graph
- Transferring Data to a Graph

Additional Graphing Conventions

Cumulative Graphs

Bar Graphs

Summary

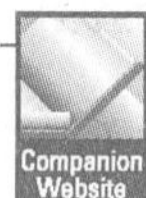

To increase your overall understanding of graphing, go to the "Supplementary Lecture Notes" module for Chapter 4 of the Companion Website.

Data collection, as you can imagine, results in a pile of data sheets. For data to be useful, the contents of those sheets must be rearranged in a way that allows them to be easily read and interpreted. The most common method of arranging and presenting data is to use a graph. A properly drawn graph provides a picture of progress across the time of instruction or intervention. Graphs should be simple and uncluttered but provide sufficient information to monitor progress. For step-by-step instructions for using the computer to create graphs, refer to Cihak, Alberto, Troutman, & Flores (in press). This is a webtext that is available through the website for this text.

To learn how to use the computer to generate graphs refer to the Webtext (Cihak, Alberto, Troutman, & Flores, in press) available on the Companion Website.

Purposes for graphs.

Graphs serve at least three purposes. First, they provide a means for organizing data during the data collection process. Tallies on sheets of paper or coded entries on data collection forms are difficult, if not impossible, to interpret. Translating raw data into a graph provides an ongoing picture of progress (or lack thereof) that is easier to understand than thumbing through piles of data sheets. Second, an ongoing picture makes possible formative evaluation, the ongoing analysis of the effectiveness of an intervention. Formative evaluation makes it possible to see how well a procedure is working and to make adjustments if it is not working well. When the intervention is finished, inspecting a graph allows for summative program evaluation, the end result of an intervention or series of interventions. Third, graphs serve as a vehicle for communication among teacher, student, parents, and related service professionals. A properly constructed graph shows all the information about how the target behavior changes during an intervention. One should be able to read and understand the graph without having to read a prose explanation. The information shown on graphs can be used to write and evaluate progress reports, individualized education plans, and behavior management plans.

For more information on graphing, go to the "Web Links" module for Chapter 4 of the Companion Website.

The Simple Line Graph

Basic Elements of the Line Graph

Line graphs are commonly used to display data in a serial manner across the duration of instruction or intervention. This allows for ongoing monitoring of the behavior and evaluation of the instruction or intervention. Graphs can be constructed using graph paper or a computer program. The grid on the graph paper or the computer software makes it possible to plot data accurately, ensuring proper alignment and equal intervals among data points. When data are presented formally, as in publications, the grid is usually omitted. The following is a description of basic elements and conventions for constructing a simple line graph (*Journal of Applied Behavior Analysis,* 2000; Poling, Methot, & LeSage, 1994; Tawney & Gast, 1984). These are illustrated by the two graphs in Figure 4–1.

Axes

These axes don't chop wood.

A graph is constructed within a set of boundaries. These boundaries are called *axes* (*axis,* singular). A line graph has two axes: the horizontal **abscissa,** or *x axis,* and the vertical **ordinate,** or *y axis*. When the graph is completed, these axes are drawn in a ratio of 2:3. Thus, if the *y* axis is 2 inches long, the *x* axis should be 3 inches. If the *y* axis is 4 inches, the *x* axis should be 6 inches.

1. *Abscissa:* The abscissa is the horizontal line that serves as the bottom boundary of the graph. It shows how frequently data were collected during the period represented on the graph. It may be labeled as, for example, days, dates, or sessions. If sessions are used, it is helpful to provide some definition of the session, for exam-

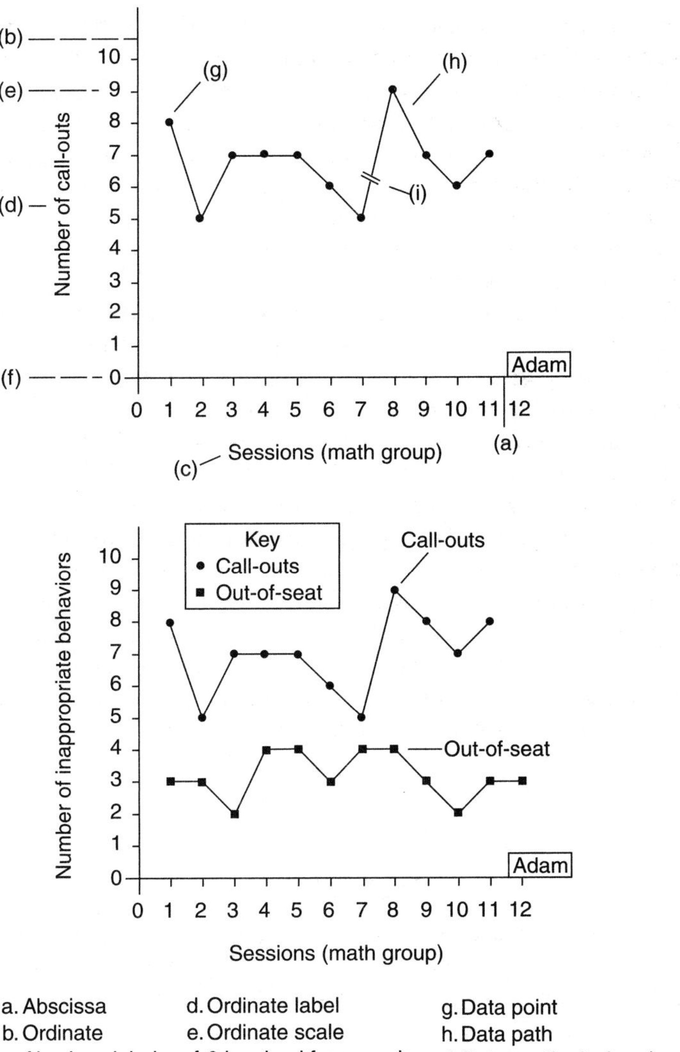

FIGURE 4–1 ***Basic elements and conventions for time graphs.***

ple, "sessions (9–9:40 a.m.)" or "sessions (math group)." The right boundary of the graph ends at the last session number.

2. *Ordinate:* The ordinate is the vertical line that serves as the left-hand boundary of the graph. The label on the ordinate identifies the target behavior and the kind of data that is being reported. For example, a label might read "number of occurrences of cursing," "rate of cursing," "number of intervals of cursing," or "percent of intervals of cursing." Standard data conversion procedures are presented in Table 4–1.

   (a) Ordinate scale: The scale on the *y* axis, used to record the performance of the target behavior, always begins at 0. If one is reporting the number of occurrences of the behavior or number of intervals during which the behavior occurred, the scale begins at 0 and goes as high as needed to accommodate the

An advantage to computing percentage.

TABLE 4–1
Summary of data conversion procedures.

Type of Recording	Data Conversion	
Permanent product recording	Report number of occurrences . . .	if both time and opportunities to respond are constant.
Event recording	Report percentage . . .	if time is constant (or not of concern) and opportunities vary.
	Report rate . . .	if both time (which is of concern) and opportunities vary, OR if time varies and opportunities are constant.
Interval recording	Report number of intervals . . .	if constant.
Time sampling	Report percentage of intervals . . .	during or at the end of which behavior occurred.
Duration	Report number of seconds/ minutes/hours . . .	for which the behavior occurred.
Latency	Report number of seconds/ minutes/hours . . .	between antecedent stimulus and onset of behavior.

x axis = abscissa y axis = ordinate

largest number. This number is sometimes difficult to predict, and the researcher may have to redraw the graph if data are being plotted before the intervention is completed. If percent is being reported, the scale always goes from 0 to 100%. The scale may progress by single digits or by twos, fives, tens, or other multiples in order to accommodate the data. It makes the graph easier to read if the beginning point of the scale (the zero value) is raised slightly from the abscissa; data points are more easily discerned when they do not rest on the *x* axis.

(b) Scale break: Occasionally, the ordinate scale may not be continuous. For example, if all the data points are above 40%, the bottom part of the graph will be empty and the top will be unnecessarily crowded. It is permissible to begin the scale at 0, draw two horizontal parallel lines between the first and second lines on the graph paper, and label the second line 40%.

Data

1. *Data point:* Small geometric forms, such as circles, squares, or triangles, are used to represent the occurrence of the target behavior during a time segment. For example, in the first graph shown in Figure 4–1, the student engaged in cursing eight times during session one; therefore, a data point is placed at the intersection of 8 on the *y* axis and 1 on the *x* axis. Each data point is independently plotted on the graph. The placement or value of one data point does not affect the placement or value of the next data point.

2. *Data path:* When a solid line is drawn connecting the data points, it forms the data path.
   (a) A single geometric form is used to represent each point on a single data path.
   (b) When more than one set of data appears on a graph, each is represented by a different geometric symbol. Which behavior is represented by each symbol and data path may be shown in one of two ways, both of which can be observed on the second graph of Figure 4–1. Each path may be labeled and an arrow drawn from the label to the path, or a legend (or key) may be provided listing each geometric symbol and the behavior it represents. No more than three different data paths should be plotted on a single graph. Additional graphs should be used when more than three data paths are necessary.
   (c) The solid line of a data path implies continuity in the data collection process. If there is a break in the expected sequence of intervention (a student is absent; a special event occurs) and a regularly scheduled session does not occur, two parallel hash marks are placed on the data path to indicate the continuity break.
3. *Student (participant) identification:* The name of the student(s) is placed in a box in the bottom right corner of the graph.

Graphs with more than three data paths look cluttered.

Transferring Data to a Graph

Transferring Permanent Product Data to a Graph

Graphing permanent product data.

Permanent product data are reported as a number of items or a percentage of items resulting from behavior. For example, a teacher might record the number of math problems completed, the percent of correctly spelled words, the number of cans placed on a display shelf, or the number or dirty clothes placed in the hamper. If the number of opportunities for responding remains constant—as in spelling tests that always have 20 items or in a series of math worksheets that always have 10 problems—the data may be graphed simply as the number of items. If the number of opportunities varies—different numbers of test items or math problems—the teacher must calculate percentages (see Figure 4–2). We calculate the percentage of correct responses by dividing the number of correct responses by the total number of responses and multiplying the result by 100, as shown:

$$\frac{\text{Number of correct responses}}{\text{Total number of responses}} \times 100 = \text{percentage of correct responses}$$

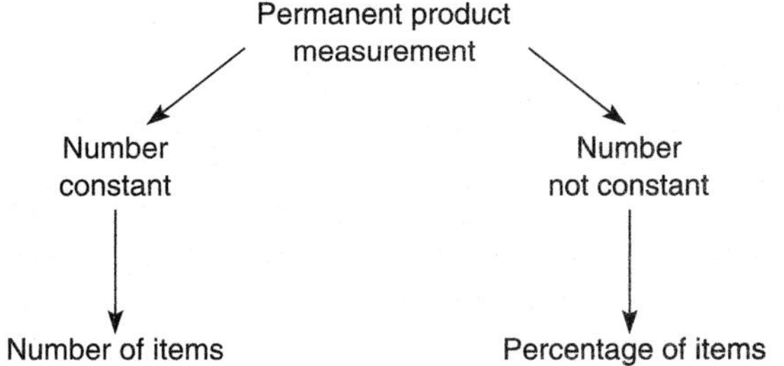

FIGURE 4–2 **Choosing measurement conversion for permanent product data.**

FIGURE 4–3
Transferring permanent product data to a graph.

Student	Catherine		
Behavior	writing paragraphs of 30 words given title and topic sentence		
Date	**Number of Words**	**Date**	**Number of Words**
1 3/16	16	6 3/27	18
2 3/18	24	7 3/30	24
3 3/20	20	8 4/2	20
4 3/23	20	9 4/4	24
5 3/25	22	10 4/7	25

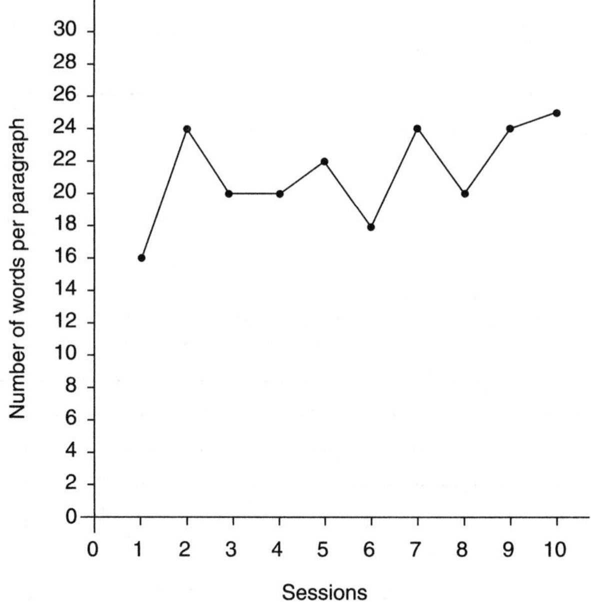

Figure 4–3 is used to record Catherine's performance of paragraph writing. Recorded on the data sheet is the number of words Catherine wrote in each paragraph. Below the data sheet is a simple line graph on which the data have been plotted.

Transferring Event Data to a Graph

Graphing event data.

Event data may be reported as (a) the number of occurrences of a behavior if the amount of time is consistent across sessions, as in the number of times the student was out of seat during the 40-minutes math group: (b) the number correct or a percentage if there are a consistent number of opportunities to respond, as in how many sight words out of 10 the student recognized; (c) a percentage correct if the number of opportunities to respond varies, as in the number of times a student complies with a teacher's instruction when the number of instructions varies from session to session.

Figure 4–4 is used to record Michael's talking out during a class activity scheduled from 10:20 a.m. to 11:00 a.m. daily. The teacher tallied the number of times Michael called out without raising his hand. Below the data sheet is a graph representing the data. Figure 4–5 is used to record Tasha's recognition of her list of 10 sight words. Below the data sheet, her performance is transferred onto a graph in two ways—as the number of words read correctly and as the percentage of words read correctly.

Student	Michael	
Behavior	calling out without raising hand	
Observation Period	10:20 a.m.– 11:00 a.m. (whole class activity)	
Days	**Instances**	**Total**
1 Monday	///	3
2 Tuesday	/	1
3 Wednesday	~~////~~ //	7
4 Thursday	///	3
5 Friday	//	2
6 Monday	~~////~~	5
7 Tuesday	////	4
8 Wednesday	////	4
9 Thursday	~~////~~ //	7

FIGURE 4–4 ***Transferring event data to a graph.***

FIGURE 4–5 ***Transferring event data to a graph.***

Student	Tasha				
Behavior	sight word reading				
	Monday	**Tuesday**	**Wednesday**	**Thursday**	**Friday**
mother	✓	✓	✓	✓	✓
father	✓	✓	✓	✓	
sister					
brother		✓	✓	✓	✓
school	✓	✓	✓	✓	✓
grocery					
hospital			✓	✓	✓
police	✓	✓	✓	✓	✓
church					✓
station					✓
Total Correct	4	5	6	6	7

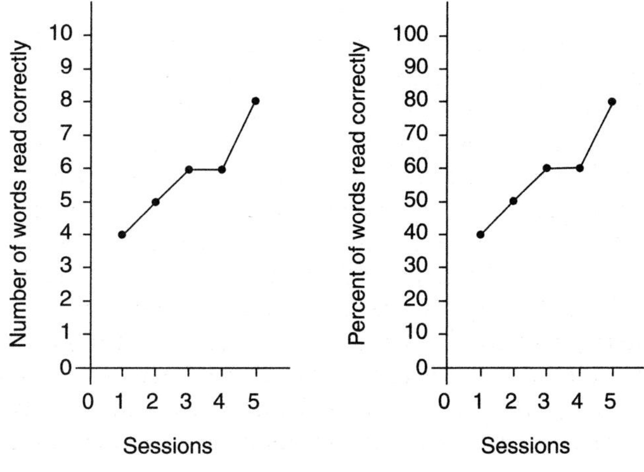

Transferring Rate Data to a Graph

Graphing rate data.

Conversion to rate data is required when the teacher is concerned with both accuracy and speed. Rate data reflect fluency of performance and allow judgments about the development of proficiency. If the time allowed for the response(s) is the same across all sessions, simply reporting frequency is all that is necessary. Such is the case when each day the student has 20 minutes to complete a set of 14 math problems. If, however, the time allocated for responding varies from session to session, rate must be calculated so that the data can be compared. Computation of rate is reviewed in Figure 4–6.

Figure 4–7 is used to record Steven's performance during vocational training at the local Red Cross office. Steven was learning to assemble packets of materials used during the blood drive. Because this was vocational training, his teacher was interested in both the number of packets he completed and how long it took him. She was interested in the rate at which Steven assembled packets. Below the data sheet is a graph displaying Steven's rate per minute of assembling packets.

FIGURE 4–6
Computing rate of correct or error responses.

Computing Rate

A rate of correct responding is computed by dividing the number of correct responses by the time taken for responding:

$$\text{Correct rate} = \frac{\text{Number correct}}{\text{Time}}$$

For example, if on Monday Kevin completed 15 problems correctly in 30 minutes, his rate of problems correct would be 0.5 per minute.

$$\frac{\text{15 problems correct}}{\text{30 minutes}} = \text{0.5 problems correct per minute}$$

If on Tuesday he completed 20 problems correctly in 45 minutes, his rate per minute would be 0.44.

$$\frac{\text{20 problems correct}}{\text{45 minutes}} = \text{0.44 problems correct per minute}$$

If Kevin's teacher had simply recorded that Kevin completed 15 problems on Monday and 20 problems on Tuesday, the teacher might think that Kevin's math was improving. In reality, though the number of math problems increased, the rate decreased, and Kevin did not do as well on Tuesday as on Monday.

Computing a rate of error may be done by dividing the number of errors by the time. For example:

$$\text{Session 1: } \frac{\text{12 spelling errors}}{\text{20 minutes}} = \text{0.6 errors per minute}$$

$$\text{Session 2: } \frac{\text{10 spelling errors}}{\text{30 minutes}} = \text{0.33 errors per minute}$$

These rate computations provide the teacher with the numbers of correct or incorrect responses per minute (or second or hour).

Student	Steven		
Behavior	packet assembly		
Observation Period	vocational training at Red Cross		
Day	**Number Completed**	**Amount of Time**	**Rate per Minute**
4/16 Monday	45	30′	1.5
4/18 Wednesday	40	25′	1.6
4/20 Friday	45	25′	1.8
4/24 Tuesday	40	20′	2.0
4/26 Thursday	50	25′	2.0
4/30 Monday	48	20′	2.4
5/2 Wednesday	54	20′	2.7

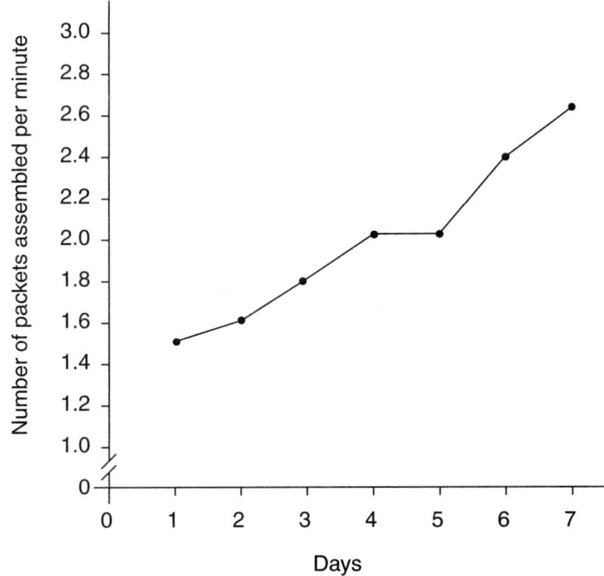

FIGURE 4–7 ***Transferring rate data to a graph.***

Transferring Interval and Time Sampling Data to a Graph

Graphing interval and time sampling data.

Interval and time sampling data are reported as the number or percent of total observed intervals during which the behavior occurs. They are usually reported as percentages.

Figure 4–8 shown Omar's out-of-seat behavior during the first 6 minutes of center time. The teacher recorded interval data. She constructed the data sheet to show the 6 minutes divided into 20-second intervals and made an X if Omar was out of his seat at any time during the interval. Below the data sheet, the data are transferred onto one graph indicating the number of intervals during which out-of-seat behavior was observed and another graph indicating the percentage of intervals during which Omar was out of his seat at some time.

FIGURE 4–8
Transferring interval data to a graph.

Student	Omar
Behavior	out-of-seat (X = out of seat)
Observation Period	6 minutes (first 6 minutes of center time)

	20"	40"	60"	20"	40"	60"	20"	40"	60"	20"	40"	60"	20"	40"	60"	20"	40"	60"
Mon	—	X	X	X	—	—	X	—	—	—	—	—	X	X	X	—	X	X
Tues	X	X	X	X	—	X	—	—	—	—	X	—	—	—	—	—	X	—
Wed	—	—	—	—	X	X	—	—	—	—	—	—	—	X	X	—	—	—
Thur	X	—	X	X	—	X	X	—	—	—	X	X	—	X	—	—	—	X
Fri	—	X	—	—	—	X	—	X	—	X	X	—	—	X	X	X	—	X

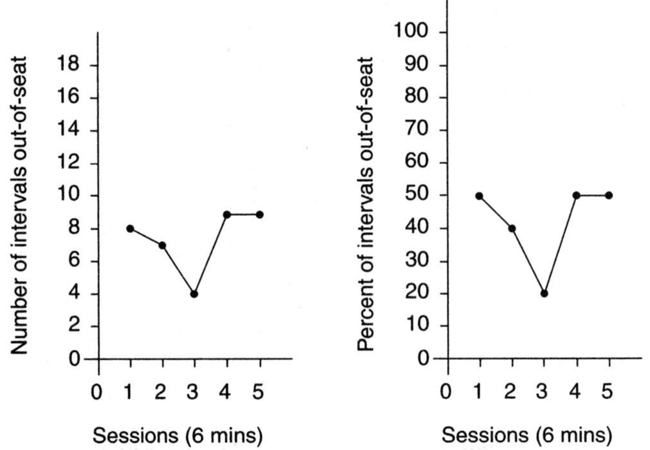

Figure 4–9 presents the data sheet on which the teacher recorded whether Leann was engaged in self-talk or peer-directed talk during 20-minute play periods. The teacher chose to use time sampling; she recorded the type of talk in which Leann was engaged at the end of each interval. Below the data sheet, the data are transferred onto one graph indicating number of intervals and another indicating percent of intervals. Note that each graph uses a different identification system to indicate the behavior associated with a data path.

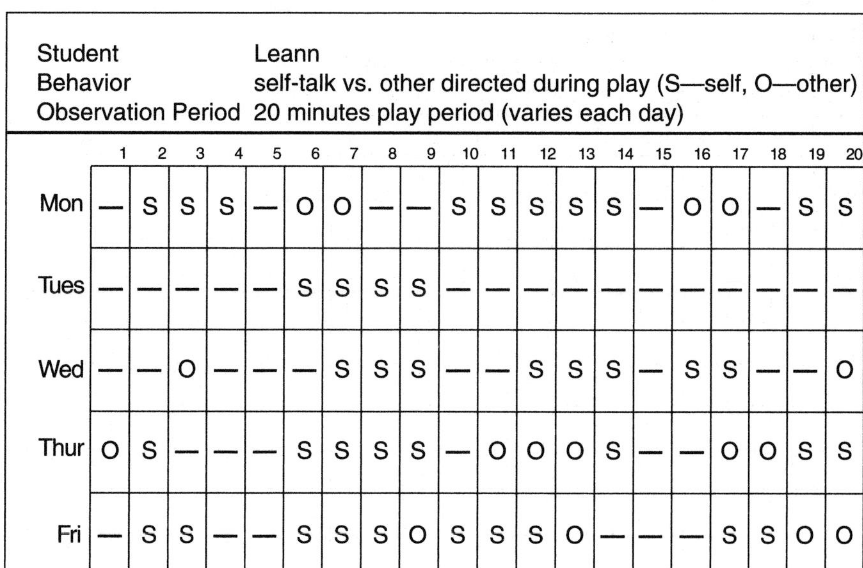

Student Leann
Behavior self-talk vs. other directed during play (S—self, O—other)
Observation Period 20 minutes play period (varies each day)

	1	2	3	4	5	6	7	8	9	10	11	12	13	14	15	16	17	18	19	20
Mon	—	S	S	S	—	O	O	—	—	S	S	S	S	S	—	O	O	—	S	S
Tues	—	—	—	—	—	S	S	S	S	—	—	—	—	—	—	—	—	—	—	—
Wed	—	—	O	—	—	—	S	S	S	—	—	S	S	S	—	S	S	—	—	O
Thur	O	S	—	—	—	S	S	S	S	—	O	O	O	S	—	—	O	O	S	S
Fri	—	S	S	—	—	S	S	S	O	S	S	S	O	—	—	—	S	S	O	O

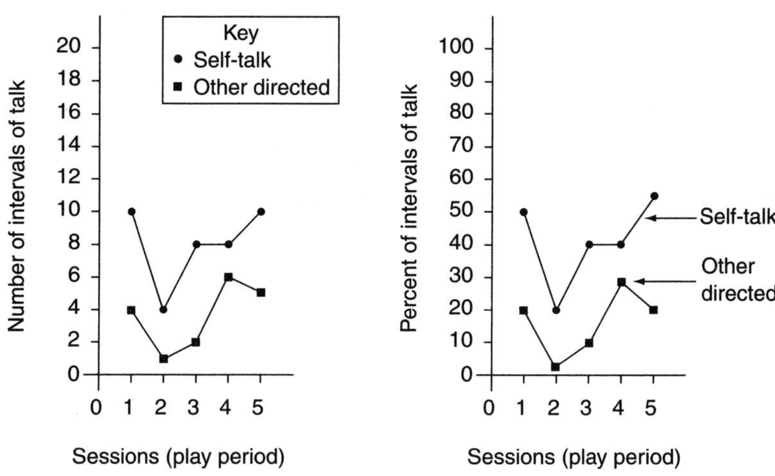

FIGURE 4–9
Transferring time sampling data to a graph.

Figure 4–10 presents a differently arranged data sheet for time sampling. On this data sheet the teacher indicated the nature of Kosh's off-task behavior during the time allocated for independent writing. Each of the two types of off-task behavior would have been properly operationalized before data collection. Below the data sheet are two ways of graphing these data and two ways of keying a graph.

FIGURE 4–10
Transferring time sampling data to a graph.

Student	Kosh			
Behavior	off-task (T—talking, D—daydreaming)			
Observation Period	independent writing (10:15–10:55)			
Monday	T 5′	T 10′	— 15′	— 20′
	— 25′	D 30′	T 35′	T 40′
Tuesday	T 5′	T 10′	D 15′	T 20′
	T 25′	— 30′	T 35′	T 40′
Wednesday	T 5′	T 10′	— 15′	— 20′
	D 25′	D 30′	T 35′	T 40′
Thursday	— 5′	— 10′	T 15′	T 20′
	— 25′	— 30′	— 35′	— 40′
Friday	T 5′	D 10′	T 15′	T 20′
	— 25′	— 30′	— 35′	T 40′

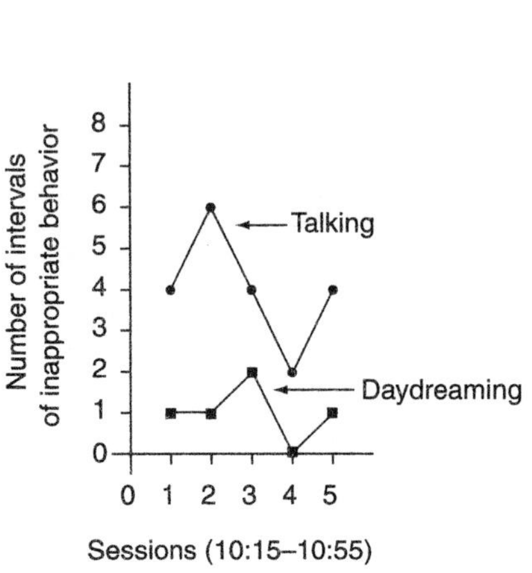

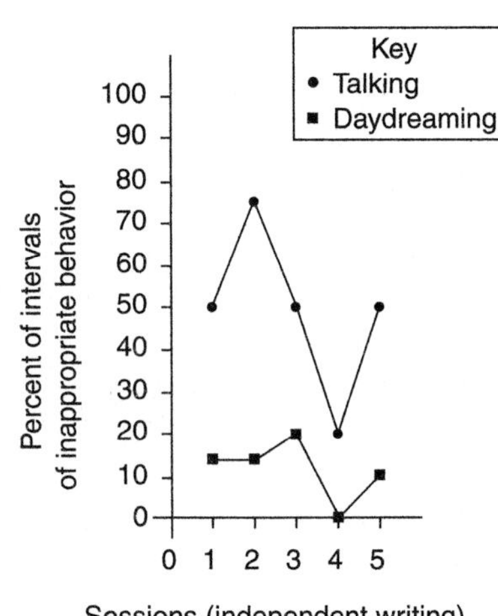

Graphing duration data.

Transferring Duration Data to a Graph

Duration data may be collected and reported either as the number of minutes or seconds it takes a student to complete a behavior or as how much of a specified period of time a student spent engaging in a particular behavior. A teacher might record, for example, the total amount of time it took a student to finish an assigned task. Another teacher might record how much of a 20-minute science lab a student spent engaged in the lab project. The second example could be reported as the number of minutes of engagement or as the percentage of available time spent engaged in the project.

Student Behavior	Casey time spent toileting			
Monday	1	12 minutes		
	2	8 minutes	➜	average = 9 minutes
	3	7 minutes		
Tuesday	1	11 minutes		
	2	16 minutes		
	3	9 minutes	➜	average = 12 minutes
Wednesday	1	15 minutes		
	2	10 minutes	➜	average = 11 minutes
	3	8 minutes		
Thursday	1	14 minutes		
	2	10 minutes		
	3	12 minutes	➜	average = 12 minutes
Friday	1	9 minutes		
	2	11 minutes		
	3	10 minutes	➜	average = 10 minutes

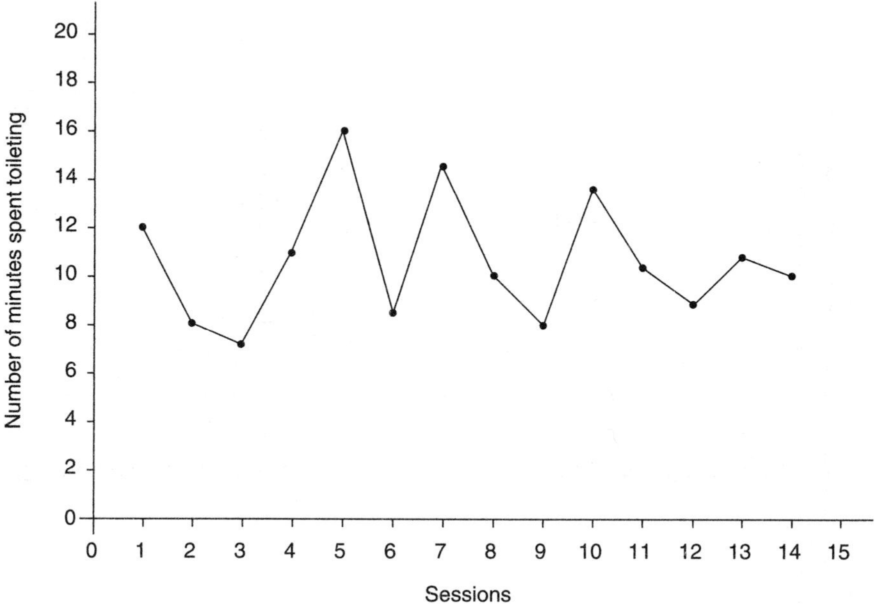

FIGURE 4–11
Transferring duration data to a graph.

Figure 4–11 shows how long it takes Casey to complete toileting. The graph below the data sheet is drawn to indicate the number of minutes he spent each time he went to the bathroom.

Transferring Latency Data to a Graph

Graphing latency data.

Latency data are reported as the number of minutes or seconds that elapse before a student initiates a behavior following a request for the behavior to be performed or for a natural occasion for its performance to occur (for example, answering a ringing telephone).

FIGURE 4–12
Transferring latency data to a graph.

Student	DuShawn	
Behavior	delay beginning of morning paragraph writing	
Observation Period	each morning—8:45 a.m.	
Day	**Number of Minutes**	**Comments**
Monday	6	pencil sharpening
Tuesday	5	roaming
Wednesday	6	pencil sharp
Thursday	2	chat
Friday	4	chat
Monday	5	pencil sharp
Tuesday	7	pencil sharp
Wednesday	5	coat-pencil
Thursday	4	roaming
Friday	5	pencil sharp

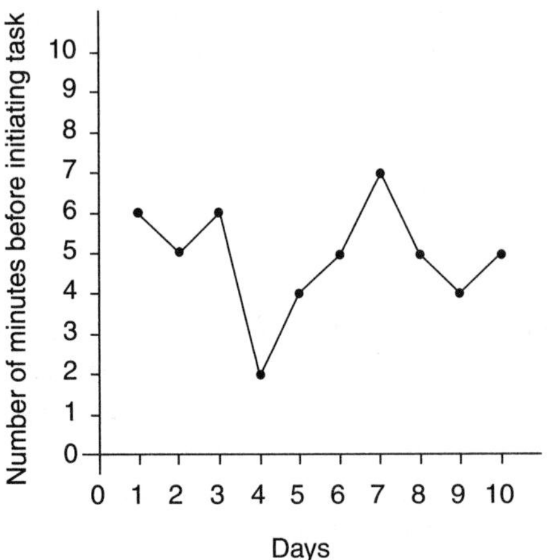

Figure 4–12 shows DuShawn's latency in beginning his daily journal-writing exercise. After giving the class the instruction to begin, the teacher recorded how many minutes elapsed before DuShawn began the task and noted what he was doing before beginning the task. Below the data sheet is a graph that represents these data.

ADDITIONAL GRAPHING CONVENTIONS

More complex graphs than the ones in this chapter will be illustrated in Chapter 6. Some additional conventions that will help you understand them are described in Figure 4–13.

Conditions are phases of an intervention during which different approaches or techniques are used. A teacher who wanted to reduce the occurrence of an inappropriate behavior might first record the current level of the behavior for several sessions or days–called **baseline data**—and then he would use some strategy to assist the student to decrease her performance of the behavior—called **intervention.** You need a clear indicator on the graph of which condition is in effect during each session. This is

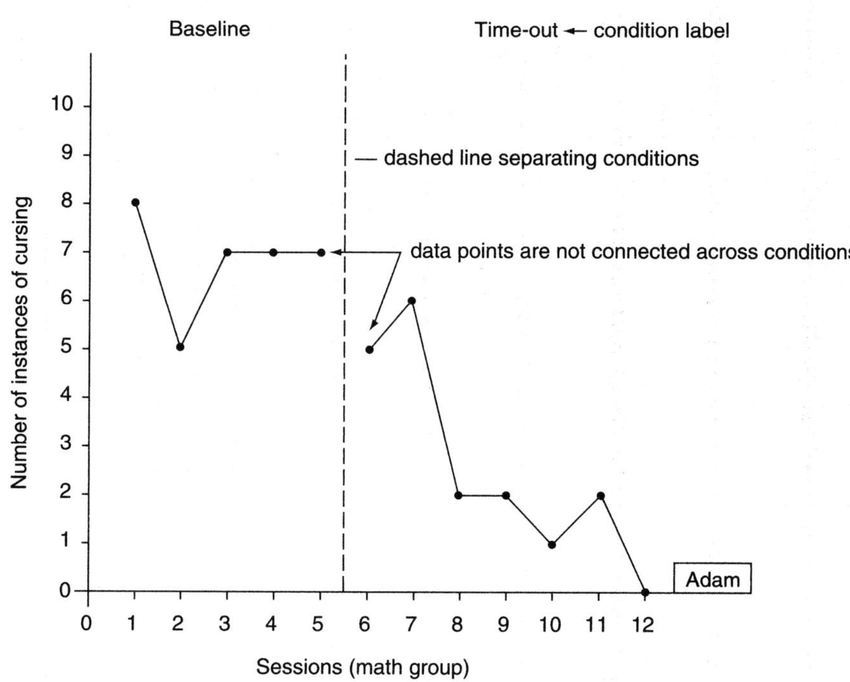

FIGURE 4–13
Conventions for conditions represented on a graph.

provided by drawing a vertical dashed line from the top to the bottom of the graph. This line is drawn between the lines on the graph paper between the last session of one condition and the first session of the next. For example, if baseline occurred for five sessions and intervention began on the sixth session, the condition line would be drawn between sessions 5 and 6 (represented on the abscissa). Data points are not connected across conditions. To identify what procedure is represented, a brief, descriptive condition label is placed above the data path for each condition, centered between the vertical dashed lines. For example, if a teacher is using a time-out procedure to reduce a student's cursing, he would print "time-out" centered above the part of the graph on which these data are placed.

CUMULATIVE GRAPHS

On a simple line graph, data points are plotted at the appropriate intersections without regard to performance during the previous session. On a **cumulative graph,** the number of occurrences observed in a session is graphed after being added to the number of occurrences plotted for the previous session. The occurrences recorded for each session include those of all previous sessions. A cumulative graph presents an additive view of a behavior across sessions, providing a count of the total number of responses. The hypothetical graphs in Figure 4–14 shows the same raw data plotted on a line graph and on a cumulative graph.

Bar graphs are clearer for young students.

Cumulative graphs always demonstrate an upward curve if any behavior at all is being recorded (Ferster, Culbertson, & Boren, 1974). This form of data illustration provides a continuous line with a slope that indicates the rate of responding. A steep slope

Raw Data

Session	Occurrences
1	1
2	1
3	1
4	2
5	0
6	0
7	1
8	3
9	3
10	1

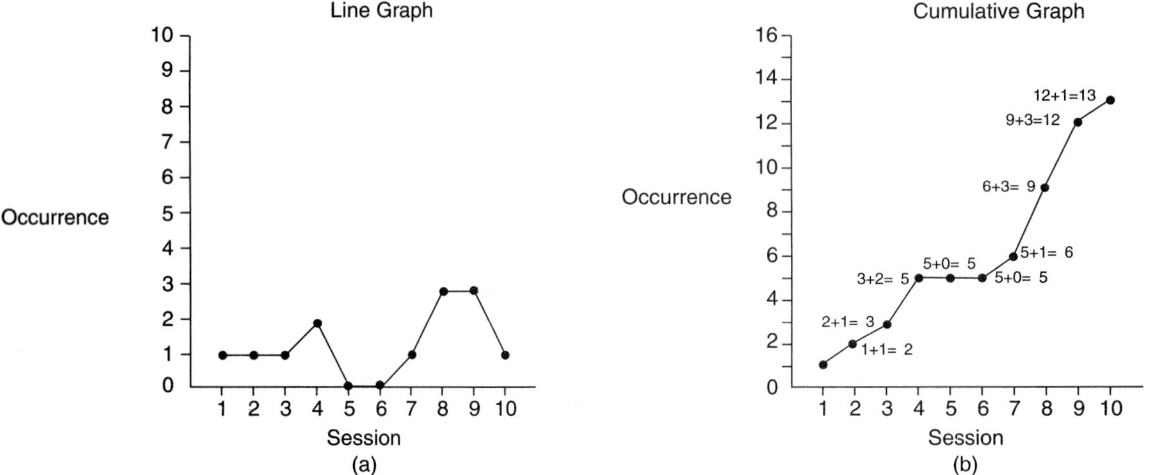

FIGURE 4–14 ***Comparison of plotting data points on line and cumulative graphs.***

indicates rapid responding, a gradual slope indicates slow responding, and a plateau or straight line indicates no responding. Each of these slope variations can be seen in the results of the study by Wilson, Majsterek, and Simmons (1996). These authors compared the use of teacher-directed instruction (TDI) with computer-assisted instruction (CAI) on the acquisition of multiplication facts by elementary students with learning disabilities. Under TDI, flashcards were used, correct responses were verbally praised, and errors were corrected immediately by repeating a three-step instructional sequence (teacher alone, student and teacher together, student alone). Under CAI, a popular computer math software program was used that delivered a brief praise statement for correct responses, indicated errors, and provided a second attempt to answer.

If the second attempt was incorrect, the software provided the correct answer and the student was instructed to repeat the answer. All students mastered more facts in the teacher-directed condition. The authors attribute the greater success of TDI to "the flexible and responsive nature of the teacher-directed condition (that) allowed teachers to move at a quicker pace, remediate errors more immediately and differentially, and build fluency through greater opportunities for practice" (p. 389). Figure 4–15 presents the graphed data of the four participating students. The authors chose to design the graph so that readers could see students' cumulative acquisition of multipli-

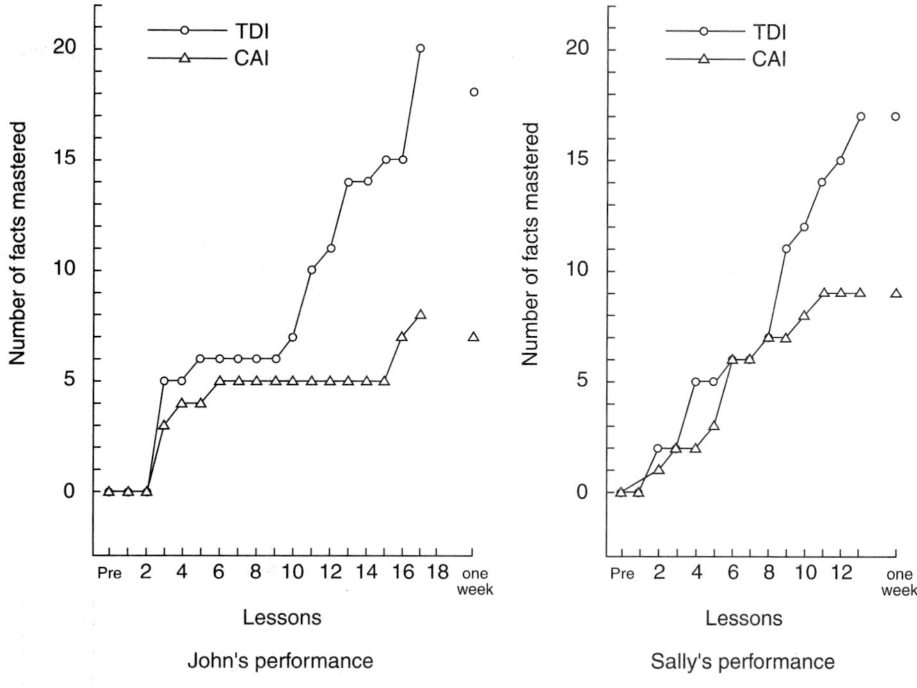

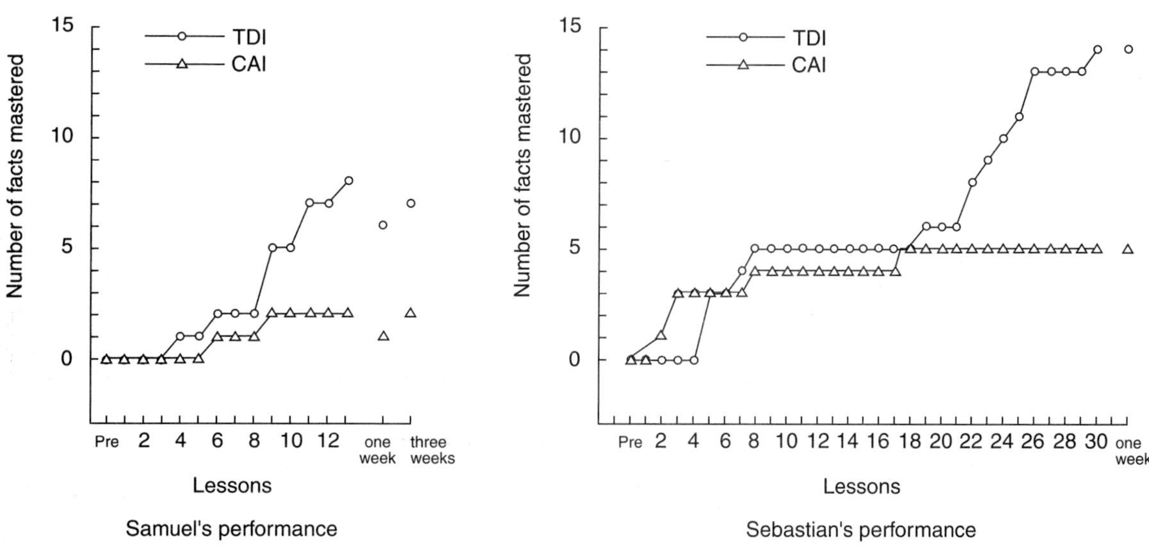

FIGURE 4–15 ***Examples of cumulative graphs.***

Note: From "The effects of computer-assisted versus teacher-directed instruction on the multiplication performance of elementary students with learning disabilities," by R. Wilson, D. Majsterek, & D. Simmons, 1996, *Journal of Learning Disabilities, 29* (4), 382–390. Reprinted by permission.

You can't ski this slope.

cation facts. Several examples of the three types of slopes described above can be clearly seen in these graphs. Examine, for example, the steep slope indicating rapid responding on John's graph for lessons 10 through 13 of TDI, the gradual slope indicating slower responding on Samuel's graph for lesson 9 through 13 of TDI, and the plateaus or straight lines indicating that Sebastian mastered no new facts during lessons 18 through 30 under the CAI condition.

BAR GRAPHS

A **bar graph,** or histogram, is yet another means of displaying data. Like a line graph, a bar graph has two axes, the abscissa (sessions) and the ordinate (performance). As its name implies, a bar graph uses vertical bars rather than data points and connecting lines to indicate performance levels. Each vertical bar represents one observation period. The height of the bar corresponds with a performance value on the ordinate. A bar graph may be better for displaying data in situations where clear interpretation of the pattern of behavior plotted on a line graph is difficult. Such confusion may result when several data paths are plotted on a single line graph, as when a teacher chooses to include data from several students or from multiple behaviors. In such cases, plotted lines may overlap or appear extremely close together because data points fall at the same intersections. Figure 4–16 offers an example of the same data plotted on a line graph and on a bar graph. The bar graph is plainly much clearer. A classroom teacher might use a bar graph to display daily the number of correct responses from each member of a small group.

Another use of the bar graph is to summarize student performance data (Tawney & Gast, 1984). This may be done for a single task, such as the mean number of science tasks completed across multiple students (Figure 4–17), or to summarize a single student's performance across multiple tasks. (Figure 4–18).

FIGURE 4–16
Comparing line and bar graph.

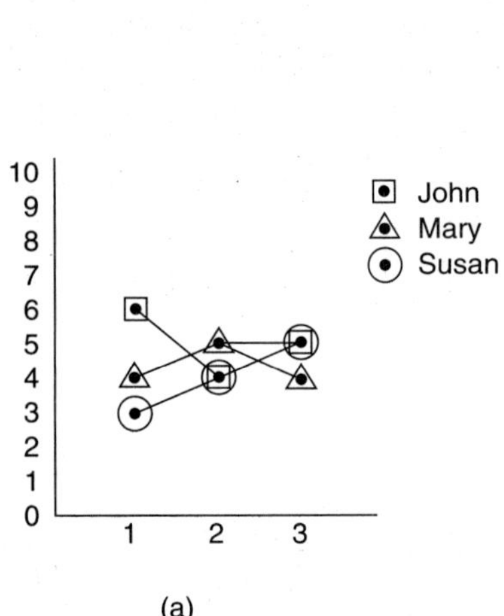

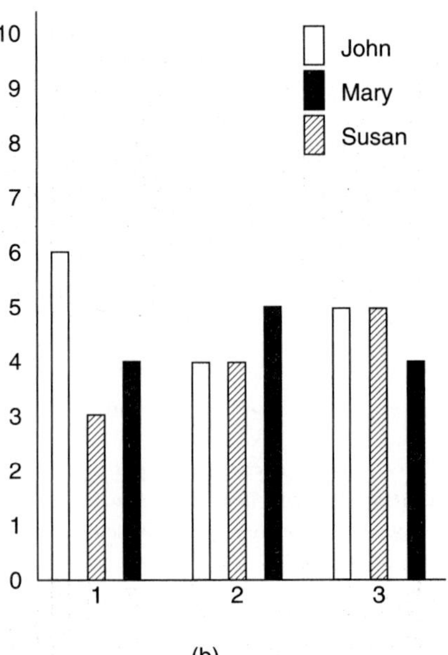

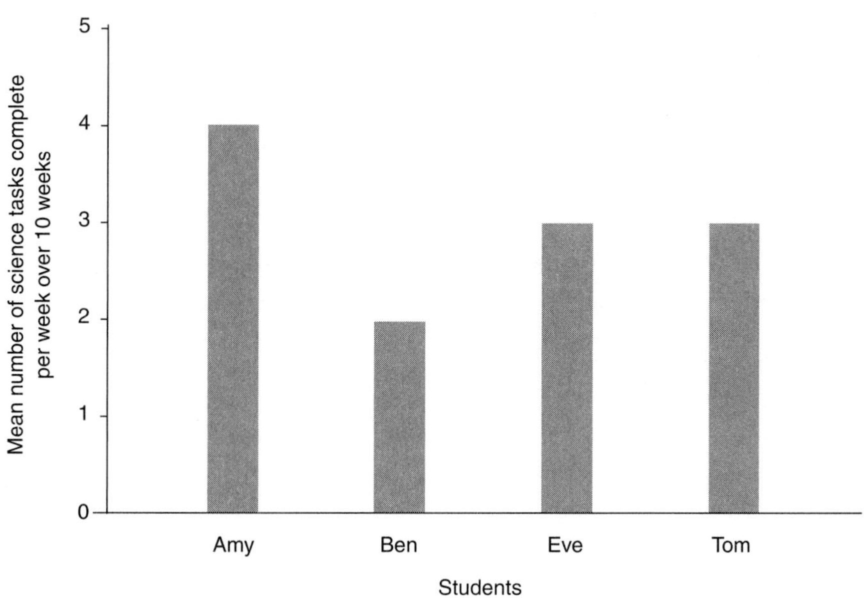

FIGURE 4–17 **Bar graph of summary of task performance of multiple students.**

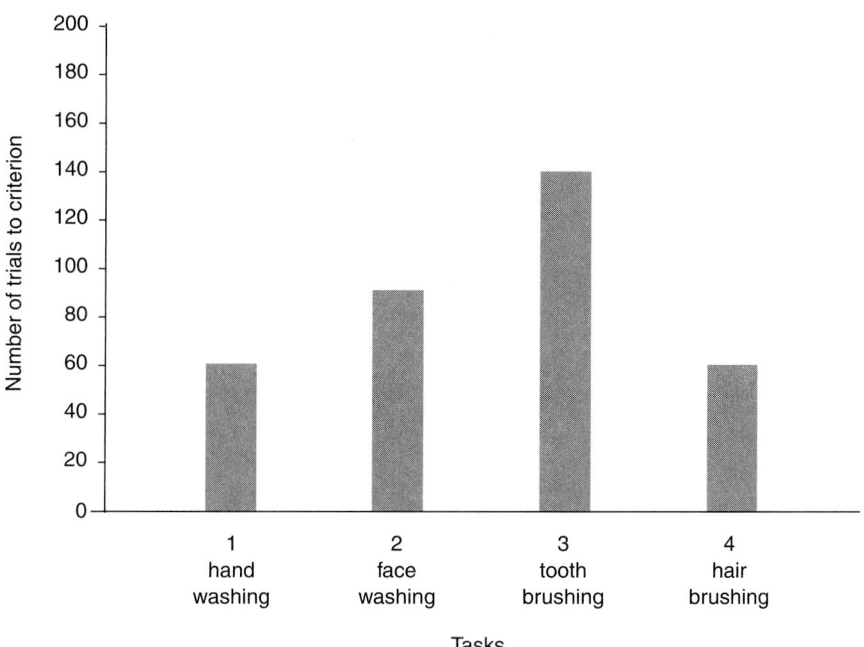

FIGURE 4–18 **Bar graph of summary of student performance across tasks.**

SUMMARY

We discussed the basic reasons for graphing data, including monitoring of student performance, formative and summative evaluation, and graphs as a tool for communicating among educators, students, and parents. We described three basic methods of graphing data: line graphs, cumulative graphs, and bar graphs. We outlined the basic conventions for drawing line graphs and provided examples of transferring various types of observational data from data sheets to graphs.

Key Terms

abscissa
ordinate
conditions
baseline data
intervention
cumulative graph
bar graph

Discussion Questions

1. How can graphs be used to (a) summarize and report student progress and (b) communicate with students, parents, and related service professionals?
2. What is the difference between frequency data and rate data? When is using each most appropriate?
3. Develop a data sheet and a graph (with hypothetical data) for the following: How much of a 20-minute science lab does Cary spend on the assigned project rather than being off task?
4. Are line graphs or bar graphs a better mechanism for monitoring ongoing student performance?
5. How and with whom can graphs be used as a communication tool?

Chapter 5

Single-Subject Designs

Did you know that . . .

- Not all sixth graders should use the same math text?
- Not every behavior change is functionally important?
- A success is truly a success only when you can replicate it?
- Single-subject research is an instructional tool?
- Big changes can happen in small steps?

Chapter Outline

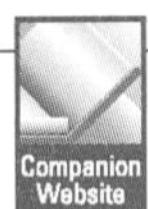

To enhance your overall understanding of single-subject designs, go to the "Supplementary Lecture Notes" module for Chapter 5 of the Companion Website.

Data collection allows teachers to make statements about the direction and magnitude of behavioral changes. Data collection alone, however, does not provide sufficient information to indicate a functional relationship between an intervention and the behavior in question. To make assumptions about functional relationships, data collection must be conducted within certain formats, or designs. A design is a systematic pattern for collecting data that enables the collector to make confident statements about the relationship between interventions and behaviors.

In this chapter we will describe a number of experimental designs used in applied behavior analysis that enable teachers and researchers to determine relationships between interventions and behavior change. Each design has a particular graphic format. The various formats are what allow visual inspection and analysis of the data. Graphs can be made with paper, a ruler, and a pencil; in most cases, however, the result will look like part of a middle school project. Such graphs do not present the image a teacher wants for a meeting with parents and other professionals gathered to evaluate the progress of student learning. For a professional appearance, standardized graphs can be made using computer software such as Microsoft Excel. To assist in creating graphs with computers, Cihak, Alberto, Troutman, & Flores (in press) provide step-by-step instructions, with picture prompts, for creating graphs for classroom use and for publication. This is a webtext that is available through the website for this text.

Teachers who can read and understand experimental research reported in professional journals can remain up to date on innovative techniques and procedures. Learning about these designs may also encourage them to become teacher-researchers who can systematically evaluate their own instruction and share their results with others. The ability to conduct classroom-based research will increase teachers' confidence, effectiveness, and credibility.

Research applications, taken from professional journals, accompany the description of each design. Each design is also applied to a classroom problem to demonstrate the utility of applied behavior analysis designs in the classroom.

VARIABLES AND FUNCTIONAL RELATIONSHIPS

We will define some terms basic to experimental investigation before discussing specific designs. The term **variable** is used to refer to any number of factors involved in research. These may include attributes of individuals being studied (age, test scores), conditions associated with the setting in which the study is done (number of students, noise level), or the nature of an intervention, which might be an instructional strategy (direct instruction phonics, cooperative learning), instructional material (counting chips, computer), or behavior management technique (tokens, self-recording). In research, the goal is to control for the presence or absence of variables that may affect outcomes. An unforeseen or uncontrolled variable (illness, for example), is referred to as a confounding variable. If a teacher is using a new program to teach a student long division, and the student's father coincidentally begins reviewing long division with the student for an hour every evening, it will be impossible to determine whether the teacher's variable (new math program) or the uncontrolled variable (home instruction) was responsible for the student's learning long division. With experimental designs researchers can control for many confounding variables.

Experimental design differentiates between two types of variables: dependent and independent. The term **dependent variable** refers to the behavior targeted for change. The term **independent variable** refers to the intervention being used to change behavior. In the following sentences, the independent variable is *italicized* and the dependent variable appears in (parentheses).

Following a student's (oral reading), the teacher provided *corrective feedback*.

Picture prompts are used when the student is engaged in (buying groceries).

Coworker modeling is provided when the student is (shelving books) in the library.

Verbal praise is contingently presented when the student (remains on task for 15 minutes).

Contingent upon (a temper tantrum), the student is placed in *time-out*.

For each (math problem completed correctly) the student earned *one token*.

Experimental designs allow researchers to demonstrate a tentative cause-effect relationship. This **functional relationship** between the independent variable and the dependent variable exists when interventions have been systematically replicated one or more times. When interventions and their outcomes have been repeated a number of times, the researcher can have confidence that the behavior changed as a function of the intervention because with each replication only the independent variable is changed or manipulated. Repeated manipulation allows the teacher-researcher to rule out confounding variables as agents of behavior change.

Basic Categories of Designs

Group designs versus single-subject designs

A research design is a format that structures the manner in which questions are asked and data are collected and analyzed. Two categories of research designs are **group designs** and **single-subject designs.** Each provides a plan and a means for demonstrating the effectiveness of an intervention on a behavior. As indicated by their names, group designs focus on questions and data related to groups of individuals; whereas single-subject designs focus on questions and data related to a particular individual.

Group designs are used to evaluate the effects of an intervention on a behavior of a whole population (for example, all the second graders of a school district or of a school building) or of a representative sample of a population. In order to determine the effectiveness of an intervention, the population (or a randomly selected sample) is, also randomly, divided into two groups: an experimental group and a control group. (It is this random selection and division that allows generalization from a sample to an entire population.) Members of the experimental group receive the intervention. This provides multiple replications of the effect of the intervention. Members of the control group do not receive the intervention. Measurements of the behavior (averages in performance) are made before intervention and at the conclusion of intervention for each group. Average changes in behavior of the two populations are compared subsequent to the intervention. This comparison is made through use of statistical procedures, the purpose of which is: (a) to verify a difference in the change in average scores between the two groups, (b) to verify that the difference is significant and therefore possibly worthy of being acted upon, and (c) to verify that the differences between groups are more likely the result of the intervention than of chance or some unknown source.

For example, the curriculum committee of Fulton County Public Schools is considering changing their sixth-grade math text. Currently they use the text by Jones & Jones. The committee randomly selects 200 students from among all the sixth graders in the district. These students are then randomly assigned to either the experimental group (100 students) or the control group (100 students). During the first week of the school year all 200 students are tested on sixth-grade math objectives. Then during the school year the experimental group receives instruction using the Smith & Smith math text, while the control group continues to receive instruction using the Jones & Jones math text. At the end of the school year each group is tested again on sixth-grade math objectives. The average gain in performance (number of objectives met) for the groups is compared. This is done to determine: (a) if there is no difference in gain in scores of the two groups, (b) if there is a difference, is this difference significant, and (c) is it reasonable to assume that a greater or lesser gain in score by the experimental group is due to using the Smith & Smith text.

Applied behavior analysts prefer multiple measurements of behavior in order to provide a detailed picture of the behavior before and during the course of intervention. They also prefer to record information specific to individuals rather than information about average performance of groups. Examining average performance may obscure important information, as illustrated in the following anecdote.

Ms. Witherspoon Orders Reading Books

Ms. Witherspoon, a third-grade teacher, was urged by her principal to order new reading books at the beginning of the school year. Being unfamiliar with her class, Ms. Witherspoon decided to use a reading test to determine which books to order. She administered the test and averaged the scores to determine the most appropriate reader. She came up with an exact average of third grade, first month, and ordered 30 readers on that level.

When the books arrived, she found that the reader was much too hard for some of her students and much too easy for others. Using an average score had concealed the fact that, although the class average was third grade, some students were reading at first-grade level and others at sixth-grade level.

SINGLE-SUBJECT DESIGNS

Single-subject designs often compare the effects of different conditions on the same individual.

Applied behavior analysis researchers prefer to use single-subject designs. Single-subject designs provide structures for evaluating the performance of individuals rather than groups. Whereas group designs identify the effects of variables on the average performance of large numbers of students, single-subject designs identify the effects of variables on a specific behavior of a particular student. These designs monitor the performance of individuals during manipulation of the independent variable(s). Certain techniques, described later in the chapter, are used to verify that changes in the dependent variable result from experimental manipulations and not from chance, coincidence, or confounding variables.

Single-subject designs require repeated measures of the dependent variable. The performance of the individual whose behavior is being monitored is recorded weekly, daily, or even more frequently over an extended period of time. The individual's performance can then be compared under different experimental conditions, or manipulations of the independent variable. Each individual is compared only to himself or herself, though the intervention may be replicated with several other individuals within the same design. Single-subject research emphasizes clinical significance for an individual rather than statistical significance among groups. If an intervention results in an observable, measurable improvement in functioning, often referred to as **enhanced functioning,** the results of the experiment are considered to have clinical significance.

Certain components are common to all single-subject designs. These include a measure of baseline performance and at least one measure of performance under an intervention condition. Single-subject research designs require at least one replication of the use of the intervention within the design. This replication allows for the assumption of a functional relationship.

Applied behavior analysts do not assume generality of research results based on a single successful intervention. When a functional relationship is established between an independent variable (intervention) and a dependent variable (behavior) for one individual, repeated studies of the same intervention are conducted using different individuals and different dependent variables. The more frequently an intervention proves effective, the more confidence is gained about the generality of the results of the intervention. That systematic teacher praise increases one student's rate of doing math problems may not be a convincing argument for the use of praise. Documentation that such praise increased production of not only math problems but also other academic and social behaviors with numerous students is more convincing. Using systematic replication, applied behavior analysts gradually identify procedures and techniques effective with many students. Others can then adopt these procedures and techniques with considerable confidence that they will work.

Sidman (1960) suggested that it would be an error to view single-subject research as simply a microcosm of group research. Repeated measures of a dependent variable when the independent variable is applied and removed demonstrate a continuity of cause and effect and the relationship of one data point to another that would not be seen when comparing the effect of the independent variable across separate groups. He contends that individual and group curves do not provide the same information "for the two types of data represent, in a very real sense, two different subject matters" (p. 54).

Baseline Measures

The first phase of single-subject design involves the collection and recording of **baseline data.** Baseline data are measures of the level of behavior (the dependent variable) as it occurs naturally, before intervention. Kazdin (1982, 1998) stated that baseline data serve two functions. First, baseline data serve a *descriptive function*. These data describe the existing level of student performance. When data points are graphed, they provide a picture of the student's behavior—his current ability to solve multiplication problems or his current rate of talk-outs. This objective record can assist the teacher in verifying the existence and extent of the behavior deficit (lack of ability to do multiplication) or behavior excess (talking out).

Second, baseline data serve a *predictive function*. "The baseline data serve as the basis for predicting the level of performance for the immediate future if the intervention is not provided" (Kazdin, 1982, p. 105). To evaluate the success of an intervention (the independent variable), the teacher must know what student performance was like before the intervention. Baseline data serve a purpose similar to that of a pretest. "The predication is achieved by projecting or extrapolating into the future a continuation of baseline performance" (p. 105). It is against this projection that the effect of an intervention is judged.

The baseline phase continues for several sessions before the intervention phase begins. In most instances, at least five baseline data points are collected and plotted. The extent of baseline data collection is affected by certain characteristics of these data points.

Baselines should be stable.

Because baseline data are to be used to judge the effectiveness of the teacher's intervention, it is important that the baseline be *stable,* providing a representative sample of the natural occurrence of the behavior. The *stability* of a baseline is assessed by two characteristics: variability of the data points and trends in the data points.

Variability of data refers to fluctuations in the student's performance. "As a general rule, the greater the variability in the data, the more difficult it is to draw conclusions about the effects of the intervention" (Kazdin, 1982, p. 109) and to make projections about future performance. When baselines are unstable, the first thing to examine is the definition of the target behavior. A lack of stability in the baseline may suggest that the operational definition of the target behavior is not sufficiently descriptive to allow for accurate and consistent recording or that the data collector is not being consistent in the procedure used for data collection.

See Chapter 2 for suggestions on writing operational definitions.

In laboratory settings, other sources of variability can often be identified and controlled. In classrooms, attempts to control variability are desirable if the sources of variability can be identified—for example, if fluctuations are caused by inconsistent delivery of medication. In cases of temporary fluctuations caused by such unusual events as a fight or a problem at home, the teacher may just wait for the fluctuation to pass. However, in classrooms, unlike laboratories, "variability is an unavoidable fact of life," and in such settings there are seldom "the facilities or time that would be required to eliminate variability" (Sidman, 1960, p. 193).

Where variables can be rigorously controlled, a research-oriented criterion for the existence of variability would be data points within a 5% range of variability (Sidman,

Session	Data Points
1	14
2	10
3	20
4	16
5	11

Baseline mean (arithmetic average) = 14.2 = 14
50% of mean = 7
Acceptable range of data points = 7 − (14 ± 7)
This baseline is stable because no data point varies more than 50% from the mean.

FIGURE 5–1
Computing baseline stability.

1960). A therapeutic criterion of 20% has been suggested (Repp, 1983). However, in classrooms where pure research concerns might be less important than rapid modification of the behavior, we suggest a more lenient parameter of 50% variability. If variability exceeds 50%, statistical techniques for performance comparisons must be used (Barlow & Hersen, 1984). A baseline may be considered stable if no data point of the baseline varies more than 50% from the mean, or average, of the baseline. Figure 5–1 illustrates a procedure for computing the stability of a baseline based on this criterion.

A **trend** in the data refers to an indication of a distinctive direction in the performance of the behavior. A trend is defined as three successive data points in the same direction (Barlow & Hersen, 1984). A baseline may show no trend, an increasing trend, or a decreasing trend. Figures 5–2 and 5–3 illustrate two types of trends—increasing and decreasing.

An *ascending baseline* denotes an increasing trend. Teachers should initiate intervention on an ascending baseline only if the objective is to decrease the behavior. Because the behavior is already increasing, the effects of an intervention designed to increase behavior will be obscured by the baseline trend.

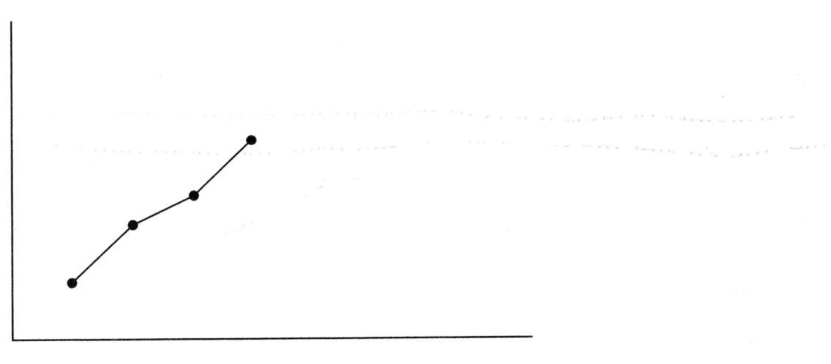

FIGURE 5–2
Increasing trend (ascending baseline).

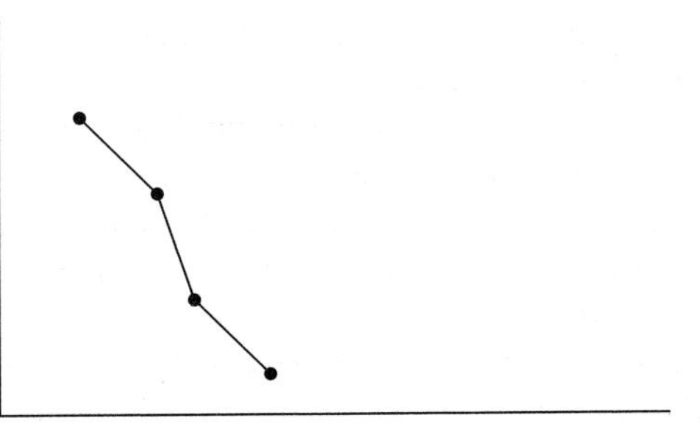

FIGURE 5–3
Decreasing trend (descending baseline).

Take baseline trends into account before intervention.

A *descending baseline* includes at least three data points that show a distinctive decreasing direction or trend in the behavior. Teachers should initiate intervention on a descending baseline only if the objective is to increase the behavior.

Intervention Measures

The second component of any single-subject design is a series of repeated measures of the subject's performance under a treatment or intervention condition. The independent variable (treatment or intervention) is introduced, and its effects on the dependent variable (the student's performance) are measured and recorded. Trends in treatment data indicate the effectiveness of the treatment and provide the teacher or researcher with guidance in determining the need for changes in intervention procedures.

Experimental Control

Professor Grundy encounters a confounding variable when he again visits Miss Harper in this chapter.

Experimental control refers to the researcher's efforts to ensure that changes in the dependent variable are in fact related to manipulations of the independent variable—that a functional relationship exists. The researcher wants to eliminate to the greatest extent possible the chance that other, confounding variables are responsible for changes in the behavior. Confounding variables are those environmental events or conditions that are not controlled by the researcher but may affect behavior. For example, if a teacher institutes a behavioral system for reducing disruptive behavior in a class after the three most disruptive students have moved away, she really cannot be sure that the new system is responsible for the lower levels of disruption. Removal of the three students is a confounding variable.

The designs discussed in this chapter provide varying degrees of experimental control. Some, called here *teaching designs,* do not permit confident assumption of a functional relationship. They may, however, provide sufficient indication of behavior change for everyday classroom use, particularly if the teacher remains alert to the possibility of confounding variables. Other designs, called *research designs,* provide for much tighter experimental control and allow the teacher or researcher to presume a functional relationship. Researchers usually demonstrate experimental control by repeating an intervention several times and observing its effect on the dependent variable each time it is repeated. Research designs may be used in classrooms when a teacher is particularly concerned about possible confounding variables and wants to be sure that intervention has had the desired effect on behavior. The teacher who is interested in publishing or otherwise sharing with other professionals the results of an intervention would also use a research design if at all possible. In the following sections on specific research designs, both a research and a classroom application are described for each design whenever possible.

AB Design

The AB design is a teaching design.

The **AB design** is the basic single-subject design. Each of the more complex designs is actually an expansion of this simple one. The designation AB refers to the two phases of the design: the A, or baseline, phase and the B, or intervention, phase. During the A phase, baseline data are collected and recorded. Once a stable baseline has been established, the intervention is introduced, and the B phase begins. In this phase, intervention data are collected and recorded. The teacher can evaluate increases or decreases in the amount, rate, percentage, or duration of the target behavior during the intervention phase and compare them with the baseline phase. Using this information to make inferences about the effectiveness of the intervention, the teacher can make decisions about continuing, changing, or discarding the intervention.

IMPLEMENTATION

Table 5–1 shows data collected using an AB design. The teacher in this instance was concerned about the few correct answers a student gave to questions about a reading assignment. For 5 days, she collected baseline data. She then made 2 minutes of free time contingent on each correct answer and continued to record the number of correct responses. As shown in Table 5–1, the number clearly increased during the intervention phase. The teacher could make a tentative assumption that her intervention was effective.

GRAPHIC DISPLAY

Data collected using an AB design are graphed in two phases: A, or baseline, and B, or intervention. A broken vertical line on the graph separates the two phases and data points between phases are not connected. The graph (Figure 5–4) shows a clearer picture of the effectiveness of the intervention than do the data in table form.

TABLE 5–1
Sample data from an AB design.

	Baseline Data
Day	**Number of Correct Responses**
Monday	2
Tuesday	1
Wednesday	0
Thursday	2
Friday	1
	Intervention Data
Day	**Number of Correct Responses**
Monday	6
Tuesday	6
Wednesday	4
Thursday	8
Friday	6

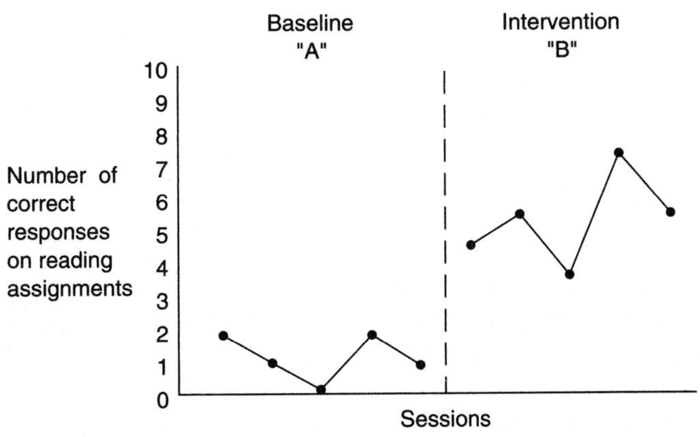

FIGURE 5–4 ***Graph of AB design data from Table 5–1.***

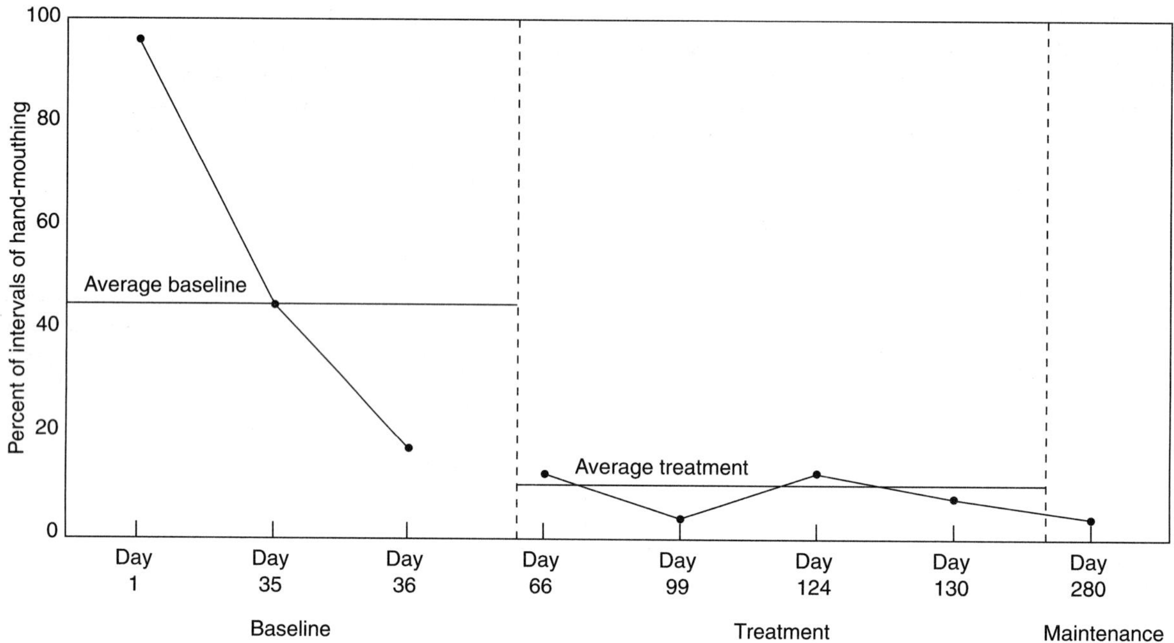

FIGURE 5–5 Use of an AB design.

Note: From "Using nonaversive techniques to reduce self-stimulatory hand-mouthing in a visually impaired and severely retarded student," by D. Miner. *RE:view, 22* (4), p. 190, 1991. Reprinted with permission of the Helen During Reid Educational Foundation. Published by Heldref Publications. 1319 Eighteenth St., N.W., Washington, D.C. 20036-1802. Copyright © 1991.

Design Application

The basic AB design is not often found in the research literature because it cannot assess for a functional relationship. The design does not provide for the replication within an experiment that establishes a functional relationship. Miner (1991) used an AB design to illustrate the results of an intervention designed to reduce the hand-mouthing behavior of a 12-year-old boy with profound retardation and visual impairments. The boy was reinforced with food and praise for assembling tubes and bolts instead of having his hands in his mouth. Figure 5–5 illustrates a steady decline in the percent of intervals of hand mouthing from the baseline to the intervention phase. One cannot, however, assume a functional relationship between the dependent variable (hand mouthing) and the independent variable (reinforcement of an incompatible activity) because the AB design does not provide for repeated manipulation of the independent variable. As Miner noted, "Unfortunately, the design of this study (AB) allows for only incomplete inference about the cause of the reduction in the target behavior" (p. 191). The following example demonstrates the use of an AB design in a classroom setting.

Jack Learns to Do His French Homework

Mr. Vogl had difficulty working with Jack, a student in the fourth-period French class. Jack was inattentive when homework from the previous evening was reviewed. Closer investigation revealed that Jack ignored the review sessions because he was not doing the assignments. To increase the amount of homework completed, Mr. Vogl decided to use positive reinforcement. To evaluate the effectiveness of the intervention, he selected the AB design using the number of homework questions completed correctly as the dependent variable.

Over a baseline period of 5 days, Jack did 0 out of 10 (0/10) homework questions correctly each day. Because Jack frequently asked to listen to tapes in the French lab, Mr. Vogl decided to allow Jack to listen to tapes for 2 minutes for each correct homework question. Data collected during the intervention phase indicated an increase in the number of questions Jack answered correctly. Data analysis suggested that the intervention technique was effective.

Advantages and Disadvantages

Many teachers use AB designs to evaluate their students' progress.

The primary advantage of an AB design is its simplicity. It provides the teacher with a quick, uncomplicated means of comparing students' behavior before and after implementation of some intervention or instructional procedure, making instruction more systematic.

The disadvantage of the AB design is that it cannot be used to make a confident assumption of a functional relationship. Although the data may show an increase or decrease in the behavior during the intervention phase, thus indicating effectiveness of the intervention, this design does not provide for a replication of the procedure. Therefore, the AB design is vulnerable to confounding variables or coincidental events. This is illustrated in the following example.

Miss Harper Conducts Research

As part of her initial student teaching assignment, Miss Harper was required to carry out a simple research project using an AB design. She decided to use Ralph's staying in his seat as her dependent variable. (Remember Ralph from Chapter 1?) Miss Harper collected baseline data for several days and determined that Ralph stayed in his seat for periods varying from 20 to 25 minutes during the 1-hour reading class. She prepared to intervene, choosing as her independent variable points exchangeable for various activities that Ralph enjoyed. When Professor Grundy made a visit soon after intervention began, Miss Harper met him at the door in a state of high excitement.

"It's working, Professor!" gloated Miss Harper. "Look at my graph! Ralph was absent the first 2 days of this week, but since he's been back and I've been giving him points, he's been in his seat 100% every day. Do you think I'll get an A on my project?"

"It's working professor. He's staying in his seat!"

Professor Grundy inspected Miss Harper's graph and agreed that her procedure appeared to be effective. He then sat down in the rear of the classroom to observe. After a few minutes, during which Ralph indeed stayed in his seat, Professor Grundy attracted Miss Harper's attention and called her to the back of the room.

"Miss Harper," he asked gently, "did it not occur to you that the heavy cast on Ralph's leg might have some effect on the amount of time he spends in his seat?"

REVERSAL DESIGN

ABAB is a research design. A functional relationship can be demonstrated.

The **reversal design** is used to analyze the effectiveness of a single independent variable. Commonly referred to as the **ABAB design,** this design involves the sequential application and withdrawal of an intervention to verify the intervention's effects on a behavior. By repeatedly comparing baseline data to data collected during application of the intervention strategy, the researcher can determine whether a functional relationship exists between the dependent and independent variables.

IMPLEMENTATION

The reversal design has four phases: A, B, A, and B:

- A (baseline 1): the initial baseline during which data are collected on the target behavior under conditions existing before the introduction of the intervention.
- B (intervention 1): the initial introduction of the intervention selected to alter the target behavior. Intervention continues until the criterion for the target behavior is reached or a trend in the desired direction of behavior change is noted.
- A (baseline 2): a return to original baseline conditions, accomplished by withdrawing or terminating the intervention.
- B (intervention 2): the reintroduction of the intervention procedure.

Data collected using a reversal design can be examined for a functional relationship between the dependent and independent variables. Figure 5–6 demonstrates a functional relationship between the dependent and independent variables, said to exist if the second set of baseline data returns to a level close to the mean in the original A phase or if a trend is evident in the second A phase in the opposite direction of the first B phase. Figure 5–7 does not demonstrate the existence of a functional relationship.

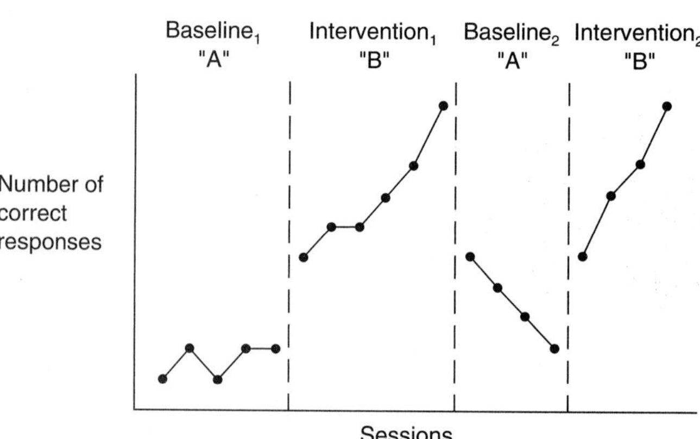

***FIGURE 5–6* Reversal design graph that demonstrates a functional relationship between variables.**

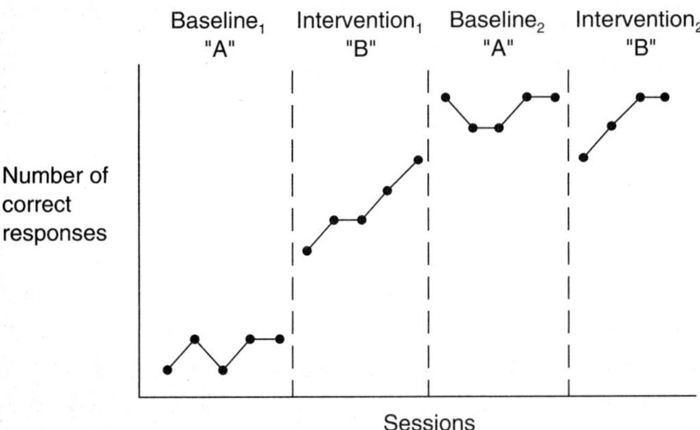

FIGURE 5–7 **Reversal design graph that does not demonstrate a functional relationship between variables.**

Note that a second B phase (intervention phase) is also desirable for verification of a functional relationship. Cooper (1981, p. 117) stated that researchers need three pieces of evidence before they can say that a functional relationship is demonstrated: (1) *prediction:* the instructional statement that a particular independent variable will alter the dependent variable—for example, the contingent use of tokens to increase the number of math problems Michael completes; (2) *verification of prediction:* the increase (or decrease) in the dependent variable during the first intervention phase, and the approximate return to baseline levels of performance in the second A phase; and (3) *replication of effect:* the reintroduction of the independent variable during a second B phase resulting again in the same desired change in behavior.

The reversal design is a research design that allows the teacher to assume a functional relationship between independent and dependent variables. The second baseline and intervention phases, with conditions identical to those of the first, provide an opportunity for replication of the effect of the intervention on the target behavior. It is unlikely that confounding variables would exist simultaneously with repeated application and withdrawal of the independent variable. The reversal design, however, is not always the most appropriate choice. The reversal design should not be used in the following cases:

It would be unethical to withdraw, for purposes of research, an intervention that stopped a student with severe disabilities from banging her head on the floor.

1. When the target behavior is dangerous, such as aggressive behavior directed toward other students or self-injurious behavior. Because the reversal design calls for a second baseline condition to be implemented after a change in the target behavior rate, ethical considerations would prohibit withdrawing a successful intervention technique.
2. When the target behavior is not reversible. Many academic behaviors, for example, are not reversible, because the behavior change is associated with a learning process. Under such conditions, a return to baseline performance is not feasible. Knowledge that $4 \times 3 = 12$, for example, is not likely to be "unlearned." At least, we would like to think not.

Graphic Display

The reversal design calls for four distinct phases of data collection. Figure 5–8 illustrates the basic reversal design. (Note that ABAB is derived from the labeling of each baseline period as an A phase and each intervention period as a B phase.)

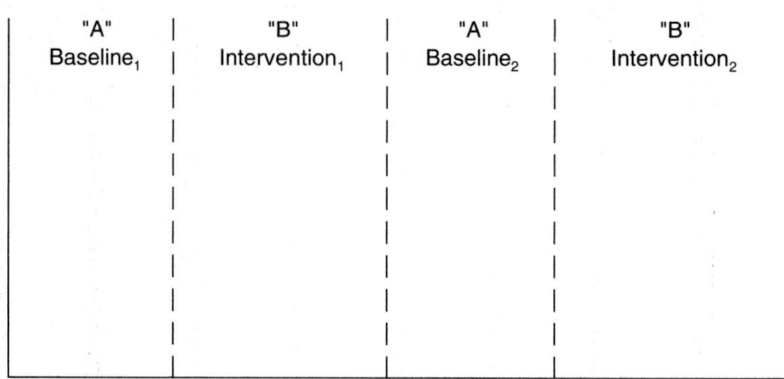

***FIGURE 5–8* Basic reversal design format.**

Design Variations

Variations of the reversal design can be found in the literature. The first variation does not involve a change in the structure of the design, but simply shortens the length of the initial baseline (A) period. This format of the design is appropriate when a lengthy baseline period is unethical, as when the behavior is dangerous, or not called for, in the case of a student who is not capable of performing the target behavior to any degree.

A second variation of the reversal design omits the initial baseline entirely. This BAB variation is considered if the target behavior is obviously not in the student's repertoire. When this design is used, a functional relation between the dependent and independent variables can be demonstrated only in the second intervention (B) phase.

Research Application

Researchers often use the ABAB design. Levendoski & Cartledge (2000) employed it to determine the effectiveness of a self-monitoring procedure for time on task and academic productivity with elementary-age students with emotional disturbance. The four boys were given self-monitoring cards at the beginning of each math period. They were told that each time they heard the bell (every 10 minutes), they should "Ask yourself. . . am I doing my work?" They were then to mark yes or no on their card. Figure 5–9

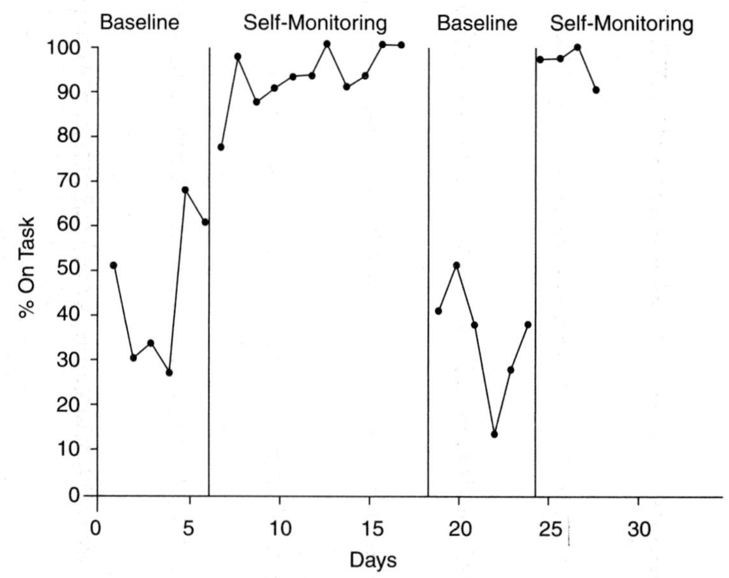

FIGURE 5–9
Research application of the reversal design.
Note: From "Self-monitoring for elementary school children with serious emotional disturbances: Classroom applications for increased academic responding." By L. Levendoski & G. Cartledge. *Behavioral Disorders, 2000.* Copyright 2000 by Council for Children with Behavioral Disorders. Reprinted by permission.

shows the results of this intervention for time on task for one of the boys. During the baseline condition when the self-monitoring card was not being used, he was on task an average of 45%. Once the intervention was in place, his time on-task average increased to 93%. During the return to baseline phase, his on-task average returned to 34%; and then increased again to an average of 96% during reintroduction of the self-monitoring card. Examination of the graph clearly shows that when the student was using the self-monitoring card, his time on task increased. Note that phases one and two are replicated by phases three and four, allowing a determination of a functional relationship.

Umbreit, Lane, & Dejud (2004) used an ABAB design to evaluate the effects of an intervention to increase on-task behavior of a general education fourth-grade student. During independent work assignments, Jason's off-task behavior included talking to other students, kicking his seat or the one in front of him, or wandering around the room. The teacher determined this behavior occurred when he completed his assignment. Jason said he finished quickly because his assignments were "almost always too easy." During baseline phases, Jason received the same math and reading assignments as the rest of the class. During intervention phases, he received assignments that were more challenging (assignments approximately two weeks further along in the curriculum). Data for his on-task behavior were recorded using thirty-seconds interval recording. As seen in Figure 5–10, during the first baseline condition (typical task), on-task behavior occurred approximately 50% of the intervals in both math and reading. During the first intervention phase, on-task behavior increased to an average of 89% in math and 92% in reading. During the second baseline phase, on-task behavior decreased to 63% during math and 65% during reading. In the final phase, on-task behavior increased to an average of 91% during math and reading. Comparison of the first baseline and first intervention phases show an increase in on-task behavior when the challenging tasks were assigned. This effect was replicated during the second baseline and second intervention phases. This replication allows the assumption of a functional

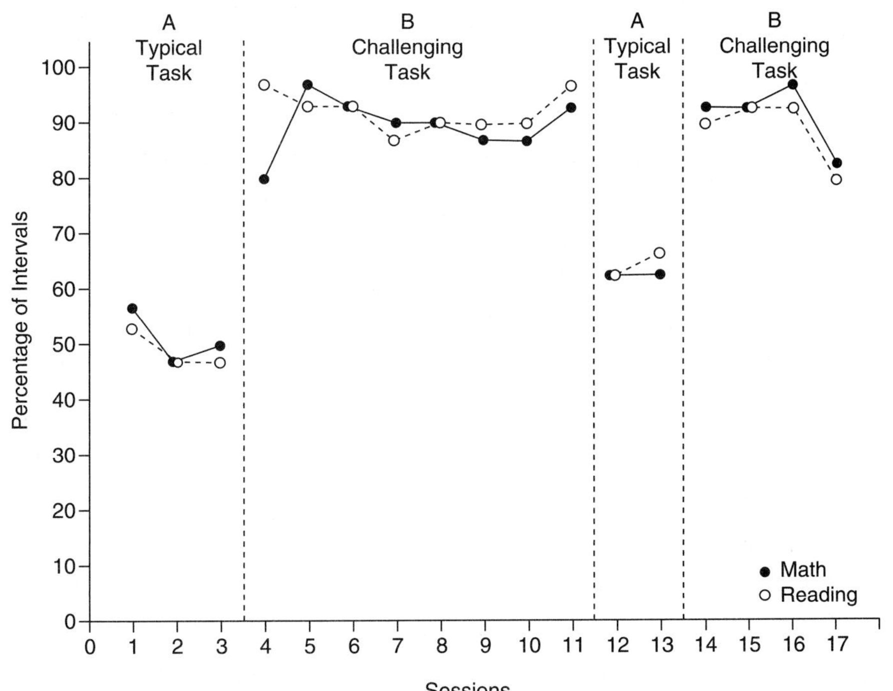

FIGURE 5–10
Research application of the reversal design.
Note: From "Improving classroom behavior by modifying task difficulty: Effects of increasing the difficulty of too-easy tasks," by J. Umbreit, K. Lane, & C. Dejund (2004), *Journal of Positive Behavior Interventions, 6,* 13–20. Copyright 2004 by PRO-ED, Inc. Reprinted by permission.

relationship between the challenging tasks (independent variable) and on-task behavior during independent academic work (dependent variable).

Teaching Application

The following vignette illustrates the use of an ABAB design in the classroom.

> ***Jill Learns Not to Suck Her Thumb***
>
> Ms. Kimball, a kindergarten teacher with 27 pupils, recently designed an effective intervention program to reduce her student Jill's thumb sucking. She decided that a reversal design would allow her to determine the existence of a functional relationship between the change in behavior and the selected intervention procedure. Ms. Kimball chose a time sampling observation procedure. She looked at Jill every 10 minutes and marked a 1 on the data sheet if Jill was sucking her thumb and a 2 if she wasn't.
>
> During the baseline condition (the first A phase), Ms. Kimball noted that Jill had her thumb in her mouth an average of 8 out of the 12 observations during a 2-hour period. Ms. Kimball decided to make a chart for Jill and to put a "smelly sticker" on the chart whenever Jill was not sucking her thumb at the end of an interval. After the intervention was applied (the first B phase), thumb sucking occurred at the end of only three intervals, on average. To determine if a functional relationship existed between the intervention and the behavior, Ms. Kimball returned to baseline (A) conditions. Jill no longer got smelly stickers, and the target behavior immediately returned to its previous level. Reinitiating the B condition immediately brought the behavior back to the lower level. Ms. Kimball felt confident the intervention had changed Jill's behavior.

Advantages and a Disadvantage

ABAB designs allow for precise analysis, but require an effective intervention to be withdrawn.

As the preceding applications show, the reversal design offers the advantages of simplicity and experimental control. It provides for precise analysis of the effects of a single independent variable on a single dependent variable.

The primary disadvantage of this design is the necessity for withdrawing an effective intervention in order to determine whether a functional relationship exists. Even if the target behavior is neither dangerous nor irreversible, it often seems foolish to teachers to stop doing something that is apparently working.

For more information on each design, go to the "Web Links" module for Chapter 5 of the Companion Website.

Changing Criterion Design

The **changing criterion design** evaluates the effectiveness of an independent variable by demonstrating that a behavior can be incrementally increased or decreased toward a terminal performance goal. This design includes two major phases. The first phase (as in all single-subject research designs) is baseline. The second phase is intervention. The intervention phase is composed of subphases. Each subphase has an interim criterion toward the terminal goal. Each subphase requires a closer approximation of the terminal behavior or level of performance than the previous one. The student's performance thus moves incrementally from the baseline level to the terminal objective.

The changing criterion design is particularly appropriate when the terminal goal of behavior change is considerably distant from the student's baseline level. For example, if the goal is for the student to read 60 sight words, and her baseline level of performance is 5 words, it is probably unreasonable for the teacher to instruct and for her to learn all 55 words at once. It is better instructional and reinforcement practice for her to acquire a smaller number of words at a time. Similarly, if the goal is for the student to remain in his seat for 40 continuous minutes so he can be successful in an inclusive class, and his baseline level of performance is 5 continuous minutes, it is probably unreasonable to expect him to be able to master the entire 40 minutes at one time. It is more within his reach, and will provide many more opportunities for reinforcement, if he is brought gradually to the terminal goal of 40 continuous minutes in his seat.

The changing criterion design is well suited for measuring the effectiveness of a shaping procedure (see Chapter 9). This design is also useful when the teacher wants to accelerate or decelerate behaviors measured in terms of frequency, duration, latency, or force.

IMPLEMENTATION

The first step in implementing the changing criterion design is to gather baseline data in the same manner used in other single-subject designs. After a stable baseline has been established, the teacher must determine the level of performance change that will be required for each subphase during intervention. The choice of the first interim level of performance may be determined using one of several techniques:

1. The interim criterion for performance can be set at, and then increased by, an amount equal to the mean of the stable portion of the baseline data. This technique is appropriate when the goal of the behavior-change program is to increase a level of performance and when the student's present level is quite low. For example, if a teacher wants to increase the number of questions a student answers and the student's mean baseline level of correct responses was two, that teacher might set two correct answers as a first interim criterion. Each subsequent subphase would then require two additional correct answers.
2. Interim criteria for performance can be set at half the mean of the baseline. If during the first intervention subphase raising the criterion by the mean of the baseline would make the task too difficult for the student, then raising it half that much may be appropriate. If the student's performance during the first intervention subphase is higher than a criterion equal to the mean of the baseline, the interim criterion may be raised by a level twice that of the mean of the baseline.
3. Interim criteria can be based on selecting the highest (or lowest, depending on the terminal objective) level of baseline performance. This is probably most appropriate for use with social behavior, such as out-of-seat or positive peer interactions, rather than for an academic behavior. The assumption is that if the student were able to perform at that high (or low) level once, the behavior can be strengthened (or weakened) and maintained at the new level.
4. Interim criteria can be based on a professional estimate of the student's ability. This procedure is particularly appropriate when the student's present level of performance is zero.

Regardless of the technique a teacher uses to establish the initial criterion, the data collected should be used to evaluate whether the amount of criterion change for each subphase is appropriate for a particular student.

The next step in implementing the changing criterion design is to begin the intervention phases. In each phase, if the student performs at least at the level of the interim criterion, the teacher provides reinforcement. It is important for the teacher to analyze the appropriateness of the selected interim level of performance during the initial intervention phase. If the student does not meet the criterion after a reasonable number of trials, the teacher should consider decreasing the interim level of performance required for reinforcement. Conversely, the teacher should consider adjusting the interim level of performance required for reinforcement if the student attains the goal too easily.

After the student has reached the established level of performance in a predetermined number of consecutive sessions (usually two, or in two out of three consecutive sessions of a subphase), the level of performance required for reinforcement should be adjusted in the direction of the desired level of performance for the overall behavior-change program. Each successive interim level of performance should be determined using the same mathematical difference established at the first interim level of performance. That is, the behavior-change program should reflect a uniform step-by-step increase or decrease in criterion level. This process is continued until

1. The behavior is increased to a 100% level or decreased to a 0% level of performance, or
2. The final goal established by the teacher in the behavioral objective is attained.

Changing criterion designs enable teachers and researchers to establish functional relationships.

A functional relationship between the dependent and independent variable is demonstrated if the student's performance level matches the continually changing criterion for performance and reinforcement specified by the teacher (Kazdin, 1998; Richards, Taylor, Ramasamy, & Richards, 1999). This method of assessing a functional relationship is based on the view that repeated matching to a changing criterion represents instances of replication. Each subphase with its interim criterion serves as the baseline for the increased (or decreased) criterion of the next subphase (Hartmann & Hall, 1976). Generally, a student must meet the established criteria in at least three consecutive phases before the assumption of a functional relationship is valid.

Graphic Display

The basic changing criterion design format is similar to the one used for the AB design. A baseline phase is followed by the intervention phase, with a dashed vertical line separating the two conditions and each subphase. Figure 5–11 shows that the data for the intervention phase are identified according to the level of performance selected for reinforcement. The procedure for graphing the data calls for connecting data points within each subphase. Data points collected in different interim phases or subphases are never connected. The magnitude of student behavior necessary for consequation (delivery of reinforcement) should be clearly identified at each level of the intervention phase (see Figure 5–11).

Research Application

Hall and Fox (1977) used the changing criterion design to increase the number of math problems correctly solved by a child with a behavior disorder. Under baseline conditions, the student demonstrated a mean level of performance of one math problem.

FIGURE 5–11 ***Basic changing criterion design format.***

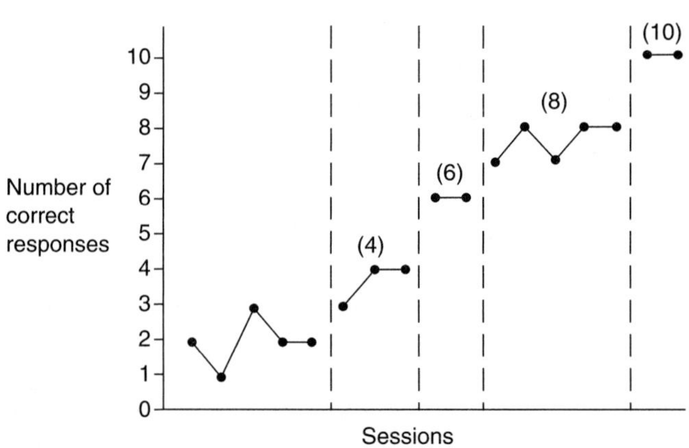

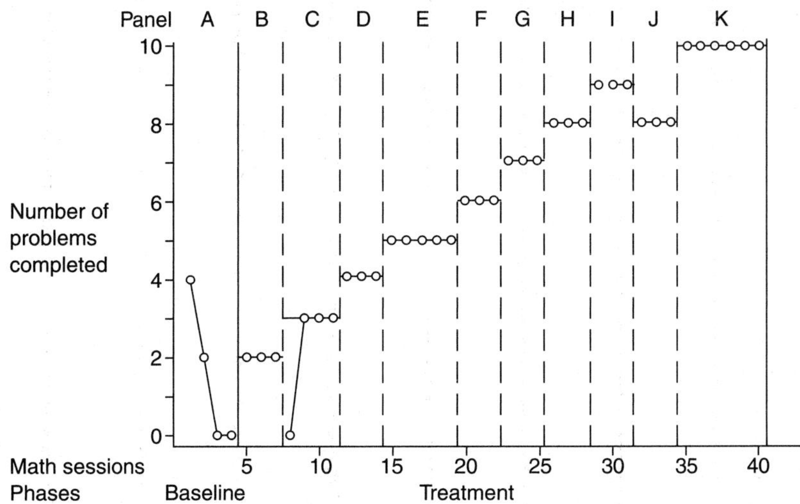

FIGURE 5–12
Research application of the changing criterion design.
Note: From "Changing criterion designs: An applied behavior analysis procedure," by R. V. Hall & R. G. Fox, in B. C. Etzel, J. M. LeBlanc, & D. M. Baer (Eds.), *New developments in behavioral research: Theory, method and application.* Copyright 1977 by Lawrence Erlbaum Associates, Inc., Publishers. Reprinted with permission of the authors and the publishers.

The first interim level of performance was established at the next whole number greater than the mean baseline performance (2) If the student met this level of performance, he was allowed to play basketball. If the student failed to reach the criterion, he had to stay in the math session until the problems were solved correctly. Figure 5–12 shows that this process was continued until 10 math problems were solved correctly.

Ellis, Cress, & Spellman (1992) used a changing criterion design to demonstrate an increase in self-managed independent exercise by students with moderate and severe mental retardation. Three of the students were taught to use a treadmill. The student whose graph is presented in Figure 5–13 was a 16-year-old girl. Following a baseline taken during unsupervised sessions held twice a week for two weeks, durations were

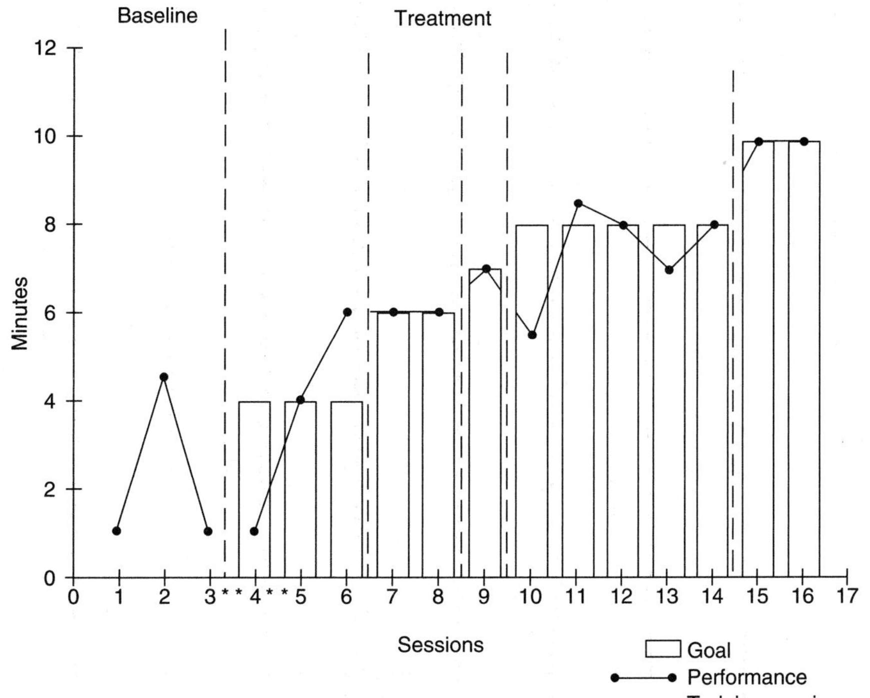

FIGURE 5–13
Application of the changing criterion design.
Note: From "Using timers and lap counters to promote self-management of independent exercise in adolescents with mental retardation," by D. Ellis, P. Cress, & C. Spellman. *Education and Training in Mental Retardation,* 1992. Copyright 1992 by the Council for Exceptional Children. Reprinted by permission.

determined for the intervention subphases. Initial durations were near or slightly longer than the longest baseline performance. Interim criteria were then increased generally by 2 minutes once the previous goal was achieved in one or more sessions. (The interim criterion was raised by only 1 minute during one subphase to further demonstrate control over the behavior by the independent variable.) Students were taught to set a digital kitchen timer, and stickers served as token reinforcers for meeting interim criteria. Students used the tokens to purchase exercise-related items (e.g., T-shirts, sweatbands, shorts) on a 5:1 ratio. The students displayed a systematic increase in the number of minutes of self-managed exercise from one subphase and interim criterion to the next. The authors attributed those sessions in which the student whose graph is presented did not reach her interim criterion to student errors in timer activation or lags between timer activation and exercise.

Certain procedural elements may increase the research credibility of the changing criterion design.

1. Altering the number of sessions in some subphases

In Figure 5–12, three sessions at each interim criterion were generally maintained; however, this number of sessions was changed in some subphases. The lengths of subphases may vary with the behavior's remaining at criterion level as long as the criterion is in effect (Cooper, Heron, & Heward, 1987; Richards et al., 1999).

2. Continuing with a subphase until a stable rate has been established

For classroom use, maintaining a behavior at the interim criterion for two sessions (or two out of three sessions) before moving to the next subphase demonstrates sufficient control. Because, for research purposes, each subphase is seen as the baseline for the following subphase, the subphase may be continued until a stable rate has been established before starting the next subphase (Richards et al., 1999).

3. Varying the increase (or decrease) in performance required in subphases

In Figure 5–13, the third subphase criterion was set at an increase of 1 minute rather than 2 minutes. That the behavior changed only enough to meet this criterion provides a more credible demonstration of experimental control than requiring the same performance level change across all subphases (Kazdin, 1998).

4. Requiring a change in a direction opposite to the terminal goal in one or more phases

In Figure 5–12, in subphase J, a change in the criterion for reinforcement was made in the direction opposite the terminal objective. Returning the student's performance level to a previously mastered criterion demonstrates a reversal effect similar to that of a return to baseline condition in an ABAB design.

Teaching Application

Here is a teaching application of a changing criterion design to compare with the research application.

Claudia Learns to Sort by Color

Claudia was a student in Mr. Carroll's intermediate class for students with moderate mental retardation. Mr. Carroll was trying to teach Claudia to sort objects rapidly by color. Claudia could perform the task, but she did it too slowly. Mr. Carroll decided to use a changing criterion design to evaluate the effectiveness of a positive reinforcement procedure. He established that Claudia's average baseline rate of sorting was 4 objects per minute. He set 6 per minute as the first interim criterion and 30 per minute as the terminal goal. Claudia earned a poker chip exchangeable for a minute's free time when she met the criterion. When Claudia met the criterion on two consecutive trials or opportunities, Mr. Carroll raised the criterion required for reinforcement by two. He continued to do this until Claudia sorted 30 objects per minute in order to earn her poker chip. Mr. Carroll concluded that there was a functional relationship between the dependent and independent variables, because Claudia's behavior changed quickly each time the criterion was changed but did not change until then.

Advantage and Disadvantage

The advantage of the changing criterion design is that it can establish a functional relationship while continually changing the behavior in a positive direction. There is no need to withdraw a successful intervention. Using the changing criterion design, however, necessitates very gradual behavior change. It may therefore be inappropriate for behaviors that require or lend themselves to rapid modification.

Multiple Baseline Design

When to use a multiple baseline design.

As indicated by its name, the **multiple baseline design** permits simultaneous analysis of more than one dependent variable. A teacher may experimentally test the effects of intervention (the independent variable) on

1. two or more behaviors associated with one student in a single setting, such as John's out-of-seat and talking-out behaviors in social studies class (*multiple baseline across behaviors*).
2. two or more students exhibiting the same behavior in a single setting, as in the spelling accuracy of Sara and Janet in English class (*multiple baseline across individuals*).
3. two or more settings in which one student is exhibiting the same behavior, such as Kurt's cursing during recess and in the school cafeteria (*multiple baseline across settings*).

The multiple baseline is the design of choice when the teacher is interested in applying an intervention procedure to more than one individual, setting, or behavior. The multiple baseline design does not include a reversal phase; therefore, it may be used when the reversal design is not appropriate: when the target behavior includes aggressive actions or when academic learning is involved.

Implementation

A teacher using the multiple baseline design collects data on each dependent variable simultaneously. The teacher collects data under baseline conditions for each student, on each behavior, or in each setting. In establishing the data collection system, the teacher should select an ordinate scale that is appropriate for each of the variables involved in the program. To make data analysis possible, the same scale of measurement (for example, number of math problems completed correctly or percent of on-task behavior) should be used for each dependent variable.

After a stable baseline has been achieved on the first variable, intervention with that variable can be started. During the intervention period, baseline data collection continues for the remaining variables. Intervention on the second variable should begin

"Baseline, directionality, stability, control—is this teaching or tennis?"

when the first variable has reached the criterion established in the behavioral objective or when the data for the first variable show a trend in the desired direction as indicated by three consecutive data points. The intervention condition should be continued for the first variable, and baseline data should still be collected for any additional variables. This sequence is continued until the intervention has been applied to all the variables identified for the behavior-change program.

The data collected in a multiple baseline design can be examined for a functional relationship between the independent variable and each of the dependent variables. The introduction of the intervention with the second and subsequent dependent variables constitutes a replication of effect. For example, after taking baseline data on Matt's on-task behavior in the special education resource class and in environmental science class, the teacher begins intervention in the resource class. Matt is presented with the contingency that if he is on task 85% of the times the teacher looks over at him, he will be able to reduce his homework assignment by 20%. The contingency goes into effect on Tuesday and continues for 4 days until his behavior meets this criterion. During these same 4 days the teacher has continued to take baseline data in the science class. Once Matt has reached the criterion in the resource class, the contingency is put into effect in the science class and continues to be in effect in the resource class. If Matt's on-task behavior is increased in the resource room and then increased in the science class, the teacher can say there is a functional relationship between Matt's on-task behavior and earning a reduction in homework. There is a functional relationship because the effect was first seen in the resource class and then replicated across settings in the environmental science class. A functional relationship is assumed if each dependent variable in succession shows a change when, and only when, the independent variable is introduced.

Adjacent graphs should be examined to be sure that each successive intervention has an independent treatment effect on the appropriate dependent variable. Only the first independent variable should be affected by the first intervention. A change in the second and succeeding dependent variables should be seen only when the intervention is

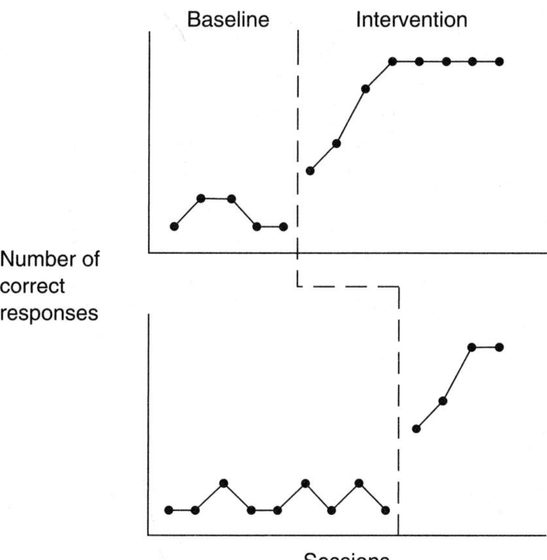

FIGURE 5–14 ***Data from a multiple baseline design that reflect a functional relationship.***

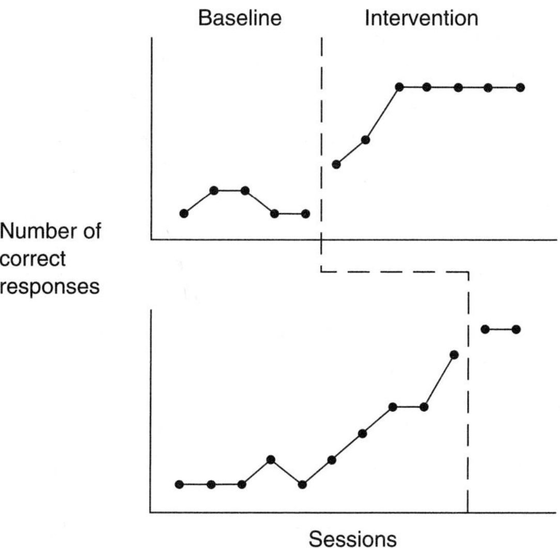

FIGURE 5–15 ***Data from a multiple baseline design that do not reflect a functional relationship.***

applied to them as well. Figure 5–14 shows an example of a functional relationship, whereas Figure 5–15 does not. In Figure 5–15, the second dependent variable begins an upward trend when the intervention is introduced for the first variable, showing that the relationships between variables are not discrete, or independent.

Graphic Display

When using the multiple baseline design, the teacher should plot the data collected using a separate axis for each of the dependent variables to which intervention was applied (individuals, behaviors, or situations). Figure 5–16 shows a composite graph of a multiple baseline design.

FIGURE 5–16 **Basic multiple baseline design format.**

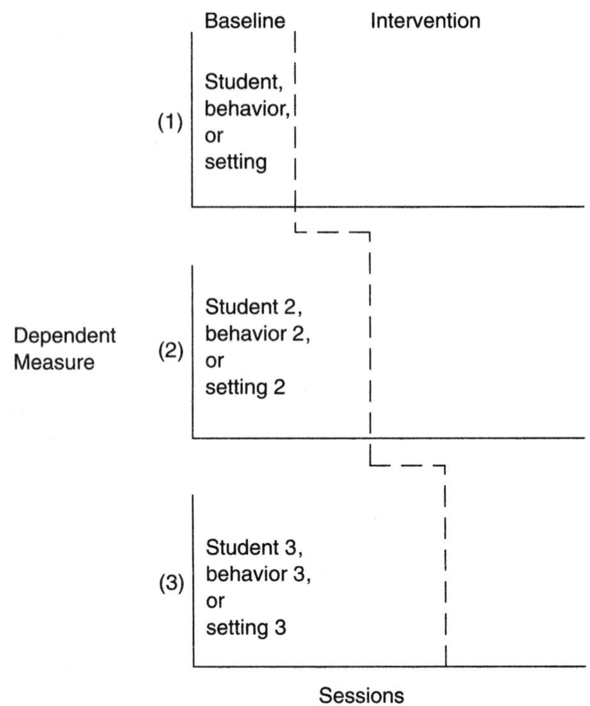

Research Applications

Across Behaviors

Higgins, Williams, and McLaughlin (2001) used a multiple baseline design across behaviors to determine if a token reinforcement program could decrease the high rates of three inappropriate behaviors of an elementary student with learning disabilities. The three behaviors were out of seat, talking out, and poor seat posture. The student earned tokens for not exhibiting the three behaviors during daily independent work sessions. The contingency was first in effect for his talking-out behavior, then placed on his out-of-seat behavior, and finally on his seat posture. Figure 5–17 indicates that the reinforcement program was effective for reducing each behavior in succession. A functional relationship between each dependent variable (the behaviors) and the independent variable (the token economy) can be said to exist because the successful use of the token economy was replicated across the three behaviors.

Across Individuals

Morin & Miller (1998) used a multiple baseline design across individuals to evaluate the effectiveness of a direct instruction format for teaching multiplication skills to four seventh graders with mild mental retardation. Figure 5–18 displays the data for this study. The dependent variable was scored on daily practice sheets that followed each 35-minute lesson. Each scripted lesson contained: (a) an advance organizer that introduced the lesson, (b) the teacher's modeling the skill or strategy being taught, (c) guided practice during which the teacher prompted student responses, and (d) independent practice. The 10 computation skills lessons progressed from those based on concrete instruction (manipulatives) to the representational level (pictures), to the abstract level (just numbers). Lessons on solving word problems followed. When baseline

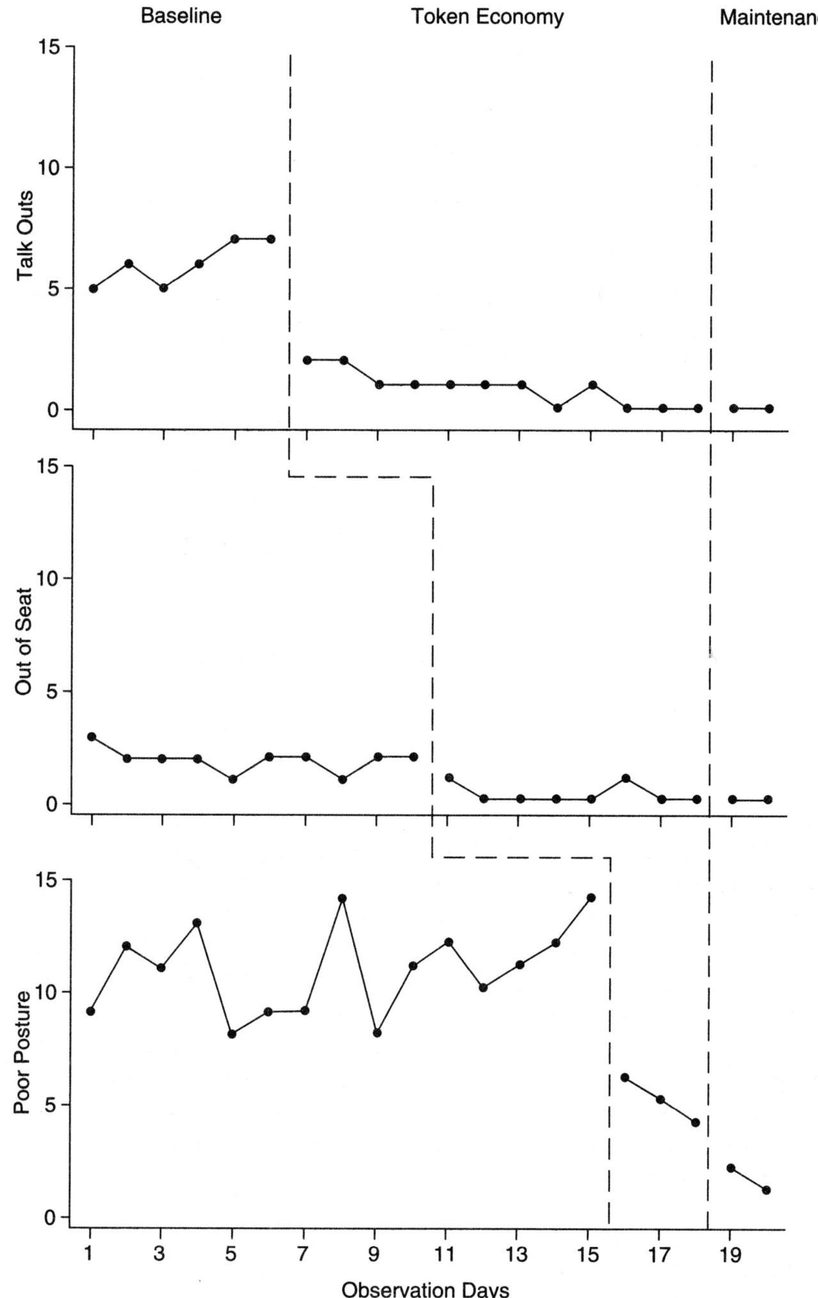

FIGURE 5–17 ***Graph of multiple baseline design across behaviors.***

Note: From "The effects of a token economy employing instructional consequences for a third-grade student with learning disabilities," by J. Higgins, R. Williams, & T. McLaughlin. *Education and Treatment of Children,* 2001. Copyright 2001 by Family Services of Western PA. Reprinted by permission.

FIGURE 5–18 **Graph of a multiple baseline design across individuals.**

Note: From "Teaching multiplication to middle school students with mental retardation," by V. Morin & S. P. Miller. *Education and Treatment of Children, 21,* 1998. Copyright 1998 by Family Services of Western PA. Reprinted by permission.

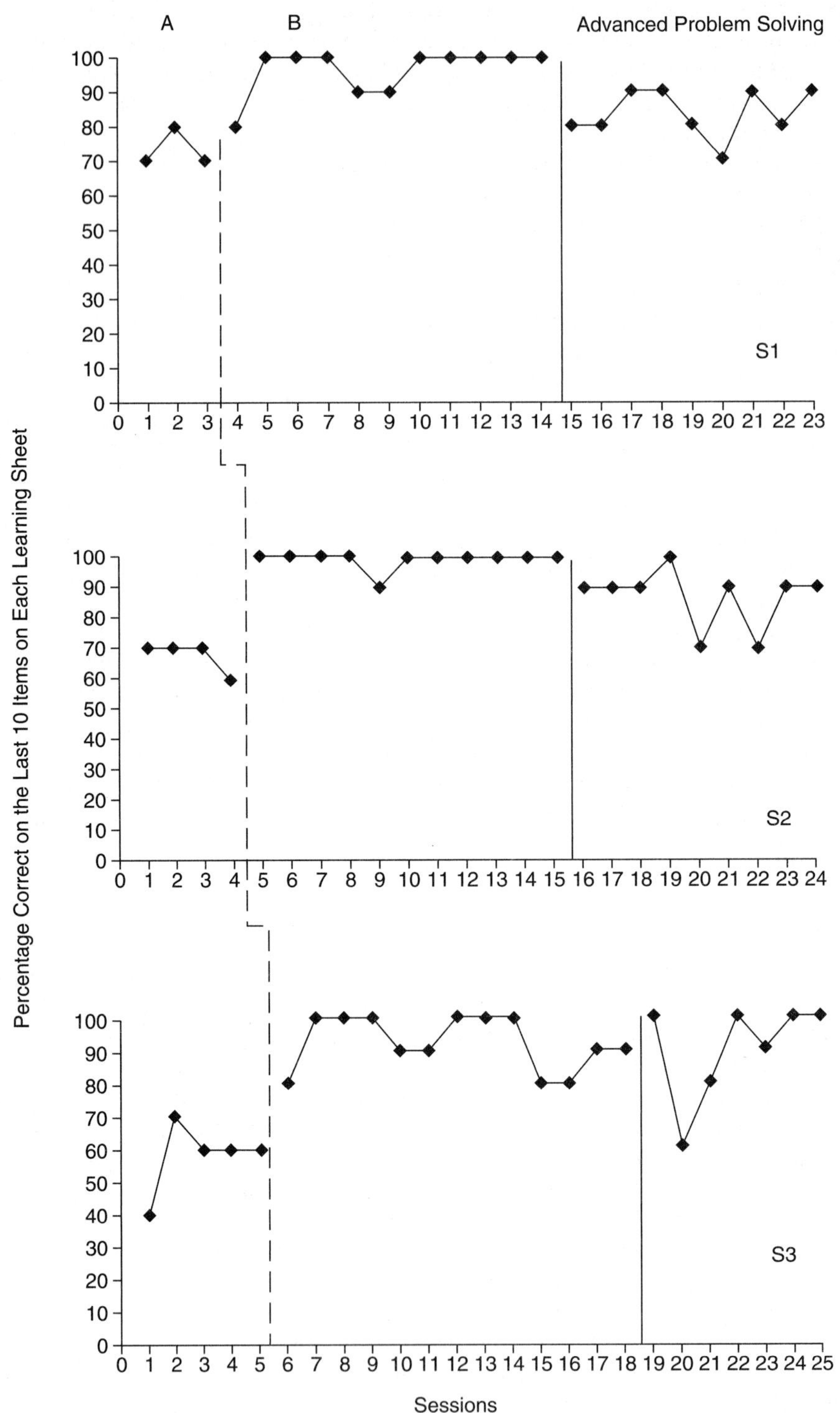

performance was stable, the direct instruction of multiplication skills was introduced to student 1. Baseline conditions were maintained for the other two students. When student 1 obtained the 80% accuracy criterion on the first learning sheet, the intervention was introduced to student 2. Baseline conditions were maintained for student 3 until subject 2 obtained the 80% accuracy criterion on the first learning sheet. As shown in the intervention phase of the graph, each student increased the percent of correct scores. Student 1 went from a mean score of 73.3% correct during baseline to a mean score of 90.5% correct during intervention. Student 2 went from a mean score of 67.5% during baseline to a mean of 93.5% during intervention. Student 3 went from a mean score of 58% during baseline to a mean of 91.5% during intervention. The success of the first student with the direct instruction strategy was replicated with the second and third students. Therefore, one can say there was a functional relationship between the dependent and independent variables.

Researchers have also used the multiple baseline across individuals design identifying pairs of students as "an individual" (Duker, Hensgens, & Venderbosch, 1995), identifying small groups of students as "an individual" (Fueyo & Bushell, 1998), and identifying an entire class as "an individual" (Kohler, Strain, Hoyson, & Jamieson, 1997; White & Bailey, 1990). White and Bailey (1990) assessed the effectiveness of a "sit and watch" procedure, a form of time-out, on the disruptive behavior (noncompliance, aggression, and throwing objects) of 30 regular fourth-grade students and 14 students in an alternative education class for fourth- and fifth-grade boys with severe behavior problems. Students who engaged in disruptive behavior were required to sit and watch the other students playing for 3 minutes. During each observation interval, the observers recorded each instance of disruptive behavior on hand counters. Figure 5–19 shows data for both classes. The numbers above the data points represent the number of times "sit and watch" was implemented. A functional relationship is assumed because the disruptive behavior decreased for each group of students when the intervention began.

Across Settings

Dalton, Martella, & Marchand-Martella (1999) used a multiple baseline design across settings to evaluate the effects of a self-management program on the off-task behavior of two eighth-grade boys with learning disabilities. Off task was operationally defined as (a) not in seat (buttocks were not on the seat of chair, feet did not have to be on the floor), (b) talking with others (student talking, whispering, or mouthing to others without permission), (c) interrupting others (passing a note, touching another student's body or possessions), (d) not working on assigned task (scribbling or doodling instead of writing, reading a magazine instead of the text), and (e) engaging in bodily movements unrelated to or interfering with assigned task (playing with pencil or ripping paper). Figure 5–20 presents Peter's graphed data. During baseline, "normal classroom procedures" were in place. These consisted of redirection, reprimand, removal from class, or detention. Peter's off-task behavior averaged 79% in science class, 87% in language arts, and 97% in learning opportunity center (study hall). The self-management program was first introduced in science class where time off task was reduced to an average of 17%, then in language arts where it was reduced to an average of 21%, and finally in study hall where his off-task behavior decreased to an average of 16%. Notice that the self-management program was initially used in science class, then replicated in language arts, and replicated a second time in learning opportunity center. These successful replications allow for a conclusion that there was a functional relationship between the dependent variable and the independent variable.

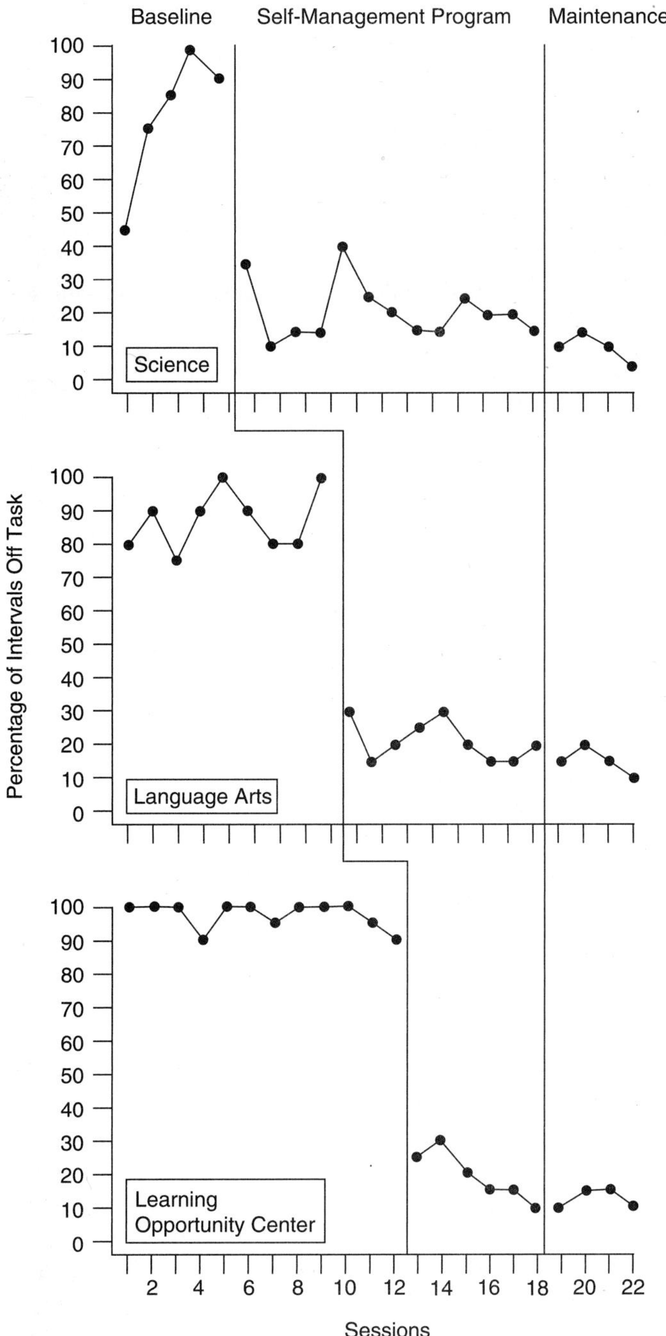

FIGURE 5–20 ***Graph of a multiple baseline design across settings.***

Note: From "The effects of a self-management program in reducing off-task behavior," by T. Dalton, R. Martella, & N. Marchand-Martella. *Journal of Behavioral Education,* Vol. 9, issue 3, pp. 157–176, 1999. Copyright 1999 by Human Sciences Press. Reprinted by permission.

Teaching Application

This vignette illustrates the use of a multiple baseline design in the classroom.

Students Learn to Come to Class on Time

Ms. Raphael was a middle-school English teacher. The students in all three of her morning classes consistently came late. She began to record baseline data on the three classes. She recorded the number of students in their seats when the bell rang. She found that an average of five students in the first class, four in the second, and seven in the third class were in their seats. Ms. Raphael then began recording an extra-credit point in her grade book for each student in the first class who was in his or her seat when the bell rang. Within a week, 25 students were on time and in their seats. The baseline data for the other classes showed no change during this first intervention. When she began giving extra-credit points in the second class, the number of students on time increased immediately and dramatically. After a week, she applied the intervention in the third class with similar results. Ms. Raphael had accomplished two things: she had succeeded in getting her classes to arrive on time and she had established a functional relationship between her intervention (the independent variable) and her students' behavior (the dependent variable).

Advantages and Disadvantages

A problem with the multiple baseline design—and a suggested solution.

The multiple baseline design can establish a functional relationship without withdrawing the intervention, as is necessary in a reversal design, and without gradual alteration, as is required in a changing criterion design. These advantages make it a particularly useful design for classroom use. The multiple baseline design does, however, have some limitations. This design requires that the researcher apply the intervention to several students, behaviors, or settings, which may not always be practical. The multiple baseline design also requires collecting baseline data over extended periods, particularly baseline data for the second and subsequent dependent variables. When the student cannot perform the behavior at all or access to additional settings is not available or practical, collecting daily baseline data may take more time than is actually warranted or may not be possible. The multiple probe technique has been suggested as a reasonable solution to this situation (Horner & Baer, 1978; Poling, Methot, & LeSage, 1995). In this variation of the multiple baseline design, data are not continuously collected on the behaviors (or students or settings) on which intervention is not being conducted. Rather, probe trails (single trials under baseline conditions) or a probe session (more than one trail under baseline conditions) are conducted intermittently on these subsequent behaviors to verify that the student still cannot perform the behavior or to record any changes in his ability before intervention. While using the intervention with behavior 1 (or with student 1 or in setting 1), the teacher intermittently probes behaviors 2 and 3. When behavior 1 reaches the criterion, one or more probe sessions are conducted on all three behaviors. Then intervention is begun on behavior 2. Postcheck probes are conducted on behavior 1 to establish that the change in behavior is being maintained, and baseline probes continue on behavior 3. When behavior 2 reaches the criterion, one or more probe sessions are conducted on all three behaviors. Then intervention is begun on behavior 3, while postcheck probes are conducted on behaviors 1 and 2.

Cade and Gunter's (2002) use of a multiple probe is presented in Figure 5–21. In this study three students, ages 12 to 14, diagnosed with emotional or behavioral disorders were taught to use a mnemonic to solve basic division calculations. Permanent product data were collected on a worksheet of 24 division-by-7 facts. Initially, baseline data were collected on all three students. Sammy quickly established a stable trend (after 3 consecutive days), and baseline sessions for the other two boys were continued as

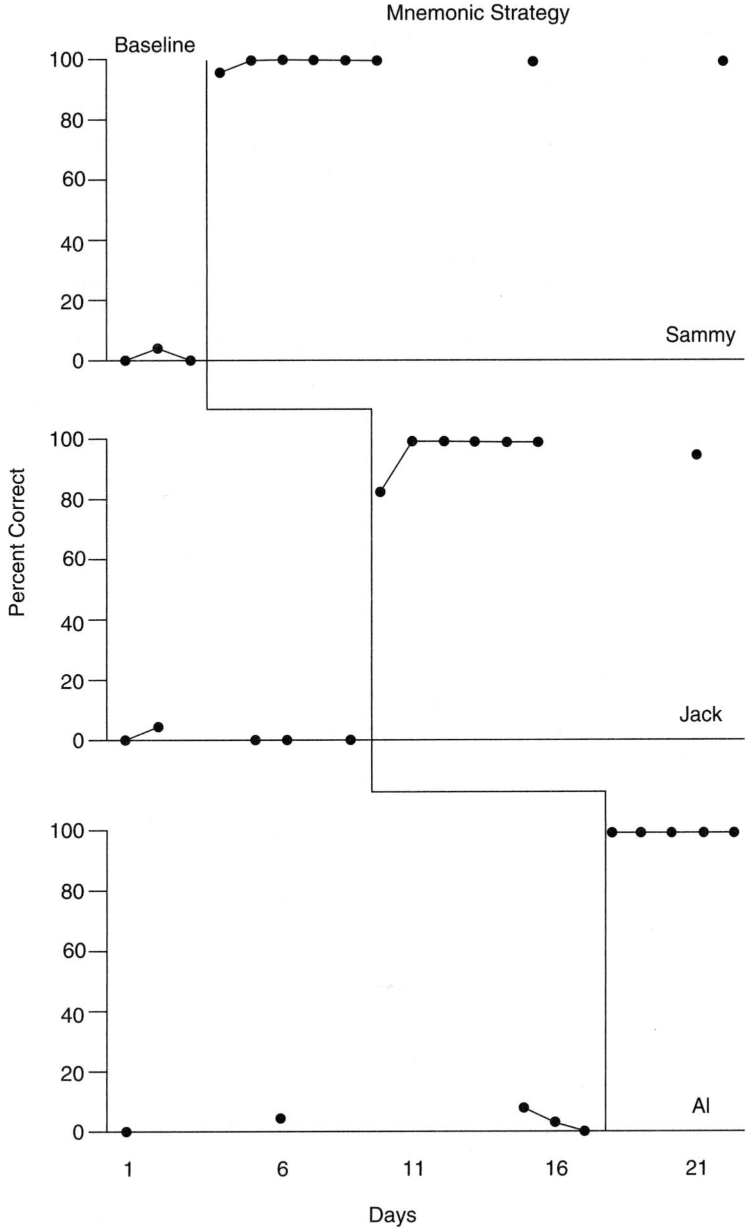

FIGURE 5–21 **Use of a multiple probe design.**
Note: From "Teaching students with severe emotional or behavioral disorders to use a musical mnemonic technique to solve basic division calculations," by T. Cade, & P. Gunter. *Behavioral Disorders,* 2002. Copyright 2002 by the Council for Children with Behavioral Disorders. Reprinted by permission.

probes. For Jack, baseline probes were taken on days 1, 2, 5, and 6. For Al, baseline probes were taken on days 1, 6, 15, 16, and 17. Use of the mnemonic was begun with each successive student as the previous student reached a criterion of five sessions at 100% correct. The use of baseline probes eliminated the necessity of recording a continuous baseline for Jack and Al on a behavior it was known they could not perform, but allowed for monitoring any potential change in their behavior before intervention.

The multiple baseline design is inappropriate in two specific situations:

1. when the target behavior calls for immediate action. The multiple baseline design calls for a considerable delay in delivery of the intervention procedure for the second and subsequent dependent variables.

2. when the behaviors selected for intervention are not independent. In such a case, intervention with one behavior will bring about a change in the related behavior; therefore, the teacher will be unable to evaluate clearly the effects of the procedure. For example, if two behaviors targeted for a student are cursing and fighting, the teacher might find that after the student's cursing decreases, fewer fights occur. In this case, the two behaviors are clearly not independent.

Alternating Treatments Design

In contrast to the multiple baseline design, which uses a single independent variable and multiple dependent variables, the **alternating treatments design** (Barlow & Hayes, 1979; Richards et al., 1999) allows comparison of the effectiveness of more than one treatment or intervention strategy on a single dependent variable. For example, using this design, the teacher can compare the effects of two reading programs on a student's reading comprehension ability or the effects of two behavior-reduction procedures on a student's talking out. The teacher can also examine the efficiency of three different types of symbols on a student's communication board. A number of different terms have been used to describe this design: multiple schedule design (Hersen & Barlow, 1976), alternating conditions design (Ulman & Sulzer-Azaroff, 1975), and multi-element baseline design (Sidman, 1960).

Implementation

The first step in setting up an alternating treatments design is to select the target behavior and two or more potential treatments. If the target behavior is social (for example, asking appropriate questions or remaining on task), it should be operationally defined. If the target behavior is academic, two or more representative samples of the behavior (for example, two or more equally difficult sets of division problems) should be selected, each designated for one of the intervention or treatment strategies.

As the name of this design implies, the treatments are implemented alternately or in rotation. The presentation of the treatments may be in random order, such as ABBABAAB (Barlow & Hersen, 1984). When two treatments are used, the student should be exposed to each treatment an equal number of times. If there are three treatments, a block rotation may be used. Each block consists of one presentation of each treatment; for example, ABC, BCA, CAB, ACB, BAC, CBA. If data are collected long enough, each possible order of presentation should be used at least once.

The alternating treatments can be used sequentially within a single session (A followed by B), or from one session to the next (A in the morning, B in the afternoon of the same day), or on successive days (A on Monday, B on Tuesday). The scheduling should be counterbalanced; that is, the treatment that was employed first in one session should be used second in the next session, the treatment employed in the morning on the first day should be used in the afternoon on the second day, and the treatment that was used on Monday the first week should be used on Tuesday of the second week. (In research situations, similar counterbalancing is used to minimize the effects of other potential confounding variables such as the person administering the treatment and the location of the treatment.) This counterbalancing should control for the possibility of carryover and sequencing effects (Barlow & Hayes, 1979). In other words, by presenting the treatments in random order, the possible effects each treatment may have on the others will be minimized.

A distinctive discriminative stimulus, signal, or cue immediately preceding each treatment will make it clear to the student which condition is in effect. For example, the teacher might say, "This is treatment A" and "This is treatment B," or "Now we are going to use a number line" and "Now we are going to use counting chips." The teacher might also color code worksheets to indicate a particular condition is in effect.

To learn how to use the computer to generate graphs refer to the Webtext (Cibak, Alberto, Troutman, & Flores, in press) available on the Companion Website.

Graphic Display

The basic form of graphing the alternating treatments design is shown in Figure 5–22. As in all designs, baseline data are plotted first and separated from intervention data by a vertical broken line. The graph for the alternating treatments design differs from others in that several curves may be shown on each graph. The points for each treatment

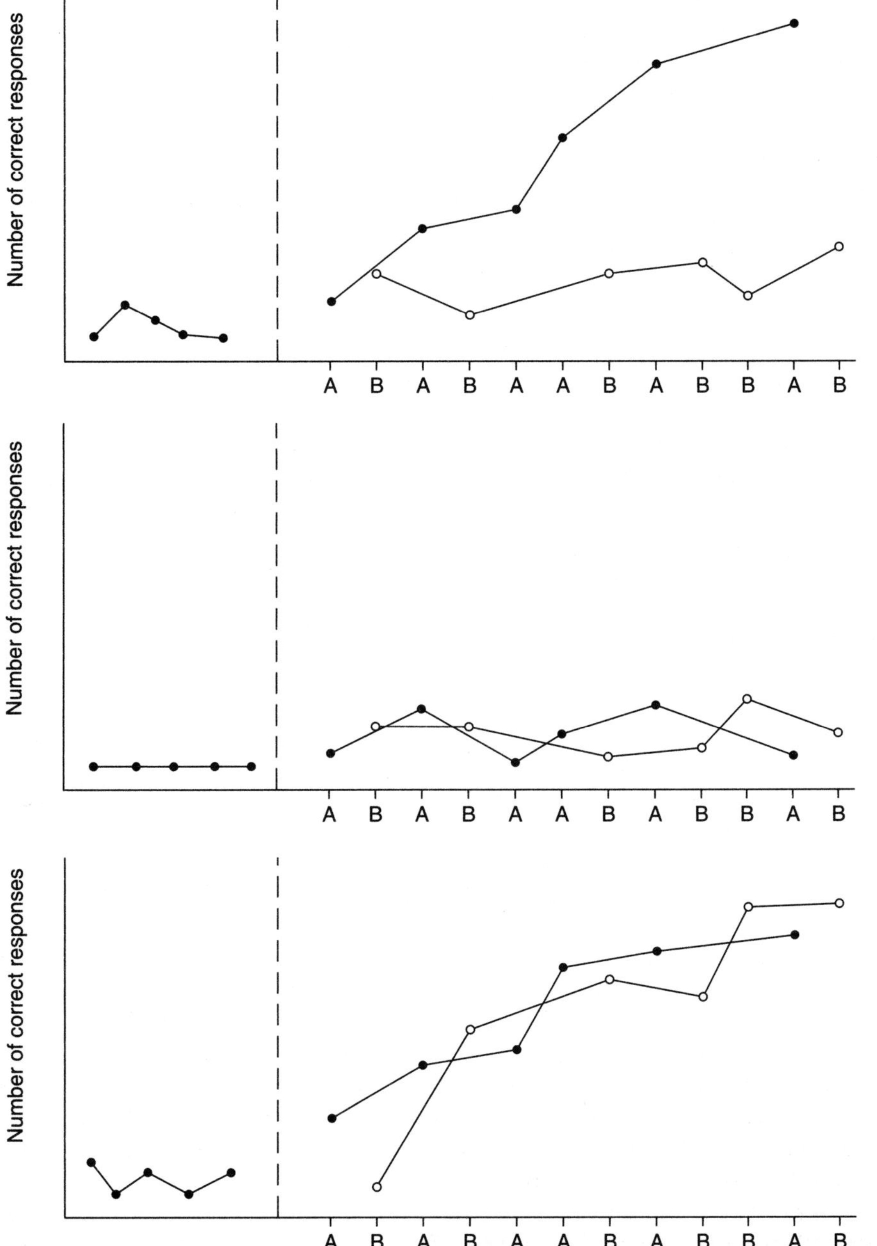

FIGURE 5–22 ***Graphs of data collected using an alternating treatments design. Top graph indicates treatment A is the more effective treatment. Middle and bottom graphs indicate no difference between treatments.***

are connected only to other points for that treatment so that the data for each are displayed as separate lines, or curves.

If the data curve of one treatment is vertically separated from the other curves, it is said to be *fractionated*. This fractionation indicates that the treatments are differentially effective (Ulman & Sulzer-Azaroff, 1975).

The top graph in Figure 5–22 shows data that demonstrate an effective treatment. Treatment A is the more effective of the two treatments. The data curves are separated; they do not cross at any point other than at the very beginning of the intervention phase. The two curves are fractionated. Figure 5–22 also shows data that are not significantly different from one another. The middle graph shows two treatments, neither of which demonstrates control over the dependent variable; thus, neither is effective. The bottom graph shows two treatments that both demonstrate control over the dependent variable; thus, either is equally effective.

By visual inspection of the graphs, we may infer experimental control between one or more of the independent variables and the dependent variable.

> Because confounding factors such as time of administration have been neutralized (presumably) by counterbalancing, and because the two treatments are readily discriminable by subjects through instructions or other discriminative stimuli, differences in the individual plots of behavior change corresponding with each treatment should be attributable to the treatment itself, allowing a direct comparison between two (or more) treatments. (Barlow & Hayes, 1979, p. 200)

As described thus far, the alternating treatments design does not include a replication phase. Therefore, the case for the existence of a functional relationship is relatively weak. To make a stronger case, a third phase can be instituted. In this phase the more effective of the treatments is applied to the behavior (or behavior sample) that was treated with the ineffective treatment during the intervention phase. If the second behavior then improves, a replication of the treatment has been accomplished and a functional relationship demonstrated. Figure 5–23 shows such a three-phase variation of the design.

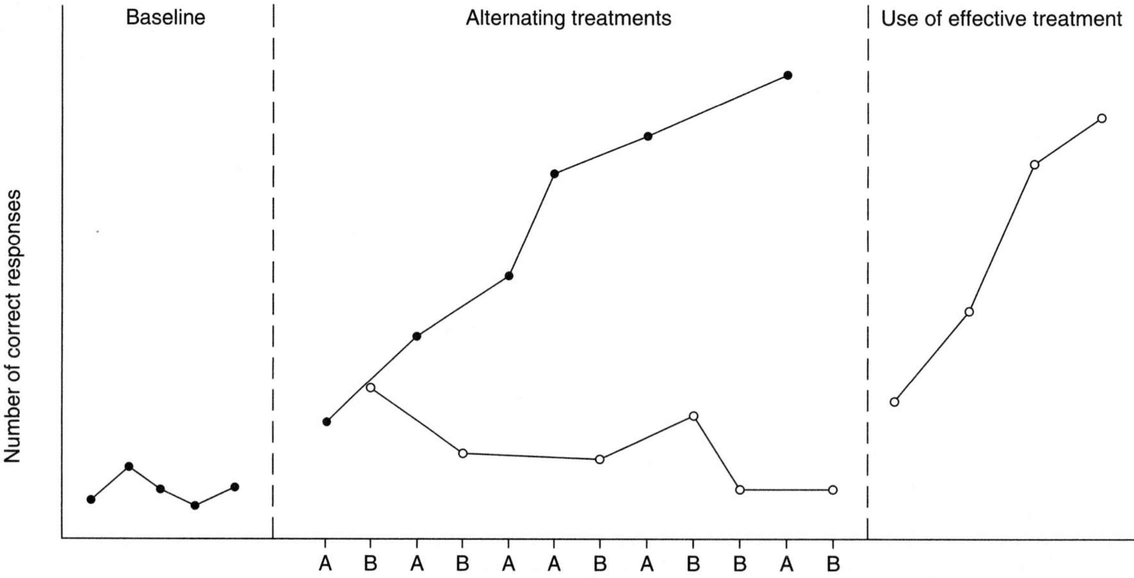

FIGURE 5–23 ***Three-phase alternating treatments design demonstrating functional relationship.***

Research Application

Singh (1990) used an alternating treatments design to measure the comparative effectiveness of two error-correction procedures in reducing oral reading errors of students with moderate mental retardation. Students read an unfamiliar 100-word passage orally three times each day. The correction procedures were word supply (the teacher supplied the correct word, the student repeated it once and continued to read) and sentence repeat (the student repeated the correct word after the teacher, read the rest of the sentence, then reread the entire sentence). As shown in Figure 5–24, the sentence-repeat procedure was more effective than the word-supply procedure (or a control—no correction) for each of the three students. In the third phase of the design the more effective procedure was used in all three daily sessions. This provided the replications needed to assess the presence of a functional relationship.

Miller and Test (1989) used an alternating treatments design to compare the effectiveness of two instructional strategies. Constant time delay and most-to-least prompting were used to teach four high school students with moderate mental retardation to use a washing machine and dryer. Figure 5–25 shows the data for the percent of steps of the task analysis performed correctly by each student. Data displayed on the graphs were taken during probes before each daily training session during which the student

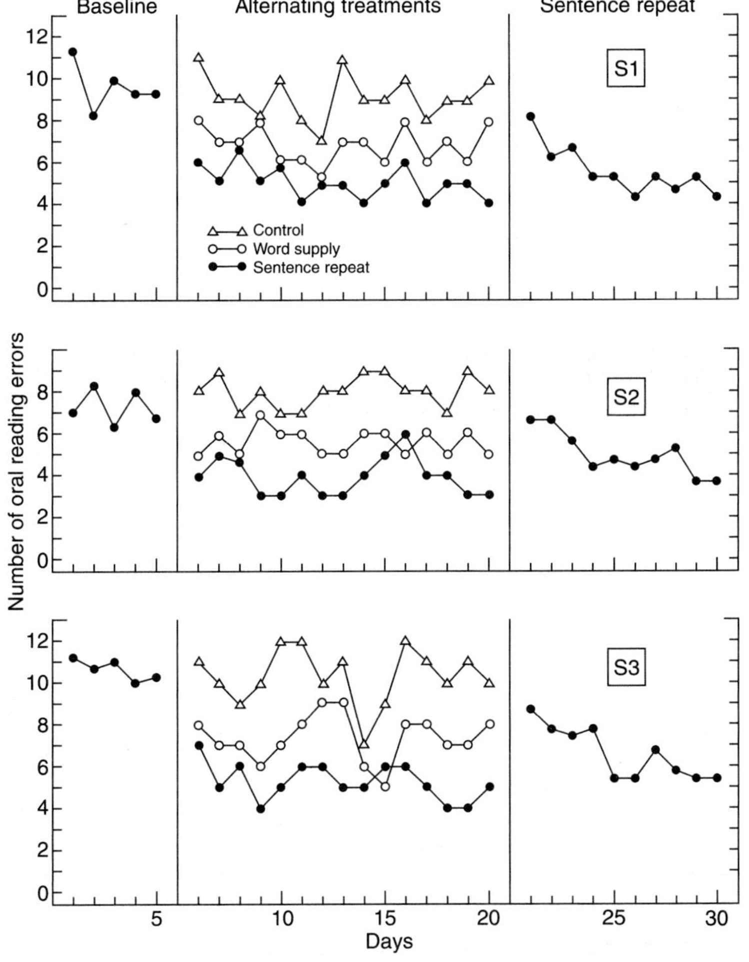

FIGURE 5–24
Research use of an alternating treatments design demonstrating a functional relationship.
Note: From "Effects of two error-correction procedures on oral reading errors," by N. Singh, *Behavior Modification,* 1990. Copyright 1990 by Sage Publications, Inc. Reprinted by permission.

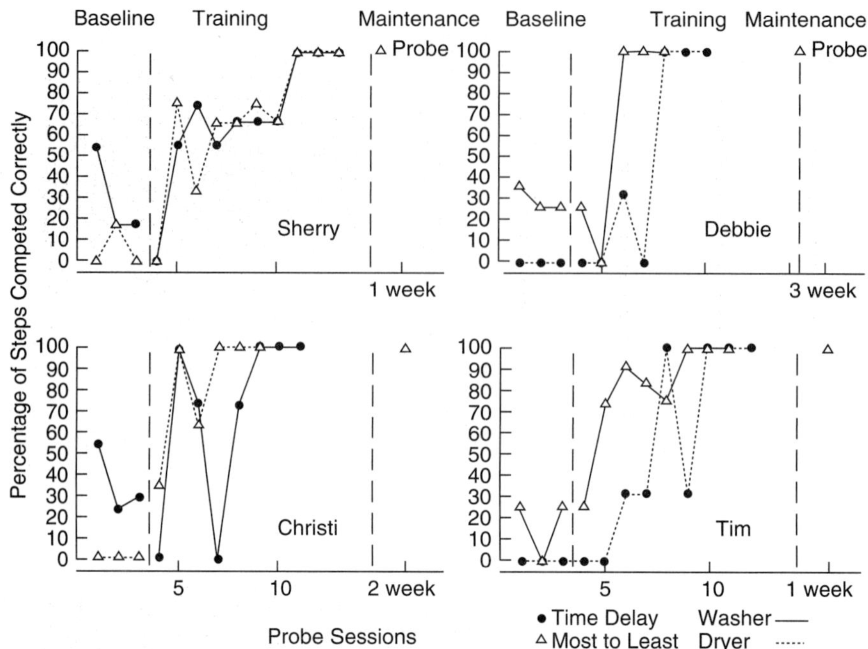

***FIGURE 5–25* Use of an alternating treatments design.**
Note: From "A comparison of constant time delay and most-to-least prompting in teaching laundary skills to students with moderate retardation," by U. Miller & D. W. Test. *Education and Training in Mental Retardation,* 1989. Copyright 1989 by the Council for Exceptional Children. Reprinted by permission.

was asked to perform the steps in the task analysis for each machine. The order of interventions and tasks was counterbalanced across students. Instruction ended when each student successfully performed the tasks without assistance over three consecutive probe sessions. Once the students reached criterion, the two strategies were compared on various measures of effectiveness and efficiency. The graphs show that student performance on both machines before intervention remained low. Both skills were taught to criterion and maintained at 100% accuracy. Both time delay and most-to-least prompting strategies were effective in teaching each student to operate a washer and dryer. Time delay, however, was more efficient than the most-to-least prompting procedure in terms of instructional time required and number of errors. In this study there is not a third phase for replication of effect. The counterbalancing of strategies and tasks across the four students may be seen as representing replications.

Using an alternating treatments design can help teachers individualize instruction.

Teaching Application

For teachers, the alternating treatments design can provide rapid and accurate feedback about the comparative effectiveness of various teaching techniques, as the following example shows.

Marcia Learns Sight Vocabulary

Mr. Hagan was a resource teacher for elementary students. He wanted one of his students, Marcia, to learn basic sight vocabulary on a first-grade level. He chose 15 words and established that Marcia's baseline rate for reading them was zero. Mr. Hagan then divided the words into three sets of five. One set he printed on cards accompanied by an audio recording tape that Marcia could use to hear the words pronounced. He assigned a peer tutor to work with Marcia on the second set, and the teacher worked with Marcia on the third set. Mr. Hagan recorded and graphed the number of words Marcia pronounced correctly each day for each set. Within a week, Marcia was pronouncing correctly the group of words learned with the peer tutor at a higher rate than either of the other sets. Mr. Hagan concluded that, for Marcia, peer tutoring was the most efficient way to learn sight vocabulary.

Advantages and Disadvantages

The alternating treatments design is an efficient way for teachers to answer one of the most important instructional questions: Which method is most likely to be successful with this student? Once clear fractionation appears, the teacher can select the most successful method using as few as three to five data points. One disadvantage is the necessity to institute a replication phase in order to establish a clear functional relationship. However, this is likely to be of little practical importance to teachers.

Changing Conditions Design

The changing conditions design reflects reality—teachers keep trying different techniques until they find one that works.

A **changing conditions design** is used to investigate the effects of two or more treatments (independent variables) on the behavior of a student (dependent variable). Unlike the alternating treatments design, the treatments in this design are introduced sequentially. The changing conditions design is also referred to as a multiple treatments design, or an ABC design, because each new treatment phase is given an identifying letter (Cooper, 1981; Kazdin, 1982; Richards et al., 1999).

The design is useful for the teacher who finds it necessary to try a number of interventions before finding one that is successful with a particular student. The teacher is changing the conditions (for example, environmental conditons, instructional conditions, reinforcement conditions) under which the student is expected to perform the behavior.

Implementation

The first step in implementing a changing conditions design is to collect baseline data to assess the student's present level of performance. Once a stable baseline is established, the teacher can introduce the selected intervention and measure its effectiveness through data collection. If the data for the first intervention do not demonstrate a change in the student's performance or if the change is not of a sufficient magnitude or in the desired direction, the teacher may design a second intervention. This second intervention can be either a complete change in strategy or a modification of the earlier intervention. This process of redesigning intervention conditions is repeated until the desired effect on the student's behavior is achieved. The teacher should expect to see some evidence of a change in the student's behavior within five intervention sessions.

The changing conditions design has three basic variations: (1) ABC, (2) ABAC, and (3) ABACAB (see Figure 5–26).

1. *ABC design:* The ABC design is used when the teacher is trying to judge the effectiveness between treatments, is trying to put together an instructional package that will facilitate a student's performance, or is trying systematically to remove forms of assistance to bring a student to a more independent performance.
   (a) Judging between treatments: This is the design a teacher is using when an intervention she tries does not work satisfactorily and she then tries another. The teacher takes baseline data, implements the first treatment, then implements the second treatment (which may or may not include elements of the first). Treatments are introduced consecutively (each with its own phase) until the desired effect on the behavior is achieved. This design is simply an extended AB design. As in an AB design, there is no replication of the effect of either intervention and there can be no assumption of a functional relationship.
   (b) Building an instructional package: Starting from a student's current performance, the teacher adds new strategies, cumulatively increasing assistance, until the student's performance is successful. As each piece is added to the instructional

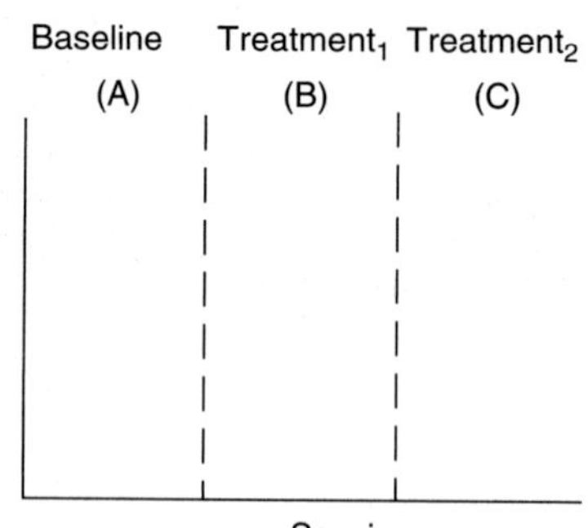

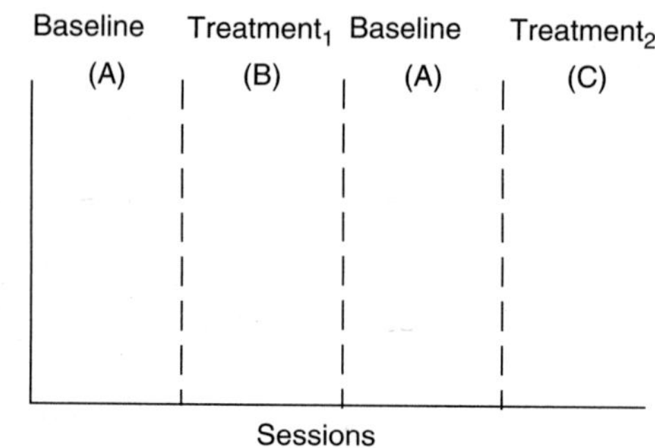

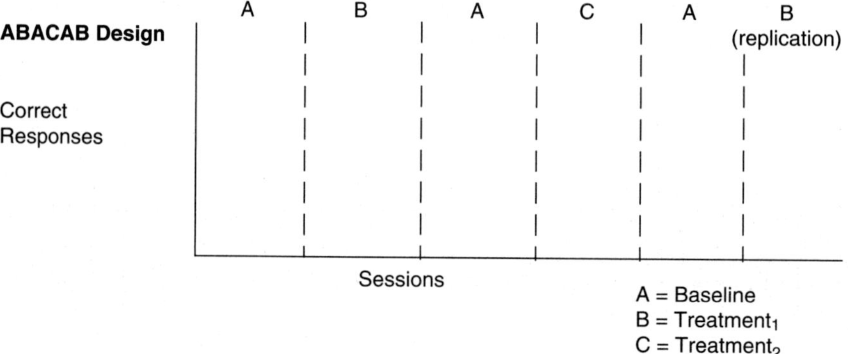

package, a new phase is identified. The study by Smith (1979) in Figure 5–27 is an example of this variation of the design.

(c) Fading assistance: The teacher systematically reduces the amount of assistance being provided a student in order to identify the least amount needed for ongoing successful performance. Each reductive change is considered a new phase. Reductive changes might include reducing the intensity of antecedents, such as providing a student who is learning to print letters to trace in the first phase, densely spaced dots to connect in the second phase, more sparsely spaced dots in subsequent phases, and eventually to writing in the presence of just a line on the paper. Other changes might include reducing the amount of reinforcement or the frequency (schedule) of the delivery of reinforcement. Reducing the number of components of an instructional package is also an example of fading assistance. If, in order to be successful in writing a paragraph,

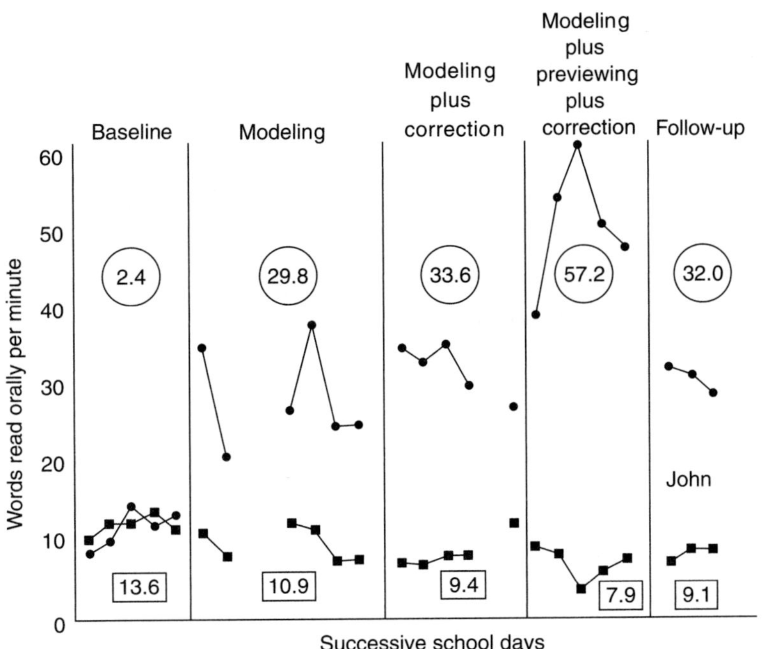

FIGURE 5–27
Research application of a changing conditions design.
Note: From "The improvement of children's oral reading through the use of teacher modeling," by D. D. Smith, *Journal of Learning Disabilities,* 1979. Copyright 1979 by the *Journal of Learning Disabilities*. Reprinted by permission.

a student initially needs to be given the topic, a picture depicting the topic, guidance through a verbal description of the picture, and a topic sentence, the teacher systematically removes each until the student is able to write a paragraph given just a topic. Examples of the use of fading in this design may be seen in studies by Ardoin, Martens, & Wolfe (1999), Boyle & Hughes (1994), and Oliver, Hall, Hales, Murphy, & Watts (1998).

2. *ABAC design:* In this design the teacher's implementation of two or more interventions is separated by additional baseline conditions: baseline, treatment 1, baseline, treatment 2, and so forth. The treatments may be completely different or variations of one other. Separating the treatments by intervening baseline conditions prevents one treatment's continuing to affect the student's behavior while another treatment is being used, thus providing a clear picture of the effect of each of the treatments. This design may be seen as a variation of an ABAB design. It is, however, not considered definitive in establishing a functional relationship (Richards, et al., 1999; Tawney & Gast, 1984). The study by Handen, Parrish, McClung, Kerwin, & Evans (1992) presented variations of this design, as illustrated in Figure 5–28.

3. *ABACAB design:* The data resulting from an ABC or ABAC design do not allow for a determination of a functional relationship between the dependent variable and any of the independent variables. As is the case with an AB design, the data can give only an indiction of the effectiveness of a particular intervention. The design can, however, be refined in order to demonstrate a functional relationship. To assess the presence of a functional relationship, there should be a replication of the effect of the intervention; therefore, following phases for each of the potential treatments, the one whose data indicate it is most successful is reimplemented after another baseline condition. If the treatment is successful again, this is a replication of its effect, and therefore a functional relationship is demonstrated. This design may also be seen as a variation of an ABAB design. A variation of this design may be seen in the studies by Cole, Montgomery, Wilson, & Milan (2000), who used an ABACAD, and Falk, Dunlap, & Kern (1996), who used an ABABCB.

Use of
ditions

guided compliance versus time out to promote child compliance: A preliminary comparative analysis in an analogue context," by B. Handen, J. Parrish, T. McClung, M. Kerwin, & L. Evans. *Research in Developmental Disabilities*. Copyright 1992 with kind permission from Elsevier Science Ltd, The Boulevard, Langford Lane, Kidlington OX5 1GB, UK.

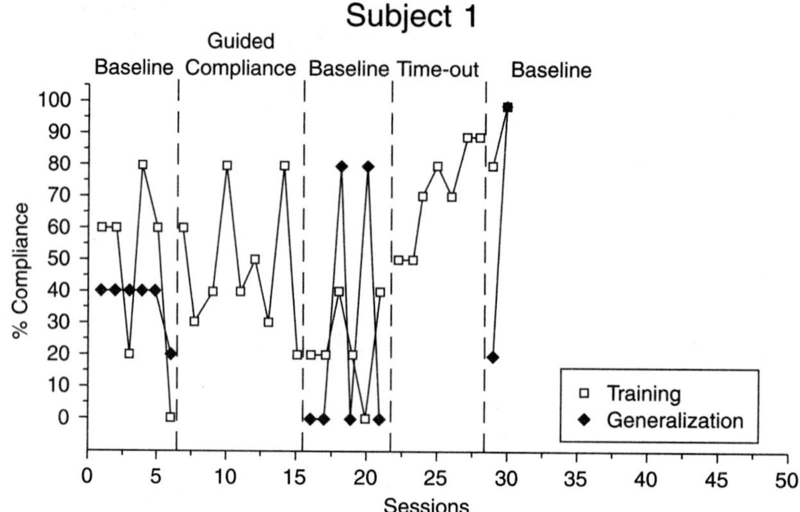

Graphic Display

The format for the changing conditions design is similar to that of the previous designs. A baseline phase is followed by the intervention phases, with a dashed vertical line separating the sessions and data associated with each specific intervention. Figure 5–26 illustrates the three basic formats: ABC, ABAC, and ABACAB.

Research Application

Smith (1979) used a changing conditions design to measure the effect of a number of teaching conditions on a 12-year-old boy's oral reading (see Figure 5–28). The dependent variable measured was the number of words read orally by the student (per minute) and the number of reading errors made. (Note that the numbers in the circles represent the average number of words read per phase. The numbers in the rectangles represent the average number of errors per phase.) Figure 5–28 presents the data recorded under each of the following conditions:

1. *Baseline*. John was asked to read from his book.
2. *Modeling*. The teacher read the first page of a new story from the child's text. John was then asked to read orally.
3. *Modeling plus correction*. The previous condition was altered by adding a correction procedure. The teacher corrected John when he made an error and offered the correct word if he did not know it.
4. *Modeling plus previewing and correction*. After the teacher read, John reread the same passage and continued reading until the instructional time (5 minutes) elapsed. The correction procedure remained in effect.
5. *Follow-up*. Baseline conditions were reinstituted.

Handen et al. (1992) used a changing conditions design with repeated baseline to examine the relative efficacy of guided compliance and time-out as a method of increasing adherence to adult requests by young children with mild mental retardation. The following conditions (phases) were included in the study. In all phases, each child was presented with 10 requests (five targeted and five generalization probes). Compli-

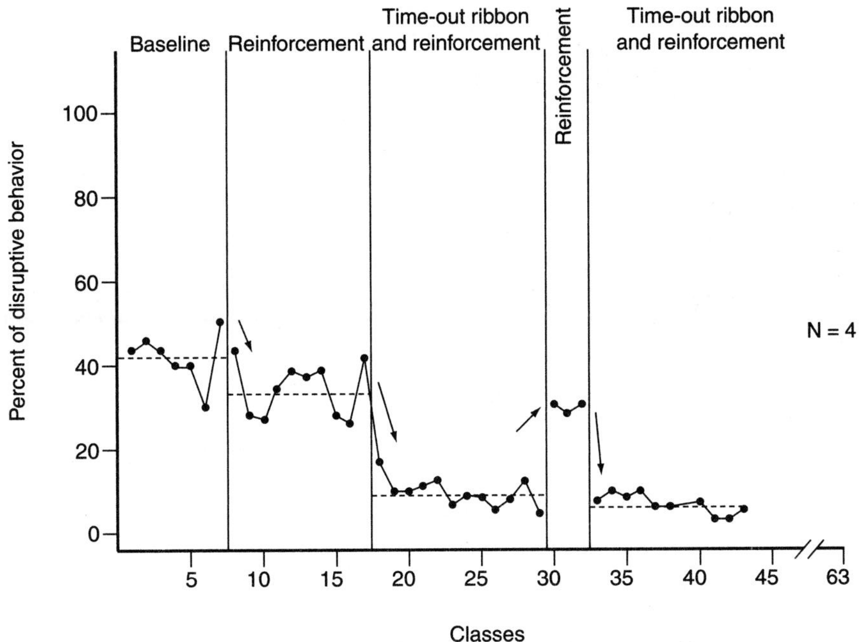

FIGURE 5–29 **Graph for visual inspection of data.**

Note: From "The timeout ribbon: A nonexclusionary timeout procedure," by R. Foxx & S. Shapiro, *Journal of Applied Behavior Analysis,* 1978. Copyright 1978 by The Society for the Experimental Analysis of Behavior. Reprinted by permission.

ance within 10 seconds was followed by praise. Figure 5–29 presents the data recorded for one of the children.

1. *Baseline.* Noncompliance was ignored and compliance praised.
2. *Guided compliance.* Noncompliance within 10 seconds resulted in the adult's guiding the child to complete the task using hand-over-hand assistance. Praise was withheld if assistance was provided.
3. *Baseline condition.*
4. *Time-out.* Noncompliance within 10 seconds resulted in placement of the child in a chair facing a corner of the room for 30 seconds (the child was held gently in the chair if he or she refused to remain seated).
5. *Baseline condition.*

Teaching Application

Here's how a changing conditions design can be used in teaching.

Roberta Learns to Shoot Baskets

Baseline.

Mr. Woods was recently hired to teach physical education at an elementary school. When he arrived at work, Mr. Woods was approached by the special education teacher, Ms. Jones. She was concerned about Roberta, a student with physical disabilities who would be in Mr. Woods's gym class. Roberta, who used a wheelchair, had difficulty with eye-hand coordination. Ms. Jones hoped the student could learn to throw a basketball. Learning to play basketball would provide coordination training and a valuable leisure skill for Roberta. Mr. Woods agreed that the basketball skill seemed appropriate.

First condition.

Mr. Woods decided to use a systematic approach to instruction. He asked Roberta to throw the basketball 20 times to see how often she could place the ball through a lowered hoop. This procedure was followed for five gym periods with no additional instruction until a baseline performance rate was

. Mr. Woods then decided to use a modeling technique. He showed Roberta how to throw the ball and o imitate him. Very little improvement was noted in five class periods. Mr. Woods met with the special eacher to determine what could be done.

Second condition.

Ms. Jones carefully reviewed all the data and suggested changing the conditions. She explained that a change in intervention seemed necessary and that a modeling procedure could be used in combination with keeping score on a chart.

Third condition.

Mr. Woods agreed to try this. In 2 weeks, Roberta showed improvement but still missed more baskets than she hit. A final condition was implemented using modeling, scorekeeping, and a correction procedure. Mr. Woods now showed Roberta how to throw, recorded her score, and showed her exactly what she did wrong when she missed. This combination of procedures resulted in Roberta's being able to throw a basketball through a hoop 15 out of 20 times. A suggestion was made to Roberta's parents that a hoop be constructed at her home so that she could enjoy her new skill after school.

Advantages and Disadvantages

Changing conditions is a teaching design.

The changing conditions design with a single baseline allows the teacher to compare the effects of a number of interventions on student behavior. Although no functional relationship can be established, recording data in this format allows the teacher to monitor the effects of various procedures on student behavior. The teacher should be aware, however, that what she may be seeing is the cumulative effects of the interventions rather than the effects of any one intervention in isolation. Individual analysis of the effects of the interventions can be made using the repeated baselines format of the changing conditions design. The teacher who records data systematically in a changing conditions design will have a record of the student's progress and a good indication of what procedures are effective with that student. The six single-subject designs we described were the AB, ABAB (reversal), changing criterion, multiple baseline, alternating treatments, and changing conditions. A summary of the uses, formats, and types of questions answered by each of these designs is presented in Table 5–2.

Evaluating Single-Subject Designs

Analysis of Results

Companion Website *For more practice using single-subject designs, go to the "Activities" module for Chapter 5 of the Companion Website.*

The purpose of using applied behavior analysis procedures in the classroom is to achieve, and verify, meaningful changes in a student's behavior. The effectiveness of an intervention can be judged against both an experimental criterion and a clinical criterion. The *experimental criterion* verifies that an independent variable (an intervention) was responsible for the change in the dependent variable (a behavior). Single-subject designs demonstrating within-subject replications of effect satisfy this criterion (Baer, Wolf, & Risley, 1968; Barlow & Hersen, 1984; Kazdin, 1998; Poling et al., 1995; Richards et al., 1999).

The *clinical criterion* is a judgment as to whether the results of the teacher's intervention are "large enough to be of practical value or have impact on the everyday lives of those who receive the intervention, as well as those in contact with them" (Kazdin, 2001, pg. 153). For example, the teacher should ask herself whether it is truly meaningful to increase a student's grade from a D− to a D (Baer et al., 1968), or to decrease a student's self-injurious behavior from 100 to 50 instances per hour (Kazdin, 2001), or to reduce a student's off-task behavior in the special education class while it remains high in a general educational class. The teacher should ask if the student's behavior has decreased sufficiently so as to no longer interfere with other students' learning, or with the ability of her family to carry out its activities at home and in the community.

TABLE 5–2
Summary of single-subject research designs.

Design	Use	Format	Example Questions
AB	To document changes in behavior during baseline and intervention. Does not allow for determination of a functional relationship — lacks a replication of the effect of the independent variable (intervention) on the dependent variable (behavior).	*Two Phases* 1. Baseline 2. Intervention	1. Will Sam's mastery of sight words increase when I use a time delay procedure for instruction? 2. Will Sam's call-out behavior decrease when I reinforce hand raising with tokens?
ABAB Reversal	To determine if a functional relationship exists between an independent variable and a dependent variable by replicating the baseline and intervention phases.	*Four Phases* 1. Baseline 2. Intervention 3. Return to baseline 4. Return intervention	1. Could the number of words Sam writes in a paragraph increase due to use of a point system? 2. Could Sam's off-task behaviors decrease due to use of a self-recording procedure?
Changing Criterion	To increase or decrease a behavior in systematic increments towards a terminal criterion. Allows for determination of a functional relationship if performance level matches the continually changing interim criteria.	Baseline plus an intervention phase for each interim criterion towards the objective; e.g., 10 phases of interim criteria raising 5 words per phase until criterion of 50 words.	1. Can I use a time delay procedure to systematically increase the pool of Sam's sight words to a criterion of 100 words? 2. Can I use token reinforcers to systematically decrease the number of times Sam runs in the hall during change of class to a criterion of no occurrences?
Multiple Baseline	To determine if a functional relationship exists between an independent variable and a dependent variable by assessing replication/generalization across: a) behaviors, b) individuals, or c) settings.	Baseline and staggered intervention phase for each replication/generalization, e.g., across behaviors: baseline and intervention for Sara's callouts *and* then out-of-seat behaviors; across students: baseline and intervention for cursing by Bob *and* then Ted; across settings: baseline and intervention in the resource class *and* then consumer math class.	1. a) Will the use of reinforcement of Linda's hand raising result in a decrease in the number of occurrences of both call-outs and out-of-seat without permission? b) Will the use of a learning strategy such as content mastery increase Linda's completion of American history assignments and biology assignments? 2. a) Will the use of points to earn the opportunity to be a team captain result in decrease in cursing by Bob, Ted, and Linda? b) Will the use of a calculator increase the accuracy of grocery purchasing by both Bob and Ted? 3. a) Will the use of self-recording result in a decrease in the occurrences of out-of-seat by Linda in the resource room, consumer math class, and music class? b) Will the use of tokens increase the number of math problems completed by Linda in both the resource class and consumer math class?

Continued

TABLE 5–2
Continued.

Design	Use	Format	Example Questions
Alternating Treatments	To determine which of two or more independent variables is more effective for increasing or decreasing occurrences of a dependent variable. Has the ability to determine the existence of a functional relationship by replicating use of the more effective independent variable in an additional phase.	*Three Phases* 1. Baseline 2. Intervention phase in which each independent variable is applied on alternating days, or alternating sessions during the same day. 3. A functional relationship may be determined by replication of the more effective intervention with the content taught by the less effective; or at the time period in which the less effective intervention was used.	1. Will the use of number line or counting chips increase Jane's accuracy in addition? 2. Will the use of earning points or losing points prove more effective in decreasing Jane's off-task behavior?
Changing Conditions Multiple Treatments ABC	To determine which of two or more independent variables is more effective for increasing or decreasing occurrences of a dependent variable. Functional relationship may be determined by replication of more effective independent variable following an additional baseline.	Multiple phases: e.g., Baseline First independent variable Baseline Second independent variable Baseline Possible replication of more effective independent variable.	1. Will oral and written practice increase Jane's spelling accuracy on test, or will oral practice alone be just as effective, or will written practice alone be just as effective? 2. Will point loss or point loss plus verbal reprimand be more effective in decreasing Jane's tardiness to classes?

A third criterion for evaluating the outcome of an intervention is its *social validity*. Those involved with the student's educational program should be concerned about and evaluate the social acceptability of an intervention program and of its outcome (Kazdin, 1977, 2001; Wolf, 1978). Social validity will be discussed at length in Chapter 12.

VISUAL ANALYSIS OF GRAPHS

Intervention effects in applied behavior analysis are usually evaluated through *visual analysis* of the graph displaying the plotted data points of the various phases (conditions). Certain characteristics of the data paths within and across phases are examined in order to judge the effectiveness of the intervention. These characteristics include the *mean* of the data points in the phase, the *levels* of performance from one phase to the next, the *trend* in performance across phases, the *percentage* of data that overlap in adjacent phases, and the *rapidity* of behavior change within phases (Kazdin, 1998, 2001; Poling et al., 1995; Richards et al., 1999).

1. Evaluation of changes in means focuses on the change in the average rate of student performance across the phases of a design. Within each phase, the mean (average) of the data points is determined and may be indicated on the graph by drawing a horizontal line corresponding to the value on the ordinate scale. Visual inspection of the relationship of these means will help determine if the intervention resulted in consistent and meaningful changes in the behavior in the desired direction of change. In Figure 5–29, Foxx and Shapiro (1978) supplied such indicators of means. The viewer can easily see the relative position of the students' disruptive behavior across the various design phases.
2. Evaluation of the level of performance refers to the magnitude and direction of the change in student performance from the end of one phase to the beginning of the next phase. "When a large change in level occurs immediately after the introduction of a new condition, the level change is considered abrupt, which is indicative of a powerful or effective intervention" (Tawney & Gast, 1984, p. 162). Tawney and Gast suggested the following steps to determine and evaluate a level change between two adjacent conditions: (1) identify the ordinate value of the last data point of the first condition and the first data point value of the second condition, (2) subtract the smallest value from the largest, and (3) note whether the change in level is in an improving or decaying direction (p. 162). In Figure 5–29, the arrows have been added to indicate level changes.
3. Evaluation of a trend in performance focuses on systematic and consistent increases or decreases in performance. Data trends are most often evaluated using a procedure known as the *quarter-intersect method* (White & Liberty, 1976). Evaluation of trends is based on lines of progress developed from the median value of the data points in each phase. The use of a trend line increases the reliability of visual analysis among people looking at a graph (Bailey, 1984; Ottenbacher, 1993; Ottenbacher & Cusick, 1991). This is of particular importance as teams of teachers, students, parents, and other concerned individuals review student data to assess progress and make decisions about future instruction or intervention. Steps for computing lines of progress are illustrated in Figure 5–30. Trend lines can provide (1) an indication of the direction of behavior change in the past and (2) a prediction of the direction of behavior change in the future. This information can help the teacher determine whether to change the intervention.

   Taking this process one step further will yield a split-middle line of progress (White & Haring, 1980). This line of progress is drawn so that an equal number of data points

FIGURE 5–30 **Steps for computing lines of progress.**

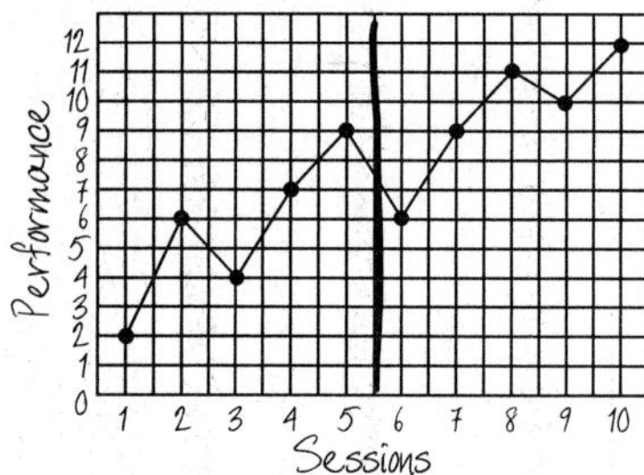

1. Divide the number of data points in half by drawing a vertical line down the graph.

In this example, there are 10 data points: therefore, the line is drawn between sessions 5 and 6. If there had been an odd number of data points, this would have been drawn through a session point.

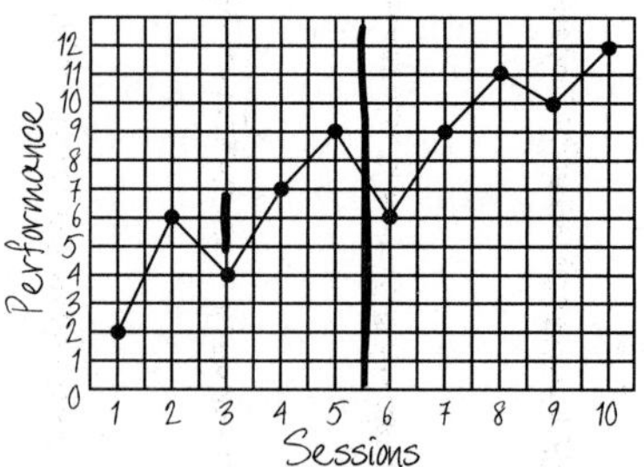

2. On the left half of the graph, find the midsession and draw a vertical line.

In this example, there are five data points; therefore, the line is drawn at session 3.
If there had been an even number of sessions, this line would have been drawn between two session points.

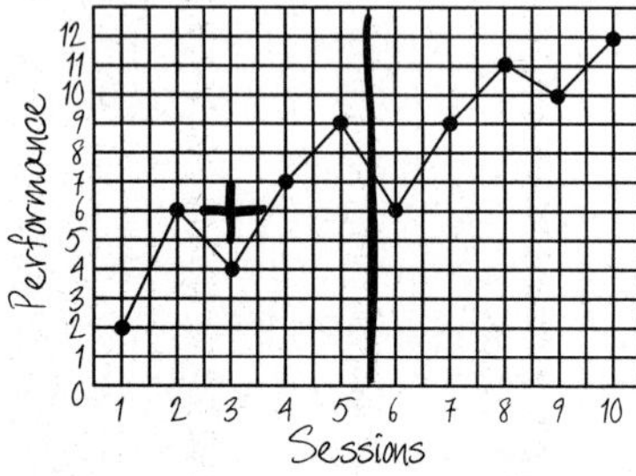

3. On the left half of the graph, find the mid-performance point and draw a horizontal line.

In this example, the data point at performance value 6 is the midperformance point because there are two data points below it and two data data points above it. If there had been an even number of data points, this line would have been drawn between the two media points.

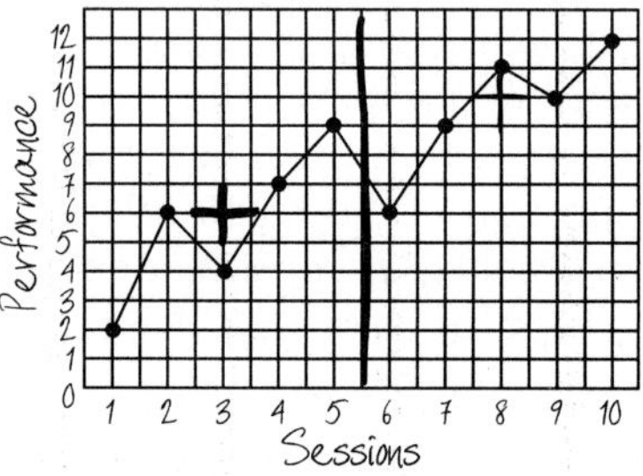

4. Repeat steps 2 and 3 on the right half of the graph.

In this example, session 8 is the midsession, and the data point at performance value 10 is the midperformance point.

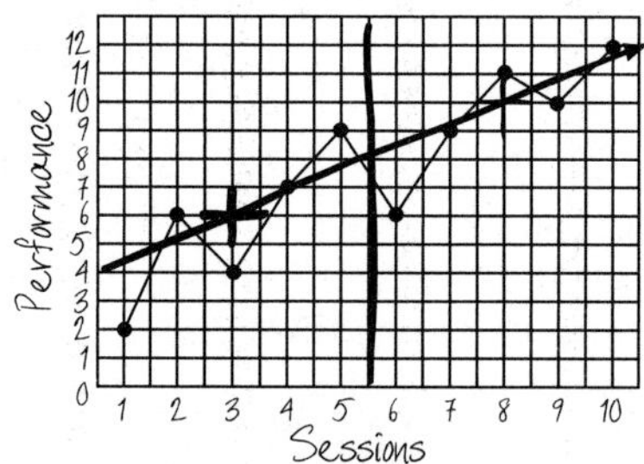

5. Draw a line connecting the intersections of both halves of the graph. This is the trend line for the data.

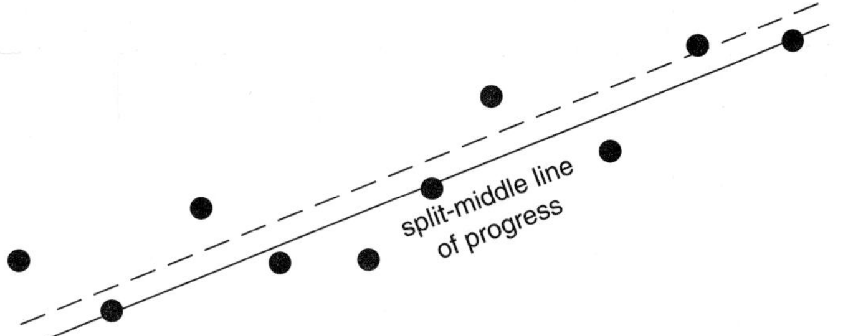

FIGURE 5–31
Split-middle line of progress.
Source: O. White and N. Haring, *Exceptional teaching* (Columbus, Ohio: Merrill, 1980), p. 118. Reproduced by permission.

fall on and above the line as fall on and below the line. As illustrated in Figure 5–31, if the data points do not naturally fall in such a pattern, the line is redrawn higher or lower, parallel to the original line, until the balance of data points is equal.

4. Evaluation of the percentage of overlap of data plotted for performance (ordinate values) across contiguous conditions provides an indication of the impact of an intervention on behavior. Percent of overlap is calculated by "(1) determining the range of data point values of the first condition, (2) counting the number of data points plotted in the second condition, (3) counting the number of data points of the second condition that fall within the range of values of the first condition, and (4) dividing the number of data points that fall within the range of the first condition by the total number of data points of the second condition and multiplying this number by 100. In general, the lower the percentage of overlap, the greater the impact the intervention has on the target behavior" (Tawney & Gast, 1984, p. 164).

   For example, in Figure 5–29, the range of data values during baseline (phase 1) is 32 to 50. In the reinforcement-only condition (phase 2), 6 of 10 data points fall within the same data value range as the baseline, yielding a 60% overlap. However, the percentage of overlap between phase 2 and phase 3 is 0%. These percentages of change indicate that the use of a time-out ribbon and reinforcement had a much greater impact on the disruptive behavior than did reinforcement alone.

5. Evaluation of the rapidity of the behavior change (sometimes called the latency of behavior change) refers to the length of time between the onset or termination of one phase and changes in performance. The sooner the change occurs after the experimental conditions have been altered (that is, after implementation or withdrawal of the intervention), the clearer the intervention effect (Kazdin, 1998). Note that "rapidity of change is a difficult notation to specify because it is a joint function of changes in level and slope (trend). A marked change in level and in slope usually reflects a rapid change" (Kazdin, 1982, p. 316).

Visual analysis is often quick and effective and is relatively easy to learn (Poling et al., 1995). This makes it useful to the teacher trying to make instructional and behavior management decisions in the classroom. The use of visual analysis encourages ongoing evaluation as data are collected and phases change, rather than reliance on pre- and postintervention data. This facilitates data-based decision making for educational programming.

Problematic in the use of visual analysis is a lack of concrete decision rules for determining whether a particular demonstration shows or fails to show a reliable effect (Kazdin, 1998). The components of visual analysis do not have agreed-upon operationalized criteria based in the research literature. Each teacher or researcher sets the standard for a component as they use it. Therefore, visual analysis may be seen as subjective and open to inconsistent application by an individual across sets of student data, or across different individuals reviewing student data. Confidence in conclusions based on visual inspection may be increased by increasing reliable use of the various components. The reliability may be increased by: (1) teacher training and repeated opportunities for use; (2) interpreting student performance data with a consistently applied standard; and (3) two or more trained individuals independently reviewing the data and drawing conclusions that can be compared (Richards et al., 1999). In special education there is at least annual interpretation and review of student data by the teacher and the IEP team. This presents an opportunity for review of data interpretation and collaboration in setting standards for data-based decision making.

It is noted that evaluation resulting from visual analysis reveals only intervention results that have a strong and reliable effect on behavior; that it may miss consistent but subtle or weak behavior change caused by some interventions. However, it may be considered a benefit for classroom use that visual analysis is more likely to identify independent variables that produce strong or socially significant results. The usual purpose of intervention is to obtain immediate and strong treatment effects. If obtained, such effects are "quite evident from visual inspection" (Kazdin, 2001, p. 150). When single-subject designs are used in classroom decision making, clinical and social validity are important criteria. The clinical criterion is a judgment as to whether the results of the teacher's intervention are large enough to be of practical value and impact on the learning or behavior of the student. They are likely to be socially valid based on the functional change in the student's performance and the social acceptance of the student.

Although visual inspection is useful, convenient, and basically reliable for identifying or verifying strong intervention effects for decision making in the classroom, educational and behavioral researchers may choose to explore statistical evaluation of single-subject data as a companion to, or comparison with, the results of visual analysis (Richards et al., 1999). This may be the case when there is concern for generalization across populations, or when seeking intervention effects so subtle as not to be clinically significant but which further research might be able to make more significant or more consistent. Kazdin (1976) offered three reasons for use of statistical techniques: (1) distinguishing subtle effects from chance occurrence, (2) analyzing the effect of a treatment procedure when a stable baseline cannot be established, and (3) assessing treatment effects in environments that lack control. Information about advanced uses of visual inspection and statistical evaluation with single-subject designs can be found in Barlow and Hersen (1984), Franklin, Allison, and Gorman (1996), Kazdin (1982, 1998), Poling et al. (1995), Richards et al. (1999), and Tawney and Gast (1984).

Summary

This summary serves as a rationale and an answer to the question: "Of what use is this to me?"

By best practice and legal mandate, data-based demonstrations of learning are required as evidence of effective instruction and of a quality education. Applied behavior analysis provides tools to meet these accountability requirements. Chapter 3 introduced methods of collecting data that provide the raw material for discussions of effectiveness. This chapter introduced single-subject designs as ways to organize the gathering and display of data. The design routinely used in the classroom is the AB design because it is a direct reflection of common classroom practice. It does not require restructuring teaching sessions. The graph of the AB design provides an uncomplicated visual format that can be used by teacher, student, parent, and supervisor to monitor, interpret, and assess learning. The other single-subject designs have specific capabilities and therefore may be used less frequently. In various ways, each design provides a database for quick, student-specific decision making. Table 5–2 summarizes the use of each and the questions they attempt to answer.

After the AB design, the changing criterion design is the most direct reflection of how a teacher manages instruction. Teachers regularly break down a goal that requires a large amount of learning into manageable units. Teaching manageable units of content, one at a time, in sequence, is the graphic picture resulting from organizing instruction and data collection within a changing criterion design. Another decision often required is which of two or more strategies will result in the most effective and efficient learning. The alternating use of strategies within the format of the alternating treatments design provides a data-based answer, usually by the end of 1 week. Given a little more time, an answer to the question can also be provided by using the ABC design. Variations of this design are used more commonly to evaluate combining several strategies in an instructional package. The multiple baseline design has gained popularity as inclusive policies are put in place in schools. Of particular interest is the multiple baseline across settings that allows tracking the effectiveness of an intervention across general education, special education, community, and home settings. The reversal design allows quick and unobtrusive evaluation of an intervention on a classroom problem that you do not want to allow to progress from being a nuisance to a spreading classroom management problem. The reversal design is appropriate for issues such as out of seat, off task, and not doing homework. Later in this text, this design is used when developing behavior management plans resulting from functional behavior assessment.

Aspects of instruction and behavior management are being continually researched and evaluated. This is especially true in ABA, which has a culture of data-based decision making. Research brings to the classroom extensions of current strategies and evaluation of proposed strategies. Teachers must be able to answer questions like: Is what I am doing still the best practice? Do the suggestions being made by colleagues, supervisors, and parents have a basis in data-based research? If educators are to be lifelong learners, they must be able to access the information provided in professional research journals. In order to read these journals, one must be literate in the type of research being published. From an ABA perspective, one must be able to read research conducted with single-subject designs. Most often found in the research journals are reversal and multiple baseline designs. The reversal design (ABAB) is frequently used because it is most powerfully able to demonstrate a functional relationship between a behavior and an intervention due to the controlled application and removal of a strategy (Kazdin, 1982). Multiple baseline designs are found frequently because they build immediate replication and therefore depth of experience with the intervention that allows broader and more confident statements of applicability to other students, behaviors, or settings.

Key Terms

variable
dependent variable
independent variable
functional relationship
group designs
single-subject designs
enhanced functioning
baseline data
trend
AB design
reversal design
ABAB design
changing criterion design
multiple baseline design
alternating treatments design
changing conditions design

Discussion Questions

1. Baseline data for Craig's self-injurious behavior indicate a mean occurrence of 17 instances per 40-minute observation period. What change in his behavior would be clinically significant (as demonstrated by enhanced functioning)?
2. Which single-subject design might a teacher use to systematically introduce and teach 30 community sight words?
3. During 3 weeks of multiplication instruction, probes of Alison's performance indicated that she still could not multiply. Her teacher wants to determine which of two alternative approaches to teaching multiplication would be most effective for Alison. Select two instructional methods. Select an appropriate single-subject design and outline the steps the teacher should follow to make this determination.
4. Outline a procedure associated with a single-subject design that would demonstrate the generalization of an intervention across settings in a high school.
5. Draw lines of progress on the two sets of data graphed below.

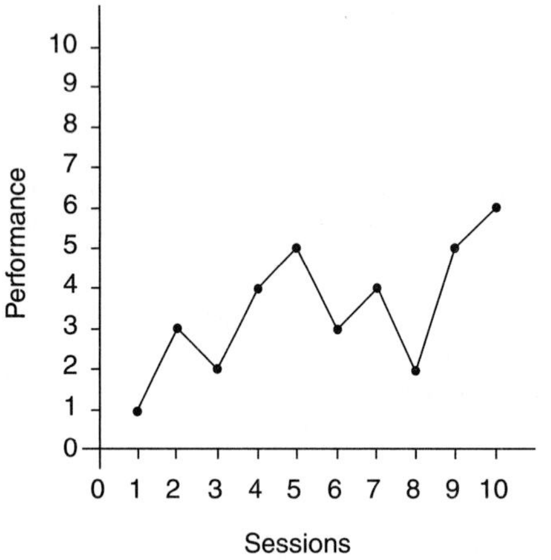

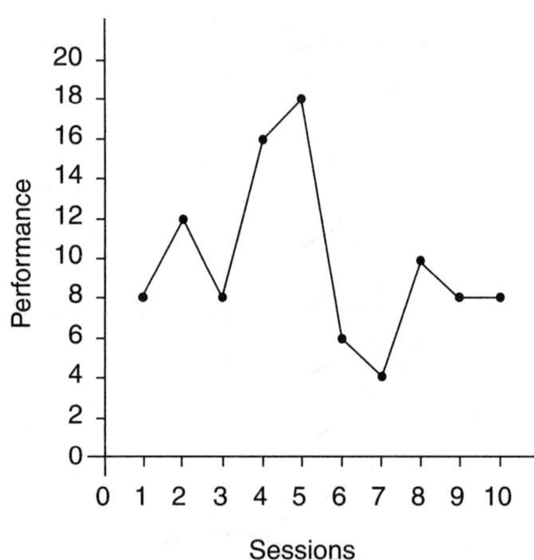

6. Many of the studies that appear in professional journals use "embedded" designs. That is, one single-subject design is embedded within another. This is illustrated in the following graph: (a) Identify the components of the multiple baseline within the graph; (b) identify the components of the reversal within the graph; and (c) identify the elements demonstrating a functional relationship.

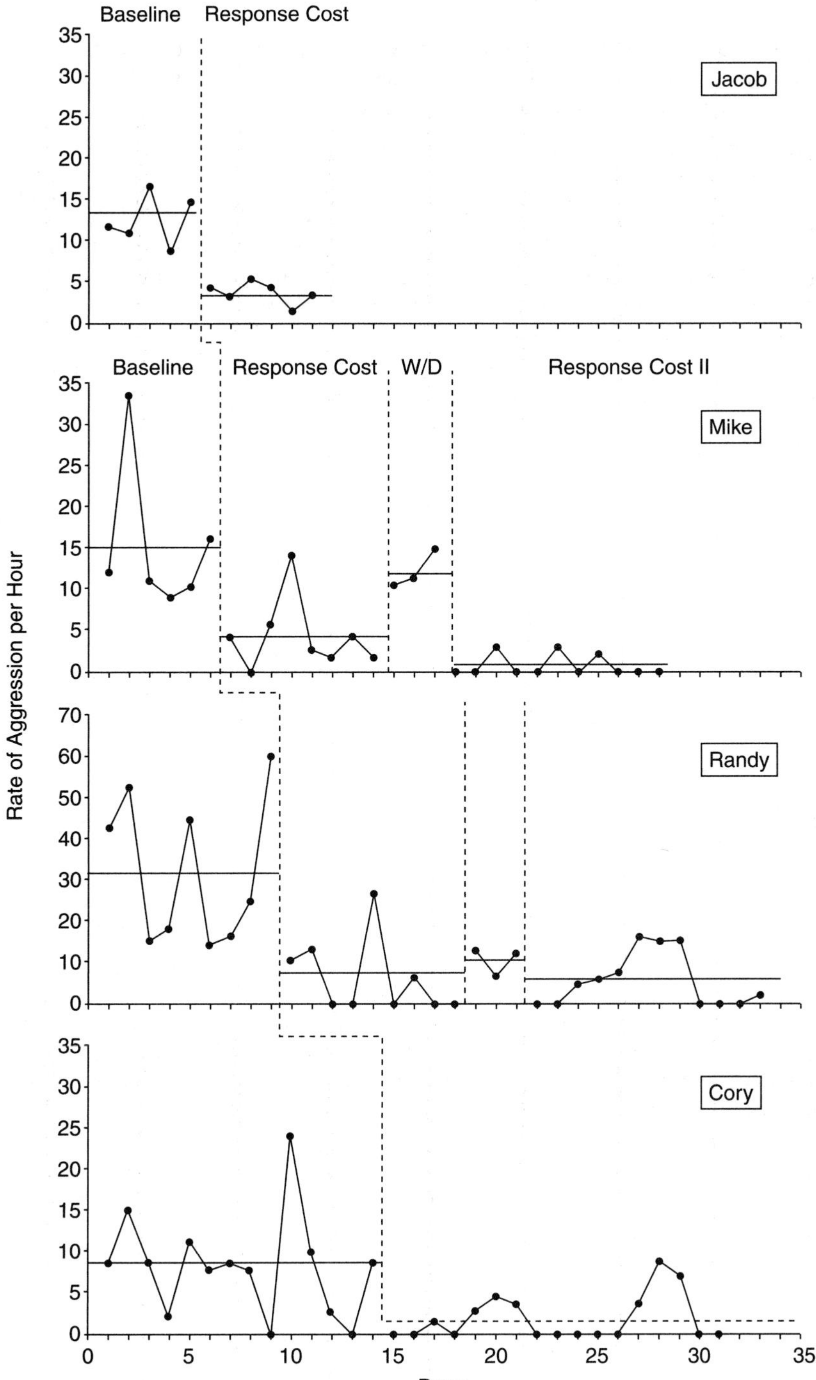

Note: From "The efficacy of a response cost-based treatment package for managing aggressive behavior in preschoolers," by L. Reynolds & M. Kelley. *Behavior modification,* 1997. Copyright 1997 by Sage Publications, Inc. Reprinted by permission.

Chapter 6

Developing a Hypothesis for Behavior Change: Functional Assessment and Functional Analysis

Did you know that . . .

- Challenging behaviors may serve a reasonable purpose?
- Multiple behaviors may serve the same purpose?
- Antecedents may influence behavior as much as consequences?
- Some students are masters of escape?

Chapter Outline

At Whittier Middle School the certain consequence for fighting is 2 days in-school suspension. During such suspension, students must labor all day at written work in individual study carrels adjacent to the principal's office, where they are not allowed to talk or socialize. Fighting has been an infrequent behavior. In these first few weeks of the school year however, Dr. Toarmina, the principal, is dealing with several fights a day. Repeated interviews with the participants have provided little information: "He just came up and hit me—I don't hardly know the dude." "The fool knocked my books out of my hand. I smacked him good." Many sixth graders have participated in the fights, but Dr. Toarmina has observed that Maurice is the only student who has participated in all of them and the only student who has endured in-school suspension more than once. Maurice is new to the school and the neighborhood. He is considered an "at-risk" student and has limited English capability. Even to a translator, however, Maurice refuses to communicate any reason for his aggression. He just shrugs and looks away. In desperation, Dr. Toarmina increases the duration of the suspension to 3 days. The fights continue. In-school suspension, an intervention that has been effective for most students in the past, is not effective for Maurice.

Angela is a new student in Mr. Gray's class for young children with developmental delays. Angela screams. Indeed, to Mr. Gray it seems that Angela screams all day. He repeatedly goes to Angela, trying to find something to pacify her. "Angela," he asks, "Do you need potty? Do you want juice? Do you want to play with Elmo? Do you hurt? Here? Here? Shall we go outside?" When he finds himself asking "Is it bigger than a breadbox?" he decides that he cannot spend so much time playing Twenty Questions with Angela and that he will use time-out to decrease her screaming. Every time Angela screams, Mr. Gray or his assistant picks her up, gently deposits her on a mat behind a screen in the classroom, and leaves her there until 1 minute after she stops screaming. Sure enough, Angela stops screaming. Suddenly, however, she starts hitting adults and other children, apparently at random, something she has never done before. Mr. Gray, not easily discouraged, begins to put Angela in time-out for hitting. Soon he observes that Angela has begun banging her head with her fists while she is in time-out. Because he obviously cannot allow her to injure herself, he does become discouraged. He abandons time-out; Angela returns to screaming; and Mr. Gray continues to play Twenty Questions.

In both these anecdotes, educators are dealing with recurring and apparently random inappropriate behavior and with students who cannot or will not provide information about the contexts within which it occurs. Attempts are made to reduce the occurrence of the behaviors with techniques that have been effective in the past, but these attempts are unsuccessful. The behavior has a familiar form or topography—it looks like behavior that has been seen before. Why, then, is the intervention strategy not working? The problem may be that in our preoccupation with the behavior's form, we have failed to determine its function. In other words, informal analysis has failed to provide an accurate determination of why the student is engaging in the behavior. In such cases, we may need more in-depth sets of procedures known as functional assessment and functional analysis (Skinner, 1953).

BEHAVIOR AND ITS FUNCTION

Things that inappropriate behaviors might serve to communicate.

When teachers ask, "Why does she do that?" we are really wondering what function the behavior serves for the student—what is her purpose for doing what she is doing. The function of a behavior is to make a desired change in the environment. If engaging in the behavior results in the change the student wants, there is an increased probability that she will engage in the behavior again. The desired change may be getting something she wants or escaping from something she does not want. This relationship between the purpose of behavior—desirable outcomes or consequences—and the maintenance of behavior is the nature of reinforcement.

Educators often focus on the physical characteristics of behavior (form or topography) because those are what we see. We develop an operational definition of the behavior that describes what we see. A quantitative measure of topography (frequency, duration, or percent of intervals during which the behavior occurs) is typically the dependent variable when we seek to change a behavior (Pyles & Bailey, 1990). We select an intervention to reduce the number of times Brett gets out of his seat during reading class, or to reduce the length of time that he remains out of his seat when he gets up, or to reduce the percentage of intervals that he is out of his seat. Focusing on a behavior's topography, however, may provide little information about factors controlling the behavior. The same behavior exhibited by two different students may be maintained for different reasons. One student's aggressive behavior may be a function of seeking teacher or peer attention. Another student may want to escape the teacher's attention because she did not do her homework or escape bullying from a peer. It is unlikely that any single intervention will have the same effect on behaviors performed for such different reasons. By neglecting to attend to a behavior's function, we may fail to see that topographically unrelated behaviors like signing "juice," pointing to a cup of juice, or banging one's empty cup on the table may serve the same function by resulting in the same outcome—getting some juice to drink (Remington, 1991).

Teachers often find that an intervention eliminates an inappropriate behavior for a short time but that the behavior soon reappears. Sometimes a new, equally or even more inappropriate behavior replaces it. If her teacher takes Sita's cup away from her every time she bangs it on the table but does not teach her to sign "juice" or to point to the juice, Sita may very well stop banging the cup for a while but start banging it again in a few days or, even worse, start screaming and banging her head as soon as she is seated at the snack table. This happens when an intervention is used simply to suppress a behavior. Unless a student has a new, more appropriate way to bring about a desired environmental change, she will continue to bring it about in ways that have been successful in the past. We often call these behaviors "challenging" both because they present major challenges to maintaining a productive learning environment and because they offer challenges to professionals trying to change them. If, by chance, the intervention selected to reduce form results in a new behavior that happens to match function, behavior management is successful. If not, we may dismiss the experience as another puzzling example of the failure of applied behavioral methods to produce lasting change. If, for example, after her teacher took Sita's cup away, Sita happened to point to the juice pitcher and get juice, Sita would probably not bang her cup anymore. She could eventually be taught to point even when holding the cup. If, on the other hand, Sita just sat and did not get juice, she would probably go back to banging the cup as soon as it was given back to her or start screaming if she did not have it. This "hit or miss" success rate characterized behavior management before we understood the need to attend to both the form and the function of behavior (Iwata, Dorsey, Slifer, Bauman, & Richman, 1982; Pelios, Morren, Tesch, & Axelrod, 1999; Repp, Felce, & Barton, 1988). It may well be that failure to consider a behavior's function is the basis for the assumption that suppression of inappropriate behavior inevitably results in "symptom substitution," or the appearance of new inappropriate behavior based on some underlying disturbance. A need for function-based intervention does not assume some internal motive for a student's behavior but focuses on the purpose of that behavior as defined by environmental events that occasion and maintain it.

TABLE 6–1
Behavior: Its functions and maintaining consequences.

Functions of Behavior		Maintaining Consequence
<u>*To gain attention:*</u> Social from adult (teacher, parent) paraeeducator, customer, etc.) Social from peer	—	<u>*Positive Reinforcement*</u> Receiving attention increases the future rate or probability of the student engaging in the behavior again.
<u>*To gain a tangible:*</u> Assistance in getting: Object Activity Event	—	<u>*Positive Reinforcement*</u> Receiving the tangible increases the future rate or probability of the student engaging in the behavior again.
<u>*To gain sensory stimulations:*</u> Visual Gustatory Auditory Kinesthetic Olfactory Proprioceptive	—	<u>*Positive Automatic Reinforcement*</u> Provision of the sensory input by engaging in the behavior itself increases the future rate or probability of the student engaging in the behavior again.
<u>*To escape from attention:*</u> Attention from peer or adult Social interaction with peer	—	<u>*Negative Reinforcement*</u> Removing the student from the interaction that is aversive increases the future rate or probability of the behavior.
<u>*To escape from:*</u> Demanding or boring task Setting, activity, event	—	<u>*Negative Reinforcement*</u> Removing the stimulus the student finds aversive increases the future rate or probability of the behavior.
<u>*To escape from sensory stimulation:*</u> Internal stimulation which is painful or discomforting	—	<u>*Negative Automatic Reinforcement*</u> Attenuation of painful or discomforting internal stimulation by engaging in the behavior itself increases the future rate and/or probability of the student engaging in the behavior again.

Companion Website

To increase your understanding of functional assessment, go to the "Activities" module for Chapter 6 of the Companion Website.

Inappropriate behaviors often serve the function of achieving a desired change in the student's environment. Table 6–1 lists six functions of behavior that appear frequently in the research literature and their relationships to reinforcing consequences that maintain the behavior. These include engaging in behavior to gain attention, to gain a tangible, to gain sensory stimulation, to escape from tasks and interactions, and to escape from internal pain or discomfort.

1. *Behavior engaged in to gain attention.* Getting the attention of an adult or peer in order to engage in social interaction is a function of behavior. The most common way to gain someone's attention is use of verbal language or some nonverbal communicative behavior. A student may raise his hand or walk up to the teacher and

engage her in conversation. When students lack the communication or social skills to gain attention, they may use behaviors considered inappropriate. The student may call out, throw items on the floor, or curse to get the teacher's attention. If these challenging behaviors succeed in getting the adult's attention (pleasant or unpleasant), the student learns that engaging in these behaviors achieves the desired result. If a student is successful in getting the teacher's attention only by raising his hand, he learns a socially appropriate behavior. Achieving the desired result increases the future rate or probability of the student's engaging in the behavior again. This is an example of positive reinforcement.

The social attention students desire may be from peers rather than adults. Dr. Toarmina, the principal of the middle school described at the beginning of this chapter, initially theorized that Maurice was initiating fights because he lacked the language and social skills to interact appropriately with his peers. She learned from the school social worker, who made a home visit, that Maurice lived with his parents in a neighborhood of older homes primarily occupied by elderly people and a few young couples. Both parents worked two jobs to save money to bring Maurice's younger brother and sister to this country. Their rental house did not allow children, so Maurice was required to stay inside at all times. He was alone much of the time and did not have an opportunity to make friends in the neighborhood. Dr. Toarmina arranged for Maurice to join an afterschool recreational program with a diverse population and a focus on appropriate social interaction. Unfortunately, although Maurice did appear to have more positive interactions with peers after a few weeks, he still started fights almost daily. Dr. Toarmina was puzzled but continued her efforts to get to the bottom of the problem.

2. *Behavior engaged in to gain a tangible.* Getting the attention of an adult or peer in order to get assistance in obtaining some tangible object, activity, or event is a function of behavior. During morning snack the student may point to or ask for some of the juice (object), or he may bang his cup on the table or throw it to the floor. A student may raise his hand and wait to be recognized, or he may call out, "Ms. Barnes I need help with question number four" (activity). A student may use an augmentative communication device to request assistance changing his position in a wheelchair or to get permission to go to the restroom (event), or he may cry, scream, or wiggle in his chair.

If a student repeatedly gets the tangible object, activity, or event by engaging in inappropriate behavior, she learns to use that behavior to achieve her desired outcome. This increases the future rate or probability that she will perform the challenging behavior again. This, too, is an example of positive reinforcement. What teachers or parents describe as inappropriate or challenging behaviors may be attempts at communication. A student without a standard form of communication might scream and hit herself because she is not able to ask, "Please change my position in my wheelchair; I'm very uncomfortable." A student may bang her cup on the table to communicate, "Please pass the juice," because she lacks the ability to sign "juice" or has not learned that she may obtain it by pointing. A student who has not been taught an acceptable way to indicate that he needs to use the bathroom may display what appears to be simply inappropriate restlessness and agitation. The assessment procedures described in this chapter enabled Angela's teacher (in the anecdote at the beginning of the chapter) to determine that she used screaming to communicate a variety of needs. When screaming became ineffective, she turned to hitting. Once the communicative content of a behavior is identified, the student should be taught a more appropriate form of behavior that serves the

It's neither fair nor ethical to punish functional behavior.

same communication purpose (Carr & Durand, 1985; Durand, 1999; Durand & Carr, 1987). Providing Angela with an augmentative communication device and the training to use it gradually reduced her screaming.

Even adults sometimes lash out when they are frustrated.

Inappropriate communicative behavior is often maintained by positive reinforcement (either consistently or inconsistently administered) resulting from the teacher's engaging in Twenty Questions when she does not know what the student is trying to tell her. Sometimes the teacher guesses correctly and the student gets what she wants. The student does not need to be successful every time to keep a behavior in her repertoire (see Chapter 7).

For more information on functional assessment, click on the "Web Links" module for Chapter 6 of the Companion Website.

3. *Behavior engaged in to gain sensory stimulation.* Getting sensory stimulation is a function of behavior. Most of us have a set of motor or communication skills that allow us to provide ourselves with sensory stimulation. We can turn on a CD player, play a video game, or take a piece of chocolate ourselves or, if need be, we can ask for assistance. If students are not able to provide themselves with appropriate sensory experiences or to ask others to provide them, they may engage in self-injurious or stereotypic behaviors. Behaviors such as humming, blowing saliva bubbles, slapping their ears, pinching themselves, flicking their fingers, mouthing objects, or rocking their bodies may provide students with the only sensory stimulation available to them. The sensory input received by engaging in the behavior increases the future rate or probability of the students' engaging in the behavior again. This is automatic positive reinforcement—the act of engaging in the behavior itself provides the desired environmental change.
4. *Behavior engaged in to escape from attention or interactions.* A behavior can serve the function of getting away from a situation one finds unpleasant or aversive. Escaping the teacher's attention when one does not have one's homework may be accomplished by using rather sophisticated social skills such as asking a question on a topic known to get the teacher distracted or by running out of the room. Overly effusive praise from a teacher may cause a middle schooler to escape so as to avoid his peers' ridicule. Escaping from an undesired social interaction with a playground bully can be achieved by communicating a need for assistance from friends or by truancy. Escaping from the repetitive activity of shelving bottles of salad dressing on a job-training site may be achieved by asking for a break or by breaking something.

Dr. Toarmina, the middle school principal, was still puzzled by Maurice's fighting. He seemed to choose his victims randomly; no pattern of events seemed regularly to occasion fighting. The only consistency was the consequence—in-school suspension. Maurice was spending most of his time at school in that environment; when released, he started another fight. She interviewed his teachers. Most of the teachers reported that Maurice was quiet and well-behaved (except when he was fighting). They indicated his English was improving rapidly and he had interesting contributions to make. Only Mr. Harris, the social studies teacher, believed that Maurice was not potentially a good student.

Students have learned that teasing from peers results from certain behaviors.

Finally, while interviewing one of Maurice's victims, she asked the right question. She asked if Maurice was having trouble in any of his classes. The student hesitated but finally stated that Mr. Harris did not seem to know that Maurice spoke very little English and kept calling on him, correcting him, and then yelling at him to pay attention and try to make sense when he talked or to shut up if he could not do any better than he was doing now. The student reported that Maurice was often close to tears. "Maybe," the student suggested, "he just gets so upset he has to take it out on somebody. He never really hurts anyone; we just fight back because that's the way it's done."

Dr. Toarmina thanked the student, dismissed him, and shut her office door. No, she thought, he's not so upset he's taking it out on other students; he's so upset that he's figured out a way to avoid being harassed and humiliated. At least nobody embarrasses him or yells at him while he's in in-school suspension. She made a note to have Maurice transferred to another section of social studies and left a note in Mr. Harris's box to see her immediately after school.

5. *Behavior engaged in to escape from tasks.* Getting out of doing a task is a function of behavior. The task can be too hard and therefore aversive, or too easy and therefore boring. Escape from a demanding task such as long division, tooth brushing, or dodge ball can be achieved by communicating the need for help, a break, or dislike for the task. If one does not have the communication or social skills to ask for a break, throwing a temper tantrum may work just as well. When the student has a tantrum and the frustrated teacher or parent just stops the task and walks away, the student learns that having a tantrum is an effective way to escape aversive tasks. In some cases the context of the task may be aversive. In school, the social embarrassment of an age-inappropriate gender-inappropriate, or culturally inappropriate task, set of materials, or setting, will cause student escape behaviors.

If a student does not have the communication skills to request escape or the social skills to remove her from an unpleasant interaction, she may engage in an inappropriate behavior. If the behavior results in escape, the environment has been changed in a way she desired. Achieving this result increases the future rate or probability of the student's using that form of escape again. This is an example of negative reinforcement. The teacher who removes the difficult task when the student throws it on the floor is teaching the student that this is what to do when you want to escape from a difficult task.

6. *Behavior engaged in to escape from internal stimulation that is painful or uncomfortable.* Escape from internal pain or discomfort is a function of behavior. Most of us can move to a more comfortable seat, get a heating pad, take an aspirin or a laxative, or tell our symptoms to a doctor. People who do not have the communication skills or cognitive ability to relate that they are uncomfortable or in pain may engage in what others view as inappropriate behavior in an attempt to reduce (attenuate) discomfort or pain. Removal of, or distraction from, pain or discomfort by engaging in the behavior increases the future rate or probability that the person will engage in the behavior again. This is automatic negative reinforcement; the act of engaging in the behavior itself provides the desired environmental change—escape from discomfort.

The following anecdote describes attempts to suppress behaviors considering only their form rather than attending to their function.

The Professor Gets a Lecture

Professor Grundy had just returned home from several days out of town at a professional conference. As he pulled his car into the driveway he heard a muffled squealing sound coming from inside the house. As he opened the back door he located the sound as coming from the laundry room.

"Minerva," he called to Mrs. Grundy. "I'm home! Is there something wrong with the washing machine? Something's making a fearful noise." Mrs. Grundy did not answer. He finally found her working at her computer in the bedroom but had to touch her on the shoulder to get her attention. She jumped and pulled something out of her ears.

"Minerva," he asked again, "is there something wrong with the washing machine? There is a horrible noise coming from the laundry room."

"That horrible noise," she retorted, "is coming from your horrible dog. He started barking and howling the day after you left. I looked in all your dog-training books and tried everything they suggested. I've thrown water on him; I've thrown aluminum cans filled with pennies; I've squirted mouthwash, hot sauce, and vinegar in his mouth."

"Perhaps," suggested Grundy, "he missed me."

"Oh, nonsense, Oliver, you've been gone for several days before since we got him and there's never been a problem," replied Mrs. Grundy. "I finally went to the pet supply store and they sold me a collar . . . "

"NOT," roared Grundy, "a shock collar!"

"No, no," soothed Mrs. Grundy, "it squirts a blast of citronella when he barks. He stopped barking, but now whenever I let him outside, he hurls himself at the fence. He's also apparently learned that he can make that awful squealing sound without setting the collar off. I'm trying to work (Mrs. Grundy wrote very popular romance novels.) and I've had to shut him in the laundry room and wear ear plugs so I can concentrate."

Grundy left her to her work and went downstairs to see about Burrhus. The dog squealed happily to see the professor, who, desirous of directly observing the behavior, took him into the yard. Burrhus squealed desperately and ran full tilt into the cedar fence between the Grundy's yard and that of their next-door neighbor, Miss Oattis.

"That's it!" Grundy exclaimed aloud, dragging Burrhus back into the house. He had remembered that Miss Oattis was a "dog person." She had three small white dogs, two of which looked pretty normal and one of which had a very peculiar hairstyle. He understood from Mrs. Grundy that Miss Oattis took her dogs, toy poodles, to dog shows and taught dog obedience classes. She would be the person to ask about Burrhus's behavior.

Miss Oattis promptly answered his knock on the front door. She was holding the dog with the peculiar hairstyle who appeared to be wearing . . . could it be a diaper? Grundy hastily averted his eyes and explained his problem.

"Well," replied Miss Oattis, "Chloe, here," she indicated the dog, "is in season, but that shouldn't bother a dog that has been neutered." Observing Grundy's confused expression, she clarified, "She's in heat, Professor, that's why she's wearing a sanitary garment. It's her first heat and probably her last. She has almost finished her championship and then she will be spayed like my other girls."

"Well," stammered Grundy, "I really didn't want to . . . "

"Are you telling me your dog has NOT been neutered?" Miss Oattis asked in an outraged tone. "He's a rescue, isn't he? Rescues," she continued firmly, "are always spayed or neutered. Didn't your vet . . . "

"Er," replied Grundy, a little overwhelmed by her forthrightness, "He did suggest, er, but it seemed, er . . . "

"Men!" snorted Miss Oattis. "It's a very simple surgery; he will never miss the equipment; and there are numerous health and behavior benefits. Make an appointment immediately! The poor boy is trying to get to Chloe; and who can blame him? For the next week or so I'll walk Chloe on leash on the other side of my house, and you walk your boy as far away from the fence as you can get. We'll just manage the environment. But you make that appointment tomorrow. If they can do the surgery in the next few days, he and Mrs. Grundy will be spared at least one day of misery while he's at the vet's."

By attending to the functions of behaviors as well as to their form, we can design interventions to enable students to meet their needs in appropriate ways. A formal document created to achieve this end is the behavior support plan.

THE BEHAVIOR SUPPORT PLAN

A plan that details an agreed-upon set of procedures for changing inappropriate behavior is the behavior support plan (BSP). In Chapter 2, we noted that IDEA uses the term behavior intervention plan. The underlying logic guiding the design of a BSP is that of replacing an inappropriate behavior with an appropriate behavior that serves the same function. The first step in designing a BSP is to form a hypothesis, based on the possible functions described above, as to what function the behavior in question serves. To form the hypothesis, we try to identify relationships among the behavior, its antecedents, the change resulting in the environment, and the reinforcement that the environmental change provides. We hypothesize that this reinforcement has maintained the inappropriate behavior and predict that the same reinforcement will maintain the more appropriate replacement behavior.

For additional information about behavior intervention plans, go to the "Web Links" module for Chapter 6 of the Companion Website.

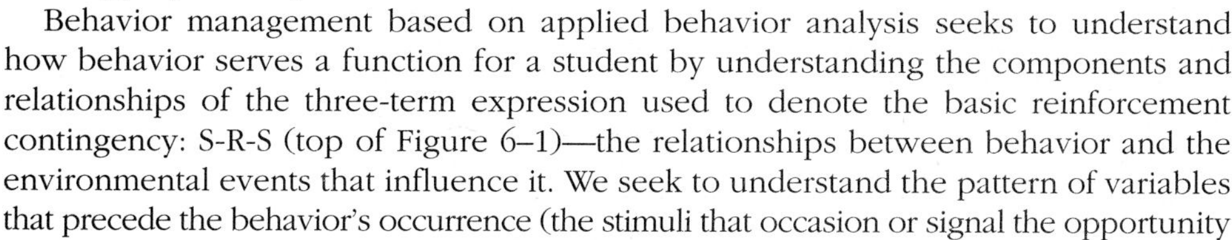

Behavior management based on applied behavior analysis seeks to understand how behavior serves a function for a student by understanding the components and relationships of the three-term expression used to denote the basic reinforcement contingency: S-R-S (top of Figure 6–1)—the relationships between behavior and the environmental events that influence it. We seek to understand the pattern of variables that precede the behavior's occurrence (the stimuli that occasion or signal the opportunity

Basic expression

S^D – *Antecedent stimulus* –	R – *Operant response* –	S *Consequence stimulus*
—Discriminative stimulus —Immediate preceding stimulus that occasions (signals) the opportunity to perform a response if you choose to—e.g.,		—Reinforcer —Punisher
—teacher asks a question	Student raises hand	
—traffic light turns green	Student crosses street	
—Terry hits Pat	Pat hits Terry	
—teacher gives worksheet	Student does math examples	
—teacher gives worksheet	Student tears it up	

Basic expression plus setting event

S^e – {S^D – R – S^r }

Setting event

—Distant antecedent event that provides the context within which the contingency exists
—Environmental, social, or physiological events

The reinforcement received when a behavior successfully serves its function—e.g.,
—student gets social attention
—student gets tangible
—student gets sensory stimulation
—student escapes task or situation
—student escapes internal stimulation

FIGURE 6–1 ***The three-term expression used to denote the reinforcement contingency.***

to perform the behavior—antecedents) and the pattern of variables that follow the behavior (those that fulfill the purpose of the behavior and therefore maintain the behavior—reinforcing consequences). An analysis of a problem behavior's function in terms of its antecedents and consequences is necessary for the selection of the most effective treatment (Crawford, Brockel, Schauss, & Miltenberger, 1992). With this analysis and an understanding of function we can select and teach an appropriate behavior to replace the inappropriate behavior. The new behavior must serve the same function as the original one and thus continue to provide reinforcement to the student. From an educational perspective the replacement behavior must also be appropriate to the student's age and contextually appropriate in the environment in which the student will use the behavior. We would not, for example, teach a young adult with retardation to wave bye-bye to indicate her desire to terminate a task. We would not send her to religious services with an augmentative communication device producing an audible "I need to go to the restroom!"

The data upon which to base a hypothesis come from conducting a **functional assessment** or a **functional analysis.** Functional assessment is a set of information-gathering strategies and instruments. Based on what precedes the behavior and what follows it, patterns are identified that lead to the hypothesis. Functional analysis, on the other hand, is a strategy of manipulating the student's environment and observing the effect on his behavior. Changes in the student's behavior lead to a hypothesis. Each of these procedures attempts to answer the following questions:

Questions that can be answered using functional assessment/analysis.

1. Is there a pattern of events or behaviors that consistently precedes the occurrence of the behavior?
2. Is there a pattern of events or behaviors that consistently follows the occurrence of the behavior? (And who engages in these behaviors?)
3. Can the student be taught an alternative, appropriate behavior to accomplish the same function as the inappropriate behavior?

In addition to these questions a fourth question is asked: What is the context within which the behavior, the antecedents, and the consequences take place? This question is asking: What are the **setting events?** Setting events refer to the setting, climate, or context within which the behavior and the contingency occur (bottom of Figure 6–1). Setting events may occur immediately before a problem behavior (proximal antecedents) or hours or days in advance (distal antecedents) and may include ongoing factors such as a student's culture, family circumstances, or medical condition. Setting events can include environmental factors (noise or temperature level, unplanned schedule changes, missing the school bus); social factors (a death or illness in the family, an encounter with a bully, receiving a bad grade in a previous class); or physiological factors (side effects of medication, illness, pain) (Kazdin, 2001). Ongoing classroom characteristics can also set a context or climate that affects the value of reinforcers and punishers. Such setting events include a classroom characterized by understimulation and student boredom (meaningless repetition of tasks, pacing instruction too slowly, lack of systematic instruction); overstimulation (large number of students, too rapid a pace of activities, inappropriate grouping of students); frustration (lack of a communication system or functional vocabulary, constant interruption of performance and goal attainment, lack of demonstrated progress); or anxiety (inconsistent management techniques, fear of failure, undiagnosed learning problems).

The information in Figure 6–2 is explained in detail in the text following.

By creating the context in which behaviors and contingencies occur, setting events influence the occurrence of the behavior and the value of the contingencies (Kazdin, 2001). They can momentarily change the value of reinforcers and punishers in an environment and therefore change the way a student responds to events and situations in the envi-

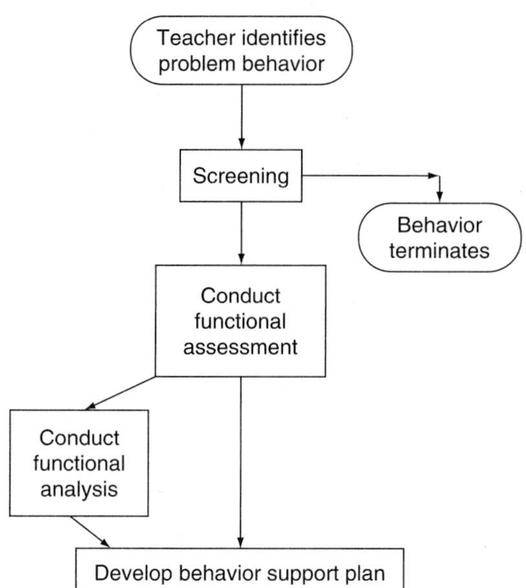

FIGURE 6–2
Development of a behavior support plan.

ronment. If, for example, a student comes to your class after receiving yet another D on an essay in her previous class, her ability to concentrate and her motivation to complete your assignment and earn the praise you provide as a reinforcer may be considerably lessened. A student who comes to school extremely overactive because her schedule of medications has been changed may be unable to control her behavior well enough to interact appropriately with her peers. If a student is repeatedly given a task she mastered weeks ago, completion of the task may not be as reinforcing as it once was.

Development of a Behavior Support Plan

A sequence of steps for developing a BSP is presented in Figure 6–2. The sequence begins with the teacher's recognizing and documenting an ongoing challenging behavior, progresses through the use of functional assessment or functional analysis procedures, and results in the implementation and monitoring of a set of intervention procedures.

Step 1: Teacher Identifies Problem Behavior

a. Develop operational definition.
b. Collect initial confirming data.
c. Notify IEP committee members.

IDEA requires development of a BSP on two occasions: (1) when a student's behavior is such that it may result in a suspension up to 10 days or a change of educational placement; and (2) when a pattern of behavior impedes the learning of the student or of another student (Turnbull, Wilcox, Stowe, & Turnbull, 2001). As educators and parents become more familiar with the procedures, collaboration, and benefits involved with the development of BSPs and their use becomes more routine in schools, BSPs are being developed for additional behaviors. These may include behaviors that: (1) are of potential harm to onself, (2) are of potential harm to others, (3) interfere with the performance of others in school, in the community, or on the job site, (4) may result in damage to property, (5) regularly require third-party intervention, (6) draw ridicule or undue negative attention to the student, (7) restrict or deny entry into current or new educational, community, or job settings, or (8) cause disruption within the family and may result in isolation within the family.

The teacher prepares an operational definition (see Chapter 2) of the inappropriate behavior targeted for reduction. The operational definition clearly states the form of the behavior. The specificity of an operational definition allows for the design of a data collection system. The teacher collects initial data with one of the data collection systems and then graphs the data (see Chapters 3 and 5). These data will be used during initial discussions of the scope and severity of the behavior in order to substantiate the existence of a challenging behavior requiring further management. The teacher notifies the members of the IEP committee of her concern and initial actions. The IEP committee (or a designated subgroup that will act as the behavior-management team) convenes, initially for two purposes. The initial purpose is to review the data collected by the teacher and to confirm that the behavior is of a nature and frequency that will require the preparation of a BSP. It may be that discussing the behavior and its occurrence with team members will provide the teacher with ideas she has overlooked and enable her to manage the behavior quickly and simply. The team will review information from the student's records to ensure that all appropriate screening measures have been conducted and that the results are up to date.

Step 2: Screening

a. Request as needed: health, medications, physical, sensory, and learning disability screenings.
b. Implement changes based on screening.

The teacher and the IEP committee may request that screening tests be conducted that might provide insight into the cause of the behavior problem and a direct solution. Toward this end the committee may request a new or updated: (1) physical health screening, (2) review of medications being taken and their interactions and side effects, (3) screening for a physical impairment or review of its current management by school personnel and family members, (4) screening for a sensory impairment or review of its current management, (5) administration of screening instruments to assess for the presence of a learning disability, whose currently unknown presence could result in inappropriate compensating behaviors by the student. Based on information from the screenings, the members can make recommendations that may terminate the behavior. A vision screening, for example, may result in a prescription for new glasses. Testing for a learning disability may result in 4 hours a week with the resource teacher. Waiting for the results of screenings need not delay the next step in the sequence, which is information gathering.

Step 3: Conduct Functional Assessment

a. Employ indirect information-gathering strategies.
b. Employ direct information-gathering strategies.
c. Formulate hypothesis of function.

Functional assessment is a set of information-gathering strategies used to formulate a hypothesis about the function of an inappropriate behavior. There are two categories of these strategies (see Table 6–2). Indirect strategies gather information from people who regularly interact with the student. This is informant assessment. Various interview forms, scales, and questionnaires are available. Direct observation strategies gather information by taking data on the behavior while the student is engaged in it. This is descriptive assessment. These strategies include: anecdotal reports, scatter plot analysis, and A-B-C descriptive analysis.

TABLE 6–2
Functional assessment strategies.

Functional Assessment Strategies: Information Gathering

A. Indirect strategies of information gathering (informant assessment)
   1. Behavioral interview
   2. Behavioral scales and questionnaires

B. Direct observation strategies of information gathering (descriptive assessment)
   1. Anecdotal reports
   2. Scatter plot analysis
   3. A-B-C descriptive analysis

Indirect Strategies: Informant Assessment

Indirect (or informant) assessment procedures involve questioning a person familiar with the student (teacher, parent, paraprofessional) or related service professional about the behavior and the circumstances surrounding its occurrence. Because this questioning necessarily takes place after the behavior has occurred, it is limited by the informant's memory, presence during the behavior, distraction by other events, potential bias, and ability to verbalize what was seen (Kazdin, 2001; Mace Lalli, & Lalli, 1991).

Behavioral Interview

The purpose of a behavioral or functional interview is to get as complete a picture as possible of the problem behavior and the environmental conditions and events surrounding it. A teacher may interview a parent about a behavior occurring at home; a special education teacher may interview a general education teacher about a behavior occurring in math class. A baffled teacher may ask a colleague or supervisor to interview him. The interview provides preliminary information to help form a hypothesis about what may be occasioning or maintaining the behavior and may be used to structure direct observation and data collection for further analysis. The interviewer wants to know, for example:

Things that can be learned by interviewing.

- the topography of the behavior
- at what times of day the behavior occurs
- during what activity the behavior often or always occurs
- in what setting the behavior often or always occurs
- with what materials the student is engaged
- what people are present
- what often or always happens right before the behavior occurs (antecedents)
- what the student does right after the behavior occurs
- what other people do right after the behavior occurs (consequences)
- what medication the student takes
- what effort have already been made to reduce the behavior

The Functional Assessment Interview (FAI) (O'Neill et al., 1997), with its accompanying forms, provides for more structured informant interviews. The FAI has 11 sections, which include:

- Describe the behavior, for example, topography, frequency, duration.
- Define potential ecological/setting events, for example, medications, staffing patterns and interactions, daily schedule.

- Define antecedents, for example, time of day, people, activity.
- Identify outcomes, for example, access to attention or tangible reinforcers, escape, or sensory consequences, how changes in routine affect behavior.
- Define efficiency of undesirable behavior, for example, slapping is very effective in getting attention.
- What functional alternative behaviors does the person already know?
- What are the primary ways the person communicates, for example, can the student say "No" meaningfully?
- What are things you should do and things you should avoid when working with this person, for example, provide positive vocal tone, avoid rapid pacing of activities?
- What are potential reinforcers?
- What previous attempts have been made at behavior reduction?

The Student Guided Functional Assessment Interview (O'Neill et al., 1997; Reed, Thomas, Sprague, & Horner, 1997) was developed with students in intermediate elementary and middle school grades. Students, as their own informants, were asked to provide the following information.

1. The behaviors that got them in trouble at school.
2. Their subjects and teachers for each class period.
3. The class periods or times of day the behaviors occur and how intensely they occur (intensity rated on a 1–6 scale).
4. What about each situation makes the behavior occur (for example, class demands that are too hard, boring, unclear, long; teacher reprimands; peer teasing or encouragement).
5. Important events, places, or activities associated with the behavior (for example, lack of sleep, illness, physical pain, hunger, trouble at home, conflict with peer, noise/distractions, activity/class).
6. What happens when they engage in the behavior? Are they removed from the situation (escape) or do they "get" something (attention, activity, or item)?

The researchers found that results of student interviews agreed closely with the results of teacher interviews. The last section of the student-guided functional assessment interview elicits student contributions regarding alternative behaviors to the behaviors that get them into trouble and strategies for a possible support plan. (Forms for recording interview data are provided in the references cited.) The Student-Assisted Functional Assessment Interview (Kern, Dunlap, Clarke, & Childs, 1994) was developed to use with elementary school students with emotional or behavioral disorders. This interview form has four sections:

- Section I has 12 questions that attempt to determine the function of a target behavior, e.g., "When you ask for help appropriately, do you get it?" (attention), "Do you think work periods for each subject are too long?" (escape).
- Section II asks about the target behavior, e.g., "When do you think you have the most problems with (target behavior) in school?"
- Section III has the student rate how much they like school subjects such as reading, math, science.
- Section IV further questions students about each subject, e.g., "What do you like about science?" "What don't you like about science?"

The authors found that information from students was useful for hypothesis development. Some responses, however, were inconsistent, vague, or "implicated variables that are not possible to modify."

In some instances an interview may be the only source of information available before forming a hypothesis and making suggestions. In the best case, however, the interview is just the first in a series of information-gathering steps.

Behavior Rating Scales

Behavior rating scales are instruments designed to obtain more quantitative information from informants. Informants are asked to respond to items describing behavior with a rating (for example, never, seldom, usually, always). The items are related to several possible functions that behavior might serve. Several individual items may elicit information about the same function. The function whose items receive the highest cumulative rating is hypothesized to be the variable maintaining the student's inappropriate behavior. Following are descriptions of four such scales.

The Problem Behavior Questionnaire (PBQ) (Lewis, Scott, & Sugai, 1994) is comprised of 15 items. These items are correlated to five potential maintaining functions (three questions per function). In responding to each of the 15 items, informants are asked to indicate the frequency with which an event is likely to be observed. The range of the item rating scale is: never, 10% of the time, 25%, 50%, 75%, 90% of the time, and always. Examples of functions and correlated items are:

1. *Access to peer attention.* "When the problem behavior occurs, do peers verbally respond to or laugh at the student?"
2. *Access to teacher attention.* "Does the problem behavior occur to get your attention when you are working with other students?"
3. *Escape/avoid peer attention.* "If the student engages in the problem behavior, do peers stop interacting with the student?"
4. *Escape/avoid teacher attention.* "Will the student stop doing the problem behavior if you stop making requests or end an academic activity?"
5. *Setting events.* "Is the problem behavior more likely to occur following unscheduled events or disruptions in classroom routines?"

The Motivation Assessment Scale (MAS) (Durand & Crimmins, 1988; 1992) is comprised of 16 items. These questions are correlated to four potential maintaining functions (four questions per function). In responding to each of the 16 items, informants are asked to indicate the frequency with which an individual is likely to exhibit an operationalized target behavior. The range of the item rating scale is: never, almost never, seldom, half the time, usually, almost always, and always. Examples of functions and correlated items are:

1. *Sensory reinforcement.* "Would the behavior occur continuously, over and over, if this person was left alone for long periods of time?"
2. *Escape.* "Does the behavior stop occurring shortly after (1 to 5 minutes) you stop working or making demands on this person?"
3. *Attention.* "Does the behavior seem to occur in response to your talking to other persons in the room?"
4. *Tangible.* "Does the behavior stop occurring shortly after you give this person the toy, food, or activity he or she has requested?"

The Functional Analysis Screening Tool (FAST) (Iwata & DeLeon, 1996) is comprised of 18 items. These items are correlated to four likely maintaining functions (five items per function, two items overlap). It is recommended that the FAST be administered to several individuals who interact frequently with the target individual. The informant is asked to indicate "yes" or "no" as to whether an item statement accurately describes the person's target behavior problem. Examples of the maintaining functions and correlated items are:

1. *Social reinforcement (attention/preferred items).* "When the behavior occurs, do you usually try to calm the person down or distract the person with preferred activities (leisure items, snacks, etc)?"
2. *Social reinforcement (escape).* "When the behavior occurs, do you usually give the person a "break" from ongoing tasks?"
3. *Automatic reinforcement (sensory stimulation).* "Does the behavior occur at high rates regardless of what is going on around the person?"
4. *Automatic reinforcement (pain attenuation).* "Does the behavior occur more often when the person is sick?"

The Questions About Behavioral Function (QABF) (Matson & Vollmer, 1995; Paclawskyj, Matson, Rush, Smalls, & Vollmer, 2000) is comprised of 25 items. These items are correlated to five potential maintaining functions (five items per function). The informant is asked to rate how often each specifically targeted behavior occurs: never, rarely, some, or often. Examples of functions and correlated items are:

1. *Attention.* "Engages in the behavior to try to get a reaction from you"
2. *Escape.* "Engages in the behavior when asked to do something" (get dressed, brush teeth, work, etc.).
3. *Nonsocial.* "Engages in the behavior even if he/she thinks no one is in the room"
4. *Physical.* "Engages in the behavior more frequently when he/she is ill"
5. *Tangible.* "Engages in the behavior when you have something he/she wants"

Special education and general education students can contribute valuable information to the development of hypotheses of behavior function. This includes information about preferences, academic difficulties, setting distractions, and conflicts with peers. There are, however, data that suggest that information gathered through interviews should be used with caution. Some responses can be inconsistent, vague, or impracticable. Type and severity of disability, as well as age, may affect the quality and reliability of a student's contribution. For both student and adult informants, there appears to be greater accuracy and consistency when the information concerns situations and classrooms that are highly likely to evoke problem behavior (Kern, et al., 1994; Kinch, Lewis-Palmer, Hagan-Burke, & Sugai, 2001; Sturmey, 1994; Yarbrough & Carr, 2000). Similar cautions are expressed about using behavior rating scales. Item ratings by teachers and parents have resulted in low percentages of reliability across items, across administrations of a scale, across rating scales, and across raters (Barton-Atwood, Wehby, Gunter, & Lane, 2003; Conroy, Fox, Bucklin, & Good, 1996; Sturmey, 1994; Zarcone, Rodgers, Iwata, Rourke, & Dorsey, 1991). These cautions suggest that, while informant information can make valuable contributions to discussions of student behavior, it should not be the sole basis for developing hypotheses. Indirectly gathered information should be supplemented with information gathered by a means of direct observation.

Direct Observation Strategies: Descriptive Assessment

Direct observation strategies are ways of describing behavior that is directly observed. They are more reliable than informant assessment. Someone who takes notes as he observes the problem behavior directly will provide a more accurate description of the context, antecedents, and consequences than someone who is working from memory. Three methods of direct observation include the use of anecdotal reports, scatter plot analysis, and A-B-C descriptive analysis (see Table 6–2). (A-B-C is an alternative way of expressing S-R-S: Antecedent stimulus—Behavior/response—Consequence stimulus.)

Anecdotal Reports

Anecdotal reports are written to provide as complete a description as possible of a student's behavior and the events surrounding it. An observer preparing an anecdotal report attempts to record in regular prose each occurrence of a target behavior and the context, activities, and interactions within which it occurs. This is done within defined observation periods, preferably over several days. (Preparation of anecdotal reports is described in detail in Chapter 3.) What makes these reports a tool of analysis is transferring the prose into a structured format that clearly identifies and labels instances of the target behavior, the immediate antecedent, and the consequence. The A-B-C formatting of this information is illustrated in Figure 3–2. This formatting facilitates identifying temporal relationship patterns among the three elements. It is the identification of patterns of particular antecedents and consequences associated with a target behavior that yields a hypothesis of function.

Scatter Plot Analysis

A scatter plot may reveal temporal patterns.

The scatter plot procedure is an assessment tool found to be easy and useful by classroom teachers (Desrochers, Hile, & Williams-Mosely, 1997; Symons, McDonald, & Wehby, 1998). The procedure can be helpful in identifying a relationship between an environmental condition and behavior that is frequent, seemingly random, but steady over long periods of time. For such behaviors, informal observations often do not suggest correspondence with particular stimuli. It is easier to isolate a particular antecedent for behavior that occurs in bursts or isolated incidents (Touchette, MacDonald, & Langer, 1985).

For scatter plot assessment, the teacher prepares a grid. Figure 6–3 shows four sample grids (A, B, C, D). On grid A, successive days or observation periods are plotted along the horizontal. Time is plotted along the vertical. Time may be divided into hours, half hours, quarter hours, and so forth, depending on the time available for observation and observation frequency. As an alternative, shown on grids C and D, time may be denoted as class periods or instructional formats.

As the scatter grid is filled in, each cell contains a designation indicating whether the behavior occurred at a high, low, or zero rate (see grid B). A cell is left blank if the behavior did not occur during the interval; a cell has a slash through it to indicate a low rate of occurrence during the interval (for example, < 4); or a cell is filled in completely to indicate a high rate of occurrence (for example, = or > 4). Inserting numbers to represent the exact number of occurrences in the cell will provide a more precise representation (Axelrod, 1987). Once the grids are completed, they can be analyzed for the presence of correlational patterns. "A pattern, should one exist, can emerge as soon as several days are plotted" (Touchette et al., 1985, p. 345). Kahng et al. (1998) cautioned that patterns may not be evident without statistical analysis, even with as much as a month's data. Touchette et al. (1985) suggested that problem behavior may be found to correlate to a time of day, the presence or absence of certain people, a social setting, certain types of activities, a reinforcement contingency, a physical environment,

SCATTER PLOT

Student: ______________ Behavior: ______________

SCORING: Blank = 0 occurrences Slash = < 4 Solid = 4/ > 4

Day/Date

Time						Activity/ Location	Comments
8:00–8:20							
8:20–8:40							
8:40–9:00							
9:00–9:20							
9:20–9:40							
9:40–10:00							
10:00–10:20							
10:20–10:40							
10:40–11:00							
11:00–11:20							
11:20–11:40							
11:40–12:00							

SCATTER PLOT

Student: Nancy Behavior: Loud vocalizations

SCORING: Blank = 0 occurrences Slash = < 4 Solid = 4/ > 4

Day/Date

Time	Mon 3–16	Tue 3–17	Wed 3–18	Thur 3–19	Fri 3–20	Activity/ Location	Comments
8:00–8:20	■	■	■	/	■	Hygiene	Hand over hand
8:20–8:40							
8:40–9:00	■	■	/	/		Snack	Hand over hand, throws food
9:00–9:20							
9:20–9:40							
9:40–10:00	/	■		■	■	Toy skills	
10:00–10:20				/			
10:20–10:40		/		■			
10:40–11:00							
11:00–11:20							
11:20–11:40	/	■	■	/	■	Hygiene	Physical resistance
11:40–12:00	■	■		■	■	Lunch	Hand over hand

SCATTER PLOT

Student: ______________ Behavior: ______________

SCORING: Blank = 0 occurrences Slash = < 3 Solid = 3/ > 3

Day/Date

Time						Activity/ Location	Comments
1-Reading: special instruction							
2-Computer							
3-Earth science							
4-Lunch							
5-Language arts: special instruction							
6-Consumer math							

SCATTER PLOT

Student: ______________ Behavior: ______________

SCORING: Blank = 0 occurrences Slash = < 3 Solid = 3/ > 3

Format/Content Area						Activity/ Location	Comments
Large group instruction							
Small group instruction							
One:one instruction							
Independent activity							
Activity transition							
Setting transition							
Hygiene							
Toileting							
Eating: lunch/snack							

FIGURE 6–3 ***Sample scatter plot grids.***

or combinations of variables. They suggested a scatter plot offers "insights into patterns of responding not readily available from graphs of daily or weekly frequency" (p. 351). Patterns may be considered to occur when three or more adjacent intervals across days contained either a low- or high-frequency occurrence of the behavior (Symons et al., 1998). Such patterns can be seen in grid B during the 8:00–8:20 interval across 5 days, the 8:40–9:00 interval across 4 days, and the 11:20–11:40 and 11:40–12:00 interval all week. Assistance in interpreting these patterns can be derived from notations of activity and location and the accompanying comments. In the example in grid B, one can begin to see correlations between the targeted behavior and, in this case, hand-over-hand techniques during hygiene and eating instruction.

There are currently no empirical data that suggest how to set a value for low or high rates of occurrence, especially across different populations of students. The value chosen will affect the cells identified as part of a pattern, and therefore any resulting hypothesis. A different picture will emerge depending on the value chosen. One suggestion is that values may be chosen by identifying rates of behavior considered disruptive by the teacher in particular settings (Symons et al., 1998). The teacher would decide how much behavior could be tolerated for a student included in a general education class, which may be less than the amount of disruption tolerated in a special education class or more than that which would be acceptable in a community setting.

Axelrod (1987) noted that a scatter plot will detect only environmental conditions that are related to behavior on a time-cyclical basis. Some events affect behavior in a noncyclical manner. For example, a student may become disruptive whenever a classmate is given a special privilege or she feels she was treated unfairly or "cheated." He suggests that it might be helpful to write comments on the data sheet to document such events.

Forms for completing functional analysis may be found on the "Web Links" module for Chapter 6 of the Companion Website.

Although a scatter plot may not be as precise or efficient as other descriptive analyses for revealing cause-effect or correlational relationships between behavior and specific environmental events (Kahng et al., 1998), it can narrow the field of analysis so closer assessment can be conducted more efficiently (Lennox & Mittenberger, 1989). It is a procedure a classroom teacher can carry out with little or no help to gather initial descriptive data of the behavior. These data can then be augmented with more precise data collection as the team decides how to proceed.

A-B-C Descriptive Analysis

A-B-C descriptive analysis provides a structure for noting behavior and the environmental events that surround it, as it is being observed, or later while viewing a videotape. Instead of the two-step anecdotal report process of writing in prose what is observed and then restructuring the notes, this procedure uses coded notations made on a prepared data sheet. The format of the data sheet imposes the A-B-C (S-R-S) structure on observations as the data are collected. Various procedures for data collection and accompanying data sheets are available. Figure 6–4 presents an adaptation of the data collection sheet by Smith and Heflin, 2001. (Alternative formats are available from Fad, Patton, & Polloway, 2000; and O'Neill et al., 1997).

The A-B-C descriptive data sheet and procedure. As seen in Figure 6–4, the form has four sections. From top to bottom, they are: (1) identification information, (2) columns and rows for data collection, (3) lists of recording codes, and (4) operational definitions of target behaviors.

Identification information. The top of the sheet provides basic identification information. This includes: (a) The name of the student for whom the observations are being made. (b) The day of the observation. At least one week of observations

STUDENT: Mona DAY/DATE: Mon 9/16 LOCATION: Classroom OBSERVATION PERIOD: 8 am – 10 am OBSERVER: MC PAGE: 1

Time/Duration	Context/Activity	Antecedent	Target Behavior	Consequence	Student Reaction	Perceived Function	Comments
8:20	1, 5	B, D	1, 4	E, A	2, 3		Hand and face washing
↓	1, 5	A, D	1, 2, 4	E, A, B	2, 1, 3		
	1, 5	A, D	1, 2, 3	E, C	2		Face slapping
8:26	1, 5	A, D	1, 3	B, C, F	1		
Recording Codes	1. Sink hygiene	A. Hand/hand	1. Scream	A. Redirect/guide	1. Stop	A. ATT	
	2. Toilet	B. Hand/arm	2. Stomp	B. "No"	2. Continue	B. ESC	
	3. Group table	C. Material	3. Slap	C. Restrain	3. Escalate	C. Stim	
	4. Snack table	D. Verbal cue	4. Resist	D. Ignore	4. New behav.	D. Tang	
	5. Teacher	E. "No"	5.	E. Calm talk	5. Move–run	E. UNK	
	6. Parapro	F.	6.	F. End activity	6.	F.	
	7.	G.	7.	G.	7.	G.	
	8.	H.	8.	H.	8.	H.	
	9.	I.	9.	I.	9.	I.	
	10.	J.	10.	J.	10.	J.	

Operational Definitions

Behavior 1: scream—high pitch vocalization above conversation level

Behavior 2: stomp—feet strike floor with force beyond used for walking

Behavior 3: slap—hand or fist strikes face or head

Behavior 4: resist—body pulling in opposition to physical prompt

(Adaptation of Smith & Heflin, 2001)

FIGURE 6–4 ***Data sheet for collection of A-B-C descriptive data.***

From: "Supporting positive behavior in public schools: An intervention program in Georgia," by M. Smith and L. J. Heflin, 2001, *Journal of Positive Behavior Interventions, 3,* pp. 39–47.

is needed in order to lead to a hypothesis of function. (c) The general location of the observation: special education classroom, general education science lab, cafeteria, Wal-Mart. (d) The beginning and ending time of the observation period. This may be an entire day, or previous data may have identified specific time periods or particular setting events. (e) The name of the person making the observations. The name of the individual doing interobserver reliability checks may also be noted when appropriate. (f) The page number. Observations of behaviors occurring at moderate to high rates across significant periods of time will require several pages.

In Figure 6–4, the data sheet is prepared for observations of Mona's behavior on Monday, September 16, from 8:00 a.m. to 10:00 a.m., in her classroom. This is page 1 of data collected by MC.

Columns and rows for data collection. Columns are provided for the following information about each instance of behavior as it occurs:

1. **Time/duration.** the beginning and ending time, and the duration of each occurrence of behavior.
2. **Context/activity.** the setting events—activity, persons, materials.
3. **Antecedent.** the stimulus event immediately preceding the occurrence of the target behavior.
4. **Target behavior.** the behavior for which the observation is designed to describe. Working operational definitions appear at the bottom of the page.
5. **Consequences.** the occurrences that immediately follow the student's engagement in the target behavior. These may include environmental events or reactions by the teacher, peers, or others in the setting.
6. **Student reaction.** What does the student do immediately following the target behavior and its consequences?
7. **Perceived function.** At the time of data collection, the observer may make note of an initial judgment of the function served by the behavior.
8. **Comments.** Notes of novel or unexpected aspect of the interaction, details for which codes are not provided, a specific material used, or some unexpected occurrence (for example, the student has a seizure, an unexpected person enters the setting).

Lists of recording codes. To assist the observer's fluency in data collection, this space allows for listing various "common" codes needed for this particular student. The lists of codes are derived from information gathered earlier and from at least one opportunity for informal observation during which the observer practices with the data sheet.

In Figure 6–4, the codes for context/activity are those that are scheduled during the observation time period; morning hygiene and toileting, group instruction of various content, and snack. Codes are also included for members of the staff who usually interact with the student. Noted under antecedents are codes for physical assistance, materials, and verbal cues. The column for target behaviors lists those previously agreed upon. This list may be expanded if additional behaviors are repeatedly observed. In this case, screaming, stomping, slapping, and resisting are Mona's target behaviors. Consequences listed are those noted during observation that the teacher uses regularly with this student. Mona's teacher regularly uses: redirection, verbal "No," restraint, ignoring, and calm talk. There is also a code to note when the teacher ends a task or activity. The next column lists codes for student reactions to the interactions occurring and the consequences. A basic list like the one on this form will be common across observations: the behavior stops, continues, escalates, a new behavior occurs, or the student moves or runs from the interaction. The next column lists four possible functions of behavior: attention, escape, stimulation, and tangible; and a code for unknown at this time. As data collection continues, the observer may add subcategories of functions such as attention from adult or peer, or escape from social interaction or academic task.

Operational definitions. For easy and repeated access for the data collector, the operational definition of each target behavior is provided at the bottom of the data sheet. In the example in Figure 6–4, "scream" is defined as occasions of high pitched vocalization above conversation level; "stomp" is defined as feet striking the floor with force beyond that used for walking; "slap" is defined as hand or fist striking face or head; and "resist" is defined as pulling any part of her body away in opposition to a physical prompt.

Data Collecting

With the prepared data collection sheet in hand, the data collector makes note of each occurrence of the behavior in the column labeled "Target Behavior." An occurrence of the behavior may be a lone occurrence or an occurrence in a cluster of behavior. A cluster is defined as individual behaviors occurring in rapid succession or simultaneously so that listing them together in a single cell provides an accurate depiction of their occurrence. (This point is also true for notations of contexts, antecedents, consequences, and reactions.) Having noted the behavior, the observer then moves his pen horizontally across the page noting the consequence provided and the student's reaction. He then moves the pen to the other side of the data sheet and notes the antecedent, the time of occurrence, and the context. If the function of the behavior for that occurrence is immediately evident the perceived, function is filled in. If not, "unknown" is written in the cell. This is one possible sequence for data collection with this data sheet. A data collector will try various sequences until he finds one with which he is comfortable and fluent, and that allows him to produce reliable data.

Data Analysis

Data analysis occurs daily and weekly. At the end of each day or observation period, the data collector (and others if possible) reviews that day's data for: (a) confirmation of the occurrence of the target behavior, (b) validity of the operational definitions, (c) occurrences of new inappropriate behaviors, antecedents, or consequences, (d) consistent relationships emerging between particular behaviors and consequences or between particular behaviors and antecedents, (e) when the student terminates the behavior, and (f) emerging functions. In addition, ongoing tallies are kept of the percent of various antecedents and consequences.

In-depth analysis of the data occurs following at least 5 days of data collection. The same questions asked of informants during interviews are now asked of these data. The purpose is to illuminate any patterns among antecedents, behavior, and consequences. These patterns are identified in part by looking horizontally across rows for consistent A-B-C relationships. It is then noted if these relationships and elements are repeated over occurrences of behavior: for example, are the same antecedents occasioning the same behaviors, resulting in the same consequences, resulting in the same student reactions. Analysis questions may include:

- Is the behavior occurring within the context of the same activity, materials, instructor, or group of peers? Does this behavior occur with both Ms. Brown and Mr. Green?
- Does the behavior consistently occur following particular antecedents? What percent of each antecedent appears in the data?

- Following instances of the behavior, is there a consistent consequence used by the teacher, peers, or other adults? What percent of each consequence appears in the data?
- Does the student terminate the behavior following a particular consequence? In what percent of occurrence does the consequence result in the student's terminating the behavior?
- When a consequence is repeatedly followed by the termination of the behavior, is there an implied function (for example, if a consistent consequence is removal of the task, and the behavior stops, does that imply an escape function, and therefore negative reinforcement as the maintaining consequence)?
- Does the same S-R-S occur repeatedly, leading to a consistent hypothesis of function across all, or almost all, occurrences of the behavior (what can you say about the occurrences that do not fit the pattern?)? What percent of this pattern appears within the data?

Figure 6–4 presents an example of data taken on Mona's behavior. It reflects a cluster of behaviors that occurred from 8:20–8:26 a.m. The notations were taken during morning hygiene when Mona was being instructed on hand and face washing. The following statements can be made based on these data:

- There is confirmation of occurrence of the target behaviors during morning instruction of hygiene skills and tasks.
- This interaction occurs entirely at the sink during instruction of hand and face washing.
- For each occurrence of the behavior, the antecedent is delivery of a verbal cue and the use of hand-over-hand prompting (with one occasion of hand-at-arm).
- The consequences used by the teacher were talking calmly to the student and redirecting to the task. As the behavior escalated, the teacher used a verbal reprimand and then restraint. There is an A-B-C pattern of hand-over-hand—target behavior—calm talk and redirection. Each occurrence of a target behavior occurs at the sink, is immediately preceded by a verbal cue and physical prompt (hand-over-hand), and is followed by calm talk and redirection. At the third occurrence of the behavior, restraint was added.
- Despite these consequences, the behavior continues and eventually escalates.
- The student reaction is continuation and escalation by adding face slapping.
- The behavior is not ended until after the fourth occurrence of the behavior, at which point the teacher stops the activity.
- This implies an escape function. The behavior is terminated once it serves its purpose. If this is escape-motivated behavior, does Mona use it with other activities she does not like in order to terminate them?

Repp et al. (1988) demonstrated that interventions based on hypotheses derived from an A-B-C descriptive analysis were more effective than those that were not. It is important to remember, however, that a relationship established as a result of A-B-C descriptive analysis is correlational, not causal, because this is a descriptive process that does not manipulate any of the variables (Lennox & Miltenberger, 1989). Once the relationship leads to a hypothesis concerning what is occasioning or maintaining the behavior, structured data collection and manipulation of the variables are possible.

Step 4: Conduct Functional Analysis

a. Systematically manipulate antecedents and consequences to determine their effect on occasioning and maintaining the target behavior—Manipulate in analog setting or natural setting.
b. Formulate hypothesis of function.

Functional analysis is a set of procedures for determining the function of a behavior by systematic manipulation of environmental variables, antecedents, and consequences and documentation of their effect on the occurrence of the target behavior. The goal is to examine the effect of each variable's presence, absence, heightening, or lessening. A functional analysis is conducted for one of the following reasons:

1. to verify a hypothesis resulting from a functional assessment. If, for example, functional assessment results in a hypothesis that the inappropriate behavior is maintained by positive reinforcement from teacher attention, the student is placed in a condition where teacher attention is provided when the behavior occurs and in a condition where teacher attention is withheld.
2. to refine the hypothesis resulting from a functional assessment. If, for example, the hypothesis is that the behavior is maintained by positive reinforcement resulting from attention, additional analysis seeks to identify the source of the attention.
3. to clarify uncertain results of a functional assessment. The data resulting from indirect and direct strategies are unclear; they do not suggest a particular function.
4. to serve as the initial step in development of a hypothesis of function.

The basic model for arranging the manipulation of environmental variables is to place the student in two or more conditions in which the settings and interactions are purposefully structured. Two conditions may be used if one variable is being assessed, or two are being compared (Karsh, Repp, Dahlquist, & Munk, 1995; O'Neill et al., 1997). If, for example, the purpose of the functional analysis is to refine an understanding of the source of attention, the student is placed in a condition in which attention is provided by an adult and one in which a peer provides attention. Two conditions may also be used if the purpose is to clarify whether the correct hypothesis of function is attention or self-stimulation. The student may be placed in a situation where attention is provided when he performs the target behavior and one where no attention is available. Four conditions are used when the function of a behavior is initially to be identified through functional analysis or when verifying the hypothesis resulting from a functional assessment. The conditions arranged represent the basic functions of behavior (or some variation) as initially discussed by Iwata et al. (1982). These conditions and functions are:

1. *Attention condition.* The function of inappropriate behavior represented in this condition is to gain positive reinforcement. This may be reinforcement in the form of social attention from another person or tangible reinforcement in the form of a preferred item or event. Often these two consequences are represented in two different conditions: one for positive reinforcement by social attention and one for positive reinforcement by a tangible reinforcer. During this condition the student has access to various activities, and the evaluator is engaged in reading or some other activity unrelated to the student. The student is not attended to (reinforced) unless the target behavior is emitted. If the function of the behavior is to gain access to positive reinforcement, the frequency of the inappropriate behavior should increase.
2. *Demand condition.* The function of inappropriate behavior represented in this condition is to escape from some demand. This represents negative reinforcement. The aversive demand being placed on the student will be removed when the inappropriate behavior occurs. The demand may take the form of an undesirable task, a difficult task, a task the student cannot do, or a social interaction. During this con-

dition the evaluator prompts the student through the task. Each time the student engages in the inappropriate behavior, the demand is briefly removed and the student is given a break from the task and allowed briefly to engage in a preferred activity. If the function of the inappropriate behavior is to escape a demand and it is thus being maintained by negative reinforcement, the frequency of the inappropriate behavior should increase.

3. *Alone condition.* The function of inappropriate behavior represented in this condition is to provide self-stimulation or automatic reinforcement. The setting contains no activities, materials, reinforcers, or other sources of stimulation. There are no externally supplied consequences for the behavior. If the function of the behavior is to provide self-stimulation and it is thus being maintained by automatic reinforcement, the occurrence of the inappropriate behavior should increase.
4. *Play condition.* This condition represents a control condition. The student is placed in an environment rich with materials and social attention from the evaluator. Under this condition the instances of inappropriate behavior should be minimal or nonexistent. If the behavior does occur, there should be no explicit consequences.

Manipulation of variables. The framework for the manipulation of variables during functional analysis is the single-subject design. Two designs are used: the multi-element design (a variation of the alternating treatments design) and the reversal design. The multi-element design allows comparison of conditions in which variables thought to occasion or maintain the behavior are presented. The reversal design is frequently used in conjunction with a multi-element design to confirm a functional relationship between the target behavior and a controlling variable.

Multi-element design. Van Camp, Lerman, Kelley, Contrucci, & Vorndran (2000) conducted a functional analysis with Rachel, a 21-year-old public school student with moderate to severe mental retardation. She was referred for aggression, defined as hitting, pinching, kicking, or pushing; and for self-injury, defined as forceful contact between one or both hands and any part of her head. The functional analysis was conducted in an unused room at the school. Rachel was exposed to a series of separate experimental conditions within a multi-element design. Three to five 10-minute sessions were conducted 2 to 5 days per week. Data were collected using frequency recording, and the data are reported as number of responses per minute. Five conditions were designed (p. 549):

1. *Alone.* No attention, leisure materials, or demands were provided; and self-injury was ignored. The purpose of this condition was to evaluate whether self-injury would persist in the absence of social consequences.
2. *Attention.* Twenty seconds of attention was delivered contingent on each occurrence of aggression or self-injury, and Rachel had noncontingent and continuous access to leisure materials. This condition was designed to identify behavior maintained by positive reinforcement in the form of attention.
3. *Tangible.* Twenty seconds of access to leisure materials was delivered contingent upon each occurrence of aggression or self-injury, and Rachel had noncontingent continuous access to attention. This condition was designed to identify behavior maintained by positive reinforcement in the form of access to tangible leisure materials.

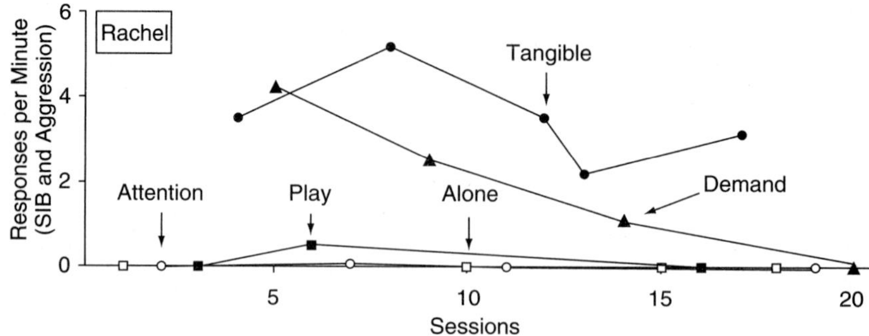

***FIGURE 6–5* Use of a multi-element design for functional analysis.**
From: "Variable-time reinforcement schedules in the treatment of socially maintained problem behavior," by C. Van Camp, D. Lerman, M. Kelley, S. Contrucci, & C. Vorndran, *Journal of Applied Behavior Analysis,* 2000. Copyright 2000 by The Society for the Experimental Analysis of Behavior. Reprinted by permission.

4. *Demand.* Twenty seconds of escape from continuous tasks was delivered contingent upon each occurrence of aggression or self-injury. No leisure materials were available. This condition was designed to identify behavior maintained by negative reinforcement in the form of escape from tasks.
5. *Play.* Rachel had continuous access to attention and preferred items, no demands were delivered, and all problem behavior was ignored. This condition served as the control for comparison with the other conditions.

In Figure 6–5, the functional analysis of Rachel's behavior suggested that the problem behavior was maintained by access to tangible reinforcement in the form of leisure materials. The effectiveness of noncontingent access to leisure materials on a continuous and noncontinuous basis during instructional sessions was evaluated. The intervention data suggested that both forms of noncontingent reinforcement (see Chapter 8) reduced Rachel's aggressive and self-injurious behaviors.

ABAB design. The ABAB design has been used alone for conducting a functional analysis (Durand & Carr, 1991; O'Neill, et al., 1997; Wacker et al., 1990). More frequently, however, it is used in conjunction with a multi-element design. When the results of the multi-element design clearly indicate a function, an ABAB design (in the form of a reversal design) can be used to demonstrate a functional relationship between the identified controlling variable and the target behavior. When the results of the multi-element design do not clearly indicate one function, an ABAB design (in the form of a withdrawal design) can be used to clarify with which variable the target behavior has a functional relationship. In the first graph in Figure 6–6 (Moore, Mueller, Dubard, Roberts, & Sterling-Turner, 2002) it was unclear following the multi-element procedure whether this young woman's self-injurious behavior was a function of positive reinforcement resulting from attention or from a tangible item (juice). The lack of clarity may be because when she engaged in the behavior and got juice, she also was spoken to—"You must want your juice." In the ABAB that followed, the tangible item was delivered with and without verbal attention. The data demonstrated that the behavior occurred at a higher level in the attention condition. As this is replicated within the design, there is evidence of a functional relationship between the self-injurious behavior and attention.

Settings for Conducting Functional Analysis

Functional analysis can be done directly in the school (Broussard & Northrup, 1995, 1997: Jones, Drew, & Weber, 2000; Karsh et al., 1995; Meyer, 1999; Mueller, Edwards, & Trahant, 2003), in community settings (O'Neill, Horner, Albin, Storey, & Sprague, 1990;

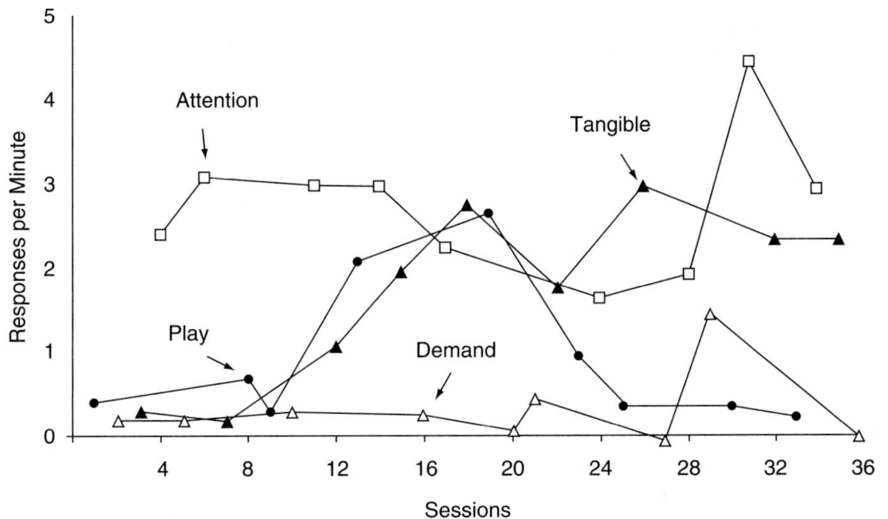

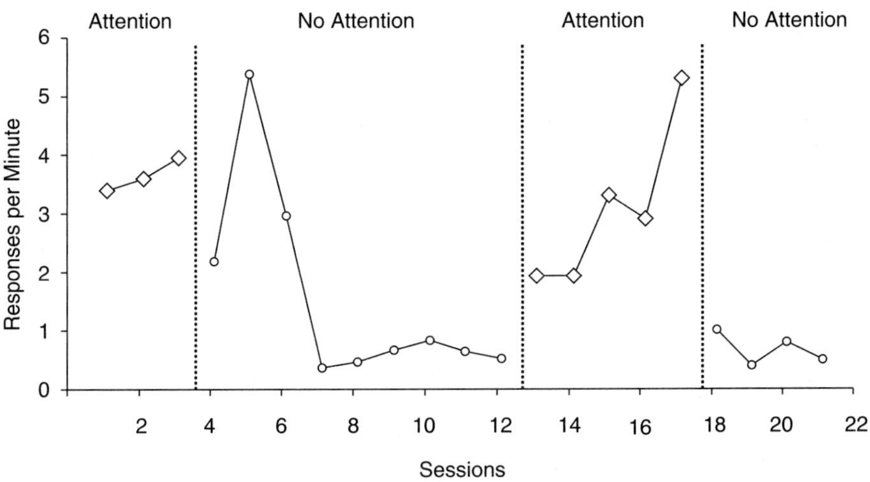

FIGURE 6–6 ***Use of a multi-element design followed by an ABAB design for functional analysis.***
From: "The influence of therapist attention on self-injury during a tangible condition," by M. Moore, M. Mueller, M. Dubard, D. Roberts, & H. Sterling-Turner. *Journal of Applied Behavior Analysis,* 2002. Copyright 2002 by The Society for the Experimental Analysis of Behavior. Reprinted by permission.

Wallace & Knight, 2003), or in the home (Arndorfer, Miltenberger, Woster, Rortvedt, & Gaffaney, 1994). In these natural settings the behavior and the usual surrounding events, people, and contingencies are in effect. A number of studies, however, have been conducted in an **analog** setting. An analog setting is an environment outside the classroom where very controlled presentation of the conditions can be managed. Analog sessions are often conducted before attempting to analyze the behavior in the natural environment. It is possible that in the controlled analog setting, the behavior may not be exposed to the same variables responsible for the behavior in the natural environment; thus in the analog one variable may be identified and in the natural setting another (Conroy, Fox, Crain, Jenkins, & Belcher, 1996; Evans & Meyer, 1985; Sturmey, 1995). The accuracy that may result from precise manipulation in a controlled environment and the rapidity of identification of controlling variables, however, may make using an analog setting more efficient in the long run (Repp & Karsh, 1994). In schools an unused classroom is often used as an analog setting. A teacher or behavior specialist conducts the functional analysis. Using the results of the functional analysis, the teacher and behavior specialist develop a treatment plan. The student is returned to the classroom where the treatment plan is implemented and carefully monitored, with adjustments if additional variables are noted. Using an analog setting requires additional personnel, either to conduct the analysis or to free the teacher to do so, and may be impractical or too expensive in some settings (Sturmey, 1995).

Sasso et al. (1992) compared the results of an investigator-conducted analysis in an analog setting and a teacher-conducted analysis in a classroom setting with two students with autism. For the analog, the teacher identified tasks and activities that were difficult for the student, a list of preferred activities, and possible social reinforcers. One student, Molly, was a 7-year-old with autism whose target behavior was aggression toward adults. She was exposed daily to four conditions, each lasting 10 minutes for 4 days. During an "ignore" condition, the investigator sat in the room with Molly and ignored all appropriate and inappropriate behavior. During a "social attention" condition, Molly sat at a table with a task. The investigator sat across the table and read a book. When aggression occurred, the investigator immediately provided attention (by saying, for example, "Please don't do that," or "Stop, you're hurting me"). All other behavior was ignored. During an "escape" condition, Molly sat at a worktable while the investigator prompted her through a demanding task. If Molly engaged in aggression, the task was immediately discontinued and removed for 15 seconds.

Appropriate behavior received no consequences. A "tangible attention" condition was similar to the "social attention" condition, except that a favorite toy, activity, or edible was provided contingent upon each occurrence of the target behavior. Finally, a "toy" condition provided an enriched environment and served as a control condition. The investigator praised appropriate behavior and ignored inappropriate behavior. The investigator provided praise and encouragement approximately every 30 seconds.

In the classroom setting, the teacher conducted an A-B-C functional assessment and a functional analysis for 15 minutes during conditions of solitary free play; low-demand, high-teacher-attention morning play; high-teacher-demand vocational tasks; and low demand and low teacher attention. The teacher recorded occurrence of the target behavior, its antecedents, and subsequent events.

The teacher also conducted a functional analysis in the classroom. Four routine tasks and activities were identified that approximated antecedent conditions described by Iwata et al. (1982). These were: "alone" (during free play), "demand" (during vocational task), "attention" (during self-help tasks), "tangible" (during individual work), and "toy" (during game activity). The teacher provided four 10-minute sessions for each condition. These sessions were identical to the investigator-conducted functional analysis except that they were conducted (a) by the teacher, (b) in the classroom, and (c) using tasks and activities that were part of the student's daily routine.

Figure 6–7 shows the results of the investigator-conducted functional analysis, the teacher-conducted A-B-C analysis, and the teacher-conducted functional analysis. Escape and tangible reinforcers apparently maintained Molly's inappropriate behavior. Intervention was designed to remove attention from inappropriate behavior and to provide a means of communication—other than hitting—to enable Molly to escape briefly from a task in order to engage in a preferred activity.

The sequence was repeated with a second teacher and second student (Tim) in a junior high school. All procedures were identical to those used with the first student. The teacher who worked with that student trained the second teacher to conduct both the A-B-C assessment and the classroom analysis. As shown in Figure 6–7, again the three methods yielded comparable findings. These comparisons suggest that functional

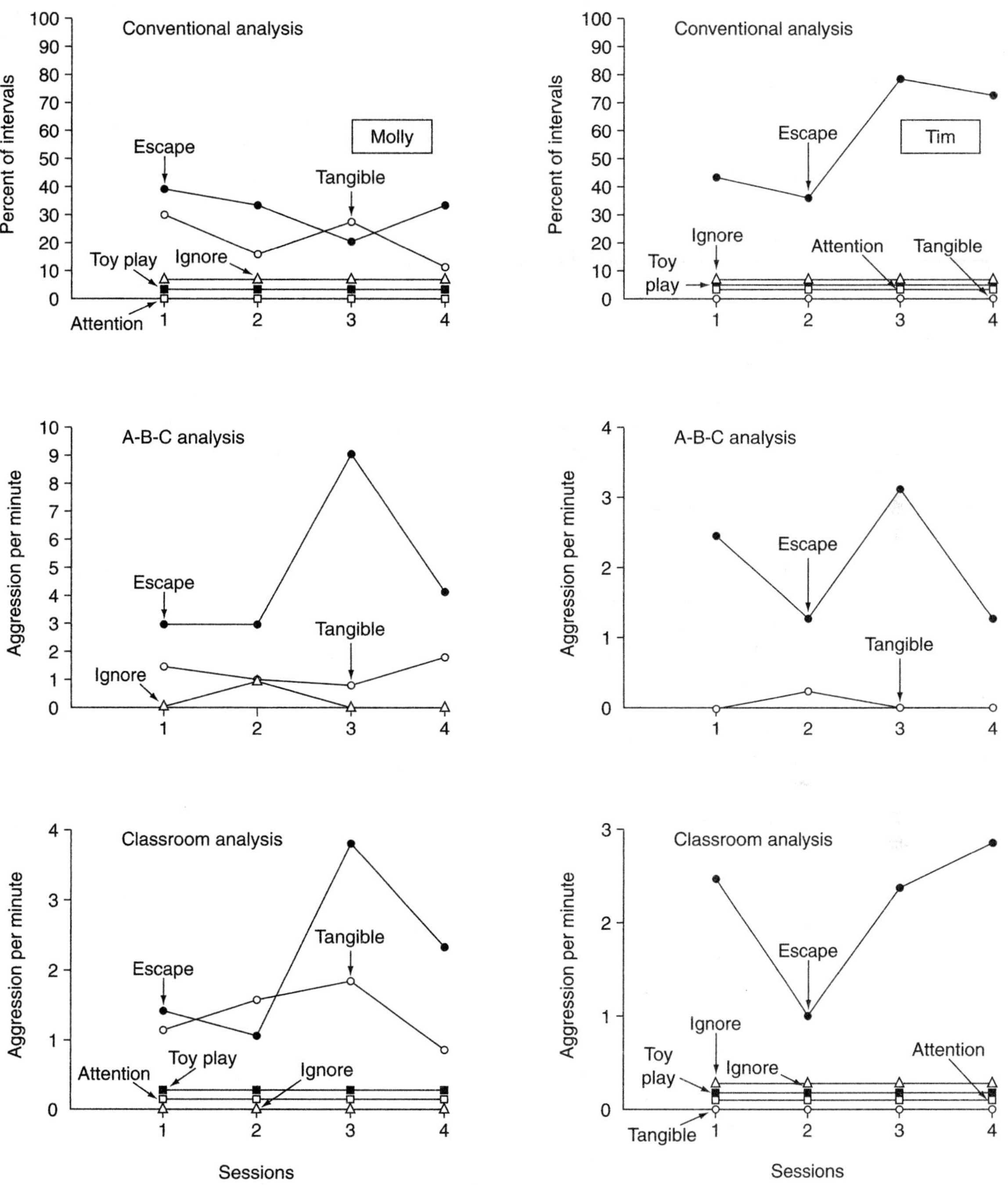

FIGURE 6–7 ***Graph of data comparing results of investigator-conducted analog functional analysis, teacher-conducted A-B-C analysis, and teacher-conducted functional analysis in classroom setting.***

Note: From "Use of descriptive and experimental analyses to identify the functional properties of aberrant behavior in school settings," by G. Sasso, T. Reimers, L. Cooper, D. Wacker, W. Berg, M. Steege, L. Kelly, & A. Allaire, *Journal of Applied Behavior Analysis, 25,* p. 816 and 817, 1992. Copyright 1992 by The Society for the Experimental Analysis of Behavior, Inc. Reprinted by permission.

analysis does not have to be conducted in analog settings by behavior specialists. Teachers can be trained to conduct valid analyses in their classrooms (Sasso et al., 1992).

Brief Functional Analysis

Adaptations to the functional analysis process have been investigated to make it more practical and efficient for use in schools with students with special needs, students at-risk, and general education students (Ellis & Magee, 1999; Northrup et al., 1991; Northrup et al., 1994; Broussard & Northup, 1995, 1997). Initially, FBA procedures involved as many as 50 to 60 sessions of up to 30 minutes to identify and verify the function of behavior. This *Extended-FBA* format could take many days (Iwata et al., 1994; Northrup et al., 1991; Steege & Northrup, 1998). The development of a *Brief-FBA* format reduced the individual sessions in which the various conditions are in place to 5 to 10 minutes, allowing completion in 90 minutes (Broussard & Northup, 1995, 1997; Sasso et al., 1992; Derby et al., 1992; Wallace & Knight, 2003). These shorter sessions yield the same interpretations leading to the same identification of functions (Wallace & Iwata, 1999). The total number of sessions conducted is also reduced. This is accomplished by not including all four conditions. The information gathered from direct and indirect methods of functional assessment is used to narrow the possible controlling variables. It must be noted that the behavior must occur at a high frequency if sufficient information is to be captured in shorter and fewer sessions (Derby et al. 1992). Studies comparing brief and extended forms of functional analysis indicate they are comparable in successfully determining function (Brown et al., 2000; Kahng & Iwata, 1999; Tincani, Castrogiavanni, & Axelrod, 1999; Wallace & Knights, 2003).

Step 5: Develop Behavior Support Plan

a. Review hypothesis and select components of a behavior support plan.
b. Collect and use data to evaluate and revise plan as necessary.
c. Maintain and generalize successful results and fade intervention as appropriate.

A behavior support plan (BSP) summarizes the information generated, presents the hypothesis of function, and details agreed-upon procedures for behavior change and support. Most state education agencies and school districts have a specific form for writing BSPs; some incorporate it as part of the IEP document. These and other published forms have various components. Figure 6–8 is a sample BSP with many components common to such forms.

Component 1 lists the behavior management team, those primarily responsible for the BSP. These members may be the entire IEP team or a subcommittee. In addition to their names and professional roles (for example, teacher, speech-language pathologist), the document also describes their specific role in this plan. The plan will identify the primary and secondary implementers of the strategies and name the person who will monitor the correct implementation of the strategies. Data collectors, members of the crisis team, and teachers in settings to which the behavior change will be generalized may also be named.

Component 2 lists the operational definitions of the target behaviors. These were previously defined by the IEP team and were used during functional assessment or functional analysis. Component 3 includes documentation of unsuccessful strategies previously used in an attempt to alter the student's behavior. This may provide some insight to the team as it designs a new course.

Components 4, 5, and 6 represent the activities for developing a hypothesis of function. Component 4 lists the types of screening examinations that were conducted, their results, and any resulting intervention. Component 5 provides information about the functional assessment. It records the indirect and direct methods of information

BEHAVIOR SUPPORT PLAN

STUDENT _______________ DOB _______________ CLASS _______________

Date of Meeting:

(1) **Team Members:**

Name	Title/Role Assigned

(2) **Operational Definition** of Target Behavior: ____

____

____

____

____

____

____

FIGURE 6–8 ***Sample behavior support plan.***

(3) Summary of **Strategies Previously Used:**

Inclusive dates of implementation:
Person(s) implementing intervention strategy:
Components of intervention strategy:

Effectiveness data (attach documentation as appropriate):

Inclusive dates of implementation:
Person(s) implementing intervention strategy:
Components of intervention strategy:

Effectiveness data (attach documentation as appropriate):

FIGURE 6–8 ***continued.***

(4) Results of **Screening:**

Health:

Medications:

Physical Disability:

Sensory Disability:

Learning Disability:

Other:

Have the results of the screening indicated some action, and has it been implemented?

(5) Complete this page if a **Functional Assessment** was conducted.

A. Was an indirect method used? YES _____ NO _____

If yes, which instrument was used? ______________________
(attach the completed instrument)
e.g., Functional Assessment Interview
Student Guided Functional Assessment Interview
Motivation Assessment Scale
Problem Behavior Questionnaire
FAST
QABF

B. Was a direct method used? YES _____ NO _____

If yes, which procedure was used? _________________________
(attach the analysis data sheets)
e.g., Analysis of Anecdotal Report
Scatter Plot Analysis
A-B-C Descriptive Analysis

C. Resulting Hypothesis.

1. Social attention seeking:	adult	_____________
	peer	_____________
2. Tangible seeking:	item/object	_____________
	activity/event	_____________
3. Self-stimulation	which sense	_____________
4. Escape/avoid:	adult	_____________
	peer	_____________
	item/object	_____________
	task/activity	_____________
5. Escape/attenuate:	internal pain	_____________

D. **SUMMARY STATEMENT OF HYPOTHESIS:**

FIGURE 6–8 ***continued.***

(6) Complete this page if a **Functional Analysis** was conducted.

A. Was the purpose to:

- verify a hypothesis resulting from a Functional Assessment?
- refine a hypothesis resulting from a Functional Assessment?
- clarify an uncertain result from a Functional Assessment?
- initial development of a hypothesis?

Purpose: ____
____

B. Was it conducted in an analog or natural setting? ____________________
____
____

C. What were the conditions used in the analysis? **(attach graph)** ____________________
____
____

D. Resulting Hypothesis.

1. Social attention seeking:	adult	________
	peer	________
2. Tangible seeking:	item/object	________
	activity/event	________
3. Self-stimulation:	which sense	________
4. Escape/avoid:	adult	________
	peer	________
	item/object	________
	task/activity	________
5. Escape/attenuate:	internal pain	________

E. **SUMMARY STATEMENT OF HYPOTHESIS:**

(7) **INTERVENTION**

(7a) Current Target Behavior(s):

(7b) Alternative/Replacement Behavior(s) to be taught: (e.g., social skills instruction, self-management training):

FIGURE 6–8 ***continued.***

(7c) Antecedent/setting event strategies (e.g., environment, routines, tasks, personnel, instructional strategy, grouping, timing, etc.):

(7d) Consequence strategies (e.g., DRA, DRO, NCR, redirection, extinction, timeout); functional equivalency training, functional communication training:

(7e) Plan for monitoring implementation:

(7f) Maintenance and generalization:

(7g) Crisis intervention: (1) What will constitute a behavioral crisis for which some intervention other than that described in this plan will be necessary? (2) What will be the crisis intervention?

(7h) Staff training, support, and resources needed:

FIGURE 6–8 ***continued.***

gathering that were used and the resulting hypothesis. Component 6 provides information about the functional analysis. It provides information about the purpose, setting, conditions of the analysis, and the resulting hypothesis. Appropriate documentation is attached to the BSP document for both functional assessment and functional analysis.

For additional practice, go to the "Activities" module for Chapter 6 of the Companion Website.

Component 7 details the elements of the resulting intervention. There are two sets of elements. One set delineates the strategies for teaching and supporting more appropriate behaviors to replace the target behavior (elements 7b, 7c, and 7d); and one set to support that implementation (elements 7e–7h).

Component 7 lists an operational definition of the alternative behavior selected to replace the inappropriate behavior. It also describes the paradigm for teaching the new behavior (for example, social skills training, self-management). Also included are changes to the contextual setting events of those settings in which the behavior occurs and alternatives to the antecedent stimuli that occasion the inappropriate behavior. Delineated are strategies for arranging consequences that will reinforce the alternative behavior and the paradigms within which they will be used (for example, functional communication training). No single intervention approach is always appropriate for a particular function across all students and circumstances. Table 6–3 provides examples of some of the successful strategies that appear in the research literature. Note that these strategies are predominantly positive, reinforcement-based approaches. As noted by Pelios et al., (1999), it appears that the use of functional analysis increases the likelihood of choosing reinforcement-based treatments for self-injurious behavior and aggression, as opposed to punishment-based treatments. Explanations of these strategies appear in the following chapters on procedures to increase behavior and procedures to decrease behavior.

The second set of elements provides for the development of further plans to support implementation. A concern of the team should be that the strategy selected is implemented correctly and consistently. A plan should be developed for periodic observation of, and assistance with, implementation. Once the intervention has been successful, you need a plan for maintenance and ongoing support for the new behavior and for its generalization into other settings at school, in the home, and in the community. The BSP acknowledges the difference between behavior management and crisis management. Behavior management, the overall purpose of the BSP, is a plan for long-lasting behavior change that systematically provides the student alternative behaviors with which to interact with those in the environment. Crisis management requires immediate stopping of inappropriate behavior when the student is out of control. This is an issue of safety rather than long-term learning. Finally, consideration must be given to staff training, new personnel, and other support in order for the plan to be successful (for example, a temporary paraprofessional, protective equipment, alternative instructional materials).

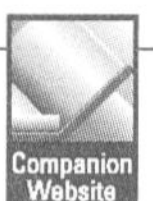

For more information, go to the "Other Resources" module for Chapter 6 of the Companion Website.

TABLE 6–3
Examples of interventions based on function.

Function: ATTENTION

DRA: Durand & Carr, 1991 (FCT); Harding et al., 2001; Meyer, 1999; Thompson, Fisher, Piazza, & Kuhn, 1998 (FCT); Zanolli, Daggett, Ortiz, & Mullins, 1999.
DRO: Kahng, Abt, & Schonbachler, 2001; Vollmer, Iwata, Zarcone, Smith, & Mazaleski, 1993
NCR: Fisher, O'Connor, Kurtz, DeLeon, & Gotjen, 2000; Jones, Drew, & Weber, 2000 (peer provided); Kodak, Grew, Northrup, 2004; O'Reilly, Lancioni, King, Lally, & Dhomhnaill, 2000.
Extinction: Hanley, Piazza, Fisher, & Eidolons, 1997.
Timeout: Mace, Page, Ivancic, & O'Brien, 1986.
Self-management: Smith & Sugai, 2000.

Function: TANGIBLE

DRA: Durand, 1999 (FCT), Vollmer, Roane, Ringdahl, & Marcus, 1999; Hagopian, Wilson, & Wilder, 2001.
NCR: Britton et al., 2000.

Function: ESCAPE

DRA: Durand & Carr, 1991 (FCT); Flood & Wilder, 2002 (FCT); Golonka et al., 2000; Lalli, Casey, & Kates, 1995 (FCT); Piazza, Moes, & Fisher, 1996.
DRO: Coleman & Holmes, 1998.
NCR: (noncontingent escape): Vollmer, Marcus, & Ringdahl, 1995.
Extinction: Mace, F. C., Page, T. J., Ivancic, M. T., & O'Brien, S. 1986. Analysis of environmental determinanats of aggression and disruption is mentally retarded children. Applied Research in Mental Retardation, 7, 203–221.

Function: SENSORY STIMULATION

DRA: Piazza, Adelinis, Hanley, Goh, & Delia, 2000; Roberts-Gwinn, Luiten, Derby, Johnson, & Weber, 2001; Shore, Iwata, DeLeon, Kahng, & Smith, 1997; Tang, Patterson, & Kennedy, 2003.
DRO: Patel, Carr, Kim, Robles, & Eastridge, 2000; Repp, Deitz, & Deitz, 1976.
NCR: Sprague, Holland, & Thomas, 1997; Carr et al., 2002.
Extinction: Kennedy & Souza, 1995.

DRA - Differential Reinforcement of Alternative Behavior
FCT - Functional Communication Training
DRO - Differential Reinforcement of Other Behavior
NCR - Noncontingent Reinforcement

SUMMARY

When students present challenging behavior that interferes with their learning and that of others and presents the possibility of a change in their educational placement, IDEA requires educators to engage in functional behavioral assessment procedures. These procedures provide a systematic means of determining the function that the behavior serves for the student. The functional assessment procedures provide direct and indirect means of information gathering that leads to a hypothesis of function. The functional analysis procedures provide for the manipulation of environmental variables that leads to a hypothesis of function. Based on the function of the behavior, it is possible to design an intervention and support plan. The BSP details changes in the environment, an alternative behavior to replace the inappropriate behavior, and strategies for teaching the alternative behavior. It has been suggested that functional behavioral assessment is not intended solely as a reaction to behavior problems that have reached a crisis point. Functional behavior assessment is most effective when problem behaviors are first exhibited (Scott & Nelson, 1999).

Companion Website

To enhance your overall understanding, go to the Supplemental Lecture Notes" module for Chapter 6 of the Companion Website.

A great deal of research and application substantiates the validity, reliability, and positive effects of these procedures, but there is still the need for further investigation to expand our knowledge of valid and effective methods that are practical in school settings (Gable, 1999; Nelson, Roberts, Mathur, & Rutherford, 1999). The need for further knowledge is especially true for populations of typical students and those with mild disabilities. For populations of students with moderate and severe disabilities, there is evidence of agreement across indirect and direct methods of functional assessment and functional analysis, and that the identification of function leads to successful intervention and support plans (Cunningham & O'Neill, 2000; Ellingson, Miltenberger, Stricker, Galensky, & Garlinghouse, 2000). Although a great deal is known about the process of functional assessment for individuals with severe disabilities, caution has been expressed due to the limited knowledge base for students with emotional and behavioral disorders (Sasso, Conroy, Stichter, & Fox, 2001).

KEY TERMS

functional assessment	setting events
functional analysis	analog

DISCUSSION QUESTIONS

1. Discuss examples of variables one might encounter in a natural setting such as a classroom, job training site, or home that may not be represented, or not comparably represented, in an analog setting.
2. In the study by Sasso et al. (1992), the teacher was asked to select tasks or activities in her usual classroom schedule that corresponded to antecedents outlined by individuals such as Iwata et al. (1982). Engage in the same task for an elementary, middle, and high school class and for a community and home setting.
3. Many teachers of typical students and those with mild disabilities attempt to determine the function of their students' behaviors by interviewing the students. They repeatedly ask students "why" they perform certain behaviors. Why is this unlikely to be effective?
4. If a functional analysis confirms a hypothesis that a student is engaging in an inappropriate behavior in order to (a) escape from demand or (b) gain social attention, what components might be included within a treatment plan?

5. Anecdotal reports are one means of direct information gathering for functional assessment. The following is an anecdotal report of one session of community-based vocational instruction. Todd, his classmate Lucy, and their teacher were at Pets-Are-Us. The session's task was to move 4-pound bags of birdseed from the storeroom to the shelves at the front of the store. Convert this report into the structure for analyzing anecdotal reports as shown in Chapter 3, Figure 3–2.

   May 3, 9:20 a.m. Teacher, Todd, and Lucy are in the storeroom. Teacher explains the task. She tells both students to pick up a bag and follow her. They do, and place bag on proper shelf. She leads them back to storeroom. Teacher tells Todd to pick up a bag of seed; he walks away. She tells him a second time. Teacher picks up a bag and takes Todd by the hand and walks out to the shelf. She hands him the bag and points to where it belongs, he puts the bag on the shelf. She tells him to go back to storeroom for another. In the storeroom she tells him to pick up a bag from the pile. The third time he is told, he picks one up and goes out front and puts the bag on the shelf. On the way out to the floor with the next bag Todd stops at a birdcage, drops bag, and begins to talk to birds. Several minutes later teacher comes for him. He ignores her. She puts his hands on bag then leads him to shelf. She then takes him to storeroom. He refuses to lift a bag. She hands him one. He drops it on floor. This is repeated twice. She takes a bag and leads him back out to the shelf. Together they put bag on shelf. She tells him to go back to the storeroom. She goes to check on Lucy. Eight minutes later she finds Todd sitting on floor eating a candy from his fanny-pack. She takes the candy, tells him it is for later. She tells him again to go to the storeroom. When she looks for him again, he is at the rabbit cage. She leads him back to storeroom. Tells him to pick up bag. After third delivery of instruction, teacher holds bag in front of him; he doesn't move his arms. She places his arms around the bag. He lets it drop through his hands, and it splits open. She scolds. She goes to get broom. She returns and he is sitting down eating the birdseed. Teacher tells Todd "Your behavior is not acceptable. Therefore, you will no longer be allowed to work today. Sit over there and time yourself out until we leave. I am very disappointed in your work behavior today."

Chapter 7

Arranging Consequences That Increase Behavior

Did you know that . . .

- Applied behavior analysts did not invent positive reinforcement?
- Candy may not be a positive reinforcer?
- Sometimes it is better not to reinforce every instance of appropriate behavior?
- Negative reinforcement is not punishment?
- You do not need a lawyer to write a contract?

Chapter Outline

The term *reinforcement,* used to describe pleasant events or rewards given to a person who complies with the demands of some behavior-change agent, has become part of the vocabulary of the general public. It has thus become associated with a stereotypic, manipulative view of behavior modification, conceptualized as an artificial tool created to make people engage in behaviors chosen by others. Although applied behavior analysts use the principles of reinforcement to change behavior, it is not true that they invented them. Reinforcement is a naturally occurring phenomenon. Applied behavior analysts have simply applied the effects of reinforcement in a thoughtful and systematic manner.

Reinforcement describes a relationship between two environmental events, a behavior (response) and an event or consequence that follows the response. The relationship is termed reinforcement only if the response increases or maintains its rate as a result of the consequence. In Chapter 1, we described two types of reinforcement: positive reinforcement, the *contingent presentation* of a consequence that increases behavior, and negative reinforcement, the *contingent removal* of some unpleasant stimulus that increases behavior. Both positive and negative reinforcement increase the future probability of the event they follow.

Everyone does things because of the consequences of doing them. Every action we engage in results in some consequence. When our behavior results in a naturally occurring, desirable consequence, this experience motivates us to continue behaving that way. Consider these examples:

- An office worker goes to work each day expecting to receive a check at the end of the week. If the check is delivered on Friday in an amount the individual finds satisfying, it increases the probability that the person will return to work on Monday.
- A little leaguer hits a double and is applauded by fans and teammates. This motivates her to play again next Saturday.
- A baby coos at his mother's approach, so she cuddles him and spends more time playing with him. The mother's response increases the frequency of the baby's cooing, which increases the time spent playing, which increases . . .
- A student spends 45 minutes each night for a week studying for a history exam. If the student makes an A on the exam, this consequence will motivate her to study just as hard for her next exam.

Although many appropriate behaviors are maintained by naturally occurring reinforcers, this natural process may be insufficient to maintain all desirable behaviors. Teachers often find students for whom naturally occurring reinforcers currently fail to maintain appropriate behavior. Some students may see little immediate benefit from learning plane geometry or applied behavior analysis. Competing reinforcers stronger than those being offered by the teacher may motivate some students. These students may find the laughter of other students more reinforcing than the teacher's approval. Some students may not value the reinforcers the teacher offers. Grades, for example, may have little meaning to them. In such instances, the teacher must develop a systematic, interim program to arrange opportunities for students to earn reinforcers they value. When naturally occurring reinforcers are not sufficiently powerful, the wise teacher looks for more powerful ones.

We shall describe procedures for the effective use of reinforcement in changing classroom behavior. The majority of the chapter examines the use of positive reinforcement, whereas the final section describes classroom applications of negative reinforcement. Suggested categories and examples of potential reinforcers are summarized in Table 7–1. This table is not designed as a scheme for ordinal selection of reinforce-

TABLE 7–1
Categories and examples of reinforcers for classroom use.

Class	Category	Examples
Primary reinforcers	1. Edible reinforcers	Foods, liquids, such as pieces of cracker, sips of juice, pudding
	2. Sensory reinforcers	Exposure to controlled visual, auditory, tactile, olfactory, or kinesthetic experience: face stroked with furry puppet, taped music through headphones
Secondary reinforcers	3. Tangible (material) reinforcers	Certificates, badges, stickers, rock star posters, balloons
	4. (a) Privilege reinforcers	Monitorships, team captain, excused from homework
	(b) Activity reinforcers	Play activities, special projects, access to media
	5. Generalized reinforcers	Tokens, points, credits
	6. Social reinforcers	Expressions, proximity, contact, words and phrases, feedback, seating arrangements

ment categories on a contrived to natural continuum. One might be tempted to identify, for example, the use of edible reinforcers in the classroom as contrived or artificial. Such a designation, however, depends on the target behavior, the setting, and the age of the student.

Any category or specific stimulus could be described as a contrived or natural reinforcer. Food as a reinforcer while teaching a student to feed himself or access to the water fountain as a reinforcer for properly lining up after a PE period may be considered natural consequences of the target behaviors. It may be helpful to distinguish among items or events ordinarily available in a given environment (that is, natural) and those temporarily added to the environment for increased consequence intensity (that is, contrived).

POSITIVE REINFORCEMENT

For more information on this topic, go to the "Web Links" module for Chapter 7 of the Companion Website.

Positive reinforcement (S^{R+}) is the contingent presentation of a stimulus, immediately following a response, that increases the future rate or probability of the response. There are three operative words in this definition. The word *increases* makes it clear we are dealing with some form of reinforcement, because the stimulus will have the effect of increasing the probability that the response will reoccur. The second operative word is *presentation*. When we use positive reinforcement, we intentionally present the student with a stimulus following the production of a response. The third operative word is *contingent*. The teacher will not present the consequence to the student unless and until the requested response is produced. If a teacher states the contingency, "Marcus, when you finish all your math problems, you may play with the airplane models," the teacher is using positive reinforcement if airplane models are reinforcing to Marcus. The reinforcing stimulus (playing with airplane models) will be presented to the student contingent on production of the requested behavior (completion of math problems). The examples in Table 7–2 illustrate the principle of positive reinforcement.

TABLE 7–2
Examples of positive reinforcers.

	Stimulus	Response	S^{R+}	Effect
Example 1	Statement of the contingency and availability of appropriate materials.	Marcus completes math problems.	He is allowed to play with model planes.	Increased probability that Marcus will complete next set of problems on time.
Example 2	—	John sits upright in his seat.	Teacher presents him with a smile and words of praise.	Increased likelihood that John will continue to sit appropriately.
Example 3	—	Sara brings in her homework each day this week.	She is appointed board monitor for next week.	Increased probability that Sara will continue to bring her homework every day.

Whereas *positive reinforcement* refers to the relationship between a behavior and a consequence, the term **positive reinforcer** describes the consequent event itself. A positive reinforcer is a consequential stimulus (S^{R+}) that

1. increases or maintains the future rate or probability of occurrence of a behavior;
2. is administered contingent upon the production of a desired or requested behavior;
3. is administered immediately following the production of the desired or requested behavior.

Choosing Effective Reinforcers

The reinforcing potential of an item or event depends on reinforcement history and deprivation.

Because a stimulus is defined as a positive reinforcer only as a result of its effect on behavior, no item or event can be termed a positive reinforcer until this relationship has been established. It follows, therefore, that a teacher cannot state with any real degree of certainty—in advance of evidence of such a relationship—what will or will not be a reinforcing consequence for any given student. What serves as a reinforcer for a particular student depends on several factors, including the student's reinforcement history (what has motivated her in the past), the student's deprivation state (what she wants but does not get easily or frequently), the perceived value of the reinforcer (whether it is worth performing the behavior to get it), consistency (whether reinforcers have been reliably delivered in the past), and age appropriateness (whether the reinforcer, even if the student might enjoy it, is more suitable for a younger child and thus embarrassing to her).

What will serve as a reinforcer may be different for each student. Preconceived notions of what should be reinforcing are frequent reasons for the failure of intervention programs. When the desired behavior change does not occur, the teacher's first reaction is often to assume the reinforcement procedures have not worked, when in fact one of the fundamental notions of reinforcement has been violated: the *individualization of reinforcers*. One way to individualize reinforcers is by using **reinforcer sampling.** Systematic sampling has been found to be more reliable than teachers' or caregivers' predictions or guesses for identifying items that will function as reinforcers when applied contingently (Daly, Jacob, King, & Cheramie, 1984; Green, Reid, White, Halford, Brittain,

& Gardner, 1988). There is also evidence that a reinforcer chosen by the individual receiving it rather than by someone else may be more effective (Fisher, Thompson, Piazza, Crosland, & Gotjen, 1997; Lerman et al., 1997; Thompson, Fisher, & Contrucci, 1998).

The method of reinforcer sampling will vary depending on students' level of functioning. Students can often be asked what they would like as a result of their effort or achievement. This can also be done using a prepared survey such as the School Reinforcement Survey Schedule (Holmes, Cautela, Simpson, Motes, & Gold, 1998) that was developed for use with students in the 4th through 12th grades. The results of asking the student, like any source of information concerning a potential reinforcer, must be taken with a grain of salt until the effect on behavior is seen (Cohen-Almeida, Graff, & Ahearn, 2000; Northup, 2000).

Another strategy for reinforcer sampling is using a prepared reinforcer menu like the one shown in Figure 7–1 in which items are named or pictured. Students are asked to rank-order the potential reinforcers in order of preference. A reinforcer menu should include a variety of items the teacher can reasonably make available. A variety of choices is necessary because what is reinforcing to some students may not be reinforcing to others. The presentation of limited choices will prevent unrealistic selections (such as CD players, video game machines, and trips to Cancun) that students might

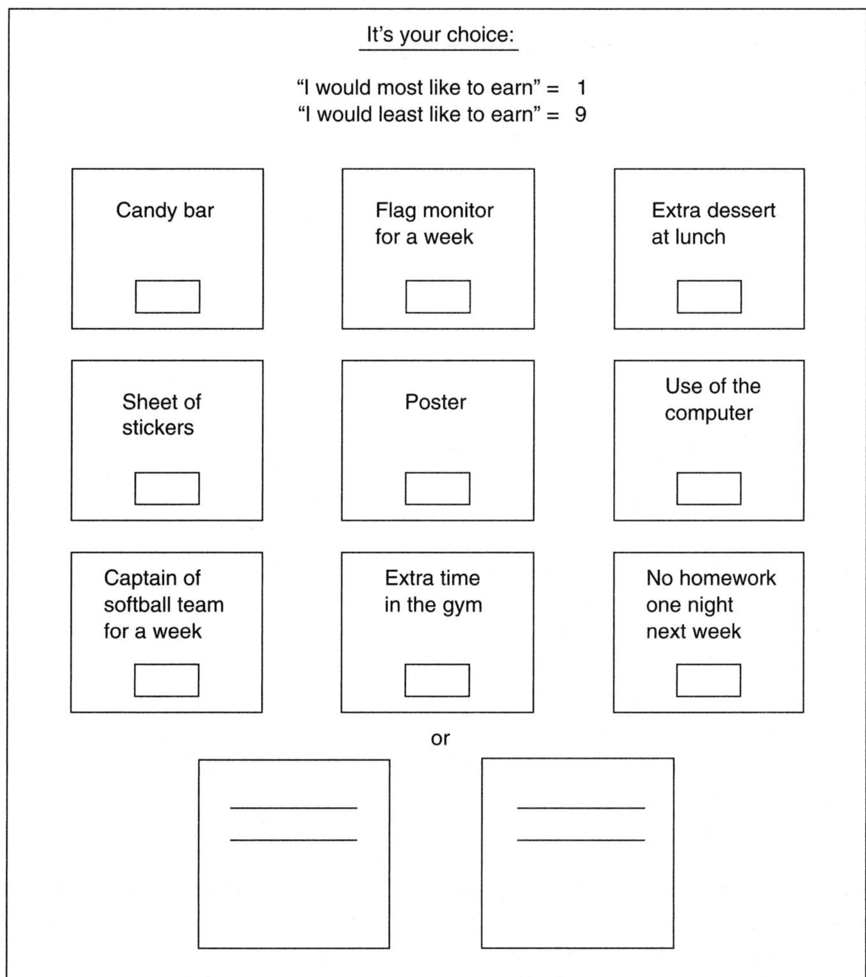

FIGURE 7–1
Reinforcer menu.

suggest. Teachers, however, may still wish to offer the opportunity for an open-ended response following some forced choices. An alternative suggestion is to offer, rather than a long list of items to be rank-ordered, a choice between two items or two categories of items (either verbally or with pictures). For example, the teacher might ask, "Which would you do a lot of hard work to get, things to eat, like chips, cookies, or popcorn, or get to do things like art projects, play computer games or go to the library." (Northup, George, Jones, Broussard, & Vollmer, 1996, p. 207).

Reinforcer sampling for students with severe disabilities must be concrete.

To determine reinforcer preferences of students whose abilities to respond are more limited, it may be necessary to conduct the reinforcer sampling with actual objects or events. Although stimuli such as photographs can be used, tangible stimuli are more reliable predictors of subsequent reinforcement effects (Higbee, Carr, & Harrison, 1999). It is usually best to bring to a sampling session up to six items the teacher thinks are potential reinforcers based on past history of reinforcer effectiveness and interviews with parents and past teachers. The items should include items from a variety of categories, such as edible items, sensory items, toys, or items that affect the environment (a fan, for example).

Three alternative reinforcer sampling procedures have been suggested: (1) Single-item presentation, in which one item at a time is presented to the student (Pace, Ivancic, Edwards, Iwata, & Page, 1985). This procedure provides an indication of whether an item is preferred or not preferred but lacks the ability to rank-order preferences. (2) Choice or forced choice presentation, in which items are presented in pairs from which the student is to select the preferred item (Fisher et al., 1992). Each item is presented at least once with every other item so preference for each relative to the others can be determined. The left or right position of the items in an array should be randomly positioned for each opportunity. There are data to suggest that this procedure better predicts subsequent reinforcement effects than does the single-item presentation method. (3) Multiple stimulus presentation, in which all items are presented simultaneously (DeLeon & Iwata, 1996; Windsor, Piche, & Locke, 1994). Once an item is selected and experienced, it is removed. This continues until all items are selected or a period of no responding passes. This process is usually repeated several times to confirm a student's preferences. With any of these methods there may be practical limits on the teacher's ability to provide an opportunity for an activity to be one of the options. Also, with these populations of students it may be difficult to determine whether the selection of a ball is due to its tactile character, its color, or the activity associated with it.

The teacher must decide which student response she will record as an item selection. Depending on the students' functioning level, they may pick up an item, point to or gaze at it, indicate the item using a less articulated approach (Pace et al., 1985), or access and select it using microswitches (Leatherby, Gast, Wolery, & Collins, 1992; Wacker, Berg, Wiggins, Muldoon, & Cavanaugh, 1985).

Preference for potential reinforcers may also be conducted based on duration of engagement (DeLeon, Iwata, Conners, & Wallace, 1999; Harding, et al., 1999; Kennedy & Haring, 1993; Parsons, Reid, & Green, 2001; Worsdell, Iwata, & Wallace, 2002). The basis for identification is the comparative amount of time the student engages in a task or with materials. The task or material is presented to the student for a specific period of time, such as 5 minutes. The options may be presented individually in sequence and duration data collected, or the student may be presented with arrays of two or more options and duration data collected for each option. This procedure can also be conducted by structuring a comparison between items identified as potential reinforcers and those identified as items of neutral value to the student. In all cases, the student should have an opportunity to experience each item before making a choice. The student must be allowed to taste, feel, or manipulate each item. As noted by Ayllon and Azrin (1968), the experiencing or sampling of the item "does not guarantee that the event will, in fact, be reinforcing to the individual; rather the sampling allows any reinforcing properties to be exhibited if the event has any potential reinforcing properties. If the individual does not seek the event after it has been sampled, it will not be because of a lack of familiarity with it" (p. 92).

Hall and Hall (1980, pp. 15–17) suggested the following nine-step sequence for selecting potential reinforcers:

Step 1: "Consider the age, interests, and appetites of the person whose behaviors you wish to strengthen." The teacher should select potential consequences that attempt to correspond to the student's chronological age and social background. Fruit Loops or an opportunity to work puzzles will probably have little motivational value to an adolescent.

Step 2: "Consider the behavior you wish to strengthen through reinforcement." The teacher should select potential consequences that attempt to correspond to the value, or effort required to produce the response. "If an employer offered to buy an employee a cup of coffee for working all weekend on a special job, it would be unlikely that any worker would accept the offer." Similarly, offering a student 5 additional minutes of free time for completion of an entire day's written assignment is an opportunity the student will probably pass up.

Step 3: "List potential reinforcers considering what you know of the person, his or her age, interests, likes and dislikes, and the specific behavior you have defined." This step allows the teacher to organize the potential reinforcers she is considering in an orderly and objective manner. Hall and Hall (1980) suggested that the potential reinforcers be organized according to categories, such as material reinforcers, activity reinforcers, and social reinforcers.

Step 4: "The Premack principle." When selecting potential reinforcers, the teacher should consider watching the student and noting activities in which he likes to engage. David Premack (1959) systematized the use of preferred activities as reinforcers. A discussion of the Premack principle follows later in this chapter.

Step 5: "Consider asking the person." The teacher should remember that the best authority on the likes and dislikes of a student is that student. The mechanism most often used to determine a student's potential reinforcers is the previously mentioned reinforcer menu. For alternative forms of reinforcer menus, see Raschke (1981).

Step 6: "Consider novel reinforcers." With this step, Hall and Hall (1980) reminded teachers that "varying the reinforcers is more effective than using the same reinforcers over and over." Repeated use of the same reinforcer can lead to boredom and satiation, lessening the motivating effectiveness of a consequence.

Step 7: "Consider reinforcers that are natural." Hall and Hall (1980) suggested three advantages to the use of natural reinforcers. First, natural reinforcers such as recognition and privileges can be provided more easily and at lower cost than most edible and material consequences. Second, natural reinforcers are more likely to be available to the student after the behavior has been established. "In a natural situation, even though you discontinue to systematically reinforce the behavior you wanted to strengthen, the natural positive consequence you provided is more likely to be available on at least some occasion in the future." Third, natural reinforcers automatically occur on a contingent basis. Praise for a homework assignment well done will not naturally occur unless the behavior was performed.

Step 8: "Select the reinforcer or reinforcers you will use." Once the teacher has considered Steps 1–7, Hall and Hall (1980) suggested selecting the reinforcers that will most likely have the desired effect on the target behavior.

Step 9: "Make a record of the behavior." The teacher is reminded that the only way to confirm a consequence as a reinforcer is to observe its effect on the behavior. To verify this effect, the teacher should systematically document the change, if any, in the production of the behavior. Various methods for providing such documentation are presented in Chapter 4 of this text.

Periodic reassessment of any reinforcer is important (Mason, McGee, Farmer-Dougan, & Risley, 1989; Stafford, Alberto, Fredrick, Heflin, & Heller, 2002). This is especially true if a single item or small set of items is used. When behavior change slows down, it may simply be because a student is tired of the reinforcer.

Making Reinforcers Contingent

It may also be necessary to be sure parents or other caregivers don't make potential reinforcers available noncontingently.

If reinforcement is to be effective, the student must receive the reinforcer only after performing the target behavior. An "if. . . then . . . " statement is in place. Such a statement establishes a clear and explicit relationship between performing the behavior and receiving the reinforcer. If Clara finds, regardless of whether she has performed the target behavior, she can get a lollipop at the end of the day when the teacher is tired and has a few pops left over, Clara may decide the teacher does not mean business: No contingency is actually in force. Implied in such a contingency and explicit in reinforcer delivery is that the teacher or some other specifically designated person is the source of the reinforcer. If the student can go to the classroom assistant or some other adult during the day and get the same promised reinforcer without having performed the desired behavior, that student will quickly determine there is no need to comply with the contingency.

Making Reinforcement Immediate

To be effective, a reinforcer should initially be delivered immediately after the target behavior is performed. This timing convinces the student of the veracity of the contingency and underlines the connection between a particular behavior and its consequence. Immediacy of delivery is also necessary to avoid the hazard of inadvertently reinforcing an intervening behavior. The longer the delay between the desired behavior and receipt of the reinforcer, the greater the possibility the student may engage in a behavior not under the contingency or not desired. Eventually the teacher will want to introduce a delay between the behavior and the reinforcer. This systematically arranged delay is known as a schedule of reinforcement and is discussed later in this chapter.

Ms. Troutman Reinforces Chaos

Ms. Troutman was a teacher of students with severe social maladjustments. She taught in a self-contained special class. It was the first week of her first year in this setting, and she was determined to make it a success. She had taken a course in applied behavior analysis and decided to set the following contingency for her students:

If you complete at least 20 assignments during the week, then you may participate in a class party at 2:15 on Friday.

The students worked busily, and Ms. Troutman glowed with satisfaction as she wondered why people thought these students were difficult to teach. At 11:00 on Friday morning, the first student completed his 20th assignment. By noon, all seven students had fulfilled the contingency. The remaining hours before 2:15 were among the longest Ms. Troutman had ever spent. Even though the students yelled, fought, cursed, ran around, and generally created havoc, the party was held as scheduled. (Ms. Troutman at least had sense enough to know that if she failed to live up to her end of the contingency, the students would never believe her again.) Monday morning the class came in yelling, fighting, cursing, and running around. Ms. Troutman had reinforced chaos, and that's what she got.

TYPES OF REINFORCERS

Two major varieties of reinforcers are available to teachers: *primary reinforcers* and *secondary reinforcers.*

Primary Reinforcers

Primary reinforcers can be powerful tools for changing behavior.

Primary reinforcers are stimuli that have biological importance to an individual. We can assume that they are innately motivating because they are necessary to the perpetuation of life. Therefore, primary reinforcers are described as natural, unlearned, or unconditioned reinforcers. Given their biological importance, we may expect that they will be highly motivating to individual students. The major types of primary reinforcers include foods, liquids, sleep, shelter, and sex (the last reinforcer is most commonly used in the form of entry to social activities). Obviously, the two most common and appropriate primary reinforcers for the classroom are food and liquids. Edible reinforcers are used mainly when teaching new behaviors to younger students and students with severe disabilities. Because of their high motivational value, they quickly affect behavior.

Different strokes for different folks.

In spite of the almost mystical association between behavior modification and M&M candy, teachers rarely find it necessary to use edible reinforcers with older students and students with mild disabilities. In many settings edible reinforcers may not be used because of concerns about infection, pests, or allergies. An imaginative teacher can choose from a great many other potential reinforcers. Reinforcing some students' behavior with candy or other treats is an example of behavioral overkill. Besides being unnecessary, primary reinforcers may be perceived by students as insulting. A ninth grader could hardly take seriously a teacher who said, "Great job on that algebra assignment, Casey. Here's your cookie." This is not to imply that teachers of older students should never use food as a reinforcer. An occasional treat may be very effective, when appropriately presented. For example, a popcorn party for students who have met some contingency may be perfectly appropriate. It is amazing to observe how rapidly second or third graders complete assignments once the smell of the popping corn begins wafting about the room.

Deprivation is a condition that must be met if primary reinforcers are to be effective.

For primary reinforcers to be effective, the student whose behavior is to be reinforced must be in a state of deprivation in relation to that reinforcer. Using an edible reinforcer with a student who has just returned from lunch is less likely to be effective because the student is not hungry. This by no means suggests that students should be starved so that food will be an effective reinforcer, but the necessity for a state of deprivation is a drawback to the use of primary reinforcers. A student need not be hungry, however, for limited amounts of special foods such as potato chips, raisins, ice cream, or candy to be effective reinforcers.

The opposite of deprivation is **satiation.** Satiation occurs when the **deprivation state** that existed at the beginning of an instructional session no longer exists, and the student's cooperation and attention have worn thin. A teacher of students with severe disabilities who conducts a training session lasting perhaps 30 minutes may come to a point in the session when the primary reinforcer loses its effectiveness. The teacher will know this when the student's rate of correct responding slows down or—in the case of more assertive students—when the student spits the no-longer-reinforcer at the teacher. There are at least seven ways a teacher may plan to prevent or delay satiation:

1. There is evidence to suggest that reinforcers selected by a student are more motivating than those chosen by the teacher. Data also indicate substantially more responding when choices among items occur during instructional sessions than before instruction (Graff & Libby, 1999). The teacher should have available an array of three or four edible reinforcers for the student to select from following correct responses.

2. Assign a particular reinforcer to each task or behavior. There is no need to use a single reinforcer all day, in all content areas, or across all behaviors. To do so is to build in the potential of satiation.
3. At the onset of satiation, when the student becomes less cooperative or errors increase, try switching to an alternative reinforcer. As a result of the reinforcer sampling that was conducted, an ordered list of several potential reinforcers is available so that more than one can be used during the day.
4. Shorten the instructional session in which the edible reinforcer is being used. Shorter sessions with fewer trials (controlled presentations) decrease the chance of satiation. Several short sessions may be held during the day.
5. Decrease the size of the pieces of the edible reinforcer given for correct responses. Smaller portions also disappear more quickly, thus not creating artificially long periods between trials as the student continues to savor the reinforcer.
6. Do not provide a reinforcer for every correct response. Require more performance from the student for a reinforcer. This changes the schedule on which reinforcers are delivered (Schedules of reinforcement are discussed later in this chapter). Combining this strategy with the availability of more than one reinforcer produces more stable responding than constant use of the same reinforcer.
7. Use multiple reinforcers, preferably those that occur naturally. For example, Carr, Binkoff, Kologinsky, and Eddy (1978) delayed the onset of satiation and tied their use of reinforcers directly to the concepts they were teaching students with autistic behaviors. While teaching the students manual signs for the words milk, apple, cookie, candy, and banana, the teacher reinforced a correctly formed sign with a piece of the food indicated. A problem with satiation is illustrated by the following story.

Mr. Alberto Eats Ice Cream

Jeff was a student with severe retardation whose behavioral repertoire seemed to consist mainly of throwing materials and chairs. He sometimes varied this by hitting teachers and other students. In an effort to control this behavior, Mr. Alberto had tried more than a dozen potential primary reinforcers—from potato chips to candy—with no success whatsoever. Appropriate behavior stayed at a low rate and inappropriate behavior at a high rate.

In desperation, Mr. Alberto asked Jeff's mother if there was anything Jeff liked. "Of course," she said. "Jeff loves butter pecan ice cream."

One quick trip to the grocery store later, Mr. Alberto began to make progress. By the end of a week, Jeff's behavior was under reasonable control, and Mr. Alberto thought his troubles were over. Before long, however, the inappropriate behavior was back in full force. Once again, Mr. Alberto questioned Jeff's mother. Could she explain why butter pecan ice cream wasn't working any more?

"Well, maybe," she said, "it's because he gets so much at home. I learned long ago that it was the only way to make him behave. I give him a whole carton some days."

Mr. Alberto solaced himself with the remaining pint of butter pecan; he prepared once again to go in search of the elusive reinforcer that would work with Jeff.

Conditions of deprivation and satiation may occur naturally, as in the case of food deprivation just before lunch period, or they may be arranged, for example, by restricting access to a particular reinforcer to one specific behavior or activity. Deprivation is a condition that establishes potentially increased effectiveness for a reinforcer. Satiation is a condition that establishes potentially decreased effectiveness of a reinforcer. Vollmer and Iwata (1991), comparing the effectiveness of reinforcers when students were in a state of deprivation to their effectiveness when students were in a state of satiation, found that the reinforcers were more effective during deprivation states.

Edibles provide the teacher with a wide range of potential reinforcers, for example, pieces of cookie (Hanley, Piazza, & Fisher, 1997), pudding (Green, Gardner, Canipe, & Reid, 1994), pretzels and candy (DeWitt, Aman, & Rojahn, 1997), chips, popcorn, and cheese doodles (Ross & Greer, 2003), licorice and fruit (Carr, Nicolson, & Higbee, 2000), gummi bears, goldfish crackers, and Reese's Pieces (Lerman, Vorndran, Addison, & Kuhn, 2004), crispy rice treats (Binder, Dixon, & Ghezzi, 2000), waffles, and cheese and crackers (Fiscus, Schuster, Morse, & Collins, 2002), soft drinks (Duker & Jutten, 1997), juice (Carr, et al., 2000), lemonade (Sigafoos, Couzens, Roberts, Phillips, & Goodison, 1996), and chocolate milk (Schepis, Reid, & Behrman, 1996). The recent fad for tiny little candies makes delivering small quantities much easier and saves the mess of trying to break larger pieces up with the one thumbnail kept a little long for that express purpose.

Common sense also suggests some precautions in selecting reinforcers. A teacher conducting language training would not use peanut butter as a reinforcer, because it is difficult to imitate sounds with your tongue stuck to the roof of your mouth. Liquid reinforcers may increase the number of toileting breaks necessary, unduly delaying the session.

Teachers should also note that the strong motivational property of certain reinforcers, especially edible reinforcers, has the potential to encourage responses that are incompatible with the target response. Balsam and Bondy (1983) illustrated this point with the example of using ice cream as a reinforcer for a young child. They suggested that the ice cream itself might stimulate so much approach behavior (that is, staring, reaching) that it interferes with the child's attending to the relevant antecedent and response requirement of the contingency. Similarly, if a teacher tells the students that if they are good, they will be allowed a special treat at lunchtime, they may become increasingly fidgety and inattentive in anticipation of the reinforcement. (For a full discussion of the theoretical and operant negative side effects of reinforcement, see Balsam & Bondy, 1983.)

Sensory reinforcers, often categorized as primary reinforcers, include:

Auditory: tones, voices, music, environmental (music through headphones)

Visual: black/white or colored lights (with or without blinking); pictures, books, magazines, slides, videos; movement (battery-operated toys, soap bubbles, slinky); mirror, kaleidoscope

Olfactory: sweet, pungent (cinnamon, clove, orange, inexpensive perfume)

Taste: solids or liquids (sweet, sour, salty, sharp, bitter)

Tactile: smooth/rough, soft/hard, warm/cold, wet/dry, movement (vibrators, fans, various textures such as fur)

Proprioceptive: bounce, swing, rock (trampolines, swings, rocking chairs, rocking horses)

Sensory events can be used individually or in combination (Dewson & Whiteley, 1987). It is important to select events that are age appropriate. Sensory reinforcers have been successfully used with nondisabled persons (Sigueland, 1968; Stevenson & Odom, 1964) and with young children with developmental disabilities (Cicero & Pfadt, 2002; Summers, Rincover, & Feldman, 1993). They have most frequently been used with students with severe and profound disabilities (Bailey & Meyerson, 1969; Gutowski, 1996; Lancioni, O'Reilly, & Emerson, 1996; Summers, Rincover, & Feldman, 1993; Smith, Iwata, & Shore, 1995). There are indications that naturally occurring sensations may be reinforcing stimuli for stereotypic or self-injurious behavior (Durand, 1990; Iwata et al., 1994; Sprague, Holland, & Thomas, 1997).

Secondary Reinforcers

No teacher wants to make students dependent on primary reinforcers for working or behaving appropriately. Primary reinforcers, even for very young or severely disabled students, are temporary measures to enable rapid acquisition of appropriate behavior. The teacher cannot send a student into a general education classroom expecting a Tootsie Roll each time he can identify the word "dog" or to a job site expecting a chocolate cake or side of beef at the end of the work week. **Secondary reinforcers** should eventually replace primary reinforcers. Secondary reinforcers include social stimuli, such as words of praise or the opportunity to engage in preferred activities, and a symbolic representation, such as a token exchangeable for another reinforcer. Unlike primary reinforcers, secondary reinforcers do not have biological importance to individuals. Rather, their value has been learned or conditioned. Thus, secondary reinforcers are often called **conditioned reinforcers.** Some students have not learned to value secondary reinforcers and must be taught to do so before secondary reinforcers will be effective.

Pairing

Pairing teaches students to value secondary reinforcers.

Students for whom secondary reinforcers have no value often need primary reinforcement to acquire appropriate behavior. To avoid dependence upon primary reinforcers, however, their use should always be in conjunction with some secondary reinforcer. The combined use of primary and secondary reinforcers is known as **pairing.** For example, when Jake behaves appropriately, his teacher may give him a bite of food and simultaneously tell him what a good job he has done. Through pairing, we condition or teach the student to be motivated by the secondary reinforcer alone. Once this association has been established, the secondary reinforcer may be as effective as the primary reinforcer. The teacher may then gradually withdraw the primary reinforcer. Some students, of course, have a reinforcement history including paired association, allowing for the use of secondary reinforcers without the need for primary reinforcers.

Tangible reinforcers and privileges are concrete and can have immediacy. There is a wide range of potential tangible reinforcers, from awards, such as certificates and badges of merit, to age-appropriate items, such as small toys, coloring books, and stickers for young children (DeLeon, Anders, Rodrigues-Catter, & Neidert, 2000; Dunlap, Koegel, Johnson, & O'Neill, 1987; McDowell & Keenan, 2001) or posters of rock stars, sports magazines, and video games for adolescents and young adults (Carr et al., 2000; Grace, Thompson, & Fisher, 1996; Sarokoff et al., 2001). Sometimes not knowing exactly what the reinforcer is can be enticing. Baer, Blount, Detrich, and Stokes (1987) and Dahlquist and Gil (1986) successfully used a grab bag. Privileges such as monitorships, being excused from homework, or caring for a class pet can earn status among the student's peers (Sainato, Maheady, & Shook, 1986).

Activity Reinforcers

An activity is the secondary reinforcement perhaps most often used by teachers. The systematic use of such activity reinforcers was described by Premack (1959) and is referred to as the **Premack principle.** The Premack principle states that individuals engage in certain behaviors at low frequencies, so these behaviors have a low probability of occurrence. Other behaviors are engaged in at high frequencies and therefore have a high probability of occurrence. When low-frequency behaviors are followed by high-frequency behaviors, the effect is to increase the probability of the low-frequency behavior. In other words, any activity a student voluntarily performs frequently may be used as a reinforcer for any activity he seldom performs voluntarily. When a teacher tells a student she may work on her airplane model in the back of the room when she

TABLE 7–3
Examples of privileges and activities available in a classroom that may be used as secondary reinforcers.

- Select and plan next field trip or class party.
- Lead a class activity (unit activity, Fun Friday, morning circle time, making popcorn).
- Choose a partner for a task.
- Put on a skit or direct the next class play.
- Decorate a bulletin board.
- Create a learning center.
- Edit class newsletter.
- Set schedule of day's lessons and activities.
- Participate in a peer tutoring program.
- Conduct a class lesson on a topic of your choice.
- Study driver education manual.
- Be excused from a night's homework.
- Be excused from a test.
- Be excused from an activity of choice.
- Write essay question for next class exam.
- Have points added to grade.
- Drop lowest quiz grade.
- Spend time on the computer.
- Make a video.
- Lead problem-solving team.
- Have access to gym or library.
- Watch a music video.
- Be first in lunch line.
- Get tickets to high school football game.
- Be classroom librarian or game manager.
- Become a member of the safety patrol.
- Be a monitor (of chalkboard, messages, pets, plants, playground equipment).
- Be a class officer.
- Have student of the week privileges.
- Be captain of sport team or reading group.
- Use media equipment (video camera, tape recorder).
- Play with games or toys.
- Use arts and crafts materials.

has finished the math assignment, or when a mother tells her child he may play outside when he has finished eating his brussels sprouts, they are using the Premack principle. The student can himself set the sequence of preferred and less preferred activities, thus choosing the sequence in which he or the class will engage in specified tasks (Kern, Mantegna, Vorndran, Bailin, & Hilt, 2001). The student may schedule two or three tasks or the tasks and activities for the entire day. (Suggestions for secondary reinforcers are shown in Table 7–3.)

Another source of ideas for secondary activity reinforcers is illustrated in the following anecdote.

Watch 'em Like a . . .

Mr. Hawk was a teacher in a short-term rehabilitation class for 10- to 13-year-old students with serious behavior problems. His job was to get his students' academic skills as well as their behavior up to snuff and very quickly reintegrate them into general education classrooms. He provided behavioral consultation to the classroom teachers and continued help with academics as necessary. Some of his students remained with him full time for several months; others began attending some general education classes within a week. Mr. Hawk used a token reinforcement system (see the discussion beginning on page 225 about token reinforcers) and prided himself on finding unusual, but effective, activity reinforcers simply by listening to students, asking what they wanted to do, or watching what they chose to do when they had free time.

Some of his students, for example, used their points to spend 10 minutes sitting on Mr. Hawk's motorcycle, safely parked in the faculty parking lot with the ignition key in Mr. Hawk's pocket. Some students helped the building engineer empty trash; others played with games or toys in the classroom. One boy, who showed some characteristics of autism, preferred to straighten and reorganize various manipulatives and teaching materials; Mr. Hawk was going to be sorry to lose Richard.

One day Mr. Hawk got a new student. In an effort to give him some immediate academic success and to provide an opportunity for reinforcement, Mr. Hawk gave Jordan a math assignment on the computer. The format was colorful, highly interactive, and entertaining. Mr. Hawk chose a level that he knew would be fairly easy for Jordan. After a few minutes, Jordan blurted out, "Wow, this is baaad!" whereupon the young man at the next computer leaned over toward him and said softly, "Careful, man, you let him find out you like something, next thing you know, you'll be earnin' it doin' something you don't like."

Kazdin (2001) suggested some limitations to the use of activity reinforcers. First, access to some high-preference activities cannot always immediately follow the low-preference behavior, thereby reducing the effectiveness of the high-preference behavior as a reinforcer. For example, scheduling problems might prevent students' using the gym right after doing their math. Second, an activity may often be an all-or-nothing enterprise. It is either earned or not earned. This may limit flexibility in administration of the reinforcer. For example, a student either earns the right to go on a field trip or he does not earn it. Such activities cannot be proportionally awarded depending on the degree of acceptable performance. This limitation, however, is not invariably true with activity reinforcers. Some activities may be earned in increments of time. For example, the consequence of 1 minute of shooting baskets in the gym for each correctly spelled word is easily administered if the minutes earned are banked until a designated time.

A third limitation on activities as reinforcers is that many activities must be freely available to students without reference to their performance. Examples include lunch periods, physical education, or art and music classes. Finally, the use of an activity reinforcer may cause an interruption in the continuous performance of the target behavior. For example, a teacher would not want to allow a student to go to the gym and shoot a basket after each correctly spelled word. Some students, however, may not continue to perform the target behavior unless some reinforcement is available after each response. In cases where the effectiveness of activity reinforcers seems lessened by such factors, the use of generalized conditioned reinforcers may be considered.

Generalized Conditioned Reinforcers

When a reinforcer has been associated with a variety of other primary or secondary reinforcers, it may be termed a **generalized conditioned reinforcer,** or simply a *generalized reinforcer*. Social reinforcers such as attention or praise are one kind of generalized reinforcer. These generalized reinforcers get their value by association with other reinforcers. Praise from the teacher after a difficult work assignment, for example, has been paired with an opportunity to use the computer, praise from a spouse for a delicious dinner has been paired with affection and physical contact, or praise from a parent for picking up dirty clothes has been paired with milk and cookies.

A second type of generalized reinforcer includes those that are exchangeable for something of value. Money is the most obvious example. Money, which has little or no intrinsic value, can be earned in a variety of ways and is associated with access to many types of reinforcers: food, shelter, a ticket to the Super Bowl, or a Mercedes. The effectiveness of generalized conditioned reinforcers is not dependent on a single type of deprivation (Ferster & Culbertson, 1982), and they are less susceptible to satiation than other types of reinforcers.

The use of generalized reinforcers has a number of advantages. Kazdin and Bootzin (1972) suggested the following advantages.

1. As opposed to certain edible or activity reinforcers, generalized reinforcers permit the reinforcement of a response at any time and allow sequences of responses to be reinforced without interruption.
2. Generalized reinforcers may be used to maintain performance over extended periods of time and are less subject to satiation effects due to their reinforcing properties and their relative independence of deprivation states.
3. Generalized reinforcers provide the same reinforcement for individuals who have different preferences.

Token Reinforcers

Because the use of money is unrealistic in most school settings, a generalized reinforcer known as a *token reinforcer* has become widely used. Token reinforcers are symbolic representations exchangeable for some reinforcer of value to students. This relationship is depicted in Figure 7–2. Originally, Ayllon and Azrin (1968) described procedures for using a token reinforcement system in a hospital for the mentally ill. Variations have been used in residential settings for disturbed and delinquent adolescents and those who are emotionally disturbed (Wood & Flynn, 1978), sheltered workshops (Welch & Gist, 1974), and hospital settings (Carton & Schweitzer, 1996).

For more practice with token systems, go to the "Activities" module for Chapter 7 of the Companion Website.

Token systems are used in most special education self-contained classes and resource rooms (Buisson, Murdock, Reynolds, & Cronin, 1995) and many general education classes (Carpenter, 2001; McGinnis, Friman, & Carlyon, 1999; Vaughn, Bos, & Schumm, 2000). Tokens are used by teachers and paraprofessionals when teaching academic skills (Connell & Witt, 2004; Lannie & Martens, 2004; Schuster & Griffen, 1993), conversational skills (Ross, 2002), and play skills (Arntzen, Halstadtro, & Halstadtro,

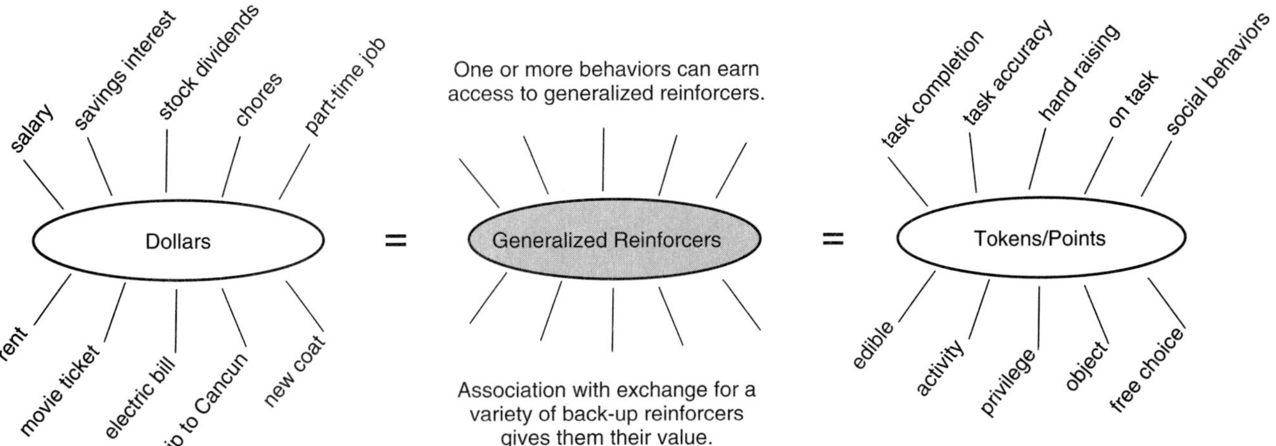

FIGURE 7–2 ***Tokens and dollars as generalized reinforcers.***

2003); when teaching students to manage their own behavior (Cavalier, Ferretti, & Hodges, 1997; Newman, Buffington, & Hemmes, 1996); for general classroom management and task engagement (Adair & Schneider, 1993; Higgins, Williams, & McLaughlin, 2001; Mueller, Edwards, & Trahant, 2003); to deal with specific challenging behaviors (Kahng, Boscoe, & Byrne, 2003; Luiselli, 1996); in managing the inclusion of students with disabilities into general education classes (Lyon & Lagarde, 1997); and in coordinating behavior-change programs between school and home (Trovato & Bucher, 1980). Peers have even been taught to evaluate behavior and distribute tokens (Stern, Fowlers, & Kohler, 1988). If you are earning points for exams, papers, and projects which you will trade in for a final grade in your behavior management course, you are participating in a token reinforcement system. The use of tokens is analogous to the use of money in general society; token reinforcers are exchangeable for a wide variety of primary and secondary reinforcers, just as money is. They are used as a transition between primary reinforcers and the natural community of secondary reinforcers. A token system may be adapted for use with a single student and a single behavior, one student and several behaviors, groups of students and a single behavior, and groups of students and several of the same or different behaviors.

Tokens won't work unless they can be exchanged for something.

A token reinforcement system requires two components: the tokens themselves and **backup reinforcers.** The tokens themselves should have no innate value; the backup items should have the value to the students. The teacher explains or demonstrates that tokens are needed to acquire the backup reinforcers. The goal is to earn enough tokens to access the backup reinforcers. The tokens are a means to an end. Tokens are delivered following the students' responses. Access to the backup reinforcers is allowed at a later time. The token can be an object, such as a poker chip, sticker, or coupon. It can also be a symbol, such as a check mark, a hole punched in a card, or the ubiquitous happy face. In general, tokens should be portable, durable, and easy to handle.

The teacher and the students should keep accurate records of the number of tokens earned. When the token is an object, like a poker chip, a token box or some other receptacle can be designated for storing the tokens in an assigned location or at each student's desk. With younger students, chaining necklaces with tokens or building towers will help to control token loss. A dot-to-dot representation of the backup reinforcer may be drawn. In this system, as each response occurs, two dots are connected. When all dots are connected, the picture is complete and the student has earned the backup reinforcer (Trant, 1977). Students may accumulate puzzle pieces that depict the backup reinforcer when all have been earned. Token cards with blank circles to be filled in with a smiley face for each point earned (Odom & Strain, 1986) may be used, or holes may be punched in a card (Maher, 1989). When the tokens are points earned, stamps, or check marks, a chart in the front of the classroom or some recording card similar to those displayed in Figures 7–3 and 7–4 may be used. The collaborative use of point cards among general education and special education teachers as students attend various classes has been successful in maintaining appropriate student behavior. The student manages the process by asking the teacher to record a symbol at the end of each class to indicate performance on each target behavior listed on the card (Carpenter, 2001).

The use of token systems requires precautions against counterfeiting or theft. Any student with 79 cents can buy 100 paper clips, thus debasing the value of paper clip tokens and thereby the effectiveness of the system. One of us once consulted with a residential treatment center that used holes punched on cards as tokens. When the residents went home on weekend passes, many of them informed their parents that their teacher wanted them to bring a hole punch back to the hospital. A simple preventive measure is to mark tokens, objects, or symbols with a code that allows validation of their source or confirmation of their ownership by a particular student. If check marks

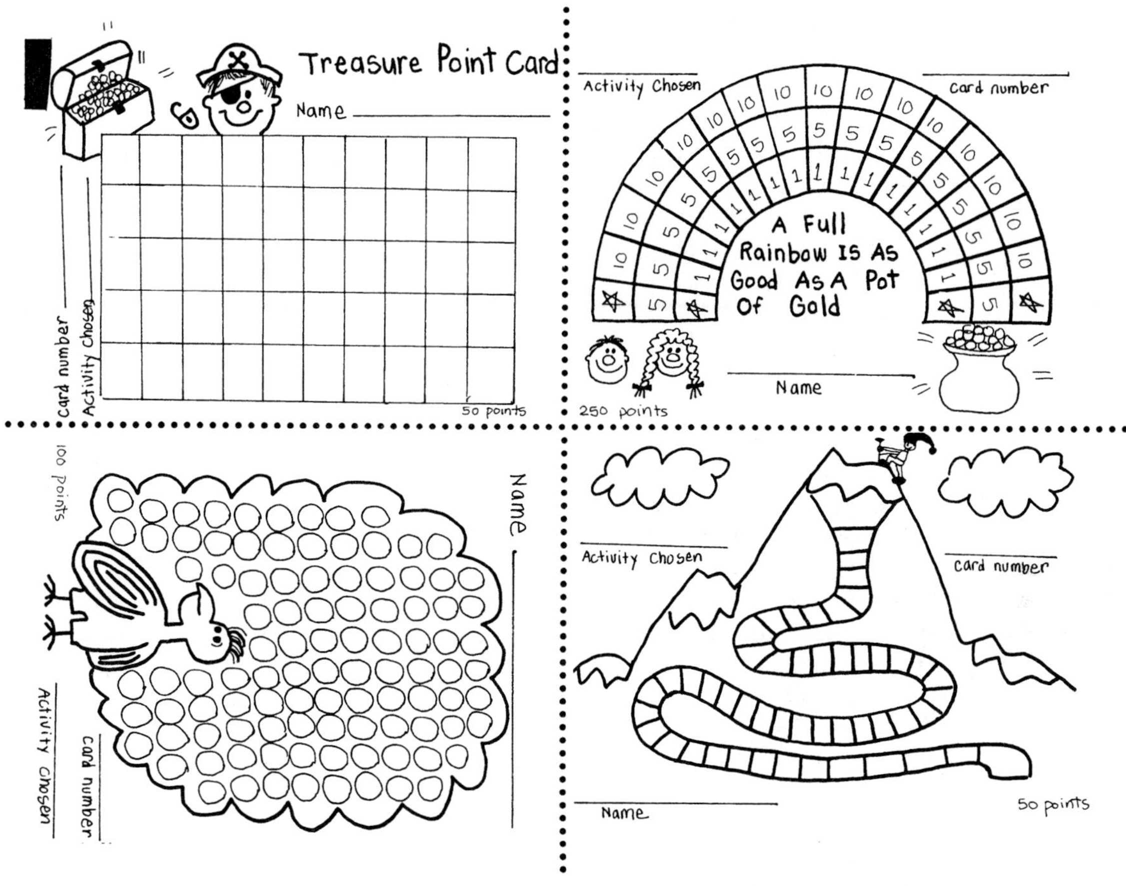

FIGURE 7–3 ***Point cards for token reinforcement systems with elementary students.***
Note: From *It's positively fun: Techniques for managing learning environments,* by P. Kaplan, J. Kobfeldt, & K. Sturla (Denver: Love Publishing, 1974). Copyright 1974 by Love Publishing. Reprinted by permission.

on a card are used, the teacher can randomly use different-colored markers on different days. The chances of a student's having a puce-colored marker at school on the day the teacher chooses that color are minimal. (The teachers at the residential center found hole punches with different shapes.)

Tokens in and of themselves are unlikely to have reinforcing power. They attain their reinforcing value by being exchangeable for items that are reinforcing. Therefore, the students must clearly understand they are working for these tokens to exchange them, at some point, for the second component of the token system, the backup reinforcer.

The selection of the backup reinforcer is probably the most difficult aspect of the token system, especially if the system is being used with a group of students or an entire class. The teacher must select a wide enough variety of backup reinforcers to provide a motivating item for each member of the class. Therefore, teachers should try to include an assortment, such as edibles (cereals, crackers, juice), activities (going to the library, listening to music), objects (game, notebook, or crayons), and privileges (being first in line, being collector of lunch money).

When a teacher announces the initiation of a token system to a class or to an individual, students will want to know at least four things immediately. First, they will want

FIGURE 7–4 **Point cards for token reinforcement systems with secondary students.**
Note: Bottom card from: "Tokens for success: Using the graduated reinforcement system," by C. Lyon & R. Lagarde. *Teaching Exceptional Children 29*(6), 1997. Copyright 1997 by The Council for Exceptional Children. Reprinted by permission.

POINT CARD

Student: Date:
Points earned for:

1	2	3	4	5	6	7	8	9	10
11	12	13	14	15	16	17	18	19	20
21	22	23	24	25	26	27	28	29	30
31	32	33	34	35	36	37	38	39	40
41	42	43	44	45	46	47	48	49	50

Total number of points earned:

Total daily points ____________ Name ____________
Date ____________

	Period 1	Period 2	Period 3	Lunch Period 4	Period 5	Period 6	Period 7
on task most of the time							
attitude							
completes work							
good relations w/ staff/peers							
keeping to yourself							

Homework: Comments:

Period 1 ____________

Period 2 ____________

Period 3 ____________

Period 4 ___ LUNCH ____________

Period 5 ____________

Period 6 ____________

Period 7 ____________

Parent Signature ____________

What students need to know about a token system.

to know what behaviors are required. As always, the contingency (if. . . , then. . .) should be clearly stated by the teacher and understood by the students. The description of each behavior to be performed and the parameters of acceptability should be clearly stated or posted.

Second, the students will want to know what backup reinforcers their tokens will buy. It is a good idea to keep representations of the backup reinforcers, if not the items themselves, in full view in the classroom.

The third question might involve the cost of each backup reinforcer in tokens. Based on their evaluation of the expense and desirability of the backups, the students will decide whether the reinforcer is worth the required behavior change. To get the process working initially, the teacher may price reinforcers to allow everyone to quickly acquire some. Students should learn at this very first exchange that if they earn a certain number of tokens, they may trade them for a certain backup reinforcer. Stainback, Payne, Stainback, and Payne (1973) suggested that prices of items, such as edibles, posters, and toy soldiers, should be in proportion to their actual monetary value. The pricing of activities and privileges is difficult to judge. Students should neither earn backups too quickly nor should they be required to work inordinately hard. It will take awhile for the teacher to judge the value of backup reinforcers based upon their perceived desirability among class members.

Finally, the students will want to know when they can exchange the tokens for the backup reinforcers. It is most common for an exchange period to take place at the end of each day or week. In the early stages of a token system, especially with young students or those with disabilities, the period before the first exchange should be very short. It would be unwise to start a token system on Monday and schedule the first exchange period on Friday. Students need to see quickly how the exchange process works and that the teacher is indeed telling the truth. Therefore, we suggest that the first exchange period be either at lunch, at the end of the school day, or even at the morning break (using a cookie exchange, for example). Stainback et al. (1973) suggested that tokens be paid frequently in the early stages and that exchange times be held once or twice a day for the first 3 to 4 days and then gradually decreased in frequency until they are held only once a week by the third week.

Exchanging tokens for backup reinforcers may take place in a variety of formats. The most common is the classroom store. In this format, the price-labeled backup reinforcers are located on shelves in a corner of the classroom. During the designated exchange period, students may enter the store and purchase any item they can afford. An interesting variation on the exchange is the class auction (Polloway & Polloway, 1979). In this format, the students are allowed to bid for each of the backup reinforcers. Students may bid as high as they choose, up to the number of tokens they have earned.

One potential impediment to an effective token system occasionally arises as a result of exchange procedures. It is illustrated by the following case.

The Case of Charlie the Miser

Charlie was a student in Mr. Thomas's class for children with learning disabilities. He was a very intelligent boy with severe reading problems and many inappropriate behaviors. Like Mr. Thomas's other students, he responded well to a token reinforcement system. The students earned check marks on a card exchangeable for a variety of backup reinforcers, including toys and privileges. The most expensive item cost three cards, and many were available for one or two cards.

After several months, Mr. Thomas noticed that both Charlie's behavior and his academic work had deteriorated drastically. This deterioration seemed to have happened overnight. Mr. Thomas could see no reason for it so he decided to do a very sensible thing. He asked Charlie what had happened. Charlie grinned and opened his work folder. "Look here," he chortled. "I got 11 cards saved up. I don't have to do anything for weeks, and I can still get anything I want from the store."

It is wise, as Mr. Thomas learned, to think through your token system to prevent the accumulation of tokens that Charlie demonstrated. There are various strategies for avoiding this problem. For example:

1. Instead of having a designated day for exchanging tokens, an exchange may be allowed as soon as the student has earned enough tokens for a particular item. This ongoing exchange will encourage students to plan for specific items and exchange their tokens rather than save them.

2. Immediate and delayed exchange may be combined. Students are allowed immediate exchange when they have earned sufficient tokens for a particular reinforcer. They may bank all tokens earned or tokens left over after an exchange for major items or events in the future. There should be a substantial penalty for early withdrawal of banked tokens.
3. The color or some other characteristic of tokens can be changed monthly or quarterly. All students understand that when the tokens change, old tokens become worthless.
4. Extremely well-organized managers can limit the number of tokens a student can accumulate and enforce this limit. This requires careful and accurate record keeping. Any token system that takes too much of a teacher's time and energy to implement and maintain is doomed to be abandoned.

See pages 394–397 for Professor Grundy's advice.

It is feasible to use token systems with an entire class or only with selected students. If only some children earn tokens, others may question why. Professor Grundy's advice in Chapter 12 should help the teacher deal with this problem.

A backup reinforcer that may encourage spending tokens is "time." Students may use their accumulated tokens to earn additional minutes to engage in preferred activities. A student may exchange the required number of tokens for the opportunity to work at the computer for 10 minutes. The student is allowed to spend an additional five tokens for an additional 5 minutes or ten tokens for 10 minutes. Within such an exchange there can be a direct, easy-to-understand proportional relationship established between a number of tokens or points and the amount of time that can be bought to engage in an activity. This also allows the student to decide on the value or extra value they associate with a particular reinforcing activity.

When using a system with an entire class, it is easiest to begin with some behavior that is a target for change for the entire class. For example, the teacher might initially give points for academic assignments finished or hands raised during class discussions. Once students have become familiar with the exchange system, the program can be individualized. While still distributing tokens for the initially targeted behavior, the teacher can integrate many academic tasks and social behaviors into the system. For example, Marty might earn tokens for neatness, Debbie for increased speed, and Sara for speaking loudly enough to be heard. Or, instead of this individual focus, the teacher might expand the initial system for classroom behavior management to include additional behaviors that are appropriate for all class members. The following is an example of a teacher's criteria for classroom points (Schumaker, Hovell, & Sherman, 1977, p. 453).

When a discussion is held:

4 pts.: Student listens and contributes three times to discussion.

3 pts.: Student listens and contributes twice to discussion.

2 pts.: Student listens and contributes once to discussion.

1 pt.: Student pays attention and listens to discussion.

0 pt.: Student does not listen to discussion.

When in-class assignment is given:

4 pts.: Student works all of class time on assignment.

3 pts.: Student works 3/4 of class time on assignment.

2 pts.: Student works 1/2 of class time on assignment.

1 pt.: Student starts work on assignment.

0 pt.: Student does no work on assignment.

In classes where there is no opportunity for participation (reading on own, movie, lecture):

4 pts.: Student is extremely attentive to subject throughout class.

2 pts.: Student is generally attentive to subject.

0 pt.: Student does not attend to subject.

A token system can also be used for teaching complex academic tasks. For instance, if a teacher is trying to teach a class of students to write appropriate paragraphs, instead of awarding 20 points for writing a paper on "How I Spent My Summer Vacation," the teacher might use the token system by awarding points for the following behaviors:

1 point for bringing pen and paper to class

1 point for beginning the writing assignment on time

1 point for completing the writing assignment on time

1 point for each sentence that begins with a capital letter

1 point for each sentence that ends with a period

Once the students have begun to master these items, the teacher can replace them with a point system for a more complex writing task. For example, by the fourth or fifth writing lesson, instead of awarding points for bringing paper and pen, the teacher might begin to award points for sentences using the appropriate plural suffix. Providing many alternative ways to earn a few points can be important in a token system. Some students find working toward several relatively simple objectives less frustrating and easier to undertake than attempting to earn many points for a long assignment that they may feel inadequate to complete. This approach also builds some measure of assured success into the assignment. Token exchange time can be used for direct or incidental teaching or for review and practice (Fabry, Mayhew, & Hanson, 1984; Kincaid & Weisberg, 1978). The teacher may place words, math problems, or science questions on each backup reinforcer. Students would respond to a stimulus or solve a problem before receiving the reinforcer. Be sure that students understand this contingency and perhaps even know what the question will be before the exchange takes place. Imagine your reaction if your employer suddenly refused to deposit your salary until you named the Supreme Court justices in order of appointment.

Token reinforcers can be very useful in managing a classroom. Ayllon and Azrin (1968, p. 77) suggested there are advantages to using tangible reinforcers (tokens) that may make them more effective than generalized **social reinforcers** (smiles and praise).

1. The number of tokens can bear a simple quantitative relation to the amount of reinforcement.
2. The tokens are portable and can be in the student's possession even when in a situation far removed from the classroom.
3. No maximum exists on the number of tokens a subject may possess. Their value does not fluctuate with deprivation or satiation.
4. Tokens can be continuously present during the period between earning them and exchanging them.

To enhance your understanding of token economies, go to the "Web Links" module for Chapter 7 of the Companion Website.

5. The physical characteristics of the tokens can be easily standardized.
6. The tokens can be made durable so they will not deteriorate before being exchanged.
7. The tokens can be made unique and nonduplicable so that the experimenter can be assured that they are received only in the authorized manner.
8. The use of tokens provides the student with a tangible means of continuous feedback. By having custody of the token objects or point card, the student can follow personal progress toward the criterion set in the contingency—whether it is for a behavior to be brought under control or for the acquisition of an academic objective.
9. The use of tokens enables more precise control by the teacher over administration of reinforcers. As noted by Kazdin (1977), a teacher's vocal tone will differ each time she or he says "Good work," as will the exact phrasing of "good," "pretty good," "very good," although in each instance the teacher means to convey an equal praise statement. Token reinforcement does not suffer from this subjective influence.
10. Tokens can be carried by the teacher and delivered unobtrusively. Thus, the administration of a token can be immediate without interfering with the student's performance of the target response or with other students' work.
11. A system of token reinforcement allows for differential valuing of performance. It does not require an all-or-nothing delivery of reinforcement. The student may initially be given a token for each correctly spelled word and later earn reinforcement for a 20-out-of-20 performance. The criterion for performance can be changed as performance improves.
12. A system of token reinforcement allows the student to become accustomed to delayed gratification of wants.
13. The use of a token system allows for greater versatility than is possible with other reinforcement systems. This versatility is related to the wide variety of backup reinforcers that may be selected and to the variety of behaviors that may be placed under a contingency for earning tokens.
14. The most important advantage a token system provides is its ease of generalizability. Unlike primary reinforcers or certain activity reinforcers, tokens can easily be used across settings (in other classrooms, in the cafeteria, on field trips) and with different behaviors simultaneously (in-seat behavior and correct spelling). They can also easily be administered by more than one teacher and by parents.
15. Tokens can often maintain behavior at a higher level than other secondary reinforcers such as praise, approval, and feedback (Kazdin & Polster, 1973; O'Leary, Becker, Evans, & Saudargas, 1969).

Many public school and residential programs for students with behavior disorders and learning disabilities use an adaptation of a token economy usually referred to as a levels system (Cavalier et al., 1997; Smith & Farrell, 1993). A levels system is a rigorous framework for shaping appropriate student behavior. Students are divided into groups according to their behavior and can move to higher levels as their behavior improves. Each level requires progressively more appropriate behavior and progressively more student self-management (self-recording, evaluation, and reinforcer selection). As students progress through levels, they have more rigorous standards to meet, gain access to a wider variety of backup reinforcers, and must display increased responsibility for their own behavior. Although there are various ways to set the expectations for behavior within each level and to determine progress from one level to another, at each level teachers set general behavior expectations (for example, use of appropriate language, keeping one's hands to oneself, not leaving the room without permission), and each student has a set of individual behavior requirements based on an individual assessment of academic, social, or behavior deficits. Students on the lowest level have very basic privileges and little freedom of choice or activity, and they earn from a limited range of reinforcers. After a period of behavior that meets various criteria, students move to higher levels, where they must meet increasing expectations and can earn more varied and valuable reinforcers. It is often the case that the last level is a transition stage into a more inclusive educational placement for the student. On the first level, reinforcers in the form of praise, feedback, and points are delivered frequently. As a student progresses through the levels, reinforcers are delivered less often, requiring more appropriate behavior for a reinforcer. At each level, certain behaviors, such as hitting another student or a staff member, will automatically drop a student a level. Some programs include aspects of a psychoeducational model such as log or journal keeping and personal goal setting as requirements for reinforcement (Barbetta, 1990; Bauer, Shea, & Keppler, 1986; Cruz & Cullinan, 2001; Mastropieri, Jenne, & Scruggs, 1988).

Social Reinforcers

A category of secondary reinforcers that teachers and others often use almost unconsciously (and usually unsystematically) includes demonstrations of approval or attention. The teacher's attention is usually the most readily available and potent reinforcer in a classroom. If teachers are not careful about distributing their attention, they may find that they have reinforced inappropriate behavior by paying attention to it. An example of reinforcing inappropriate behavior in another environment is provided in the following episode.

Burrhus Teaches the Professor

Professor Grundy was sitting on the sofa reading the newspaper. Burrhus padded into the room, lumbered over to Grundy, and stuck his huge head under the professor's arm between the professor and the paper. "Look, Minerva," said the professor, scratching Burrhus on the head, "he likes me. Good boy. Good boy. Aren't you a good boy?" He continued to scratch; Burrhus remained close to the professor, occasionally inserting his head and being petted and praised. Later that day the professor returned from the grocery store. Burrhus lumbered over, stuck his head between the professor and the grocery bag and precipitated the bag to the floor. "He didn't mean to," stated the professor. "He was just glad to see me. Weren't you boy?" he crooned, stepping over the broken eggs that Mrs. Grundy was cleaning up. "Want to go chase your ball?" After dinner Grundy retired to his study to complete work on an important manuscript. Burrhus accompanied him and settled in a place close to the professor's feet. All went well until Burrhus got up, inserted his head between the professor and the computer screen, drooled into the keyboard, and smeared the screen. Grundy leaped up and shouted, "Minerva, call this dog! He's driving me crazy! He's going to have to learn to leave me alone when I'm working."

"Oliver," said Mrs. Grundy tartly, "you have been reinforcing him with your attention for nudging you all day. Now you're complaining. Do you expect him to know you're working? I talked to Miss Oattis this morning. She's teaching a dog obedience class starting next week. I think the two of you need to go."

A wide variety of interactions is associated with a job well done. As shown in the following list, the range of potential social reinforcers includes various nonverbal expressions, teacher proximity to the student, physical contact between teacher and student, student privileges, and words and phrases that convey pleasure and approval of the student's performance. (Barry & Burlew, 2004; Collins & Griffen, 1996; Conroy, Asmus, Ladwig, Sellers, & Valcante, 2004; Jahr, 2001; Knight, Ross, Taylor, & Ramasamy, 2003; McDonnell, Johnson, Polychronis, & Risen, 2002; Werts, Zigmond, & Leeper, 2001).

Social reinforcers have proven effective not only for teachers in changing and maintaining student behavior but also for students in changing and maintaining teacher behavior (Gilberts, Agran, Hughes, & Wehmeyer, 2001; Polirstok & Greer, 1977).

Expressions

smiling, winking, laughing, nodding, clapping, looking interested

Proximity

sitting next to the student at lunch, sitting next to the student on bus trips, placing the student's desk next to the teacher's, sitting next to the teacher during storytime, being teacher's partner in a game

Contact

shaking hands, holding hands, pat on the back

Privileges

having good work displayed, being leader of an activity, being classroom monitor, being team captain

Words and Phrases

"I like the way you are sitting." "That is excellent work." "You should be proud of what you have done." "That is just what I wanted you to do." "You should show this to your parents."

Of these social reinforcers, words and phrases are the most often deliberately used by teachers. Words and phrases used by teachers may be affirmatively described as forms of teacher praise. O'Leary and O'Leary (1977) stated that teacher praise must have certain qualities to function effectively as reinforcement:

1. *Praise must be delivered contingent on performance of the behavior to be reinforced.* Noncontingent delivery of praise violates one of the essentials of the operational definition of reinforcement. Noncontingent delivery of praise removes the dependent relationship between student performance and teacher's affirmative attention and therefore does not increase the future probability of the behavior.
2. *Teacher praise should specify the behavior or particulars of the behavior being reinforced.* There should be no confusion on the part of the student as to why he is receiving the teacher's affirmative attention.
3. *The praise should sound sincere.* This means the teacher should avoid the use of stock phrases. The praise statement should vary in content and tone according to the situation and the preference of the student being praised. Just as a student can satiate on the unrelenting delivery of primary reinforcers, students can satiate on the unrelenting delivery of certain phrases. Such stock phrases soon lose their reinforcing quality, deteriorate into teacher patter, and are soon ignored or even resented by the student.

Clinton and Boyce (1975) differentiated the words and phrases used by teachers into two types. They referred to *affirmative reinforcers,* which are characterized by words such as *good* and *fine,* and *informative reinforcers,* which are characterized by words such as *right* and *correct.* Informative reinforcers would commonly be referred to as *constructive feedback.* When feedback is used as a reinforcer, it is almost always prefaced with an affirmative, followed by a behavior-specific praise statement that focuses on the accuracy or appropriateness of the behavior, as in "That's it, you put the puzzle piece on the table" (Parrish, Cataldo, Kolko, Neef, & Engel, 1986). Verbal feedback may also be used to reinforce an attempt or approximation (Hall, Sheldon-Wildgen, & Sherman, 1980); for example, "Good try, you got two out of three right. Now do this one the same way." Behavior-specific praise has a direct effect on student on-task and study behavior in general education and special education settings (Ferguson & Houghton, 1992; Hall, Lund, & Jackson, 1968; Sutherland, Wehby, & Copeland, 2000). Sutherland et al. (2000), for example, defined behavior-specific praise as verbal praise that specified the desired student behavior, "Mark, I like the way you are looking at me," or "You did a super job completing your work today, Christine," as opposed to non-behavior-specific praise such as "Good job" or "That's good" (p. 4). They demonstrated that student on-task behavior increased when the rate of behavior-specific praise by the teacher was increased and decreased when the rate was decreased.

Table 7–4 offers examples of constructive verbal feedback. Some forms of feedback provide the student with a more tangible measure of accuracy, as in Cronin and Cuvo's (1979) use of various-colored stars (red stars equal a performance better than last time; gold stars equal 100% accuracy). Graphs and charts alone have been used as a means of feedback and reinforcement. Seeing their individual bar graphs grow may reinforce some children. Line or cumulative graphs may be used as visual reinforcers for older students (Jens & Shores, 1969). People have used graphs to reinforce themselves (see Chapter 11). Feedback alone, however, may not be a reinforcer for all students in all situations. Depending on a student's previous experience, it may serve as a reinforcer, a punisher, or as a powerless antecedent that does not alter inappropriate behavior or result in the continuation of desired behavior (Brophy, 1981; Peterson, 1982).

CONTRACTING

It can be difficult for a teacher to use a reinforcement system serving a number of students and having a variety of objectives for managing behavior and instruction. On a hectic day, a teacher might offhandedly state a contingency for a student without thinking it through. Later the teacher may not remember the details of what was said and thus not be in a position to enforce the contingency. To complicate this uncertainty, students tend to rewrite reality to suit themselves: "You said I could go outside if I finished my math. You didn't say I had to get them right." A simple way to systematize the use of reinforcement is contracting. **Contracting** is placing the contingency for reinforcement into a written document. In the contract itself, the teacher creates a permanent product that can be referred to if questions arise.

Companion Website

To increase your knowledge of contracting, go to the "Activities" module for Chapter 7 of the Companion Website.

TABLE 7–4
Constructive verbal feedback.

Affirmative	Feedback
"Great!	(Description of correct response) You finished your work on time."
"Good try!	(Reinforcement of approximation) You almost got finished on time."
"Much better!	(Suggestion for modification) If you keep trying not to make careless mistakes, you'll finish all of them next time."

As with any contract, the classroom contract should be the product of reasonable negotiations between the parties involved—namely, the teacher and the student. In many cases these negotiations involve the collaboration of the student and all the teachers whose classes he attends (Lassman, Jolivette, & Wehby, 1999). Though the exact wording of a written contract will depend on the sophistication of the student for whom it is designed, each will contain some form of the basic "if. . . , then . . . " statement, as shown in Figure 7–5. A written contract should always contain those elements minimally necessary for any reinforcement contingency: the behavior, the conditions, the criterion, and the reinforcer.

To avoid later disagreement about what was really meant, the contract should contain precisely written statements describing the behavior required. This description should include the parameters within which the behavior is to be performed and the criterion level for meeting the contract terms. After discussion of the criterion, the student should understand the method or instruments that will be used to evaluate performance. The contract should also include the type, amount, and method of delivery of the reinforcement.

In addition to these basic items, dates for an interim and final review should appear in the contract. The interim date reminds the teacher of the need to monitor progress and allows renegotiation if the behavior required is unrealistic or if there is an instructional component to be added. Listing the final review date sets the student's time limit for fulfilling the terms of the contract.

Once the terms of the contract have been discussed and written down, the teacher should answer all questions the student may have. To ensure that the student understands the terms of the contract, he or she should read it back to the teacher and then restate the terms in different words. If this process results in a very different statement, the contract should be rewritten in easier language. Once a contract is finalized, the teacher and the student should both sign it, and each should have a copy.

Homme, Csanyi, Gonzales, and Rechs (1970, pp. 18–20) suggested basic rules for the use of reinforcers in contracting (numbers 1–5) and characteristics of proper contracting (6–10):

1. "The contract payoff (reward) should be immediate." This rule follows what has been stated as one of the essential elements of an effective reinforcer: It must be administered immediately upon performance of the target behavior.
2. "Initial contracts should call for and reward small approximations." This form of successive approximations—that is, progressive steps toward the target behavior—is particularly useful for behaviors the student has never performed before, a criterion level set too high, or a behavior category that is too broad (such as "clean your room").

See Chapter 9 for more about reinforcement of small approximations.

3. "Reward frequently with small amounts." Homme stated that experience has shown that "it is far more effective to give frequent, small reinforcements than a few large ones." Frequent delivery of reinforcement allows for closer monitoring of the progress of the behavior change by both the teacher and the student.
4. "The contract should call for and reward accomplishment rather than obedience." Homme suggested that contracts focusing on accomplishments lead to independence. Therefore, appropriate wording should be, "If you accomplish such and such, you will be rewarded with such and such," as opposed to "If you do what I tell you to do, I will reward you with such and such."

Official Contract

This is an agreement between (student name) and (teacher name). The details of this contract begin on ____________ and end on ____________.

The terms of this contract are as follows:

1. (Student name) will: ______________________________
____
____
____

2. (Teacher name) will: ______________________________
____
____

If the student fulfills his/her part of this contract, then (the student) will receive the following agreed upon reinforcer: ______________________________
____

However, if (the student) fails to fulfill his/her part of this contract, the terms of this contract will not have been met and the reinforcer will not be delivered.

Signed this date: ______________________

Student's signature: ______________________

Teacher's signature: ______________________

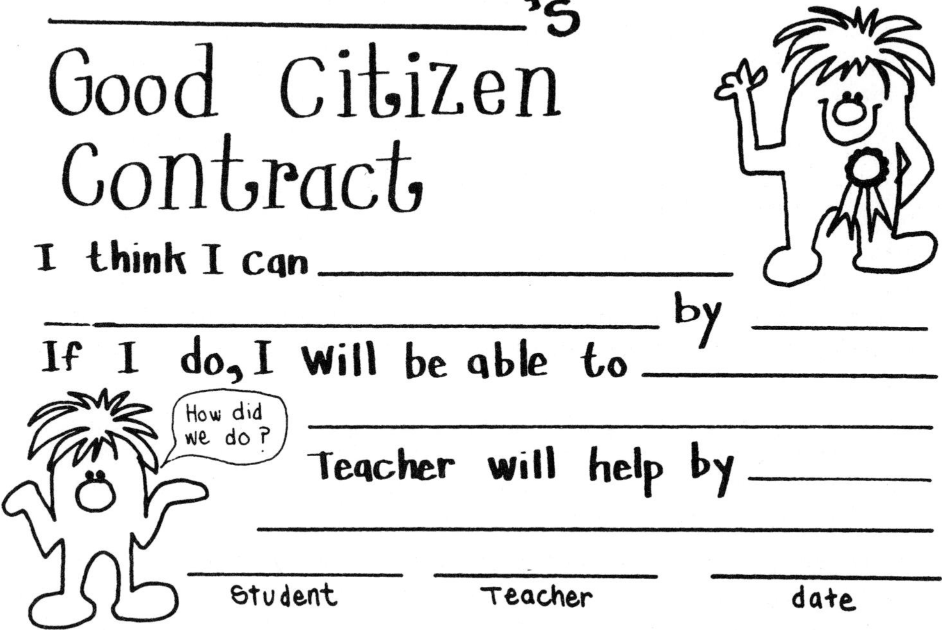

FIGURE 7–5
Formats used in contracting.
Note: From *It's positively fun: Techniques for managing learning environments,* by P. Kaplan, J. Kobfeldt, & K. Sturla (Denver: Love Publishing, 1974). Copyright 1974 by Love Publishing. Reprinted by permission.

5. "Reward the performance after it occurs." This rule restates an essential element of a reinforcer: It must be administered contingently. Inexperienced teachers sometimes state contingencies as, "If you get to go on the field trip today, you must do all your work next week." They are usually disappointed with the effects of such statements.
6. "The contract must be fair." The "weight" of the reinforcement should be in proportion to the amount of behavior required. The ratio set up in the contract should be fair to both the teacher and the student. Asking the student to finish 2 out of 20 problems correctly for 30 minutes free time is just as unfair as requiring 20 out of 20 problems correct for 2 minutes free time.
7. "The terms of the contract must be clear." Ambiguity causes disagreement. If the teacher and student do not agree on the meaning of the contract, the teacher may decide contracting is more trouble than it is worth. The student may decide neither the teacher nor the system can be trusted.
8. "The contract must be honest." According to Homme, an honest contract is one that is (a) "carried out immediately" and (b) "carried out according to the terms specified in the contract." This can be assured if the teacher and the student have freely engaged in the contract negotiation. Teachers should avoid imposing a "contract" on the student.
9. "The contract must be positive." Appropriate: "I will do. . . , if you do . . . " Inappropriate: "I will not do. . . , if you do . . . " "If you do not . . . , then I will . . . " "If you do not, then I will not . . . "
10. "Contracting as a method must be used systematically." As with any form of reinforcement strategy, if contracting is not done systematically and consistently, it becomes a guessing game: "Does she really mean it this time?"

Writing contracts brings added advantages to a reinforcement system:

1. A written contract is a permanent document that records the variables of the original contingency for consultation by the teacher and the student.
2. The process of negotiation that leads to the contract enables students to see themselves as active participants in their learning as they each take part in setting their own expectations or limitations.
3. The writing of a contract emphasizes the individualization of instruction.
4. Contracting provides interim documents that state current objectives between IEP meetings. Such information may be shared with parents.

Variations in Administration of Reinforcers

A basic reinforcement system has the following design:

- The teacher presents the antecedent discriminative stimulus.
- The student performs the requested response.
- The teacher presents the student with an appropriate reinforcer.

This basic scheme focuses on the administration of an individually selected reinforcer designed for the particular student. Reinforcement is, however, a flexible strategy that can be adapted to a number of situations that arise in the management of a

Manner of administering consequences		Type of contingencies: Individualized	Standardized	Group
	Individual	1	2	3
	Group	4	5	6

FIGURE 7–6 **Variations in administration of consequences.**
Note: From *The token economy: A review and evaluation,* by A. E. Kazdin (New York: Plenum Press, 1977). Reprinted by permission.

classroom. Based on the type of contingency and manner of administering consequences, Kazdin (2001) devised a matrix to represent these variations (see Figure 7–6). Although the matrix was originally proposed for variation in use of token systems, it is equally appropriate with any reinforcement system.

As Figure 7–6 shows, there are two options for administering consequences. First, reinforcement can be administered individually: The particular student who has performed the requested response is given the cereal, free time, or appropriate number of tokens. Second, reinforcement can be administered to students as a group: Given an acceptable performance by the whole class, for example, all 30 students earn extra time for crafts on Wednesday afternoon.

There are three options for the type of contingency a teacher may establish for receipt of reinforcement. These are represented at the top of the matrix in Figure 7–6. For the first one, *individualized contingencies,* the behavior requested and the criterion of performance required are specific to the behavior or instructional needs of a particular student. Under the second option, *standardized contingencies,* the teacher sets a requirement that is applied equally to all members of a class or to several class members. Using the third alternative, *group contingencies,* some behavior is required of a group of students and reinforcement is based on performance of the group as a whole.

Interaction among the two manners of administration and the three types of contingencies yields the six-celled matrix in Figure 7–6.

Cell 1 shows a system in which both the contingency for reinforcement and the manner of its delivery are individualized. The behavior and criterion are specific to a particular student, and the reinforcement is delivered only to that student.

1. Randy, if you complete 17 of your 20 arithmetic problems correctly, then you may use the computer terminal for 10 extra minutes.
2. Randy, for each arithmetic problem you solve correctly, you will receive one token.

Cell 2 shows a system that provides the same contingency for reinforcement for all class members (standard) but individualizes the manner of delivery to each student.

1. Class, each of you who completes 17 of your 20 math problems correctly may have an extra 10 minutes at the computer terminal.
2. Class, each of you may earn one token each time you raise your hand before asking a question.

Cell 3 shows a system that sets the same contingency for reinforcement for a particular group of students, but individualizes the manner of reinforcer delivery to each group member.

1. Math Group B, if you can develop 10 original problems that require multiplication for their solution, you may all have 10 extra minutes at the computer terminal whenever you choose and with whichever program you wish.
2. Each boy in the class may earn a token for placing his tray on the cart when he has finished eating his lunch.

Cell 4 shows a system that requires each member of a group to perform a specific behavior in order for the group as a unit to be reinforced.

1. Math Group B, you are to present a 15-minute program to the class concerning the use of multiplication. Randy, you are responsible for an explanation of the basic computation procedure. Carol, you are to explain the relationship between multiplication and addition. Nicholas, you are to demonstrate how to work problems from our math workbooks. Sandy, you are to pose three original problems for the class to solve. At the end of the presentation, the four of you may use the computer terminal together for one of the game programs.
2. The following students may go to the gym to play basketball if they write an essay on basketball: Gary, your essay must have at least four sentences. Jamie, your essay must have at least six sentences. And Cory, your essay must have at least 10 sentences.

Cell 5 shows a system that sets the same contingency for reinforcement for all class members and allows each individual who has met this standard criterion to become a member of a group to be jointly reinforced.

1. Class, for homework you are to develop a problem that requires multiplication for its solution. All students who bring an appropriate problem will be allowed to go to the math lab tomorrow morning from 10:00 to 10:30.
2. All students who receive a grade of 100 on the geography test today will be exempt from geography homework tonight.

Cell 6 shows a system that sets the same contingency for reinforcement and same manner of reinforcer delivery for a group of class members.

1. Math Group B, here are 20 problems. If you get the correct answers for all 20, you may go to the math lab for 30 minutes.
2. Redbirds, if you all remember to raise your hand before speaking during our reading lesson, you may select your own books to take home this weekend.

Following a review of studies in which contingencies were applied to more than one individual at a time, Litow and Pumroy (1975) delineated three administrative systems. They categorized these as dependent, independent, and interdependent group-oriented contingency systems.

In *dependent group-oriented contingency systems,* "the same response contingencies are simultaneously in effect for all group members but are applied only to the performances of one or more selected group members. It is the performance of the selected group members that results in consequences for the whole group" (p. 342). The teacher makes reinforcement for the entire class contingent on the performance of one or more particular students. The remaining class members are dependent on the targeted student's performance for the reinforcement.

1. The opportunity for the class to have an extra session of physical education depends on Robert's and Caroline's passing Friday's spelling test.
2. The opportunity for the class to have an extra session of physical education depends on William's and Bernice's having talked out without raising their hands no more than seven times during math class.

In *independent group-oriented contingency systems,* "the same response contingencies are simultaneously in effect for all group members but are applied to performances on an individual basis. In this type of contingency system, each member's outcomes are not affected by (are independent of) the performances of the other group members" (p. 342). The teacher makes reinforcement for each class member contingent on that class member's being able to meet the contingency criterion level of performance. Those who fail to achieve the performance criterion will not receive the reinforcer.

1. The opportunity for an extra session of physical education is available to each student who passes Friday's spelling test.
2. The opportunity for an extra session of physical education is available to each student who talks out no more than three times.

In *interdependent group-oriented contingency systems,* "the same response contingencies are simultaneously in effect for all group members but are applied to a level of group performance. Consequently, in this type of contingency system, each member's outcome depends ([is] interdependent) upon a level of group performance" (p. 343).

Litow and Pumroy (1975) listed three types of group performance levels:

1. The contingency is stated so that each group member must achieve a set criterion level. Failure to achieve this criterion level by the class results in no class member receiving the reinforcer. For example, the opportunity for an extra session of physical education is contingent on each member of the class earning at least 90% on Friday's spelling test.
2. The contingency is stated such that each group member's performance meets a criterion average for the entire group. For example, the opportunity for an extra session of physical education is contingent on a class average of 90% of written work completed.
3. The contingency is stated so the class, as a group, must reach a single highest or lowest level of performance. For example, the opportunity for an extra session of physical education is contingent on the class as a whole having engaged in no more than 12 talk-outs.

By using these variations of the reinforcer delivery system, the teacher can tailor a reinforcement system to a particular classroom. Every classroom is different: Some groups, even in general education classrooms, need a formal token system; other groups may have members who need contracting or individual systems; many general education classrooms can be managed using relatively informal arrangements of social and activity reinforcers. Teachers should use the simplest, most natural system that will be effective.

Always use the simplest effective system.

Group Contingencies and Peer Mediation

Group contingencies can be an extremely effective means of managing some students' behavior. Adolescents, particularly, may find working as a group more reinforcing. There is some evidence that both typical and disabled students rank academic work with peers very highly (Lloyd, Eberhardt, & Drake, 1996; Martens, Muir, & Meller, 1988). Lloyd et al.

(1996) also found that when compared with individual study and group study with individual reinforcement, group study with group reinforcement raised mean quiz scores, decreased the range of scores, and had substantial positive effects on the scores at the low end of the distribution. Group contingencies can foster interdependence and may result in increasing cooperative behavior among students (McCarty, Griffin, Apolloni, & Shores, 1977). Kohler et al. (1995) found that group contingencies could increase supportive prompts, such as sharing and assistance, among disabled and nondisabled peers.

Group contingencies can be accomplished through peer mediation as well as teacher-managed intervention. Pigott, Fantuzzo, and Clement (1986) successfully arranged peer tutoring and group contingencies for the academic performance of underachieving fifth-grade students. The students were divided into arithmetic drill teams. Each member of the team was assigned a role. The coach reminded the team of their group goal for the number of correct answers, the strategy they had selected (for example, "work fast," "work carefully," "don't talk"), and selected backup reinforcers from a reinforcer menu. The scorekeeper counted the number of correct answers on individual team members' papers. The referee served as the reliability checker, and the team manager compared the total team score with the goal and decided if the goal was met. In all three classes the students' math performance improved and was maintained during the 12-week follow-up when students were allowed to use teams if they wished, but no reinforcement contingency was in place. Cashwell, Skinner, and Smith (2001) taught second-grade students to record and report the prosocial behaviors of their peers that occurred during the day.

Following sessions in which prosocial behavior was defined and examples generated, the students recorded on an index card all incidents of peers helping them or other classmates. A group contingency of a cumulative goal of 100 reports was set for the class in order for them to participate in an agreed-upon activity reinforcer (e.g., extra play time). Each morning the students were told of the tally from the day before and it was entered on a ladder-like bar graph. When the class met their cumulative goal, the entire class received access to the predetermined group reinforcer. This interdependent group reinforcement procedure and publicly posted progress-feedback procedure resulted in increases in the students' prosocial behaviors. In a third example, Carpenter and McKee-Higgins (1996) combined a group contingency and individual contingencies in a first-grade classroom. Over a period of months off-task behaviors had spread from one disruptive student to most of the class members. A plan was implemented combining teacher statements acknowledging appropriate behavior and redirecting inappropriate behavior with reinforcement contingencies. The students chose an activity reinforcer in the form of chalkboard class games played by the whole class for the group contingency. They chose pieces of candy for the individual contingencies. The teacher paired the edible reinforcer with positive verbal statements to shape and maintain desired student behavior and gradually eliminated its use once student behaviors began to improve. Before each activity time, students were asked to determine an acceptable level of off-task behaviors for the group. If the students reached their goal for two of three activities, they were reinforced with a chalkboard game. At the end of each activity students placed a card in a pocket on the bulletin board if they thought they personally had used on-task behaviors during the activity. The teacher and students briefly discussed the on-task behaviors and reached consensus about the student's performance. When individual students earned 10 cards, they got a piece of candy.

Peer pressure is a powerful tool in group contingencies. Indeed, it is so powerful that group contingencies should be used with caution to avoid the negative side effect of undue pressure on some members of a group (Balsam & Bondy, 1983). Consider the following example.

Ms. Montgomery Teaches Spelling

Ms. Montgomery, a fifth-grade teacher, was concerned about her students' grades on their weekly spelling test. Some students did very well, but others spelled only a few words correctly. Ms. Montgomery came up with what she felt was a brilliant plan. She divided the students into pairs—one good speller and one poor. She then announced, "The grade that I enter in my grade book on Friday will be an average of what you and your partner make on the test." She sat back and watched the students busily drilling one another and assumed that her troubles were over.

She first began to see a flaw in her plan when she observed LeeAnn chasing Barney around the playground during recess, slapping him with her speller and yelling, "Sit down, dummy, you've got to learn these words." She knew she had blown it when she got a phone call at home that night from LeeAnn's mother protesting that LeeAnn was going to fail spelling because that dumb Barney couldn't learn the words, and one from Barney's mother asking if Ms. Montgomery had any idea what might have caused Barney to spend the entire afternoon crying in his room.

Ms. Montgomery violated one of the most important rules about setting group contingencies: *Be absolutely sure each member of the group is capable of performing the target behavior.* If this rule is violated, the teacher risks subjecting students to verbal and physical abuse by their peers. It is especially important in an era when students with disabilities and students with limited English are placed in general education classes not to put them in such a position.

Teachers sometimes think these procedures work only on American children. Saigh and Umar (1983) report that they are also effective for Sudanese students.

Another important caution is being sure some member does not find it reinforcing to sabotage the group's efforts. Barrish, Saunders, and Wolf (1969) arranged a group contingency to modify disruptive out-of-seat and talking-out behavior in a class of 24 fourth-grade students. The class was divided into two teams during reading and math periods. Each instance of out-of-seat behavior or talking out by an individual team member resulted in a mark against the entire team. The team with the greatest number of marks would lose certain privileges. Although this procedure was successful, an important modification was implemented. Two members of one team consistently gained marks for their team. During one session, one of the members "emphatically announced" that he was no longer going to play the game. The teacher and the children felt the behavior of one student should not further penalize the entire team. The saboteur was removed from the team (and the group contingency) and made into a one-person team, thus applying an individual-consequences procedure until his behavior was brought under control and he could then be returned to one of the class teams. The authors stated that it appeared the expected effects of peer pressure, instead of bringing individual behavior under group control, may have served as a social reinforcer for the student's disruptive behavior.

Finally, the system must minimize the possibility of some members' performing the target behavior for others. If these factors are taken into account, group contingencies can be a very useful management device.

Schedules of Reinforcement

Schedules of reinforcement refer to patterns of timing for delivery of reinforcers. Until now, we have described the delivery of reinforcers for each occurrence of the target behavior. Delivery of reinforcement on a continuous basis is referred to as a continuous schedule of reinforcement (CRF). That is, each time the student produces the target response, she or he immediately receives a reinforcer. This schedule has a one-to-one ratio, or response: reinforcement (R: S^R).

We call a one-to-one CRF schedule one that has a *dense* ratio of reinforcement to response; there is a lot of reinforcement relative to performance and this leads to a high rate of responding. This high rate of responding results in an increase in the number of trials or opportunities for the student to perform the response (increased practice) and to receive feedback and reinforcement from the teacher. Therefore, CRF schedules are most useful when students are learning new behaviors (acquisition). A student who is learning a new behavior should receive a reinforcer for each correct response or any response that is closer to a correct response than previous ones. The process of reinforcing closer (successive) approximations to the target behavior is called shaping and will be discussed in Chapter 9. A CRF schedule may also be useful when the target behavior initially has a very low frequency. It is most effective during the early stages of any reinforcement system. There are, however, certain potential problems when using a CRF schedule.

1. A student whose behavior is on a CRF schedule may become satiated on the reinforcer, especially if a primary reinforcer is being used. Once correct responding is frequent, the continuous receipt of an edible will reduce the deprivation state and thereby reduce motivation for correct responding.
2. Continuous delivery of reinforcers may lead to accusations that teachers are leading students to expect some type of reinforcement every time they do as they are told.
3. CRF schedules are not the most efficient way to maintain a behavior following its initial acquisition or control. First, once a behavior has been acquired, or its frequency increased, by reinforcement on a CRF schedule, teachers may terminate the intervention program. The transfer from continuous reinforcement to no reinforcement results in a rapid loss of the behavior. This rapid loss of behavior when reinforcement is withheld is called **extinction** and will be discussed in Chapter 8. Second, CRF schedules may interfere with classroom routine. How long could (or would) a teacher continuously reinforce 4, 6, 8, or 30 students for raising their hands before speaking or for making the letter "a" correctly?

Using a variety of less-than-continuous schedules may solve the problems caused by using CRF schedules beyond the point of effectiveness.

Intermittent Schedules

In **intermittent schedules,** reinforcement follows some, but not all, correct or appropriate responses (Skinner, 1953). Because each occurrence of the behavior is no longer reinforced, intermittent schedules put off satiation effects. Behaviors maintained on intermittent schedules are also more resistant to extinction. Intermittent schedules require greater numbers of correct responses for reinforcement. The student learns to delay gratification and to maintain appropriate behavior for longer periods of time.

The two categories of simple intermittent schedules most often used to increase frequency of response are **ratio schedules** and **interval schedules** (Ferster & Skinner, 1957; Skinner, 1953). To increase the duration of a response, the teacher may use **response-duration schedules** (Dixon et al., 1998; Stevenson & Clayton, 1970).

Ratio schedules. Under ratio schedules, the number of times a target behavior occurs determines the timing of reinforcer delivery. Under a **fixed-ratio schedule (FR),** the student is reinforced on completion of a specified number of correct responses. A behavior on an FR3 schedule would be reinforced immediately following the occurrence of every third correct response, a contingent ratio of three correct responses to each reinforcer (R, R, R:S^R). A student who must complete eight math problems correctly to earn

"No, Mrs. Cole, a VR10 schedule does not mean 10 cookies every time Ralph gets it right."

the right to work the puzzles or who must correctly point to the blue object on eight trials before getting a bite of pretzel would be on an FR8 schedule of reinforcement.

Behaviors placed on FR schedules have particular characteristics. The student generally has a higher rate of responding than on CRF schedules because increases in rate result in increases in the frequency of reinforcement. Because the time it takes the student to perform the specified number of correct responses is not considered when delivering reinforcers, FR schedules may result in inappropriate fluencies for a given behavior. For example, to earn a reinforcer, a student may work math problems so rapidly that he makes more mistakes and his handwriting deteriorates. In addition to inappropriate fluency, FR schedules may cause another type of problem. As the schedule ratio increases (from FR2 to FR10, for example), the student will often stop responding for a period of time following delivery of the reinforcer, taking what is termed a postreinforcement pause.

The problems of fluency and postreinforcement pause are eliminated by transition to a variable-ratio schedule (VR). Under a VR schedule, the target response is reinforced on the average of a specified number of correct responses. A behavior on a VR5 schedule would be reinforced on the average of every fifth correct response. Therefore, in a teaching or observation session, the student may be reinforced following the third, eighth, fifth, and fourth correct responses.

After the occurrence of a behavior on the FR schedule has been established at the criterion level (as stated in the behavioral objective), the VR schedule will maintain a moderate and consistent rate of correct responding. The unpredictability of reinforcer delivery on a VR schedule causes the student's rate of responding to even out, with little or no postreinforcement pausing. "The probability of reinforcement at any moment remains essentially constant, and the 'student' adjusts by holding to a constant rate" (Skinner, 1953, p. 104).

Interval schedules. Under interval schedules, the occurrence of at least one correct or appropriate response plus the passage of a specific amount of time are the determinants for delivery of the reinforcer. Under a **fixed-interval schedule (FI),** the student is reinforced the first time he or she performs the target response following the elapse of a specified number of minutes or seconds. A behavior on an FI5-minute schedule may be reinforced 5 minutes after the last reinforced response. The first correct response

For more information, go to the "Web Links" module for Chapter 7 of the Companion Website.

that occurs after the 5 minutes has passed is reinforced. Following the delivery of that reinforcer, the next 5-minute cycle begins. Because a single instance of the behavior after the end of the interval is reinforced, instances that may occur before the interval ends are not reinforced. It is this phenomenon that defines a fixed-interval schedule as intermittent reinforcement.

Behaviors placed on FI schedules also have particular characteristics. Because the only requirement for reinforcement on an FI schedule is that the response occur at least once following each specified interval, behaviors occur at a relatively low rate as compared with behaviors on ratio schedules. This is especially true if and when the student becomes aware of the length of the interval and, therefore, aware of when reinforcement is possible. The length of the interval will affect the rate of responding (Skinner, 1953). If reinforcement is available every minute, responding will be more rapid than if it is available every 10 minutes. Behaviors on FI schedules also have a characteristic that parallels the postreinforcement pause of FR schedules. A student eventually realizes additional correct responses before the interval ends do not result in reinforcement. It also becomes apparent that responses immediately after reinforcement are never reinforced. The rate of responding eventually is noticeably lower (or ceases) for a short time after each reinforcement (the initial portion of the next interval). This decrease in correct responding is termed a *fixed-interval scallop,* because of the appearance of the data when plotted on a cumulative graph.

Lee and Belfiore (1997, p. 213) cautioned teachers that FI schedules may not be the best choice if the goal is to increase student time on task. If secondary English students, for example, are assigned to work on writing a paper and the teacher habitually reinforces those who are writing when the end-of-period bell rings by excusing them from homework, the teacher should expect a typical FI pattern of responding: that is, a long period of inactivity followed by a slight increase in writing rate just before the bell rings—the end of the interval. If the teacher's goal was to increase the amount of time students were engaged in writing, her goal was not met. Her program increased time on task only shortly before the bell. A similar pattern would emerge if a teacher placed students on an FI5-minute schedule when they were assigned the vocational task of assembling packets for distribution by the Red Cross. The work would proceed at low rates with only a slight increase toward the end of each interval, resulting in low productivity.

The effects on rate of responding resulting from FI schedules are eliminated by transition to a **variable-interval schedule (VI).** Under a VI schedule, the intervals are of different lengths, but their average length is consistent. A behavior on a VI5-minute schedule would have a reinforcer available for the target response on the average of every 5 minutes. As in use of VR schedules, the unpredictability levels out student performance. Behaviors under a VI schedule are performed at moderate, steadier rates across intervals without the appearance of fixed-interval scallops, because the student can no longer predict the length of the interval following delivery of a reinforcer and therefore cannot predict which response will be reinforced.

A technique for increasing the rate of responding under an interval schedule is use of a **limited hold (LH)** contingency. A limited hold restricts the time the reinforcer is available following the interval. That is, when the interval has elapsed and the next correct response will be reinforced, the reinforcer will remain available for only a limited time. In this case, students must respond quickly to earn reinforcers, whereas under a simple interval schedule, they may delay responding and still be reinforced. An F15-min/LH5-sec schedule would make a reinforcer available for 5 seconds following each 5-minute interval. For example, when a student is being taught to ride a bus, he learns that the bus comes every 15 minutes and that he must step in quickly when the doors open (naturally occuring reinforcement) for only 30 seconds (FI15 min/LH30 sec).

Response-duration schedules. Under response-duration schedules, the continuous amount of time of a target behavior is the determinant for delivery of the reinforcer. Under a fixed-response-duration schedule (FRD), the student is reinforced following completion of a specified number of minutes (or seconds) of appropriate behavior. A behavior on an FRD 10-minute schedule would be reinforced immediately at the end of each 10 minutes of continuous appropriate behavior. A student whom the teacher wants to remain seated during reading period and whom the teacher verbally praises for in-seat behavior every 10 minutes is under an FRD 10-minute schedule. Timing is restarted if the behavior stops occurring at any point during the time period.

As in FR and FI schedules, a pause following reinforcement may be seen under FRD schedules. In this case, the pause appears to be related to the length of the required time period for appropriate behavior. The longer the time period, the longer the pause. It may be expected if the time period is too long or is increased too rapidly, the behavior will either decrease or stop occurring altogether. Varying the length of the time periods required for reinforcement, using a **variable-response-duration schedule (VRD),** minimizes these problems. Under a VRD schedule, continuous appropriate behavior is reinforced on the average of a specified time period. A behavior on a VRD 10-minute schedule would be reinforced on the average of every 10 minutes.

Thinning Schedules of Reinforcement

A formal classroom reinforcement system should be viewed as a temporary structure used to produce rapid behavior change. Most teachers eventually plan to bring students' behavior under the control of more natural reinforcers. Schedule **thinning** helps decrease dependence on artificial reinforcers and helps students learn to delay gratification. In thinning, reinforcement gradually becomes available less often or, in other words, becomes contingent on greater amounts of appropriate behavior.

In the real world, the ability to delay gratification is necessary.

In thinning reinforcement schedules, the teacher moves from a dense schedule (continuous) to a sparse schedule (variable). The ratio between correct responding and reinforcement is systematically increased. The following examples illustrate this concept.

1. A student may be on a CRF schedule (1:1) for correctly identifying vocabulary words on flash cards. As the student approaches the criterion of 90% accuracy, the teacher may move the student to an FR3 schedule (R, R, R:S^R) and then to an FR6, to a VR8, and to a VR10. With each schedule shift, the teacher requires the student to perform more correct responses to receive a reinforcer.
2. A student may be on an FRD5 for sitting in her seat during the time she is to work in a workbook. Once the student has been able to meet this criterion, the teacher may move her to an FRD10, FRD20, and FRD30 schedule. With each schedule shift, the teacher is requiring the student to maintain longer periods of appropriate behavior to earn reinforcement.

Figure 7–7 presents a model of a schedule thinning. As schedule shifts are made from a continuous schedule to a fixed schedule to a variable schedule, a point is finally reached where predetermined timing of reinforcer delivery is no longer required. At this point the behavior is under the control of naturally occurring reinforcers.

Thinning schedules of reinforcement should result in

1. higher, steadier levels of responding as a result of moving to variable schedules
2. decreasing expectation of reinforcement
3. maintenance of the behavior over longer periods of time as the student becomes accustomed to delayed gratification

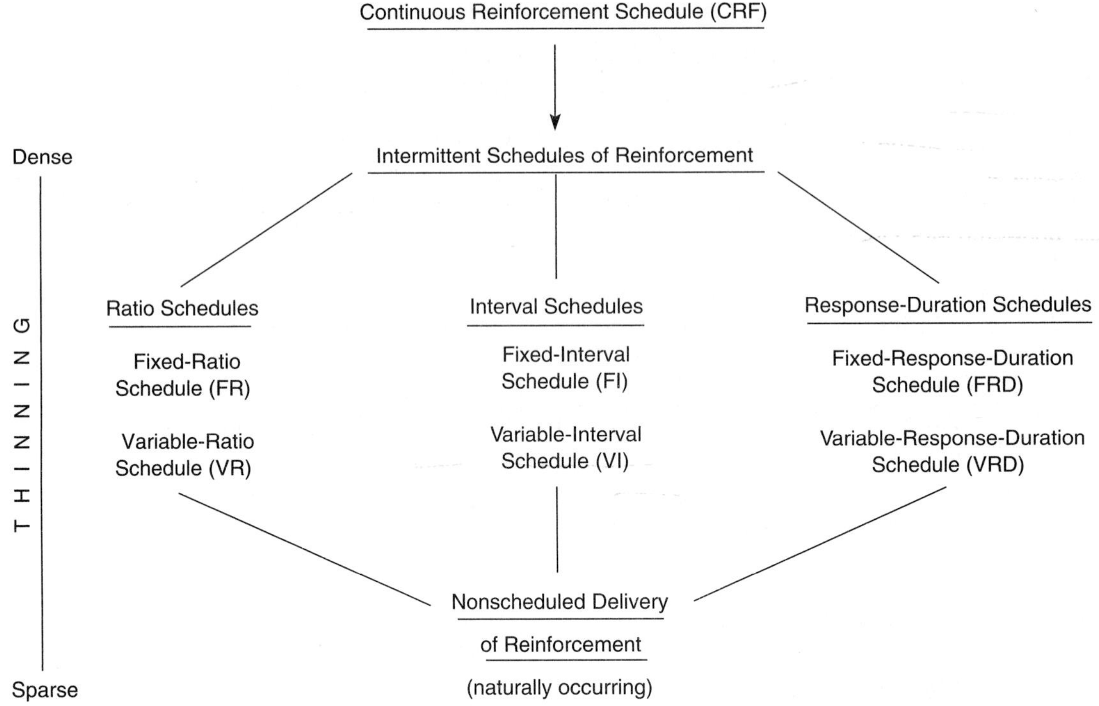

FIGURE 7–7 ***Schedules for delivery of reinforcers.***

4. removal of the teacher as a necessary behavior monitor
5. transfer of control from the reinforcer to more traditional methods, such as teacher praise and attention (O'Leary & Becker, 1967), especially if schedule thinning is done in conjunction with pairing social reinforcers with tokens or primary reinforcers
6. an increase in persistence in responding toward working for goals (reinforcers) that require greater amounts of correct responding (work)
7. the ability in educational settings to deliver reinforcers on a relatively lean schedule so that appropriate levels of student performance can be maintained in a practical way (Freeland & Noell, 1999)

One caution should be considered when thinning schedules. Behaviors are subject to an effect known as **ratio strain.** Ratio strain occurs when the schedule has been thinned so quickly that the ratio for correct responding and reinforcement is too large. In such instances, the student does not earn a reinforcer often enough to maintain responding, and the rate decreases significantly. The student may stop responding altogether. If teachers see this effect occurring, they should return to the last schedule that resulted in an acceptable rate of responding and then thin again, but in smaller schedule shifts.

It is usually best to tell the student the schedule of reinforcement delivery that is in effect. If students do not know what the rule is, they will probably make up one of their own. They will theorize and verbalize to themselves: "I must read three words correctly in order to get another token," or "I must work for 15 minutes to get another token." If this is a self-generated rule rather than one stated or confirmed by the teacher, it may not be correct (Lattal & Neef, 1996). If students work under an incorrect formulation of the rule, their unmet expectations may interfere with their learning and their trust in the teacher's contingencies.

Professor Grundy Goes to Las Vegas

As Professor Grundy prepared to leave the house one morning, Mrs. Grundy handed him a stack of envelopes.

"Oliver, dear," she asked, "would you mind putting these in the mail for me?"

"More contests?" sneered Professor Grundy. "You've entered every contest and sweepstakes and bought every raffle ticket ever offered. And how often have you won?"

"Well," answered Mrs. Grundy, "there was the pickle dish 6 years ago, the steak knives the year after that, and last year . . . "

"Minerva," scolded the Professor, "I've heard of resistance to extinction, but your behavior is being maintained on a VI3-year schedule. I'd think that was a little lean, even for you."

Imagine the professor's surprise when he received a phone call later that morning. "Oliver," bubbled Mrs. Grundy, "I've won a trip for two to Las Vegas! How's that for a reinforcer?" The very next weekend, the Grundys flew off to claim their prize. As they walked into the lobby of their hotel, they passed a bank of slot machines.

"Just one moment, my dear," said Professor Grundy. "Let me try a couple of quarters in one of these. After all, when in Las Vegas . . . "

"Humph! Just as I thought—primary and secondary reinforcers galore!"

An hour later, Mrs. Grundy checked into their room. Three hours later, she ate a solitary dinner. At midnight, she returned to the lobby where the professor was still pulling the handle on the slot machine.

"Oliver," she insisted, "you must stop this."

"Just a few more minutes, Minerva," pleaded the professor, "I know a few more quarters will do it."

Mrs. Grundy watched for a few minutes as Professor Grundy pulled the handle. Occasionally, the machine paid off with a few quarters.

"Oliver," snorted Mrs. Grundy, as she turned on her heel and stalked off, "I've heard of resistance to extinction, but your behavior is being maintained on a VR27 schedule of reinforcement. How utterly ridiculous!"

NEGATIVE REINFORCEMENT

Although positive reinforcement is usually used when the teacher's goal is to increase the rate or frequency of a target behavior, another procedure is available. *Negative reinforcement* (S^{R-}) is the contingent removal of an aversive stimulus immediately following a response that increases the future rate or probability of the response.

The first operative word in this definition is, once again, *increases,* which implies that a form of reinforcement is taking place. The second operative word is *removal.* Whereas in positive reinforcement a stimulus is presented to the student, in negative reinforcement something is removed from the student's environment. The third operative word is *contingent.* The teacher will not remove the aversive condition (negative reinforcer) unless and until the requested response is performed. If a teacher states the contingency, "Marcus, you must stay in the room and finish all your math problems before you may join the rest of the class in the gym," that teacher is using negative reinforcement. The aversive condition of being left behind in the classroom while the rest of the class goes to the gym will be removed contingent on completion of the math assignment that Marcus should have completed earlier. His rate of completing math problems will probably increase today so he can get to the gym and may well increase tomorrow so he can avoid having to stay in the room at all.

Negative reinforcement works because the student performs the behavior to escape and thereby terminate an aversive stimulus. It is not necessary, however, for an aversive stimulus to be present for negative reinforcement to work. Negative reinforcement also works when a student performs some behavior to avoid an aversive stimulus. If Marcus indeed finishes his math quickly the day after he has to stay in the room while the other students go to the gym, he avoids that negative reinforcer. Negative reinforcement often serves to establish and maintain behaviors teachers would rather their students not demonstrate. For example, many students who engage in inappropriate behaviors during lessons do so hoping to escape from what to them is an existing aversive event.

Teachers often use negative reinforcement inadvertently. When a student engages in disruptive behavior, is off task, or whines about an assignment and her teacher removes the assignment (in hopes of stopping the behavior), the student learns that the disruptive behavior will result in the termination of the assignment (aversive stimulus). The student then whines the next time an assignment is presented in order to escape again. This repeated demonstration of the disruptive behavior indicates that the inappropriate behavior has been negatively reinforced. This is a negative reinforcement cycle:

1. student is confronted with an aversive stimulus,
2. student engages in inappropriate behavior,
3. teacher removes aversive stimulus,
4. student is negatively reinforced for the inappropriate behavior,
5. next time the student is confronted by the aversive stimulus, the cycle is repeated.

In such situations, negative reinforcement may be at work for both teacher and student. Taking the task away from the student may be negatively reinforcing for the teacher because the behavior disrupting the classroom has ceased. The degree to which this cycle can contribute to the development of spectacularly inappropriate behavior is illustrated in the following true (only the names have been changed. . .) anecdote.

The Howler

Dr. Carp was an assistant professor of special education at a large university. To supplement her income and "to keep her hand in," she tutored children who were having problems in school. Many of her clients were the children of fellow faculty members who attended an elementary school where there was virtually no direct instruction and where students were expected to learn from texts and other materials and to progress through the curriculum on their own. These children usually had only minor problems and made a lot of progress in a short time with a little direct remediation and some instruction about using study skills. The tutoring was thus positively reinforcing for the children, who experienced success, for the parents, who saw a lot of improvement, and for Dr. Carp, who received many compliments and more referrals. Therefore she eagerly accepted the request from a colleague to work with his third-grade daughter, who was, in his words, "having a little trouble with math."

Sarah was duly delivered by her mother to Dr. Carp's home one afternoon the next week. Dr. Carp greeted mother and daughter at the door and suggested that Mom return in an hour. She sat Sarah at the student desk in the den and explained brightly that she and Sarah would be doing some easy problems together to let Dr. Carp get an idea about what might be causing math to be giving her "a little trouble." As the worksheet reached the surface of the desk, Sarah suddenly erupted with a howl that would have done a coyote justice. Simultaneously, tears, nasal mucous, and saliva began to flow at an incredible rate, covering Sarah, the worksheet, and the desk, but not Dr. Carp, whose rapid movement in the face of erupting children had often been negatively reinforced in the past. The dog, banished to the kitchen for the duration of tutoring, matched the howl, ululation for ululation, and Dr. Carp's own children, banished upstairs, appeared in the doorway to check on her welfare. Muttering the words "a little trouble with math, my eye," Dr. Carp hushed the dog, rebanished the children, fetched a wastebasket, paper towels and disinfectant spray from the kitchen and waited for Sarah to stop howling. She then politely explained that she could not evaluate damp worksheets and that Sarah could start with a fresh one as soon as she had disposed of the wet one and cleaned herself and the desk up with the disinfectant. Sarah, a little startled, complied, but when the fresh worksheet reached the surface of the desk, she repeated her earlier performance. The cycle was repeated seven times.

By then the hour was almost over, and Mom's car appeared through the window. Sarah jumped up and announced she was leaving. Dr. Carp replied, "No, you'll need to work these first three problems before you go; I'll go ask your mom to wait."

"She won't make me," shrieked Sarah, throwing herself on the floor and resuming the howl. "You're so mean, she won't make me stay. She loves me."

Dr. Carp walked to the car and explained, over the audible howls from inside, that Sarah was not quite finished and that if Mom could not wait, Dr. Carp would be happy to bring Sarah home when she was done. Mom burst into tears, her loud wails immediately echoed by the infant in the car seat behind her.

"She hates math so," Mom howled. "Her teachers just let her do puzzles instead. Listen to her"—as if Dr. Carp had a choice—"I don't want her to be upset. I'll just take her home and calm her down, and we'll try again next week."

"Mrs. Howler," said Dr. Carp gently, "she's your daughter and it's your choice, but if you take her home now, I'll have to ask you not to bring her back."

Leaving Mom and the baby howling in the car, Dr. Carp returned to the desk and said cheerfully, "Mom's going to wait. Let's look at this first one—you tell me what you would do first."

One huge hiccup later, Sarah completed the first three problems and joined her mother and sibling in the car. Over the next few months there were increasingly infrequent bouts of howling as demands were increased, and Sarah reached grade level in math and performed adequately at school. Dr. Carp did not hear from Sarah's dad (she's always wondered if he ever knew what the "little trouble with math" really was) until years later when he stopped her in the parking lot and said that the family was taking a weekend trip to Sarah's very selective college, where she was about to be inducted into an academic honor society and was to receive a degree cum laude in a few weeks. In engineering. Honest. That's the kind of positive reinforcement that keeps teachers teaching.

Students may view various tasks as aversive; Sarah obviously held this view about math. As with reinforcers, what is aversive is individual to a student. In general, tasks or activities may be seen as aversive if they are too difficult, too boring and repetitive, or too embarrassing. A student given a math worksheet with problems above her current ability level, or one who did not do the homework, or one who has not benefited from effective instruction will find the task too difficult and engage in inappropriate off-task behaviors to escape the assignment. A student given yet another age-inappropriate pegboard to fill time may find the task too boring and find something much more entertaining to do with the board. Asking a poor reader to read aloud in front of the class, or a poor math student to do a problem on the board, or a student with poor coordination to climb the rope in physical education class may result in that student's trying to escape the task to avoid the ensuing embarrassment. A variety of other events may be aversive to students, such as a reading task for a student with a reading disability, being touched for a child with autism, an incorrect wheelchair position for a child with a physical disability, failure to introduce the items in her immediate environment to a student with a visual impairment, receiving excessive praise from the teacher in front of his classmates for a middle school student, or dissecting a frog for a squeamish biology student. Factors like these have been observed in special education and general education settings (Cooper et al., 1992; McComas, Hoch, Paone, & El-Roy, 2000, Moore & Edwards, 2003; Romaniuk et al., 2002; Smith, Iwata, Goh, & Shore, 1995). An additional factor influencing behavior maintained by negative reinforcement is teacher attention resulting from attempts to escape (Moore & Edwards, 2002; Moore, Edwards, Wilczynski, & Olmi, 2001). This is both negative reinforcement, because the student has gotten to stop doing the aversive task, and positive reinforcement, because the teacher's behavior is often quite entertaining.

Instead of engaging in inappropriate behavior, students can be taught appropriate means of accessing the negative reinforcement resulting from escaping a task. In place of an inappropriate behavior that results in escape, students can be taught a more standard and appropriate means of communicating the need for assistance or for a break. This is known as functional communication training (Carr, & Durand, 1985; Durand, 1999; Durand & Carr, 1992). For example, Durand and Carr (1991) worked with students whose challenging behaviors (e.g., tantrums; hitting, slapping, and pinching themselves and others) were resulting in escape from academic demands. These students were being negatively reinforced, and therefore, their inappropriate behaviors were being strengthened. In place of the inappropriate behaviors, the students were taught to use an assistance-seeking phrase (for example, "Help me," I don't understand) to provide escape and therefore negative reinforcement. As the new behaviors were used and resulted in reinforcement, the students no longer needed to use the inappropriate behaviors to achieve escape and negative reinforcement.

Students can also perceive teachers' behavior as aversive. Teacher behaviors such as nagging, unpleasant vocal tones, threatening facial expressions, sarcasm, or outright hostility may occasion student escape and avoidance. Despite this, some teachers use these behaviors to set the general tone of classroom management. Every teacher makes a decision to run a classroom in such a way that students behave appropriately to avoid unpleasantness from the teacher or in such a way that they behave appropriately because the teacher provides many opportunities for positive reinforcement. Harrison, Gunter, Reed, and Lee (1996) suggested that the way in which teachers provide instructions to students may also be aversive. They suggested that asking a student with behavior disorders to perform tasks without sufficient information is associated with higher rates of disruptive behavior. If the student does not understand the instruction, he may choose to be disruptive and thereby escape further instruction rather than risk embarrassment due to responding incorrectly.

Cipani (1995, p. 37) suggested that a teacher may be able to determine whether disruptive behavior is being negatively reinforced by answering the following questions:

1. Does the behavior result in the termination or postponement of specific teacher requests, instructional demands, or instructional tasks, activities, or materials (even temporarily)?
2. Is the student not competent with regard to the specific instructions, tasks, teacher requests, or materials identified in Question 1?
3. Does the problem behavior occur more frequently under those specific content areas, tasks, materials, or teacher requests identified in Questions 1 and 2 (in contrast to other content areas or tasks where the student is more capable academically)?

   These situations, like satiation and deprivation described earlier, may serve as setting events that interfere with the effects of planned reinforcement strategies.

Using negative reinforcement has some disadvantages. Tantrums, attempts to flee, or destruction of materials are examples of escape and avoidance behaviors. They may occur particularly if the individual is unskilled at subtler or socially acceptable forms of escape (Harrison et al., 1996; Iwata, 1987). Apparently these behaviors are especially likely to happen when difficult demands or tasks are placed on students with limited behavioral repertoires. Aggressive or self-injurious behavior may be an avenue of escape from the demands because their intensity or topography can be alarming to a teacher

Negative reinforcement can be used as a teaching strategy. Alberto, Troutman, and Briggs (1983) employed negative reinforcement for initial response conditioning of a student with profound disabilities. Following an exhaustive reinforcer sampling, the only response made by the student was to pull his hand away from an ice cube. During instruction he was taught to turn toward a source of blowing air (a fan) by simultaneously guiding his head and removing ice from the palm of his hand. He was negatively reinforced by the removal of the ice for performing the desired behavior. Steege et al. (1990) determined that escape from grooming activities (negative reinforcement) was maintaining the self-injurious biting of two young children. When the children bit themselves, efforts to comb their hair and perform other grooming were abandoned. Intervention involved substituting a more appropriate means of indicating the desire for an activity to cease. Brief escape from grooming was made contingent upon a behavior incompatible with self-biting—pressing a microswitch to activate a prerecorded message of "stop." Iwata (1987) made the point that it is often difficult to distinguish between negative reinforcement and positive reinforcement. To make the distinction, the teacher must consider the sequence of events and the existing environmental conditions. In some cases the real functional relationship may be very difficult to determine.

Negative reinforcement is often used in conjunction with behavior programs based on the results of a functional assessment. As discussed in Chapter 6, students may engage in attempts to escape and avoid demanding tasks, social interactions with adults or peers, unwanted attention, or a variety of classroom activities and events. The controlled and contingent use of opportunities to escape from, or terminate, an event may be managed by the teacher to decrease interruptive escape attempts. Escape is allowed based on a contingency set by the teacher rather than as a reaction to the student's inappropriate behavior. In this way negative reinforcement is used to establish a new more appropriate behavior. Another component of such an intervention is simultaneous positive reinforcement of an alternative means of achieving escape. The teacher may provide the student with an opportunity to escape following an appropriate, more typical request for a break (e.g., use of functional communication training), gradually increasing the amount of work required before a break is allowed, and eventually allowing breaks only after tasks have been completed.

The use of aversive stimuli in the classroom should be minimized. As we will discuss in greater detail in Chapter 8, such stimuli may lead to aggressive reactions. The child who is confined to his room until he gets "every last doll and dinosaur off the floor" is likely to kick the unfortunate cat who comes to investigate the clattering and banging. Escape and avoidance behavior may not be limited to the aversive stimulus but may result in a student's escaping (running out of the room) or avoiding the entire school setting (playing truant). Mild aversive stimuli may sometimes be justified, but positive reinforcement is the procedure of choice for increasing or maintaining behavior. For a discussion of the theoretical and applied concerns relating to negative reinforcement, see Iwata (1987).

Aversive stimuli may lead to aggressive reactions.

Natural Reinforcement

Reinforcement is a naturally occurring process. A structured reinforcement system in the classroom has at least four purposes. The first is simply to manage behavior. Second, for some students, the imposition of "artificial" high-intensity reinforcing stimuli provides highly visible connections between their behavior and its consequences. This allows them to learn a cause-and-effect relationship. Third, a classroom reinforcement system provides in microcosm a learning laboratory for how reinforcement works in the everyday world. The fourth purpose is to teach students to value a more general and natural pool of reinforcers. Students should be taught to be motivated by reinforcers that naturally occur in a situation; that is, those that will ordinarily result from their behavior in their school, home, and community settings.

Whether a reinforcer is natural depends on the situation, the setting, and the ages of the individuals. Almost any reinforcer can be natural. Most students in general education classes earn privileges for appropriate academic and social behavior—from being a lunch monitor in kindergarten to being excused from final exams in high school. Adults earn privileges as well—from a special parking place for the custodial employee of the month to access to the executive washroom. Activities are also often earned naturally, from an extra 5 minutes of recess for a hard-working kindergarten class to a trip to Bermuda for the salesperson of the year. Everyone works for tokens—gold stars for kindergartners and big bucks for some successful professionals (fortunately most teachers like gold stars). Finally, when everyone remembers his or her manners, social reinforcers abound in the natural environment. Reinforcers that are natural outcomes for a specific behavior are more effective than unrelated reinforcers (Litt & Schreibman, 1981; Williams, Koegel, & Egel, 1981). In addition, behavior reinforced naturally has an increased probability of being maintained and generalized (Haring, Roger, Lee, Breen, & Gaylord-Ross, 1986; Stokes & Baer, 1977). As students learn to anticipate and accept natural reinforcers, they are exposed to naturally occurring schedules of reinforcement. They learn that behavior in some situations results in immediate and frequent reinforcement, while in others it results in delayed and infrequent reinforcement.

To enhance your overall understanding of the information presented in this chapter, go to the "Supplemental Lecture Notes" module for Chapter 7 of the Companion Website.

Professor Grundy Teaches About Reinforcement

Professor Grundy's graduate class had turned in their observation assignments, muttering and grumbling all the while. After collecting the papers, Professor Grundy launched into his lecture on reinforcement. One of the students came up to the podium at the end of the lecture. Beaming, she said, "It's about time, Professor. I took this course to learn how to manage a classroom. For weeks, all we've talked about is history, theory, and all that technical junk. It was worth living through that just to hear tonight's lecture. I was going to drop the course, but now I won't miss a week."

"Why," asked Professor Grundy, lighting his pipe to hide the grin on his face, "do you think I wait to talk about reinforcement until after we're done with all that technical junk?"

Summary

This chapter described procedures to increase or maintain appropriate academic or social behaviors. Positive reinforcement, the preferred approach, is the presentation of a stimulus contingent on appropriate behavior. Positive reinforcers may be either primary or secondary, and the best reinforcers are natural. Negative reinforcement is the removal of an aversive stimulus contingent on the performance of the target behavior. We suggested specific ways in which students' behavior can be changed using these procedures. We hope we have also positively reinforced your reading behavior and you are now prepared to continue.

Key Terms

positive reinforcement
positive reinforcer
reinforcer sampling
primary reinforcers
satiation
deprivation state
secondary reinforcers
conditioned reinforcers
pairing
Premack principle
generalized conditioned reinforcer
backup reinforcers
social reinforcers
contracting
schedules of reinforcement
extinction
intermittent schedules
ratio schedules
interval schedules
response-duration schedules
fixed-ratio schedule (FR)
fixed-interval schedule (FI)
variable-interval schedule (VI)
limited hold (LH)
variable-response-duration schedule (VRD)
thinning
ratio strain

Discussion Questions

The following scenarios depict implementations of reinforcement strategy gone wrong. Discuss why you believe the teacher's plan is not working and what you might do to fix the situation.

1. Questions, questions, questions, etc.

   Jack and Ryan call out "all the time"—when they have answers to questions, when they have questions, when they have information they want to share with Ms. Andrews or their classmates. Ms. Andrews has been told they have "poor impulse control." She decides to reinforce them for raising their hands. Each time either of them raises his hand, she immediately calls on him and provides verbal praise. Within two days both boys have reduced their call-outs to less than one a day. Two days later Ms. Andrews is satisfied that the boys have learned to raise their hands, so she goes back to her usual procedure of randomly calling on students who have their hands up. Two days after that, the two boys' calling out is back to its original rate.

2. From minor annoyances large disturbances can grow.

   Ms. Arnold is becoming concerned with Todd's behavior. Though a minor annoyance, it is disturbing and appears to be happening more frequently. Not wanting to make a big production, she decides to place the behavior on extinction—planned ignoring. She knows she must not make a show of ignoring the behavior, so she merely makes a notation on the blackboard and shakes her head each time the student does it. To her further annoyance, the behavior continues to escalate.

3. Help from the principal.

   Ms. Taber is at her wits' end with Tracy and his aggressive verbal behavior. She has tried scolding, moving his seat, and giving him extra assignments. There has been no decrease in the frequency of his behavior. She decides she needs help. Each time the student engages in the behavior, she sends him to the principal's office to discuss his behavior. If the principal has someone with her, Tracy sits outside the office where everyone who passes talks to Tracy about his inappropriate behavior. Tracy continues his verbal aggression in the classroom.

4. Endless laughs.

   Ms. Hughes is at her wits' end with Oran and his clowning around. She has tried scolding, moving his seat, subtracting points, and giving him extra assignments. There has been no decrease in the frequency of his behavior. She decides to ignore the behavior and put it on extinction, understanding and expecting that the behavior will increase before it decreases. Oran continues the behavior; it continues to be disruptive and makes the other students laugh and talk back to him. She studiously ignores each occurrence and continues lessons and group work through the behavior. But after two weeks without any decrease in the behavior, she is giving up again.

5. Boy, he is a hard worker.

   Troy is a hard worker and took to the point system from day one. He looked over the available back-up reinforcers and immediately identified two he wanted. He needed 115 points for the two items; he earned 145. On Friday he cashed in for item one and "banked" his tokens for item two for the next Friday. During the second week Troy seemed to be in a world of his own rather than attending to math and science.

6. This is how it's going to work.

   Mr. Kana wants to start a token economy. He provides the basic information to his class: "We are going to start our economy by earning points for two general behaviors expected of all of you, and one behavior personal to each of you. On day one you can earn two points each time you raise your hand and lose one point every time you call out. The second behavior is work completion. You can earn 5 points per completed assignment. You will lose 1 point per assignment component not completed within time limits. Points lost will increase by one each day through Friday. Each personal behavior will be developed through a contract between you and me." The students were each given a written copy of the rules. Hand raising and task completion increased the first day, then showed a decreasing trend for the remainder of the week.

7. Good citizenship.

   Ms. Stafford has confirmed that her students Ali, Ben, Manny, and LaToya think cheesy fish crackers are great. She decides to use them to reinforce the eight basic "good citizen" behaviors posted in her classroom on a CRF schedule. From when she starts on Wednesday through the following Monday, the students are perfect good citizens. By Thursday, however, the chaos rate is on the rise.

8. Fishing for reinforcers

   Ms. Gonzales talked to Ms. Stafford during the early days of her cheesy fish program. By show of hands she confirms that her students think the crackers are great too. She decides to use them to reinforce hand-raising behavior during their whole class lesson each day and during small group reading. Her data indicate that she is having overall success with her management plan; however, Kyle and Rudy's data indicated they continued calling out as much as ever.

9. Sharing best practice.

   At a staff development workshop a teacher shared the idea of using stickers as tokens. Ms. Briggs decided to use seasonal sticker tokens with her third-grade class. She began using stickers for in-seat behavior during group instruction sessions and center times. The students were enthusiastic, and the roaming around the room so prevalent in her class was greatly reduced. After the weekend, however, the students were still trading in stickers but the roaming behavior was back.

10. A fraction of the skill.

    Ms. Heller introduced multiplying fractions to Eric and Anu. She understood that when teaching a new behavior, she needed to provide a reinforcer every time the behavior was performed correctly. Within nine sessions the students were accurately adding fractions with like denominators. Ms Lowell then stopped the continuous reinforcement in order to allow internal reinforcers and self-esteem to take the place of the external reinforcer. When she did the next weekly maintenance check, the students were no longer adding accurately.

11. No thank you.

    Ivan is reviewing the catalogue of back-up reinforcers that are available within the token economy at Pioneer High School. After reviewing pages containing pictures of boy-band posters, various monitorships, fast-food restaurant coupons, art materials, etc., he put his Game Boy back in his pocket and went to sleep on his desk.

Chapter 8

Arranging Consequences That Decrease Behavior

Did you know that . . .

- You can use positive reinforcement to get students to stop doing inappropriate things?
- It is easier to give than to implement advice to "ignore it and it will go away"?
- Students who are sent out in the hall often thoroughly enjoy themselves?
- The teacher who told you to "chew that gum until you are sick of it" was using a form of behavior modification?

Chapter Outline

When teachers complain about a student's misbehavior, other teachers usually offer sympathy and advice. Too often their suggestions emphasize punishment; by which they mean applying an aversive stimulus following the inappropriate behavior—for example, a rap on the back of the head, a reading of the riot act, or a prolonged visit to the principal where the student "will learn how this school is run." Using punishment can become a reflex, because it often simply and immediately stops the behavior—it works! Using punishment negatively reinforces teachers. Unfortunately that reinforcement may make teachers lose sight of the side effects or reactions that may accompany the use of punishment. This chapter describes a broad range of behaviorally based alternatives to punishment that will have the same effect of reducing the occurrence of inappropriate and challenging behavior. These alternatives are presented as a sequenced hierarchy. The sequence moves from the most positive approaches for behavior reduction (those that use reinforcement strategies) to the most aversive approaches. Although the use of aversive consequences has a conceptual place in such a hierarchy, due to ethical and professional considerations and awareness of the undesirable effects that aversive stimuli produce, these approaches are rarely, if ever, appropriate in the school setting. Indeed, in our hierarchy three levels of options are presented before aversive consequences are even mentioned. These alternatives, with their individual constraints, are presented as viable alternatives to aversive procedures, because they too have the desired effect of reducing the occurrence of inappropriate and challenging behavior.

More information may be found at the "Web Links" module for Chapter 8 of the Companion Website.

Certain principles should guide the selection of a procedure for behavior reduction. The first is the principle of the least intrusive alternative. This principle suggests that when determining which intervention to choose, an important consideration is the intervention's level of intrusiveness. When one is considering behavior reduction, the least intrusive intervention is the least aversive or the lowest on the hierarchy. The teacher should determine, based on a hierarchy of procedures from the least intrusive to the most intrusive (most positive to most aversive), an effective procedure that is in the positive range of available choices. For example, if a Level 1 procedure as shown in Figure 8–1 will accomplish the behavior change, it is neither necessary nor ethical to use a Level IV procedure. In addition, Gast and Wolery (1987) suggested that "if the choice of treatments is between procedures that are equally effective, then the least aversive (intrusive) should be selected. If the choice is between a less intrusive but in-

Procedure of choice	Level	Strategies
	Level I	**Reinforcement-based strategies**
		a. Differential reinforcement of lower rates of behavior (DRL) b. Differential reinforcement of other behavior (DRO) c. Differential reinforcement of incompatible behavior (DRI) d. Differential reinforcement of alternative behavior (DRA) e. Noncontingent reinforcement
	Level II	**Extinction (terminating reinforcement)**
	Level III	**Removal of desirable stimuli**
		a. Response-cost procedures b. Time-out procedures
	Level IV	**Presentation of aversive stimuli**
		a. Unconditioned aversive stimuli b. Conditioned aversive stimuli c. Overcorrection procedures

FIGURE 8–1 ***Procedural alternatives for behavior reduction.***

effective procedure and more aversive but effective procedure, then the effective procedure should be selected" (p. 194). Given the extensive published research and reported success with Level 1 reinforcement-based procedures during the past decade, the use of aversive procedures in schools has little support.

The second principle is that, when possible, selection of an intervention should be based on the identified function of the challenging behavior. Before the development of the procedures described in Chapter 6 that allow the identification of function, the selection of interventions was often "hit or miss." An intervention would work for many but not all students or would reduce some but not all behaviors. The behavior would eventually return or be replaced by one equally bad or even worse. This erratic success occurred because sometimes interventions selected without considering the function of the behavior, but only its form and topography, would accidentally match the function of the behavior (Carr, 1977; Iwata, Dorsey, Slifer, Bauman, & Richman, 1994). In addition, a significant component of this principle is that concurrent instruction of a functionally equivalent alternative behavior must occur. The student must learn an appropriate replacement behavior that will result in the same reinforcement as that resulting from the inappropriate behavior to be eliminated. With the recent introduction of pretreatment functional assessment/analysis, it is more likely that educators and researchers will use reinforcement-based treatments for serious behavior problems rather than punishment-based treatments or reinforcement-based treatments with a punishment component. (Pelios, Morren, Tesch, & Axelrod, 1999).

Several requirements must be met in implementing procedures for behavior reduction. The first requirement is that movement along the hierarchy must be data based. That is, before deciding that a currently employed procedure is not effective and that an alternative, possibly more intrusive, procedure should be used, the data collected during the intervention must substantiate the ineffectiveness of the procedure. The second requirement is that a point of consultation and permission must be established. At some point, the teacher must consult with her supervisor, the student's parent, or a behavior management committee to review the progress of the current intervention and agree on a further plan of action. Such a plan may include conducting a functional assessment or functional analysis and developing a behavior support plan as described in Chapter 6.

Procedural Alternatives for Behavior Reduction

The hierarchy outlined in Figure 8–1 has four levels of options for reducing inappropriate behaviors. Level I is the first choice to consider, whereas Level IV is, in most instances, the choice of last resort.

Level I offers five strategies using differential reinforcement: differential reinforcement of low rates of behavior, differential reinforcement of other behaviors, differential reinforcement of incompatiable behaviors, differential reinforcement of alternative behaviors, and noncontingent reinforcement. These are options of first choice because, by selecting them, the teacher is employing a positive (reinforcement) approach to behavior reduction.

Level II refers to extinction procedures. Using extinction means withholding or no longer delivering the reinforcers that maintain a behavior.

Level III contains the first set of options using what will be defined as a punishing consequence. However, these options—such as response-cost and time-out procedures—still do not require the application of an aversive stimulus. The administration of these options may be seen as a mirror image of negative reinforcement. In the use of negative reinforcement, an aversive stimulus is contingently removed in order to increase a behavior. Level III options require removal or denial of a desirable stimulus in order to decrease a behavior.

The options in Level IV of the hierarchy are to be selected after unsuccessful attempts at the first three levels have been documented or when the continuation of some behavior presents an imminent danger to the student or to others. The options at this level include the application of unconditioned or conditioned aversive stimuli or the use of an overcorrection procedure. Selecting one of these options is not the prerogative of a single individual. Administration of these options may be seen as the mirror image of a reinforcement procedure.

Positive reinforcement: Stimulus is contingently *presented* to *increase* a behavior.

Presentation of aversive stimuli: *Aversive* stimulus is *presented* to *decrease* a behavior.

Level I: Reinforcement-Based Strategies

In Chapter 7, reinforcement was defined as the presentation or removal of a stimulus contingent upon performance of behavior (response) that increases or maintains the future rate or probability of that behavior. A reinforcing stimulus can also be manipulated to decrease behavior. Reinforcement-based procedures to decrease behavior either contingently reinforce behavior on a differential basis or use reinforcement in a noncontingent manner. Five such reinforcement-based procedures are included in Level 1.

Differential Reinforcement of Lower Rates of Behavior

DRL schedules may be used when shaping behavior (see Chapter 9).

Differential reinforcement of lower rates of behavior (DRL) is the application of a specific schedule of reinforcement, used to decrease the rate of behaviors that, while tolerable or even desirable in low rates, are inappropriate when they occur too often or too rapidly. For example, contributing to a class discussion is a desirable behavior; dominating a class discussion is not. Doing math problems is appropriate; doing them so rapidly that careless errors occur is not. Burping occasionally, while hardly elegant, is tolerable; burping 25 times an hour is neither.

In the initial laboratory version of DRL, a reinforcer was delivered contingent on a response, provided that a minimum period of time had elapsed since the previous reinforced response. To decrease the total number of occurrences within a total time period, it is necessary only to increase the minimum period of time that must pass before another response will be reinforced. This format is referred to as *interresponse-time DRL* or *spaced-responding DRL*. This procedure was used by Singh, Dawson, and Manning (1981) to reduce stereotypic behaviors (rocking, mouthing, complex movements) of three adolescent girls who were profoundly retarded. The time required between occurrences was increased from 12 seconds to 180 seconds. The average percent of intervals of occurrence for the three girls went from 92.5% to 13%.

The DRL format more commonly used in the classroom provides for reinforcement delivery "when the number of responses in a specified period of time is less than, or equal to, a prescribed limit" (Deitz & Repp, 1973, p. 457). This DRL has two variations: full-session DRL and interval DRL.

Full-session DRL compares the total number of responses in an entire session with a preset criterion. A reinforcer is delivered if occurrences are at or below that criterion. For example, baseline data indicate that Jenny interrupts on the average of nine times per 30-minute lesson. Although not wanting to extinguish this behavior completely, the teacher wants it reduced to no more than two such interruptions per lesson. Jenny is told that she is allowed two interruptions, and if she keeps her interruptions to that level, she will be awarded an extra token for good behavior that day. If she keeps interruptions at or below two occurrences, the reinforcer is delivered. Interval DRL involves dividing a session into smaller intervals (for example, dividing the 30-minute session into six 5-minute intervals) and delivering reinforcement at the end of each interval in which responding is below or equal to a specified limit. This format may be used if the teacher believes that a more gradual approach will be more successful. If the maximum number of interruptions that can be tolerated is two per session, that number is initially allowed during each 5-minute interval. Once the behavior has stabilized, the length of the interval is increased, so that the student may interrupt, for example, only twice per 10-minute interval if she is to earn a reinforcer. The contingency might then be that to earn a reinforcer the student may interrupt twice in each of two 15-minute intervals. Finally, the student would be allowed only two interruptions during the full 30-minute session. These forms of the DRL procedure have been used to reduce a variety of behaviors, including talking out (Deitz & Repp, 1974; Hall et al., 1971); out-of-seat behaviors (Harris & Herman, 1973); self-stimulatory behavior (Rotholz & Luce, 1983); and eating rate (Lennox, Miltenberger, & Donnelly, 1987; Wright & Vollmer, 2002).

Recall the changing criterion design discussed in Chapter 5.

Finally, DRL may be arranged in a manner analogous to using a changing criterion design. If baseline levels of the target behavior are high, the teacher may successively lower DRL limits to bring the rate into an acceptable range. For example, if a student's baseline rate of out-of-seat behavior averaged 12 occurrences, he would be told that if during a lesson he got out of his seat no more than nine times, he would be allowed to select the day's free time activity. Once he had stabilized at 9 occurrences, the contingency would be changed to no more than six times, then no more than three times. When using this approach, the teacher must bear in mind when she tells a student he can do something nine times, he will (and she must congratulate him!).

In their initial experiments in the use of DRL, Deitz and Repp (1973) employed both criterion-setting strategies. In the first, an 11-year-old boy with moderate retardation had a baseline of talk-outs within a 50-minute session that averaged 5.7, with a range of 4 to 10 talk-outs per session. He was told that if he talked out three or fewer times in a 50-minute session, he would be allowed 5 minutes of free playtime at the end of the day. During this intervention, he averaged 0.93 talk-outs per session with a range of 0 to 2.

In the second experiment, 10 students with moderate retardation had an average of 32.7 talk-outs with a range of 10 to 45. The students were told that if the group talked out five or fewer times in a session, each person would get two pieces of candy. This intervention yielded an average of 3.13 talk-outs per session with a range of 1 to 6. In the third experiment, 15 high school girls in a regular class demonstrated a baseline level of 6.6 instances of inappropriate social discussion during a 50-minute class period. The intervention was planned in four phases: six or fewer inappropriate discussions, three or fewer, two or fewer, and then a zero rate in order to earn a free period on Friday.

As a guide in the use of DRL scheduling, Repp and Deitz (1979, pp. 223–224) suggested the following:

1. Baseline must be recorded to determine the average number of responses per full session or session intervals. This average occurrence may then serve as the initial DRL limit.
2. Reasonably spaced criteria should be established when using successively decreasing DRL limits to avoid too frequent reinforcement and ratio strain, and so that the program can be faded out.
3. A decision must be made as to whether or not to provide feedback to the student concerning the cumulative number of responses during the session.

See Chapter 7 for a discussion of the merits of reinforcement strategies.

The primary advantage of DRL scheduling is its peculiar ability to reduce the occurrence of the behavior through delivery of reinforcement. It, therefore, offers the same advantages of reinforcement in general. In addition, the approach is progressive, because it allows the student to adjust, in reasonable increments, to successively lower rates rather than making a drastic behavioral change. The limits chosen should be within the student's abilities and acceptable to the teacher. DRL is not a rapid means of changing behavior and, therefore, is inappropriate for use with violent or dangerous behavior.

Ms. Keel Teaches Stacy to Be Self-Confident

Stacy was a student in Ms. Keel's second-grade class. Stacy had excellent academic skills but raised her hand constantly to ask, "Is this right?" or to say, "I can't do this." If Ms. Keel had not been a behaviorist, she would have said that Stacy lacked self-confidence.

One morning, Ms. Keel called Stacy to her desk. She remembered that Stacy always volunteered to clean the blackboards after lunch. She told Stacy that she wanted her to learn to do her work herself.

"If you really need help," she assured Stacy, "I'll help you. But I think three times in one morning is enough. If you raise your hand for help three times or fewer this morning, you may clean the blackboards when we get back from lunch."

Stacy agreed to try. Within a few days, she was raising her hand only once or twice during the morning. Ms. Keel praised her enthusiastically for being so independent. The teacher noticed that Stacy often made comments like "I did this all by myself, Ms. Keel. I didn't need help once." If Ms. Keel had not been a behaviorist, she would have said that Stacy was developing self-confidence.

Differential Reinforcement of Other Behaviors

When using the procedure called **differential reinforcement of other behaviors (DRO),** a reinforcing stimulus is delivered contingent on the target behavior's not being emitted for a specified period of time (Reynolds, 1961). Whereas DRL reinforces gradual behavior reduction, DRO reinforces only zero occurrences. In fact, DRO is sometimes referred to as *differential reinforcement of zero rates of behavior* or *differential reinforcement of the omission of behavior.* In Chapter 7, reinforcement was defined as the delivery of a reinforcing stimulus contingent on the occurrence of a desired behavior. DRO involves the presentation of a reinforcing stimulus contingent on the *nonoccurrence* of a behavior.

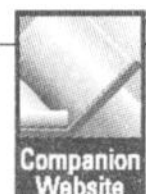

To further your understanding of this topic, go to the "Web Links" module for Chapter 8 of the Companion Website.

DRO may have at least three administrative variations, similar to those used with DRL procedures:

1. Reinforcement contingent on the nonoccurrence of a behavior throughout a specified time period. For example, reinforcement is delivered only if talking out does not occur for an entire 40-minute period (DRO 40 minutes). The student is told, "If you do not talk out during this reading period (40 minutes long), then you may be one of the captains in the gym this afternoon." If the student meets this contingency, she receives the reinforcer. Scheduling reinforcement delivery only after no instances of the behavior occur during an entire session is called full-session DRO.
2. Reinforcement contingent on the nonoccurrence of a behavior within a time period that has been divided into smaller intervals. This procedure is used when a more gradual reduction of inappropriate behavior is more practical or realistic. In some cases of very high rates of inappropriate behavior, implementation of a full-session DRO would mean that the student would never earn a reinforcer. A 40-minute session may be divided into 5-minute intervals and reinforcement delivered at the end of each 5-minute interval in which the student has not talked out. This breaking down of the time period provides the student an increased number of opportunities for reinforcement, an increased amount of feedback, and an increased number of opportunities for success. The intervals may be of equal or different lengths (that is, on the average of every 5 minutes, as is done in variable-interval scheduling). Once the student can control his behavior for these smaller intervals, the teacher increases the length of the intervals. For example, the schedule of eight 5-minute intervals is changed to four 10-minute intervals. This process continues to the point that the contingency can be met for the entire 40 minutes, the equivalent of a full-session DRO. If the teacher is having difficulty establishing the initial length of intervals, Deitz and Repp (1983) suggested using the average length of the target behavior (interresponse interval). For example, if during 100 minutes of baseline (five 20-minute sessions), Luke got out of his chair 25 times, the teacher would begin with intervals of 4 minutes or less (100 divided by 25). As an alternative, the initial interval may be set equal to the average amount of time between behaviors during baseline sessions (Repp, Felce, & Barton, 1991).
3. DRO may be used with permanent-product data. For example, the teacher may draw a happy face on every paper that does not contain doodles.

Three important factors should be considered before a teacher implements a DRO procedure. First, a "pure" DRO requires that reinforcement be delivered if the student does not perform the target behavior, no matter what else he does. In effect, the student may be positively reinforced for performing a wide range of inappropriate behaviors, as long as he does not perform the target behavior. Some students will take advantage of this loophole. They may not walk around the room but may instead throw spitballs, something they have never done before. Technically, they would still be entitled to reinforcers. For practical classroom management this cannot be allowed to happen. For this reason, DRO procedures are sometimes used in conjunction with other reduction procedures for such interfering behaviors. Sometimes, also, occurrences of the target behavior may be followed by some consequence rather than ignored as in the traditional procedure (Vollmer & Iwata, 1992).

Second, DRO reinforces the absence of a behavior. The student earns the reinforcer if the target behavior does not occur during the specified time period. For students who do not have a large repertoire of appropriate behaviors, the teacher may be creating a behavior vacuum. If a behavior is not identified to replace the targeted one, the student may soon fill that vacuum with the only behavior he knows—the one the teacher tried to reduce. It is practical and ethical to identify an appropriate behavior to replace the inappropriate one and to positively reinforce its occurrence.

Third, the effectiveness of a DRO procedure may depend on the reinforcer selected (Repp et al., 1991). The stimulus used to reinforce the student for not engaging in the inappropriate behavior must be of at least equal strength or motivating value as that which is currently maintaining the behavior (Cowdery, Iwata, & Pace, 1990). A student who is entertaining his peers with hilarious comments during math class is being reinforced by their appreciative laughter. Offering him 5 minutes to play computer games if he refrains from wisecracking for 50 minutes may not be a sufficiently powerful competing reinforcer.

DRO has been used with a variety of behaviors, such as self-injurious behaviors (Lindberg, Iwata, Kahng, & DeLeon, 1999; Patel, Carr, Kim, Robles, & Eastridge, 2000; Ringdahl, Vollmer, Marcus, & Roane, 1997); disruptive behaviors (Reese, Sherman, & Sheldon, 1998); aggression (Borrero, Vollmer, & Wright, 2002; Hegel & Ferguson, 2000); stereotypic behaviors (Haring & Kennedy, 1990); fingernail biting (Long, Miltenberger, Ellingson, & Ott, 1999); and off-task and out-of-seat behaviors (Repp, Barton, & Brulle, 1983).

Repp et al. (1974) used DRO procedures with three individuals with severe retardation. The individuals were a 12-year-old girl whose target behavior was flapping her lips with her fingers, a 22-year-old woman whose target behavior was rocking, and a 23-year-old man whose target behavior was waving a hand in front of his eyes. A kitchen timer was set to a prescheduled number of minutes (the DRO interval). The student who did not emit the target stereotypic response during the interval was hugged and praised by the teacher when the bell rang. If the target stereotypic behavior occurred, the teacher said "no" and reset the timer. Very short intervals (40 seconds) were used initially. As the rates of behavior decreased, the intervals lengthened. All the participants showed greatly decreased rates of stereotypic behaviors. Higgins, Williams, and McLaughlin (2001) used DRO to reduce the disruptive classroom behaviors of a 10-year-old third grader with learning disabilities. The student's targeted behaviors included high rates of out of seat, talking out without permission, and poor seat posture (e.g., legs splayed out, tucked underneath body, lying on the desk). During the 20-minute sessions the student earned a check mark if, at the end of each minute, appropriate behavior occurred instead of the specific targeted behaviors. By the end of the case study, three check marks could be earned per period for the absence of all three target behaviors. A piece of paper was taped to the corner of the student's desk to record check marks, enabling him to receive feedback on his behavior. At the end of the session, the check marks were counted and divided by two to determine the number of minutes available to use backup reinforces such as math worksheets, computer time, leisure reading, and playing academic games (p. 102).

As a guide to the use of DRO scheduling, Repp and Deitz (1979, pp. 222–223) and Deitz and Repp (1983) suggested:

1. Baseline must be recorded not only to measure the inappropriate behavior, but also to schedule the DRO procedure properly. Because the size of the initial DRO interval can be crucial, it should be based on data rather than set arbitrarily. From the baseline an average interresponse time (time between responses) should be determined, and a slightly smaller interval should be designated as the initial DRO interval.

2. Criteria must be established for increasing the length of the DRO interval. The basic idea is
   (a) to start at a small enough interval that the student can earn more reinforcers for not responding than he could earn for responding, and
   (b) to lengthen that interval over time. The decision to lengthen should be based on the success of the student at each interval length.
3. Possible occurrence of the undesirable behavior necessitates two additional decisions:
   (a) whether to reset the DRO interval following a response occurrence or merely to wait for the next scheduled interval, and
   (b) whether to deliver a consequence for a response occurrence in any other way or just to ignore it.
4. Reinforcement should not be delivered immediately following a grossly inappropriate behavior even if the DRO interval has expired without the target response having occurred.

To increase your understanding of differential reinforcement, go to the "Activities" module for Chapter 8 of the Companion Website.

Clarence Learns Not to Hit People

Clarence was a student in Mr. Byrd's resource class. He often hit other students in the class, usually because someone had touched some possession of his. Having observed that Clarence hit someone an average of 12 times during the 90-minute resource period, for an average interresponse time of 7.5 minutes, Mr. Byrd chose an interval of 7 minutes. He told Clarence that he could earn a card worth 5 minutes to work on an art project for each 7 minutes that elapsed without hitting. When Clarence hit someone, Mr. Byrd reset the timer. He did this rather than simply not delivering the reinforcer at the end of the interval, because he was afraid that once Clarence had "blown it," he would engage in a veritable orgy of hitting until the end of the interval.

Within a few days, Clarence's hitting rate was much lower, so Mr. Byrd lengthened the intervals to 8 minutes, then 10, then 15. Soon he was able to reinforce the absence of hitting at the end of the period and still maintain a zero rate.

Differential Reinforcement of Alternative Behavior and Incompatible Behavior

An excellent way to prevent creating a behavior vacuum is the use of **differential reinforcement of alternative behavior (DRA).** With this procedure, an inappropriate or challenging behavior is replaced by a behavior considered (by student, parent, teacher) as more appropriate, positive, or standard. DRA refers to reinforcing an alternative behavior, the performance of which decreases the likelihood that the inappropriate behavior will be performed. Selection of an alternative behavior is usually based on physical incompatibility or functional equivalence.

Differential reinforcement of incompatible behavior (DRI) is a DRA procedure that reinforces a behavior that is topographically incompatible with the behavior targeted for reduction. For example, if out-of-seat behavior is targeted for reduction, in-seat behavior is reinforced because these two behaviors cannot occur simultaneously (similarly, running and walking, normal voice and screaming, on task and off task). Such mutually exclusive behaviors are chosen so that an appropriate response makes it physically impossible for the student to engage in the inappropriate behavior. This allows for increasing the strength or rate of the appropriate behavior and decreasing the probability of the inappropriate behavior. Reinforcing a child's play with a particular toy, and her play skills in general, decreases the opportunity and probability of her engaging in stereotypic hand movements (Favell, 1973). When her hands are appropriately occupied, she cannot engage in the inappropriate behavior.

Differential reinforcement of incompatible behavior has been used to modify behaviors including: pica (Donnelly & Olczak, 1990); stereotypic behaviors (Favell, 1973); SIB (Day, Rea, Schussler, Larsen, & Johnson, 1988; Tarpley & Schroeder, 1979); off-task behavior (Lewis & Sugai, 1996; Symons, McDonald, & Wehby, 1998); and out-of-seat behavior (Friman, 1990). Ayllon and Roberts (1974) used DRI to bring the disruptive behaviors (i.e., out of seat, talking, hitting) of five fifth-grade boys under control by reinforcing their academic performance. Points for daily and weekly exchange were made contingent on the percent of correct answers in their reading workbooks during daily 15-minute sessions. This time period was just long enough for the boys to complete the assignment correctly (thus gaining access to the highly desirable backup reinforcers) if they did not waste time engaging in disruptive behavior. During baseline, the mean percentages for both disruptive behavior and academic accuracy were in the 40 to 50% range. After intervention, disruptive behavior had decreased to an average of 5% of the intervals and average academic accuracy had increased to 85%.

As a guide to the use of DRI scheduling, Repp and Deitz (1979, p. 224) suggested:

1. A behavior that is incompatible to the undesirable behavior must be chosen. If there is no appropriate behavior that is opposite to the inappropriate behavior, then a behavior that is beneficial to the student should be selected and should be reinforced.
2. Baseline should be recorded to determine: (a) how often the inappropriate behavior occurs, and (b) how often the chosen incompatible behavior occurs.
3. The schedule of reinforcement must be determined. In addition, a program for carefully thinning the schedule should be written so that the program can be phased out and the student's behaviors can come under control of natural contingencies in the environment.

Often a mutually exclusive behavior is not readily identifiable. This fact, plus the research on interventions based on functional assessment and functional analysis, has resulted in greater emphasis and use of DRA in which selection of the replacement behavior is based on the functional equivalence of the behavior, rather than physical incompatibility of the form of the behavior as is the case with DRI. In this broader approach to DRA, the alternative behavior and the inappropriate behavior are topographically dissimilar, but not necessarily physically incompatible.

With DRA, each time the student attempts the inappropriate behavior, one of two procedures is implemented: (1) performance of the inappropriate behavior is ignored (placed on extinction) and the alternative behavior is reinforced; or (2) performance of the inappropriate behavior is interrupted and redirected (with physical guidance if necessary) to performance of the alternative behavior, which is then reinforced (Piazza, Moes, & Fisher, 1996; Vollmer & Iwata, 1992). Initially the alternative behavior is placed on a CRF schedule of reinforcement, with reinforcers delivered as quickly as the original behavior occasioned them. For example, each time Anne begins to talk out to get the teacher's attention, she is redirected to raise her hand, receives praise for raising her hand, and receives the natural reinforcement of being called upon by the teacher. In some instances DRA is combined with a mild punisher (e.g., a mild reprimand or the loss of a token) for the continued use of the inappropriate behavior (Luiselli, 1980).

With older, high-functioning, or nondisabled students, DRA often involves instruction and reinforcement of more appropriate social skills (Umbreit, 1995; Vollmer, Borrero, Lalli, & Dency, 1999), work or school routine behaviors such as compliance, direction following, and task engagement (Beare, Severson, & Brandt, 2004; Blum, Mauk, McComas, & Mace, 1996; Flood, Wilder, Flood, & Masuda, 2002; Piazza et al., 1996; Umbreit, 1995; Vollmer, Roane, Ringdahl, & Marcus, 1999), or self-management skills (Gumpel & Shlomit, 2000). Frequently, for young students with significant communication disorders or severe disabilities, challenging behaviors have proven to be an effective, but inappropriate, means of communication. Therefore, the use of DRA involves instruction and reinforcement of a more standard means of communication. This is known as functional communication training (FCT) (Carr & Durand, 1985; Durand, 1990; Durand & Carr, 1991). For example, three boys who received assistance with tasks or social attention by engaging in self-injurious and aggressive behaviors were taught instead to solicit attention with verbal language, using phrases such as: "I don't understand," "Help me," and "Am I doing good work" (Durand & Carr, 1991). Four students, ages 5 to 13 years old, who also engaged in self-injurious and aggressive behaviors to gain attention or to achieve escape were taught to: manually sign "more," "play," "I want to play," "done"; or point to or touch cards that said "break, please" or "done" (Brown et al., 2000). Durand (1999) successfully implemented an FCT procedure using an alternative communication device. Five students, ages 3 to 15 years old, who engaged in various self-injurious and aggressive behaviors (face slapping, head banging, screaming, throwing objects, hitting) were taught instead to communicate with an AAC device. The Introtalker by Prentke Romich was programmed for each student based on the identified function of the challenging behavior. For the two students for whom escape from difficult tasks was the function of their behavior, the Introtalker was programmed to say "I need help." For the two students for whom gaining a tangible was the function of their behavior, the device was programmed to say "I want more please." The device was programmed to say "Would you help me with this" for the student whose challenging behavior served to gain the attention of others.

A DRA procedure in which selection of an alternative replacement behavior is based on function is referred to as *functional equivalency training* (Horner & Day, 1991). Such training takes a long-term, educational view of behavior change, rather than a short-term, crisis-management view for immediate reduction of behavior (Carr, Robinson, & Palumbo, 1990). Certain criteria should be considered when selecting an alternative behavior (Brown, et al., 2000; Carr, et al., 1990; DeLeon, Fisher, Herman, & Crosland, 2000; Durand, Berotti, & Weiner, 1993; Friman & Poling, 1995; Horner & Day, 1991; Horner, Sprague, O'Brien, & Heathfield, 1990; Lim, Browder, & Sigafoos, 1998; O'Neill et al., 1997; Richman, Wacker, & Winborn, 2000; Shore, Iwata, DeLeon, Kahng, & Smith, 1997). These criteria include:

1. The alternative behavior serves the same function as the behavior being replaced.
2. The student, parent, and general public view the alternative behavior as more appropriate, often partly because the new behavior is viewed as a more standard behavior that achieves the same function as the behavior it replaces.
3. The alternative behavior requires equal or less physical effort and complexity.
4. The alternative behavior results in the same type, quantity, and intensity of reinforcer. If the student learns that the new behavior does not result in equivalent reinforcement, he will revert to the inappropriate behavior that has resulted in reinforcement in the past.
5. The alternative behavior is reinforced on the same schedule (frequency and consistency). If the alternative behavior of raising a hand does not result in gaining teacher attention with the same consistency as the old behavior, the student will revert to screaming in order to gain attention.

6. There is no greater delay between performance of the alternative behavior and its reinforcement than there was with the original behavior. The efficiency of replacement is enhanced if a behavior already in the student's repertoire is selected. If the student can already perform the behavior, learning a new behavior is not required at the same time as learning to replace an old behavior. Finding a behavior already in the student's repertoire is difficult with a student whose existing repertoire of appropriate behaviors is limited. Shaping an existing basic motor or social behavior into a more complex behavior may be necessary.
7. The alternative behavior is eventually maintained by natural reinforcers.

Figure 8–2 summarizes and compares various options for differential reinforcement.

Noncontingent Reinforcement

Another procedure that uses reinforcers to decrease behavior is **noncontingent reinforcement (NCR).** NCR provides the student the reinforcer that is maintaining an inappropriate behavior independently of his performance of the behavior (Carr et al.,

	Purpose	Formats	Management	Provides for reinforcement of alternative behavior	Objective
DRL[1]	Reduce behavior to acceptable level	Full session Interval Changing criterion Spaced responding	Focus on reducing number of occurrences	No	Tom will talk out no more than 3 times in 40 minutes.
DRO[2]	Reduce behavior to zero occurrences	Full session Interval Permanent product	Focus on increasing time of nonoccurrence	No	Tom will have no occurrence of talking out in a 40-minute period.
DRI[3] DRA[4]	Reinforce a functional alternative behavior	Concurrent reduction and strengthening programming	Focus on developing functional alternative behavior	Yes	Tom will press a buzzer to indicate he wants the attention of an adult instead of engaging in yelling and face slapping.

[1]Differential reinforcement of lower rates of behavior
[2]Differential reinforcement of other behaviors (or of zero rates of behavior, or of omission of behavior)
[3]Differential reinforcement of incompatible behavior
[4]Differential reinforcement of alternative behavior

FIGURE 8–2 ***Summary of differential reinforcement procedures.***

2000; Tucker, Sigafoos, & Bushnell, 1998). The student receives the reinforcer not when she performs the inappropriate behavior but at preselected intervals of time. This serves to disassociate the reinforcer from the behavior and results in the behavior's decrease. While NCR is in place, the inappropriate behavior is essentially on extinction. The inappropriate behavior is ignored (not reinforced), and there is systematic delivery of reinforcers independent of performance of the inappropriate behavior. For example, if calling out is being maintained by attention from the teacher, the teacher ignores calling out but provides lots of attention throughout the class session at preselected time intervals, whatever the student is doing. If throwing tantrums is being maintained by escape from a task, the teacher ignores the tantrums but allows the student to escape the task (take a break) at intervals throughout the class.

No behavior is systematically strengthened as a result of NCR because the reinforcers are delivered at intervals regardless of what the student is doing. It is for this reason that some argue that the term NCR is not appropriate because, technically, reinforcement must result in the strengthening of a behavior (Poling & Normand, 1999; Vollmer, 1999). The procedure, however, is effective and the term communicates its implementation. Because no alternative behavior is developed using NCR, that procedure and DRA have often been used together (Tucker et al., 1998).

During NCR reinforcer, delivery is time scheduled. Access to positive reinforcement (teacher attention, for example) or negative reinforcement (a break from a task, for example) may be delivered on a fixed time schedule (FT of every 5 minutes, for example), or a variable time schedule (VT of on the average of every 5 minutes). NCR is typically administered initially on a dense, often continuous, schedule. Once the inappropriate behavior is reduced to acceptable levels, the schedule is thinned. This parallels schedule thinning as described in Chapter 7.

A potential unintended effect of NCR is adventitious, or accidental, reinforcement of the inappropriate behavior that it is the goal of the intervention to decrease (Vollmer, Ringdahl, Roane, & Marcus, 1997). It is possible for a reinforcer to be delivered right after the inappropriate behavior occurs, just as it has in the past, "One would surmise that aberrant behavior that occurs at a high frequency would be more susceptible to adventitious reinforcement than a lower frequency behavior. Using the same logic, a denser NCR schedule would be more likely to produce adventitious reinforcement than a leaner schedule" (Carr et al., 2000, p. 386).

NCR has become one of the most reported function-based interventions for challenging behavior (Carr et al., 2000). NCR has been used successfully to reduce levels of inappropriate speech (Carr & Britton, 1999); stereotypy (Luiselli, 1994; Roane, Kelly, & Fisher, 2003; Sprague, Holland, & Thomas, 1997); rumination (Wilder, Draper, Williams, & Higbee, 1997); pica (Piazza et al., 1998); aggression and disruption (Britton, Carr, Kellum, Dozier, & Weil, 2000; Coleman & Holmes, 1998; Lalli, Casey, & Kates, 1997); and self-injurious behavior (DeLeon, Anders, Catler, & Neidert, 2000; Mace, Shapiro, & Mace, 1998). Vollmer, Marcus, and Ringdahl (1995) used an NCR strategy to reduce the self-injurious behavior (head hitting and punching) of an 18-year-old student with profound mental retardation. The hypothesis resulting from functional analysis was that SIB was maintained by negative reinforcement (escape). During intervention, the student was allowed to take a 30-second break during a task of a 10-minute walk on "an FT schedule in which the student's behavior did not influence the frequency of escape. SIB no longer directly produced escape, but breaks were not delayed or withheld when SIB occurred" (p. 19). Over the course of intervention, the NCR escape schedule was faded from continuous escape to FT 10 min. The fading was conducted across sessions by adding 10 seconds to the task when the SIB rate was at or below 0.3 responses per minute during any given session. Once at an FT schedule of 1 min, the progression of schedule change was from: 1 min, to 1.5 min, to 2.0 min, to 2.5 min, to 3.0 min, to 4.0 min, to 5.0 min, and finally to 10 min. The student essentially went from a walk that was all breaks to a 10-minute walk with a break at the end.

Jones, Drew, and Weber (2000) used an NCR strategy to reduce disruptive classroom behaviors of an 8-year-old general education student with ADHD. A functional analysis confirmed that Sam's talking out and out-of-seat behaviors were maintained by peer attention following each incident. The teacher arranged for Sam and a peer to share a desk during the time for independent work on math. The two students' interactions were uninterrupted, providing Sam with ongoing attention. Sam's disruptive behaviors were reduced from a mean of 86% of independent work time to a mean of 37%.

Ms. Elliott in the Community

Toni and Jake's mothers asked that trips to stores be included in their community-based instruction. When they took their children to stores, the children would take items from shelves and throw them on the floor or themselves drop to the floor and scream. During her first trip with the two students, Ms. Elliott found that this indeed occurred. She understood the parents' frustration and embarrassment. As alternative behaviors, Ms. Elliott decided to reinforce Toni for holding onto the shopping cart while pushing it down the aisles and to reinforce Jake for holding a basket on his lap as he sat in his wheelchair. As she came to various items, she would give the students opportunities to identify the correct item from two she held up, asking them to choose the "red" box or the "bottle" or the "little one" and then guiding them into placing the items in either the cart or the basket. Once the students' behavior was consistently appropriate, Toni's mother was invited to come on a shopping trip to see how the procedure was done. Jake's mother, who was unavailable during school hours, received a videotape made during one of the shopping trips.

Level II: Extinction

For additional discussion on these procedures, go to the "Web Links" module for Chapter 8 of the Companion Website.

In contrast to Level I, which focuses on providing reinforcement, Level II, **extinction,** reduces behavior by withholding or terminating the positive reinforcer that maintains an inappropriate target behavior. This abrupt withdrawal results in the cessation or extinction of behavior. When the behavior being maintained is an appropriate one, preventing extinction is the goal. Many inappropriate behaviors, however, are also maintained by positive reinforcement. A parent who gives children cookies or candy when they cry may be positively reinforcing crying. If the cookies are withdrawn, crying should diminish.

Extinction is most often used in the classroom to decrease behaviors that are maintained by teacher attention. Teachers often pay attention to students who are behaving inappropriately, and many students find such attention positively reinforcing. This may be true even if the attention takes the form of criticism, correction, or threats. Some students' behavior may be positively reinforced by even such extreme measures as yelling and spanking.

It is often difficult for teachers to determine when their attention is positively reinforcing inappropriate behavior. Thus, a teacher may find it helpful to have someone else observe the teacher-student interaction. Once the relationship between the teacher's attention and the student's behavior is verified by this method, extinction in the classroom most often takes the form of ignoring inappropriate behavior. The teacher withholds the previously given positive reinforcer (attention), and the inappropriate behavior extinguishes or dies out.

Extinction procedures have been used to decrease the occurrence of a variety of problem behaviors, including disruptive behavior (Arndorfer, Miltenberger, Woster,

Rortvedt, & Gaffaney, 1994; Richman, Wacker, Asmus, Casey, & Andelman, 1999; Zimmerman & Zimmerman, 1962); obscene language (Salend & Meddaugh, 1985); tantrums (Carr & Newsom, 1985); sleep disturbance (France & Hudson, 1990); nonstudy behavior (Hall, Lund, & Jackson, 1968); and aggressive, self-injurious behavior and noncompliance (Iwata, Pace, Kalsher, Cowdery, & Cataldo, 1990; O'Reilly, Lancioni, & Taylor, 1999; Zarcone, Iwata, Mazaleski, & Smith, 1994). Extinction has also been used to increase the variety of types of responses within a class of behavior, such as increasing the variability in communicative gestures of individuals with severe retardation (Duker & van Lent, 1991) and the variety of responses used by young children during toy play (Lalli, Zanolli, & Wohn, 1994).

Extinction is most often used in conjunction with reinforcing other more appropriate behaviors. Combining procedures this way appears to speed extinction. When extinction is used independently, "there is little or no evidence of constructive learning. What is learned is that a certain behavior no longer provides an expected reward; the net effect is a reduction in the repertoire of behavior" (Gilbert, 1975, p. 28). If attention is given to appropriate behavior, this indicates to the student that the teacher's attention (S^{R+}) is still available, but that it is selectively available. It is not the student who is being ignored, just the inappropriate behavior.

"Just ignore it and it will go away. He's only doing it for attention." This statement is one of the most common suggestions given to teachers. In truth, extinction is much easier to discuss than to implement. It *will* go away, all right, but not necessarily rapidly or smoothly. Whatever "it" is, the teacher who decides to implement an extinction procedure should give careful consideration to the following points.

Delayed Reaction

Problems with extinction.

The effects of extinction are not usually immediate. The extinction procedure may take considerable time to produce reduction in behavior. Once reinforcement is withheld, behavior continues for an indeterminate amount of time (Ducharme & Van Houten, 1994; O'Reilly et al., 1999; Skinner, 1953). This characteristic, known as *resistance to extinction,* is particularly marked when behaviors have been maintained on intermittent reinforcement schedules. The student continues to seek the reinforcer that has eventually resulted in the past. In an initial extinction phase to reduce aggressive behavior toward peers in a preschooler, Pinkston et al. (1973) found it took 8 days to reduce the rate of behavior from 28% of total peer interactions to 6% of interactions. In a study of the effects of self-injurious behavior, Lovaas and Simmons (1969) reported that "John hit himself almost 9,000 times before he quit" (p. 146). Not all self-injurious behavior, however, is resistant to extinction (Lerman & Iwata, 1996). Iwata et al. (1990) found, after performing a functional analysis, that extinction reduced self-injurious escape behavior by the fifth 15-minute session.

Increased Rate

The teacher should expect an increase in the rate, duration, or intensity of the behavior before significant reduction occurs (Watson, 1967). It is going to get worse, in other words, before it gets better. This is often referred to as a burst of the behavior (Lerman, Iwata, & Wallace, 1999; Zarcone et al., 1993). In comments on one subject, Lovaas and Simmons (1969) stated, "Rick eventually did stop hitting himself under this arrangement (i.e., extinction) but the reduction in self-destruction was not immediate, and even took a turn for the worse when the extinction was first initiated" (p. 146). About John and

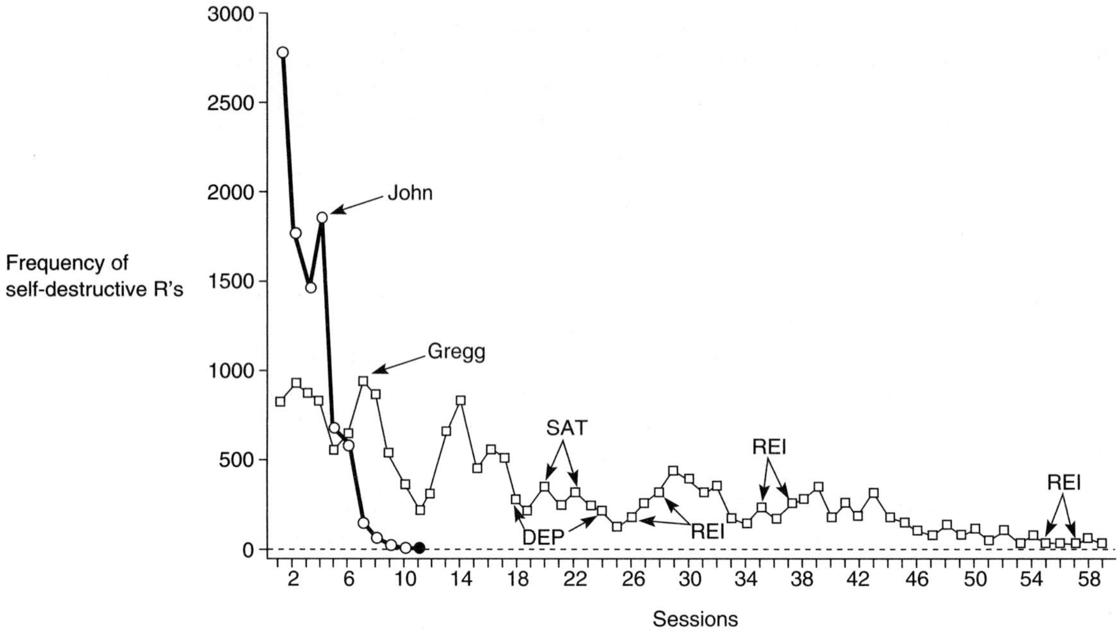

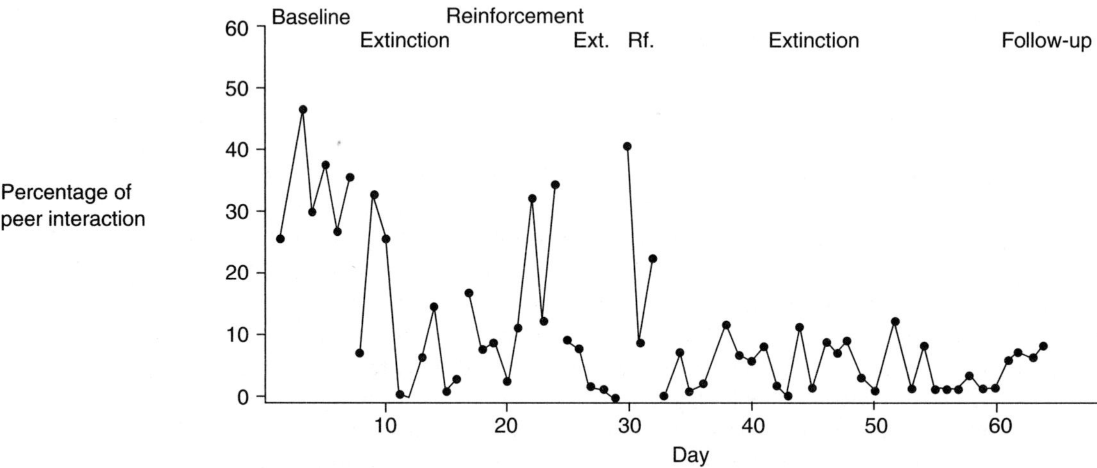

FIGURE 8–3 ***Data from studies using extinction procedures for behavior reduction.***

Note (top): From "Manipulation of self-destruction in three retarded children," by O. I. Lovaas & J. Q. Simmons, *Journal of Applied Behavior Analysis,* 1969. Copyright 1969 by the Society for the Experimental Analysis of Behavior, Inc. Reprinted by permission.

Note (bottom): From "Independent control of a preschool child's aggression and peer interaction by contingent teacher attention," by E. M. Pinkston, N. M. Reese, J. M. LeBlanc, & D. M. Baer, *Journal of Applied Behavior Analysis,* 1973. Copyright 1973 by the Society for the Experimental Analysis of Behavior, Inc. Reprinted by permission.

Gregg, two other subjects, they acknowledged "the self-destructive behavior showed a very gradual drop over time, being particularly vicious in the early stages of extinction" (p. 147). Figure 8–3 displays this phenomenon in graphic data from Lovaas and Simmons (1969) and Pinkston et al. (1973).

A common pattern is that of the teacher who decides to ignore some inappropriate behavior such as calling out. When a student finds a previously reinforced response is no longer effective, the student then begins to call out louder and faster. If, after a period of time, the teacher says, "Oh, all right, Ward, what do you want?", the teacher has reinforced the behavior at its new level of intensity and may find that it remains at this level. Once an extinction procedure has been implemented, the teacher absolutely must continue ignoring whatever escalation of the behavior occurs.

Controlling Attention

It is ridiculous to say to a student, "Can't you see I'm ignoring you?" Of course, what the student *can* see is that the teacher is *not* ignoring her. Even nonverbal indications that the teacher is aware of the misbehavior may be sufficient to prevent extinction. The teacher who stands rigidly with teeth and fists clenched is communicating continued attention to the student's behavior. It takes a great deal of practice to hit just the right note. We have found that it helps to have something else to do.

1. Become *very* involved with another student—perhaps praising the absence of the target behavior in her—"I like the way you raised your hand, Lou. That's the *right* way to get my attention."
2. Read something or write busily.
3. Recite epic poetry subvocally.
4. Carry a worry rock or beads.
5. Stand outside the classroom door and kick the wall for a minute.

Extinction-Induced Aggression

The last suggestion in the preceding section is related to another phenomenon that may occur: extinction-induced aggression by the student in the early stages of extinction procedures (Azrin, Hutchinson, & Hake, 1966; Lerman & Iwata, 1996; Lerman, et al., 1999). In search of the previously available reinforcer, the student says, in effect, "You only think you can ignore me. Watch this trick." The pattern of escalation and aggression that occurs in the early stages of extinction is illustrated by a typical interaction between a thirsty customer and a defective vending machine. The customer puts four quarters in the machine (a previously reinforced response) and pushes the appropriate button. When no reinforcer is forthcoming, the customer pushes the button again . . . and again . . . and faster . . . and harder. Before her response is extinguished, she is likely to deliver a sharp rap or swift kick to the unreinforcing machine or even to try to shake the soda out of it. Indeed, it has been reported that the abuse of soda vending machines has resulted in a considerable number of injuries. The machines fall forward onto the thirsty aggressor when rocked or tilted (Byrne, 1989; Spitz & Spitz, 1990).

Spontaneous Recovery

Teachers may also expect the possible, temporary reappearance of an extinguished behavior. This phenomenon, known as spontaneous recovery (Lerman & Iwata, 1996; Lerman, Kelley, Van Camp, & Roane, 1999; Skinner, 1953), may occur after the behavior has been extinguished for some time. The student tries once again to see if the extinction rule is still in effect or if it is in effect with all the teachers with whom she comes in contact. Ignoring this reemergence of the behavior can quickly terminate it. Failure to ignore it, however, may result in rapid relearning on the part of the student.

Imitation or Reinforcement by Others

The behavior the teacher is ignoring may spread to other class members. If other students see a particular student getting away with misbehavior and not being punished for it, they may imitate the behavior (Bandura, 1965). This may serve to reinforce the behavior. As a result, a number of students may perform the misbehavior, instead of just one, making the behavior that much harder to ignore. The use of an extinction procedure relies on the teacher's ability to terminate the reinforcing stimulus for the inappropriate behavior. This is one of the hardest aspects of conducting an extinction procedure. In a classroom setting, the best bet is that the behavior is being reinforced by attention from the teacher (yelling) or from the classmates (laughing). To determine the reinforcing stimulus, the teacher may have to test several suspicions systematically, attempting to eliminate one potential reinforcer at a time.

It is frequently difficult to control the reinforcing consequences delivered by peers. Successful approaches to this problem have been used by Patterson (1965), who reinforced peers for withholding attention when the target student was out of seat, talking, or hitting others; by Solomon and Wahler (1973), who selected five high-status peers and trained them in the use of extinction and reinforcement of appropriate behavior; and by Pinkston et al. (1973), who attended to the peer being aggressed against while the aggressor was ignored.

Limited Generalizability

Although extinction is effective, it appears to have limited generalizability. That is, the behavior may occur just as frequently in settings where extinction is not in effect. Liberman, Teigen, Patterson, and Baker (1973) reported no generalization of treatment to routine interchanges with staff on the ward. Lovaas and Simmons (1969) reported that behavior in other settings is unaffected when extinction is used only in one setting. Programming extinction may be required in all necessary environmental settings (Ducharme & Van Houten, 1994).

Benoit and Mayer (1974) suggested six considerations before making a decision to use extinction, stated here as questions to guide teachers' decision making:

Questions to ask yourself before implementing an extinction procedure.

1. Can the behavior be tolerated temporarily based on its topography (for example, is it aggressive?) and on its current rate of occurrence?
2. Can an increase in the behavior be tolerated?
3. Is the behavior likely to be imitated?
4. Are the reinforcers known?
5. Can reinforcement be withheld?
6. Have alternative behaviors been identified for reinforcement?

A social consequence, such as teacher attention, is not always the maintaining consequence of a behavior. "Some persons do things not for attention or praise, but simply because it feels good or is fun to do" (Rincover, 1981, p. 1). In such instances sensory consequences rather than teacher consequences may be maintaining the behavior. This seems to be particularly true of certain stereotypic or self-injurious behaviors. A student's stereotypic hand flapping may be maintained by the visual input resulting from the behavior. A student's self-injurious self-scratching may be maintained by the tactile input resulting from the behavior. When sensory consequences can be identified as the reinforcer of a behavior, the form of extinction known as *sensory extinction* may be employed (Rincover, 1981).

Sensory extinction attempts to remove the naturally occurring sensory consequence of the behavior. Hand flapping and head hitting have been reduced by placing weights on the student's arm, thereby making the behavior more work, reducing its frequency, and fading the reinforcer (Hanley, Piazza, Keeney, Blackeley-Smith, & Worsdell, 1998; Rincover, 1981; Van Houten, 1993). Self-scratching has been reduced by covering the area being scratched with heavy petroleum jelly, thereby eliminating the tactile consequence of the behavior. Face scratching has been reduced by placing thin rubber gloves on the individual's hands (Rincover & Devany, 1982). Hand-mouthing has been reduced by requiring students to wear mitts or soft arm restraints (Irvin, Thompson, Turner, & Williams, 1998; Mazaleski, Iwata, Rodgers, Vollmer, & Zarcone, 1994; Zhou, Goff, & Iwata; 2000). Two children's finger sucking was reduced by placing adhesive bandages on their fingers (Ellingson et al., 2000). A padded helmet has been used to reduce face slapping (Kuhn, DeLeon, Fisher, & Wilke, 1999) and head banging (Rincover & Devany, 1982). Goggles have been used to block the sensory reinforcement of eye poking (Lalli, Livezey & Kates, 1996), as has using one's hand to block an individual's hand as it approached the eyes (Smith, Russo, & Le, 1999). Difficulties may arise using sensory extinction with precision if identification of the reinforcing sensory consequence is unclear, and if there is difficulty eliminating "all the sensory consequences inherent in many commonly occurring stereotypic responses, such as rocking or clapping" (Aiken & Salzberg, 1984, p. 298).

Mr. Medlock Extinguishes Arguing

Judy was a student in Mr. Medlock's fourth-grade class. Whenever Mr. Medlock told Judy to do something, she argued with him. Mr. Medlock had found himself having conversations like this:

"Judy, get to work."

"I am working, Mr. Medlock."

"No you're not, Judy. You're wasting time."

"I'm getting ready to work."

"I don't want you to get ready. I want you to do it."

"How do you expect me to work if I don't get ready?"

He realized one day that he was having childish arguments with a 9-year-old and that his behavior was reinforcing Judy's arguing. He decided to put this behavior on extinction. The next day he said, "Judy, get to work." When Judy began to argue that she was working, he walked away.

Judy muttered to herself for a while and then said loudly, "I ain't gonna do this dumb work, and you can't make me." Mr. Medlock held on and continued to ignore her comments.

Emily raised her hand. "Mr. Medlock," she simpered, "Judy says she's not going to do her work."

"Emily," said Mr. Medlock quietly, "take care of yourself."

"But, Mr. Medlock, she said you can't make her," countered Emily.

Mr. Medlock realized that his only hope was to ignore Emily's behavior too. He got up and began to walk around the room, praising students who were working and reminding them of the math game they were going to play when the work was finished. Soon Emily went back to her work. Judy, however, began to tap her pencil ostentatiously on her desk. Mr. Medlock continued to interact with other students. Judy finally shrugged and began to do her assignment. When she had been working for several minutes, Mr. Medlock walked casually over to her and said, "Good job, Judy. You've already got the first two right. Keep it up."

It occurred to Mr. Medlock that Judy's delay in starting to do her work was probably reinforced by his nagging and that if he ignored her procrastination as well, Judy would probably begin to work more quickly.

A group of investigators has examined the use of extinction through manipulation of what is known about reinforcement schedules. In Chapter 7, we noted that once new behaviors are well established, we move from continuous to intermittent schedules of reinforcement so that behaviors become more resistant to extinction (Ferster & Skinner,

1957). The investigators wondered if inappropriate behaviors being maintained by occasional (intermittent) reinforcement would become easier to extinguish if reinforcement was temporarily delivered continuously and then withdrawn.

Neisworth, Hunt, Gallop, and Nadle (1985) investigated the efficacy of this procedure with two 19-year-old students with severe mental retardation. One student engaged in stereotypic hand flapping and one in finger flicking. "During the CRF phase of treatment, the trainer delivered a reinforcer each time the participant emitted the target behavior. During the EXT phase of treatment, the reinforcer was, of course, no longer available to the participant" (p. 105). For both students, the stereotypic behaviors were reduced to near zero levels. This remained so for one of the students at a two-week follow-up, whereas the other student's behavior returned to baseline levels. As noted by the authors, though the effects on behaviors "run close to textbook illustrations and laboratory demonstrations" (p. 111), this is a preliminary study. In addition, the necessity to increase a behavior's rate makes the selection of an appropriate target behavior an ethical question. (This study was replicated with laboratory animals by Wylie and Grossman in 1988.)

Sometimes intermittent reinforcement works to maintain inappropriate behavior. Teachers or parents who reinforce a behavior during occasional moments of weakness may maintain it forever.

Ms. Troutman's Moment of Weakness

Ms. Troutman, a teacher and parent, picked her children up at day care after her work at school was done. Her 2-year-old son always asked for a p-bo-jelly as soon as they got home. She always explained that it was too close to dinnertime for peanut butter and jelly sandwiches. He always fell to the floor and screamed. She ignored him. This pattern was repeated daily, often several times. One afternoon her 7-year-old daughter, over the sound of screaming, explained that when Ms. Troutman had an especially hard day at school, she occasionally went ahead and fixed the boy a sandwich in order to avoid the tantrums, and that's why he kept asking and screaming. Ms. Troutman, albeit not graciously, was forced to acknowledge the correctness of the fledgling behaviorist's analysis.

PUNISHMENT

The two remaining levels of the hierarchy, Levels III and IV, contain options for behavior reduction that may be termed *punishment*. As is the case with the term **reinforcer,** we use a functional definition of the term **punisher.** A punisher is a consequent stimulus (S^P) that

1. decreases the future rate or probability of occurrence of behavior;
2. is administered contingently on the production of the undesired or inappropriate behavior;
3. is administered immediately following the production of the undesired or inappropriate behavior.

It must be clearly understood that the terms *punishment* and *punisher* as used in this context are defined functionally. Any stimulus can be labeled a punisher if its contingent application results in a reduction of the target behavior. *A punisher, like a reinforcer, can be identified only by its effect on behavior—not on the nature of the consequent stimulus.* For example, if a father spanks his son for throwing toys, and the son stops throwing toys, then the spanking *was* a punisher. If the son continues to throw toys, then the spanking *was not* a punisher. If each time a student talks out, her teacher reduces her playtime by one minute or takes tokens away, and this results in the reduction or cessation of the talking out, then the consequence was a punisher. If the behavior continues, the consequence was not a punisher. Again, this is a definition of the term *punisher* from a functional perspective.

Punishers, like reinforcers, may also be naturally occurring phenomena. Punishers are not simply techniques devised by malevolent behaviorists to work their will on students. Consider the examples and label the punishers:

> Jeannie toddles into the kitchen while her father is cooking dinner. As her father's back is turned, Jeannie reaches up and touches the saucepan on the front burner. She jerks her hand away crying and thereafter avoids touching the stove.
>
> Theresa has finished her math assignment quickly. Proudly, she raises her hand and announces this fact to her teacher. The teacher assigns her 10 additional problems to work. The next day Theresa works more slowly and fails to finish her assignment before the end of math class.
>
> Gary, a student with special needs, is to attend a general education class for reading. On the first day that he attends Mr. Johnston's fourth-grade reading class, he stumbles through the oral reading passage. The other students ridicule him, and he subsequently refuses to leave the special class to attend the fourth grade.
>
> Mrs. Brice, a first-year teacher, decides to use praise with her junior-high social studies class. She greets each student who arrives on time with effusive compliments and a happy face sticker. The next day no students arrive on time.

LEVEL III: REMOVAL OF DESIRABLE STIMULI

RESPONSE-COST PROCEDURES

Response-cost occurs when reinforcers are removed in an attempt to reduce behavior. The procedure itself may be defined as the withdrawal of specific amounts of reinforcer contingent on inappropriate behavior. As implied by this definition, "some level of positive reinforcement must be made available in order to provide the opportunity for . . . withdrawing that reinforcement" (Azrin & Holz, 1966, p. 392). If the use of a response-cost procedure empirically results in the desired behavior reduction, withdrawal of the reinforcement functions as a punisher.

For more information on these procedures, go to the "Web Links" module for Chapter 8 of the Companion Website.

Response-cost may be seen as a system of leveling fines, a familiar event. A city government has, as a means of behavior control and fund raising, a whole system of fines for predefined, inappropriate behavior. We, the citizens, have possession of the pool of reinforcers—the dollar bills we have earned. The city administration withdraws specific amounts of these reinforcing stimuli contingent on such inappropriate behaviors as littering, staying too long at a parking meter, and speeding. Similarly, McSweeny (1978) reported the number of directory assistance phone calls made in Cincinnati decreased significantly when a charge for these calls was instituted. Marholin and Gray (1976) found that when cash shortages were subtracted from employees' salaries, the size of shortages was sharply reduced.

A token system can incorporate response-cost procedures. If a teacher informs students they will earn one token for each of 10 math problems they solve correctly, that teacher is employing a token reinforcement system. If, on the other hand, the teacher hands out 10 tokens to each student and informs them that, for each problem they solve incorrectly, one token will be "repossessed," that teacher is employing a response-cost procedure. In practice, a response-cost procedure is most often and effectively (Bierman, Miller, & Stabb, 1987; Kazdin, 1994) used in combination with a token reinforcement system. In such a combined format, the students concurrently earn the pool of reinforcers and lose the reinforcers as fines for misbehavior. The students have ongoing access to future reinforcers.

In classrooms, response-cost procedures have been shown to have great versatility, without the undesirable side effects usually associated with punishment (Kazdin, 1972). They have been used in modifying social behaviors such as rule violation, off-task behavior, and hyperactivity (DuPaul, Guevremont, & Barkley, 1992; Rapport, Murphy, & Bailey, 1982; Salend, 1988); aggressive and disruptive behavior (Dougherty, Fowler, & Paine, 1985; Reynolds & Kelley, 1997); disruptive and off-task classroom behaviors (Higgins, Williams, & McLaughlin, 2001; Kelley & McCain, 1995; Proctor & Morgan, 1991); disruptive and obscene vocalizations (Falcomata, Roane, Hovanetz, Kettering, & Keeney, 2004; Trice & Parker, 1983); perseverative utterances durning conversations (Ross, 2002); and food scavenging (Smith, Piersel, Filbeck, & Gross, 1983). They have also been used to improve academic performance such as completion of math problems (Iwata & Bailey, 1974) and vocational training activities in community settings (Rusch, Connis, & Sowers, 1978). The response-cost contingency has been enforced by both adults and peers (Dougherty et al., 1985) and used to coordinate between school and home (Kelley & McCain, 1995). This procedure has been used to manage groups of students as well as individuals (Mowrer & Conley, 1987; Salend & Kovalich, 1981). Salend and Lamb (1986) divided a class of students with learning disabilities into two groups during their reading periods. At the beginning of each period each group was given a preset number of tokens. Each time a group member made an inappropriate verbalization, a token was removed from the group's pool. Within a reversal design, the number of inappropriate verbalizations decreased from a mean of 50 during baseline, to a mean of 4.2 during the first intervention period, and from a mean of 34.8 to a mean of 2.9 during the second intervention period.

Problems with response-cost.

There are a number of practical cautions in the use of a response-cost procedure. First, the teacher must have the ability to withdraw the reinforcer once given. It is probably unwise to attempt to use response-cost procedures with edible primary reinforcers. The student who has at his desk a cup of candies that are to be contingently withdrawn is apt immediately to eat all the candy as his first inappropriate behavior. The slight young teacher in the secondary classroom who walks over to the football tackle and announces that he is to return five tokens may find that the student answers, "In a pig's eye" (or something to that effect). It is best in such an instance to use points, which can be withdrawn without being physically repossessed.

Careful consideration must also be given to the magnitude of the penalties—the number of tokens or points being withdrawn. Research has produced mixed recommendations. For example, Burchard and Barrera (1972) used severe fines, whereas Siegel, Lenske, and Broen (1969) used mild fines; both got good results. An important point to remember is that exacting large fines may make tokens worthless. If students learn that an entire day's work can be wiped out by a fine, they are unlikely to work very hard.

Another problem may occur when all the reinforcers have been withdrawn. Consider, for example, the substitute teacher who is assigned to a ninth-grade remedial class for the day. One of the thoughts uppermost in her mind, in addition to the educational welfare of her temporary charges, is making it in one piece to lunchtime. When the students enter the room, she announces that, if they cooperate and work hard during the morning hours, she will permit them 30 minutes of free time. If she fines them 5 minutes whenever anyone misbehaves, by 10 a.m. the students may have very little free time left. Once the reinforcement system has become debased to this extent, the student energy involved in being good far outweighs the remaining amount of the reinforcer.

When using response-cost, as with all management systems, students must clearly understand the rules of behavior and the penalties for infractions. Clear understanding will avoid lengthy conversations at the time of misbehavior, when the teacher should just describe the infraction and exact the fine.

Before selecting a response-cost procedure, the teacher should answer the following questions:

Guide to setting up a response-cost procedure.

1. Have more positive procedures, such as differential reinforcement strategies, been considered?
2. Does the student currently have, or have access to, a pool of reinforcers?
3. Have the rules of appropriate behavior and the results (fines) for infractions been clearly explained and understood?
4. Has the ratio of the size of the fine to each instance of misbehavior been thought out?
5. Can the reinforcers be retrieved?
6. Will appropriate behavior be reinforced in conjunction with the use of response-cost?

Response-Cost Coupons

In order to make a response-cost system more concrete for her class of 6- and 7-year-olds, Ms. Calabash decided to use pictorial coupons as tokens. Before leaving the classroom and entering the community, the four children were given five coupons each to keep in their waist packs. Four of the coupons had a picture of an item they could acquire while on their trip (a soft drink, a yogurt cone, a picture of a bus seat meaning they could choose where to sit, and a picture of the store where they could buy something). The fifth coupon had a picture of an activity they could choose when they got back to class (puzzle, record player). If they misbehaved while on the trip, the teacher removed one of the coupons.

Time-Out Procedures

Time-out procedures serve as punishment by denying a student, for a fixed period of time, the opportunity to receive reinforcement. **Time-out** is a shortened form of the term *time-out from positive reinforcement.* Before using time-out procedures, the teacher must be sure that reinforcing consequences for appropriate behavior are available in the classroom. These consequences might be a formal reinforcement system or simply activities that the students enjoy. Identification of available reinforcers may be relatively simple when the students in a classroom are working for a specific item, such as tokens. The specific reinforcers in many classrooms where this is not the case are more difficult to identify. In some classrooms, reinforcers are infrequent, thus limiting the effectiveness of time-out procedures. Some classrooms may be so unpleasant that students are delighted to be excluded from them.

Time-out procedures may be categorized according to the method of denying access to reinforcers. While the student is still within the classroom, the teacher may make an environmental rearrangement. These procedures may be termed **nonseclusionary time-out.** For more disruptive behaviors, the student may be denied access to reinforcers by being taken outside the classroom or activity area. This procedure is called **exclusionary time-out.** If a time-out room is used, the procedure is referred to as **seclusionary time-out.**

Nonseclusionary Time-Out Procedures

In *nonseclusionary time-out procedures,* the student is not removed from the instructional setting; instead, the teacher denies the student access to reinforcers through a temporary manipulation of the environment. Teachers use this procedure in its most common form when faced with a generalized, minor disturbance. They may tell the students to put their heads on their desks, or they may turn out the room lights (Baron, Kaufman, & Rakavskas, 1967; Higgins, et al., 2001) to eliminate the mutual reinforcers

"I don't understand it, Professor. Time-out just isn't working anymore."

of talking and laughing with one another. If during instruction students begin to act inappropriately, the teacher may remove the materials (for example, eating utensils, counting chips, frog and dissection kit), herself, and her attention for a brief period contingent on the inappropriate behavior. Similarly, time-out may be accomplished by turning off a record player during free time when jocularity gets out of hand or turning off the radio on the school bus when students are out of their seats (Ritschl, Mongrella, & Presbie, 1972). If the problem occurs while the student is getting to the bus, the teacher can place the student in nonseclusionary time-out by stopping all verbal prompting and social attention and removing from sight any reinforcers that are being delivered for appropriate walking to the bus (Huguenin, 1993).

A frequently reported form of nonseclusionary time-out is use of the time-out ribbon model. This procedure has been used with individual students (Alberto, Heflin, & Andrews, 2002; Fee, Matson, & Manikam, 1990; Huguenin & Mulick, 1981; McKeegan, Estill, & Campbell, 1984; Salend & Maragulia, 1983) and with groups of students (Foxx & Shapiro, 1978; Salend & Gordon, 1987). During a group lesson, Foxx and Shapiro had students wear a ribbon tie while behaving in a socially appropriate manner. A student's ribbon was removed for any instance of misbehavior. This removal signaled an end to teacher attention and an end to the student's participation in activities and access to reinforcers for 3 minutes. During community-based instruction, Alberto et al. had students wear an athletic wristband. The wristband was removed for instances of inappropriate behavior. When not wearing the wristband, the student was required to stay next to the teacher and was not given a task to perform. He was neither spoken to nor given social attention, and if regularly scheduled tokens were distributed, the student did not get one.

Various time-out "ribbons" have been used, including actual ribbons, badges, leather shoelaces in belt loops, and wristbands with smiling face stickers. In a study by Adams, Martin, and Popelka (1971), a misbehavior prompted the teacher to turn on a recorded tone. While the tone was audible, access to reinforcers was denied to the student. In classrooms where token systems are in effect, taking a student's point card for a specified number of minutes provides a period of time-out from reinforcement.

Another form of nonseclusionary time-out is *contingent observation,* which involves moving students to the edge of an activity so that they can still observe other students' appropriate behavior and its reinforcement. Barton, Brulle, and Repp (1987) used contingent observation with two elementary students with severe disabilities. When the students misbehaved, they were moved slightly away from the group but were allowed to observe the classroom activities. Not every instance of the behavior resulted in contingent observation. A prespecified number of occurrences were permitted within given time intervals. Time-out was used only when instances of misbehavior exceeded the maximum. Such scheduling is similar to that used for DRL procedures. White & Bailey (1990) used what they referred to as a "sit and watch" procedure during physical education classes comprised of typical fourth graders and students with severe behavior problems. During "sit and watch," the teacher removed the student from the activity and explained the reason for his removal. The student picked up an egg timer, walked to an area away from the other students, sat down on the ground, and turned the timer over. He remained in "sit and watch" for approximately 3 minutes, until all of the sand had flowed to the other end of the timer. The student was then allowed to rejoin the class. At the teacher's request, back-up procedures were available in the form of lost privileges for some students. Twyman, Johnson, Buie, and Nelson (1994) described a range of more restrictive contingent observation alternatives that were used for vocal or physical disrespect to staff or peers, noncompliance, off task, out of area, or talk-outs with elementary students with emotional or behavior disorders. Students remained in the setting at a desk, in a chair, on the floor, against the wall, or just standing. In each case, students were required to maintain "appropriate hands and feet" and to keep their heads tucked between their arms. "Although the required posture reduced the possibility of visual observation, the student was able to hear the activities of the group and reinforcement being delivered to others" (p. 247). (Note: The study in which this procedure was used found that warning students of potential point loss for inappropriate behavior during contingent observation resulted in increased negative interaction between staff and students.)

A type of nonseclusionary time-out that has been used with more severe behavior problems is known as facial or visual screening. Facial screening procedures have been successfully used with stereotypic behaviors (Jordan, Singh, & Repp, 1989; McGonigle & Rojahn, 1989; Singh, Landrum, Ellis, & Donatelli, 1993); pica (Bogart, Piersel, & Gross, 1995; Singh & Winton, 1984); self-injury (Singh, 1980; Singh, Watson, & Winton, 1986; Watson, Singh, & Winton, 1986; Winton, Singh, & Dawson, 1984); disruptive mealtime behavior (Horton, 1987); trichotillomania (compulsive hair pulling; Baumann & Vitali, 1982); and inappropriate vocalizations (Cameron, Luiselli, Littleton, & Ferrelli, 1996). This procedure involves occluding the student's eyes with a terry-cloth bib or the teacher's hand usually for a period of 3 seconds (though data by Singh, Beale, and Dawson [1981] suggest that a 1-minute duration is the most effective) following cessation of the behavior without removing him from the instructional setting. Once the bib or hand is removed, the ongoing lesson is immediately resumed. For older children a T-shirt or sweatshirt, slit up the sides, would be more age appropriate. McGonigle, Duncan, Cordisco, and Barrett (1982) used visual screening with four students engaged in various stereotypic and self-injurious behaviors. Their procedure had the "teacher placing one hand over the child's eyes so as to preclude any source of visual input, while holding the back of the child's head with the other hand. Duration of the visual screening treatment was a minimum of 5 seconds for each child. Criterion for release from visual screening was contingent upon nondisruptive behavior following expiration of the minimum time requirement" (p. 463).

Exclusionary Time-Out Procedures

Exclusionary time-out involves removing the student from an activity as a means of denying access to reinforcement. The student may be taken to another room (Luiselli, 1996; Rortvedt & Miltenberger, 1994), but it is not always necessary to remove the student from the classroom completely. Exclusion (May, Mcallister, Risley, Twardosz, & Cox, 1974) may be accomplished by removing the student from the immediate activity area to another part of the room. Observation and subsequent modeling of reinforced behavior (as with contingent observation) are not components of this procedure. The student is removed to a chair facing away from the group, facing a corner, or in a screened-off area of the room. This procedure has been used with young children (including Dennis the Menace) who display aggressive and disruptive behaviors, tantrums, and noncompliance (Handen, Parrish, McClung, Kerwin, & Evans, 1992; LeBlanc & Matson, 1995; Mace, Page, Ivancic, and O'Brien, 1986; Reitman & Drabman, 1999; Roberts, 1988). Baer, Rowbury, and Baer (1973) used a variation of such exclusion. When a student misbehaved during an activity for which she was earning tokens, she was placed in the middle of the room out of reach of the work activity, and thereby denied access to earning tokens. In another variation, a student was moved to a chair outside the play area when he displayed aggressive behavior. The teacher stood next to him until he sat quietly for 5 seconds. While in the time-out area, the student was required to perform a nonpreferred task (stringing three beads) before being allowed to return to the play area. The addition of this task was intended to decrease the potential reinforcing value of teacher attention during the time-out (Richman et al., 1997).

Seclusionary Time-Out Procedures

In most instances, time-out is a procedure associated with the use of a time-out room (Birnbrauer, Wolf, Kidder, & Tague, 1965; Lahey, McNees, & McNees, 1973; MacPherson, Candee, & Hohman, 1974). The procedure involves removing the student from the classroom itself to a room identified for total social isolation, contingent on misbehavior. In such a room, access is denied to all potential reinforcers from the teacher, classmates, or the classroom. Such a procedure is sometimes termed *seclusionary time-out*. This procedure is usually reserved for behaviors such as physical aggression, verbal aggression, and destruction of property (Costenbader & Reading-Brown, 1995; Zabel, 1986).

Unfortunately, time-out rooms have often been seriously misused or mismanaged. Their use, therefore, has been the subject of negative publicity and even litigation (Cole v. Greenfield-Central Community Schools, 1986; Dickens v. Johnson County Board of Education, 1987; Hayes v. Unified School District No. 377, 1989; Honig v. Doe, 1988). In a review of these cases, Yell (1994, pp. 296–300) extrapolated basic guidelines for the use of exclusionary and seclusionary time-out procedures:

Guidelines for seclusionary time-out.

1. Teachers should be aware of, and adhere to, local and state policies regarding time-out.
2. Written procedures for the use of time-out should be developed, and each teacher should have a copy. Parents and students must be informed of the possible use of time-out, of the procedures, and of behaviors that will lead to its use.
3. Written permission from parents should be obtained indicating informed consent.
4. According to both case law and the 1997 reauthorization of IDEA, the IEP committee should be involved in making decisions concerning the use of behavior reduction procedures such as time-out.
5. Time-out must serve a "legitimate educational function. Legitimate purposes include reducing dangerous or disruptive behavior and simultaneously teaching adaptive behavior and protecting the educational environment from disruption" (p. 297).

6. Time-out must be used in a reasonable manner and be proportionate to the inappropriate behavior and the age and physical condition of the student.
7. Thorough accurate records must be kept. Included in these records should be the student's name, date, time, behavior that precipitated the use of the procedure, specific form of time-out used, length of time the student was in time-out, student's behavior following the use of time-out, and witnesses present.
8. The results of time-out must be monitored and evaluated. Ongoing data collection should verify that the use of time-out results in a decrease in the occurrence of the target behavior.

Concern about time-out rooms arises in part because of two aspects of the use of time-out rooms: duration of time in the room and physical features of the room. Gast and Nelson (1977b, p. 463) addressed both these concerns:

> The duration of each time-out period should be brief. One to five minutes generally is sufficient. It is doubtful that time-out periods exceeding 15 minutes serve the purpose for which they are intended. If a seclusion time-out is to be employed, the time-out room should:
>
> 1. Be at least 6 by 6 feet in size.
> 2. Be properly lighted (preferably recessed, with the switch outside the room).
> 3. Be properly ventilated.
> 4. Be free of objects and fixtures with which children can harm themselves.
> 5. Provide the means by which an adult can continuously monitor, visually and auditorily, the student's behavior.
> 6. Not be locked. A latch on the door should be used only as needed, and only with careful monitoring.

A teacher should work through the following sequence of steps when using any form of time-out.

1. Before beginning to use time-out as a management procedure, identify the behaviors that will result in use of a time-out procedure. Be sure the students understand the behavior. Explain the behavior expected of students while they are in time-out. Tell them how long the time-out period will last.
2. When the misbehavior occurs, reidentify it. Tell the student in a calm manner, "That is fighting. Go to time-out for . . . minutes." No other conversation should ensue. Ignore any statements the student may make as an excuse for misbehavior or relating to feelings about time-out. If necessary, lead the student to the time-out area. If the student resists, Hall and Hall (1980, p. 11) suggested that the teacher
   (a) gently but firmly lead the student to time-out.
   (b) be prepared to add time to time-out if the student refuses to go or yells, screams, kicks, or turns over furniture.
   (c) require the student to clean up any mess resulting from resistance to time-out before the student may return to classroom activities.
   (d) be prepared to use a backup consequence for students who refuse time-out.
3. Once a student enters the time-out area, the time begins. Check your watch or set a timer. Gast and Nelson (1977a) reviewed three formats for contingent release from time-out rooms:
   (a) release contingent on a specified period of appropriate behavior (for example, 2 minutes).

(b) release contingent on a minimum duration of time-out, with an extension until all inappropriate behavior has terminated.

(c) release contingent on a minimum duration of time-out, with a specified extension (such as 15 seconds) during which no inappropriate responses are exhibited. Mace et al. (1986) found this delayed release procedure effective.

4. Once the time interval has ended, return the student to the previous appropriate activity. Do not comment on how well the student behaved while in time-out. A student should be returned to the activity he or she was engaged in before time-out to avoid negatively reinforcing an escape from that activity.

Monitoring time-out.

To monitor the effects of time-out and to substantiate proper and ethical use of the procedure, records should be kept of each time-out occasion, especially when a time-out room is used. Records should include at least the following information (Gast & Nelson, 1977b):

1. the student's name
2. the episode resulting in the student's placement in time-out (behavior, activity, other students involved, staff person, and so on)
3. the time of day the student was placed in time-out
4. the time of day the student was released from time-out
5. the total time in time-out
6. the type of time-out (contingent observation, exclusion, or seclusion)
7. the student's behavior in time-out

Before selecting a time-out procedure, the teacher should consider the following questions concerning its use:

Questions to ask before using time-out.

1. Have more positive procedures—for example, differential reinforcement strategies—been considered?
2. Have both nonseclusionary and seclusionary time-out procedures been considered?
3. Can time-out be implemented with minimal student resistance? Can the teacher handle the possible resistance?
4. Have the rules of appropriate behavior and the results for misbehavior been clearly explained and understood?
5. Have the rules of behavior while in time-out been clearly explained and understood?
6. Have district regulations concerning the use of time-out procedures been reviewed and complied with?
7. Will appropriate behavior be reinforced in conjunction with the use of time-out?

The following vignette provides an example of what might happen should a teacher fail to consider questions such as these.

Ms. Sutton Tries Time-out

Ms. Sutton, a second-grade teacher, read about time-out. She decided that she would use it to teach Aaron not to hit other students. She did not have access to a time-out room, but concluded that putting Aaron in the hall outside the classroom would be just as good.

The next time Aaron hit someone, Ms. Sutton told him, "Aaron, you hit somebody. You have to go to time-out." She sat him in a chair in the hall and went back to teaching reading. At the end of the period, about an hour later, she went to get him. He came back into the room and hit Elaine before he even got to his seat. Once again, he went to the hall. This pattern was repeated throughout the morning.

Aaron spent most of the time in the hall and the rest of the time hitting people. Ms. Sutton concluded that time-out was an ineffective procedure. Later that day, she heard Aaron say to Elaine, "Hey, I got this all figured out. If I hit you, I get to go sit in the hall. I don't have to do my work, and I get to talk to all the people in the hall. The principal even came by and asked me what I did. Boy, did I tell him!"

Time-out will not be effective if positive reinforcement is not available in the classroom, if students escape tasks while in time-out, or if reinforcing consequences are available during time-out.

Factors that may make time-out ineffective.

Level IV: Presentation of Aversive Stimuli

What makes the presentation of aversive consequences so appealing to parents and teachers?

The presentation of an aversive stimulus as a consequence of an inappropriate behavior is, in popular usage, identified with the term *punishment.* Teachers turn to this form of punishment almost by reflex. Perhaps because many people have been disciplined at home and at school by being yelled at or hit, they learn to handle other people's inappropriate behavior by yelling and hitting, especially when their opponent is physically smaller. From a more functional perspective, this form of punishment is often used because it has three powerful advantages. First and foremost, the use of an aversive stimulus rapidly stops the occurrence of a behavior and has some long-term effects (Azrin, 1960). A child throwing a tantrum who is suddenly hit across the backside will probably stop immediately; a pair of students gossiping in the back of the room will stop when the teacher screams at them. Second, the use of aversive stimuli facilitates learning by providing a clear discrimination between acceptable and unacceptable behavior or between safe and dangerous behavior (Marshall, 1965). The student who is slapped for spitting, subjected to mild shocks on the arm for self-injurious behavior, or hit by a car while dashing across the street clearly and immediately sees the inappropriateness of the behavior. Third, the aversive consequence following a student's inappropriate behavior vividly illustrates to other students the results of engaging in that behavior and, therefore, tends to lessen the probability that others will engage in the behavior (Bandura, 1965).

For more information, go to to the "Web Links" module for Chapter 8 of the Companion Website.

In listing these advantages, *we are not recommending the use of aversive consequences* (especially involving physical contact) as a routine management procedure in the classroom, in homes, or in institutions. We merely acknowledge the behavioral effects resulting from their use. Physical or other strong aversive consequences are justified only under the most extreme instances of inappropriate behavior. They are appropriate only when safety is jeopardized or in instances of long-standing serious behavior problems. Aversive consequences should be used only after considering appropriate safety and procedural guidelines. Guidelines should minimally include

1. *demonstrated* and *documented* failure of alternative nonaversive procedures to modify the target behavior;
2. informed written consent of the student's parents or legal guardians through due process procedures and assurance of their right to withdraw such consent at any time (Rimm & Masters, 1979);
3. the decision to implement an aversive procedure made by a designated body of qualified professionals;
4. a prearranged timetable for review of the effectiveness of the procedure and discontinuance of the procedure as soon as possible;

Go to the "Activities" module for Chapter 8 of the Companion Website.

5. periodic observation to ensure the staff member's consistent and reliable administration of the procedure;
6. documentation of the effectiveness of the procedure as well as evidence of increased accessibility to instruction;
7. administration of the procedure by only designated staff members (The staff member should have had instruction in the procedure, have reviewed published studies in the use of the procedure, and be familiar with procedure-specific guidelines and possible negative effects.);
8. positive reinforcement of incompatible behavior, whenever possible, as a part of any program using aversive stimuli.

Krasner (1976) pointed out an important distinction between effectiveness and acceptability. It is not the effectiveness of aversive procedures that is in question, but their acceptability to parents, the public, and many professionals. Techniques involving aversive consequences understandably cause concern to many people. As reflected by the resolutions in the Appendix, some professionals believe that aversive techniques are always inappropriate. Others believe their use may be acceptable in cases of self-injurious behavior, for example, if proper safeguards are implemented. It is doubtful, however, that such drastic measures could or even should become accepted as routine classroom management procedures.

The Professor Experiences Déjà Vu

Mrs. Grundy had made numerous inquiries about obedience training for the professor's dog. She found that Miss Oattis taught for a licensed dog club and signed Burrhus and the professor up for an 8-week series of classes. One Monday evening, therefore, the professor and the dog stood in what appeared to be a former convenience store whose fixtures had been replaced with green rubber mats. There were decrepit lawn chairs along one wall, separated from the training floor by what appeared to be baby gates.

Miss Oattis introduced herself and began by telling the group some basic school rules—where the dogs were to be taken to relieve themselves and procedures for making up missed classes. She stressed the need for each owner to maintain control of his or her dog and keep it at least 6 feet from the other dogs. The large, active, brown dog next to the professor continued to investigate Burrhus and to pull on his owner. The instructor asked the owner to control her dog and continued with the introduction.

"We will be using lots of praise and treats to help our dogs learn. In operant conditioning (the professor began to pay very close attention), we call that positive reinforcement. Operant conditioning is the latest, most modern kind of dog training. It's not hard to learn and I'm here to help you. We will also be using corrections when the dogs behave inappropriately. You will learn why both are necessary and how to use them effectively. We will also use cues, signals, and prompts as well as shaping. Don't worry about all this new terminology; you'll catch on." (The professor was all ears.) The large, brown dog finished its investigation of Burrhus and jumped on the professor. Miss Oattis said calmly, "This is the perfect opportunity to demonstrate a correction." She walked briskly over to the woman with the large, brown dog and took the leash from her. As the dog began to jump on the professor again, she snapped the leash as she said, "Off!" in a ringing tone. The dog put all four feet on the floor and regarded the instructor quizzically. "Good dog," she said, sweetly.

"You see," Miss Oattis stated, "the dog was behaving inappropriately. I snapped the leash so that his collar put pressure on his neck, and he stopped jumping. Soon we'll teach him to sit so he will know what to do instead of sniffing and jumping around people and other dogs."

The dog's owner drew herself up to her full height.

"I am appalled," she hissed, "I have been watching tapes of some of the most famous dog trainers and they say you should never, ever, correct a dog. It is inhumane and will destroy your relationship with him. You can do all the training you need with only praise and treats. You have abused my dog. I'm leaving right now and I want my money back."

The professor's mind flashed back to a confrontation he had recently witnessed at a professional conference. "Amazing," he said to himself. "The same issue and the same anger."

TYPES OF AVERSIVE STIMULI

Aversive stimuli may be categorized into two groups: unconditioned aversive stimuli and conditioned aversive stimuli. **Unconditioned aversive stimuli** result in physical pain or discomfort to the student. This class of stimuli includes anything that causes pain: naturally occurring consequences, such as contact with a hot stove, or contrived consequences, such as the application of electric shock. Because these stimuli immediately produce a behavior change without the need for any previous experience, they may also be termed *universal, natural,* or *unlearned punishers.*

Unconditioned aversive stimuli also include consequences that may be described as mild aversives (McGonigle et al., 1982; Singh, 1979; Zegiob, Jenkins, Becker, & Bristow, 1976). Rather than causing pain, these noxious stimuli result in annoyance, discomfort, or irritation (Dorsey, Iwata, Ong, & McSween, 1980; Singh, 1980; Zegiob, Alford, & House, 1978). These mild aversive consequences include the administration of substances and the use of physical control.

Substances used as aversive consequences of inappropriate behavior include water, lemon juice, and aromatic ammonia. Directing a fine mist of tap water toward a subject's face contingent on the occurrence of a targeted behavior has been employed with behaviors ranging from mouthing objects (resulting in vomiting or hand biting for some subjects), to head banging and tearing of flesh from lips and forearms (Dorsey et al., 1980; Gross, Berler, & Drabman, 1982), to other forms of self-injury and stereotypic behaviors (Bailey, Pokrzywinski, & Bryant, 1983; Fehr & Beckwith, 1989; Fisher, Piazza, Bowman, Hanley, & Adelinis, 1997; Singh et al., 1986), to pica (Rojahn, McGonigle, Curcio, & Dixon, 1987). Putting lemon juice into the subject's mouth has been used to suppress rumination—regurgitation of swallowed food (Apolito & Sulzer-Azaroff, 1981; Becker, Turner, & Sajwaj, 1978; Sajwaj, Libet, & Agras, 1974)—and self-injurious behavior (Mayhew & Harris, 1979). The strongest, and most extreme, of the substance consequences has been the use of aromatic ammonia. Aromatic ammonia in the form of capsules of smelling salts crushed and held under the subject's nose has been used to reduce self-injurious behavior (Altman & Haavik, 1978; Baumeister & Baumeister, 1978; Singh, 1979; Tanner & Zeiler, 1975), aggression toward others (Doke, Wolery, & Sumberg, 1983), and pica (Rojahn et al., 1987).

Physical control refers to procedures requiring direct, physical intervention to suppress a targeted behavior. Two such procedures are contingent exercise and immobilization or physical restraint. Contingent exercise requires the student to engage in unrelated physical activity such as push-ups or deep knee bends as a consequence for a targeted behavior. This procedure has been used with self-injurious, stereotypic, self-stimulatory, and aggressive behaviors (DeCatanzaro & Baldwin, 1978; Kern, Koegel, & Dunlap, 1984; Kern, Koegel, Dyer, Blew, & Fenton, 1982; Rolider & Van Houten, 1985; Singh et al., 1986), and behaviors of military recruits that annoy drill sergeants.

Physical restraint has been used primarily with stereotypic behaviors (Reid, Tombaugh, & Van den Heuvel, 1981) and self-injurious behaviors (Hamad, Isley, &

Lowry, 1983; Luiselli, 1986; Matson & Keyes, 1988; Pace, Iwata, Edwards, & McCosh, 1986), pica (Singh & Bakker, 1984; Winton & Singh, 1983), and feces smearing (Rolider, Williams, Cummings, & Van Houten, 1991).

Harris (1996) discussed three categories of restraint: personal restraint, mechanical restraint, and self-restraint. Personal restraint is movement suppression by the application of force or pressure by one person upon another. This may involve holding a student's hands to his side, placing pressure on the student's back or shoulders, or using an embrace or "baskethold" for immobilization. If physical restraint is necessary, most educators agree that personal restraint in a chair is more acceptable than methods involving personal restraint on the floor (McDonnell & Sturmey, 2000). Mechanical restraint involves use of a device such as arm splints or adapted clothing. Self-restraint involves actions an individual employs to restrict his or her own movements, such as pressing arms against floor or furniture, wrapping arms in clothing, and self-use of mechanical restraints (Fisher, Grace, & Murphy, 1996; Fovel, Lash, Barron, & Roberts, 1989; Foxx, 1990; Hyman, Oliver, & Hall, 2002; Isley, Kartsonis, McCurley, Weisz, & Roberts, 1991; Oliver, Murphy, Hall, Arron, & Leggett, 2003; Pace et al., 1986; Silverman, Watanabe, Marshall, & Baer, 1984; Smith, Lerman, & Iwata, 1996). For a more extensive discussion of the relationship among self-restraint, self-injury, and reinforcement, see Fisher & Iwata, 1996 or Isley et al., 1991.

Schloss and Smith (1987) suggested certain limitations to the use of physical restraint.

1. Restraint does not involve the reinforcement of an alternative behavior.
2. The inappropriate behavior may be reinforced by manual restraint, thereby increasing the probability of future occurrences.
3. Once the student learns that he will be physically blocked from performing the response, he is likely to increase his efforts to perform it.
4. Implementation may result in harm to the student or the teacher.

Given these cautions, Schloss and Smith (1987) and Ryan and Peterson (2004) suggested guidelines that include:

1. Manual restraint should be used only to prevent the student from causing harm to himself, others, or objects. It is a form of crisis management, not routine punishment for noncompliance.
2. Every opportunity should be provided for the student to control his own behavior before physical management is implemented.
3. Extreme care should be taken to provide for the safety and comfort of the student during the restraint procedure. The safest method available should be employed, using the minimal amount of force necessary to protect the student and others from physical injury or harm. The restraint should be discontinued as soon as possible.
4. No restraint should prevent a student from breathing or speaking. Personnel must have initial and ongoing specialized training.
5. Following use of a physical restraint, the person who administered it should verbally notify an administrator as soon as possible. A written report that describes the antecedents, specific aggressive responses, and outcomes or consequences should be made immediately following each incident.

The potentially harmful nature of these aversive consequences precludes their selection by any single individual. If an aversive consequence is to be used, the following are critically and ethically important elements involved in making that decision: (a) it must be made by a team of professionals directly involved

in the education of the student and the student's parent or guardian; (b) it must be made based on a review of data that substantiates the severity of the behavior and previous attempts at behavior management; (c) professionals should read the professional literature concerning a procedure before recommending and implementing its use. An understanding of procedure-specific guidelines, such as duration and schedule of administration of the consequence and, of special concern, the potential behavioral and physical negative effects, must be shared by all parties before implementation; (d) provisions must be made for initial and ongoing staff training, as well as careful monitoring of implementation; and (e) it must be made within the guidelines set out by the local school system and by the courts. [A review of cases is provided by Lohrmann-O'Rourke & Zirkel, 1998. Ongoing reviews and updates are provided in publications by organizations such as The Center for Education and Employment Law and LRP Publications.]

Although these consequences are included in the category of unconditioned aversive stimuli, they are not necessarily universal punishers. Some students may find the procedure reinforcing rather than punishing. A student may indeed like the taste of lemon juice, find it fun to have water sprayed in his face, or enjoy physical contact with the teacher. Access to restraint has actually been used as a positive reinforcer (Favell, McGimsey, & Jones, 1978; Favell, McGimsey, Jones, & Cannon, 1981).

Conditioned aversive stimuli are stimuli a person learns to experience as aversive as a result of pairing with an unconditioned aversive stimulus. This class includes consequences such as words and warnings, vocal tones, or gestures. For example, a child may have experienced being yelled at paired with being spanked. Yelling may thus have become a conditioned aversive stimulus, because experience has proven to the student that yelling is associated with pain. The pain associated with a conditioned aversive stimulus may also be psychological or social pain or discomfort, usually in the form of embarrassment or ridicule from peers.

Verbal reprimands (shouting or scolding) are the most common form of conditioned aversive stimuli used in the classroom (Heller & White, 1975; Thomas, Presland, Grant, & Glynn, 1978; White, 1975). A series of studies was conducted to identify factors that influence the effectiveness of reprimands (Van Houten, Nau, Mackenzie-Keating, Sameoto, & Colavecchia, 1982). Three such factors were identified: (1) verbal reprimands were more effective when delivered in conjunction with "nonverbal aspects of reprimands such as eye contact and a firm grasp"; (2) "reprimands were more effective when delivered from nearby the student than when delivered from across the room"; and (3) "the delivery of reprimands to one student reduced the disruptive behavior of an adjacent peer" (p. 81).

If unconditioned or conditioned aversive stimuli are to be used as consequences in a behavior-reduction program, they should be used as effectively as possible. As indicated in the functional definition, the teacher must be consistent and immediate in applying the consequences (Azrin, Holz, & Hake, 1963). The rules of behavior must be clearly associated with a contingency that has been previously stated: the "if, then" statement of cause and effect. The student must understand that the aversive consequence is not being arbitrarily applied. The immediacy of application convinces the student of the veracity of the contingency and underlines the connection between a particular behavior and its consequence.

In addition to ensuring consistency and immediacy, the teacher should avoid extended episodes of punishment. Consequences should be quick and directly to the point. Sometimes teachers become so involved in analyzing behavior and arranging consequences, they forget that for some children, a polite request to "Please stop doing that" is all that's required. If words are a punisher for a student, a few words—such as, "Don't run in the hall"—may be far more effective than a 15-minute lecture, most of which the student tunes out.

Punishment is far less effective when the intensity of the aversive stimulus is increased gradually instead of being initially introduced at its full intensity (Azrin & Holz, 1966). With a gradual increase in intensity, the student has the opportunity to become habituated or desensitized to the intensity of the previous application. Such gradual habituation may eventually lead the teacher to administer an intensity level far above what was originally considered necessary to terminate the student's misbehavior.

A desire or actual attempt to escape from an aversive condition is a natural response. If punishment is to be effective in changing undesirable student behavior, the teacher will have to arrange the environment to prevent students' escaping punishment (Azrin, Hake, Holz, & Hutchinson, 1965; Bandura, 1969).

The most important element of any program that includes punishment of inappropriate behavior is to be sure that any punishment is always used in association with reinforcement for appropriate behavior. Punishment involves very little learning. In effect, all the student learns is what behavior should not be engaged in. Reinforcing appropriate behavior instructs the student on appropriate or expected behaviors and provides an opportunity for successful or reinforced experiences.

Disadvantages of Aversive Stimuli

The disadvantages of aversive consequences far outweigh the advantages of their immediate effect. The following limitations of such procedures should make teachers stop and consider very carefully before choosing to use aversives:

1. In the face of aggressive punishers, the student has three behavior options:
   (a) The student may strike back (for example, yell at the teacher or even become physically aggressive). A reaction may be triggered that will result in escalation of the situation.
   (b) The student may become withdrawn, tune out the punisher, and remain tuned out for the rest of the day, thus learning nothing.
   (c) The student may engage in an escape and avoidance behavior. Once a student has run out of the room, a punisher in the classroom can have no immediate effect.
2. We know that a most basic and powerful form of instruction and learning takes place through modeling or imitation. Because a teacher is a figure of respect and authority, students closely observe his or her behavior. A teacher's reactions become a model of adult behavior for various situations. The teacher who yells or hits is, in effect, saying to the students this is how an adult reacts and copes with undesirable behaviors in the environment. Students may, through such a model, learn an inappropriate, aggressive form of behavior. As noted by Sobsey (1990), this punishment-induced aggression results in more inappropriate behavior and can result in harm to both the individual and to any targets of aggression.
3. Unless students are taught to understand what behavior is being punished, they may come to fear and avoid the teacher or the entire setting in which the punishment occurred. Consider
   (a) the fourth-grade teacher whose students flinch when she walks up and down between the rows of desks. She is a slapper.

(b) the little girl in an institution who suddenly would not sleep in her room at night. She cried and screamed until she was taken out in the hall. It was discovered that an attendant had been taking her into her room and paddling her for bad behaviors during the day.

4. Many interactions that teachers consider punishers function as positive reinforcers instead. A child may find making an adult lose control and look ridiculous very reinforcing.

A disadvantage of punishment is illustrated by the following vignette.

Professor Grundy Teaches Dennis a Thing or Two

Professor Grundy's 5-year-old nephew, Dennis, was spending the week at the professor's house. One of Dennis's more unpleasant habits was jumping on the bed. Mrs. Grundy had asked Dennis not to do it, but this had been completely ineffective.

Professor Grundy was sitting in his easy chair, smoking his pipe, and reading a professional journal. He heard the unmistakable "crunch, crunch, crunch" of the bedsprings directly overhead in the guest bedroom. "Minerva," he said, "the time has come for drastic action. Where is the flyswatter?"

"Oliver, you're not going to beat the child, are you?" asked Minerva.

"Certainly not, dear," replied the professor. "I shall merely apply an unconditioned aversive stimulus, contingently, at a maximum intensity."

The professor took the flyswatter in hand and tiptoed up the carpeted steps in his stockinged feet. He continued to tiptoe into the bedroom, where he observed Dennis happily jumping on the bed. Dennis did not observe the professor; his back was to the door. Grundy applied the immediate, contingent, and intense aversive stimulus saying, firmly, "Do not jump on the bed." Dennis howled.

"That, I think," said the professor to Mrs. Grundy, "will teach Dennis a thing or two." In fact, Dennis did not jump on the bed all weekend. Professor Grundy was at home all the time and knew he would have heard the springs.

"Oliver, let's first try offering him a treat if he doesn't jump on the bed."

On Monday, when the professor arrived home from the university, Minerva met him at the door. "Oliver," she said, "I don't know which thing or two you planned to teach Dennis, but the one he learned was not to jump on the bed when you were home. He's been at it all day."

Like Dennis, what students learn most often from punishment using aversive stimuli is not to perform the behavior when the person who applied the punishment is present. They learn not to get caught! They don't learn to behave appropriately.

Concern about inappropriate and excessive use of aversive interventions has resulted in position statements about their use from various advocacy and professional organizations. Several of these statements appear in the Appendix.

Overcorrection

Overcorrection was developed as a behavior-reduction procedure that includes training in appropriate behaviors. Overcorrection procedures are therefore considered educative (Azrin & Foxx, 1971). The purpose of overcorrection is to teach students to take responsibility for their inappropriate acts and to teach them appropriate behaviors. Correct behavior is taught through an exaggeration of experience. The exaggeration of experience characteristic of overcorrection contrasts with a simple correction procedure in which a student rectifies an error of behavior but is not necessarily required to follow that with exaggerated or extended practice of the appropriate behavior.

There are two basic types of overcorrection procedures. *Restitutional overcorrection* is used when a setting has been disturbed by a student's misbehavior. The student must overcorrect the setting she or he has disturbed. *Positive-practice overcorrection* is used when the form of a behavior is inappropriate. In this procedure, the student practices an exaggerated correct form of an appropriate behavior (Foxx & Azrin, 1973).

Overcorrection procedures should have the following characteristics (Foxx & Bechtel, 1982, p. 231):

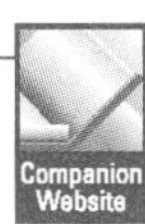

To enhance your understanding and skills in using overcorrection procedures, go to the "Web Links" module for Chapter 8 of the Companion Website.

1. The consequence (behavior) required of the student should be directly related to the misbehavior. This should reduce the likelihood of use in a punitive or arbitrary fashion and should prevent the inappropriate response from occurring.
2. The student should directly experience the effort normally required of others to correct the results of the misbehavior.
3. Overcorrection should be instituted immediately following the misbehavior.
4. The student performing the overcorrection should act rapidly so that consequences constitute an inhibitory effort requirement.
5. The student is instructed and manually guided through the required acts, with the amount of guidance adjusted on a moment-to-moment basis according to the degree to which the student is voluntarily performing the act.

Successful use of overcorrection has been demonstrated using various durations. Overcorrection periods may last anywhere from 30 seconds (Azrin et al., 1973) or 1 minute (Freeman, Graham, & Ritvo, 1975) to as long as 2 hours (Foxx, 1976), depending on the behavior involved. Successful reduction of stereotypic hand movements has been reported after requiring a student to engage in an overcorrection procedure for 2.5 minutes (Epstein, Doke, Sajwaj, Sorrell, & Rimmer, 1974) and 5 minutes (Foxx & Azrin, 1973). Carey and Bucher (1983) noted that shorter durations result in fewer instances of negative side effects such as aggression.

Restitutional Overcorrection

A restitutional overcorrection procedure requires that the student restore or correct an environment that he or she has disturbed not only to its original condition, but beyond that. For example, when the teacher catches a student throwing a spitball, she is employing simple correction when she says, "Michael, pick that up and throw it in the trash." She is employing restitutional overcorrection when she says, "Michael, pick that up and throw it in the trash, and now pick up all the other papers on the floor."

This form of environmental restoration was used by Azrin and Foxx (1971) as part of their toilet-training program. When a child had an accident, she or he had to undress, wash the clothes, hang them to dry, shower, obtain clean clothing, dress, and then clean the soiled area of the lavatory. A variation was employed by Azrin and Wesolowski (1974) when, in order to eliminate stealing, they required the thief to return not only a stolen item but also an additional identical item to the person who had been robbed.

A review of studies by Rusch and Close (1976) shows restitutional overcorrection techniques used to reduce various classes of disruptive behavior:

1. In cases where objects were disturbed or rearranged, all objects (such as furniture) within the immediate area where a disruption occurred were straightened, not merely the originally disturbed objects.
2. In cases where someone annoyed or frightened others, all persons present were to be apologized to, not just those annoyed or frightened.
3. In cases of self-inflicted oral infection, a thorough cleansing of the mouth with an oral antiseptic followed unhygienic oral contacts such as biting people or chewing inedible objects.
4. In cases of agitation, a period of absolute quiet was imposed following commotions such as shrieking and screaming.

Positive-Practice Overcorrection

With positive-practice overcorrection, the student who has engaged in an inappropriate behavior is required to engage in exaggerated or overly correct practice of the appropriate behavior. For example, if a class runs to line up for recess, the teacher who makes everyone sit back down and line up again is using simple correction. The teacher who makes everyone sit back down and then practice getting in line several times while reciting the rules for doing it the right way is using positive-practice overcorrection.

Positive-practice overcorrection of behavior that is autisticlike is sometimes called autism reversal.

To ensure the educative nature intended by this procedure, the practice should be of an alternative appropriate behavior topographically similar to the inappropriate behavior. Foxx and Azrin (1973) and Azrin et al. (1973) used this procedure to reverse the stereotypic behavior of children with autism. As shown in Figure 8–4, the researchers identified and then required the students to practice exaggerations of appropriate postures for extended periods of time. Azrin and Foxx (1971) used positive-practice procedures in their toilet-training program by artificially increasing the frequency of urinations through offering students large quantities of appealing liquids. This technique increased the opportunity for practice and reinforcement. Azrin and Wesolowski (1975) eliminated floor sprawling by requiring the student to practice sitting on several

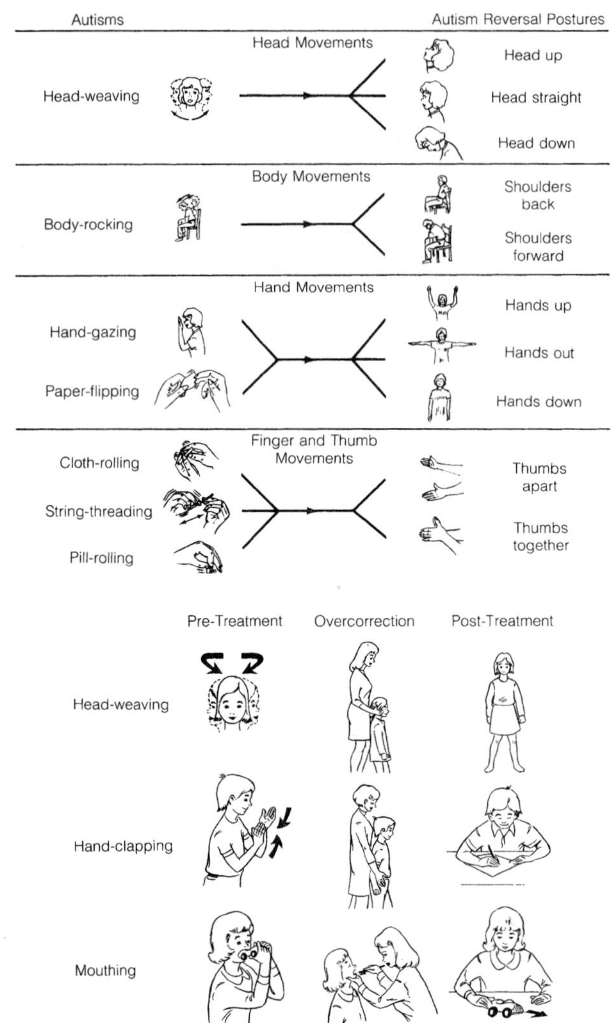

FIGURE 8–4
Positive-practice overcorrection in reducing stereotypic behaviors.
Note (top): From "The elimination of autistic self-stimulatory behavior by overcorrection," by R. Foxx & N. Azrin, *Journal of Applied Behavior Analysis,* 1973. Copyright 1973 by The Society for the Experimental Analysis of Behavior, Inc. Reprinted by permission.
Note (bottom): From "Autism reversal: Eliminating stereotyped self-stimulation of retarded individuals," by N. H. Azrin, S. J. Kaplan, & R. M. Foxx. *American Journal on Mental Deficiency,* 1973. Copyright 1973 by the Society for the Experimental Analysis of Behavior, Inc. Reprinted by permission.

chairs (one at a time, of course) for an extended time. Classroom disturbances have been overcorrected by requiring students to practice reciting correct classroom procedures to the teacher during periods such as recess (Azrin, Azrin, & Armstrong, 1977; Azrin & Powers, 1975; Bornstein, Hamilton, & Quevillon, 1977).

In addition to its use for these and other inappropriate behaviors such as bruxism (Steuart, 1993); stereotypic behavior (Denny, 1980; Doke & Epstein, 1975); aggression (Adams & Kelley, 1992; Luiselli & Rice, 1983); and self-injury (Gibbs & Luyben, 1985; Wesolowski & Zawlocki, 1982), positive-practice has been successful with various academic behaviors (Lenz, Singh, & Hewett, 1991). To improve oral reading performance, students who made an error were instructed to listen to the teacher read the word correctly while the student pointed to the word in the book. The student then said the word correctly five times and reread the sentence (Singh, 1987; Singh & Singh, 1986, 1988; Singh, Singh, & Winton, 1984). To correct spelling errors, students were instructed to listen to the word pronounced, pronounce the word correctly, say each letter aloud, and write the word correctly (Matson, Esveldt-Dawson, & Kazdin, 1982; Ollendick, Matson, Esveldt-Dawson, & Shapiro, 1980; Stewart & Singh, 1986). Positive-practice has also been used with cursive writing (Mabee, 1988; Trap, Milner-Davis, Joseph, &

Cooper, 1978) and manual communication (Hinerman, Jenson, Walker, & Peterson, 1982; Linton & Singh, 1984). In their review of academic remediation and the use of overcorrection, Lenz et al. (1991) suggested that overcorrection procedures used for academic remediation be called "directed rehearsal" because they found that the procedures did not totally meet the criteria set by Foxx and Bechtel (1982; for example, use of manual guidance or prompt administration) and that their major components were rehearsal and attention directed to the learning task.

Overcorrection procedures should not themselves be allowed to become positively reinforcing. Indeed, a quality of aversiveness is involved in their use. Restitutional or positive-practice overcorrection procedures usually include the following components (Epstein et al., 1974; Rusch & Close, 1976):

Guidelines for using overcorrection.

1. telling the student she or he behaved inappropriately;
2. stopping the student's ongoing activity;
3. providing systematic verbal instructions for the overcorrection activity in which the student is to engage;
4. forcing the practice of correctional behavior (manually guiding the desired movements, using as much bodily pressure as necessary, but reducing such pressure immediately as the person begins to perform the movement with verbal instruction alone);
5. returning the student to the ongoing activity.

Before using an overcorrection procedure, teachers should consider the following management concerns:

1. Implementation of overcorrection requires the full attention of the teacher. She must be physically close to the student to ensure that he complies with the overcorrection instruction and be ready to intervene with physical guidance, if necessary.
2. Overcorrection procedures tend to be time consuming, sometimes lasting 5 to 15 minutes and possibly longer (Foxx & Azrin, 1973; Ollendick & Matson, 1976; Sumner, Meuser, Hsu, & Morales, 1974). Studies suggest, however, that short-duration implementation may be at least as effective as longer durations in facilitating behavior changes, especially when appropriate alternative behavior is being taught emphasizing the educative rather than punishment potential of the procedure (Carey & Bucher, 1983; Cole, Montgomery, Wilson, & Milan, 2000; Conley & Wolery, 1980).
3. Because physical contact with the student is involved in the use of overcorrection, the teacher should be aware of the possibility of aggression by the student (Carey & Bucher, 1983; Rollings, Baumeister, & Baumeister, 1977) or attempts to escape and avoid the aversive situation.
4. During long periods of overcorrection the student may become so disruptive that the teacher cannot guide him through the overcorrection procedure (Matson & Stephens, 1977).
5. Because overcorrection often involves physical guidance for extended periods, it may be a very aversive procedure to the adults implementing it (Repp, 1983).
6. If students are reinforced for correct responses during positive practice, they may misbehave in order to perform the procedure and receive reinforcers (Foxx & Bechtel, 1982). This probably will not happen often, and using reinforcement is generally the better course. In comparing positive practice with and without reinforcing correct responses, Carey & Bucher (1986) found that use without reinforcement "showed no advantages over the reinforced variation, and resulted in a greater incidence of undesirable side effects such as aggression and emotionality" (p. 85).

Overcorrection may provide an alternative to aversive consequences in the classroom. It is important to remember that overcorrection procedures, although they have some aversive features, are to be used not as retaliative but as educative tools. The teacher's tone and manner make a difference in the way the procedures will be received by students. A teacher who uses an angry or haranguing tone of voice or unnecessary force when guiding students through overcorrection procedures may increase the probability of resistance. Firmness without aggression is the aim here.

Occasionally, two procedures that result in behavior reduction may be misidentified as a form of overcorrection or confused with those procedures. These other approaches are *negative practice* and *stimulus satiation*. The confusion may occur because, as in overcorrection, these procedures involve providing an exaggeration of experience.

Negative practice (Dunlap, 1928, 1930, 1932) may be confused with positive practice. Negative practice requires that the student repeatedly perform the *inappropriate* behavior. There is no pretense that the procedure is educative. The procedure is based on the assumption that repeated performance will result in response fatigue or satiation. For example, if a certain student's inappropriate behavior is getting up and running around the room during a lesson, positive practice might involve extended time periods sitting in various chairs, whereas negative practice might involve requiring the student to run and run and run and run.

Negative practice has been used to reduce small motor behaviors (Dunlap, 1928, 1930). A limited number of studies report the use of this procedure. Those that have been published have dealt with tics (Walton, 1961; Yates, 1958), smoking (De Lahunt & Curran, 1976), grimacing and unusual body movements made by children with cerebral palsy when speaking (Rutherford, 1940), self-injurious behavior (Mogel & Schiff, 1967), and teeth grinding (Vasta & Wortman, 1988).

Negative practice depends on response fatigue or satiation. **Stimulus satiation,** on the other hand, depends on the student's becoming satiated with the antecedent to the behavior. Ayllon (1963) used stimulus satiation with an individual who hoarded large numbers of towels and stored them in her room in a psychiatric hospital. To reduce this hoarding behavior, nurses took towels to the woman when she was in her room and simply handed them to her without comment. The first week she was given an average of 7 towels daily; by the third week, the number was increased to 60 towels. When the number of towels kept in her room reached 625, she started to take a few out. Thereafter, no more towels were given to her. During the next 12 months, the average number of towels found in her room was 1 to 5 per week, compared with the baseline range of 13 to 29.

SUMMARY

To enhance your overall understanding of the topic presented in Chapter 8, go to the "Supplemental Lecture Notes" module of the Companion Website.

This chapter reviewed a number of procedures to decrease or eliminate inappropriate or maladaptive behaviors: differential reinforcement, reinforcement of incompatible behaviors, extinction, punishment, and overcorrection. These procedures are most usefully and constructively viewed as a hierarchy of approaches, from those emphasizing reinforcement to those having aversive features (Figure 8–1).

We stressed throughout the chapter that procedures to decrease behaviors should be chosen only when the behaviors in question are clearly interfering with a student's ability to learn or are presenting a danger to the student or to other people. Positive reinforcement of appropriate behavior should always be combined with any procedure to decrease or eliminate behavior.

KEY TERMS

differential reinforcement of lower rates of behavior (DRL)
differential reinforcement of other behaviors (DRO)
differential reinforcement of alternative behavior (DRA)
differential reinforcement of incompatible behavior (DRI)
noncontingent reinforcement (NCR)
extinction
reinforcer
punisher
response-cost
time-out
nonseclusionary time-out
exclusionary time-out
seclusionary time-out
aversive stimuli
unconditioned aversive stimuli
conditioned aversive stimuli
overcorrection
negative practice
stimulus satiation

DISCUSSION QUESTIONS

For each of the following scenarios, decide what has gone wrong and suggest ways to improve the intervention.

1. Can he sit and work?

   Morse, a student in Mr. Sharpton's special education class, has the opportunity to attend a seventh-grade computer class during the second period each day. The teacher who has agreed to this said that before he can come to her class, Morse, who can barely sit still for 15 minutes, must be able to stay in his seat for 40 consecutive minutes. Mr. Sharpton spoke to Morse about this opportunity and Morse indicated he wanted to be in the class. So Mr. Sharpton told him if he would sit and work for 40 minutes for a whole week in Mr. Sharpton's class, the following week he could be a member of the computer class. Alas, Morse never became a member of the computer class.

2. What, what, what!

   Jade is a question asker. She asks questions all the time. She raises her hand and asks questions, she calls out questions, and she asks her neighbors questions. While question asking is important, and her teacher, Mr. Cibak, does not want to punish it or get rid of it totally, he does want to reduce its occurrence from the current 23 questions per class period. Mr. Cibak decides to reinforce a gradual reduction in Jade's question asking, beginning during his Environmental Science class each day. His plan is to reinforce Jade's asking 20 or fewer questions, then 17 or fewer questions, then 14 or fewer, and so on. He reduces the allowed number of questions by 3 after the third day at each interim criterion. Mr. Cibak and Jade reviewed the first criterion and the contingency attached. The science class progresses and Jade does fine. She does fine the next day, too. The fourth day she asks nine questions in a row at the very end of class. Mr. Cibak, exasperated, scolds her for this. On day five he begins to scowl each time Jade asks a question but he answers them. As the days progress, he allows her to ask her questions, he continues to scowl, and the frequency of question asking is unchanged.

3. Six of one, half a dozen of the other.

   Deon is a 7-year-old student with severe mental retardation and autism. He has no standard form of communication. It is believed that his self-injurious behavior, such as face slapping, is a form of communication used to gain adult attention. Each time he slaps his face, his teacher holds his hand and tells him to stop. His teacher and the behavior-management team selected a replacement behavior for gaining teacher attention: grasp a large red chip and raise it in the air. For days the behavior specialist or paraprofessional was at Deon's side to block attempts at face slapping and to redirect his hand to the chips. They used hand-over-hand prompting to help him raise a chip. When he did so, if the teacher noticed the chip, she came over to him and put some of his favorite "slime" in his hands. The team felt good that the teacher was catching him more than 75% of the time, but the data on his face slapping seemed to have plateaued.

4. Around and around. . . faster and faster.

   Dave runs around the room often, and he runs with such force that sometimes he runs into the walls and into chairs. Ms. Wyatt's immediate concern is the potential for Dave to run into one of the three students in wheelchairs. She provides Dave with numerous models of appropriate walking behavior. She reinforces walking behavior of other students, and ignores Dave's running. His behavior continues and escalates. Later in the morning, Dave finally does knock over an empty wheelchair. Ms. Wyatt yells: "See what you did! What if Joan was in her chair, she would be on the floor and hurt." Dave is startled, but soon resumes his running at an even more frantic pace.

5. Clowning around.

   Bart, the self-proclaimed class clown, makes ongoing comments about each student's reading as they take turns reading orally. It becomes more and more disruptive as students giggle, hiss, and talk back. The teacher sees that scolding Bart is not producing noticeable results. She decides to put the behavior on extinction. But the behavior does not decrease with this strategy, either.

6. I don't want to do that any more, any more.

   The hypothesis evolving from a functional assessment is that Calvic engages in self-injurious behaviors to escape tasks with significant motor demands. Ms. Parker decides to redirect Calvic's hand to task materials each time his hand rises above his shoulder. He is reinforced each time he touches the material. After six days of this intervention, Calvic's SIB was not decreasing.

7. There are limits.

   Mrs. Clinton has a token economy in her fourth-grade class. Students can both earn points and lose them (response-cost). After two weeks, she needs to adjust for the amount of carryover points the students can keep and use. She sets a ceiling on the number of points an individual student can earn in any given week not to exceed 5% in excess of the most "expensive" item on the reinforcer menu. For the next week, students earn points within this new limited number of points available while continuing to lose the usual number of points for misbehavior. By Thursday lunchtime, the students no longer seem to be engaged in their work.

8. Continued, and continued, and continued.

   Ms. Cohen says the following two behaviors will result in a fine: getting out of your seat without permission and calling people names. That afternoon Steve gets out of his seat without permission. Ms. Cohen goes over and asks for three tokens. Ms. Cohen says, "Steve, your being out of your seat will cost you three tokens". Steve says, "I wasn't really out of my seat because it was for a good reason, Ron's money fell and I had to give it to him." "Steve we did not say there were good and bad reasons for being out of your seat." Steve adds, "Besides, that is too many tokens because I was out of my seat for a good reason and only for just a second." "Steve, I am sure I said that will cost you three tokens. Three tokens now." "I understand you said that. But you need to understand that I really wasn't out of my seat except for a very good reason." This exchange continued, and continued, and continued.

9. Amphibian competition.

   Mr. Morris set up a math competition between the Frogs and the Toads. The two groups earn points for the number of math problems solved correctly. They lose points for grabbing papers and for yelling. Mr. Morris fined the Frogs a point the first time they yelled. He fined them a point again the next time. When the Toads yelled, he fined them two points more than the Frogs because they yelled louder. When it occurred again, the Toads lost three points and the Frogs lost one. Then the Toads lost an additional point for "grousing" about the point loss. The Toads eventually lost the competition by a considerable margin, mainly because of the very few points earned for completion and accuracy.

10. In the community.

    Mrs. O'Hara has designed a time-out ribbon procedure to use during community-based instruction. Before each session in the community, she and three students review what are good and bad behaviors and what happens when you engage in a bad behavior: "I will take your sweatband off your wrist, and for the next 5 minute you cannot earn tokens for dessert." While out in the community, each time someone commits an infraction, she takes the three students' wristbands and does not return them for 5 minutes.

11. The scales of justice.

    At the lunch table the students in Mr. Brown's class are talking about the token economy in their class. The first Monday morning of each month Mr. Brown announces the items that will earn or lose points for the month. Then in the afternoon the class discusses and finalizes the rules for the month. During the month of October, they will be getting one point for bringing in their homework, one point for subject-verb agreements in their paragraph writing each morning, and one point for each library book they read. They will lose two points for each pencil they sharpen over two a day, two points for a dropped piece of paper, and three points for whispering to a neighbor. The students say that it seems unfair, but they cannot put their fingers on exactly why.

12. A walk together.

    John is a 6-year-old with autism. He always seems to be in such distress, whining and thrashing his arms around. So when the teacher asks the paraeducator to walk him to the time-out room, she walks with him, talking to him in a soothing manner, and hands him his favorite keys. Three weeks of data indicate no decrease in John's inappropriate behavior.

Chapter 9

Differential Reinforcement: Antecedent Control and Shaping

Did you know that . . .

- Not all discrimination is the concern of the Equal Employment Opportunity Commission?
- Not all prompters work in theater?
- Applied behavior analysts shape up behavior rather than ship out students?
- You can teach anybody anything?

CHAPTER OUTLINE

In Chapters 7 and 8, we described some ways to increase appropriate behavior and to decrease inappropriate behavior. That solved a number of problems having to do with behavioral deficits and excesses. Not all problems, however, can be solved simply by increasing or decreasing the frequency of behaviors. Many behaviors are defined as appropriate or inappropriate based not on their frequency but on the circumstances under which they occur. Running, for example, may be viewed very differently by the track coach and the teacher with hall duty. What makes running appropriate or not depends not on how often or how fast someone runs but on the circumstances under which someone runs. It is very appropriate to run on the track during practice but very inappropriate to run in the halls of the school. Yelling is perfectly acceptable, even admirable, when the team scores a touchdown but considered a problem behavior when it occurs in the cafeteria. Many academic skills are acquired when a student learns, for example, to say a word he knows in response to printed letters (we call that reading) or to write a numeral he knows how to write on a worksheet with examples like "2 +1 = " (we call that math). Bringing responses the learner already knows under the control of the appropriate cue or signal is called *stimulus control.* There are many other antecedent influences on behavior that must also be considered when implementing behavior-change procedures.

When people learn about reinforcement procedures, they often protest that the behavior they are looking for cannot be reinforced because it never occurs. How can one increase something that does not exist? How does a teacher reinforce talking when a student never talks? sitting when a student never sits? or anything at all when a student appears to do absolutely nothing? One way of teaching students to do new things is by **shaping.** The teacher literally molds or shapes an existing response into the desired behavior.

Stimulus control and shaping are often used together to teach students academic and social behaviors. For that reason, and because both make use of differential reinforcement procedures, they are both described in this chapter. The first part of the chapter describes in detail the phenomenon of stimulus control and stimulus control procedures for use in the classroom.

Antecedent Influences on Behavior

In Chapters 7 and 8, when we talked about arranging consequences to increase or decrease behavior, we were concerned with what happens after a behavior is performed—with the effects of behavior on the environment. In this chapter, our concern will be with what happens before the behavior is performed—with the effects of the environment on behavior. We will describe some influences that may be distant in time and space from the behavior we observe as well as those closely associated.

Applied behavior analysts have traditionally focused on antecedent conditions and events that occur and can be observed immediately before a given behavior. In recent years, there has been an increasing emphasis in examining the influence of conditions and events that exist or occur at times or settings outside the environment being observed (Luiselli & Cameron, 1998). As we discussed in Chapter 6, functional analysis to assess the influences on challenging behaviors must consider such setting events in addition to immediately observable factors. **Setting events** may be environmental (including instructional and physical aspects of the environment and environmental changes), physiological, or social (Bailey, Wolery, & Sugai, 1988; Kazdin, 2000). Setting events may also be manipulated to bring about desired changes in behavior. This may be accomplished by removing or preventing the occurrence of a setting event, reducing the effects of the setting event if it cannot be eliminated entirely, or satiating the student with a reinforcer when she is in a state of deprivation in regard to it (Kennedy & Meyer, 1998). If, for example, a student frequently comes to school cranky from sleep deprivation (physiological setting event) and refuses to work and has tantrums on those days, a conference with parents or other caregivers about an earlier or more consistent bedtime might have excellent results. The reinforcers available for appropriate behavior will be more powerful when the student is not sleep deprived and cranky. Carr, Smith, Giacin, Whelen, and Pancari (2003) provided pain-relieving medication and other palliatives to three women with mental retardation whose challenging behaviors were related to menstrual discomfort. It was impossible to prevent or remove the discomfort entirely, but reducing it resulted in positive changes in behavior. There are numerous examples in Chapter 8 of the use of noncontingent reinforcement. In these interventions, students are provided, at no charge as it were, with large amounts of the reinforcer maintaining a challenging behavior. A student, for example, who avoids tasks and wants only to play games on the computer, may be allowed to play on the computer for an extended time before being asked to perform tasks.

Other antecedent manipulations may involve changes to the environment when setting events are known to be in effect. Dadson and Horner (1993), for example, changed classroom expectations for a young woman with severe disabilities who displayed challenging behaviors when she had less than 8 hours sleep or when her bus was late. They provided extra attention from teachers and paraprofessionals on those days, allowed the student to substitute a preferred activity for one she disliked, and allowed her more opportunities to make choices about the order in which she would do tasks. Her behavior improved significantly. It seems self-evident that teachers who are aware of setting events beyond their control should manipulate those that are within their control. If a teacher is aware that a student is undergoing a family trauma, he can take care to decrease demands and increase the availability of powerful reinforcers. The same kinds of modifications might be made for a student whose medication is being adjusted, whose household size has been significantly increased by the arrival of immigrating relatives, whose placement has or is about to be changed, or who is simply unnerved by the presence of a young lady upon whom he has a crush.

Differential Reinforcement for Stimulus Control

Operant and respondent conditioning are contrasted on page.

When describing events that affect operant behavior, it is important to remember the distinction between operant and respondent behavior described in Chapter 1. Respondent conditioning involves stimuli that elicit reflexive behavior—for example, the puff of air (unconditioned stimulus) that results automatically in an eye blink (response). This automaticity is absent in operant behavior; the relationship between antecedent events and behavior is learned rather than reflexive. Although antecedent events do not elicit operant behavior, they do exert considerable influence over such behavior.

Principles of Discrimination

Students learn to discriminate as a result of differential reinforcement.

Discrimination is the ability to tell the difference between environmental events or stimuli. Discrimination develops as a result of differential reinforcement. A certain response results in positive reinforcement (S^{R+}) in the presence of a given stimulus or group of stimuli that are said to be discriminative stimuli (S^Ds) for the response. The same response is not reinforced in the presence of a second stimulus or group of stimuli, referred to as **S-deltas (S^Δs).** After a period of time, the response will occur reliably in the presence of S^D and infrequently, if at all, in the presence of S^Δ. The S^D is then said to occasion the response (Holland & Skinner, 1961). This relationship between the S^D and the response is different from that between the unconditioned stimulus and response in respondent conditioning. The S^D does not elicit the response; it just sets the occasion for it, or to use the technical terminology, it **occasions** it. The response that occurs in the presence of S^D, but not in its absence, is said to be under stimulus control. A behavior under stimulus control will continue to occur in the presence of the S^D even when reinforcement is infrequent. Michael (1982) suggested care be taken to avoid saying an event is an S^D for reinforcement—it is the behavior that is occasioned, not its reinforcement. The development of discrimination is an important factor in much human learning. A baby learns that saying "mama" is reinforced in the presence of the adult with the glasses and the curly hair, but usually results in the disappearance of the adult with the beard. Glasses and curly hair are an S^D for the response "mama." A beard is an S^Δ. The first grader learns that saying "went" in the presence of a flash card with the letters *w-e-n-t* (S^D) results in praise, but that the same response to a flash card with the letters *c-a-m-e* (S^Δ) does not. A group of junior-high students learns that obscene language and disruptive behavior get their math teacher's (S^D) attention, but that the social studies teacher (S^Δ) attends only to raised hands and completed assignments. "Mama" is the right response to the adult with the curly hair and glasses and the wrong response to the adult with the beard. "Went" is the right response to the flashcard with the letters *w-e-n-t* and the wrong response to a flashcard with any other set of letters. Obscene language and disruptive behavior are the right way to get the math teacher's attention but not that of the social studies teacher. Many teachers unwittingly make themselves into S^Ds for inappropriate behavior by giving it their attention.

Much of the everyday behavior of adults is a result of discrimination learning. We answer telephones when they ring, not when they are silent. We drive through intersections when lights are green, not when they are red. Discriminations based on relatively informal or imprecise patterns of reinforcement develop slowly and are often imperfect. For example, babies may, for a while, call all men with beards "daddy." First graders may say "went" when they see a flash card with the letters *w-a-n-t* or *w-e-t*. Junior-high students may occasionally raise their hands in math class or utter obscenities in social studies class. Adults sometimes pick up the phone when the doorbell rings.

The imperfect stimulus control exerted by traffic signals provides employment for numerous police officers, tow-truck drivers, and ambulance attendants. Van Houten and Retting (2001) recently reported a study that added a light-emitting diode (LED) sign showing eyes looking right and left and a "LOOK BOTH WAYS" legend to a traditional stop sign at a busy intersection, thus reducing " conflicts between vehicles on the major and minor road" (p. 185). The use of prompts like this one will be described in detail later in this chapter.

Discrimination Training

Teaching students to respond appropriately to specific stimuli is the teacher's basic job. As teachers, we want our students to obey rules, follow instructions, and perform specified academic or functional skills at the appropriate time, in the appropriate place, and in response to specified instructions or other cues. A major part of the teaching task is establishing specific times, places, instructions, and other antecedent events as discriminative stimuli for various student behaviors.

To increase your understanding of stimulus control, go to the "Web Links" module for Chapter 9 of the Companion Website.

Simple Discrimination

When establishing simple discriminations, we want a student to differentiate something—his name, for example, from other things that are not his name. The teacher presents a flash card with the student's name on it and a flash card with an unrelated word. The teacher says, "Point to your name." If the student responds by pointing to the correct card (S^D), he receives a reinforcer. If he responds to the other card (S^Δ), no reinforcer is delivered. The ability to read means the ability to distinguish each combination of letters constituting a word from all other combinations. A student may use the word "went" in conversation but not say "went" when shown a flash card with the letters *w-e-n-t* and asked, "What is this word?" The teacher wants to bring saying "went" under stimulus control of the letters *w-e-n-t*.

In this example, the teacher established the letters *w-e-n-t* as the S^D for the response "went" through the process of differential reinforcement. The response is reinforced in the presence of *w-e-n-t* (S^D) and not in the presence of *g-o* or any other combination of letters (S^Δ). With sufficient repetition, the student should reliably respond correctly and could then be said to have formed a discrimination. Note that *g-o,* which functions as S^Δ in this example, will be the S^D for responding with "go." The definition, as always, depends on the function. To state with any degree of confidence that the response "went" is under stimulus control, the teacher will have to establish that no other combination of letters occasions the response, including combinations such as w-a-n-t and w-e-t, whose shape and spelling (topography) closely resemble that of the S^D. The teacher will also want to determine that w-e-n-t is a reliable S^D for "went" when it is written in places other than on the original flash card. Students can be taught discriminations using only repeated presentation of S^D and S^Δs with reinforcement for correct responding, but that is a very inefficient teaching method. We will discuss ways to increase teaching efficiency when we describe prompts and errorless learning strategies later in this chapter.

It is important to be sure that students are responding to salient features of the stimulus. One first-grade teacher thought she had finally taught one of her students to read the word "come" only to learn that the real S^D was a smudge on the flash card. Many beginning readers identify words by their first letters alone. This strategy works well as long as "went" is the only word in the reader that starts with w. When the teacher introduces the word "what," however, the student can no longer discriminate reliably. Students may respond either to some totally irrelevant stimulus, like the smudge on the flash card, or to only one aspect of the stimulus, like the first letter of a word. This tendency toward **stimulus overselectivity** (Lovaas, Schreibman, Koegel, & Rhen, 1971) is a characteristic of some student with disabilities.

The teacher tells the student what the word is before asking for the discrimination to be made.

Many things that teachers want students to learn involve multiple simple discriminations. Students must discriminate each letter of the alphabet from all the other letters and from stimuli that do not represent letters of the alphabet. Each numeral must be discriminated from all the others and all other stimuli. Chemistry students must discriminate each element of the periodic table from the others and from stimuli that do not represent elements.

Concept Formation

A **concept** is a class of stimuli that have characteristics in common (Becker, Engelmann, & Thomas, 1975a). All members of the class should occasion the same response. There are many stimuli properly identified as person, mammal, prime number, honesty, and so forth. Each of these words, and hundreds of thousands of others, represents a class of stimuli having common characteristics, or a concept. In order to learn a concept, a student must discriminate based on specific characteristics common to a large number of stimuli, thus forming an abstraction (Ferster, Culbertson, & Boren, 1975).

Such learning may be accomplished by providing many samples of positive and negative instances of the concept or abstraction and reinforcing correct responses. Using such a procedure, Herrnstein and Loveland (1964) were able to teach pigeons to respond differently to pictures that included people and to pictures that did not. They simply reinforced pecking only on pictures containing people. Basic concepts, those that cannot be fully described with other words (other than synonyms; Engelmann & Carnine, 1982, p. 10), must be taught in almost the same way to people.

Try to think of a way to teach a 3-year-old child the concept "red" by describing it. Obviously, it is impossible. What most parents do is provide many examples of red things, label them, and provide strong reinforcement when the child points and says "red" appropriately or when the child responds correctly to the instruction "Give me the red block." Most children learn thousands of basic concepts in this informal manner before ever entering school. Children who do not must be taught them systematically. For these children, we do not wait for casual opportunities to introduce "red" into conversation. We get some red objects and some not-red objects and proceed to label, instruct, and ask for responses until the student demonstrates mastery of the concept.

Concepts may often be taught more efficiently by using additional antecedent stimuli. If the common elements of a stimulus class can be listed—if the concept can be verbally defined—it may be more efficient to provide a set of rules for identifying instances and then reinforcing correct responses. Concepts that can be verbally defined need not be taught using only differential reinforcement. Most students, unlike pigeons, have some verbal skills that enable a teacher to use sets of rules as shortcuts in teaching them concepts or abstractions.

PROMPTS

This kind of prompting will be discussed later in the chapter.

A **prompt** is an additional stimulus that increases the probability that the S^D will occasion the desired response. Prompts are offered after an S^D has been presented and has failed to occasion the response. Most people are familiar with the use of prompts in the theater. An actor who fails to respond to his cues (the preceding lines, for example) is prompted from the wings. The use of the word "prompt" in applied behavior analysis has a similar meaning. Students who fail to respond to S^Ds are prompted. Prompts can be in the form of assistance with a response (response prompts) or by making temporary changes to the stimulus (stimulus prompts). Wolery and Gast (1984) provided a thorough review of both kinds of prompts as well as suggestions for fading them. Prompts may be presented verbally, visually, or physically. The desired response may also be demonstrated or modeled. The reading teacher who holds up a flash card with the letters *w-e-n-t* and says, "Not came, but . . . " is providing a verbal prompt. The kindergarten teacher who puts photographs as well as name tags on her students' lockers is providing a visual prompt. The mother who says to her child, "Wave bye-bye to Granny," while vigorously flapping the infant's hand, is furnishing a physical prompt. Each hopes that control will eventually be attached to the S^D "went," the student's name, or "wave bye-bye." The prompt is a crutch to be gradually withdrawn (faded) as soon as the need for it no longer exists. Prompts increase teaching efficiency. Rather than waiting for the student to emit the desired behavior, the teacher uses extra cues to increase the number of correct responses. The more correct responses that occur, the more there are to be reinforced, and the faster the behavior will be learned. When prompting is used, a reinforcer is usually delivered just as if the student had not needed prompting.

Rules as Verbal Prompts

The English teacher who wants students to identify nouns and verbs correctly will probably not simply give students numerous chances to respond with "noun" or "verb" when they read sentences with the S^D underlined. Because most people have the ability to use verbal rules or definitions to form concepts, the English teacher might define noun, then present students with sentences and ask, "Is the underlined word a noun?" (S^D). "Is it the name of a person, place, or thing? Then it's a noun" (prompt). "Right, John, it's a noun" (S^{R+}). Prompting using rules or definitions is not confined to academic tasks. By defining honesty, politeness, kindness, or any other concept related to social behavior, a teacher can prompt students until they can identify instances of each behavior. This, of course, does not ensure that students will engage in the behaviors, merely that they can label them.

Instructions as Verbal Prompts

Instructions are often a means of prompting behavior. If, when the teacher says, "Get ready for reading," the children do not move, the teacher will probably add, "Put your materials away and go to the reading circle." If the S^D does not occasion correct responding, the teacher may provide step-by-step instructions. The teacher who uses instructions as prompts is making two assumptions. The first is that the instructions offered are accurate. It is not easy to give clear, verbal instructions for a complex task. If people who ask you for directions to get from one place to another by car usually become hopelessly lost, do not be surprised if students fail to follow your instructions. The second assumption is that the student's behavior is under stimulus control of the general S^D, "Follow instructions." Many students do not follow instructions, as any experienced teacher will attest. Before depending on instructions as prompts, the wise teacher will determine that students do indeed follow them. It may be necessary to bring this response under stimulus control first. Becker et al. (1975a) suggested that teachers reinforce following instructions to the most specific detail. Practice in this skill can be provided by specifying details arbitrarily, such as telling students to line up with their toes on a crack in the floor or to perform activities in a specified order even though no specific order is required. This kind of practice can become a game. The traditional Simon Says game provides practice in following instructions.

It's not easy to give instructions.

Another technique for teaching students to follow instructions more reliably is to issue a series of instructions with which students are likely to comply (high-probability or high-p instructions) followed rapidly by an instruction with which they are less likely to comply (low-probability or low-p instruction). This has been shown in increase compliance with the low-p instruction. One might say to a group of students, for example, "Touch your head, touch your nose, clap your hands, get out your math books." The behavioral momentum created by compliance to the high-p instructions carries students through the low-p instruction. (Ardoin, Martens, & Wolfe, 1999).

Hints as Verbal Prompts

Many verbal prompts are less elaborate and more informal than rules or instructions. A reading teacher might prompt the correct response to the S^D, *dog,* by saying, "This is an animal that says 'bow-wow'." When a teacher tells the class to line up, then adds, "Quietly," this too is a prompt. Such reminders or hints increase the probability that the correct response will be emitted, thus supplying an opportunity for reinforcement.

Self-Operated Verbal Prompts

For practice identifying how prompts are used, go to the "Activities" module for Chapter 9 of the Companion Website.

Several studies have demonstrated that recorded verbal prompts can enable students with disabilities to acquire vocational skills (Alberto, Sharpton, Briggs, & Stright, 1986; Briggs et al., 1990; Mitchell, Schuster, Collins, & Gassaway, 2000; Steed & Lutzker, 1999; Taber, Alberto, & Fredrick, 1998). A complex task is broken into its component steps and a teacher records an instruction for each step on audiotape. Students use portable tape players with headphones and are taught to operate the player and to follow instructions. The student is instructed to listen to each step and to turn off the tape to perform it. When the student turns the player back on, the next step is prompted. The student is periodically asked to evaluate her progress and to ask for assistance if necessary. Self-operated recorded prompts have also been used to increase fluency of task performance (Davis, Brady, Williams, & Burta, 1992). Students are allowed to choose music to listen to; the teacher superimposes verbal prompts such as "Keep on working" on the musical selection. A major advantage of this procedure is that it is by no means unusual in many workplaces for employees to wear portable tape players and headphones on the job. The apparatus, therefore, does not draw undue attention to the workers with disabilities even if the prompts are needed for a long period of time or even permanently (Davis et al., 1992).

Visual Prompts

Many teaching strategies involve some form of visual prompting. The illustrations in most beginning readers are designed to aid students in identifying the printed word. Teachers may give examples of correctly completed math problems to prompt students. Students may be allowed to use a matrix of multiplication facts when learning complex computational procedures. A number line may be used when students are learning to add or subtract (Fueyo & Bushell, 1998). Rivera, Koorland, and Fueyo (2002) used picture prompts to teach sight words to a student with learning disabilities. The student drew his own representations for the words and gradually made the pictures smaller and less vividly colored. Picture prompts have been used to help teach a wide variety of behaviors to learners with disabilities, particularly complex daily living and vocational tasks. Martin, Rusch, James, Decker, and Trtol (1974) taught adults with moderate and severe disabilities to prepare complex meals independently by using sequenced picture prompts. Wilson, Schepis, and Mason-Main (1987) taught an adult with moderate retardation to perform food-service tasks independently at a restaurant with the owners ultimately providing his only supervision. Frank, Wacker, Berg, and McMahon (1985) taught students with mild mental retardation selected microcomputer skills. Schmit, Alper, Raschke, and Ryndak (2000) used photographs to assist a student with autism to handle transitions. Kimball, Kinney, Taylor, and Stromer (2003) used Microsoft PowerPoint® to create individual, interactive, activity schedules for young students with autism. Wacker and Berg (1983) taught high school students with moderate and severe retardation complex vocational tasks. They provided the students with books of pictures illustrating the successive steps in performing a complex assembly task and trained them to use the books, that is, to turn a page after each step and to match the correct object to its illustration. The authors found that the books greatly improved students' performance. The students were able to learn new tasks using picture prompts more quickly than they learned the initial task. Students were able to perform tasks without the books after training had been completed. A procedure using a combination of picture cues and other prompts enabled students with autism to choose and engage in leisure and after-school activities more independently (MacDuff, Krantz, & MacClannahan, 1993). Copeland and Hughes (2000) used picture prompts to teach high school students with severe disabilities to complete vocational tasks. They added a self-monitoring component requiring the students to touch each picture before starting and to turn it over when finished. This increased the students' independent task completion. Many employers use picture prompts to train both disabled and nondisabled workers. Figure 9–1 is a picture prompt like those used to train workers at fast-food restaurants to prepare basic hamburgers and cheeseburgers. Some restaurants now print these prompts directly on the wrappers for the sandwiches. One advantage of picture prompts is that once students have been taught to use them, they can do so independently, just as adults use maps or diagrams to prompt themselves. Many educators, in fact, consider such prompts as examples of self-management of behavior rather than merely as teaching tools (Hughes et al., 2000; Lancioni & O'Reilly, 2001; Rodi & Hughes, 2000). Berg and Wacker (1989) illustrated the endless creativity required of those who work with students with disabilities by providing similar prompts for a student who was blind. Instead of pictures, they used a book with sandpaper numbers (tactile cues) and taught the student to match the numbers to those on bins of materials.

Visual prompts can save a lot of teacher time. Bulletin boards in classrooms can easily be used to provide picture prompts. Line drawings or photographs of the correct procedure for accomplishing some task, or a picture of the way desks should look before leaving the room, or a photograph of the class in a nice straight line on the way to the cafeteria posted just inside the doorway could all be used to prompt correct responding.

Other visual prompts are provided in written form. Classroom schedules and rules are often posted to serve as reminders of cues. Many students are easily prompted to do complex new tasks by written instructions. Think of all the tasks you do that depend on written instructions and think of how important it is that the instructions are clear and accurate. Anyone who has tried to assemble children's toys late at night before a holiday can attest to the importance of clarity and accuracy. Of course, written instructions are technically verbal prompts, because the written word is a form of verbal (though not vocal) communication. Because they are processed visually, however, it seems logical to consider them here.

Krantz and McClannahan (1993) used a written script to prompt a child with autism to interact with peers. Kate was given a written list of statements and questions relevant to school activities. She was taught (using physical prompts) to pick up a pencil, point to an item, and move the pencil along below the text. She was then physically prompted to face a classmate and instructed to ask the question or issue the statement. The physical guidance was faded first and Kate continued to use the

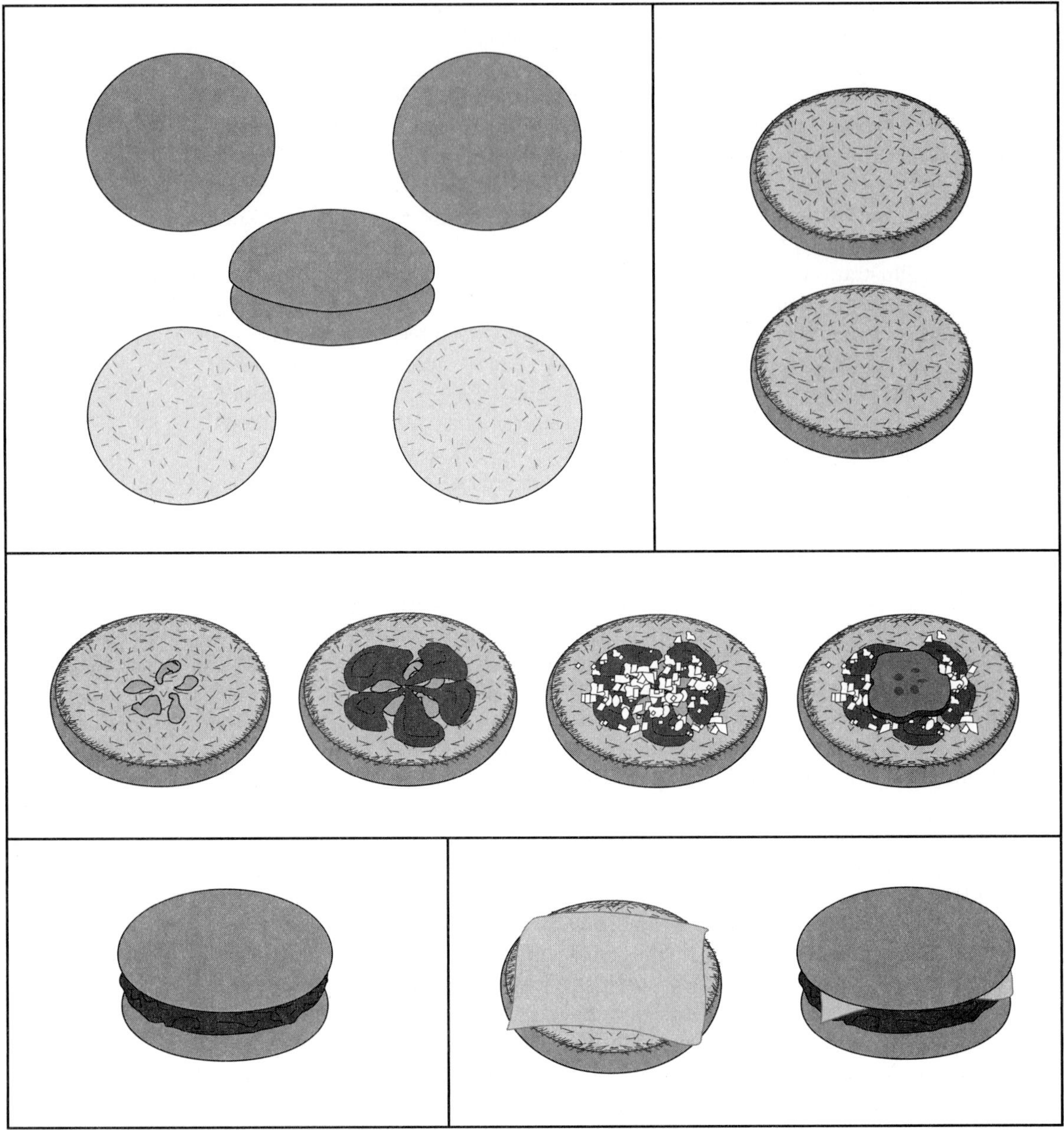

FIGURE 9–1 ***Picture prompt for preparing hamburgers.***

script independently. Even after the script was faded, Kate continued to interact with her peers more frequently. A similar study used a combination of picture prompts and very simple words to increase interaction with adults in young children with autism who had very limited reading skills. The students learned to read "Look" and "Watch me," and cards with these words were interspersed with pictures in their activity schedules. They were prompted to read the words aloud when they appeared, thus asking for adult attention. As any parent knows, that is an extremely typical behavior of young children. The students' verbal interactions with adults increased and spontaneous requests for attention occurred (Krantz & McClannahan, 1998).

Teachers often provide such prompts for themselves as well as for their students. A road map help the itinerant consulting teaching who is given the S^D, "Go to Oakhaven School." Some teachers post reminders to themselves to help them remember to reinforce certain student behaviors. Other adults use prompts as well: hand-held computers, calendars, address books, tickler files, and sticky memos often remind us of tasks or information we knew but would not have remembered without a prompt.

MODELING

"Watch me, I'll show you," says the teacher. This teacher is using yet another kind of prompt. When verbal instructions or visual cues are insufficient, many teachers demonstrate, or model, the desired behavior. In many cases, demonstration may be the procedure of choice from the start. A home economics teacher attempting to tell the class how to thread a sewing machine provides a convincing example of the superiority of demonstration.

The majority of students, including those who have mild disabilities, easily imitate the behavior of a model. Many explanations of this phenomenon have been offered (see Bandura, 1969, for a complete discussion), but the simplest is that most students' history of reinforcement includes considerable reinforcement of imitative behavior, resulting in a generalized imitation response. In other words, "Do it like this" has become an S^D for imitation in virtually any setting.

Origin of the generalized imitation response.

Most individuals reinforced for imitating various responses will eventually also imitate unreinforced responses (Malott, Whaley, & Malott, 1997). Anyone observing a parent interacting with an infant has seen examples of positive reinforcement of imitation. Such reinforcement occurs throughout the preschool years so that most children come to school already accustomed to responding to the S^D, "Do it like this" or "Do it like Mary." Of course, children are as likely to imitate inappropriate behavior as appropriate behavior. Many a parent has at some point been startled at how quickly children imitate less admirable parental habits.

Students also imitate the behavior of their classmates. Kindergarten students spontaneously play Follow the Leader. Nonacademic behaviors, such as speech patterns, are frequently imitated. It is amazing how quickly a new student with a distinctive regional accent begins to sound exactly like his or her peers. The tendency to imitate peers perhaps reaches its zenith in the secondary school. Adolescents tend to dress alike, talk alike, and engage in the same activities.

Furnishing appropriate models for students with disabilities is one of the primary goals of the current trend toward placement of such students in settings with as many typical students as possible. It is hypothesized that the students with disabilities will imitate and thus learn from their nondisabled peers. This may happen in an informal way but may also be programmed. Werts, Caldwell, and Wolery (1996), for example, taught nondisabled peers to model and verbally describe a complex behavior for children with disabilities included in their classroom. The nondisabled peers were able to model the behaviors effectively, and the students with disabilities learned to perform them.

In using demonstration techniques to prompt behavior, a teacher may choose to model the behavior personally, to allow another student to be a model, or to bring in someone from outside the group. The choice of a model is important, as certain characteristics increase models' effectiveness. Students are most likely to imitate models who

- are similar to themselves
- are competent
- have prestige (Sulzer-Azaroff & Mayer, 1986)

A very promising modeling technique has recently become possible because of video technology. Video self-modeling (Buggey, 1999; Dowrick, 1999) uses edited video recordings to show students themselves performing a behavior correctly. It is even possible with more sophisticated editing to show students themselves engaged in behaviors they have never actually performed. Seeing a model that is not just similar to herself, but is herself, who is competent (at least on the tape) and who certainly must be prestigious (she's on TV!) has promise for changing a wide variety of social and academic behaviors.

Modeling may be used to prompt simple or more complex behaviors. A teacher may use modeling to prompt speech in a student with severe disabilities. A math teacher may task a competent student to demonstrate a problem on the board before other students are expected to work similar problems on their own. A physical education teacher may demonstrate a complex gymnastic performance. Hunter (1984) described a procedure that combines verbal and physical modeling. She suggested that the teacher first perform the skill while describing the actions involved, then perform the skill while the students provide the verbal prompts, then ask students to perform it while the teacher provides verbal guidance. Students are then asked to perform the skill on their own. There is some evidence that a verbal description of what is being demonstrated makes modeling more effective (Hay, Murray, Cecire, & Nash, 1985; Hunter, 1984). Most of us can intuitively confirm that by remembering a high school or college mathematics instructor who demonstrated highly involved proofs or algorithms on the board while saying not a word, then turned to the class and asked, "Everyone got that?" The following anecdote illustrates a procedure combining modeling with verbal instructions.

The Students Learn to Polka

Some children with poor gross-motor skills were enrolled in an after-school program designed to improve motor coordination. Their teacher decided that, because the students had mastered skipping and hopping, they would enjoy learning to polka. "Let's polka!" said the teacher. "Watch what I do. Step-together-step-hop! Now you do it. Step-together-step-hop." Soon, when the teacher said, "Let's polka!" the students produced the desired movement. Many of them, incidentally, continued to whisper "step-together-step-hop" as they danced.

Self-instruction is discussed in Chapter 11.

Modeling can be an effective prompting procedure, but it does have limitations. Some behaviors are difficult to imitate. Some students, particularly those who have severe disabilities, have not acquired a generalized imitation response and do not respond to verbal cues. Although it is possible to teach students to respond to modeled prompts by reinforcing imitation, other forms of prompting may be required. Many teaching procedures involve combining various kinds of prompts.

PHYSICAL GUIDANCE

When students fail to respond to less stringent forms of prompting, they may be physically prompted. Such a procedure, often called *putting-through,* is useful for teaching many motor behaviors and some vocal behaviors that may be manually guided (Karen), 1974). Physical prompting may be a first step in the development of a generalized imitation response. Streifel and Wetherby (1973) taught a student with severe retardation to follow instructions, such as "Raise your hand," by using a physical guidance procedure. The teacher first gave the verbal instruction, then guided the student so that the instruction was followed. Eventually, the student's behavior was under the control of

The teacher puts his or her hand on the student's hand and pulls it up.

the instructions. The implications of bringing the behavior of students with severe disabilities under stimulus control of imitation and instructions are enormous. Students who will imitate a model and follow instructions can be taught many things. Physical guidance procedures are by no means limited to use with students with disabilities. Most teachers routinely use such procedures when teaching beginning handwriting skills, for example. Music teachers may guide their students' fingering. Many athletic skills are most easily taught using physical guidance. It is difficult to imagine any other way of teaching anyone to change gears in a car with a four-speed manual transmission. When using physical guidance, teaching need to be sure that the student is cooperative. Such a procedure will be unpleasant (possibly to both parties) if it is performed with a resisting student. Even cooperative students may have a tendency to tighten up when physically prompted.

Other Tactile Prompts

Advances in technology have made it possible to prompt students using paging devices more commonly used by very busy and important people who are considerate enough to turn them to "vibrate" when in public. Researchers have used a pager that can be activated by remote control (Shabani et al., 2002) or one that can be preset to activate at specified intervals (Taylor & Levin, 1998) to prompt students with autism to initiate interaction with peers. This technology appears to have promise for other students and behaviors.

Fading

A prompted response is not under stimulus control. Prompts must be withdrawn, and the response must be occasioned by the S^D alone. Too abrupt removal of prompts, however, may result in termination of the desired behavior. Gradual removal of prompts is referred to as **fading.** Any prompt may be gradually faded so that the response occurs and is reinforced when the S^D alone is presented. Considerable skill is involved in determining the optimum rate of fading: too fast, and the behavior will not occur frequently enough for reinforcement to be effective; too slow, and students may become permanently dependent on the prompt. Prompts can be faded in a number of different ways. Billingsley and Romer (1983) reviewed systems for fading prompts and suggested four major categories: decreasing assistance, graduated guidance, time delay, and increasing assistance.

Decreasing Assistance

When using decreasing assistance (sometimes called most-to-least prompts) for fading prompts, the teacher begins with a level of prompting that virtually assures that the student will produce the appropriate response. The amount of assistance is then systematically reduced as the student becomes more competent. This procedure can be used to fade a wide variety of prompts. The English teacher using rules to help her students identify nouns might start the S^D, "Is this a noun?" and the prompt, "If it's the name of a person, place, or thing, it's a noun." When her students respond reliably, she might say:

Is this a noun? (S^D)

Is it the name of a person, place, or thing? (prompt)

then

Is this a noun? (S^D)

Remember, person, place, or thing. (prompt)

then

Is this a noun? (S^D)

Remember your rule. (prompt)

and finally

Is this a noun? (S^D, no prompt)

The math teacher using the decreasing assistance procedure to fade a visual prompt might allow students a complete multiplication matrix to help them work problems and systematically remove easier combinations as they are mastered. The teacher who fades a modeling prompt may demonstrate less of the behavior, perhaps fading from full demonstration to only partial demonstration of the response (Wilcox & Bellamy, 1982) and finally providing only a gesture. The following anecdote illustrates such a fading procedure.

The Children Learn to Hula Hoop

Coach Townsend was an elementary school physical education teacher. He decided to teach the first graders to hula hoop so they could perform at open house. He began by demonstrating. "Watch me!" he said and proceeded to show the students how to do it. When the giggles died down, he handed each first grader a hula hoop. "Ready," he said, "hoop!" Twenty-six hoops hit the floor clattering and banging. The children looked discouraged. The coach took a hoop from one student. "Okay," he said, "start it like this." He pushed his hoop with his hands. "Now do this." He rotated his hips. When the giggles died down, he said, "Again, just like this!" Coach Townsend gave the hoop back to the student and just demonstrated the movements. He eventually faded the hand movement to a flick of the wrist and the hip movements to a mere twitch. Before long, the cry "Ready, hoop!" was enough.

The great day finally arrived. Twenty-six first graders equipped with hula hoops stood in the gym. Their parents sat in the bleachers. Coach Townsend started the music and said, "Ready, hoop!" He stood to one side of the group. The children did him great credit, but he heard suppressed giggling from the audience. The coach finally realized that, in his enthusiasm, he had gone back to modeling the necessary hip movements.

Csapo (1981) illustrated a system of decreasing prompts when using a physical guidance procedure to teach students with severe disabilities a discrimination task. The verbal instruction was initially followed by a full physical prompt, then by a partial prompt, and then by a gesture.

Stimulus shaping should not be confused with the shaping procedures described later in this chapter.

The system of decreasing prompts may also be used when combinations of prompts are used. If teachers initially provide students learning a new math skill with a demonstration, a sample problem, and step-by-step instructions, these three different kinds of prompts may be removed one by one until the students are responding simply to the incomplete example.

The most refined form of decreasing prompts results in virtually **errorless learning.** Many procedures termed errorless learning use alterations within the stimuli (S^Ds or S^Δs) to prompt correct responses. These prompts are often called **stimulus prompts,** and the procedure itself is sometimes called stimulus shaping. To enable students to make a discrimination more easily, some features of the S^D, the S^Δ, or both are changed. Malott et al. (1997) described a procedure by which Jimmy, a student with developmental delay, learned to discriminate his name from another by pasting the name *Susan* in white letters on a black card and the name *Jimmy* in white letters on a white background. Reinforcing the choice of *Jimmy* established the correct card as the

S^D. The background color on the *Jimmy* card was gradually darkened until both names were printed in white on black. The student made no incorrect choices and eventually made the discrimination based on the relevant stimulus properties.

Haupt, Van Kirk, and Terraciano (1975) used two decreasing prompts fading procedures to teach math facts. In one procedure, the student was asked to provide the answer to subtraction problems on flash cards. At first, the answers were visible, but they were gradually covered with colored cellophane. Eventually, there were 32 pieces of cellophane over the answer. The student learned and remembered the facts. The second procedure required written answers to multiplication facts. Successive thicknesses of tracing paper covered the initially visible answers. This procedure, too, was successful.

Another example was described by Ayllon (1997). A teacher was trying to teach a group of young children to discriminate their right from their left hands. On the first day of training, each child's right hand was labeled with an x made by a felt-tipped marker. This enabled the students to discriminate the S^D (right hand) from the S^Δ (left hand) when asked to raise their right hands. On the second day, the plan was again to mark right hands, but because of the permanence of the marker (or the personal habits of the children), each child still had a visible mark. As the training proceeded during the week, each child's mark gradually faded, and by week's end, each child consistently raised the right hand when asked. Mosk and Bucher (1984) used stimulus alteration to teach students with moderate and severe mental retardation to hang toothbrushes and washcloths on the correct peg. At the beginning of instruction, only one peg was on the board. Distractor pegs were introduced, one at a time. At first, each distractor peg was too short to hang the item on; longer pegs were gradually introduced.

Evidence indicates (Schreibman & Charlop, 1981; Stella & Etzel, 1978) that errorless learning is most efficient if the features of only the S^D are altered and the S^Δ is held constant. Although it is possible to provide for learning without errors with other prompting systems, the technical term errorless learning is most often used when systematic alteration of the discriminative stimulus is the primary form of prompting.

Fading for errorless learning provides for development of stimulus control without practicing incorrect responses and without occasioning inappropriate behavior that some students display when they make errors (Dunlap & Kern, 1996; Munk & Repp, 1994). Providing a completely error-free learning environment, however, may not always be desirable. Spooner and Spooner (1984) suggested that optimal learning may occur when initially high error rates decrease quickly and correct responding accelerates rapidly. Terrace (1966) pointed out that a lack of frustration tolerance may result from errorless training. In the real world, some errors are inevitable, and students must learn to handle mistakes. Krumboltz and Krumboltz (1972) suggested gradually programming students to persist after errors. Rodewald (1979) suggested that intermittent reinforcement during training may mitigate possible negative effects of errorless learning. Such intermittent reinforcement may help develop a tolerance for nonreinforcement of responses.

Graduated Guidance

Graduated guidance is used in fading physical prompts (Foxx & Azrin, 1972). The teacher begins with as much physical assistance as necessary and gradually reduces pressure. The focus of the guidance may be moved from the part of the body concerned (spatial fading), or a shadowing procedure may be substituted in which the teacher's hand does not touch the student but follows his movement throughout the performance of the behavior (Foxx & Azrin, 1973). Juan learns by a graduated guidance procedure in the following vignette.

Juan Learns to Eat with a Spoon

Juan was a student with severe mental retardation. His teacher, Ms. Baker, believed that he could eat lunch with his typical peers if he could learn to use a spoon instead of his fingers for eating. She equipped herself with a bowl of vanilla pudding and a spoon, hoping that the pudding, which Juan loved, would be a positive reinforcer for using the spoon and that vanilla would make a less visible mess than chocolate on Juan, herself, the table, and the floor. (Teachers have to think of everything!) Ms. Baker sat next to Juan, put her hand over his right hand, and guided it to the spoon. She helped him scoop up some pudding and guided his hand toward his mouth. When the spoon reached his mouth, he eagerly ate the pudding. Ms. Baker then removed Juan's left hand from the pudding dish and wiped it off with the damp cloth that she had thoughtfully provided. She repeated this procedure a number of times, praising and patting Juan whenever the spoon reached its goal. As she felt Juan making more of the necessary movements on his own, she gradually reduced the pressure of her hand until it was merely resting on Juan's. She then moved her hand away from his—to his wrist, to his elbow, and finally to his shoulder. Eventually, she removed her hand entirely. Juan was using the spoon on his own.

Time Delay

Time delay differs from other fading formats in that the form of the prompt itself is not changed, just its timing. Rather than presenting the prompt immediately, the teacher waits, thus allowing the student to respond before prompting. Delays are usually only a few seconds. Time delays can be constant (the delay remains the same length) or progressive (the interval before the prompt becomes longer as the student gains competence; Kleinert & Gast, 1982). Time delay procedures can also be used with a variety of prompting formats. Many teachers use them instinctively. Let's go back to our English teacher. She asks, "Is this a noun?" and waits a few seconds. Finding no response forthcoming, she prompts, "If it's the name of a person, place or thing, it's a noun." Textbooks about teaching often include a discussion of wait time (Kauchak & Eggen, 1998), encouraging teachers to give students up to 3 seconds to answer before providing assistance or calling on another student. Luciano (1986) used a systematic variation of this informal procedure to teach children with mental retardation to produce appropriate verbal responses.

Time delay can also be used to fade visual prompts. A teacher working on sight vocabulary might cover up the picture on the flash card and wait a few seconds to allow students to identify the word without seeing the picture. If they fail to respond within the latency the teacher has established, the picture is uncovered. Stevens and Schuster (1987) used a similar procedure to teach 15 spelling words to a student with learning disabilities.

Touchette and Howard (1984) used a progressive time delay to fade a modeled prompt. Students were asked to point to a specific letter or word printed on one of four cards. Initially, the teacher pointed to the correct card immediately on presentation of the verbal S^D. The teacher's pointing was gradually delayed to provide an opportunity for the student to respond without prompting. Touchette and Howard's results also indicated that responding to the S^D alone was learned somewhat more efficiently when responses made before the prompt were reinforced more heavily than responses occurring after the prompt. Time delay is easily implemented when using a physical prompt. A teacher working with a student on a dressing skill might say, "Pull up your pants," and then wait for the student to perform the behavior without assistance before providing it.

Morse and Schuster (2000) used time delay and other procedures to teach elementary students with moderate and severe disabilities to shop for groceries. Students were initially prompted immediately as they performed the steps required to complete the shopping task. Subsequently, a delay of 4 seconds was introduced before a prompt was given.

Increasing Assistance

Billingsley and Romer (1983) described increasing assistance as "similar to the reverse application of the decreasing assistance approach" (p. 6). Increasing assistance is also referred to as the *system of least prompts,* or *least-to-most prompts.* When using this procedure, the teacher starts with the S^D, moves to the least intrusive prompt in her repertoire, and gives students an opportunity to respond. Many teachers use a verbal least prompts procedure without being aware of the terminology. The English teacher says, "Is it a noun?" and gets no response. She prompts, "Remember your rule," and gets no response. She says, "Remember, person, place, or thing, " and gets no response. She prompts "Is it the name of a person, place, or thing?" and gets no response. She whimpers, "If it's the name of a person, place, or thing, then it's a noun." It is sometimes difficult to implement a verbal increasing assistance procedure without sounding either strident or whiny.

An increasing prompts procedure can be used to fade a visual prompt. A beginning reading teacher using a set of flash cards might first show a card with just the word boy and then a card with a stick figure, finally moving to a card with a representational drawing of a boy. To use the procedure with modeling, one could first provide a gesture and move toward a full demonstration. To use increasing prompts with physical guidance, one would also start with a gesture and then move toward a full putting-through procedure.

Increasing prompts may also be implemented with combinations of prompt modalities. Test, Spooner, Keul, and Grossi (1990) taught two adolescents to use the public telephone to call home. Four levels of prompting were used: "(a) independent, the participants performed the required task within the given time limit without any prompt from the trainer; (b) verbal, if the participant did not perform the correct response under the independent condition, the trainer verbally instructed the client how to perform the required task; (c) verbal plus gesture, if the participant did not correctly respond to verbal instructions, the trainer provided verbal instructions and demonstrated the required task; and (d) verbal plus guidance, if the other levels of prompts were not successful, the trainer physically guided the client in performing the required task while providing verbal instructions" (p. 162). Le Grice and Blampied (1997) used a similar procedure to teach four adolescents with mental and physical disabilities to use video recorders and personal computers.

Effectiveness of Methods for Fading Prompts

The majority of the literature on fading prompts has examined the efficacy of their use with students who have moderate or severe disabilities. Caution should be observed in generalizing the results to other populations. Some researchers suggest that time delay may be a more efficient and economical alternative than either increasing or decreasing assistance procedures (Bradley-Johnson, Johnson, & Sunderman, 1983; Touchette & Howard, 1984); others (Etzel & LeBlanc, 1979) disagree. Researchers who have reviewed many studies have suggested that "decreasing assistance training may be more effective than increasing assistance training at least for severely handicapped subjects in the acquisition phase of learning, and that progressive time delay procedures are no less effective, and may in some cases be more effective, than increasing assistance methods" (Billingsley & Romer, 1983, p. 7). Others (Le Grice & Blampied, 1997) argue that increasing assistance can be effective, is less intrusive, and requires less teacher effort. This lack of agreement need not overly concern the classroom teacher. "Each has been shown to produce errorless learning under some circumstances and each should be considered as an alternative when the other fails" (Touchette & Howard, 1984,

p. 187). It is interesting in the light of these tentative conclusions that teachers of average students and those with mild disabilities according to our observations almost routinely use increasing assistance procedures, perhaps because they require less teacher effort. It would be interesting to see the results of a systematic study of increasing assistance and other prompting procedures with these populations.

Summary Chart for Fading Prompts

Increasing Assistance (Least Assistance, Least-to-Most Prompts). Start with the least intrusive prompt, provide more intrusive prompts if necessary.

Graduated Guidance. Reduce full physical guidance to "shadowing," (following movement but not touching the student), a light touch at a distance from the part of the body performing the behavior.

Time Delay. May be constant or progressive. Wait several seconds before prompting to allow the student to respond.

Decreasing Assistance (Most-to-Least Prompts). Start with the most powerful prompt available. When the target behavior occurs reliably, move to the next less intrusive prompt.

Procedures for establishing and maintaining stimulus control are powerful tools. Once all prompts have been withdrawn and behaviors are under stimulus control, they will continue to occur, sometimes for years, without any reinforcement except that naturally available in the environment, and even when the person knows no reinforcement will be forthcoming. Have you ever sat at a red light at 3 a.m. at a deserted intersection and waited for the light to change? If you have, you have some idea of the power of stimulus control.

It appears that stimulus control procedures have great promise in facilitating not only the acquisition of behaviors but also their generalization and maintenance. Stimulus control has recently emerged as one of the most powerful potential tools for programming generalization—for ensuring that the skills acquired by students are performed in settings other than that in which they were taught and that the skills will continue to be performed long after the original programmer is gone (Halle, 1989; Halle & Holt, 1991; Schussler & Spradlin, 1991). Generalization and maintenance, and their relationship with stimulus control, are discussed at length in Chapter 10.

In the following anecdote, Professor Grundy illustrates the power of stimulus control in maintaining behaviors—be they appropriate or not.

A Smoke-Free Environment

Ms. Cadwallader, who had been a university departmental secretary for over 20 years, returned from a campuswide clerical staff meeting with her arms full of signs and a smile on her face. "They didn't believe the memos and announcements," she chortled to herself, "but these they'll believe." As she entered the department, the atmosphere of pipe and cigarette smoke assailed her nostrils. "Whew," she said aloud, "I'll be glad to be rid of this." She busied herself removing ashtrays from the public areas and posting signs on all the outside doors and inside walls—big, shiny signs with the international symbol for forbidden behavior and the legend "THIS IS A SMOKE-FREE BUILDING."

An hour or so later she looked up from her desk and observed Professor Grundy standing outside the glass front door of the building, holding his smoking pipe and staring fixedly at the new sign. She kept her head down over her computer terminal and watched from the corner of her eye as he shrugged and deposited the smoking mess from his pipe into the ashtray she had placed outside the building, "Good," she thought, "stimulus control gets even professors. He's minding the sign."

She greeted the professor cheerily, "Good morning, Professor, I hope the new policy is not going to be a problem for you."

"Certainly not," growled Grundy, "do you think a professor has habits he can't control?" Grundy picked up his mail and phone messages and proceeded to his office. He settled in his chair, put his pipe in the tray on his desk, and prepared to go about his business. He read the first phone message and reached for the phone. As he finished dialing the number, his hand automatically reached for the pipe. He quickly withdrew the hand, completed the call, and began to read his mail. As he opened a large envelope containing an eagerly awaited research report, he settled back in his chair, put his feet up, and automatically reached for the pipe.

"This," he admitted to himself, "may be a little more difficult than I had anticipated. It appears that many of the routine actions that I perform have become S^Ds for smoking." By noon he had identified a number of other stimuli—advising students, conferring with colleagues, making last-minute preparations for class—that occasioned the reaching response. He determined that he needed a substitute response and stopped at a local market during his lunch break for a supply of candy.

During the afternoon he happily reached for a piece of candy instead of the pipe. As he left for the day, he cheerfully assured Ms. Cadwallader that for professors who understood applied behavior analysis, control of even their own behavior was no problem.

Effective Prompting

To make the most effective use of prompts, teachers need to attend to the following guidelines:

Guidelines for using prompts.

1. Prompts should focus students' attention on the S^D, not distract from it. Prompts that are spatially or otherwise distant from the stimulus may be ineffective (Schreibman, 1975). Cheney and Stein (1974) pointed out that using prompts unrelated to the stimulus may be less effective than using no prompts or trial-and-error learning. The well-meaning teacher who encourages beginning readers to use the illustrations in the preprimer as clues to the words on the page may find that overemphasis on such prompts may result in some children's developing an overdependence on the illustrations at the expense of the written word. For some students, such dependence may be so well developed as to require the use of reading materials without illustrations in order to focus attention on the relevant S^D.

2. Prompts should be as weak as possible. The use of strong prompts when weak ones will do is inefficient and may delay the development of stimulus control. The best prompt is the weakest one that will result in the desired behavior. Strong prompts are often intrusive. They intrude on the environmental antecedent, the S^D, and drastically change the circumstances or conditions under which the response is to be performed. Every effort should be made to use the least intrusive prompt possible. Visual and verbal prompts are, on the whole, less intrusive than modeling, and all are less intrusive than physical guidance. This may not always be the case. A gentle push on the hand to help a young child slide in a recalcitrant puzzle piece is probably less intrusive than yelling "Push it the other way." Inefficiency is not the only undesirable effect of prompts that are stronger than necessary. Many students react negatively to strong or unnecessary prompts (Krumboltz & Krumboltz, 1972). When students say, "Don't give me a hint. I'll figure it out myself!" the wise teacher listens.

3. Prompts should be faded as rapidly as possible. Continuing to prompt longer than necessary may result in failure of the S^D to acquire control. The efficient teacher uses prompts only as long as necessary and fades them quickly, thus avoiding students' becoming dependent on prompts rather than S^Ds. Students who are allowed to use a matrix of multiplication facts for extended periods may never learn their multiplication facts.
4. Unplanned prompts should be avoided. Anyone who has observed a large number of teachers has seen students watch the teacher carefully for clues to the correct answer. A teacher may be completely unaware that students are being prompted by a facial expression or vocal inflection. Neither is an inappropriate prompt when used intentionally. But the teacher who asks, while shaking her head, "Did Johnny really want to go to the park in the story?" in such a tone that all the children answer "no" is fooling herself if she thinks that the students necessarily comprehended what they read.

Teaching Complex Behaviors

So far we have discussed bringing behavior under stimulus control as if all behaviors consisted of simple, discrete actions that may be occasioned by a discriminative stimulus, using prompts if necessary, and reinforced. Much of what we want students to learn involves many such discrete behaviors, to be performed in sequence on presentation of the S^D. Most functional, academic, and social skills are of this complex nature. Before even considering teaching such sequences of behaviors, the exact nature of the complex task must be analyzed.

Task Analysis

To task analyze, pinpoint the terminal behavior and list necessary prerequisite skills and component skills in sequence.

For more practice, go to the "Activities" module for Chapter 9 of the Companion Website.

The most exacting task facing the teacher who wants students to acquire complex behavioral chains is determining exactly what steps, links, or components must be included and their sequence. Breaking complex behavior into its component parts is called task analysis. **Task analysis** forms the basis of many of the teaching strategies used to teach individuals with disabilities to perform complex behaviors and sequences of behaviors. Before the teacher can select instructions, cues, prompts, or other teaching tools, he must decide exactly what he is teaching and break the task down into manageable components. Tasks with many steps or components may be divided into phases for teaching purposes. Smith, Collins, Schuster, and Kleinert (1999), for example, broke the task of cleaning tables into three phases: preparing materials, cleaning table, and putting away materials. Each phase was taught separately.

Task analysis requires considerable practice but can be applied to behaviors ranging from eating with a spoon, to shopping for groceries (Morse & Schuster, 2000), to writing a term paper. It is perhaps easier, in general, to analyze motor tasks than those related to academic and social behavior, but the analysis is equally important for teaching all complex behaviors. Teachers and researchers originally used task analysis to break basic skills into small steps in order to teach them—one step at a time—to learners with severe and profound disabilities. It proved such a valuable tool that it has been used not only for this population but to help teachers of all kinds of students to analyze all kinds of tasks.

To acquire a general idea of what is involved in task analysis, take a simple task, such as putting on a jacket, and list its component parts in the correct sequence. Then read your steps, in order, to a tolerant friend while she or he does exactly what you have written. Don't worry; you'll do better next time. One of the authors assigns this task as part of a midterm exam. Failing grades are given only to task analyses that result in feet being placed through armholes.

Task analysis is the basis for programs teaching complex functional and vocational skills to people who have severe and profound disabilities. It is theoretically possible, by breaking a task into sufficiently small components, to teach anybody anything. Time limitations make it impractical to teach some students some things. Nevertheless, the technology exists. Teachers can even teach students to perform behaviors that those teachers cannot perform, so long as the teachers can recognize and reinforce the terminal behavior and its components (Karen, 1974). One is reminded of the middle-aged, overweight gymnastics coach cheering on his adolescent charges as they perform incredible feats of agility—feats that he has taught them but that it is laughable to picture him performing.

Moyer and Dardig (1978) provided a basic framework for analyzing tasks. The first step is always to determine what skills or concepts the learner must already have in order to learn the task at hand. These are known as the prerequisites for learning the skill. Anyone who has tried to teach a child who does not know how to hold a pencil to print her letters, or a child who does not know basic multiplication facts to find the least common multiple is aware of the folly of these endeavors. When analyzing any new task, it is important to ask, "What does the learner already need to know in order to learn this?" If more teachers asked themselves that simple question before beginning a lesson, fewer children would be chronic failures in school. Although it is wise to attempt to list prerequisite skills before beginning a task analysis, many teachers find that one of the most valuable aspects of the analysis itself is that additional prerequisites are identified as they go through the process.

Before analyzing the task, the teacher also lists any materials that will be required to perform it. Again, others may show up as necessary as the analysis progresses. Finally, the analyst must list all the components of the task in the order in which they must be performed. Although it is possible to do this simply from experience, many people find that watching someone competent (a master of the skill) perform the task (Moyer & Dardig, 1978) is helpful. It may be valuable to ask the "master" to list the steps verbally as he performs them.

Test et al. (1990) asked an adult to perform the steps of using a touch-tone public telephone in order to derive the task analysis presented in Table 9–1. They then used

TABLE 9–1
Task analysis and time limits for performing each task for using the public telephone.

	Step	Time Limit
1.	Locate the telephone in the environment	2 minutes
2.	Find the telephone number	1 minute
3.	Choose the correct change	30 seconds
4.	Pick up receiver using left hand	10 seconds
5.	Put receiver to left ear and listen for dial tone	10 seconds
6.	Insert first coin	20 seconds
7.	Insert second coin	20 seconds
8.–14.	Dial seven-digit number	10 seconds per
15.	Wait for telephone to ring a minimum of five times	25 seconds
16.	If someone answers, initiate conversation	5 seconds
17.	If telephone is busy, hang up phone and collect money	15 seconds

Note: From "Teaching adolescents with severe disabilities to use the public telephone," by D. W. Test, F. Spooner, P. K. Keul, & T. Grossi, *Behavior Modification, 14,* Copyright 1990. Reprinted by permission.

TABLE 9–2
Task analyses for food preparation.

Kool-Aid	Crackers
1. Get spoon	1. Get plate
2. Get Kool-Aid	2. Get table knife
3. Get pitcher	3. Get crackers
4. Get cup	4. Get aluminum foil
5. Put 2 scoops in pitcher	5. Get 2 spreadables from refrigerator
6. Take pitcher and lid to sink	6. Take 10 crackers out of box
7. Fill pitcher to line	7. Spread one spreadable on half of the crackers
8. Put lid on	8. Wipe off knife with wash cloth
9. Take pitcher back to table	9. Spread the other spreadable
10. Take off the lid	10. Put away spreadables
11. Stir Kool-Aid	11. Put away crackers
12. Put lid on	12. Put knife in sink
13. Put spoon in sink	13. Tear off piece of aluminum foil
14. Put Kool-Aid mix away	14. Place all but 2 crackers in foil
15. Pour Kool-Aid into cup	15. Wrap crackers in foil
16. Put pitcher of Kool-Aid away	16. Place foiled crackers in frig

Note: From "Accepting specific versus functional student responses when training chained tasks," by C. W. Wright & J. W. Schuster, *Education and Training in Mental Retardation and Developmental Disabilities, 30.* Copyright 1994. Reprinted by permission.

the task analysis as a basis for designing an instructional program used to teach adolescents with disabilities to perform the task. Table 9–2 presents two task analyses for food preparation derived by the authors of they study (Wright & Schuster, 1994). The following anecdote illustrates the derivation of a task analysis by "watching a master perform" and asking him to list the steps.

Ms. Cadwallader Analyzes a Task

The consultant from Computer Services stood in Ms. Cadwallader's office waiting to get her attention. "Excuse, me, er, Ma'am," he said diffidently, "I'm here to install your new computer."

"Yes, indeed," answered Ms. Cadwallader cheerfully, "I can hardly wait." The consultant looked dubious; his experience had been that most clerical workers were attached to their current systems and highly resistant to new technology. He had not met Ms. Cadwallader.

As the young man unplugged and plugged, he muttered continuously about microprocessors, memory, bits, chips, viruses, spreadsheets, interfaces, buffers, and other esoteric lore. Ms. Cadwallader ignored him and continued working. Soon he happily announced that her system was "up" and prepared to leave.

"One moment, young man," said Ms. Cadwallader firmly, removing a pencil from her bun and a notebook from her pocket, "although you may safely assume that I have the necessary prerequisite skills to operate this system, I will need for you to show me exactly what steps to take in order to activate and operate the word-processing program. Please be good enough to describe exactly what you are doing at each step. You may begin now."

"But, lady," protested the consultant, "this is a state-of-the-art system; you can surf the Net, access the mainframe, download updates, burn CDs . . ." The expression on Ms. Cadwallader's face silenced the consultant.

"Step one?" She prompted. As the consultant listed and performed the steps in order (Ms. Cadwallader had noticed before that most computer programmers were quite good at this if pressed), Ms. Cadwallader carefully wrote them down. She knew that this task analysis would be useful not only for herself but for teaching the professors in the department how to use their new computers. As she thanked the somewhat chastened young man, she sighed quietly.

"As I expected," she thought, "nothing much to it. Most of my professors will pick it up quickly with a little coaching. After all, most of them have been using less efficient word processors for years. But, oh my, wait until Professor Grundy finds out that there's no more typing from longhand and he really has to learn word processing at last."

We suggest that you begin acquiring the skill of task analysis by breaking down simple motor tasks into their prerequisites and components. A number of examples are provided in the following section when we discuss teaching behavioral chains. For those who are accomplished cooks, many recipes provide models of task analysis. An understanding of the importance of prerequisite concepts and skills is easily understood by those of us less accomplished. When confronted by a recipe beginning, "First, bone a young hen," we have questions about prerequisite skills and concepts: "Bone? It looks pretty bony already. Young? Its date of birth isn't on the package. Is it young if today is the day before the 'Use or freeze by' date? Hen? How the heck would I know?" When informed that "to bone" to the well-informed means to remove the bones, a serious question about component skills arises. The task of removing the bones from a chicken (of either sex) is one that itself requires analysis. However, the analysis is not enough. Simply reading the steps or even watching Julia Child (certainly a master of the skill) perform them is not sufficient. We, at least, will have to be taught. Someone will have to help us learn each component and perform them all in sequence. Only then can we incorporate that task into the even more complex task that will produce the delicious chicken cassoulet. We may send out for pizza instead, a task the components of which we have thoroughly mastered.

Chaining

The components of a task analysis form what applied behavior analysts call a *behavioral chain.* The ideal task analysis would break a task down into components that the learner could already perform with a verbal instruction or a demonstration. When teaching typical students and those with mild disabilities, this is often possible. Even more frequently the chain may consist primarily of behaviors learners can perform with instruction (behaviors under stimulus control) but incorporate one or two behaviors that must be taught. The major focus when teaching chains whose components are already part of student repertoires is their learning to perform the behaviors in sequence with the presentation of only one S^D. Consider, for example, a classroom teacher who gives the instruction, "Get ready for math practice." The result is vague shuffling and furtive looking around among the students. Some students locate their math workbooks; others imitate them. "Come on," prompts the teacher, "hurry up now." One or two students locate pencils; some students still appear completely confused. The process of getting ready for math practice is actually a series of behaviors performed in a sequence.

A behavior chain.

1. Clear desk of other materials.
2. Locate math workbook.
3. Locate pencil.
4. Wait quietly for instructions.

The students in this class are probably able to perform each of these behaviors, but the behaviors are not under the control of the S^D presented ("Get ready for . . . "). The teacher must establish a series or chain of behaviors that will occur when the instruction is given. The teacher might proceed by giving each instruction separately and reinforcing compliance, always starting with "Get ready for math practice." Soon two steps could be combined, and reinforcement would follow only after completion of the two-part chain. Finally, the teacher would need to provide only the S^D. The students would have acquired a behavioral chain.

A behavioral chain is a sequence of behaviors, all of which must be performed to earn a reinforcer. Many complex human behaviors consist of such chains—often with dozens or even hundreds of component steps. Usually, reinforcement occurs only when the final component is performed. The instructional procedure of reinforcing individual responses occurring in sequence to form a complex behavior is called **chaining.**

To understand the process involved in the development of behavioral chains, first recall that any stimulus must be defined in terms of its function and that identical stimuli may have different functions. Similarly, behaviors included in chains may simultaneously serve multiple functions. Consider the behaviors in the get-ready-for-math-practice chain. When the chain is fully established, reinforcement occurs only after the last link. The last link in the chain, however, is paired with the reinforcer and thus becomes a conditioned reinforcer, increasing the probability of occurrence of the preceding link. Each link is subsequently paired with its preceding one: each link serves as a conditioned reinforcer for the link immediately preceding it.

We can also look at the behavior chain from another perspective: each link also serves as an S^D for the link immediately following it. Consider again the getting-ready-for-math-practice chain:

1. Clear desk of other materials (S^D for 2).
2. Locate math workbook (S^{R+} for 1; S^D for 3).
3. Locate pencil (S^{R+} for 2; S^D for 4).
4. Wait quietly for instructions (S^{R+} for 3).

Each link increases the probability of the one it follows and specifies, or cues, the one it precedes (Ferster et al., 1975; Staats & Staats, 1963). Test and Spooner (1996) illustrated this with an everyday example. They described a set of directions for reaching a house to which one has been invited to dinner. The instructions read: "(a) From your house go north to the first stop sign; (b) turn right (immediately after you turn right, you will see a bright yellow house on the left); (c) go two stoplights (not stop signs); (d) turn left at the second light; (e) turn right on Independence Boulevard . . ." (p. 12). Figure 9–2 illustrates how a link in the chain serves both as a reinforcer and an S^D (the authors use "cue" as a synonym for S^D).

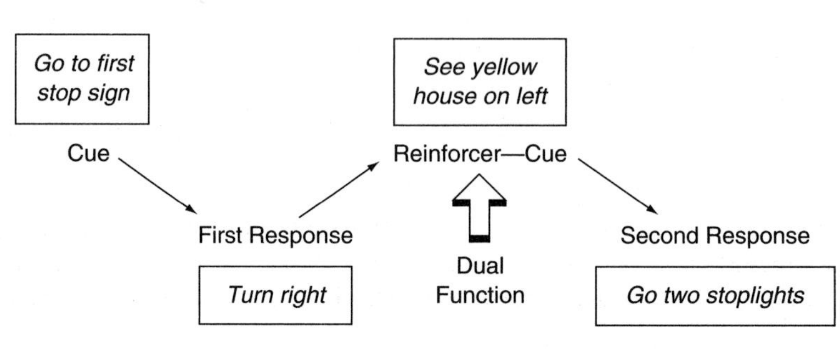

***FIGURE 9–2* A practical example of a diagrammed chain.**
Source: From *Community-based instructional support* by D. W. Test and F. Spooner. Washington: American Association on Mental Retardation. Copyright 1996 by the American Association on Mental Retardation. Reprinted by permission.

On another level, each of the component links of a chain, as in our classroom example, can in turn be described as a chain; that is, clearing one's desk includes picking up books and papers, opening the desk, and putting books in the desk. Picking up books is also a chain of behaviors—raising the arm, extending it, opening the hand, grasping the books, and raising the arm. Grasping books, in fact, is still another chain, including placing the thumb . . . but wait. We can go on this way in both directions—toward increasing specificity in behaviors and toward increasing complexity. Later in the school year, the teacher in our example may say, "Boys and girls, for math practice I want you to do the first 10 problems on page 142," whereupon the students promptly

1. get ready for math practice,
2. open their books,
3. pick up their pencils, and
4. complete the assignment.

The original chain has now become merely a link in a more complex chain. The process of chaining simple behaviors into longer and more complicated sequences results in production of the most elaborate and sophisticated forms of human behavior. For some students, behavioral chains can be acquired by having each step in the chain verbally prompted or demonstrated. The prompts can then be faded and the links combined (Becker, Engelmann, & Thomas, 1975b). For other students, some or all of the separate steps of the chain may have to be taught using more elaborate prompting procedures as the chain is developed. When working with students with severe physical or cognitive disabilities, the teacher may identify links in the chain that must temporarily or permanently be performed by someone else. Such partial participation enables these students to do as much as possible for themselves. The same thing, of course, can be true of anyone. One is reminded of an elderly, but fiercely independent, neighbor who insisted upon mowing her own lawn but accepted assistance starting the mower. Several procedures may be used to teach chains of behavior to students who do not necessarily know how to perform any or more than a few of the links. Those most commonly used are backward chaining, forward chaining, and total task presentation.

Backward Chaining

When backward chaining is used, the components of the chain are acquired in reverse order. The last component is taught first, and other components are added one at a time. Delbert and Harmon (1972) described a backward chaining procedure for teaching a child to undress himself. The child is given the instruction, "Timmy, take your shirt off," and his shirt is pulled over his head until his arms are free and the neckband is caught just above his eyes. If the child does not automatically pull the shirt off, he is physically guided to do so. Primary and social reinforcers are then given. Training on this step continues until mastery is achieved. During the next training step, the neckband is left at his neck; in subsequent sessions, one arm, then both arms, are left in the sleeves. The S^D, "Timmy, take your shirt off," is always presented and reinforcers given only when the task has been completed. The removal of each garment is taught in this manner; then the component steps are combined until the instruction, "Take your shirt off," has acquired stimulus control. Backward chaining is intuitively appealing because the reinforcer is always delivered at the most natural point—when the task is completed.

To increase your understanding and use of chaining, go to the "Activities" module for Chapter 9 of the Companion Website.

Forward Chaining

When forward chaining is used, the teacher starts with the first link in the chain, teaches it until it is mastered, and then goes on to the next link. The student may be required to perform all the steps previously mastered each time, or each step may be separately taught to the criterion and then the links made (Patterson, Panyan, Wyatt, & Morales, 1974). To use forward chaining to teach undressing skills, the teacher would start with the student fully dressed, deliver the instruction, "Timmy, take your shirt off," and then provide whatever prompting was required to get Timmy to cross his arms and grab the bottom of his T-shirt. When Timmy reliably performed this behavior, she would add the next step until Timmy's shirt was off. Many academic applications of forward chaining come to mind. The first-grade teacher who wants students to print the letters of the alphabet in sequence may start with A and add a letter a day until the children can print all 26 capital letters in sequence. The chemistry teacher who wants students to know the elements on the periodic table in order starts with a few at a time and adds a few each day. A teacher who wants students to recite a poem may have them recite the first line until it is mastered and then add a line at a time until they can recite the entire poem. A conscientious teacher who requires students to write a report (an extremely complex chain) teachers them to find references, then take notes, then outline, then prepare a rough draft, and then turn in a final copy.

Total Task Presentation

Combine verbal instructions, modeling, and chaining.

When using total task presentation, the teacher requires the student to perform all the steps in sequence until the entire chain is mastered. Total task presentation may be particularly appropriate when the student has already mastered some or all the components of a task but has not performed them in sequence. It is also possible, however, to teach completely novel chains in this manner (Spooner, 1981; Spooner & Spooner, 1983; Walls, Zane, & Ellis, 1981). Total task presentation is generally considered the most appropriate and effective method for teaching students with disabilities to perform functional skills (Gaylord-Ross & Holvoet, 1985; Kayser, Billingsley, & Neel, 1986; Spooner & Spooner, 1984).

Many academic chains are forged using a total task presentation. The arithmetic teacher working on long division usually requires her students to solve an entire problem, with whatever coaching is required, until they have mastered the process. Students practice the entire process of finding the longitude and latitude of a given location in geography until it is mastered, as do biology students learning to operate a microscope.

Although total task presentation appears to be more effective then either forward or backward chaining to teach functional skills to students with moderate to severe disabilities (Test et al., 1990), forward and backward chaining are certainly useful in some instances. Classroom teachers are again advised to try what seems, in their professional judgment, to be the best procedure, and if that does not work, to try something else. This may be a good place to repeat that a teacher must regularly read the professional literature. New conclusions about effective management and instructional techniques are published constantly.

How to Manage Teaching Chains

Whatever method a teacher chooses when teaching chained behavior, some organization will be required in order to manage the process efficiently and, of course, to keep accurate and precise data showing progress toward mastery of the chain. The teacher will need a list of the steps to be taught and a way to mark correct or incorrect responses. Most teachers find it more convenient to include the list of steps on the data sheet itself. One can either make and duplicate a sheet for a specific chain or make a generic data sheet on which the steps for any task can be written.

Figure 9–3 is arranged for recording dichotomous data on the instruction of chained tasks. The data sheet is arranged for tasks with up to 25 steps, indicated by the numbers on the far left. The response required for each step is written next to the number.

Student Hisa Task hand washing Criteria 100% of steps-1 wk

	Step/Response	DATE	9-6	9-6	9-8	9-8	9-10	9-10	9-13	9-15	9-17	9-20	9-22	9-24	9-27	9-29	10-1	10-3	10-5	10-8	10-10	10-12
25.			25	25	25	25	25	25	25	25	25	25	25	25	25	25	25	25	25	25	25	25
24.			24	24	24	24	24	24	24	24	24	24	24	24	24	24	24	24	24	24	24	24
23.			23	23	23	23	23	23	23	23	23	23	23	23	23	23	23	23	23	23	23	23
22.			22	22	22	22	22	22	22	22	22	22	22	22	22	22	22	22	22	22	22	22
21.			21	21	21	21	21	21	21	21	21	21	21	21	21	21	21	21	21	21	21	21
20.			20	20	20	20	20	20	20	20	20	20	20	20	20	20	20	20	20	20	20	20
19.			19	19	19	19	19	19	19	19	19	19	19	19	19	19	19	19	19	19	19	19
18.			18	18	18	18	18	18	18	18	18	18	18	18	18	18	18	18	18	18	18	18
17.			17	17	17	17	17	17	17	17	17	17	17	17	17	17	17	17	17	17	17	17
16.			16	16	16	16	16	16	16	16	16	16	16	16	16	16	16	16	16	16	16	16
15.			15	15	15	15	15	15	15	15	15	15	15	15	15	15	15	15	15	15	15	15
14.			14	14	14	14	14	14	14	14	14	14	14	14	14	14	14	14	14	14	14	14
13.	Throw towel in trash		13	13	13	13	13	13	13	13	13	13	13	13	13	13	13	13	13	13	13	13
12.	Rub hands		12	12	12	12	12	12	12	12	12	12	12	12	12	12	12	12	12	12	12	12
11.	Pull one towel		11	11	11	11	11	11	11	11	11	11	11	11	11	11	11	11	11	11	11	11
10.	Go to towel dispenser		10	10	10	10	10	10	10	10	10	10	10	10	10	10	10	10	10	10	10	10
9.	Turn off cold water		9	9	9	9	9	9	9	9	9	9	9	9	9	9	9	9	9	9	9	9
8.	Turn off hot water		8	8	8	8	8	8	8	8	8	8	8	8	8	8	8	8	8	8	8	8
7.	Rub hands 3 times		7	7	7	7	7	7	7	7	7	7	7	7	7	7	7	7	7	7	7	7
6.	Place hands under water		6	6	6	6	6	6	6	6	6	6	6	6	6	6	6	6	6	6	6	6
5.	Press pump		5	5	5	5	5	5	5	5	5	5	5	5	5	5	5	5	5	5	5	5
4.	Hand under soap pump		4	4	4	4	4	4	4	4	4	4	4	4	4	4	4	4	4	4	4	4
3.	Turn on hot water (red)		3	3	3	3	3	3	3	3	3	3	3	3	3	3	3	3	3	3	3	3
2.	Turn on cold water (blue)		2	2	2	2	2	2	2	2	2	2	2	2	2	2	2	2	2	2	2	2
1.	Approach sink		1	1	1	1	1	1	1	1	1	1	1	1	1	1	1	1	1	1	1	1
			1	2	3	4	5	6	7	8	9	10	11	12	13	14	15	16	17	18	19	20

FIGURE 9–3 **Data sheet for use with chained tasks.**

Note. Adapted from *Vocational Habilitation of Severely Retarded Adults: A Direct Technology,* by G. T. Bellamy, R. Horner, & D. Inman (Baltimore: University Park Press, 1979). Copyright 1979 by University Park Press, Baltimore. Reprinted with permission.

The 20 columns to the right represent 20 trials or opportunities for performance of the task. Each column has 25 numbers representing up to 25 potential steps. Each trial consists of an opportunity for the student to perform all the steps that make up the chained task. For each trial, the teacher records the accuracy of the student's performance of each step, using the simple circle and slash procedure (see Figure 3–7); or as seen in this figure, by noting an error by putting a slash through the step number and leaving untouched the step number for a correct response. This format allows for graphing directly on the sheet. The number corresponding to the number of correctly performed steps is indicated by placing a filled-in circle in each trial column. Then the circles are connected across trials to create the graph line. Hisa's performance, depicted on the data sheet, indicates she correctly performed 2 of the 13 steps on the first trial of the hand-washing task analysis being used by the teacher. She also correctly performed 7 steps on trial 7, and 11 steps on trial 17.

Figure 9–4 is arranged for recording coded data on the instruction of chained tasks. The data sheet is arranged for tasks with up to 25 steps, indicated by the numbers on the far left. The response required for each step is written next to the number. The columns on the right represent 16 trials or opportunities for performance of the task. For each step the teacher records the type of prompt the student required for performance. On this graph the data for the first trial on September 6th indicate Hisa independently performed steps 5 and 12, required a verbal prompt on step 1, a gesture prompt on steps 4, 6, 7, 9, 10, 11, and 13, and required full physical assistance on steps 2 and 3. A graph can be created directly on this data sheet also. Use the numbers on the left (the step numbers) as the ordinate of the graph. For each trial, count the number of steps the student performed independently and place a data point on the line representing that number. On the graph presented, the data path rises from 2 steps performed independently to 11 steps performed independently. If the objective defines a level of assistance that allows recording a correct response, the graph is created by counting responses with the allowed level of assistance and all lesser levels. If, for example, the objective allows for performance with a verbal prompt, steps performed independently or with a verbal prompt are counted for graphing.

It is helpful to provide spaces on data sheet to record the level of any prompts. Snell and Loyd (1991) found that teachers were more consistent in assessing students' performance and that the teacher made more correct instructional decisions when they had that information.

Differential Reinforcement for Shaping

The behavioral procedures described in this chapter assume that students are able to perform with some degree of prompting the components of the target behavior. The emphasis has been on differential reinforcement to bring the desired behavior under the control of a specified stimulus. Many behaviors that teachers want students to perform are not a part of the students' behavioral repertoire. For such behaviors, a different approach, called shaping, is required. **Shaping** is defined as differential reinforcement or successive approximations to a specified target behavior. Becker et al. (1975b) listed two essential elements of shaping: differential reinforcement and a shifting criterion for reinforcement. Differential reinforcement, in this case, requires that responses that meet a certain criterion are reinforced, whereas those that do not meet the criterion are not. The criterion for reinforcement shifts ever closer to the target behavior.

For further explanation, go to the "Web Links" module for Chapter 9 of the Companion Website.

Student: Hisa   Instructor: Ms. Ebenezer   Location: 1st floor bathroom

Objective: will independently complete 100% of steps for hand washing for 1 week

PROMPT CODES: I V g P

(e.g. I=independent, V=verbal cue, G=gesture, P=physical assist)

Steps:

Steps																
25.																
24.																
23.																
22.																
21.																
20.																
19.																
18.																
17.																
16.																
15.																
14.																
13. throw towel in trash	g	g	I	I	I	I	I	I	I	I	I	I	I	I	I	I
12. rub hands	I	I	I	I	I	I	I	I	I	I	I	I	I	I	I	I
11. pull one towel	g	g	V	V	I	I	I	I	I	I	I	I	I	I	I	I
10. go to towel dispenser	g	g	g	g	g	g	V	V	V	V	g	V	g	V	V	I
9. turn off cold water	g	P	P	P	P	P	P	g	P	P	P	P	g	g	g	g
8. turn off hot water	P	P	P	P	P	P	P	P	g	g	g	g	g	g	g	I
7. rub hands 3 times	g	g	V	V	V	I	I	I	I	I	I	I	I	I	I	I
6. place hands under water	g	g	I	I	I	I	I	I	I	I	I	I	I	I	I	I
5. press pump	I	I	I	I	I	I	I	I	I	I	I	I	I	I	I	I
4. hand under soap pump	g	g	g	V	I	I	I	V	V	I	I	I	V	I	I	I
3. turn on hot water (red)	P	P	P	P	P	P	P	P	g	V	V	V	I	g	g	g
2. turn on cold water (blue)	P	P	P	P	V	V	V	V	V	V	V	V	I	I	I	I
1. approach sink	V	V	V	V	V	V	V	V	I	I	I	I	I	I	I	I
Date	9/6	9/6	9/8	9/8	9/10	9/10	9/13	9/15	9/17	9/20	9/22	9/24	9/27	9/29	10/1	10/3

Comments:

FIGURE 9–4 ***Data sheet (showing prompt levels) for use with chained tasks.***

Although the term differential reinforcement is used in both stimulus control and shaping, the usage is somewhat different. In developing stimulus control, a response in the presence of the S^D is reinforced; the same response in the presence of S^Δ is not reinforced. The differentiation of reinforcement depends on the antecedent stimulus. In shaping procedures, differential reinforcement is applied to responses that successively approximate (or become increasingly closer to) the target behavior. It is easy to confuse shaping with fading, because both involve differential reinforcement and gradual change. The following guidelines should clarify the differences:

1. Fading is used to bring an already learned behavior under the control of a different stimulus; shaping is used to teach a new behavior.
2. The behavior itself does not change when fading is used; only the antecedent stimulus varies. In shaping, the behavior itself is changed.
3. In fading, the teacher manipulates antecedents; in shaping, consequences are manipulated.

Shaping is not a stimulus control procedure; it is included in this chapter because it is an integral part of many teaching strategies that combine elements of stimulus control, prompting, fading, and chaining.

To design successful shaping programs, the teacher must first clearly specify the **terminal behavior,** the desired goal of the intervention. This will be a behavior that is not currently in the students' repertoire. Then the teacher will identify an **initial behavior,** a behavior that resembles the terminal behavior along some significant dimension and that is in the students' repertoire. The teacher may also identify **intermediate behaviors** that represent successive approximations toward the terminal behavior (Malott et al., 1997). Each intermediate step in the sequence will be reinforced until established; then the criterion for reinforcement will be shifted to the next step.

Panyan (1980) described a number of *dimensions* of behavior along which behavior may be shaped. These dimensions are similar to those we described in Chapter 3. Most basically, the *form* or *topography* of the behavior may be considered. Other dimensions include *duration,* the length of time a student spends responding; *latency,* the length of time between the S^D and the response; *rate,* the speed or fluency of the behavior; and force, the intensity of the response.

An example of shaping along the dimension of topography, or form, would be teaching vocal imitation to a child with severe disabilities. The teacher would present the S^D—"ah," for example—and reinforce successive approximations to correct imitation. The teacher might reinforce any vocalization (initial behavior) at first, then only vowel-like sounds (intermediate behaviors), then only close sounds, and finally exact imitations of "ah" (terminal behavior). In the heat of a language-training session with a child with autism, it is frequently difficult to determine whether a given vocal utterance is closer to the target behavior than the preceding one. Only extended practice, supervised by an instructor who shapes the teacher's behavior, will result in the development of such a skill. Coaches who reinforce successive approximations to correct swings in baseball or golf, correct posture in gymnastics or fencing, or correct form in dance or ice skating are equally concerned with the shaping of topography.

Many teachers have concerns about the duration of behaviors. So many students are described as hyperactive or as having deficits in attention that teaching students to stay in place and on task for extended periods of time is a major part of assisting them to be functional students. Suppose his teacher wants Harold to remain in his seat for an entire 20-minute work period. She has observed that Harold has never remained in his seat longer than 5 minutes, with an average of 2 minutes. A program in which Harold earns a rein-

"I wonder how he'll react when he finds out about our class behavior-shaping project."

forcer for remaining in his seat for 20 minutes is doomed—Harold will never come into contact with the reinforcer. Instead, the teacher defines her target behavior as Harold's remaining in his seat for the full 20 minutes but sets up a graduated sequence of criteria.

1. Harold remains in his seat for 3 minutes.
2. Harold remains in his seat for 5 minutes.
3. Harold remains in his seat for 10 minutes.
4. Harold remains in his seat for 15 minutes.
5. Harold remains in his seat for 20 minutes.

This example illustrates another aspect of shaping that requires great skill on the part of the teacher: determining the size of the steps toward the goal. If the steps are too small, the procedure is needlessly time consuming and inefficient. If the steps are too large, the student's responses will not be reinforced and the behavior will be extinguished. Finally, the teacher must consider how long to remain at each plateau—just long enough to establish the behavior solidly, but not so long that the student becomes stuck at that level.

It is not always possible to make all these decisions before beginning a program. For example, Harold's teacher might find that even after Harold has consistently remained in his seat for 5 minutes for a full week, he fails to meet the criterion of sitting for 10 minutes. The teacher would then have to drop back to 5 (or even 4) minutes and gradually work back up to 10, using smaller increments this time. The ability to evaluate and adjust ongoing programs is vital to the success of shaping procedures.

Most concerns about latency, the period of time between the presentation of an S^D and a student's response, are about decreasing it. For example, when a teacher says, "Get ready for math practice," he usually wants students to do so quickly. Teachers want students to respond to sight words or math facts on flash cards more and more quickly as training proceeds. Sometimes, however, a teacher might want to shape longer latencies for some responses. This would be particularly true in the case of children often called impulsive, who need to stop and think before they respond. In either case, shaping latency proceeds as in shaping any other dimension: Start with a latency the student demonstrates and shorten or lengthen the response time that receives reinforcement until the desired latency is achieved.

Shaping fluency, rate, or speed of responding is often critical. Many children with disabilities fail to perform adequately in general education classrooms, not because they cannot perform certain behaviors, but because they cannot perform them fast enough to meet standards set in those classrooms. Fluency is shaped, for example, when students are given timed tests and expected to steadily increase the number of correct responses from test to test. Examples of performances whose fluency has been shaped to astounding rates abound in everyday life. Think of an experienced cashier or bank teller counting money, an expert chef cutting an onion, or any master of a craft at work. One of us recently encountered a gentleman who was a master of the task of filling a soft drink vending machine. Upon noticing open-mouthed admiration, he grinned and stated, "Yup! Three hundred plus cans a minute. They use me to show trainees how it's done." Admiration and respect were clearly continuing to reinforce a high rate of behavior developed by shaping.

Force, or intensity, may refer to the volume of a student's voice, to the pressure she exerts when writing on paper, or to the tightness with which a student learning an assembly task holds onto parts. Any of these behaviors, along with countless others, may need shaping in either direction of force.

Shaping is an extremely useful teaching tool. It provides a means of developing new behaviors in students with all levels of ability. Used alone, however, it may be less efficient than procedures using it combined with other tools.

As we stated earlier, shaping and fading are often used in combination. The following example illustrates a combined procedure.

Ms. Wallace's Class Learns to Print the Letter A

Ms. Wallace was trying to teach her students to print the letter A. At first she just told them, "Make a capital A." They did not respond to this S^D. "Look at the one on the chart," she said. "Make it just like this one." Some of the students responded to this visual prompt by producing a creditable A.

But, "Does this look like the one on the chart, Harold?" asked Ms. Wallace. She then tried some verbal instructions: "Make two slanted lines that look like a teepee; then make another line across the middle."

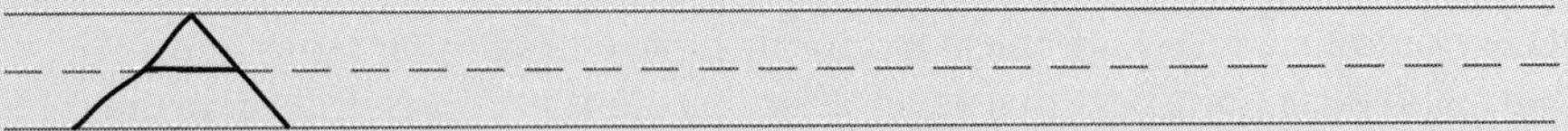

This verbal prompt resulted in success for some students. But, "Ralph, your teepee is a little flat," sighed Ms. Wallace. In desperation, Ms. Wallace walked around the room, guiding her students' hands through the correct movements. Physical prompting resulted in success for many students. But, "Melissa, relax your hand, for heaven's sake. I'm only trying to HELP you," wailed Ms. Wallace.

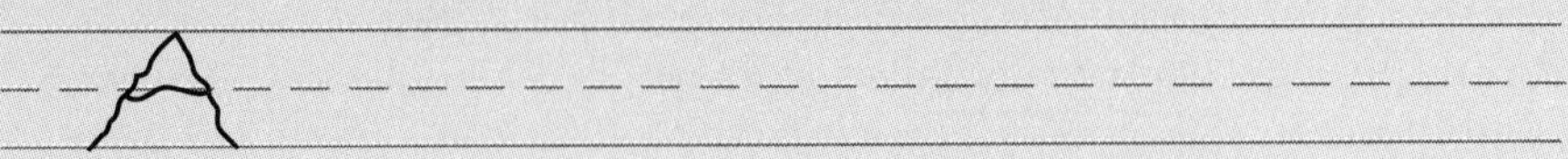

In the teachers' lounge that afternoon, Ms. Wallace sobbed, "I can't go through this 25 more times." An unkind colleague pointed out that she had forgotten the lowercase letters, making 51 more to go. Before Ms. Wallace became completely hysterical, an experienced first-grade teacher showed her a worksheet like this:

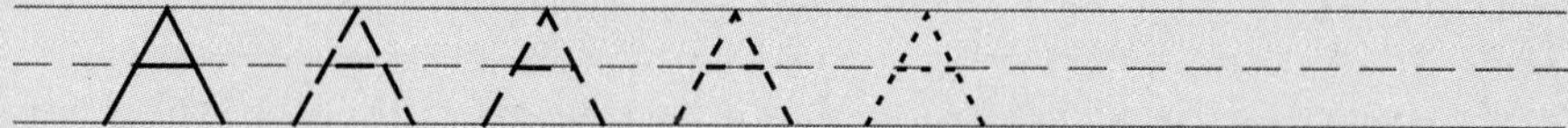

"You see," said Ms. Weatherby, "you just reinforce successive approximations to the terminal behavior of writing an A independently, tracing with fewer and fewer cues until the prompt just fades away."

SUMMARY

You have learned a variety of skills that will help you to teach students to perform behaviors, simple and complex. We have discussed the process of differential reinforcement for bringing students' behavior under stimulus control and the process for bringing simple and complex behaviors under the control of antecedent stimuli. Verbal, visual, modeling, and physical prompts have been discussed, as well as systematic procedures for fading these prompts. Task analysis, backward chaining, forward chaining, and total task presentation have been described. Finally, procedures for shaping behaviors that students cannot initially perform were suggested.

To enhance your overall understanding of the information presented in Chapter 9, go to the "Supplemental Lecture Notes" module for Chapter 9 of the Companion Website.

KEY TERMS

shaping
setting events
S-deltas (S^{Δ}s)
occasions
stimulus overselectivity
concept
prompt
fading
errorless learning
stimulus prompts
task analysis
chaining
shaping
terminal behavior
initial behavior
intermediate behaviors

DISCUSSION QUESTIONS

1. Describe stimuli in your environment that evoke certain appropriate and inappropriate behaviors in you.
2. Anything can be taught to anybody if it is broken into small enough tasks. True or false? Explain.
3. Design a plan for teaching a complex task using shaping, fading, and chaining.
4. Design a series of prompts to facilitate acquisition of a concept.
5. As a group, design a task analysis for an everyday task. Give your analysis to another group and see if they can perform it. Determine whether any difficulties they have require improvement to the task analysis or one of the teaching procedures described in this chapter.

Chapter 10

Providing for Generalization of Behavior Change

Did you know that . . .

- It takes a long time and a lot of hard work to decide which of a student's behaviors to change?
- Planning a program to change those behaviors takes a lot of research and considerable creativity?
- Carrying out that program is time consuming and demanding?
- Teachers become frustrated if, as soon as the program has been completed and the contingencies withdrawn, the student goes right back to behaving the way he did before the program was started? The potential for this kind of disappointment emphasizes the importance of programming for generalization?

Chapter Outline

Behavior change that doesn't last is useless.

Preceding chapters described principles and procedures related to strengthening appropriate behaviors, reducing or eliminating maladaptive behaviors, and teaching new behaviors. The technology of behavior change presented in earlier chapters has been thoroughly investigated and its efficacy demonstrated beyond doubt. Applied behavior analysts have not, however, been as thorough in demonstrating that behaviors changed using their technology are changed permanently or, indeed, that the changed behaviors are displayed in any setting except that in which training programs are executed. It is meaningless to change behavior unless the change can be made to last and unless behavior will occur in settings other than the original training site and in the absence of the original trainer.

Ways that behavior change can generalize.

Many criticisms of applied behavior analysis have resulted from the short-lived results of many behavior-change programs. Fortunately, these criticisms have resulted in a radical increase in concern for documenting generalization of behavior change. To program meaningful behavior change, teachers must use the behavioral principle of generality. Baer, Wolf, and Risley (1968), in their classic essay defining applied behavior analysis, stated: "A behavioral change may be said to have generality if it proves durable over time, if it appears in a wide variety of possible environments, or if it spreads to a wide variety of related behaviors" (p. 96). Baer and his colleagues describe three ways a behavior may show generality: over time, across settings, and across behaviors. Each of these types of **generalization** will be discussed in more detail later in this chapter. The following examples illustrate behavior changes that do not have generality:

> The students at the Foxwood Youth Center have a very structured program during both the school day and in their dormitories. Most of them have been referred because of serious behavioral problems that have brought them in contact with the judicial system, but under the point and level system of the center they display very few problem behaviors. When discharged, however, many of them go right back to the same behaviors that caused them to be referred. A significant percentage of the discharged students are back at Foxwood or in another correctional facility within a few months.
>
> Ms. Kitchens is a consultant teacher for children with learning disabilities. She spends approximately half an hour a day working directly with clusters of her students and their peers in the students' general education classes. Ms. Kitchens has noticed that, although her students do very well when she is there, they do not perform academic tasks that she knows they can do when only the general education class teacher is present.
>
> Mr. Fonseca's first graders have learned to recognize a large number of words using flash cards and a sight word approach. When confronted with an unfamiliar word, however, the students just guess. They have not learned to decode new words based on relationships between symbols and sounds.

The preceding examples describe situations in which some academic or social behavior has been successfully changed. The change, however, was accomplished only for as long as the contingencies were in effect, or only in the presence of the initial trainer, or only for very specific behaviors that were trained. There is no question that applied behavior analysis procedures often cause situation-specific behavior changes.

Indeed, several of the research designs described in Chapter 5 depend on this phenomenon (Hartmann & Atkinson, 1973). The classic ABAB (reversal) design demonstrates functional relationships between behavior and consequences by successfully applying and withdrawing such consequences and demonstrating that the dependent variable (the behavior) changes according to the condition. If the behavior failed to return to its baseline rate under one of these designs, the experimenter would have failed to demonstrate a functional relationship.

The multiple baseline design enables an experimenter to demonstrate functional relationships by successfully applying contingencies to several different behaviors, to behavior in several different settings, or to the same behavior displayed by different students. A functional relationship is shown only when the behaviors are not changed until contingencies are implemented. Baer et al. (1968) stated, "generalization should be programmed rather than expected or lamented" (p. 97). The experimenter attempting to establish functional relationships between procedures and behavior may, indeed, lament the occurrence of generalization. The classroom teacher is more likely to expect it and to lament its absence. With few exceptions (Kifer, Lewis, Green, & Phillips, 1974), it is the professional expecting generalization who will be disappointed. If generalization does not automatically result when behavior is changed, does that mean applied behavior analysis procedures are useless? If you have stuck with us this far, you know that we do not think so. To most behavior analysts, the lack of automatic generalization indicates the need for developing a technology of generalization as efficient as the technology of behavior change. Such a technology need not interfere with the necessity for demonstrating functional relationships; it may be applied after these relationships have been established (Kallman, Hersen, & O'Toole, 1975).

As Baer et al. (1968) suggested, generalization must be programmed. This chapter describes the principles of generalization that are the foundation of this programming and suggests specific ways that teachers can increase the odds that the behaviors their students learn will be maintained even when all the charts, graphs, and reinforcers have been discarded.

GENERALIZATION

How to write objectives for generalization and maintenance. There are several kinds of generalization.

In Chapter 2, we described a response hierarchy for designing objectives. It included response levels of acquisition, fluency, maintenance, and generalization. It is important that the IEP for each student with a disability includes objectives for the levels of maintenance and generalization (Billingsley, 1987). Haring and Liberty (1990) suggested that maintenance and generalization objectives differ from acquisition objectives in two ways: the conditions under which the behavior is to be performed and the criteria defined for performance. The conditions specified should be those that exist in the setting or settings in which the behavior will ultimately be performed. For example, if our generalization objective for a student is that he or she will order food at a fast-food restaurant, we might begin instruction in the classroom under simulated conditions. Numerous prompts and reinforcers would probably be provided. However, in a real restaurant the student will have to function with only a cue such as "May I help you?" or "Help you?" or "What do you want?" or, conceivably, "Would you like to try our roasted buffalo burger special today?" Neither the order taker nor another customer is likely to say "Good ordering," "Nice waiting," or "Good getting your money out," or to provide hugs, tokens, or points as a consequence. These prompts and reinforcers may be perfectly appropriate during the acquisition phase, but the conditions specified in a generalization objective should reflect conditions in the real-life environment.

Criteria specified in a generalization objective should reflect performance that is good enough, a phrase that occurs frequently in popular self-help literature. As we stated in Chapter 2, performance for some behaviors, like looking both ways before crossing the street, is good enough only if it is perfect—one must look both ways every time. For other behaviors we might ask, for example, if the student can wash, dry, and fold towels at the laundromat well enough that the towels can be stored in the linen closet at the group home. During the acquisition phase the instructor might insist that towels be folded with corners exactly square and stacked precisely. If that same instructor, however, were to permit us a peek at his linen closet, we might find that he, too, settles for "good enough" performance in towel folding.

Trask-Tyler, Grossi, and Heward (1994) defined cooking as good enough if the result could be eaten. The evaluation of generalization objectives is also critical (Billingsley, 1987). We must consider both where the behavior is to be evaluated and who is to do the evaluation. If we want George to be able to get a soft drink from any machine he encounters, we might begin instruction on the vending machine in the community center where he goes swimming twice a week. It is important to be aware that even though we may pat ourselves on the back because we are conducting instruction in the community, this skill is no more likely to generalize than if we brought a vending machine into the classroom (Haring, 1988). After we have taught George to use various vending machines in various locations, we can assess generalization. It is obviously impossible to take George to every vending machine in his community, so we conduct *probes*. We select several vending machines in different locations and check to see whether George gets a soft drink—without prompts and with no reinforcer except the soda. If we really want to be certain that George has a generalized skill, it will be important that his teacher or another adult he knows not be standing near him with a clipboard. Generalization probes are best taken by someone unfamiliar to the student or at least someone who would normally be in the environment in which generalization is to be assessed.

Before suggesting guidelines for facilitating generalization, we need to differentiate several types. The first of these occurs when a response that has been trained in a specific setting with a specific instructor occurs in a different setting or with a different instructor. This phenomenon, called *generalization* (Koegel & Rincover, 1977), *transfer of training* (Kazdin, 2001), or *stimulus generalization* (Barton & Ascione, 1979), should be distinguished from *response maintenance* (Kazdin, 2001), which refers to the tendency of a learned behavior to occur after programmed contingencies have been withdrawn. Response maintenance may also be labeled *maintenance* (Koegel & Rincover, 1977), *resistance to extinction, durability,* or *behavioral persistence* (Atthowe, 1973). Finally, the term *response generalization* is used when referring to unprogrammed changes in similar behaviors when a target behavior is modified (Twardosz & Sajwaj, 1972). This phenomenon may also be termed *concomitant* or *concurrent behavior change* (Kazdin, 1973). It is easy to see why some confusion may result from varying terminology or from researchers' failure to differentiate among the varieties of generalization. In this chapter, the term *generalization* will refer to any of the three types, and the terms *stimulus generalization, maintenance,* and *response generalization* will be used when distinctions are made among them. Table 10–1 illustrates the relationships among the terms used to describe generality of behavior change.

Stimulus Generalization

Not all generalization is a good thing.

Stimulus generalization occurs when responses that have been reinforced in the presence of a specific stimulus (S^D) occur in the presence of different but similar stimuli. Sometimes this is a good thing. Parents and teachers, for example, spend a lot of time

TABLE 10–1
Terminology used to describe types of generalization.

	Generalization		
	Stimulus Generalization	**Maintenance**	**Response Generalization**
Synonyms	Generalization Transfer of training	Response maintenance Resistance to extinction Durability Behavioral persistence	Concomitant behavior change Current behavior change

teaching young children concepts such as colors and shapes. We do not expect to have to teach every example of "red" or "triangle." The children will eventually identify shades of red we have not taught or triangles that look different from those used in teaching. A group of stimuli that should occasion the same response may be considered members of a **stimulus class.** The more similar the stimuli, the more likely it is stimulus generalization will occur. The students described at the beginning of this chapter who performed differently in the presence of their consulting teacher have not learned that all teachers should occasion academic performance. The student who stands befuddled when the fast-food worker asks, "What'll it be?" instead of "May I help you?" has not learned that there is a class of questions that should occasion the ordering response.

Stimulus overgeneralization (described in Chapter 9) can be a problem. Children who are learning colors often identify objects that are pink or orange as red, or shapes with more than three sides as triangles. Remember the baby who called all bearded adults with glasses "Daddy." Some stimuli are in a class by themselves.

MAINTENANCE

Most behaviors that teachers want students to perform should occur even after systematic applied behavior analysis procedures have been withdrawn. This continued performance over time is **maintenance.** Teachers want their students to read accurately in class and also to continue reading accurately after they are no longer in school. Math problems in school are merely a means to an end—we want students eventually to balance checkbooks, fill out income tax forms, or multiply measurements in recipes. Appropriate social behaviors, although adaptive in the classroom, are also necessary when a specific program for their systematic reinforcement no longer exists. Chapter 8 detailed what happens when positive reinforcement is abruptly withdrawn from a behavior that previously has been reinforced on a continuous schedule: The behavior decelerates and is eventually extinguished. Extinction may be a very useful phenomenon when a teacher withdraws attention from a maladaptive behavior. On the other hand, it may be frustrating when the teacher has systematically developed some appropriate behavior only to see that it has disappeared when the student is observed a year later.

If you were unable to remember this, perhaps your behavior, when no longer reinforced by passing tests, has undergone extinction.

Ensuring that behavior will be maintained is an important part of teaching. It is impossible for the teacher to follow students around forever, reinforcing them with cereal or smile and praise. Behaviors that extinguish rapidly when the artificial contingencies used to develop them are withdrawn can hardly be considered learned in any meaningful sense. Most experimental evidence indicates that extinction occurs unless specific measures are taken to prevent it (Kazdin, 2001; Kazdin & Bootzin, 1972; Rincover & Koegel, 1975; Stokes, Baer, & Jackson, 1974).

Response Generalization

Sometimes changing one behavior will result in changes in other, similar behaviors. Such similar behaviors are often referred to as a *response class,* and changes in untrained members of the response class as **response generalization.** For example, if students receive reinforcers for completing multiplication problems and subsequently increase their rates of completing both multiplication and division problems, response generalization has occurred to untrained members of the response class: completion of arithmetic problems. Unfortunately, this kind of generalization does not happen often. Usually only the specific behavior reinforced will change. "Behavior, unlike the flower, does not naturally bloom" (Baer & Wolf, 1970, p. 320).

Training Generalization

For practice promoting generalization, go to the "Activities" module for Chapter 10 of the Companion Website.

Ensuring the generality of behavior change is particularly important to the teacher of students with disabilities. Because legislation requires that all such students be educated in the least restrictive environment, large numbers of students with disabilities are educated entirely in general education classes or are in special classes only temporarily or for only part of the school day. The special educator cannot count on being able to apply systematic applied behavior analysis procedures for extended periods of time or even for the entire school day. Even the teacher of students with pervasive disabilities must be aware that these students, too, will be living, learning, and working in an environment that is least restrictive—that is, one that as much as possible resembles that of their typical peers. Special educators must prepare their students to perform in situations where systematic contingency management programs may not be available.

General education teachers also must be aware of techniques for promoting generalization. These teachers will serve large numbers of students with disabilities who have been taught appropriate academic and social behaviors using applied behavior analysis procedures. To help these students perform optimally in their classrooms, general education teachers must know not only the techniques used to teach these students but also techniques that will encourage generalization to less-structured settings. The current emphasis on increasing integration of students with disabilities in the regular programs makes awareness of this technology more important for all teachers.

The procedures for prompting generalization described in the following sections include some that do not meet more stringent or technical definitions of generalization of behavior change (Johnston, 1979; Skinner, 1953). Traditionally, generalization has been noted only when behavior occurs spontaneously in circumstances where no contingencies are in effect. For practical purposes, we shall also consider behavior changes that can be facilitated by relatively minor changes in the setting in which generalization is desired. If such changes can be made fairly effortlessly and if gains made in the training setting can be maintained, for all practical purposes the behavior has generalized. Haring and Liberty (1990) suggested a number of questions that instructors should ask to help make decisions about programming for generalization. In simplified form, questions that a teacher might ask when assessing and programming for generalization include:

1. Has the skill been acquired? Unless the student can perform the skill fluently, accurately, and reliably in an instructional setting, it is useless to hope that she will perform it in any other setting.
2. Can the student acquire reinforcers (natural or otherwise) without performing the skill? If, when George stands helplessly in front of a soft drink vending machine at

the local miniature golf course, typical peers kindly (or impatiently) take his change and get him a drink, he is unlikely to be motivated to get it for himself.

3. Does the student perform part of the skill? When the student performs part of a skill in a generalization setting, the teacher's job is to go back to his task analysis, assess the antecedent and consequent stimuli for the missing or nonperformed component, provide more effective ones during retraining, and identify potentially effective stimuli in the generalization environment.

Zirpoli and Melloy (1933, p. 192) provided the following general guidelines to facilitate generalization:

- Teach desired behaviors, whether they are social or academic, within the natural setting where they should occur.
- Employ a variety of caregivers for training (for example, several teachers, parents, peers). This decreases the probability that the behavior will become situation specific.
- Train in a variety of settings.
- Shift as quickly as possible from artificial cues and reinforcers to more natural ones.
- Shift from continuous reinforcement to intermittent reinforcement.
- Gradually increase delays in the delivery of reinforcement.
- Reinforce instances of generalization.

Stokes and Baer (1977, p. 350), in a more detailed analysis, reviewed the literature on generalization assessment and training in applied behavior analysis and categorized the techniques for assessing or programming generalization as follows:

Train and hope.

Sequentially modify.

Introduce to natural maintaining contingencies.

Train sufficient exemplars.

Train loosely.

Use indiscriminable contingencies.

Program common stimuli.

Mediate generalization.

Train to generalize.

The following sections review relevant research on each of the techniques described by Stokes and Baer (1977) and provide examples illustrating possible classroom uses.

Train and Hope

Unplanned generalization does sometimes happen. It may be likely to happen in cases where the skill trained is particularly useful to the student or where the skill becomes reinforcing in itself. For example, Patterson (1965) used a DRO procedure to eliminate aggressive and disruptive classroom behavior in a boy who behaved hyperactively. The inappropriate behavior was reduced on the playground and at home (where no formal contingencies were in operation) as well as in the classroom. Other researchers have reported that students who are given token reinforcers for appropriate behavior during some part of the school day may show changes in that behavior during other parts of the day or even in other classrooms (Walker, Mattsen, & Buckley, 1971).

Appropriate behaviors may also last after programs are withdrawn. Many behaviors taught to typical children and those with mild disabilities do generalize. Students who learn to read in school delight their parents (and sometimes drive them to distraction) by reading street signs. This spontaneous generalization, however, is much less likely to occur with students with more severe disabilities (Horner, McDonnell, & Bellamy, undated).

In spite of reported evidence that some behaviors are automatically generalized, it is important to remember that most are not. When they are, we usually do not know why (Kazdin, 2001). It has been suggested that some aspect of the generalization setting may have acquired conditioned reinforcing characteristics (Bear & Wolf, 1970; Chadwick & Day, 1971; Medland & Stachnik, 1972). Another possibility is that the behavior of teachers or parents has been permanently altered by the implementation of the applied behavior analysis procedure and that reinforcing consequences, though no longer formally programmed, may still occur more frequently than before intervention (Greenwood, Sloane, & Baskin, 1974; Kazdin, 2001).

Remember that changes in children's behavior may change adult's behavior, too.

Although there is hope that behaviors acquired or strengthened through formal contingency management programs may generalize, there is no certainty. Hoping will not make generalization happen. The teacher who expects it should be prepared to monitor students' behavior closely and to instigate more effective procedures immediately upon learning that early hopes have been dashed. The following example illustrates a behavior that generalized for no discernible reason.

Ms. Andrews Works a Miracle

Ms. Andrews, who did private tutoring at home to supplement her income, was asked to work with Brandon, who had completed the first semester of the seventh grade with 2 Cs, 2 Ds, and an F. Because Brandon had previously been an excellent student, his parents were frantic. Ms. Andrews tested Brandon, found no learning problem, and decided that Brandon simply had a particularly bad case of seventh-grade slump. He was not doing homework or classwork, and he didn't study for tests. He seemed to have efficient study skills—he just wasn't using them. Ms. Andrews suggested that once-a-week tutoring was not the answer and urged the parents to implement some contingency management. She explained the low probability that study behavior would generalize beyond her living room. They insisted on tutoring and implemented no program.

For two weeks, Ms. Andrews worked with Brandon on grade-level materials—not the books he was using at school because he, naturally, forgot to bring them. She provided very high rates of verbal praise for reading, studying, and completing math problems, as well as access to a gamelike vocabulary development program if Brandon completed other tasks.

During the third week, Brandon's mother called. Three of his teachers had written notes indicating that Brandon's work in their classes had improved dramatically. Tests and papers from all classes were As and Bs. Ms. Andrews, said Brandon's mother, had worked a miracle. Agreeing modestly before hanging up, Ms. Andrews spent the next few minutes staring into space and wondering, "Did he just coincidentally decide to kick into gear, or was it really something I did?"

SEQUENTIALLY MODIFY

A procedure that allows stimulus generalization or transfer of training across settings is *sequential modification*. In this procedure, generalization (in the practical sense) is promoted by applying the same techniques that successfully changed behavior in one setting to all settings where the target behavior is desirable. Exactly the same process is undertaken when using a multiple-baseline-across-settings design to demonstrate a functional relationship between independent and dependent variables. For example, for a student who learned to behave appropriately and complete academic tasks in a resource room but did not perform in any general education classrooms, the teachers involved might set up a reinforcement system similar to that used in the resource class in each general education classroom. A similar procedure to promote maintenance

Review Chapter 5 for an extended discussion of the multiple baseline design.

would necessitate training those responsible for the student's education and care after the student has been dismissed from a special training program. Teachers, parents, or other caregivers would be trained to carry out the same applied behavior analysis procedures employed in the training situation. In some cases, it may be unrealistic to program exactly the same contingencies in the generalization setting. For example, a general education classroom teacher may not be able to monitor disruptive behavior as closely, or deliver reinforcers as often, as a special-class teacher. Similarly, parents may be unable or unwilling to structure programs as closely as may be done in residential settings. In such cases, modified versions of programs may still provide enough environmental control to maintain the target behaviors at rates close to those established during training.

Homes may be harder to structure than schools or other institutions.

Examination of any published study using a multiple-baseline-across-settings experimental design provides an example of sequential modification

To increase your understanding of this topic, go to the "Activities" module for Chapter 10 of the Companion Website.

Trask-Tyler et al. (1994) taught three young adults with developmental disabilities and visual impairments to prepare three different recipes using tape-recorded instructions. After sequential training on these recipes, cooking skills generalized to untrained recipes requiring similar skills (simple generality) and to more difficult untrained recipes requiring a combination of skills learned during instruction (complex generality).

Drasgow, Halle, and Ostrosky (1998) taught three children with language delays to substitute an appropriate form of request (signing "please") for one that was inappropriate (leading an adult to an object, reaching for the object, or screaming.) The initial training was conducted in an isolated setting. The students learned the appropriate request but never used it in other settings until they were trained in each setting. They then used the appropriate request in all settings that were observed.

A study by Lovaas, Koegel, Simmons, and Long (1973) demonstrated the effectiveness of applying sequential modification in ensuring both transfer and maintenance. Parents whose children with autism had acquired basic communication self-care, and social skills in a special program were trained to reinforce these skills with their children. On a 1- to 4-year follow-up, children who had remained at home and whose parents had continued to reinforce appropriate behavior had maintained the gains made in the special program and in some cases had made additional progress. Those children who had been institutionalized where personnel were not trained in applied behavior analysis procedures had lost all the gains made in the special program.

It is not always necessary to employ identical procedures to obtain stimulus generalization or maintenance. Walker and Buckley (1972) studied the effects of several ways of promoting maintenance in students whose behavior was changed in a special class setting using a token economy. After 2 months in the special class, the students were divided into four groups and sent back to general education classes. For one group, the authors used a procedure they referred to as *peer reprogramming*. Each experimental subject had the opportunity to earn points for appropriate behavior during two 30-minute periods a week. The points could be exchanged for prizes such as field trips, which were then awarded to the entire class. An interesting double contingency was in effect, because the target student had to earn the right to the 30-minute reinforcement period by appropriate behavior during the rest of the week. A rather elaborate electronic signaling system involving lights and buzzers was used during the reinforcement period to indicate to the subject and classmates that points were or were not accumulating. The authors theorized that, because the student's peers were being rewarded for appropriate behavior, the peers would reinforce such behavior rather than disruption or inattentiveness.

The procedure described by Walker and Buckley (1972) for the second group was more closely related to exact sequential modification. This procedure used a duplication of many conditions in the special class. The same curriculum materials, systematic social reinforcement, and token economy were implemented in the general education class. The only procedural difference was the absence of time-out and response-cost contingencies, which the authors feared might be used punitively by inexperienced teachers. An adapted rating system was used when the students were in classes other their homeroom, and the homeroom teacher awarded points based on ratings.

For the third group, the classroom teachers in whose classes the target students were to be placed received systematic training in applied behavior analysis. The teachers' implementation of the procedures in their classrooms was monitored, and course credit and free tuition for graduate credit for the teachers was contingent on correct implementation (another double contingency). A final group of students was returned to the general education class.

The authors reported that peer reprogramming and similar reinforcement procedures maintained the students' appropriate behavior at over 70% of the rate shown in the special class. The teacher-training and no-treatment procedures were less effective, though still maintaining over 60% of the gains. A reanalysis of the data by Cone (1973) showed smaller percentages of maintenance and no clear difference among the three treatment procedures, which were, however, all more effective than simply training and hoping—the no-treatment procedure. In addition, students who received the programmed maintenance procedures continued to show more appropriate behavior 4 months after all modifications were withdrawn.

Anderson-Inman, Walker, and Purcell (1984) used a procedure they call *transenvironmental programming* to increase generalization from resource rooms to general education classrooms. Transenvironmental programming involves assessing the target environment, providing students in the resource room with skills identified as critical in the general education classroom, using techniques to promote transfer of the skills acquired, and evaluating student performance in the general education classroom. Specific techniques for facilitating transfer included reinforcing the newly acquired skills in the general education classroom.

Browning (1983) used taped reminders of appropriate behavior to maintain the improved behavior of six adolescents with autism. Their inappropriate verbalizations and angry outbursts were brought under control in a highly structured setting using time-out and response-cost. When the students were integrated into a less restrictive setting, they heard 10- to 30-second messages reminding them of appropriate verbal behavior and giving them directions for coping with anger or difficult situations. The program was effective for all the students.

The transfer and maintenance of behaviors by sequential modification may not technically qualify as generalization, as we discussed earlier. The provision of identical or similar applied behavior analysis procedures in alternate settings, however, is practical and frequently successful. Even if the alterations are necessary for extended periods, their effectiveness may make their implementation well worth the trouble. The following vignette illustrates the use of sequential modification.

Whose behavior has generalized here?

Connie Learns to Do Her Work

Connie was a second-grade student in Ms. Gray's resource room for children with learning disabilities. Connie performed very well in the resource room, where she earned points exchangeable for free time when she completed academic tasks, but did no work in the general education classroom, where she spent most of the school day. Instead, she wandered around the classroom bothering other students. After conferring with the general education classroom teacher, Ms. Gray provided her with slips of paper preprinted with Connie's name, a place for the date, and several options to check regarding Connie's academic work and classroom behavior (see Figure 10–1). Ms. Gray then awarded Connie bonus points for her work in the general education classroom. Although Connie continued to be less productive in the general education classroom than in the resource room, her behavior was acceptable, and the amount of academic work completed was comparable to that of most students in the class. The general education classroom teacher was so impressed with the procedure that she made rating slips for several of her problem students and awarded them special privileges when they completed their work and behaved properly.

Connie	Date: _____
Assignments complete:	Behavior:
Yes _____	Good _____
No _____	Fair _____
Partly _____	Poor _____
	_____ Initials

FIGURE 10–1
Connie's chart.

Introduce to Natural Maintaining Contingencies

An ideal applied behavior analysis program seeks to change behaviors that receive reinforcement in the student's natural environment. Baer (1999) suggested "A good rule is not to make any deliberate behavior change that will not meet natural communities of reinforcement" (p. 16). He added that this rule should be broken only if there is a commitment to provide follow-up for as long as necessary. Ideally, as a result of the program, the student would behave appropriately for the same reasons that motivate students who were never referred because of inappropriate behavior. The student would work hard at academic tasks to earn good grades, behave well in the classroom to receive the approval of the teacher, or perform a job for money. It may be possible to accelerate the process of making the natural reinforcers more powerful (Horcones, 1992). If a teacher points out how a student's hard work on a math paper resulted in a big red A+, or how proud a resource student's general education teacher has been of his good behavior, or how terrific it is to be able to spend money one earns by working hard, these natural reinforcers become more noticeable. For example, although fairly complicated procedures—including shaping, chaining, and graduated guidance—may be necessary to teach students with severe disabilities to feed themselves, feeding themselves may generalize to other settings and be durable after training is withdrawn (Browning, 1980). Such a skill has a built-in positive reinforcer in that children who feed themselves efficiently can control their own intake of food. Toilet training of persons with mental retardation (Azrin, Sneed, & Foxx, 1973) and nondisabled young children (Foxx & Azrin, 1973) may be maintained after contingencies are withdrawn because discomfort is avoided. Similarly, students who are taught such skills as reading or math may maintain these skills without programmed generalization because the skills are useful. Some social behaviors may also generalize.

An increasing emphasis in the education of persons with severe disabilities has been on training functional skills—that is, skills useful to the individual in his school or workplace and community (Brown, Nietupski, & Hamre-Nietupski, 1976). Rather than teach these students meaningless school skills like sorting blocks by color, we teach them skills they need for maximum independence: riding the bus, using the laundromat, cooking a meal, even using an automated bank teller machine (Shafer, Inge, & Hill, 1986). O'Reilly, Lancioni, and Kierans (2000) taught four adults with retardation to order their own drinks in a bar and to interact with other patrons. These skills, by their nature, are more prone to be maintained by the natural environment. One of the most

We try to teach functional skills—those that are useful to the student.

important reasons for teachers to know about their students' lifestyles, customs, and cultures is so they will know what behaviors those students' environments will maintain. Choosing behaviors to change that will be maintained by the natural environment applies the Relevance of Behavior Rule. Ayllon and Azrin first described this rule in 1968. Baer and Wolf (1970) conceptualized the Relevance of Behavior Rule as a form of *trapping*. They asserted that if applied behavior analysts can generate behaviors that are reinforced by the natural environment, a situation analogous to catching a mouse in a trap will be created. The mechanism of trapping works this way:

> Consider, for example, that very familiar model, the mouse trap. A mouse trap is an environment designed to accomplish massive behavior modification in a mouse. Note that this modification has thorough generality: The change in behavior accomplished by the trap will be uniform across all environments, it will extend to all of the mouse's behaviors, and it will last indefinitely into the future. Furthermore, a mouse trap allows a great amount of behavioral change to be accomplished by a relatively slight amount of behavioral control. A householder without a trap can, of course, still kill a mouse: He can wait patiently outside the mouse's hole, grab the mouse faster than the mouse can avoid him, and then apply various forms of force to the unfortunate animal to accomplish the behavioral change desired. But this performance requires a great deal of competence: vast patience, supercoordination, extreme manual dexterity, and a well-suppressed squeamishness. By contrast, a householder with a trap needs very few accomplishments: If he can merely apply the cheese and then leave the loaded trap where the mouse is likely to smell that cheese, in effect he has guaranteed general change in the mouse's future behavior. The essence of a trap, in behavioral terms, is that only a relatively simple response is necessary to enter the trap, yet once entered, the trap cannot be resisted in creating general behavioral change. For the mouse, the entry response is merely to smell the cheese. Everything proceeds from there almost automatically. The householder need have no more control over the mouse's behavior than to get him to smell the cheese, yet he accomplishes thorough changes in behavior. (Baer & Wolf, 1970, p. 321)

Some behaviors do lend themselves to trapping. If behaviors can be generated that result in increased peer reinforcement, they are particularly likely to be maintained in the natural environment. Social and communication skills, grooming skills, and even assertiveness may only need to be generated to be maintained (Bourbeau, Sowers, & Close, 1986). The network of reinforcement available for such behaviors may form an irresistible environmental trap that, like the mouse trap, once entered is inescapable. Unfortunately, it is often difficult to pinpoint behaviors that will be reinforced by the natural environment (Kazdin, 2001). Most natural environments seem to ignore appropriate behavior and concentrate attention on inappropriate behavior. Few drivers are stopped by police officers for compliments; workers are seldom praised for getting to work on time and attending regularly. Even in the classroom, teachers tend to pay little or no attention to students who are doing well but instead correct students whose behavior is disruptive or inattentive. It is unwise for the applied behavior analyst to assume that any behavior will be maintained by the student's natural environment. We can say, however, that the maintenance or transfer of behaviors to reinforcement contingencies in the natural environment may be facilitated by:

1. Observing the student's environment. What parents, teachers, or other adults describe as desirable behavior for the student may or may not be what they reinforce.
2. Choosing behaviors that are subject to trapping as determined by observation. For example, if teachers in a given school heavily reinforce pretty handwriting, a consulting teacher may teach students pretty handwriting, even if it would not otherwise be a priority.

3. Teaching students to recruit reinforcers from the environment (Seymour & Stokes, 1976). Students can be taught to call adults' attention to appropriate behavior and thus to receive praise or other reinforcers. Craft, Alber, and Heward (1998) taught fourth graders in a special class to ask, "How am I doing?" or make statements like, "Look, I'm all finished!" an appropriate number of times during a class session. The students were able to perform the skill in their general education class. Praise from their teachers increased and so did their academic performance.
4. Teaching students to recognize reinforcement when it is delivered. It has been the authors' experience that many students who have difficulty in the general education classroom may not recognize more subtle forms of social reinforcement. This may be a function of what Bryan and Bryan (1978) called a lack of social perception. Some students cannot pick up subtleties of nonverbal communication that may be the only reinforcers available. Teaching students to recognize such subtleties may increase the reinforcing potential of the natural environment.

Ways to promote generalization.

The teacher who wants the natural environment to take over reinforcement should be aware that this is by no means an automatic process. Careful monitoring should take place to assess the natural environment and to determine how well the behavior change is being maintained. The first vignette illustrates a behavior that is maintained because it receives naturally occurring reinforcers. The second anecdote illustrates a failure of the environment to provide sufficient reinforcers.

Not all teachers believe in praising children.

Alvin Learns to Read

Alvin was an adjudicated juvenile delinquent in Mr. Daniel's class at the detention center. He was a virtual nonreader when he came into the class, but with a systematic direct instruction (Adams & Engelmann, 1996) reading method using token reinforcement for correct responses, Mr. Daniel taught Alvin to read phonetically regular one- and two-syllable words. Mr. Daniel wondered whether Alvin would ever read after being released from the center, because the boy certainly showed little enthusiasm for any of the high-interest, low-vocabulary books available in the classroom for recreational reading. Alvin appeared to read only when the token condition was in effect. About a year after Alvin's release, however, Mr. Daniel happened to meet him emerging from an adult bookstore. He had several paperback books under his arm, one open in his hands, and a look of intense concentration on his face.

Marvin Fails the Sixth Grade

Mr. Cohen, a consulting teacher, had worked with Marvin for 2 years, while he was attending fourth- and fifth-grade classes. He spent time in Marvin's classroom with small groups of students and sometimes scheduled Marvin and others for more intensive work outside the general education classroom. Marvin had done well in fourth and fifth grades because his teachers had used high rates of verbal praise and free time contingent on completion of work. Marvin was dismissed from special education at the end of fifth grade. Mr. Cohen had not even considered that Marvin might have trouble in sixth grade, but the sixth-grade teacher, Ms. Roach, was, to put it bluntly, a hardnose. She did not believe in praising students for good behavior or in providing any consequence for academic work except grades. As she put it, "That's why they come to school. I don't believe in coddling them." Marvin went back to the behaviors that had resulted in his original referral: He disrupted the classroom, did not complete assignments, and ultimately failed the sixth grade. Mr. Cohen felt he had learned two things at Marvin's expense: Never assume that the same conditions exist in all classrooms, and always follow up on students whose behavior appears to have been permanently changed.

Train Sufficient Exemplars

Most academic and social behaviors that we want to teach our students to perform are members of various response classes. That is, there is seldom a single behavior that is always performed in exactly the same way in exactly the same place. For example, when we teach a student to read, we expect that she will eventually apply her reading skills to decoding and comprehending material she was never read. We would certainly not expect her to do that after learning one or two words with the same beginning sound or after one example of how to use the context to derive the meaning of an unfamiliar word. We would provide lots of examples and lots of lessons; we would provide sufficient exemplars. Similarly, we would not expect a student with severe disabilities to use any vending machine in the city after learning to use only the one in community center, or a student who had learned to great his teacher in the morning to greet any adult. Again, we would train sufficient exemplars.

General Case Programming

General case programming promotes generalization by training sufficient exemplars. It was developed to teach language, academic, and social skills to young children at risk (Becker & Engelmann, 1978). General case programming emphasizes using sufficient members of a class of stimuli to ensure that students will be able to perform the task on any member of the class of stimuli. If we want a child to identify red objects, we do not have to expose him to every red object in the world to ensure that he can perform this task. We just have to expose him to enough red objects having enough variety in their redness, and he will reliably identify any red object as red. For many children it is not necessary to be very systematic in picking the red objects—we just label whatever objects come our way. With learners who have disabilities, however, careful attention must be given to selecting objects that will facilitate their acquisition of this skill. Horner, Eberhard, and Sheehan (1986) stressed the importance of defining the range of characteristics across which members of the class stimuli may vary and the range of different behaviors that may be required and ensuring that teaching examples include these variations.

Engelmann and Carnine (1982) stated that examples used to train the general case must teach *sameness*—the characteristics of a stimulus that are the same for all members of a class—and *difference*—the range of variability within the members of a class. In other words, what do all red things have in common and how different can things be and still be red? The selection of the training stimuli is the critical factor in general case programming. If all the stimuli used in training sessions are red plastic objects of the same shade, the student asked to fetch the red book from the teacher's desk (it's her copy of Engelmann and Carnine's *Theory of Instruction*) may very well fail to do so because the book is an orangy red, not the pinkish red of the training stimuli. General case programming has been very successful in teaching academic behaviors to students with and without disabilities. It has also been used to teach appropriate social behaviors (Engelmann & Colvin, 1983).

General case programming has also been used to teach prelanguage and language skills to learners with severe disabilities. The study discussed in Chapter 9 in which students were taught a generalized imitation response is an example. You will remember that the students, systematically taught to imitate movements made by the trainer, also imitated movements whose imitation was never reinforced. Similar training (Garcia, Baer, & Firestone, 1971) has resulted in generalized correct use of many verbal responses including plurals (Guess, Sailor, Rutherford, & Baer, 1968) present and past tense (Schumaker & Sherman, 1970), and appropriate syntax (Garcia, Guess, & Byrnes, 1973)

More recent applications of general case programming emphasize teaching functional skills to learners with severe disabilities (Wilcox & Bellamy, 1982). If, for example, a teacher wanted to teach a student to use any vending machine in a section of a city, the teacher would have to determine what variations in vending machines existed (where coins are put, how the machine is activated, and so on) and provide training on machines having all these variations (Sprague & Horner, 1984). The procedure has been equally successful in teaching telephone skills (Horner, Williams, & Stevely, 1984), street crossing (Horner, Jones, & Williams, 1985), using different soap dispensers in handwashing (Pancsofar & Bates, 1985), sorting mail by zip code (Woolcock & Lengel, 1987), bussing cafeteria tables (Horner et al., 1986), and many other skills. The use of simulations, including those provided by videotape, may enable teachers to train more exemplars without actually traveling to as many locations as would be necessary without the use of these procedures (Haring, Breen, Weiner, Kennedy, & Bednersh, 1995).

It would be wise to prepare students for vending machines that talk, which can startle even those of us without serious disabilities.

Using Multiple Settings, Teachers, and Activities

Another approach to using sufficient exemplars is to train the behavior in a number of settings or with several different trainers. Such a practice often results in generalization of the behavior change into settings where no training has taken place. Considerable evidence exists to indicate that training novel responses under a wide variety of stimulus conditions increases the probability of generalization under conditions where no previous training has occurred. This procedure differs from sequential modification in that change is targeted and assessed with settings, individuals, or activities in which no intervention has taken place. For example, Stokes et al. (1974) determined that a greeting response occurred only in the presence of the trainer who had systematically reinforced the response. The introduction of a second trainer resulted in the generalization of the response to 14 staff members.

Emshoff, Redd, and Davidson (1976) trained adolescent students who were delinquent to use positive interpersonal comments. Students trained under multiple conditions (activities, trainers, locations) showed greater generalization in a nontreatment setting than did those trained under constant conditions. Ducharme and Holborn (1997) taught social skills to preschool children with hearing impairments. Students taught multiple activities with multiple peers were able to use their skill with new teachers, play activities, and peers.

Many studies have demonstrated that the effects of suppressing deviant behaviors in individuals with severe disabilities are situation- and experimenter-specific unless trained across several conditions (Corte, Wolf, & Locke, 1971; Garcia, 1974). The effects of punishment contingencies are apparently even less likely to generalize than behavior changes resulting from positive reinforcement.

The training of sufficient exemplars is a productive area for teachers concerned with increasing generalization. It is not necessary to teach students to perform appropriate behaviors in every setting or in the presence of every potential teacher or other adult. The teacher need train only enough to ensure that a generalized response has been learned. Neither is it necessary to teach every example of a response class that we want students to perform. Imagine the difficulty of teaching students to read if this were so. We expect students to generalize letter or syllable sounds and thus to decode words they have never read before. Most teaching of academic skills is based on the assumption that students will be able to use these skills to solve novel problems or to perform a variety of tasks. The following examples show how teachers may use training a number of exemplars to program response generalization and generalization across trainers and across settings.

See Chapter 8 for a discussion of generalization after punishment.

Carol Learns to Use Plurals

Carol was a 5-year-old student with a language delay in Ms. Sims's integrated preschool class. Carol had learned the names of many common objects but did not differentiate the singular from the plural forms. Ms. Sims made a point of labeling single and multiple examples of objects frequently during the school day: "Look, Carol, coat" (as Carol took hers off); "Carol, coats" (as she ran her hand over all the students' coats in the cloakroom); "Say coat" (as Carol hung up hers); "Say coats" (as she moved Carol's hand along all the coats). Using a discrimination training procedure, she brought Carol's verbal responses under stimulus control of the correct form of a number of singular and plural pairs:

cow	cows
shoe	shoes
dog	dogs
bird	birds
plane	planes

She then tested for generalization. She showed Carol a new set of pictures:

chair	chairs

Carol responded correctly. Her response using singular and plural forms had generalized to an untrained example. Carol used singular and plural forms correctly in a variety of untrained examples. Her response generalization was so broad that when the principal and superintendent visited the class, Ms. Sims heard Carol say to another student, "Mans come." Ms. Sims restrained herself from tearing her hair out by remembering that such overgeneralization is not uncommon among young children and that she would just have to teach irregular plurals as a separate response class.

This is the same phenomenon that causes a typical city 2-year-old to call the first cow she sees a "doggie."

In the following anecdote, DeWayne helps out Professor Grundy and illustrates the effectiveness of general case programming.

The Professor Goes High-Tech

After ignoring numerous memos and announcements regarding the importance of integrating technology into his classes, Professor Grundy reluctantly agreed to videotape some student presentations. The students were to include the tapes in portfolios they were required to compile before student teaching. He attended a seminar during which he received instruction on how to operate a video camera, but when he arrived at his class, he observed that the camera that had been delivered looked very much unlike the one on which he had received training. He circled the equipment slowly and poked several buttons to no avail. Just as he was about to announce that the presentations would not be taped after all, DeWayne jumped out of his seat and approached the camera.

"Don't worry, Professor," he announced. "This is one of the new cameras. I've never seen one either, but I worked in the lab for a while and I'll figure it out. The university gets bids on equipment and buys it from the lowest bidder. It seems like that's never the same vendor so there's no two pieces of equipment of the same make or model."

"Let's see," he mumbled, "there's usually a power switch up near the top. Yep, here it is. Now let's see if I can find the 'pause' button; it's usually red or orange and in a good place for a right-handed person who's looking at the LED screen. Oops! Almost forgot; you always have to take off the lens cap. Here it is, Professor," Dewayne announced proudly, "all you have to do is push this red button to stop and start. Look at this little screen and you'll see either a green light or the word 'record' when it's on."

Train Loosely

Teaching techniques based on principles of behavior have usually emphasized tight control of many teaching factors (Becker, Engelmann, & Thomas, 1975; Stephens, 1976; White & Haring, 1980). Teaching procedures for students with disabilities are often rigidly standardized: adhering to the same format, presenting items in a predetermined sequence, and requiring mastery of on skill before training on another has begun. Although this may be an efficient means of instruction, and although it is the way that most special educators were taught to teach, especially those training to work with populations having more severe disabilities, there is increasing evidence that it may not always be the best way to ensure that skills will be generalized. What began in the early 1970s as an investigation of alternating or rotating various stimuli or responses in highly structured training sessions resulted in a major change in the instruction of individuals with disabilities in the 1990s. Schroeder and Baer (1972) found that vocal imitation skills were better generalized to untaught members of the response class when the training stimuli were varied within sessions rather than when each skill was taught to mastery before instruction on another was begun. Rather than tightly restricting the vocal skills being taught (serial training), the researchers allowed a number of different imitations to be taught within a single session (concurrent training).

Sometimes too much structure interferes with generalization.

In an example of response alternation, Panyan and Hall (1978) investigated the effects of concurrent as opposed to serial training in the acquisition, maintenance, and generalization of two different response classes: tracing and vocal imitation. The serial training procedure required mastery of one response class (tracing) before instruction began on a second response class (vocal imitation). In the concurrent training procedure, training on the two different response classes was alternated in a single training session before either task was mastered. The procedure used did not affect the time required for acquisition or maintenance of the response trained, but generalization to untrained responses was greater under the concurrent training condition. These studies have definite implications for the teacher. Apparently, it adds no efficiency to train students to master one skill before beginning instruction on another, unless of course the first skill is prerequisite to the second. Alternating teaching within sessions not only does not interfere with learning but, on the contrary, leads to greater generalization. Thus, statements like "I can't worry about Harold's match until I get him reading on grade level" may not be justified.

For practice promoting generalization, go to the "Activities" module for Chapter 10 of the Companion Website.

Investigations of "loose training" have showed great promise in a wide variety of settings and for many behaviors. Variously termed *incidental teaching, naturalistic teaching, nonintensive teaching,* or *minimal intervention,* strategies that incorporate instruction for individuals with disabilities into less structured activities have been successful in promoting acquisition of behaviors and even more successful in promoting generalization.

Campbell and Stremel-Campbell (1982) taught two boys with moderate to severe disabilities to use various statements and questions while they were being taught academic and self-help skills. The target verbal skills were reinforced when they were emitted spontaneously or when their use was prompted. Both boys acquired the verbal skills along with the academic and self-help skills, and generalization also occurred. Using a procedure they called *nonintensive,* Inglesfield and Crisp (1985) compared the effects of teaching dressing skills 10 times a day for 3 days (an approach many special educators might choose for initial skill acquisition) to the effects of teaching the same skills twice a day for 15 days (an approach that would occur in the natural environment). They found the twice-daily procedure more effective for both initial learning and generalization.

Several other studies have indicated that less intensive, more natural instructions promote generalization with little or no loss of efficiency in acquisition. Success has been demonstrated in teaching receptive object labels (McGee, Kkrantz, Mason, & McClannahan, 1983), expressive language (Koegel, O'Dell, & Koegel, 1987; Woods, 1984), sign language (Carr & Kologinsky, 1983), and reading (McGee, Krantz, & McClannahan, 1986).

The use of naturalistic or loose training represents a departure from tradition in special education teaching. Its success suggests again the importance of teachers' maintaining their skills and keeping up with current research. Although most special educators continue to use structured teaching during the acquisition of new skills, they rapidly begin to incorporate teaching and assessing these skills more informally.

Use Indiscriminable Contingencies

As we described in Chapter 7, resistance to extinction or maintenance of behavior is greatly prolonged by intermittent reinforcement schedules. Intermittent reinforcement may be used to maintain behaviors at a high rate, or it may be a step toward eliminating reinforcement entirely. It is possible to thin a reinforcement schedule to such a degree that few reinforcers are used. If reinforcement is then withdrawn altogether, the behavior will continue. This resistance to extinction is not permanent, because behavior, if unreinforced, will eventually be extinguished. It may be possible, however, that "eventually" will be so far in the future as to make no practical difference. The behavior will be maintained as long as necessary.

Considerable evidence indicates that intermittent reinforcement schedules lead to increased maintenance of behavior change (Kazdin & Polster, 1973; Phillips, Phillips, Fixsen, & Wolf, 1971). Teachers should consider this evidence when planning and implementing behavior-change strategies. Even if intermittent reinforcement must be continued indefinitely, if schedules are very lean this may be a fairly efficient and economical means of providing for maintenance.

Other procedures besides intermittent reinforcement make it difficult for students to discriminate which responses will be reinforced. One strategy that may lead to generalization across settings is delaying the delivery of reinforcers. Schwarz and Hawkins (1970) videotaped the behavior of a student during math and spelling classes. After the end of the school day, the student was shown the videotape, and appropriate behaviors in math class were reinforced. In the next days, a behavior change was evident in spelling class as well as math class. The authors hypothesized that the generalization across settings was due to the delayed reinforcement, which made it more difficult for the student to determine when contingencies were in effect.

Fowler and Baer (1981) used a delayed reinforcement procedure to modify various behaviors of preschool children. The children received tokens exchangeable for toys either immediately after the period during which they earned them or at the end of the day, after other periods during which no tokens were available. The children generalized the appropriate behavior; that is, they behaved better all day when the reinforcer was not given until the end of the day. Similarly, Dunlap, Koegel, Johnson, and O'Neill (1987) used delayed reinforcement to maintain the work performance of students with autism in community settings.

Another way of delivering reinforcers that resulted in decreased discriminability of contingencies was demonstrated by Koegel and Rincover (1977). The authors taught children with autism to perform simple nonverbal imitations or to follow simple instructions. After the behavior was learned (using continuous reinforcement), schedules were thinned. Once training was concluded, the children were observed to allow researchers to assess maintenance of behavior change. The behaviors were ultimately extinguished. (The thinner the schedule during training, the more responses occurred before extinction.) The use of noncontingent rewards after extinction, however, resulted in recovery of the behavior. At random intervals, the children were given candy identical to that earned in the original training setting—whether their responses were correct or not. The noncontingent rewards delayed extinction considerably. Apparently, the reinforcer had acquired the properties of a discriminative stimulus. It served as a cue to the students that, in this setting, reinforcement was available. The students were unable to discriminate which responses would be reinforced, so they produced larger numbers of the correct (previously reinforced) responses before extinction. This procedure also illustrates aspects of contriving common stimuli discussed later in this chapter.

Thin intermittent reinforcement schedules are the most frequently used means of making reinforcement contingencies indiscriminable. Evidence indicates, however, that any procedure that makes it difficult for students to determine when contingencies are in effect is likely to result in greater durability of behavior change, either in the original training setting or in other settings. The following example illustrates a procedures that make it difficult for students to make such determinations.

Ms. Bell's Class Learns to Complete Assignments

In the morning group in her intermediate-level resource room, Ms. Bell's students with mild retardation consistently failed to complete their assignments. Each student was expected independently to complete a reading comprehension, a math, and a spelling activity, while Ms. Bell worked with small groups on other academic skills. Ms. Bell began giving her students tokens worth 5 minutes of free time to be exchanged at the end of the morning for each assignment completed. This resulted in almost 100% completion of assignments. Ms. Bell then announced that tokens would not be given until the end of the morning and that only two assignments could earn tokens. She put the words reading, spelling, and math on slips of paper and allowed a student to draw two slips. The students did not know until the end of the morning which two assignments would earn free time but continued to complete their assignments. Ms. Bell, who wanted to move to a lean reinforcement schedule, then announced that there would be the possibility of two drawings daily: one for a "yes/no" card, which would determine whether reinforcement would be available, and a second if the "yes" card was drawn. The second drawing would determine which assignment would earn free time. At first, one "yes" and one "no" card were available. She then gradually added "no" cards to the pool until there was only a 20% probability that free time would be available. The students continued to complete their assignments in all three subject areas and seemed to enjoy the suspense of never knowing when free time would be available or for which specific behavior.

Program Common Stimuli

Walker and Buckley (1972) asserted "intra-subject behavioral similarity across different settings is probably a function, in part, of the amount of stimulus similarity which exists between such settings" (p. 209). Kirby and Bickel (1988) suggested that stimulus similarity, and thus stimulus control, is the major factor in any generalization. A possible method of achieving either maintenance or stimulus generalization is deliberate programming of similar stimuli in the training setting and in the setting in which generalization is desired. This may be accomplished by either increasing the similarity of the training situation to the natural environment or by introducing elements of the training situation into the natural environment.

Several studies have investigated the effects of introducing elements of the natural environment into the training situation to increase the probability of generalization. For example, Ayllon and Kelly (1974) restored speech in a girl who was electively mute. After speech occurred frequently in the training situation (a counselor's office), elements similar to those present in the classroom were introduced. Other children, a blackboard, and desks were installed in the room; and the trainer began to function more as a traditional teacher by standing in the front of the room, lecturing, and asking questions. Training was also continued in the classroom. Increases in speech occurred in the classroom, and a follow-up a year later indicated that speech was maintained in several novel settings. Although the specific effects of the increase in similarity between training and natural settings are difficult to assess because of the package of treatments employed, generalization to the classroom did occur and was maintained.

Jackson and Wallace (1974) used tokens to increase vocal loudness in an adolescent girl with retardation. After satisfactory levels of loudness were achieved within the training setting, procedures similar to those employed by Ayllon and Kelly (1974) were introduced. Generalization to the classroom setting occurred.

Koegel and Rincover (1974) trained children with autism to respond to instructions in a one-to-one situation. Generalization to a classroom setting was programmed by gradually introducing more children into the training situation, so that it resembled the classroom. Livi and Ford (1985) found that domestic skills generalized from a training site to each student's home much more efficiently when stimuli similar to those in each home were used. (Every effort should be made to teach those skills in the students' homes.) In general, using discriminative stimuli during training that are similar to those in the setting where generalization is desired has proven to be a very effective technique (Stainback, Stainback, & Strathe, 1983). Woods (1987) suggested that such a procedure is an adaptation of the naturalistic procedures discussed previously, in that the stimuli in the generalization setting are natural ones.

Stimulations may be more practical than always teaching every skill in the natural environment.

One way of attempting to introduce natural stimuli into training settings is through the use of simulations. For example, van den Pol et al. (1981) successfully used pictures of fast-food items to teach students with moderate retardation to use community fast-food establishments. Simulated instruction for students with more severe disabilities is generally less successful (Foxx, McMorrow, & Mennemeier, 1984; Marchetti, McCartney, Drain, Hooper, & Dix, 1983). Horner et al. (undated) suggested that simulations employing real, rather than representational, items from the environment may be more successful. When real telephones are used, for example, students learn a generalized telephone response (Horner, Williams, & Stevely, 1984). Simulations using real stimuli have been used to teach numerous generalized skills, including comprehension of category labels (Hupp, 1986), video game use (Sedlack, Doyle, & Schloss, 1982), and menstrual care (Richman, Reiss, Bauman, & Bailey, 1984). They have, in general, proved more effective than procedures using pictures.

A limited number of studies have attempted to increase generalization by introducing elements of the training situation into the setting where generalization was desired. Rincover and Koegel (1975) taught children with autism to imitate nonverbal behaviors modeled by a therapist. When the children responded correctly on 20 consecutive trials without a prompt, a transfer test was made. For children who emitted no correct responses on the transfer test, an assessment of stimulus control was made. Stimuli from the training environment were introduced into the extratherapy setting, one at a time. If the child did not respond correctly in the presence of the first stimulus, that stimulus was removed and another one introduced. This process was continued until the stimulus controlling the behavior was identified and the responses occurred in the extratherapy setting. It was found that each of the children was responding selectively to some incidental stimulus in the treatment room. When this stimulus was provided in the extratherapy setting, each child responded correctly. The amount of responding in the extratherapy situation was, however, consistently less than in the training situation.

Baer (1999) suggested the use of a contrived common stimulus. A functional and portable object was introduced from the training setting into the setting in which generalization was desired. Trask-Tyler et al. (1994) suggested that a portable tape player with audio instructions for task completion is such a contrived common stimulus that may have great promise for improving generalization for students with severe disabilities. Many of the procedures described in Chapter 9 using schedules, picture cues, and other relatively unobtrusive items are equally useful. Troutman (1977) used an analogous procedure to program generalization from resource rooms to general education classrooms. Six students with learning disabilities showed high rates of academic task completion and low rates of disruptive behavior in the resource room but did not perform appropriately in the general education classroom. Each student was allowed to bring from home some object, such as a figurine, to decorate his or her desk in the resource room, where points were earned for completing academic tasks and for behaving appropriately. After a few weeks, the students were instructed to take their objects to the general education classroom. The resource teacher suggested that the object would remind the students to work hard. Both academic task completion and appropriate behavior increased in the general education classroom.

Several researchers have investigated the use of students' peers as stimuli common to the training and generalization settings. Stokes and Baer (1976) taught word recognition to students with learning disabilities through a peer-tutoring procedure. The students did not display the skills in other settings until the peer tutor and pupil were brought together. Then both students showed increased generalization.

Johnston and Johnston (1972) used a similar procedure to maintain and generalize correct articulation in two students. Each was trained to monitor and correct the other's speech, and monitoring was reinforced with tokens. The students consistently showed more correct speech when the monitor was present, even when monitoring no longer occurred.

A logical extension of programming common stimuli may change completely the approach to providing services for persons with severe and profound disabilities. The setting with the most stimuli common to the setting where generalization is desired is that setting itself. If we want behavior to occur in the classroom, why not teach it in the classroom rather than an isolated treatment room or corner (Horner & Budd, 1985)? If the behavior should occur in the community (Bourbeau et al., 1986) or in an employment site (Dehaven, Corley, Hofeling, & Garcia, 1982), why not teach it there? Miltonberger et al. (1999) taught sexual abuse prevention skills to women with mental retardation. The skills did not generalize until they were taught in the community. Community-based programming for persons with disabilities is now accepted practice.

The potential effectiveness of stimulus control for stimulus generalization and maintenance is a factor that should be considered by all teachers. Relatively simple and economical measures can help ensure reliable generalization in many settings and help maintain gains long after training has been terminated. The following vignettes illustrate generalization achieved by increasing stimulus similarity.

Ms. Statler's Students Get Ready for Supported Employment

Ms. Statler was a teacher of secondary students with moderate to severe retardation and other disabilities. Some of her students were receiving instruction that would enable them to gain independence in employment, and others were preparing for employment in a more supportive environment. For these students, supported employment in a local nursery greenhouse with a full-time job coach on site was the goal. Because of transportation and other logistical problems, it was possible to take the students to the nursery for instruction only once a week.

Although Ms. Statler could teach relevant skills in the classroom, she was concerned that the environment was not very similar to that of the nursery and was much less visually and aurally distracting. To solve these problems, she borrowed a number of props from the nursery, including a bench like the one at which the students would eventually work, and created a minienvironment in one corner of her classroom. She also made an audiotape of the nursery environment. While she played this tape, she arranged for as many people as possible to visit her classroom for a minute or two and to walk through the minienvironment examining plants and communicating with the students.

Sammy Learns to Behave in the Second Grade

Sammy was a student in Mr. Reddy's class for students who were developmentally delayed. His academic work was superior, but he displayed bizarre behavior, such as shouting gibberish and making strange movements with his hands and arms. This behavior was controlled in the special class by positive reinforcement on a DRO schedule, but Mr. Reddy had noticed that outside the special class Sammy continued to shout and gesture. Because the goal of the special program was to return students to the general education classroom as quickly as possible, Mr. Reddy was concerned about Sammy's behavior outside the special class.

Mr. Reddy decided to borrow a second grader from Sammy's class. After getting parental permission, he invited Brad, a gifted student, to visit his class for half an hour three times a week. He taught Brad basic learning principles to help with a project Brad was doing for his enrichment class. He also allowed Brad to give reinforcers to Sammy during his observation periods. When Sammy began spending short periods of time in the general education class, Brad came to get him and brought him back. Sammy consistently behaved appropriately in the second-grade class, even though no reinforcers were ever given there. Brad's presence had become an S^D for appropriate behavior for Sammy.

Mediate Generalization and Train to Generalize

We can teach students to generalize some skills.

We shall consider together these last two procedures for facilitating generalization: *mediating generalization* and *training to generalize*. It is possible to increase the probability of generalization by reinforcing generalization as a response class (Stokes & Baer, 1977). In other words, if students receive reinforcers specifically for displaying behavior in settings other than the training setting, performing learned behaviors in a novel setting may become a generalized response class. The students have thus been taught to generalize. If the student has sufficient receptive verbal ability, it is appropriate to explain the contingency to the student; that is, students may be told that if they perform a particular behavior in a new setting, reinforcement will be available (Mastropieri & Scruggs, 1984).

In mediating generalization, students are taught to monitor and report on their own generalization of appropriate behavior. Such a program involves self-control or self-management, possibly the most promising of all techniques for ensuring the generalization and maintenance of behavior change. If you check the dates on many of the studies discussed in this chapter, you will find that many date from the 1970s and 1980s. Although those procedures are still valuable, most researchers are currently focusing on self-management training to facilitate generalization. Ways of teaching these skills will be described in Chapter 11. For many students, the ultimate objective of the applied behavior analyst is to bring behavior under the control of self-monitoring, self-administered contingencies, and even self-selected goals and procedures.

Summary

We have investigated many techniques for promoting stimulus generalization, response generalization, and maintenance of behavior. In the first edition of this text, we stated that the technology of generalization was in its infancy. In the second edition, we suggested that it had reached the toddler stage. With increased emphasis on theoretical and practical analysis of generalization, there is reason to hope that the technology will continue to mature. Every year there is more emphasis on generalization in the literature. Its status, however, was well described by Buchard and Harig (1976):

To enhance your overall understanding of Chapter 10, go to the "Supplementary Lecture Notes" module of the Companion Website.

> Formulating questions about generalization is somewhat like a game that might go something like this: At the start, there are two things to worry about. Will the behavioral change be maintained in the natural environment or won't it? If it won't, then there are two more things to worry about. Does the lack of generalization reflect the type or level of the reinforcement schedule that produced the behavioral change in the first place, or did the behavior fail to generalize because of a lack of supporting contingencies in the community? If the problem pertains to the schedule, you have little to worry about. You go back to the treatment setting and strengthen the desirable behavior, preferably through a positive reinforcement schedule. However, if the problem is with the supporting contingencies in the natural environment, then you have to more things to worry about. Should you reprogram the natural environment to provide supporting contingencies through intermittent reinforcement, fading, or overlearning? And so on . . . (pp. 428–429)

Obviously the game is one in which these questions can be formulated ad infinitum. With generalization, the unfortunate part is that there will probably always be something to worry about; this is the nature of the beast! It is hard enough to try to determine whether or not behavior has changed, and if so why, let alone trying to determine whether or not the change also occurred in a completely different setting. Applied behavior analysts who are also teachers may never stop worrying about generalization. Given the techniques described in this chapter and the next, however, there appears to be less and less excuse for mere worrying. If applied behavior analysis procedures are to become an accepted part of the repertoire of every teacher, it is time, as Baer et al. (1968) suggested, "to stop lamenting and start programming."

Key Terms

generalization
stimulus generalization
stimulus class
maintenance
response generalization

Discussion Questions

1. Part-time resource services for students with mild handicaps who spend most of their time in the general education classroom have not been as successful as most educators hoped. What have you learned about generalization that may explain this? Give some suggestions that might increase the success of resource programs.
2. Providing services to children and adults with severe disabilities in community settings seems to increase their successful functioning in those settings. How can you explain this? What are some advantages and disadvantages to this approach?

Chapter 11

Teaching Students to Manage Their Own Behavior

Did you know that . . .

- Someone is the only person who will be with a student through his or her entire educational experience, in school and out?
- Someone is most tuned in to a student's day-to-day behavior and learning?
- Someone knows best what kind of reinforcement a student wants?
- So someone should learn to bear the primary responsibility for monitoring, reinforcing, and maintaining behavior?

Chapter Outline

The "someone" in the preceding four questions is "the student." The best person to manage a student's behavior is the student. We call this kind of behavioral intervention *self-management.* Your grandmother called it self-control or self-discipline. Anyone who is to function independently to any extent must learn to manage their own behavior. There is considerable interest among theorists about the development of self-control or self-discipline among people in general (Lloyd & Hughes, 1993) and in the processes and mechanisms that enable some people to be more responsible and productive than others. Such theoretical concerns are beyond the scope of this text; we will confine our discussion to relatively simple procedures that teachers can use to help students progress toward independence. There is also considerable speculation as to why some of the procedures, singly or in combination, are effective. Although many researchers offer theories, at this point we really do not know why they work (Hughes & Lloyd, 1993), just that they often do. As teachers, we will do what we always do—try something, make data-based decisions as to its effectiveness, and either continue to do it if it works or discard it and try something else if it does not.

Throughout this book, we have described procedures for teachers to use to change their students' behavior. In Chapter 10, we discussed many ways to increase the generalizability of behavior change and thus minimize the necessity for continued teacher support. This chapter further examines techniques that enable teachers to make students less dependent on teachers' environmental manipulation. The procedures discussed place the responsibility for change on the student. The focus in all the approaches is on teaching students to become effective modifiers of their own behavior. John Dewey (1939) suggested many years ago that "the ideal aim of education is the creation of self control" (p. 75). Students who have self-control can learn and behave appropriately even when adult supervision is not available.

Lovitt (1973) noted that "self-management behaviors are not systematically programmed [in the schools] which appears to be an educational paradox, for one of the expressed objectives of the educational system is to create individuals who are self-reliant and independent" (p. 139). If we, as teachers, agree that our goals include independence for our students, then we must teach students to be independent. Although total independence is not possible for all students, most can be taught to be more self-reliant. Kazdin (2001, pp. 302–303) offered several additional reasons for preferring self-management to that controlled by external change agents:

- The use of external change agents sacrifices consistency, because teachers or others may "miss" certain instances of behavior.
- Problems associated with communication between agents in different settings (such as teachers and parents) can also undermine the success of a program.
- The change agents themselves can become an environmental cue for the performance or lack of performance of a behavior.
- An individual's contribution to the development of a personal behavior-change program may increase performance.
- External agents are not always available in the environment where the target behavior is occurring or should occur.

Self-management usually comes in packages.

Both typical learners and those with disabilities can be taught to monitor and change their own behavior. We will describe several aspects of self-management, including goal setting, self-recording, self-evaluation, self-reinforcement, and self-instruction. Students can use any technique to change their own behavior that a teacher can use to change it for them. Students can be taught to set their own goals and objectives, to record data about their behavior, to evaluate their behavior, and to provide their own consequences through self-reinforcement and even self-punishment. Students can also learn to manipulate behavioral antecedents by using self-instruction.

Although each of these self-management techniques is described separately, in practice they have most often been employed in packages. In other words, combinations of the procedures were used—for example, self-recording with self-reinforcement or self-instruction with self-reinforcement. Although we will discuss goal setting, self-monitoring or evaluation, self-recording, and self-instruction separately, these procedures have been used almost universally in combination with one another and with other procedures such as direct instruction and modeling. It is often impossible to identify which components of such packages are actually influencing behavior. Some efforts have been recently made to examine the differential effects of the various procedures (Haisten, 1996). We will describe the use of several self-management packages in some detail.

A Common Experience

Self-management procedures are as much a part of the natural environment as are all the behavioral procedures described in this book. Many people use goal setting, self-recording, self-reinforcement, self-punishment, and self-instruction in managing their everyday behavior.

Many popular self-help and self-improvement programs are commercially available to adults who wish to change their lives for the better financially, emotionally, romantically, or in the area of productivity. Virtually all of these programs begin by encouraging their users to set goals, to put them in writing, and to use them to change behavior. As we write this section, a new year is approaching and millions of people are engaged in **goal setting** in the form of making New Year's resolutions. Some of the strategies we suggest might help them to stick to these resolutions more successfully.

Many self-employed or freelance workers use **self-recording** as a means of maintaining productivity. Author Irving Wallace (1977) described how he and other authors, including Anthony Trollope and Ernest Hemingway, have practiced self-recording techniques. Trollope, a Victorian novelist, described the reactivity of such self-recording rather graphically: "There has ever been the record before me, and a week passed with an insufficient number of pages has been a blister to my eye and a month so disgraced would have been a sorrow to my heart" (p. 518).

The use of **self-reinforcement** is also familiar to most people. Consider the following teacher's internal monologue as she heads home from a day at school:

What a day! Bus duty at 7:00 a.m. . . .

Jenny Lind fell, sprained her ankle, screamed like a banshee, and her mother says she's going to sue . . .

Clifford refused to believe that 6 times 4 was 24 today just because it was yesterday . . .

Two fights over whose turn it was to use the blue paint in art class. Tran ended up with the blue paint; Mark ended up blue . . .

The picture money didn't balance . . .

Why does that Velma Johnson always sit next to me at lunch and talk my ear off?

I kept my temper all day though—I deserve a stop at Baskin Robbins!

If the same teacher also practices **self-punishment,** she may remember the three scoops of rocky road at lunchtime tomorrow and restrict herself to two pieces of lettuce and a diet drink.

Many of us also practice **self-instruction,** providing ourselves with verbal prompts. We talk to ourselves, sometimes aloud, as we do complex or unfamiliar tasks. Many children also use such self-instruction naturally. For example, Kohlberg, Yaeger, and Hjertholm (1968) recorded the self-instruction processing of a 2-year-old child during solitary play with a set of Tinker Toys.

> The wheels go here, the wheels go here. Oh, we need to start it all over again. We have to close it up. See, it closes up. We're starting it all over again. Do you know why we wanted to do that? Because I needed it to go a different way. Isn't it pretty clever, don't you think? But we have to cover up the motor just like a real car. (p. 695)

B. F. Skinner, the founder of behaviorism, was a master of self-management techniques (Epstein, 1997). Using goal-setting, environmental management, self-recording, self-assessment, and reinforcement, he was able to be incredibly productive and to maintain this productivity until the day before his death at 84. He even produced a book about using self-management techniques to overcome the difficulties presented by old age (Skinner & Vaughan, 1983). The book is out of print but available used from Internet sources. We read it as an amusing curiosity when it was initially published; we are now seriously considering ordering two copies.

Teaching students to manage their behavior is a mechanism for systematizing and making more powerful these naturally occurring phenomena. Some students may be effective self-managers without training, others may be unready to manage their own behavior to even a small extent. Diminished ability for self-regulation has been found in students with mental retardation (Whitman, 1990), learning disabilities (Baker, 1982; Short & Weissberg-Benchell, 1989), and emotional disturbance (Kern-Dunlap et al., 1992). The wise teacher will remain alert for signs that students are ready to begin managing their own behaviors and will take advantage of this readiness. The strategies discussed in this chapter are sometimes called cognitive training strategies (Hallahan, Kneedler, & Lloyd, 1983) or metacognitive strategies (Borkowski, 1992). Along with other strategies less closely related to applied behavior analysis, they are ways to help students think and solve problems more productively.

PREPARING STUDENTS TO MANAGE THEIR OWN BEHAVIOR

The teacher who uses some systematic behavior-management program can try a number of techniques to increase students' potential for taking the responsibility for managing their own behavior.

- Teachers may ask students to set goals. "Sammy, you did 7 problems correctly in 10 minutes yesterday; how many do you think you can do today?"
- Teachers may ask students to evaluate their performance. "Sammy, check your problems with the answer sheet. How many did you do correctly?"
- When delivering reinforces, the teacher may explain to the student what behavior resulted in reinforcement. "Sammy, you did 10 math problems correctly. You get 10 points—1 for each problem."
- The teacher may ask the student to relate part of the contingency. "Sammy, you get 10 points. Why do you get 10 points?" or "Sammy, you did 10 problems right. How many points have you earned?"
- The teacher may ask the student to state the entire contingency. "Sammy, how many points? Why?"

- The teacher may involve students in choosing reinforcers and in determining their cost in terms of behavior.

Students who have been exposed to such techniques will frequently volunteer statements about their behavior and its consequences. It is a small step from asking a student how many points he has earned and why to allowing him to record the points himself with teacher supervision. Ultimately, Sammy may be allowed to check his own answers, count the number of problems he has done correctly, and record his points on his card.

Goal Setting

We addressed the issue of teachers' and students' negotiating goals and contingencies when we described the use of contracts in Chapter 7. People usually believe that teachers set goals for students as part of the educational process. This is certainly true in some cases, but students can be taught to set their own goals. There is clear evidence that students who set their own goals perform better than those whose goals are simply assigned by others (Johnson & Graham, 1990; Olympia, Sheridan, & Andrews, 1994). Barry & Messer (2003) used a combination of goal setting, self-chosen reinforcement, and self-reinforcement to increase on-task behavior and academic performance and decrease disruptive behavior in students with ADHD. Lee and Tindal (1994) taught low-achieving Korean students to set goals for themselves for completing math problems. Students were provided with graphs reflecting their performance in a previous session and asked to write the total number of additional problems they would complete and the additional number they would complete correctly during the current session. Goal setting produced improvement in productivity and accuracy as great as that produced by cued self-recording. The students preferred the goal-setting procedure because it was less intrusive than cued self-recording. Grossi and Heward (1998) taught adults with developmental disabilities enrolled in a community-based restaurant training program to set goals as part of a self-management package. Each trainee was encouraged to set goals regarding speed and duration for tasks such as pot scrubbing, dish racking, sweeping and mopping floors, and bussing and setting tables. Trainees were encouraged to set goals that were higher than their baseline means but not higher than the highest performance during baseline. As goals were met, trainees were encouraged to increase their goals to approximate a competitive standard established by observing the performance of nondisabled employees. Along with self-evaluation, this procedure enabled the trainees to improve performance significantly.

When teaching students to set goals, it is important to help them set goals that are specific, challenging but achievable, and whose attainment, in the early stages, is immediate rather than distant. It is also helpful to provide feedback about the success or failure to achieve goals (Johnson & Graham, 1990).

Self-Recording of Data

Chapter 3 describes techniques for data collection.

Students may be asked to keep a record of their behavior rather than having it recorded by an observer as described in Chapter 3. Having students record data is sometimes called self-monitoring, but the latter term is also sometimes used when students are asked to evaluate their performance rather than simply making a record of it. We prefer to use the terms self-recording (students are making a record) and self-evaluation (students are asked to compare their work to a standard) to distinguish

FIGURE 11–1
Student self-monitoring form.
Note: From "Self-monitoring for elementary school children with serious emotional disturbances: Classroom applications for increased academic responding," by L. Levendoski, & G. Cartledge, *Behavioral Disorders, 25,* p. 214, 2000. Copyright 2000 by Council for Children with Behavioral Disorders. Reprinted by permission.

Name: ____________________

Date: __________

* At this exact second am I doing my work?

	Yes		No	
Day	1st Bell	2nd Bell	1st Bell	2nd Bell

between the two procedures. We also distinguish between cued self-recording, when students are given a signal (usually a recorded tone) and asked to indicate whether they were performing the behavior when they heard the tone, and noncued self-recording, when students are asked to make a notation each time they perform the target behavior. Figure 11–1 provides an example of a data collection sheet that students might use.

Self-recorded data provide the student and teacher with concrete feedback regarding behavior. This information may be used to determine what reinforcers are available. In some cases, collecting data on a behavior may have a *reactive effect* on the behavior. The behavior may change in the desired direction as a function of the self-recording process alone. In this capacity, self-recording functions as a behavior-change technique (Rosenbaum & Drabman, 1979). In some cases, it is as effective as an external cue or reminder (Hayes & Nelson, 1983). If you have ever tried to budget money by writing down every penny you spend in a little notebook, you have probably experienced this reactivity. If, while reading a chapter on self-management, you start recording every instance of daydreaming with a tally mark on a 3 × 5 card, you will probably daydream less. (If 3 × 5 cards are unavailable, just make a pencil mark in the margin.) Freeman & Dexter-Mazza (2004), however, found that adult feedback increased the effectiveness of self-recording with an adolescent with disruptive behavior.

The reactive effect of self-recording may be only temporary.

As a self-management and behavior-change technique, self-recording has been successfully used in a variety of settings, with a wide variety of behaviors, and with learners with and without disabilities (Dalton, Martella, & Marchand-Martella, 1999; Digangi, Maag, & Rutherford, 1991; Hughes & Boyle, 1991; Hughes & Hendrickson, 1987; Hughes, Korinek, & Gorman, 1991; Hutchinson, Murdock, Williamson, & Cronin, 2000; Kasper-Ferguson & Moxley, 2002; Koegel, Harrower, & Koegel, 1999; Levendoski & Cartledge, 2000; Prater, Joy, Chilman, Temple, & Miller, 1991; Reinecke, Newman, & Meinberg, 1999; Shimabukuro, Prater, Jenkins, & Edelen-Smith, 1999; Webber, Scheuermann, McCall, & Coleman, 1993; Wolfe, Heron, & Goddard, 2000; Wood, Murdock, & Cronin, 2002; Wood, Murdock, Cronin, Dawson, & Kirby, 1998). It has been least successful in changing behavior in students with emotional and behavioral disorders (Hughes, Ruhl, & Misra, 1989), a finding possibly related to the questionable efficacy of self-management for people who do not want to change their behavior (Hughes & Lloyd, 1993). Although self-recording may change behavior when first used, changes may dissipate over time unless supported with additional self-management procedures, such as self-reinforcement (Kanfer, 1975; McLaughlin, 1976). Although self-recording has been used for initial behavior-change programs, it appears to be most effective in maintaining behavior changes resulting from traditional, teacher-managed strategies. A recent body of research has focused on the differential effects of teaching students to monitor their attention to task as opposed to their rate of task completion, accuracy, or productivity (Harris, Graham, Reid, McElroy, & Hamby, 1994; Maag, Reid, & DiGangi, 1993; McCarl, Svobodny, & Beare, 1991). The question posed is whether it is more effective for students to record that they are "paying attention" or "working hard" or to keep track of how much academic work they have completed or done correctly. It appears that both procedures are effective but that many students prefer to record tasks accomplished. Many teachers may also prefer this approach; we are sometimes reluctant to encourage students to give themselves credit for merely looking busy. Teaching students to use self-recording should include the following components:

- selecting a target behavior
- operationally defining the behavior
- selecting an appropriate system of data collection (Successful data collection systems include adaptations of event recording, time sampling, and permanent-product recording; notation methods include tally sheets, wrist counters, graphs, and charts. Figures 11–2 and 11–3 provide examples of charts that may be used.)
- instructing the student in the use of the data collection system selected
- monitoring at least one practice data-recording session
- allowing students to use self-recording independently and monitoring the results

The following vignette shows how one teacher used cued self-recording to help her students learn self-management.

Ms. Dietrich's Students Learn To Work Independently

Ms. Dietrich was a resource teacher for elementary students with learning problems. She arranged her schedule so that each group of students received direct instruction for the first 20 minutes of each scheduled resource hour. That group then worked independently while Ms. Dietrich taught another group. She was concerned that she could not give tokens to the groups working independently without disrupting the lesson she was teaching. She decided to teach the students self-recording. She acquired a child's noisemaker, a "cricket." At first, she observed the students working independently and clicked the cricket only if all of them appeared on task. They awarded themselves a point when they heard the click. After a while, she just clicked randomly during her direct teaching and told the independently working students to give themselves a point if they were working hard when they heard the sound. She found her procedure very effective. It was almost as good as being in two places at once.

Two reasons for the success of self-recording procedures.

Several suggestions have been made as to why self-recording changes behavior (Hayes & Nelson, 1983; Kanfer, 1975; Rachlin, 1974). All agree that self-recording forces students to monitor their behavior. Kanfer emphasized self-reward and self-punishment, which, he states, inevitably accompany self-monitoring. Thus, a student who indicates on a chart that he has completed his daily tasks or reviews his tally of hand raising may, by his act of self-recording, be saying to himself, "I am a good boy" (Cautela, 1971). Rachlin, Hayes and Nelson, and Baer (1984) emphasized that self-monitoring provides environmental cues that increase the students' awareness of potential consequences. As the preceding examples show, self-recording alone has some reinforcing qualities if there is a behavior change in the desired direction.

FIGURE 11–2 **Self-recording checklist for a language arts activity.**

Name: ______________________ Date: ______________

	Check yourself off
Have I capitalized the correct letters?	_____
Have I put a period at the end of sentences?	_____
Have I spaced between words?	_____
Have I put my name on the paper before handing it in to the teacher?	_____
Have I answered all the questions?	_____
Have I checked my answers in the paragraphs I read?	_____

FIGURE 11–3 **Self-recording checklist for home use.**

Have I?	Terry	Todd
1. Washed my face and hands?	_____	_____
2. Brushed my teeth?	_____	_____
3. Brushed my hair?	_____	_____
4. Picked up my dirty clothes?	_____	_____
5. Made my bed?	_____	_____
6. Put my lunch money in my pocket?	_____	_____
7. Gotten my homework and my books?	_____	_____

But won't they

An issue often raised when considering a self-recording procedure is the accuracy of students' records. Efforts to increase the accuracy of student data collection have not been very successful (Marshall, Lloyd, & Hallahan, 1993), but most studies find that students' self-recording is quite accurate when compared with records kept by teachers or others. It appears, in reality, that the accuracy of students' records has little effect on behavioral changes; even inaccurate record keeping may result in positive behavior change (Marshall et al., 1993; Reinecke et al., 1999; Rosenbaum & Drabman, 1979).

Self-Evaluation

To increase your understanding of self-management procedures, click on the Activities module on the Companion Website and complete the first activity.

Asking students to evaluate their performance may take many forms. Students may be asked to compare their responses on a worksheet to an answer key prepared by the teacher or provided in a teacher's edition of a textbook (most students find it reinforcing merely to have access to the teacher's edition). Occasional spot checking and, of course, eternal vigilance will reduce students' temptation to record their answers *after* referring to the answer key rather than before. Shimabukuro et al. (1999) taught students with ADD/ADHD to self-correct their work in reading comprehension, mathematics, and written expression. The students recorded accuracy and productivity (comparing the number of items completed to the number assigned). They recorded their scores and plotted them on graphs. Self-correction of spelling (Morton, Heward, & Alber, 1998) and multiplication facts (Bennett & Cavanaugh, 1998) enabled students to receive immediate feedback (after each word or math problem) rather than waiting for feedback from a teacher. Immediate feedback resulted in improved performance. More complex procedures may require students to rate less easily evaluated products against standards. Sweeney, Salva, Cooper, and Talbert-Johnson (1993), for example, taught secondary students to evaluate the legibility of their handwriting on the basis of shape, spacing, slant, size, and general appearance. The legibility of the students' handwriting improved significantly as a result of this self-evaluation and other elements of a treatment package.

Teaching students to evaluate their own behavior requires teaching them to discriminate between acceptable and inappropriate behavior. Dalton et al. (1999) used direct instruction to teach two adolescents with learning disabilities to identify on-task and off-task behaviors. The teacher randomly provided examples of each and asked the students to label them as on or off task. Training may also include a teacher or peer modeling examples of either appropriate behaviors or, in some cases, inappropriate behaviors and teaching students to discriminate between them. Videotapes of students modeling appropriate or inappropriate behavior may be useful in helping students form these discriminations. Embregts (2000) used videotaping to improve social behavior in students with mild retardation. Tapes were made during lunch, dinner, and group meetings. The students watched the tapes (as much as a week later) with an instructor. The tape was stopped every 30 seconds and the students were asked to record whether their behavior was appropriate or inappropriate. When their evaluation matched that of the instructor 80% of the time, a comparison was made only at the end of the session. The students earned tokens for accurate identification. Kern et al. (1995) found that self-evaluation was facilitated by the use of videotaping in a population (severe emotional disturbance) that has been resistant to self-management procedures.

Self-Reinforcement

In most classrooms, teachers arrange contingencies. They specify what behaviors are expected and the consequences for performing those behaviors. Contingencies are

stated in the form of "if . . . , then . . . " statements: "If you complete your composition, then you may have 5 minutes extra free time." "For each correct answer to the reading comprehension questions, you will earn one token." Students may be involved in contingency management in a number of ways. They may be allowed to choose reinforcers, to assist in determining the cost of the reinforcers in relation to behavior, or even to choose behaviors to be modified. The ultimate goal in allowing students to participate in contingency management is to encourage their use of the procedures they have been taught to manage their own behavior. As with self-recording, the transition from teacher-managed to student-managed programs must be gradual, and students must be explicitly taught to use self-reinforcement or self-punishment.

Start with teacher-controlled contingencies.

It has been repeatedly demonstrated that self-determined contingencies and teacher-determined contingencies can be equally effective in producing behavior change. In fact, self-determined standards and reinforcers may sometimes be more effective than those externally determined (Hayes et al., 1985). Lovitt and Curtiss (1969) compared the academic response rate of a 12-year-old student under a teacher-determined contingency for reinforcement with his rate under a self-determined contingency for reinforcement. The self-selected contingencies resulted in a 44% increase in academic response rate. The teacher-selected contingencies had been explained, written out, and attached to the student's desk. As he completed each academic assignment, the student was shown how many responses had been made and was asked to calculate the corresponding points he had earned. The teacher had set the following reinforcement value for each assignment:

Math:	10 problems	1 minute free time
Reading:		
(no errors)	1 page	2 minutes
(errors)	1 page	1 minute
Spelling:	18 words	1 minute
Writing:	20 letters	1 minute
Language arts:	10 answers	1 minute
Library book:	1 story	3 minutes
	3 questions	1 minute

Under the self-determined contingency for reinforcement, the student was asked to specify his own reinforcer in each area and to record his selections on a card that was then attached to his desk. The student selected the following reinforcers for each task:

Math:	10 problems	2 minutes free time
Reading:		
(no errors)	1 page	3 minutes
(errors)	1 page	2 minutes
Spelling:	5 words	1 minute
Writing:	10 letters	2 minutes
Language arts:	10 answers	2 minutes
Library book:	1 story	6 minutes
	3 questions	2 minutes

Rhode, Morgan, and Young (1983) used a self-reward system to generalize appropriate behavior from resource rooms to regular classrooms. Students were taught first to evaluate their own behavior in the resource room and then asked to do so in the regular classroom. O'Brien, Riner, and Budd (1983) successfully taught the parent of a disruptive child to implement a self-reward system and thus to teach her child to evaluate his own behavior.

When allowing students to select their own contingency for tasks to be completed, specific instructions should be given as to the procedure to be followed. The following set of instructions (Felixbrod & O'Leary, 1974, p. 846) has served as a model for many investigations of self-reinforcement:

1. When people work on a job, they get paid for what they do. I am going to pay you points that you can use to buy these prizes (pointing to prizes and point-exchange values). YOUR job is to answer these arithmetic questions. Answer the questions in order. In order to earn the points, only correct answers will count (repeated). You will have 20 minutes to do these. But you can stop before 20 minutes are up if you want to. . . .
2. I am going to let YOU decide how many points you want to get paid for each right answer. Take a look at the numbers on the next page (pointing to a separate page on which the subject is to choose a performance standard). I want YOU to decide how many points you want to get paid for each right answer. (Experimenter points to each possible choice in a list of 10 possible performance standards: "I want to get paid 1 point; 2 points . . . 10 points for each right answer.") After I leave the room, draw a circle around the number of points you want to get paid for each right answer.

Several studies conducted in classrooms (e.g., Felixbrod & O'Leary, 1974; Fredericksen & Fredericksen, 1975) have shown that students tend to select more lenient performance standards than those selected by teachers. Because stringent standards—whether self-determined or teacher determined—produce significantly better academic performance than do lenient standards, students should be taught to set fairly stringent standards for themselves. A prompt for selecting stringent standards can be used successfully if it is followed by social reinforcement. The following instructional prompt, or variations of it, has often been used to encourage students to select stringent standards:

To increase your skills using these procedures, go to the Activities module for Chapter 11 of the Companion Website.

> If you pick 10 points per problem and you do 2 problems, then you get 20 points. But, if you pick 2 points per problem and you get 10 problems correct, you still get 20 points and the same good prize. So, if you pick a lower number, you can get the same good prize just doing more problems. We would really like you to pick 1, 2, or 3 points per problem. Let's take a look at the prizes and I'll show you what I mean. (Starting with the lowest value prize, describe to the child how much each prize is worth, and then concentrate on the highest.) Now, this prize costs 250 points. If you pick 1 point per problem, then you have to do more than 12 pages of problems to win this prize. But, if you pick 2 points per problem, then you only have to do 6 pages of problems to get the same prize. Do you understand? I'll leave the room and you circle one of these numbers. Remember, we would like you to pick 1, 2, or 3 points. (Brownell, Coletti, Ersner-Hershfield, Hershfield, & Wilson, 1977, p. 445)

Contingency-management systems are most often implemented with the teacher controlling the selection and administration of reinforcers. A period of teacher-controlled contingency management should precede any effort to teach students self-reinforcement (King-Sears, 1999; O'Brien et al., 1983). After the students become accustomed to the mechanics of the system, the students themselves can manage contingencies effectively. Drabman, Spitalnik, and O'Leary (1973) and Turkewitz, O'Leary, and Ironsmith (1975) used the following successive steps to transfer gradually both recording and reinforcement responsibilities from the teacher to the students in a token economy.

- Teachers initially awarded and recorded points and determined reinforcement.
- Students recorded points awarded by the teacher.

- Students awarded themselves points and earned bonus points for matching teacher ratings.
- Matching was gradually faded, and students ultimately rated their own behavior and determined their own reinforcement independently (Drabman et al., 1973, p. 11).

Desired changes in behavior were maintained throughout the transfer process. In addition, behavior changes generalized to control periods in which token reinforcement was not in effect. Drabman and his colleagues suggested several factors that may have contributed to the maintenance of the desired changes in behavior. Continuous teacher praise for appropriate student behavior may have become more reinforcing over the course of the investigation. Peer reinforcement for appropriate behavior also increased. Accurate self-evaluation was praised by the teacher and may have acquired conditioned reinforcing properties, thereby strengthening appropriate behavior. Improved academic skills incompatible with inappropriate behavior were developed.

The following vignette illustrates a combined self-recording and self-reinforcing procedure.

DeWayne Passes Intro to Behavior Mod

DeWayne was panic stricken. At midterm, his average in his behavior mod course was 67. If he failed, his grade point average would drop below the point where he would be retained in college. After listening to a lecture on self-reinforcement, he decided to try it on himself.

"What do you mean you have other plans? I didn't know until just now if I'd have enough cards to go out tonight."

DeWayne acquired an inexpensive kitchen timer and a supply of 3 × 5 cards. He decided that he needed short-term and long-term reinforcers. He began setting the timer for an hour and making a check on a 3 × 5 card whenever he sat at his desk or in the library without getting up or talking to anyone for the entire hour. He then allowed himself a 10-minute break for talking to his roommate, making a cup of coffee, or taking care of bodily necessities. When he had four checks, he decided to allow himself to go out with his friends for pizza and a soft drink. He saved the cards, and when he had accumulated five cards with at least four checks, he called his girlfriend and asked her to go to a movie. Although he was somewhat skeptical about the effectiveness of his plan, he found it worked. When he studied for an average of 4 hours a day, his grades began to improve. He finished the semester with a 3.0 grade point average and a conviction that applied behavior analysis was more than a gimmick for getting students to stay in their seats.

Self-Punishment

Most self-management procedures have emphasized self-reinforcement. Some investigations, however, have analyzed the effectiveness of teaching students to punish rather than reinforce behaviors. Fans of Harry Potter (Rowling, 1998) may remember Dobby, the house elf, who regularly punished himself by banging his head on the wall, beating himself with a desk lamp, twisting his ears, and even slamming his ears in the oven door. In classrooms, not surprisingly, self-punishment is rather different. The form of self-punishment most often investigated has been the use of response-cost in conjunction with token reinforcement systems (Humphrey, Karoly, & Kirschenbaum, 1978; Kaufman & O'Leary, 1972).

Self-reinforcement is more effective than self-punishment.

Humphrey and his colleagues (1978) worked in a second-grade reading class that was "initially a chaotic one as evidenced by the teacher's having referred 13 of 22 children to a special program for children with behavioral problems" (p. 593). A self-reinforcement system and a self-punishment system were put in place to compare their relative effectiveness and also to assess potential side effects of self-punishment. The students using reinforcement placed tokens from banks into cups kept at their desks, contingent on accurate performance on reading assignments. The criteria for reinforcement were printed on the answer keys accompanying each reading paper. The teacher checked the work of six randomly selected students each day to minimize inaccuracy and cheating. The students using response-cost began each morning with their cups filled with the maximum number of tokens that could be earned that day. They fined themselves for inaccurate work by referring to the response-cost criteria printed on the answer keys. Students also fined themselves for failing to complete the daily allotment of reading assignments. Under both self-management systems, the students did more reading assignments and maintained the accuracy of their work. In addition, disruptive behaviors, which were not under the contingencies, decreased slightly. Although self-punishment (response-cost) was effective, self-reinforcement appeared to be more effective. Several explanations for the relative superiority of self-reinforcement to self-punishment are possible (Humphrey et al., 1978, p. 599). Self-response-cost may have been more difficult to use because it required children to subtract rather than add. A second possible explanation is that concern about losing reinforcers may have caused a fear of failure. Response-cost may maximize fear of failure. If response-cost accentuated children's awareness of failure, the children may have evaluated their behavior more negatively. Negative self-evaluation or selective attention to failures or inadequacies can result in abandonment of behavior strategies.

In the following vignette, observe the combination of self-recording, self-reinforcement, and self-punishment.

Professor Grundy Completes a Book

Professor Grundy was panic stricken. He had just received a telephone call from the editor in charge of production on his textbook manuscript (which, as you may remember, was considerably overdue). Because he had heard the words "breach of contract" and "by the end of the month" used in the same sentence, he concluded he had best accelerate his writing rate. He decided that he needed to write at least 10 pages every day and that he would need some motivation for doing so. He had bought a personal computer for word processing but had spent hours surfing the net and communicating with others in chat rooms and very little time processing words. He therefore provided himself with a nutrition bar cut neatly into 10 pieces, two styrofoam cups, and a number of marbles borrowed from his nephew Dennis. Before he sat down to work, he filled one styrofoam cup with marbles and put the other next to it. He placed the pieces of the bar on a saucer. Mrs. Grundy agreed to cooperate by keeping his coffee cup constantly full. (She was motivated by the hope that her living room decor might eventually consist of something besides stacks of books and reprinted articles, note cards, and crumpled multicolor sticky notes.)

Professor Grundy's preparations for writing had consumed almost an hour. He was tempted to take a break before beginning but restrained himself. He began putting words on the screen and at the end of each page ate 1 of the 10 pieces of his bar. Whenever he found his mind wandering, he transferred a marble from the full to the empty cup. He had decided he would have to write an extra page for each marble over 10 that accumulated in the previously empty cup.

Professor Grundy was very pleased with the effectiveness of his self-management system. "It's amazing," he thought to himself. "I've been using applied behavior analysis procedures on other people for years and even teaching students to do it. Why didn't I ever think to try it on myself?" He spent considerable time in self-congratulation and then, with a guilty start, transferred a marble and got back to work.

For more information on these procedures, click on the Weblinks module on the Companion Website and then the Nichcy website.

Self-Instruction

Self-instruction is a process of providing one's own verbal prompts. Prompting, as we discussed in Chapter 9, is necessary when discriminative stimuli are insufficient to set the occasion for the required response. Prompts are often supplied by others; self-instruction involves providing prompts for oneself. Many adults give themselves prompts when they engage in difficult or unfamiliar tasks. We talk ourselves through such activities as starting a new car or performing a complicated dance step. We use prompts such as "i before e except after c" when we encounter a hurdle in letter writing. Some of us still sing the "ABC" jingle when looking for a name in the phone book. Teaching students to use self-instruction tactics enables them also to provide verbal prompts for themselves, rather than to remain dependent on others.

Self-instruction enables students to identify and guide themselves through the process necessary to solve problems. Training in self-instruction occurs before students are given problems to solve, questions to answer, or tasks to perform. Students who are taught self-instruction procedures may be able to generalize these strategies to other settings: for example, from one-to-one tutoring to the classroom (Bornstein & Quevillon, 1976). They may also be able to generalize across tasks: for example, from arithmetic or printing tasks to a phonics task not specifically trained but requiring similar process management for completion (Burgio, Whitman, & Johnson, 1980).

Teaching students self-instruction tactics has been effective in

1. teaching children who are hyperactive and impulsive to increase their attending and on-task behaviors (Barkley, Copeland, & Sivage, 1980; Meichenbaum & Goodman, 1971; Peters & Davies, 1981).

2. increasing students' ability to demonstrate academic skills (Borkowski, 1992; Bryant & Budd, 1982; Burgio et al., 1980; Callicott & Park, 2003; Case, Harris, & Graham, 1992; Leon & Pepe, 1983).
3. increasing appropriate social behaviors (Burron & Bucher, 1978; O'Leary, 1968).
4. teaching a wide variety of skills to persons with moderate, severe, and profound disabilities (Browder & Shapiro, 1985; Lagomarcino, Hughes, & Rusch, 1989).

Most studies investigating self-instruction have used adaptations of a training sequence developed by Meichenbaum and Goodman (1971). A five-step training program for self-instruction successfully increased the self-control of second graders who had been labeled hyperactive and thus increased their ability to attend to a task and to decrease errors. Students were taught individually using the following sequence (Meichenbaum & Goodman, p. 117):

1. An adult model performed a task while talking to himself aloud (cognitive modeling).
2. The student performed the same task under the direction of the model's instructions (overt, external guidance).
3. The student performed the task while instructing himself aloud (overt self-guidance).
4. The student whispered the instructions to himself as he went through the task (faded, overt self-guidance).
5. The student performed the task while guiding his performance via private speech (covert self-instruction).

For more practice using these procedures, click on the Activities module on the Companion Website and complete the third activity.

The following example shows the cognitive model provided by the teacher and then rehearsed, overtly and covertly, by the student. The task requires copying line patterns:

> Okay, what is it I have to do? You want me to copy the picture with the different lines. I have to go slowly and carefully. Okay, draw the line down, down, good; then to the right, that's it; now down some more and to the left. Good. I'm doing fine so far. Remember, go slowly. Now back up again. No, I was supposed to go down. That's okay. Just erase the line carefully. Good. . . . Even if I make an error, I can go on slowly and carefully. I have to go down now. Finished. I did it! (Meichenbaum & Goodman, 1971, p. 117)

For students to learn to imitate an effective and complete strategy, the teacher must include in the initial modeling several performance-relevant skills that guide the task process. These skills (Meichenbaum, 1977, p. 123) include:

1. problem definition ("What is it I have to do?")
2. focusing attention and response guidance ("Carefully . . . draw the line down.")
3. self-reinforcement ("Good, I'm doing fine.")
4. self-evaluative coping skills and error-correction options ("That's okay. . . . Even if I make an error, I can go on slowly.")

The same basic strategy has been used to teach kindergarten children with handwriting deficiencies to print the letters of the alphabet (Robin, Armel, & O'Leary, 1975), and fifth- and sixth-grade students with learning disabilities to solve word problems in arithmetic (Case et al., 1992). Burgio et al. (1980) used a similar procedure to increase on-task behavior for students with mild retardation.

To help impulsive students to be more reflective and thus better able to finish a matching task, a teacher modeled the following strategy:

> Now let's see, what am I supposed to do? I have to find which of these (pointing to the six alternatives) goes into this space (pointing to the blank space in the rectangular figure). Good.

> Now I have to remember to go slowly and be sure to check each one of these carefully before I answer. Is this the one (pointing to the first alternative)? It's the same color but it looks different because the lines are thicker. Good, now I know it isn't this one. Now I have to check this next one (pointing to the second alternative). It looks different because there aren't any lines on it and this one (pointing to the standard) has lines on it. Good, now I know it isn't this one. Next I have to check this one (pointing to alternative three). It looks the same to me. The colors are the same and the lines are the same too. I think it might be this one but I have to check the other ones slowly and carefully before I choose . . . (continues to check remaining three alternatives one at a time). Good, I have checked them all and I have gone slowly and carefully. I think it is this one (points to the correct variant). (Peters & Davies, 1981, p. 379)

In a study to develop self-control for boys with chronic behavior problems during math and reading lessons, Barkley et al. (1980) added a group modeling process to self-instruction training. The teacher presented a problem and modeled its solution via self-instruction. She then divided the group of boys into smaller groups and presented a series of similar problems for each boy to solve using self-instruction techniques. The teacher and the other boys thus provided models of self-instruction.

Four similar self-instruction steps were used in teaching 9-year-old boys who were under psychiatric care for hyperactive behavior (Palkes, Stewart, & Kahana, 1968). With these students, visual cues were added to encourage and remind them to use the self-instruction statements. These cues consisted of four 5 × 7-inch cards printed with instructions and self-directed commands (see Figure 11–4) and kept on the student's desk in front of him during task performance.

Self-instruction can be a useful procedure for helping students become more independent and for maintaining and generalizing behavior change. Several factors appear to influence the effectiveness of self-instruction.

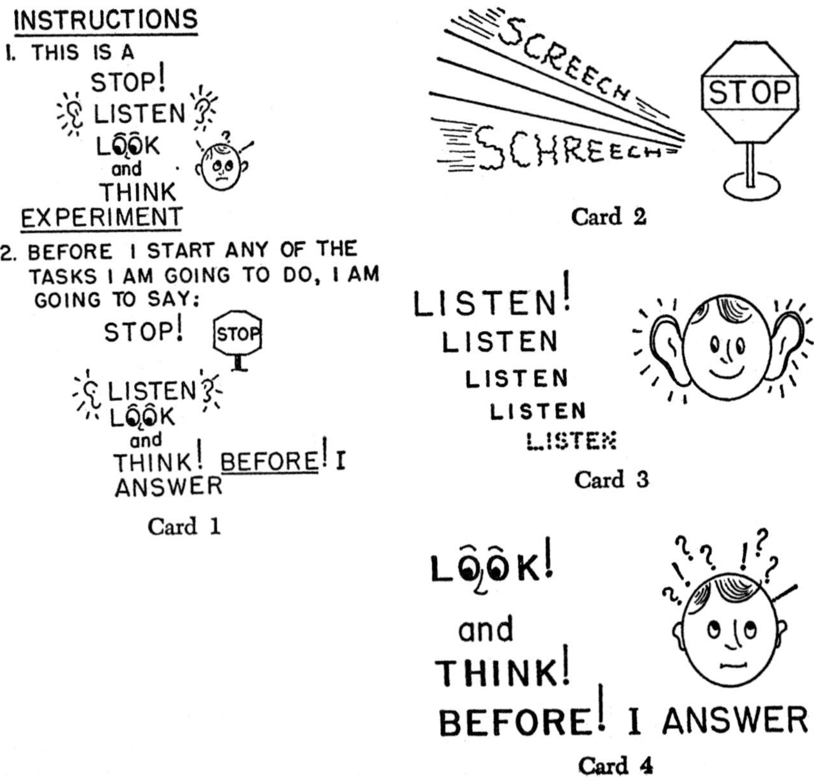

FIGURE 11–4 ***Self-instruction cuing cards.***
Note: From "Porteus maze performance of hyperactive boys after training self-directed verbal commands," by H. Palkes, M. Steward, & K. Kahana, 1968, *Child Development, 39,* p. 819. Copyright 1968 by Child Development. Reprinted by permission.

Factors influencing the effectiveness of self-instruction.

1. Actual implementation of the procedure during task performance. Roberts, Nelson, and Olson (1987), however, found no difference in performance between students who used self-instruction and those who had merely been taught a self-instructional strategy. They suggest that, at least in some cases, training in self-instruction to solve specific kinds of problems may be good academic instruction rather than a modification of cognitive processing.
2. The ability of the students to perform the response in question. Higa, Tharpe, and Calkins (1978) found that unless kindergartners and first graders had practiced making a motor response, self-instructions actually interfered with performance. No amount of self-instruction will enable students to perform tasks not in their repertoire.
3. Reinforcement for adhering to self-instructions.
4. Making the focus of instructions specific. For example, Mishel and Patterson (1976) found nursery school children were better able to resist talking to a puppet if they specifically instructed themselves not to talk to the clown than if they reminded themselves with general instructions to work on their assigned tasks.

Results of self-instruction training have been somewhat inconsistent. Billings and Wasik (1985) failed to replicate the results of Bornstein and Quevillon's (1976) study cited earlier. Bornstein (1985) suggested that differential effects of the procedure may result from age, gender, intelligence, race, history, or attributional or cognitive style. Whitman (1987) suggested that self-instruction may be most successful with young children and persons with mental retardation who "have developed some language proficiency but have difficulty processing information given them by socialization agents and subsequently using this information in the absence of these socialization agents to regulate their behavior independently" (p. 216). Bornstein pointed out, "Quite simply, it appears that self-instructional programs can be effective, although obviously they are not always effective" (p. 70). As we have said before, "Nothing always works."

Efforts to teach persons with moderate and severe disabilities to use self-instruction have included the use of picture prompts as described in Chapter 9 (Pierce & Schreibman, 1994; Steed & Lutzker, 1997). Students are provided with books of pictures portraying various tasks performed in sequential order. Students refer to the books, after being taught to use them, without needing a teacher, job coach, or employer to provide constant supervision, just as teachers refer to lesson plans, lecturers to lecture notes, and physicians to the *Physician's Desk Reference.*

Most self-instructional procedures are taught in combination with self-monitoring and self-reinforcement. Thus, students provide for themselves both antecedents to behavior and consequences for correct performance. The following sections describe several studies that examined the effects of implementing intervention packages including several types of self-management.

SELF-MANAGEMENT FOR LEARNERS WITH SEVERE DISABILITIES

Descriptions of self-management procedures might lead one to believe that only high-functioning individuals could use such techniques. On the contrary, many students with relatively severe disabilities, including mental retardation and autism, have been taught to use self-management procedures (Agran, Fodor-Davis, & Moore, 1992; Dixon et al., 1998; Hughes & Agran, 1993; Mancina, Tankersley, Kamps, Kravits, & Parrett, 2000; Newman, Buffington, & Hemmes, 1996; Newman et al., 1995; Reinecke et al., 1999).

Stahmer and Schreibman (1992) used a package of both traditional and self-management techniques, including prompting and differential reinforcement (delivered by the experimenter) and self-evaluation, self-recording, and self-reinforcement, to increase appropriate play in children with autism.

Three children with autism who displayed very little appropriate toy behavior were taught to discriminate appropriate toy play by observing the experimenter who displayed examples of appropriate play (putting a puzzle together, for example) and inappropriate play (spinning or throwing the pieces of the puzzle), asking the children if what the experimenter was doing was "right," and reinforcing correct responses. Each child was then provided with an alarm wristwatch and record sheets containing boxes to be filled in with pencil if they had played "right" during the (initially very short) interval before the alarm. Students received edible or tangible reinforcers if they both played and recorded appropriately but only praise for correct reporting if they indicated they had played inappropriately. The watches and recording sheets were eventually removed (because they might function as cues and inhibit generalization) and students were asked if they had played right during intervals when the experimenter left the room. All the students increased their rates of appropriate play, even in settings outside the training setting and when they were unsupervised (and observed through one-way mirrors).

To increase your understanding of the use of self-management procedures, click on the Activities module on the Companion Website and complete the fourth activity.

Self-management procedures show great promise in providing skills to students with significant disabilities to participate fully in inclusive settings (King-Sears, 1999; Koegel et al., 1999). Callahan and Rademacher (1999) used self-management to help Seth, an 8-year-old with autism who had good academic skills to participate 100% of the time in a second-grade general education classroom. The researchers defined on-task behaviors and used direct instruction to teach Seth to discriminate them. They made an on-task poster for Seth's desk, and he circled a happy or sad face when prompted by a beep from a nearby tape recorder. Seth's full-time paraprofessional recorded behavior as well, and Seth was reinforced for both on-task behavior and accurate recording. Seth's on-task behavior increased and his classroom behavior also improved.

SELF-MANAGEMENT FOR LEARNERS WITH MILD DISABILITIES

Cassel and Reid (1996) used both direct instruction and a package of self-management techniques, including self-instruction, self-evaluation, and self-reinforcement, to teach two students with mild retardation and two students with learning disabilities to use a structured, seven-step strategy to solve arithmetic word problems. The experimenter taught students the strategy using direct instruction and modeled the strategy using prompt cards with the seven steps listed. Students were also asked to generate statements they might use for self-instruction during each step and statements they might use as verbal self-reinforcers. Students were asked to check off each step of the strategy as they used it to solve the problems. All the students improved their performance in solving word problems.

Self-management strategies can also improve the performance of students with mild disabilities in general education settings (Dalton et al., 1999; Todd, Horner, & Sugai, 1999). Todd et al. taught Kyle, a fourth-grade student with learning disabilities, to use self-management in his classroom. Kyle used a Sony Walkman tape recorder with a cassette that prompted him to record a + if he was on task and behaving appropriately and a 0 if he was not. Role playing and simulation were used to teach Kyle to discriminate appropriate and on-task behavior. Kyle was also taught to raise his hand or approach his teacher, depending on the classroom activity, after giving himself three pluses, thus recruiting praise. The researchers reported decreases in problem behaviors, increases in on-task behavior, increases in overall teacher perception, increases in work completion, and increases in teacher praise.

SELF-MANAGEMENT FOR AT-RISK STUDENTS

To enhance your overall understanding of self-management, click on the Supplemental Lecture Notes module on the Companion Website and review the Powerpoint overheads.

Some studies have described the use of self-management strategies with students who are not identified as disabled, but who are at risk of school failure because of poor academic work and disruptive behavior (McDougal & Brady, 1998; Mitchem, Young, West, & Benyo, 2001; Ninness, Ellis, & Ninness, 1999; Wood et al., 1998). Mitchem et al. developed a class-wide peer-assisted self-management (CWPASM) program. A combination of self-recording, peer monitoring, and reinforcement produced improvement in academic performance and behavior.

SUMMARY

This chapter has described a number of techniques for transferring behavior management from teachers to students. Several advantages come with such transfer. Students become more independent. Their behavior may be maintained and generalized in settings where no intervention is in effect. The emphasis is changed from short-term intervention designed to change a single target behavior to the acquisition of strategies that may be used to change many behaviors over the long term. Discussion of self-management procedures may seem contradictory to the emphasis on overt, observable behavior throughout this book. Some of the processes described in this chapter, such as covert self-instruction, are not directly observable. However, the emphasis, as always, is on changes in behaviors that are observable. For example, although we cannot observe students' covert self-instruction, we can observe that they perform academic tasks more rapidly and more accurately than before they were taught to use the procedure.

KEY TERMS

goal setting
self-recording
self-reinforcement
self-punishment
self-instruction

DISCUSSION QUESTIONS

1. Design a self-management program for yourself. Include self-recording, self-monitoring, and self-reinforcement.
2. Implement the program and see if you can change your own behavior. Describe the change process.

Chapter 12

Responsible Use of Applied Behavior Analysis Procedures

Did you know that . . .

- Some people think behavior modification and brain surgery are the same thing?
- It's possible to be both a humanist and a behaviorist?
- It isn't always ethical to follow the rules?
- Effective procedures scare some people?
- Applied behavior analysis can make students more creative?

Chapter Outline

This chapter addresses many of the issues raised by those who practice applied behavior analysis and those who believe that its practice is, at best, inappropriate and, at worst, morally reprehensible. First, we will consider some of the concerns often expressed and some possible causes of these concerns. Then we will examine and respond to some of the specific criticisms of behavioral procedures, particularly as these methods are used in educational settings. We will suggest ethical guidelines for using procedures, Professor Grundy will answer some common questions asked by uninformed people, and we will submit reasons for thoroughly understanding procedures and principles.

Concerns About Applied Behavior Analysis

Some people believe that changing behavior invariably infringes on personal freedom.

Resistance to the use of operant procedures to change behavior has come from several sources. The term behavior modification, which is most commonly used to describe such techniques, has caused some confusion. Because the word modification is synonymous with change, the term behavior modification has often been misused to refer to any procedure that has the potential to change behavior. This contamination of the term is one reason that we prefer the term **applied behavior analysis.**

Other objections to operant procedures have come from those who feel that any systematic effort to change behavior is coercive and, thus, inhumane. Those who take this position often describe themselves as "humanists." Their objections are based on a rejection of a deterministic viewpoint and advocacy of free will and personal freedom. The intuitive appeal of these humanistic values makes humanists' rejection of behavioral procedures a formidable objection, although as we shall see, such objections frequently rely on a rather shaky logical foundation.

The very effectiveness of applied behavior analysis procedures is one source of much concern about this approach. It is ironic that many people are comfortable with ineffective techniques or with techniques whose effectiveness at least lacks verification. The same people often reject other procedures—such as those based on applied behavior analysis—because their use results in predictable, consistent behavior change.

The battle to bring about "the destruction of the behaviorist evil and the hegemony of the cognitive good" (Schnaitter, 1999, p. 209) reached its peak in the 1970s and 1980s and the fervor of the criticisms is well-characterized by Schnaitter's description. Applied behavior analysis was virtually ignored by researchers and teachers outside of special education during the 1980s (Axelrod, Moyer, & Berry, 1990), perhaps because its critics perceived that the battle had been won and "behaviorism" defeated. We were in graduate school when the debate was in full swing and one of our fellow students was confronted with the statement "behaviorism is dead!" "What?" she replied, "Have they repealed the laws of behavior?" Applied behavior analysis has recently again become a target for attack (Haberman, 1995; Kohn, 1993), even by some special educators (Pugach & Warger, 1996). Axelrod (1996) suggested several possible reasons for this:

- Behavioral approaches are too much work and provide too little reinforcement.
- Behaviorism contradicts the popular developmental views of education and psychology.

- Behavior analysis is a threat to the prevailing power structures in education and psychology.
- Positive reinforcement is a practice that often lacks social acceptability.
- Behavior analysis fails to glorify human beings as do other psychologies and philosophies (pp. 248–253).

To increase your understanding of Ethics, click on the Activities module on the Companion Website and complete the first activity.

Anyone who has ever taught reading using a Direct Instruction (Engelmann et al., 1988) approach, derived from behavioral principles, can attest that it is a lot more work than, for example, providing students with a literacy-rich environment and waiting for literacy to emerge. Implementing behavior support plans is a lot harder than sending students to the principal's office and subsequently suspending or expelling them. Axelrod's (1996) statement that behavioral approaches provide little reinforcement is based on the fact that most applied behavior analysts are in relatively low-paying occupations, such as teaching. Fortunately, there are other reinforcers for using applied behavior analysis that may be more important than money. Most teachers are reinforced when children learn to read and to behave appropriately.

We described the developmental theories that are currently popular and institutionalized in schools and university teacher education programs in Chapter 1. They are certainly maintained by existing power structures. Axelrod (1996) indicated that, even after many years at one university, he must still "endure snide comments of long-time colleagues when the topic of behavior analysis is raised" (p. 247). One of us works in a very large department where there are only two faculty members who identify themselves as behavior analysts. At a recent faculty meeting a suggestion was made to add the statement "grounded in a constructivist paradigm" to the department's mission statement. Neither of us was sure exactly what that meant (can one be grounded in a paradigm?) but we were pretty sure it did not apply to us. Fortunately, someone changed the subject before we had to ask.

In addition to addressing Axelrod's (1996) concerns, we will discuss some other reasons why applied behavior analysis continues to be controversial.

Confusion with Other Procedures

Much of the public outcry against what is popularly called *behavior modification* results from the use of this term to describe procedures that are totally unrelated to applied behavior analysis. Popular journalists (Holden, 1973; Mason, 1974; Wicker, 1974) and even behavior modification professionals (McConnell, 1970) have done incalculable harm to the image of applied behavior analysis during the years when its use with human beings was in its developmental phase by including unrelated treatment procedures under the heading of behavior modification. Hypnosis, psychosurgery, brain implants, drug therapy, and electroconvulsive shock treatment have all been lumped under this label. Such procedures undoubtedly change behavior, but they are not related to the systematic changing of behavior by application of behavioral principles. It would be equally logical and equally erroneous to list under the title of behavior modification the entire array of therapeutic interventions including "psychoanalysis, Gestalt therapy, primal screams, lectures, books, jobs and religion" (Goldiamond, 1975, p. 26). Although many criticisms of applied behavior analysis were reactions to its use many years ago, more recent publications have blamed behavioral procedures for everything from the failure of public education to teach large numbers of children to the destruction of the American work ethic (Haberman, 1995; Kohn, 1993).

Applied behavior analysis certainly does not include such treatments as electroconvulsive therapy or brain surgery; neither does it involve the use of drugs. The effective

Applied behavior analysis is not hypnosis, prefrontal lobotomy, brain implants, drug therapy, or shock treatment.

application of appropriate behavioral procedures often reduces the need for such drastic interventions. This has been strongly demonstrated in studies using positive reinforcement as an alternative to medication for children labeled *hyperactive* (Ayllon, Layman, & Kandel, 1975) or as having *attention deficit disorder* (Rapport, Murphy, & Bailey, 1982). It is possible that behavior modification, in the proper sense of the term, will ultimately diminish the use of surgery, drugs, and other such behavior-change techniques. It is, therefore, particularly unfortunate that the improper use of the term has caused so much public hostility to a technology that is so potentially benign.

Used correctly, the term behavior modification refers only to procedures derived from the experimental analysis of human behavior. Unfortunately, the term has become so unalterably linked with other procedures in the minds of the public that its use is best avoided. Teachers who tell parents that they use behavior modification must be prepared for negative reactions. By no means do we advocate abandoning the technology of behavior modification: We simply suggest that teachers avoid using the term with uninformed or misinformed people. In many cases, other professionals, including administrative staff and fellow teachers, may be as confused as parents and school board members. Some textbooks and other materials widely used in preservice teacher education programs may well contribute to this confusion. It may be as necessary to educate fellow professionals as it is to teach children. The use of terminology has consistently caused problems for behaviorally oriented practitioners. It may be that it is not what behaviorists do that disturbs people but the way they refer to it. Teachers should be careful how they talk about procedures, even among themselves. Problems may arise because of the way programs are described, even when the programs themselves are appropriate.

Risley (1975) described a time-out procedure that was disallowed primarily because staff members referred to the free-standing structures built for short-term exclusion as "boxes" and to the procedure as "putting him (the resident) in the box." That the "boxes" were large, adequately lighted structures made no difference. The use of the wrong words resulted in withdrawal of approval for the program. Those of us who tend toward flippant labels would be especially wise to guard our tongues when discussing procedures with people who might misunderstand.

For a greater understanding of the controversy surrounding the use of Applied Behavior Analysis, go to the "Activities" module for Chapter 12 of the Companion Website.

Carr (1996) suggested that we modify our language even more drastically when addressing the general public, including parents and educators who are not behavior analysts. He advocated using the language of ethics, focusing on values such as compassion, dignity, and honesty rather than the language of technology. In other words, rather than saying that we use positive reinforcement to increase the future probability of behavior, we should say that we use it because "it is a humane procedure (compassion) that can help individuals lead better, more fulfilling lives (dignity), and we offer it sincerely (honesty) as feedback. . . " (p. 266). This is certainly not an attempt at deception; we believe that most behavior analysts are honest, compassionate, and supportive of the dignity of every individual.

Reaction to Controversial Procedures

Not all misunderstanding or hostility has resulted from those outside the field. Both professionals and the public frequently reject procedures derived from the experimental analysis of behavior. Some parents and educators even reject the use of positive reinforcement, stating that students should be intrinsically motivated and that systematic positive reinforcement reduces intrinsic motivation (Balsam & Bondy, 1983; Kohn, 1993). There is actually very little evidence for this claim (Cameron, Banko, & Pierce, 2001). Cameron and Pierce (1994) examined 96 published studies and found that intrinsic motivation is more often increased than decreased when positive reinforcement is used.

It is easier to understand people's rejection of procedures that cause pain or discomfort and the use of exclusion. Although these are only a few of the tools of the applied behavior analyst, their use has received a disproportionate share of attention from the press, the public, and the judiciary (Stolz, 1977). It is sufficient to note that aversive or exclusionary procedures may create problems in two ways:

Guidelines for the use of aversive and exclusionary procedures are provided in Chapter 4.

1. Their misuse is common and often described by users as behavior modification.
2. Their use, even when appropriate, causes more concern than other behavioral procedures.

Unfortunately, there have been many abuses. Risley (1975) described a "behavior modification" program in a Florida institution where bizarre punishments were used. The mildest of these was washing residents' mouths out with detergent when they spoke, in the staff members' opinions, inappropriately. One of us was recently asked to work with a student who, while a resident in a "behavior modification unit" in a for-profit facility, had been in what was called *time-out* for several weeks. Time-out, used properly, is measured in minutes. Isolation for days or weeks is more properly called *solitary confinement* and is certainly not an applied behavior analysis procedure. It is fully understandable that procedures causing pain or discomfort to any individual, but particularly one who is disabled, are reasons for concern. However, many, but not all, professionals believe certain controversial procedures are sometimes justified, just as many, but not all, parents believe spanking children is sometimes appropriate. The controversy about aversive procedures was discussed in Chapter 8.

Concerns About Coercion

The notion that applied behavior analysis is inhumane rests on the assumption that each human being should be free to choose a personal course of behavior. It follows, for those who criticize behavioral procedures, that any systematic attempt to alter the behavior of another human being is coercive and thus inhumane.

A belief that behavior is lawful does not imply that human beings are not free to choose what they will do.

This criticism of behavioral techniques is based on the philosophic concept of free will. Advocates of the assumption of free will tend to attribute human behavior to forces arising from within the individual and, thus, not subject to prediction or control. This is an example of the glorification of human beings described by Axelrod (1996). In other words, people are different from animals in that they just do what they do because they decide to do it. A deterministic position, on the other hand, holds that even human behavior is **lawful behavior** (subject to prediction) and its causes can be identified in environmental events. A determinist recognizes systematic relationships among such events (Mahoney, Kazdin, & Lesswing, 1974) and considers human behavior as part of the system. This contrasting view concludes that human behavior is subject to lawful prediction. People do things, or decide to do things, because of past events and present circumstances. It is important to distinguish between the use of the term lawful, in the sense of an orderly relationship between events, and any implication of authoritarian control. Many criticisms of applied behavior analysis are predicated on a misunderstanding of that simple concept (Dollard, Christensen, Colucci, & Epanchin, 1996; Nichols, 1992). *Lawful,* in the sense used here, refers to relationships among events that occur naturally, not to attempts to legislate human behavior.

Applied behavior analysts, by definition, are also determinists. Their position is predicated on solid evidence that "the assumption of **determinism** is both justified and essential in dealing with human behavior" (Craighead, Kazdin, & Mahoney, 1976, p. 172). This confirmation has come from a large body of psychological research, some but by no means all of it conducted by those who call themselves applied behavior analysts.

The assumption of lawful relationships among events and behavior does not imply a rejection of human freedom. For the applied behavior analyst, "freedom is defined in terms of the number of options available to people and the right to exercise them" (Bandura, 1975, p. 865). It is unfortunate that because of "misunderstandings of Skinner's thought, it is believed that, somehow, behavior analysis has the power to remove the ability of the individual to choose alternative responses" (Newman, Reinecke, & Kurtz, 1996, p. 277). The goal of the behavior analyst is to increase, not decrease, such options or alternative responses and thus to increase the freedom of the individual. The high school student who repeatedly fails English is not free to attend college. The child who is afraid to interact with peers is not free to make friends. People who have severe behavioral deficits may have no options at all; they cannot move around, take care of their basic needs, or control their environment in any way.

Behaviorists define freedom in terms of a person's ability to make choices and to exercise options.

The last example points out a crucial concept in understanding the deterministic position. The relationship between behavior and the environment is reciprocal (Bandura, 1969; Craighead et al., 1976). Environmental events control behavior, but behavior inevitably alters the environment as well. This reciprocal relationship exists between people. The behavior modifier's behavior is changed by the actions of the subject of the modification. Thus, everyone influences and controls others' behavior. It is impossible to abandon control; we inevitably influence the behavior of other people (Bandura, 1975; Rogers & Skinner, 1956). For example, a child who seldom smiles is not very pleasant to be around, so teachers and other children may avoid him. If his teacher systematically reinforces his occasional happy facial expressions, the child will smile more. Because a smiling child is pleasant to be around and to interact with, he will himself become more reinforcing to others, including his teacher. She will then have more opportunities to reinforce smiling.

Seen in this context, behavioral technology is neither dehumanizing nor inhumane. When goals are **humane,** we must offer the most effective means available to reach them. In many cases, the proven effectiveness of applied behavior analysis procedures makes them the most humane choice.

The following anecdote illustrates a clash between humanists and behaviorists. We urge you to consider the values being practiced on each side of this particular example. The episode is almost 40 years old; applied behavior analysis was in its infancy. There are now much more sophisticated procedures, such as functional analysis, that are implemented before aversive control is even considered. We think, however, the story is so vivid that it should be included here.

> A colleague at a different university showed us a deeply moving film. The heroine was an institutionalized primary-grade girl. She was a head banger, so a padded football helmet was put on her head. Because she could take it off, her hands were tied down in her crib. She kept tossing her neck and tore out her hair at every opportunity. She accordingly had a perpetually bruised face on a hairless head, with a neck almost as thick as that of a horse. She was nonverbal.
>
> My colleague and his staff carefully planned a program for her, using all kinds of reinforcers. She was remanded to their program but persisted in her typical behavior. In desperation, the ultimate weapon was unwrapped. When she tossed her head, my colleague yelled "Don't!" simultaneously delivering a sharp slap to her cheek. She subsided for a brief period, tossed again, and the punishment was delivered. My colleague reports that less than a dozen slaps were ever delivered and the word "Don't!" yelled even from across the room was effective. Its use was shortly down to once a week and was discontinued in a few weeks. In the meantime, the football helmet was removed and the girl began to eat at the table. She slept in a regular bed. Her hair grew out, and she turned out to be a very pretty little blond girl with delicate features and a delicate neck. In less than a year, she started to move toward joining a group of older girls whose behavior, it was hoped, she would model. She smiled often.
>
> The initial institution and her parents discovered that she had been slapped. They immediately withdrew her from the custody of my colleague's staff. The last part of the film shows

her back at the institution. She is strapped down in her crib. Her hands are tied to a side. She is wearing a football helmet. Her hair is torn out, her face is a mass of bruises, and her neck is almost as thick as that of a horse. (Goldiamond, 1975, pp. 62–63)

ETHICAL USE OF APPLIED BEHAVIOR ANALYSIS PROCEDURES

All teachers—whether or not they are also applied behavior analysts—are concerned with ethics. Before describing ways in which teachers can behave ethically, we will discuss the concept of ethics itself. A decision or action is ethical if it is right. That, of course, is a deceptively simple statement. The determination of what is right, according to whom it is right, and how we decide it is right has occupied philosophers and others since the days of Aristotle. Very simply stated, a teacher who is doing the right thing is behaving ethically. Doing the right thing, however, means far more than avoiding censure or even complying with some set of ethical guidelines. We are not "more concerned that . . . teachers follow the rules than that . . . teachers become ethical beings" (Watras, 1986, p. 14). Simply because something is accepted practice does not ensure that it is right (Kitchener, 1980). People following rules have done some very wrong things over the centuries, and no set of rules can ever cover every eventuality. Teachers must be prepared to act ethically in the absence of guidelines and even when their actions are in conflict with guidelines or instructions.

Awareness of potential criticism may help avert interference from uninformed persons.

The ways prospective teachers become ethical beings is the subject of intense interest among teacher educators. A volume of the *Journal of Teacher Education* (1986) was almost entirely devoted to the issue. The consensus appears to be that discussing ethical dilemmas in a forum of other interested prospective and practicing professionals best develops ethical reasoning. Ethics should not be addressed in a single course but should permeate all courses. If ethical issues do not arise and are not discussed in your classes, we suggest you bring them up.

Although the primary reason to behave ethically is to act consistently with what one believes is right, there is another reason. Teachers must always be aware that other people are concerned with teachers' doing the right thing. Previous sections have acknowledged that people are especially apt to worry about ethics when behavioral techniques are used. Unless teachers take particular care to act ethically and to assure others that they do, they may find noneducators seeking and acquiring more and more control over what may and may not be done in classrooms.

For more information related to Code of Ethics, click on the Weblinks module on the Companion Website and then the websites listed under this topic.

A number of factors must be considered when attempting to determine whether a proposed intervention is ethical. These include "community standards, laws, prevailing philosophies, individual freedom and responsibility of the clients through informed consent as well as the clients' attitudes and feelings" (Sulzer-Azaroff, Thaw, & Thomas, 1975). In the case of schoolchildren or residents of an institution, it is important to seek the opinions of the parents or guardians of the students to ask them how they feel about procedures being used or proposed for use with their children. It may seem strange for behaviorists to concern themselves with such subjective criteria as attitudes and feelings, but Wolf (1978) made a strong case for considering these factors. If participants do not like a program, he said, "They may avoid it, or run away, or complain loudly" (p. 206). Wolf suggested that social validity should be established for goals, procedures, and outcomes. **Social validity,** or consumer satisfaction (Holman, 1977), is simply the acceptability of a program or procedure to its consumers. Assessing social validity requires applied behavior analysts to rely on sources of data that have not traditionally been used in this field, including questionnaires, interviews, and surveys. It is possible that reliance on such data makes many conclusions about social validity invalid. However, "it is entirely possible that even quite invalid queries into social validity are better than no queries at all: Giving consumers any opportunity to express complaints and discontents that otherwise would go unnoticed may save at least some programs from fatal backlashes, at least if the offended consumer is moved enough by simply the existence of an otherwise inadequate social-validity assessment form to write in its margins or talk to the appliers" (Baer, Wolf, & Risley, 1987, p. 323).

Stainback and Stainback (1984) suggested that increased attention be given to qualitative research methods that provide "more attention to the social and educational relevance of research efforts" (p. 406). Simpson and Eaves (1985) urged that attempts be made to quantify such subjective measurements. It is clear that teachers using behavioral procedures must concern themselves with factors in addition to those within their classrooms. Goals, procedures, and outcomes must be acceptable to the consumers of education—students, parents, and the community. It is critically important for teachers and researchers to be attentive to the wide cultural diversity present in most communities and to select goals, procedures, and outcomes congruent with that diversity.

Misunderstanding of behavioral procedures and concern about their misuse have resulted in increasing pressure for mandatory guidelines for the use of applied behavior analysis procedures. Such mandatory guidelines and restrictions are becoming increasingly common, especially in institutional settings (Martin, 1975). Particularly likely to be restricted are aversive or exclusionary procedures and items or events that may be used as positive reinforcers. It is not generally permissible, for example, to require residents of institutions to earn the right to food, privacy, or basic activities (Wyatt v. Stickney, 1972).

We hope we have convinced you that it is in your best interests to behave ethically. Although we acknowledged earlier that guidelines are necessarily incomplete, we believe it would be unethical not to provide some. It would be difficult to imagine an ethical position that did not focus on protecting students' rights. A statement approved by the Executive Council of the Association for Behavior Analysis (ABA) includes a list of individual rights that provides teachers with the basis for making ethical decisions about many issues. We will elaborate on each part of the statement in an effort to give concrete examples of instances in which each individual right should be protected.

The statement begins: "We propose that individuals who are recipients or potential recipients of treatment designed to change their behavior have the right to (1) a therapeutic environment, (2) services whose overriding goal is personal welfare, (3) treatment by a competent behavior analyst, (4) programs that teach functional skills, (5) behavioral assessment and ongoing evaluation, and (6) the most effective treatment procedures available" (Van Houten et al., 1988, p. 111).

A Therapeutic Environment

A therapeutic environment is "safe, humane, and responsive to individual needs" (Van Houten et al., 1988, p. 111). It is also enjoyable. The environment for students with disabilities must also be the least restrictive environment for those individuals. The least restrictive environment is not necessarily the regular classroom or even a regular school for all students. It is that environment that "imposes the fewest restrictions necessary, while insuring individual safety and development. Freedom of individual movement and access to preferred activities, rather than type or location of placement, are the defining characteristics of a least restrictive environment" (p. 112).

Recently some educators have suggested that the only appropriate environment for any child, however severe the disability, is in a regular classroom, with peers of the same chronological age. Discussions of this practice, known as *full inclusion* (Stainback & Stainback, 1992), should certainly include the issue of whether it is possible to provide a safe, humane environment that is responsive to individual needs for every child with a disability in a regular classroom. Those who advocate full inclusion of students with disabilities argue that the effects, positive or negative, it will have on typical students or those with disabilities are not an issue. Separate classes for students with disabilities constitute segregation. Inclusion is a civil right and it is *unethical* to exclude any student (Laski, 1991).

Providing a safe environment is unarguably necessary. Doing so requires such simple and obvious, but too often neglected, steps as removing any potentially dangerous items or storing them so students do not have access to them. When a student stabs another student with the teacher's 4-inch pointed scissors, our first question is why, in a classroom where some students are known to have violent outbursts, the scissors were not locked away.

Students' safety outside the classroom must also be assured. Students with disabilities are especially vulnerable, for example, to verbal, physical, and sexual abuse from their peers. Students' safety must be monitored in halls, restrooms, cafeterias, playgrounds, and buses. Peers are not the only ones who may abuse or neglect students, and regular schools and classrooms are not the only places where abuse or neglect can occur. Recently, in the city in which one of us lives, a student living in a residential treatment facility was left on a school bus overnight. His parents thought he was at the facility and the staff at the facility assumed his parents had taken him home for a visit, as they sometimes did. Someone should have checked.

Providing a humane environment means more than refraining from neglecting or abusing students. Every human being has a right to be treated with dignity. "Minimally dignified treatment requires sanitation, cleanliness, comfort, and attempts at respectful communication and consent" (Schroeder, Oldenquist, & Rohahn, 1990, p. 105). This means, among many other things, not talking about students' problems in front of them, even if they are too young or too low functioning to understand. It means not having a student "do his thing" for visitors, even if his "thing" is funny. It also means not treating older students with disabilities like babies by, for example, changing their clothing in front of others. An attempt was made recently to introduce one of us to a 20-year-old man who was seated on a portable toilet shielded from the rest of the classroom by a screen. That was a violation of dignity both inhumane and unethical.

An environment sensitive to individual needs provides each individual with a comfortable place or places to sit, interesting things to look at and do, and opportunities to engage in age-appropriate and functional activities. It allows students some choices about what they will do, when they will do it, and how they will do it. Of course, children will inevitably have to do things they do not want to do. These tasks should lead to positive reinforcement and a feeling of accomplishment. After all, adults often do things they dislike, but are glad they did them. For example, we, like Dorothy Parker, loathe writing but love having written.

Services Whose Overriding Goal Is Personal Welfare

It may seem obvious that the behaviors targeted for change should be those whose change will benefit the student. Nevertheless, accusations have been made that residential institutions (Wyatt v. Stickney, 1972) and schools (Winett & Winkler, 1972) use behavior-change programs primarily to reduce behaviors that disrupt the smooth functioning of the institution or school but are not detrimental to residents or students. Winett and Winkler examined articles detailing behavior-change programs in the *Journal of Applied Behavior Analysis* from 1968 through 1970. They stated that the majority of the articles concerned the attempted suppression of talking, moving around, and such disruptive behaviors as whistling, laughing, and singing. Winett and Winkler concluded that the technology of applied behavior analysis was being used merely to establish "law and order" (p. 499) rather than to serve the best interests of students. They further mentioned that similar goals were set in residential institutions.

Although O'Leary (1972) agreed with Winett and Winkler (1972) that careful examination of goals is important, he disagreed with their conclusions. He cited numerous studies that demonstrated the researchers' concern with such behaviors as academic response rates, talking, prosocial interactions, and language and reading skills. O'Leary did agree with Winett and Winkler's call for "extensive community dialogues concerning those behaviors and values we wish to develop in our children" (p. 511).

Applied behavior analysis procedures may be abused if students' rights and best interests are not considered.

Applied behavior analysis procedures may be used to decrease or increase any behavior. Even such behaviors as creativity (defined in terms of observable behavior, of course) have been increased using this technology (Malott, Whaley, & Malott, 1997). There is no justification for asserting that the procedures, in and of themselves, contribute to maintenance of behaviors for the convenience of those other than students. Appropriate goal selection should prevent the use of such institution-oriented criteria for change as "be still, be quiet, be docile" (Winett & Winkler, 1972, p. 499).

For selected goals to be in the best interests of the students, they or their parents must voluntarily agree to the goals. Federal legislation requires that parents consent to programs planned for their children with disabilities. If parents are not available, an advocate must be named to determine that any proposed program is in the best interest of the child. Such a requirement is intended to ensure that participation in programs is voluntary. It is not necessary to acquire parental consent for all aspects of a teaching program, however. Martin (1975) suggested that widely accepted strategies for overall classroom management and student motivation do not require anyone's consent, even if the teacher decides to change from one strategy to another. Consent is required for procedures not yet widely accepted and for those applied only to individual students.

The consent that ensures voluntary participation in behavior-change programs must be both informed and voluntary (Rothstein, 1990). **Informed consent** is based on full understanding of the planned program. Informed consent does not occur unless parents or other advocates demonstrate that they comprehend all aspects of the program, including possible risks. If necessary, information must be provided in the native language of those involved.

Voluntary consent may be obtained only if neither threats nor rewards are used to acquire such consent (Martin, 1975). It is not acceptable, for example, to tell parents that unless a particular procedure is used, their child will need residential treatment. Nor is it ethical to assure parents that if a procedure is used, their child will no longer require placement in a special class. Sulzer-Azaroff and Mayer (1977) suggested that the voluntariness of students' participation in behavior-change programs should also be considered. Voluntary participation is facilitated by avoiding threats and incentives that are too powerful and by involving the subjects of the programs in selecting as many aspects of the program as possible. Such involvement leads naturally to eventual self-management—the ultimate goal for most students.

Treatment by a Competent Behavior Analyst

Because many applied behavior analysis procedures seem so simple, persons who do not adequately understand them often misuse them. A common example is the teacher who attends a short workshop on applied behavior analysis techniques, buys a bag of candy, and proceeds to hand out "reinforcement" indiscriminately. A common result is that the teacher in question concludes, as have many others, that behavior modification does not work. An unfortunate side effect is that the children treated in this manner may become more disruptive than ever because they do not understand why they got candy or why they stopped getting it. Moreover, parents become upset because their children's teeth are decaying and their appetites are spoiled; the principal expresses annoyance because she receives numerous irate phone calls from those parents; other teachers become enraged because their students demand candy, too; and the escutcheon of applied behavior analysis suffers another blot.

Implementing these procedures is not always as easy as it sounds.

It is not possible to learn in a few days enough about applied behavior analysis to implement ethical, effective programs (Franks & Wilson, 1976). One of the authors attended a meeting several years ago during which she was asked to develop a packet for other faculty members that would enable them, after a few hours' reading, to include behavior management techniques in their methods courses. When she retorted that she had taken eight courses in applied behavior analysis, had a background in animal research, had been practicing the procedures for 17 years, and was still learning, the reaction was typically: "But behavior mod is so simple!"

Good supervision includes training, observation, and evaluation.

The principles of applied behavior analysis are indeed easy to understand. Their effective implementation, however, is not so simple. In addition to a thorough understanding of the principles, acquired from qualified instructors, supervised practice is desirable. This is particularly important for difficult procedures, such as shaping, or procedures subject to abuse, such as aversive or exclusionary techniques.

Initial training must always be followed by adequate supervision. Martin (1975) suggested that such supervision include formal and informal in-service training and regular evaluation. Ongoing supervision will continuously upgrade the performance of competent staff. It is equally important to ensure that incompetent staff members do not implement procedures that may be detrimental to students or fail to follow through with procedures that are in the students' best interests.

Programs That Teach Functional Skills

Students need to learn skills that will enable them to function effectively in their environment. Teaching those skills should be the primary focus of every student's educational program. What skills are functional will be different for each student. It is functional for some students to learn algebra so they can learn geometry and trigonometry. It is functional for others to learn household skills so they can be contributing members of their families. In every case the choice of skills must be based on the assumption that "unless evidence clearly exists to the contrary, an individual is . . . capable of full participation in community life and [has] a right to such participation" (Van Houten et al., 1988, p. 113).

This assumption is a cornerstone for educators. It means, in our opinion, that it is unethical to believe that any young child, even if poor, at risk, or even disabled, is not capable of learning academic and preacademic skills. As a resource teacher and friend said, "I teach as if every one of my 6-year-olds will be going to Harvard." We believe equally strongly that it is unethical to waste the time of students for whom there is clear evidence that they are not capable of mastering traditional academics. An individual with a disability who can take care of her personal needs, help around the house, do simple shopping, entertain herself, behave appropriately in public, and perform routine tasks, including those related to paid employment, if possible, has functional skills. Such skills should be the focus of her education. It is of great importance that the particular environment in which an individual lives be considered when decisions about functional skills are made (Schroeder et al., 1990). The customs and values of a given community are as important as the resources available.

It is sometimes necessary to eliminate or reduce the rate of some student behaviors. A child who bites himself must be stopped from doing so. A student who hurts others cannot be allowed to continue. Students who are so disruptive that they cannot be maintained in a classroom must learn to stop running, screaming, or destroying property. Merely eliminating such behavior, however, is indefensible in the absence of a plan to develop constructive behavior. A student who just sits quietly doing nothing is not much better off than she was before intervention. Teachers must pay attention to developing behaviors in the student that will lead to improved learning or social interaction. Attention to functional assessment and analysis, as discussed in Chapter 6, will enable teachers to substitute appropriate behaviors for those that are disruptive or dangerous.

In some cases, inappropriate behavior may be decreased by reinforcing constructive behavior rather than by directly attempting to decrease destructive behavior. For example, decreasing disruptive behavior does not automatically result in improved academic performance (Ferritor, Buckholdt, Hamblin, & Smith, 1972), whereas increasing academic output may result in decreased inappropriate behavior (Ayllon & Roberts, 1974; Kirby & Shields, 1972). In general, for students who display any appropriate behavior at all, the teacher should try reinforcing such behavior and monitoring the effects of this procedure on the inappropriate behavior. Some students' repertoires of appropriate behavior are so limited and their performance of inappropriate behavior so continuous that there is little or no opportunity for a positive-reinforcement approach. In such cases, the teacher may first have to undertake elimination of the maladaptive behavior. This should be only a first step, however, and should never be undertaken without a detailed functional analysis. As soon as possible, the student must be taught to substitute constructive behaviors that lead to the acquisition of functional skills.

Behavioral Assessment and Ongoing Evaluation

Information for goal setting comes from many sources: tests, records, observation, parents, teachers, and the students themselves.

Ethical teachers cannot and do not arbitrarily decide what to teach students to do or to stop doing. Goals and objectives for each student must be based on careful observation of what the student does under a variety of conditions. After goals are selected and programs implemented, the ethical teacher keeps track of how the program is going. It is wrong to make statements like "I started using counters to help Ben with his math and he seems to be doing better." We want you to be able to say, "I observed that for 4 days Ben got only 2 to 3 of 10 one-digit addition problems right. I gave him 20 bottle caps and showed him how to use them as counters. He got 6 right that day, 7 yesterday, and 9 today. When he gets all 10 right for 3 days in a row, I'll go on to subtraction." We taught you how to say that in "behavioriese" in Chapter 3, which covers using data collection to assess and evaluate the results of procedures.

The Most Effective Treatment Procedures Available

"Before behavior analysis, custodial care was often the best anyone could do. But that's not true anymore. Generally, a right to effective intervention now means a right to a behavioral intervention . . . (Malott et al., 1997, p. 414). We believe this statement, which the authors made about persons in residential treatment, has broad application. There is no excuse for programs, in schools or elsewhere, in which the goal is merely to keep students from harming themselves or others.

A primary consideration that guides professionals and parents in designing a program to change a student's behavior is the proven effectiveness of a technique in changing similar behaviors in similar students. The most ethical and responsible procedure to use in changing both academic (Heward, 2003) and social behavior is one that has been established as most effective. Throughout this text, we have reviewed literature related to changing specific behaviors and provided suggestions about effective procedures. Teachers who plan behavioral programs should also continually review current professional journals in order to keep abreast of new developments. Many journals provide information on behavior-change procedures for use with students who have specific disabling conditions and with students in general education classes who display certain deficits or excesses.

In some cases, it may not be possible, ethical, or legal to use a procedure that has been proven effective (Lohrmann-O'Rourke & Zirkel, 1998). The use of aversive procedures—specifically including contingent electric shock—though proven effective in eliminating some very maladaptive behaviors, such as self-injury, has been restricted (Wyatt v. Stickney, 1972). Such procedures may now be used only if consent has been obtained from the subject (or parents or advocate) and a supervisory committee has confirmed that less drastic procedures have not eliminated or sufficiently decelerated the maladaptive behavior (Martin, 1975). Limitations have also been placed on the use of time-out from positive reinforcement, a technique that may involve seclusion (confining a student in an isolated area) or exculsion (removing a student from a potentially reinforcing situation). Seclusionary time-out is particularly subject to regulation (Morales v. Turman, 1974). Before using any aversive or seclusionary procedure, teachers should examine their employers' guidelines or regulations pertaining to such procedures, because rules may vary considerably. The unauthorized use of even short-term seclusion, a relatively mild but effective technique, may result in criticism or misunderstanding.

To enhance your knowledge of this topic, click on the Activities module on the Companion Website and complete the second activity.

The use of aversive or seclusionary interventions should, in any event, be reserved for severely maladaptive behaviors that have not been successfully modified using positive means. Many behaviors targeted for deceleration may be eliminated using reinforcement of incompatible behavior, differential reinforcement of other behavior (DRO), or extinction.

Techniques for decreasing behavior were described in Chapter 8.

ACCOUNTABILITY

Accountability implies publication of goals, procedures, and results so that they may be evaluated. Applied behavior analysis lends itself easily to such accountability. Goals are stated behaviorally, procedures described clearly, and results defined in terms of direct, functional relationships between interventions and behaviors. It is impossible to conduct applied behavior analysis as described by Baer, Wolf, and Risley (1968) without being accountable. The entire process is visible, understandable, and open to evaluation. The result of such accountability is that parents, teachers, administrators, and the public can judge for themselves whether an approach is working or whether a change is needed.

Teachers should not view the requirement of accountability as negative or threatening. It is to a teacher's advantage to verify the effectiveness of his or her teaching. This approach enables teachers to monitor their own competence and to demonstrate this competence to others. It is much more impressive to face a supervisor at a yearly evaluation conference armed with charts and graphs showing increases in reading ability and decreases in disruptive behavior than it is to walk in with only vague statements about a pretty good year.

To whom are teachers accountable? In terms of ethical behavior, the answer is "to everyone." Teachers are accountable to their profession, the community, their administrative superiors, the parents of their students, those students, and themselves.

The teacher who follows the suggestions provided in this chapter should avoid many problems associated with the use of applied behavior analysis procedures in the classroom. Table 12–1 summarizes these suggestions. No amount of prevention can forestall all criticism; nor can a teacher avoid making mistakes. Systematic attention to the ethical standards in the ABA's statement, however, can minimize criticism and enable teachers to learn from mistakes rather than become discouraged by them.

Accountability is a major benefit of applied behavior analysis.

TABLE 12–1
Suggestions for ethical use of applied behavior analysis.

Assure competence of all staff members.
Choose appropriate goals.
Ensure voluntary participation.
Be accountable.

Let's listen in on Professor Grundy, whose workshop discussion may address concerns you have. All the questions the professor answers here are inevitably addressed to everyone who undertakes a career as an applied behavior analyst.

Professor Grundy Conducts a Workshop

The superintendent of schools in a large metropolitan area near the university asked Professor Grundy to conduct a 2-hour workshop on behavior modification for elementary and secondary teachers. Although aware of the limitations of such short-term workshops (Franks & Wilson, 1976), Grundy concluded that if he confined himself to a description of basic learning principles, no harm would be done. On the appointed day, Grundy, dressed in his best tweed coat with leather elbow patches, stood before 700 teachers and wondered how he got himself into this mess.

After a slow start, during which several teachers fell asleep and numerous others openly graded papers, Grundy hit his stride. He delivered a succinct, snappy talk full of humorous anecdotes and sprinkled with just enough first-name references to his friends, all "biggies" in applied behavior analysis and all totally unfamiliar to the teachers. As Grundy reached the conclusion of his presentation, glowing with satisfaction, he noticed to his horror that he was coming up about 45 minutes short of the amount of time agreed to in his contract. Over the thunderous applause (resulting at least partially from the fact that the teachers thought they were going to be released early), Grundy called faintly for questions. There was considerable rumbling and shifting about, but when the superintendent mounted the stage and glared fixedly at the audience, the hands began to go up. The nature of the questions made Grundy vow never to be caught short again, but he did his best to answer each.

Question: Isn't what you're suggesting bribery?

Answer: I'm glad you asked that question. Webster's Third New International Dictionary (1986) defines a bribe as something given to pervert the judgment or corrupt the conduct of a person. In that sense, the use of the principles I have described is certainly not bribery. Teachers use the principles of learning to motivate their students to do things that will benefit them—things such as reading, math, and social skills.

A second definition is that a bribe is anything promised or given to induce a person to do something against his or her wishes. Some people might say that's exactly what I'm advocating. As a behaviorist, I have some difficulty with the word wishes, because I cannot see wishes but only actions. It appears to me that students have a free choice as to whether they will perform a behavior for which they know they will receive a reinforcer. My interpretation is that if Joanie, for example, chooses to perform the behavior, she has demonstrated her "wishes." The word bribery definitely implies something underhanded. I prefer to think of applied behavior analysis procedures as open, honest attempts to change students' behavior in a positive direction. Any other questions? If not . . .

Question: But shouldn't children be intrinsically motivated? Surely they don't have to be rewarded for learning. They should want to learn.

Answer: Madam, why are you here today? I'm sure that given the choice of spending the day at the mall or coming to an in-service session, your intrinsic motivation for learning might have wavered just a little. All of us here are being paid to be here; most adults, even those who enjoy their work enormously, would not continue to perform it in the absence of some very concrete application of the law of positive reinforcement. Why should we expect children to perform difficult tasks for less than we expect of ourselves?

Question: But won't our students expect rewards for everything they do?

Answer: Certainly. And why not? However, as your students become more successful, they will begin to respond to the reinforcers available in the natural environment—the same reinforcers that maintain the appropriate behavior of students who are already successful. Good students do not work without reinforcers. Their behavior is reinforced by good grades, by parental approval, and, yes, by the love of learning. When doing good work has been consistently reinforced, it eventually does become a secondary, or conditioned, reinforcer. We cannot, however, expect this to happen overnight with students who have had very little experience with success in learning tasks. Does that answer your questions? Thank . . .

Question: At our last in-service session, the speaker told us that using rewards will decrease intrinsic motivation.

Answer: That's a rather widespread notion nowadays (Kohn, 1993). Not everyone agrees, however, and many question the validity and interpretation of the studies cited as evidence for it (Chance, 1992; Slavin, 1991). There's so much evidence of the effectiveness of behavioral procedures that, in my opinion, it is unethical not to implement them.

Question: Doesn't this kind of behavior management just suppress the symptoms of serious emotional problems without getting at the root cause?

Answer: Oh, my. That's a very complicated question. Behaviorists don't accept the concept of emotional problems caused by some underlying root cause. We have found that if we deal with the problem behaviors, the roots just seem to die out. Human beings are not like weeds whose roots lurk under the surface of the ground waiting to send up shoots as soon as it rains.

Question: Yes, but everyone knows if you suppress one symptom, a worse one will take its place. Doesn't that prove there are underlying problems?

Answer: No, sir, everyone does not know that. Human beings are no more like piston engines than like weeds. Just because one symptom "goes down," another one will not necessarily "pop up." My colleagues (Baer, 1971; Bandura, 1969; Rachman, 1963; Yates, 1970) have reported extensive research indicating that removal of so-called symptoms does not result in the development of new ones. As a matter of fact, when children's inappropriate

"With automotive 'behavior,' prof, you gotta get right to the cause. Now, after you had the oil changed in 1953 . . . "

behaviors are eliminated, they sometimes learn new, appropriate behaviors without being taught (Chadwick & Day, 1971; Morow & Gochors, 1970; O'Leary, Poulos, & Devine, 1972). Even if new maladaptive behaviors do occur—and they sometimes do (Balson, 1973; Schroeder & MacLean, 1987)—there is no evidence to show they are alternative symptoms of underlying deviance. Functional analysis generally indicates that those behaviors served a communicative function for the individual and that new behaviors are a continued attempt to communicate some need. If appropriate behaviors are taught that meet the same communicative purpose, the inappropriate ones will go away. Now if . . .

Question: Isn't what you're talking about based on the behavior of animals such as rats and monkeys? That's how you train a dog, for heaven's sake: Give him a treat when he does a cute trick and hit him with a rolled-up newspaper when he's bad. Isn't it unethical to treat our kids like animals?

Answer: Early research studying the laws of behavior was conducted with animals. This doesn't mean we control human beings as if they were nothing but white rats or pigeons, or even dogs. Such animal research—also called analogue research (Davison & Stuart, 1975)—provides only a basic foundation for studying human behavior. The applied behavior analyst uses procedures tested with human beings in real-world conditions, not in laboratories. These procedures take into account the complexity of human behavior and the undeniable freedom of human beings to choose their course of action. What's unethical is not learning and applying all we can from whatever source. And, by the way, there is no reason to hit your dog with a newspaper; there are much more . . . sorry, that's a little off the subject.

Question: This stuff may work on those special education kids, but my students are smart. Won't they catch on?

Answer: Good heavens, of course they'll catch on. The laws of behavior operate for all of us. We can change behavior in youngsters with very severe disabilities, but it's a very complex process. With your students, you can shorten and simplify the procedure. You just tell them what the contingencies are. You don't have to wait for the students to learn from experience. Applied behavior analysis procedures work on everyone, even professors. Take punishment, for example. If I ever agree to do another workshop, it'll be a cold day in . . . . Pardon me. Any more questions?

Question: But how can behavior mod work with my kids? I don't care how much candy you gave them, they still couldn't read.

Answer: Perhaps, madam, you missed some of my presentation during your nap. Applied behavior analysis is not just giving students candy. If your students do not respond verbally to the written word, then you must bring their responses under stimulus control. That's applied behavior analysis. If they have no vocal language, you shape it; that's applied behavior analysis. If they just sit there and do nothing, you get their attention. AND THAT'S APPLIED BEHAVIOR ANALYSIS! ARE THERE ANY MORE QUESTIONS?

Question: I think the whole thing sounds like too much work. It seems awfully tedious and time consuming. Is it really worth the trouble?

Answer: If . . . it's . . . not . . . worth . . . the . . . trouble, . . . don't . . . do . . . it. Behaviors that are serious enough to warrant more complicated procedures take up an enormous amount of your time. You don't use a complicated procedure to solve a simple problem. Try timing yourself with a stopwatch. How much time is this problem taking the way you're handling (or not handling) it now? Try applying systematic contingencies and keeping records. Then compare the amount of time you've spent. You might be surprised! Now, I really must . . .

Question: I have only one student with really serious problems. If I use some systematic procedure with him, won't the others complain? What do I say to them?

Answer: The problem will not occur as often as you think. Most students know that a student who is not performing well needs extra help and are neither surprised nor disturbed when he gets it. Few students will even ask why that student is treated differently. If they do, I suggest you say to them, "In this class everyone gets what he needs. Harold needs a little extra help remembering to stay in his seat." If you consistently reinforce appropriate behavior for all your students, they will not resent it when a more systematic procedure is implemented for a student with special problems. If that's all, I . . .

Question: Most of my students with problems can't learn much because they come from very bad home situations. There's just nothing you can do in such cases, is there?

Answer: Madam, pigeons can learn to discriminate between environments and to perform the behaviors that will be reinforced in each. Are you implying your students are less capable than birds? Such an assumption is inhumane. Blaming poor learning or inappropriate behavior on factors beyond your control is simply a refusal to accept responsibility. You may have very little influence on your students' environment outside your classroom, but you have an enormous influence on that classroom environment. It is your job to arrange it so your students learn as much as possible, both academically and socially. What do you think teaching is, anyway? *Teach* is a transitive verb. You're not teaching unless you're teaching somebody something.

Question: Have you ever taught school?

At this point Professor Grundy became incoherent and had to be helped from the podium by the superintendent. As he drove home, he realized he had made a number of mistakes, the first of which was agreeing to do the workshop. He had assumed that teachers expecting to receive concrete help with classroom management problems would be interested in a theoretical discussion of learning principles. He had also assumed that the teachers would immediately see the relationships between these principles and the behaviors of their students. Grundy realized it was unreasonable of him to expect this. He did decide, however, that he needed to include more practical applications in his courses on applied behavior analysis.

Theory or Recipes?

Professor Grundy was undoubtedly correct in his belief that the effective use of applied behavior analysis requires knowledge of the basic principles. Teachers often reject theory and seek immediate practical solutions to specific problems. Such a cookbook approach, however, has serious limitations. Although students supplied with cookbook methods may acquire competencies more quickly, the students who are required to spend more time on basic principles tend to show more competence in the long run (White, 1977).

Summary

This chapter described several objections to the use of applied behavior analysis techniques. These techniques have been criticized on the basis that they interfere with personal freedom and that they are inhumane. We have described our reasons for disagreeing with these objections. Properly used, applied behavior analysis procedures enhance personal freedom by increasing options. Applied behavior analysis procedures are humane because they are an effective tool for increasing options and teaching appropriate skills.

Applied behavior analysis procedures will be used ethically if the program includes a therapeutic environment, services whose overriding goal is personal welfare, treatment by a competent behavior analyst, programs that teach functional skills, behavioral assessment and ongoing evaluation, and the most effective treatment procedures available. Teachers who choose applied behavior analysis procedures and consider these factors know they are acting in the best interests of their students.

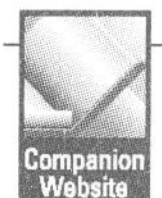

To enhance your overall understanding of the ethical use of Applied Behavior Analysis, go to the "Supplemental Lecture Notes" module for Chapter 12 of the Companion Website.

KEY TERMS

applied behavior analysis
lawful behavior
determinism
humane
social validity
informed consent
voluntary consent
accountability

DISCUSSION QUESTIONS

1. If, as a teacher, you decided to use applied behavior analysis procedures to teach your students, how would you justify or describe their use to parents? to school administrators? to students?
2. Would changing the terminology—avoiding the word "punishment", for example—change the acceptability of applied behavior analysis to professionals and the public? Can you think of alternative terms?
3. Is it ever ethical to use aversive procedures? If so, under what circumstances is their use justified?
4. At what point should the attempt to teach academic or preacademic skills to students with disabilities be abandoned? Should the attempt even be made with some students?

Chapter 13

Putting It All Together

In the first 12 chapters of this text we described numerous procedures for examining and changing students' behavior. We considered those procedures as separate techniques, but in reality, of course, teachers and other professionals use them all together. The following anecdotes give you some examples of what an environment looks like when teachers implement the principles and practices of applied behavior analysis. We will visit several teachers, all applied behavior analysts, teaching in several different settings. We will look at everything from their room arrangements to their daily schedules to see how they implement the principles they have learned and practiced.

Remember Miss Harper?

Miss Harper's second student teaching placement is in an integrated preschool setting. Because she is seeking a minor in early childhood special education, Professor Grundy feels that this will be perfect for her. Miss Harper is not so sure. She has been informed that about one fourth of her prospective students are developmentally delayed, and she knows that could mean anything.

On her first day Miss Harper approaches the classroom tentatively. As she walks through the open door into a large, airy room, she is struck by the appearance of the classroom. There are a few tables with tiny little chairs, but most of the room is divided into large areas containing various collections of what she characterizes as toys—blocks, both sand and water tables with buckets and other utensils, colorful construction materials, dolls and furniture, and a miniature collection of kitchen and other household furniture. She also observes easels and paints, displays of children's art, and modeling clay, along with numerous riding toys, smaller toy vehicles, and what appears to be a huge number of very young children. As she attempts to identify those "developmentally delayed" ones, she is approached by a smiling young woman wearing cropped pants and tennis shoes, who Miss Harper assumes must be an assistant.

"Miss Harper?" she inquires, "I'm Amy Somerville, the lead teacher. Welcome to our class." She looks dubiously at Miss Harper's tailored suit, midheel pumps, and wary expression, but continues, "Come on over and meet the other teachers; we're really looking forward to working with you."

"Michael," she states firmly to a tot in a tiny electric wheelchair speeding perilously close to Miss Harper's pumps, "look where you're going, kiddo."

As they make their way through the mass of children, Miss Harper spots two children with Down syndrome and two more with braces. They appear to be engaged in playing with other children. As they approach the other teachers, Ms. Amy asks, "What's your first name, Miss Harper? We're very informal here." "Michelle," gasps Miss Harper, as she is introduced to four other adults. No distinction is made as to status, but Barry, Lisa, Bonnie, and Lucille apparently have responsibility with Ms. Amy for the 25 (could there really be only 25?) 3- and 4- year-olds in the classroom.

Lisa takes charge of Miss Harper, "We've already done circle this morning, and most of the children are getting ready to work in the centers." Her pitying look at Miss Harper's outfit is undisguised. "Perhaps you'd like just to observe for a while." She guides Miss Harper to an adult-sized chair at a worktable and hurries away to take a shovel away from a child at the sand table.

"Sand," she states firmly, "is for building, not for throwing." She sinks to the floor at the sand table and begins asking the children about their activities. She encourages the children to work together and praises a student who gets a dump truck in order to move the sand more efficiently. Meanwhile Ms. Bonnie gathers three children and settles them at one of the tiny tables. She pulls objects from a box and asks the students to identify them, tell what color they are, and answer other questions about them. A young man whom Miss Harper recognizes as a fellow university student arrives to work with one of the children with autism who is receiving intensive one-on-one instruction for part of the time he is at school.

As Miss Harper watches the activities in the room, a pattern begins to emerge. In addition to the direct instruction activities, she sees many small groups of children who are playing—working, she remembers—at the various centers. She decides to watch one center for a while to zero in on what is going on. She picks the block center. Four children are building a series of structures and chattering about their activities. One child sits by himself. Barry is seated on the floor nearby. "Mr. Barry," insists one of the children, "Charlie's hogging the big blocks." Indeed, Charlie appears to be simply collecting the largest blocks and keeping himself between them and the other children.

"Maybe you should ask him to share, DeJohn," suggests Barry. "No way, man," objects DeJohn, "he'll hit me." Miss Harper begins to suspect that Charlie, too, may be "developmentally delayed."

"Charlie," suggests Barry quietly, "I think DeJohn doesn't know how hard we've been working on sharing. Remember, you earn computer time. Go on," he adds more loudly, "DeJohn, ask—you remember how."

"Charlie," says DeJohn, "we need big blocks. Come help us." With a glance at Barry, Charlie pushes several blocks from his hoard toward DeJohn and moves slightly toward the group. Barry quickly hands Charlie a token that Charlie slips into his pocket. "Good job, Charlie; you too, DeJohn."

Miss Harper turns her attention to the area where students are playing—working, working—with water. Both Ms. Lisa and Ms. Lucille are there with six children. One of them is Maria, a child with Down syndrome. The children are pouring water from smaller into larger containers, and yes, from larger into smaller containers. Miss Harper admires both the ingenious design of the table and the presence of two adults. Both adults converse with all the children. She notices that Maria answers with monosyllables when a teacher asks a question but does not initiate interaction. The other students talk among themselves but ignore Maria. Miss Harper begins, however, to pick up a pattern. Casually, Ms. Lucille suggests, "Melanie, ask Maria to hand you that yellow cup, please. Good job saying thank you, Melanie."

A few minutes later, Ms. Bonnie says, "Toshi, would you ask Maria if she would like to be a cleanup helper? You can be the leader." Miss Harper is impressed that the teachers are encouraging the typical students to interact with their peers with disabilities. She realizes that a setting using developmentally appropriate practices can adapt those practices to a wide variety of developmental levels, even those considered "delayed."

By the end of the day Miss Harper, having observed indoor work, outdoor work, lunchroom work, and quiet-time work, is convinced that this is exactly the right placement for her. She leaves the preschool headed for the mall. She needs cropped pants and a pair of tennis shoes. What else would Miss Michelle wear?

Ms. Mitchell's Self-Contained Class

Ms. Mitchell teaches eight 6- to 9-year-olds. All have severe developmental disabilities. Three students use wheelchairs; one student has braces and crutches. Some of the students have few verbal skills; others can talk fairly well. Ms. Mitchell shares a two-room suite with a resource teacher. She has a full-time assistant and works with a speech and language therapist, a physical therapist, and an occupational therapist, all of whom work in several schools. Her room is arranged so that her students with wheelchairs and crutches can move about easily and safely. There is a table where all the children and several adults can sit, areas where students can sit or lie on the floor, and a number of adapted seating and standing devices designed for specific children. There is also a screened area where students' clothing can be changed when necessary.

Ms. Mitchell's daily and weekly schedules are quite complex. She must arrange the schedules to take maximum advantage of the professional and paraprofessional help available and to see that all students have opportunities to be with their typically developing and less disabled peers. Perhaps the best way to show how Ms. Mitchell puts it all together in her classroom is to spend an entire day with her class. All Ms. Mitchell's students ride buses to school. Either she or Ms. Post, her assistant, meets each bus to help the drivers and the assistants who ride the busses get the students off and to help the students get to the classroom. Several student volunteers from regular classrooms also meet their "buddies" and provide assistance. As little assistance as necessary is provided; indeed, the teachers have recently started just shadowing Malcolm as he makes his own way to the classroom. Because the buses arrive at considerable intervals, there is plenty of time to spend with individual students as they arrive in the classroom. Part of what makes Ms. Mitchell's planning so complex is that, in getting coats and boots off and hung up, she must constantly remember that, for example, Malcolm is working on colors, Trish is working on counting objects, and Steven is working on responding to his name. As they arrive in the classroom, each student is prompted as necessary to go to his or her own coat hook. Students' names and pictures are posted by each hook.

"Take off your coat, Trish. That's good, Malcolm, you took off your coat. Now hang it up. Good, Malcolm. Take off your coat, Trish." Ms. Mitchell puts her hand over Trish's and helps her through the unbuttoning process.

"How many buttons, Trish? Let's count. One, two, three; three buttons. Take off your coat." As Trish begins to comply, Ms. Mitchell asks, "Is your shirt red, Malcolm?" Malcolm nods. "Speak up, Malcolm, say 'yes.' Good, Malcolm. Good girl, Trish, you took off your coat. How many coats this morning? Good job, Trish, three coats. Steven!" As Steven turns his head, he is rewarded with a tickle and "Good, Steven, let's go to the circle."

Ms. Mitchell likes to start the day with a variation of "show and tell" as in most primary classes. The speech and language therapist is here on Monday mornings so today she leads the session, asking each student to respond verbally or with a communication device.

"Tell me something you did yesterday. Malcolm, what did you do yesterday? Did you watch TV? Tell me, 'I watched TV.' Good, Malcolm. Hannah, did you watch TV? Good, Hannah (when Hannah points to the TV on her communication board). What did you watch, Trish? Pokemon? I watched that, too." Ms. Mitchell moves among the children, prompting responses and patting students who respond on the shoulder. Steven, who has the fewest language skills, responds to "TV" by laughing. Ms. Post, who is standing behind him, provides another tickle and asks, "Do you like TV, Steven?" He giggles again.

After the circle activity, it is time for Malcolm to change to go to PE with the second grade. Ms. Post works on his dressing skills, helping him take off his red shirt and put on his blue shorts, while Ms. Mitchell and the speech and language therapist engage the other students in rearranging and putting things on and under the bookshelves, asking Trish to count the books, and occasionally attracting Steven's attention.

A second grader comes to get Malcolm. Ms. Mitchell and Ms. Post work intensively with individuals and small groups on various skills while other students work by themselves for short periods. When Malcolm returns in about 45 minutes, he tells Ms. Mitchell all about kickball (it was a red ball) while he changes into his regular clothes. Several of the children help Ms. Post prepare the morning snack. Malcolm gets the cups and hands the red one, the yellow one, and the blue one to Ms. Post. Trish counts two cookies for each student. After the snack has been cleaned up (surely, by now you can guess who washes the red cup and who counts the cups to be sure they were all washed), six of the children and Ms. Post join the resource class for a math activity, and Ms. Mitchell, Hannah, and Trish put on coats and go for a walk. Most of Hannah's neighbors walk to school and Ms. Mitchell's goal is for Hannah to learn to cross streets safely so she can join them. Trish lives too far away to walk, but is also ready to learn the skills. Ms. Mitchell talks with the girls as they walk, identifying things they see and asking them to do the same. She asks Trish to count several things during the walk. They walk to Hannah's house and back, looking both ways even after the light is green.

Several of the students eat lunch with regular classes, each with a lunch buddy to be sure that all goes well. Ms. Post takes several others, who still need a little more help and supervision, to the cafeteria as a group. Ms. Mitchell helps Steven in the classroom; he becomes very excited and displays some self-injurious behavior if he has to cope with the cafeteria. Ms. Mitchell plans to start taking him by himself in a few weeks.

After lunch, as in most primary classrooms, there is a quiet story and music listening time. Ms. Post and Ms. Mitchell each take charge of half the time so the other can eat lunch peacefully in the teachers' lounge. Ms. Mitchell times her lunch so she can eat with a friend and, for a change, have somebody tell her that she's doing a good job.

After quiet time, Malcolm goes to the resource room for reading readiness activities. Ms. Post, Ms. Mitchell, and the physical therapist help the others change for PE. The physical therapist has helped develop a plan for gross-motor activities for each student and also helps implement it. By the time the children have finished PE, it is time to start getting ready for the buses. Ms. Mitchell used to be frustrated at the amount of time spent in her classroom on routines, until she realized how much she could teach during those routines.

Ms. Washington's Resource Room

Ms. Washington is a resource/consulting teacher in a large, suburban middle school. She works with about 30 sixth- and seventh-grade students who have learning disabilities or mild mental retardation or whose behavior problems have earned them the label "emotionally disturbed." Being a behaviorist, she does not worry too much about their disturbed emotions but concentrates on their academic and social behavior. All Ms. Washington's students spend at least half their day in a regular classroom. A few are with her for as much as 3 hours every day; some come only when they encounter a problem in the regular classroom; and others are maintained fulltime in the regular classroom. Ms. Washington is responsible, with a multidisciplinary team, for developing an individualized education program (IEP) for each of her students and for coordinating the implementation of that IEP with regular classroom teachers. She regularly consults with the teachers who have "her" students on a fulltime basis. She has a half-time assistant who comes in the afternoons.

It usually takes Ms. Washington several weeks to get her weekly and daily schedule coordinated. She has to work around art, music, physical education, and lunch schedules for many classes; she must also be sure that her students do not, for example, miss math, which they are good at, to come to her for reading, which they are not good at, meanwhile sitting in a reading class in which they are totally lost and getting behind in math. If that sounds very confusing, think how Ms. Washington feels. She does not try to schedule her students by grade level or type of disability but tries to schedule students who are working at about the same level in a subject area at the same time. She often has several subclasses in her room at a given time; for example, five students working on reading and one needing help with math. She does what all teachers do: She provides independent work for some students while she works with others. She schedules her largest groups and her most difficult students in the afternoon when the assistant will be available to monitor and help with independent work. This year she has two boys who spend all morning with her; she is responsible for their instruction in reading, math, and social studies. She has scheduled an additional five students for each hour of the morning, thus having seven students in her room at any given time. Three students spend 2 hours each afternoon with her, and she schedules five others during each of those 2 hours. Ms. Washington eats lunch from 11:30 to noon and keeps the hour from noon to 1:00 for observations and conferences. She has found that many working parents prefer to have meetings during the lunch hour. She requires students to be in their seats at their scheduled time and provides a small clock face with the time they need to leave the regular class for those students who need a prompt.

Ms. Washington uses a formal token system in her classroom. Each student has a point card and earns points for being on time, completing assignments, and behaving appropriately. Many students also bring less elaborate point cards from their regular teachers and earn additional points for having completed assignments and behaved appropriately in the regular classroom. She provides what her students call the "store" on Fridays; students may trade filled cards for food items, school supplies, and small toys. Ms. Washington, like many teachers, buys the items for her store herself. She maintains that it is cheaper than the psychiatric treatment she would require without the token system. She also has a time-out area where disruptive students can be separated from the group.

All instruction in Ms. Washington's classroom is individualized. Contrary to what some teachers apparently believe, this means neither that all instruction is one-on-one nor that each student has his own personal packet of worksheets that he works on without interaction with the teacher. It means that each student's lesson for each day is designed to help master the goals and objectives written in the IEP. Some children may have the same goals; they can often receive instruction as a group. Ms. Washington posts the daily schedule with what each child will be doing on a bulletin board that is convenient to her and her assistant.

Ms. Washington has arranged her room so that she has two teaching and work areas as far apart as possible. Most of the students sit at tables instead of desks. She provides separate desks for a few students to prevent them from bothering other students. Two of her students do some of their work at a study carrel that she has created with a bookcase.

Let's visit Ms. Washington first thing Monday morning. At 8:30 on the dot, having said the "Pledge of Allegiance" and paid for lunch in the regular classroom, Alvin and Tyrone, two children who stay all morning, along with Melanie, Michael, Donna, Charlie, and Harold, have picked up their point cards and are sitting in their assigned seats. Ms. Washington greets them only after they are seated. "Good morning, Alvin; it's good to see your smile on this rainy Monday. You're right on time. You're already earned 10 points for that and 2 bonus ones for getting started on your task" Each student's place has a simple paper-and-pencil task that reinforces following instructions. Each student is greeted and given points.

As the students finish their order tasks (usually in less than 5 minutes), Ms. Washington puts a large A on each one, gives more points, and continues: "Alvin, we're going to be doing reading first. While I get the others started, you get three red books and bring them here." She gets four of the students started on a written reading comprehension activity based on a story they read yesterday, reminds them that they can raise their red (cardboard) flag if they need help, and sits down at the table with Alvin, Tyrone, and Harold. "Alvin, thank you for bringing our books. You did a great job. No talking and fooling around on the way. That's worth another 3 bonus points." After a brisk 10-minute drill, during which the students respond chorally identifying words and sounds, Ms. Washington says, "Now I'm going to put the title of the story we're going to read today on the board. I'll bet somebody can read it easily because it has a lot of the clusters we've been working on." She prints the title "The Fantastic Voyage" on the board and, sure enough, all three students are eager to read it.

"Marvin, you try." Marvin reads the title as "The Fantastic Voyeur." Suppressing a giggle, Ms. Washington prompts, "What sound do the letters a-g-e make? Right! Now try it. Great! Harold, what does fantastic mean? It's a word we might use about science fiction. Right! It means strange or hard to believe. Very good!"

Ms. Washington continues to present vocabulary words, prompting and reinforcing correct responses. She avoids getting sidetracked or slowing down, but keeps the group on task and her pace brisk. She starts the group silently reading the first paragraph and goes to check the students working independently. No one has raised a flag, but Melanie has not started. She is staring out the window.

"Melanie, take your work into the carrel, please. It will be easier for you to concentrate. I expect that work to be finished before it's time for you to read."

Ms. Washington's reading lesson is finished in about 20 minutes. She gives the boys an assignment and points for paying attention and participating. She then checks the other students' work, gives more points, and asks Charlie to get the blue books for his group. She determines that Melanie (who is a group unto herself) is working and spends about 2 minutes going over her assignment while Charlie distributes the blue books. She also gives Melanie fewer points than she could have earned "because you had a little trouble getting started today." The reading lesson has the same format as the first group's. As the group starts to review vocabulary. Alvin, who should be working independently, leans over and says something to Tyrone, who tries to ignore him.

"Excuse me for interrupting our lesson, Group. Alvin, you need to do your own work and leave Tyrone alone, please."

When this group is finished, Ms. Washington spends 10 uninterrupted minutes with Melanie, who is still having trouble with the short vowel sounds. She is frustrated that she has so little time to spend with each child, but she tries very hard to make the independent work meaningful and to make every minute of instruction count. She spends the last 5 minutes of the hour helping students total their points and decide what kind of day they had. She dismisses the students and reminds them pleasantly that their teachers expect them back right on time.

Ms. Washington repeats the cycle four more times. During the afternoon, with the help of her assistant, she is able to give her undivided attention to each instructional group. For that reason, she also tries to use her afternoons to help most of the children with serious learning problems and all of the children with serious behavior problems.

Who Needs Behavior Mod?

Ms. Samples is a 30-year veteran fifth-grade teacher at the middle school where Ms. Washington teaches students with mild disabilities. She is somewhat of a legend—never sends children to the office and only reluctantly sends them to the resource room. At the beginning of the year she listened doubtfully to Ms. Washington's explanation of her token system. "Good heavens," she declared, "you young teachers with your newfangled notions. All those points and charts. Coddling them with bribes. I've been tough as nails for 30 years and that's what works for me."

Mr. Jackson, the principal, is somewhat in awe of Ms. Samples. Her tough talk worries him, but her students seem happy and parents clamor to get their children into her class. In spite of the fact that she ridicules each successive wave of reform in curriculum and methodology, her students do well on standardized tests and are well prepared for seventh grade. Mr. Jackson generally leaves Ms. Samples alone and guiltily tends to assign her more than her share of children with learning and behavior problems. When he does observe in her classroom, he sees a variety of activities. Ms. Samples appears to use frequent episodes of rather intense direct instruction with either the whole class or some part of it. During these episodes the students have many opportunities to respond individually and chorally. Although this kind of instruction, which Mr. Jackson himself thinks rather old-fashioned, does not coincide with the activities recommended by the local curriculum development council, he sometimes wonders if other classes would do better on standardized tests of achievement if they had some of it. Ms. Samples sometimes groups students to complete tasks, and her students often work with manipulatives and do projects. Tyrone, Harold, and Melanie are all members of her class, along with several other children who attend the resource class.

Ms. Samples accosted Ms. Washington in the teacher's lounge one Monday morning.

"Listen," she said, "I really need to keep all the kids all this week. I've got important stuff to teach, and if they miss parts of it, they'll get behind." Ms. Washington, having recently attended a seminar on inclusion, agreed to this temporary arrangement. She asked with some trepidation if she could observe how her children functioned under this arrangement. "Come any time," said Ms. Samples. "I've got nothing to hide. Just don't expect to see any of your individualized education or whatever it is . . . nor any of your foolish behavior mod either."

Ms. Washington rearranged her schedule to free up a full hour Friday afternoon. She approached the door of Ms. Samples' class, firmly closed as usual, and quietly entered. To her immense surprise, the children were not seated quietly at their desks watching Ms. Samples at the board. She did not, in fact, see Ms. Samples right away because the teacher was sitting on the floor surrounded by a group of children engaged in attaching curtain hooks to a 6-foot length of burlap with brightly colored pieces of felt glued to it. Other groups of children were occupied framing printed documents and arguing about the distance between cup hooks on a long piece of wood. Desks and tables were pushed aside or arranged in clusters with several children working on other apparently nonacademic tasks. Ms. Washington sat down at an empty desk and tried to make some sense of the seemingly chaotic activity. Tyrone approached her and asked what she was doing. When she stated that she had wanted to see him and the others working in their "other" classroom, he gloated, "Oh, we haven't done any work all week. We all worked hard last 6 weeks and brought the class report card average up a whole letter grade, so we've just been making our tapestry about the American Revolution." Tyrone explained that he had been on the team that researched the battle of Bunker Hill and decided what scene to cut from felt and glue on the wall hanging.

"It was fun," he stated, "Amanda helped with the hard words, and I even got to measure the felt." Ms. Washington immediately realized that Ms. Samples' teaching methods, whatever her statements about newfangled notions, were right up to date. When Tyrone went back to his group, she examined the classroom carefully. One bulletin board was labeled CLASSROOM POLICIES. Children's work was posted on another. She asked a student about it and was told that it was not really work, just copies of the best short reports about the Revolution that were being framed to accompany the mural.

"It's awesome to have your work on that board," she said. "It has to be like totally perfect. I rewrote mine three times and got help from my spelling partner before it was good enough." She proudly pointed out her essay. Ms. Washington was interested to see Melanie's essay, right next to it, much shorter, but neatly written and bearing the same big, red A+. The heading attributed the essay to Melanie, as told to Lee Anne. Ms. Samples had gotten up from the floor. "Thanks, guys" she said to two boys who had each given her a hand, "it's nice to know that you apply our class policy on helping others to me, too." She began to move around the room.

"Melanie," she asked, "have you finished cutting the mats? Remember, your group depends on you. Mike, watch Harold carefully—he's really an expert framer." Harold grinned hugely. A stranger to Ms. Washington muttered. "That retard's an expert?" to a friend, who snickered. Ms. Samples took each boy's arm, marched them to an unoccupied area of the room and quietly, but with steel in her voice, reminded them that another class policy was respect for others and that each of them was to copy that policy from the board and write an essay on how it makes others feel when you call them names.

Suddenly there was a commotion at one end of the room. Tyrone pushed a chair over and cocked his fist at another student. Ms. Samples had both his arms by the elbow before he could carry out the act.

"Tyrone, that is totally unacceptable. Hitting is not the solution to any problem. You will have to sit out for 15 minutes." Tyrone sullenly but obediently went to a chair behind a file cabinet and sat down. Ms. Washington noticed while Tyrone was "sitting out," Ms. Samples spoke with the other boy, reminding him that Tyrone was sometimes volatile and that the kind of teasing other children take in stride was apt to make him blow.

Ms. Samples rang a bell on her desk. There was instant silence and all eyes turned to her. "We have only 30 minutes left, boys and girls," she said to accompaniment of groans, which she ignored, "We'll have to finish up next week. Let's clean up now so our room will be a pleasure to enter on Monday. Think how proud we're all going to be when the students, teachers, and parents see our tapestry in the cafeteria. I can't wait, and I'll bet you can't either."

As the students efficiently put away supplies and restored order to the room, Ms. Washington reflected that for a real tough teacher who did not believe in behavior mod, Ms. Samples certainly seemed to understand clearly the benefits of applying learning principles. She also decided to talk with her about placing some of her students with mild disabilities in her class on a full-time basis.

Mr. Boyd's Math Classes

Mr. Boyd teaches math in a large, urban high school. He has a homeroom, three sections of ninth-grade arithmetic, and two sections of tenth-grade consumer math. Most of his students score below grade level on achievement tests, and each of his sections contains several students who have been classified as having special education needs. His class sizes range from 22 to 25. At the beginning of the year Mr. Boyd, using the diagnostic tests provided with the textbooks issued to the students, divided each class into four teams. He composed teams carefully so that each has a mixture of more and less competent students. One year he tried forming teams each week based on the past week's performance but found that to be a logistical nightmare. He now keeps the teams intact for a 6-week grading period. Each team has a captain, who is in charge of overall management, and an accountant, who is in charge of record keeping. These jobs rotate weekly. Each team is allowed to choose a name.

Mr. Boyd follows the same weekly schedule as much as possible because he has found that things run more smoothly when he does. When the schedule will not be followed, he tries to let the students know in advance. On Mondays and Wednesdays he presents new concepts and teaches new skills using large-group direct instruction. Tuesdays and Thursdays are team days. The students work together on assignments, helping one another as necessary. Mr. Boyd circulates, being sure that peer tutors are providing correct information and working with individuals and small groups when necessary. Fridays are test and reward days. Students receive grades for individual work, but all activities also earn points for their team. Teams receive points when members are present and on time, have necessary materials, complete homework and class assignments, perform well on tests and other activities, and behave appropriately. Teams lose points when members are disruptive or noncompliant. Expectations are explained at the beginning of the school year, and each student has a copy of the class rules and procedures in a required notebook. Every team can be a winner every week if enough points are earned. Each team's scores are posted on a bulletin board, and the team with the highest score is named Team of the Week. Mr. Boyd was afraid that high school students might find this system too childish, but the students seem to enjoy it. There is a good bit of friendly competition and lots of encouragement to bring supplies, be on time, behave appropriately, and learn the material. Let's look at a typical Monday in Mr. Boyd's first-period arithmetic class.

Mr. Boyd stands in the doorway as the students enter. He greets each one by name, with a positive comment about appearance, or at least with a smile and eye contact. Because many of his students are athletes, he attends many games and keeps track of all of them. He often offers a word of congratulation or commiseration. He also remembers birthdays and writes them on his lesson plans so he can acknowledge them—quietly, of course, because he knows adolescents are easily embarrassed. This greeting routine also allows him to determine whether any students are obviously intoxicated or under the influence of drugs and to be forewarned about any student whose body language clearly indicates that she or he is angry or upset.

As students enter the room, they go immediately to their assigned seats, which are arranged in rows so that all can see the chalkboard. There are several review problems on the board, and all students except the accountants begin work immediately. The accountants, who are excused from the review activity (they get plenty of math practice keeping up with all those points), move down their team's row with a clipboard and a data sheet on which they record whether students have supplies. Mr. Boyd ignores team members' surreptitiously lending one another supplies; that is what teamwork is all about.

As soon as the bell rings, Mr. Boyd takes roll by referring to his seating chart. Each team captain also notes absences; captains are encouraged to find out why their team members are not at school. Although teams are not penalized for excused absences, a member who is not present cannot earn bonus points. Within 5 minutes, the students have completed the review activity. Team members check one another's work, and the papers are passed to the front and collected.

Mr. Boyd begins the lesson on equivalent fractions by donning a pizza deliverer's hat and asking how many students would like to order a pizza. All raise their hands eagerly, and Mr. Boyd passes out photocopies of a pizza he has drawn and cut into pieces. There is some good-natured muttering about the inedibility of this pizza and the pitifulness of Mr. Boyd's drawing, a standing joke.

Mr. Boyd raises his hand in his established signal for quiet and the students stop talking. He asks, "How many pieces do you have? Marvin? Sara? Hey, that's not fair, Marvin has eight pieces and Sara has only four! Marvin, you'll have to give Sara some of yours." When Marvin protests that Sara's pieces are bigger than his, Mr. Boyd is well launched into his lesson. He uses larger cardboard pizzas to illustrate that 1/2, 2/4, and 4/8 all represent the same amount of pizza.

"What about 500,000/1,000,000?" he asks, writing it on the board. Marvin quips, "You're gonna have to eat that pizza with a spoon." There is general laughter. Mr. Boyd laughs, too, but soon raises his hand again. All students become quiet except two who are repeating the joke. Mr. Boyd says matter-of-factly, "ShaqAttack just lost two points," and continues his lesson. The other members of the team glare at the malefactors and the room is again quiet.

Mr. Boyd models the procedure for determining equivalency, brings students to the board to work problems, and assigns a short written assignment to be sure students understand the concept and can do the computation. He moves constantly about the room as students work independently, providing frequent positive comments, pointing out errors, and reteaching when necessary. He notes students who are having difficulty to be sure that they are assigned a peer tutor tomorrow.

Ten minutes before the end of the period, Mr. Boyd has students exchange papers again and goes over the correct answers. He reminds them not to panic if they are having trouble because they will get help tomorrow. He announces the number of points earned by each team and congratulates them. When the bell rings, Mr. Boyd dismisses this class and gets ready to do it all again with the next one.

On Tuesday the homeroom class rearranges the room into clusters of desks for each team. The procedure for doing this quickly and quietly was taught at the beginning of the year. Mr. Boyd gives each team captain his team's papers from yesterday, and the captains themselves work out how to ensure that each team member masters the material. Some captains assign individual tutors; some assign several students to one tutor; one looks at her team's papers and tells Mr. Boyd that they all need help. He makes sure all the teams are functioning efficiently and sits down to work with the "trouble team." He reminds himself to distribute the members of this team differently during the next grading period. The two strongest members of the original team have moved away and their replacements are weak. The in-class assignment for today will earn a grade for each student as well as points for the team.

After working with the weak group for several minutes, he tells them to continue working on the assignment and monitors the class to be sure that team members are working together but not doing one another's work. He answers questions, makes suggestions to tutors, and provides an enrichment activity for bonus points to one team whose members have all completed the assignment correctly. Several times the "busy hum" of the classroom approaches a roar. Mr. Boyd raises his hand and, because not all the students are facing him, snaps his fingers twice. Team members shush one another and the noise never becomes a serious problem.

Ten minutes before the end of the period, Mr. Boyd asks the class to turn around and look at him. He collects the papers of students who are finished, reminds those who are not finished that their work must be turned in tomorrow, and gives a short homework assignment. He announces points earned for appropriate behavior, reminds the students that he will announce points for the in-class assignment when it has been graded, and allows students to begin their homework assignment. The chairs remain as they are until sixth period when that class rearranges them in rows. Mr. Boyd at one time thought it might be more efficient to do 2 days of group work in a row to avoid all the furniture moving but was quickly informed by the building engineer that it is impossible to clean any room whose desks are not in rows.

Ms. Michaels Has It in the Bag

Ms. Michaels teaches a group of students with moderate to severe disabilities. Her students range in age from 17 through 20. She shares responsibility for 24 students with another licensed teacher and two paraprofessionals. Her job has changed dramatically over the years. She started her career in a state-run residential institution and is now working with a similar population of students located at a regular suburban high school. Her students spend a great deal of time outside school learning skills they will need as adults.

Today she plans to take three of her students into the community for several hours. This requires a great deal of advance planning. She and her colleagues determine that the other teacher and one assistant will work on domestic skills, simulated shopping skills, and prevocational skills, with most of the students remaining at school. The classroom contains a fully equipped kitchen and laundry room, and the students will prepare lunch for themselves, wash and fold towels from the school gym, and prepare brochures from a local health club for mailing. In return, the health club has agreed to allow class members to use the facility. The classroom also has an area that can simulate a grocery, drug, or convenience store so that students can practice shopping using lists or picture cues. Four highly verbal students will accompany the assistant to the resource room, where the teacher is working on appropriate social skills on the job. They will eat lunch with some of the resource students and return to their classroom for the shopping simulation.

The students who are to be in the community will work at a job site for an hour, eat lunch at a cafeteria, and shop for clothing at a local discount department store. The students accompanying Ms. Michaels today are Sam, 17 years old with good verbal skills and excellent behavior, Kimberly, 18, who uses a communication device and behaves well unless frustrated or confused, and Ricardo, 19, who has some verbal skills but is prone to violent outbursts.

Ms. Michaels first checks to see that all three students are present and feeling well, then spends some time previewing the trip, using pictures. Sam and Kimberly are old hands at the grocery store where they are learning job skills. They have also eaten at the cafeteria and shopped at the department store several times. Ricardo has less experience at the grocery store but has eaten and been shopping alone with a teacher. This will be his first group experience at these sites. Ms. Michaels has specific objectives for each student at each site. After the preview, which serves as a language lesson, Ms. Michaels checks to see that everyone has their identification, that everyone has used the restroom, that Kimberly's device has been programmed correctly for the various activities, and that she, herself, has everything she needs. (She occasionally indulges in a sigh of nostalgia for the simplicity of her work at the residential institution.) Everyone makes fun of the large satchel she carries into the community, but she has learned to be prepared. She picks up the bag, as she calls it, as she leaves the room.

The bus stop is right outside the school. While waiting for the bus, each student counts out the correct change from his or her coin purse—they have been riding the bus since elementary school. The bus is right on time and the students put their coins in the container and greet the bus driver. Ricardo begins humming with excitement but subsides immediately when Kimberly touches him on the shoulder and shakes her head. Ms. Michaels decides that Ricardo is going to need support today from the token system that they are trying to phase out. She pulls some chips from her bag and puts them in her pocket. She will give them throughout the trip on a random schedule based on good behavior. Ricardo is familiar with the chips, their value, and the expected behaviors, so no explanation will be required. Ricardo can keep the chips in his pocket until they return to school, where he can exchange them for tangible rewards or time for preferred activities. Ms. Michaels will try to keep the process as unobtrusive as possible.

After an uneventful ride (Sam takes charge of watching for the approach of the right stop and pulling on the cord), the students and Ms. Michaels exit at the stop near the supermarket. Sam and Kimberly immediately go to the time clock, followed by Ricardo after a reminder from Ms. Michaels. All three don red aprons with nametags. Kimberly makes her way independently to the deli, greets Ms. Phelps, her supervisor, with a smile and is greeted in return. Today she will be filling containers with the various dips and spreads made in the deli. Ms. Phelps puts a poster from Ms. Michaels' bag, showing pictures of each step of the task, on the wall over the work area. She has asked for extras of the various posters Kimberly and other students use. She believes they will help many of her nondisabled employees. Ms. Phelps gives Kimberly instructions, watches her go through this new task several times as she would with any employee, and shows her where she can get more containers from the storeroom if she runs out. She has agreed to keep track of the number of times Kimberly either gets new materials or asks for assistance (her communication device will audibly say "I need help, please," when she pushes the right button) rather than whining or shouting in frustration.

Ms. Michaels accompanies Sam and Ricardo to the checkout area where they will be bagging groceries. Sam will also accompany customers to their cars and unload groceries. On his next visit he will begin learning to stock shelves and replenish the produce counters. This particular chain of grocery stores has an excellent history of hiring persons with disabilities, and Sam will have a summer job this year with the possibility of permanent employment when he finishes school. He greets his friend Stan, an older individual with retardation, who is employed full time at the store. They chat as they bag groceries quickly and efficiently. At one point they become excited about an upcoming sports event and are reminded by the checkout clerk to "Keep it down, guys." They comply immediately.

Ms. Michaels meanwhile works directly with Ricardo and the assistant manager who trains the bag persons. They work on correctly loading sacks and being careful with fragile items. The students all take a break and get a soft drink from the machine in the break room. They interact with other employees, disabled and nondisabled, and groan like the others when the break is over. Sam and Kimberly can read the passage of 15 minutes on the clock. Ricardo carries a small timer that he is learning to set for various spans of time. Ms. Michaels observes and records on a small clipboard from her bag the number of times Sam appropriately interacts with a coworker, her main objective for him on this part of the trip.

After about an hour the students remove their aprons and clock out. Calling and waving their farewells, they leave the supermarket. The cafeteria is within walking distance, and Ms. Michaels has planned the excursion so that the restaurant will not be crowded. Sam asks for what he wants; Kimberly points. Ms. Michaels stays close to Ricardo, who is showing signs of agitation. Recognizing a potential crisis, Ms. Michaels decides to abandon education for expedience and begins rewarding with chips and praise any semblance of OK behavior. She pulls from her bag Ricardo's list (made during the rehearsal this morning) of what he wants for lunch.

"Ricardo," she says cheerfully, "I like the way you're walking."

She pops a chip in his pocket.

"Fish," mutters Ricardo as she orders for him.

"Good talking quietly, Ricardo," she says quickly, popping another chip. Ricardo begins to appear less agitated.

"Would you like to order your tea? Tell the lady 'I want tea, please'." Ricardo complies.

"Good ordering, Ricardo," she says, hoping the danger of Ricardo's blowing it has passed.

"Can you carry your tray?" Ricardo picks up the tray and follows Sam. Ms. Michaels picks up his check—she is not about to remind him at this point—along with hers. She is disappointed because she had planned to collect data on his independent accomplishment of getting through the line, a task that she has broken into small steps and that Ricardo has practiced in the school cafeteria.

The students make it to an empty table without mishap and unload their trays. Ricardo suddenly announces loudly that he has to "GO." Ms. Michaels reminds him to announce that quietly in the future and directs him to the men's room. (She feels that she knows the location of every public restroom in the city.) She also reminds herself that she and her colleagues need to work on getting Ricardo to communicate his needs before they become urgent and thus cause him to become agitated.

After a lunch spent discussing the upcoming shopping trip, the students prepare to pay for their meals. Each reads the number on the bottom of the ticket and gets out one more dollar. They hand their ticket and the money to the clerk and hold out their hands for change. Ms. Michaels jots down that Sam, for the first time, responds, "Thanks, you too," to the clerk who encourages him to "Have a nice day." She is really pleased with Sam's social skills.

After another bus ride, they arrive at the department store. All three students need to buy sweats to wear to the health club they will begin using next week. The unisex sweats are in large bins. Kimberly finds the "M" bin, Sam finds the "L" bin, and Ms. Michaels helps Ricardo find the "S" bin. He wants red sweats but sees only black in his bin. He begins to shout and wave his arms. Ms. Michaels hands the bag to Kimberly, instructs Sam and Kimberly to "Come with me, please," and (thankful that Ricardo is "S") hustles him into the gardening equipment area at the back of the store, which she knows from previous trips will be virtually unpopulated. She instructs Ricardo to "Settle down," meanwhile holding him firmly against a wall to prevent his flailing.

An elderly lady, looking horrified, says, "Young lady, you're abusing that poor, afflicted child. I'm going to report this."

Ms. Michaels says, through her gritted teeth, "Kimberly, give the lady a blue card, please." Kimberly reaches into a side pocket and hands the woman an official-looking card explaining Ms. Michaels's qualifications and position, the special needs of her students, and the purpose for their presence in the community. The card invites anyone who has concerns to call Ms. Michaels' supervisor and provides the telephone number. Ricardo, meanwhile, does settle down and apparently no one else has noticed the episode. They return to the shopping floor, pick out sweats (the red ones are in the ***other*** "S" bin), check the label for the correct letter, pay for them, and exit.

Ms. Michaels is delighted that she had earlier decided to put off until later in the week her students' prewashing the sweats at a local group home while they worked on kitchen cleaning. Breathing a sigh of relief, she arrives with her charges at the bus stop. Her sense of relief begins to wane when several minutes pass without the arrival of the bus. Even Sam begins to shift restlessly on the bench and demand, "Where's the bus?" Ms. Michaels reaches into her bag and offers each student a choice of a magazine or a handheld video game. They sit quietly for the remaining 20 minutes of their wait.

Appendix

Professional Resolutions Regarding the Avoidance of Aversive Behavioral Intervention

Several major associations of professionals involved in education and the use of behavioral change procedures have adopted policies recommending that aversive behavioral intervention be avoided. Three of their statements follow. The first is a joint statement by The Arc (Association for Retarded Citizens) and AAMR (Amercian Association on Mental Retardation).

The Arc and AAMR Joint Position Statement on Behavior Supports[1]

Policy Statement

People with mental retardation and related developmental disabilities[2] should have access to behavioral supports that are individually designed, positive, help them learn new skills, provide alternatives to challenging behaviors, offer opportunities for choice and social integration, and allow for environmental modifications.

Issue

Our constituents are frequently subjected to aversive and deprivation procedures[3] that may cause physical and/or psychological harm and are dehumanizing. Furthermore, aversive procedures result in a loss of dignity and inhibit full participation in and ac-

---

[1] Copyright 2002 by The Arc. Reprinted by permission

[2] "People with mental retardation and related developmental disabilities" refers to our constituency, *i.e., those defined by the AAMR classification and the DSM IV. In everyday language they are frequently referred to as people with cognitive, intellectual and developmental disabilities although the professional and legal definitions of those terms both include others and exclude some defined by DSM IV.*

[3] Aversive refers to noxious, painful, or intrusive stimuli or activities applied in response to a behavior that result in physical or psychological pain; as illustrated by, but not limited to, ammonia spray, electric shock, water spray to the face, pinches and deep muscle squeezes, etc. Psychological pain results from verbal abuse, including the ongoing use of stigmatizing language and outwardly aggressive interactions, including tone of voice and body posture. Deprivation refers to such actions as withholding, withdrawing, or delaying visitation or private communication with family and friends, adequate sleep, shelter, bedding, bathroom facilities, and food or drink or subjecting the person to prolonged periods of isolation and seclusion.

ceptance by society. Finally, as more of our constituents move into or remain in the community, there is an urgent need to provide positive behavioral supports in natural settings including the family home.

Position

Considerations before applying a behavioral intervention:

- The nature and extent of the perceived behavior problem and what the person is trying to communicate through this behavior.
- Perspectives from the individual, his or her family, their social/cultural background, and the circumstances in which the behavior occurred.
- Contributing factors such as physical or medical conditions, social and environmental influences, and inappropriate programming as determined through a comprehensive functional analysis[4].

Considerations for acceptability of a behavioral invention:

- Its proven effectiveness.
- Potential secondary effects and risks associated with the intervention.
- Legal, social, and ethical implications.
- Ease and practicality of implementation.

Consideration for designing behavioral supports:

- Determined within the broader context of providing quality medical, psychological, educational, and habilitative services.
- Designed in a person-centered process and applied in a humane and caring manner respecting individual dignity with informed consent[5].
- Systematic in approach, based upon a formal functional analysis, a thorough assessment of each individual's unique abilities and contributions, an understanding of how previous interventions worked, and the least restrictive strategy described in a written plan.
- Based on procedures adequately documented in the clinical and educational research literature.
- Intended to replace challenging behavior with adaptive and socially productive behavior.

Considerations for implementing behavioral supports:

- Implemented in positive and socially supportive environments, including the home.
- Carried out by individuals (staff, family members and others) who have been trained and are qualified to effectively apply positive, non-aversive approaches. Positive interventions for behavioral change should include adaptations to the environment and reinforcers that our constituents and their families identify as "extraordinarily" posi-

[4] A functional analysis involves the observation of how a behavior is affected by both internal (e.g., illness) and external (e.g., social interactions) influences. Such analyses should include an evaluation of factors contributing to the occurrence of the behavior and the consequences resulting from the behavior. The intent of such an analysis is to identify environmental, medical, social, and psychological factors which point to the origin, contribute to the exhibition, and maintain the behavior.

[5] A functional analysis involves the observation of how a behavior is affected by both internal (e.g. illnesses) and external (e.g. social interactions) influences.

tive. Interventions ***must not*** withhold essential food and drink, cause physical and/or psychological pain, uses drugs as restraints, or produce humiliation or discomfort.

- Monitored continuously and systematically to ensure that the approach is consistent with individual needs, positive in its methods, successful in achieving established goals, and changed in a timely fashion if success is not evident or occurring at an appropriate rate.

Adopted: Board of Directors, AAMR

May 28, 2002

Congress of Delegates, The Arc of the United States (Provisional two-year adoption)

November 9, 2002

Council for Exceptional Children Policy on Physical Intervention[6]

The Council recognizes the right to the most effective educational strategies to be the basic educational right of each special education child. Furthermore, the Council believes that the least restrictive positive educational strategies should be used, as they relate to physical intervention, to respect the child's dignity and personal privacy. Additionally, the Council believes that such intervention shall assure the child's physical freedom, social interaction, and individual choice. The intervention must not include procedures which cause pain or trauma. Lastly, behavior intervention plans must be specifically described in the child's written educational plan with agreement from the education staff, the parent, and when appropriate, the child.

The Council recommends that physical intervention be used only if all the following requirements are met:

- The child's behavior is dangerous to herself/himself or others or the behavior is extremely detrimental to or interferes with the education or development of the child.
- Various positive reinforcement techniques have been implemented appropriately and the child has repeatedly failed to respond as documented in the child's records.
- It is evident that withholding physical intervention would significantly impede the child's educational progress as explicitly defined in his/her written educational plan.
- The physical intervention plan specifically will describe the intervention to be implemented, the staff to be responsible for the implementation, the process for documentation, the required training of the staff and supervision of staff as it relates to the intervention and when the intervention will be replaced.
- The physical intervention plan will become part of the written educational plan.
- The physical intervention plan shall encompass the following provisions:
  1. A comprehensive analysis of the child's environment including variables contributing to the inappropriate behavior;
  2. The plan to be developed by a team including professional and parent/guardians, as designated by state/provincial and federal law;
  3. The personnel implementing the plan shall receive specific training congruent with the contents of the plan and receive ongoing supervision from individuals who are trained and skilled in the techniques identified in the plan;

[6] CEC Policy on Physical Intervention, April, 1993. Reprinted by permission.

4. The techniques identified in the physical intervention plan are approved by a physician to not be medically contraindicated for the child (a statement from the physician is necessary); and
5. The impact of the plan on the child's behavior must be consistently evaluated, the results documented, and the plan modified when indicated.

The Council supports the following prohibitions:

- Any intervention that is designed to, or likely to cause physical pain;
- Releasing noxious, toxic or otherwise unpleasant sprays, mists, or substances in proximity to the child's face;
- Any intervention which denies adequate sleep, food, water, shelter, bedding, physical comfort, or access to bathroom facilities;
- Any intervention which is designed to subject, used to subject, or likely to subject the individual to verbal abuse, ridicule or humiliation, or which can be expected to cause excessive emotional trauma;
- Restrictive interventions which employ a device or material or objects that simultaneously immobilize all four extremities, including the procedure known as prone containment, except that containment may be used by trained personnel as a limited emergency intervention;
- Locked seclusion, unless under constant surveillance and observation;
- Any intervention that precludes adequate supervision of the child; and
- Any intervention which deprives the individual of one or more of his or her senses.
- The Council recognizes that emergency physical intervention may be implemented if the child's behavior poses imminent and significant threat to his/her physical well-being or the safety of others. The intervention must be documented and parents/guardians must be notified of the incident.
- However, emergency physical intervention shall not be used as a substitute for systematic behavioral intervention plans that are designed to change, replace, modify or eliminate a targeted behavior.
- Furthermore, the Council expects school districts and other educational agencies to establish policies and comply with state/provincial and federal law and regulations to ensure the protection of the rights of the child, the parent/guardians, the education staff, and the school and local educational agency when physical intervention is applied.

Association for Persons with Severe Handicaps (TASH) Resolution on Positive Behavioral Supports[7]

Statement of Purpose

The purpose of this resolution is to affirm the rights of people with disabilities to receive interventions that are respectful, free of pain and produce positive change for the individuals. TASH's resources, expertise and advocacy are dedicated to the development, implementation, evaluation, and dissemination of positive educational and behavioral support practices that are appropriate for use in typical community settings and are consistent with the commitment to a high quality of life and personal satisfaction with life for individuals with severe disabilities.

[7] Adopted October 1981, Revised November 1986, Revised March 2000. Reprinted by permission.

Rationale

Educational and other habilitative services must employ instructional and support strategies which are consistent with the right of each individual with severe disabilities to effective support without compromising their equally important right to freedom from harm. Access to strategies that humanely assure physical safety is an important part of this right.

Current research and practice have demonstrated the practical efficacy and benefits of functional behavioral assessment and positive interventions for helping to resolve the challenges of problem behavior affecting people with severe disabilities. Individuals with severe disabilities have the right to equal access to medication, emergency, and safety procedures available to individuals not labeled with a disability, according to legal, regulatory, personal, family, and community standards. THEREFORE BE IT RESOLVED, THAT TASH, an international advocacy association of people with disabilities, their family members, other advocates and people who work in the disability field calls for the cessation of the use of any educational, psychological, or behavioral intervention that exhibits some or all of the following characteristics:

1. dehumanization through the use of procedures that are normally unacceptable in community environments for persons who are not labeled with a disability;
2. obvious signs of physical pain experienced by the individual;
3. physical injury and potential or actual side effects such as tissue damage, physical illness, and/or severe physical or emotional stress;
4. effects which would require the involvement of medical personnel, and/or other health care authorities;
5. ambivalence and/or discomfort on the part of the individual, family, staff, and/or caregivers regarding the use of interventions or their own involvement in such interventions;
6. signs of community or peer repulsion or stress from witnessing procedures that are widely divergent from the standard of acceptable practice;
7. the use of physical restraint for any purpose other than crisis intervention to protect individuals from imminent harm; and/or
8. the use of sedative drugs (chemical abuse or restraint) for the sole purpose of behavior management.

BE IT FURTHER RESOLVED, THAT TASH, calls for all persons with severe disabilities to have access to approaches that enable them to positively affect their lives in ways that are meaningful to them.

Therefore, educational and other support services applied in situations involving problem behavior must:

1. be developed in collaboration with the individual in a respectful and culturally sensitive manner that facilitates self-determination;
2. be based on a functional behavioral assessment of the internal and external variables that may be affecting the person's behavior; and
3. use the findings of the aforementioned analysis to develop constructive and comprehensive approaches—including medical, education, communicative, and environmental interventions—to assist the individual to address the circumstances that adversely affect his or her behavior. Further, supports should be provided in a manner that maximizes access to, and participation in, the full range of typical home, school, and community settings, in order to maximize the individual's personal well being.

Glossary

AB design A format for graphing single-subject data which allows for monitoring behavior change. The AB design has two phases: baseline (A) and treatment (b). This design cannot demonstrate a functional relationship between dependent and independent variables because it does not include a replication of the effect of the independent variable. Single-subject experimental designs, which allow for a determination of functional relationship, are extensions of this foundational design.

ABAB design An extension of the AB design in which the independent variable is withdrawn and then reapplied. This reversal design can demonstrate a functional relationship between dependent and independent variables.

ABC design See changing conditions design.

A-B-C assessment A form of information gathering for functional assessment through direct observation of behavior.

abscissa The horizontal or *x* axis of a graph. The time dimension (sessions) is represented along the abscissa.

accountability In education, the assessment of students' progress on a regular basis and the publication of this assessment, as well as goals, objectives, and procedures, to parents, school administrators, and other parties with a right to the information.

acquisition The basic level of student response competence. It implies the student's ability to perform a newly learned response to some criterion of accuracy.

activity reinforcement See Premack principle.

alternating conditions design See alternating treatments design.

alternating treatments design A single-subject experimental design that allows comparison of the effectiveness of two or more treatments. It differs from other single-subject designs in that treatments (sometimes including baseline) are alternated randomly rather than presented sequentially (also known as multiple schedule design, multi-element baseline design, alternating conditions design).

analog A setting sufficiently similar to a natural setting, such as a classroom or work site, to allow inferences that what occurs in the analog setting may occur in the natural setting. Analog settings are often used for functional analysis.

anecdotal reports Written continuous data recording that provides as much information about the behavior and environmental surrounding as possible. The events contained in the report are then sequenced, identifying each behavior, its antecedent, and its consequence.

antecedent stimulus A stimulus that precedes a behavior. This stimulus may or may not serve as discriminative for a specific behavior.

applied behavior analysis Systematic application of behavioral principles to change socially significant behavior to a meaningful degree. Research tools enable users of these principles to verify a functional relationship between a behavior and an intervention.

aversive stimulus A stimulus that decreases the rate or probability of a behavior when presented as a consequence; as such, it is a type of punisher. Alternatively, an aversive stimulus may increase the rate or probability of a behavior when removed as a consequence; as such, it is a negative reinforcer.

backup reinforcer An object of event received in exchange for a specific number of tokens, points, etc.

bar graph A graph that employs vertical bars rather than horizontal lines to indicate levels of performance (also called a histogram).

baseline data Data points that reflect an operant level of the target behavior. Operant level is the natural occurrence of the behavior before intervention. Baseline data serve a purpose similar to that from a pretest, to provide a level of behavior against which the results of an intervention procedure can be compared.

behavior Any observable and measurable act of an individual (also called a response).

behavior support plan A plan for behavior change which (a) summarizes information gathered through various functional assessment strategies, (b) states the hypothesis of function of a target behavior, and (c) details agreed-upon procedures for behavior change and support. (also called Behavior Improvement Plan, Behavior Intervention Plan).

behavioral objective A statement that communicates a proposed change in behavior. A behavioral objective must include statements concerning the learner, the behavior, the conditions under which the behavior will be performed, and the criteria for evaluation.

chaining An instructional procedure that reinforces individual responses in sequence, forming a complex behavior.

changing conditions design A single-subject experimental design that involves successively changing the conditions for response performance in order to evaluate comparative effects. This design does not demonstrate a functional relationship between variables. Also called ABC design.

changing criterion design A single-subject experimental design that involves successively changing the criterion for reinforcement. The criterion is systematically increased or decreased in a stepwise manner.

concept A set of characteristics shared by all members of a set and only the members of that set.

conditioned aversive stimulus A stimulus that has acquired secondary aversive qualities through pairing with an unconditioned aversive stimulus, such as pain or discomfort.

conditioned reinforcer A stimulus that has acquired a reinforcing function through pairing with an unconditioned or natural reinforcer; includes most social, activity, and generalized reinforcers (see secondary reinforcers).

conditions Naturally existing or teacher-created circumstances under which a behavior is to be performed.

consequence Any stimulus presented contingent on a particular response.

continuous behavior A behavior with no clearly discriminable beginning and ending.

continuous schedule of reinforcement (CRF) A schedule of reinforcer delivery that rewards each correct response. The ratio between responses and reinforcement is 1:1.

contracting Placing contingencies for reinforcement (if . . . , then statements) into a written document. This creates a permanent product that can be referred to by teacher and student.

controlled presentations A variation of event recording. A method of predetermining the number of opportunities to respond. This method often involves presenting a specific number of trials per instructional session.

cumulative graph A graph on which the number of occurrences of behavior observed in a given session is added to the number of occurrences of previous sessions in order to derive the data points to be plotted.

dependent variable The behavior to be changed through intervention.

deprivation state A condition in which the student has not had access to a potential reinforcer.

determinism A philosophical belief that events, including human behavior, follow certain fixed patterns.

differential reinforcement of alternative behavior (DRA) Reinforcing a more appropriate form of a behavior than the one in which the student is currently engaged. DRA is often used in conjunction with redirecting behavior.

differential reinforcement of incompatible behavior (DRI) Reinforcing a response that is topographically incompatible with a behavior targeted for reduction.

differential reinforcement of lower rates of behavior (DRL) Delivering reinforcement when the number of responses in a specified period of time is less than or equal to a prescribed limit. This maintains a behavior at a predetermined rate, lower than at its baseline or naturally occurring frequency.

differential reinforcement of other behaviors (DRO) Delivering reinforcement when the target behavior is not emitted for a specified period of time. Reinforcement is contingent on the nonoccurrence of a behavior.

directionality A distinctive ascending or descending trend of data plotted on a graph.

discrete behaviors Behaviors with a clearly discriminable beginning and ending.

discrimination The ability to differentiate among stimuli or environmental events.

discriminative stimulus (S^D) See stimulus control.

duration recording Recording the amount of time between the initiation of a response and its conclusion; an observational recording procedure.

educational goals Statements providing the framework for planning an academic year or an entire unit of learning. It sets the estimated parameters of anticipated academic and social development for which educators are responsible (also called long-term objectives).

enhanced functioning An observable, measurable improvement in functioning, indicating that an intervention has been successful.

errorless learning An instructional procedure that arranges S^DS and prompts to evoke only correct responses.

establishing operations See setting events.

event recording Recording a tally or frequency count of behavior as it occurs within an observation period; an observational recording procedure.

exclusionary time-out Denying access to reinforcement by removing a student from an ongoing activity.

extinction Withholding reinforcement for a previously reinforced behavior to reduce the occurrence of the behavior.

fading The gradual removal of prompts to allow the S^D to occasion a response independently.

fixed-interval schedule (FI) See interval schedules.

fixed-ratio schedule (FR) See ratio schedules.

fixed-response-duration schedule (FRD) See response-duration schedules.

fluency The second level (after acquisition) of student competence. Fluency describes the rate that students accurately perform a response.

frequency The number of times a behavior occurs during an observation period.

functional alternative A less inappropriate behavior that replaces and serves the same communicative or other purposes as a dangerous or maladaptive behavior.

functional analysis Procedures (usually reversal design or multi-element design) that test a hypothesized relationship by manipulating the variables thought to occasion or maintain a behavior in order to verify a functional relationship.

functional assessment Gathering information in order to form a hypothesis as to variables occasioning or maintaining a behavior. May be done by interview, checklist, or direct observation.

functional communication training (FCT) A DRA procedure for replacing an inappropriate communicative behavior with a more standard behavior.

functional equivalency training The process of (a) conducting a functional assessment/analysis of a problem behavior and (b) teaching a socially appropriate behavior to replace it.

functional relationship A quasi-causative relationship between the dependent and independent variables. This relationship is said to exist if the dependent variable systematically changes in the desired direction as a result of the introduction and manipulation of the independent variable.

generalization Expansion of a student's capability of performance beyond those conditions set for initial acquisition. Stimulus generalization refers to performance under conditions—that is, cues, materials, trainers, and environments—other than those present during acquisition. Maintenance refers to continued performance of learned behavior after contingencies have been withdrawn. Response generalization refers to changes in behaviors similar to those directly treated.

generalized conditioned reinforcer A reinforcer associated with a variety of behaviors or with access to a variety of other primary or secondary reinforcers; may simply be called generalized reinforcer.

goal setting A process through which students, in collaboration with teachers or other adults, are encouraged to participate in choosing goals they wish to achieve.

group designs Experimental investigations that focus on data related to a number of individuals.

histogram See bar graph.

humane Marked by consideration for others. In education, providing a safe, comfortable environment, treating all individuals with respect, and providing effective interventions.

independent variable The treatment or intervention that the experimenter manipulates in order to change a behavior.

Individual Transition Plan (ITP) A written plan describing goals for postsecondary vocational or educational placement. The plan includes services to be delivered to facilitate achievement of goals.

Individualized Education Program (IEP) A written educational plan developed for every school-aged student eligible for special education services.

individualized family service plan (IFSP) A written plan describing the needs of infants and toddlers and their families. The plan specifies the goals to be achieved and the services children and their families will receive.

informed consent A legal term meaning that the parents (or surrogates) and the student, if appropriate, have been fully informed, in their native language or other mode of communication, of all information relevant to the activity for which consent is sought and have agreed to the activity.

initial behavior A behavior that resembles the terminal behavior (the ultimate goal of the intervention) along some significant dimension and that the student is already capable of performing (used with shaping).

intermediate behavior Behaviors that represent successive approximations toward the terminal behavior (used with shaping).

intermittent schedules Schedules in which reinforcement follows some, but not all, correct or appropriate responses or follows when a period of appropriate behavior has elapsed. These schedules include ratio, interval, and response-duration schedules.

interobserver agreement See reliability.

interval recording An observational recording system in which an observation period is divided into a number of short intervals. The observer counts the number of intervals when the behavior occurs rather than instances of the behavior.

interval schedules Schedules for the delivery of reinforcers contingent on the occurrence of a behavior following a specified period or interval of time. In a fixed-interval (FI) schedule, the interval of time is standard. For example, FI5 would reinforce the first occurrence of behavior following each 5-minute interval of the observation period. In a variable-interval (VI) schedule, the interval of time varies. For example, VI5 would reinforce the first response that occurs after intervals averaging 5 minutes.

intervention Any change in a person's environment that is designed to change that person's behavior.

latency recording Recording the amount of time between the presentation of the S^D and the initiation of a response.

lawful behavior Behavior that can be predicted by knowledge of antecedent events and a history of reinforcement.

limited hold (LH) A procedure used with interval schedules of reinforcement that restricts the time during which the reinforcer is available.

long-term objectives See educational goals.

maintenance The ability to perform a response over time, even after systematic applied behavior procedures have been withdrawn. See generalization.

modeling Demonstrating a desired behavior in order to prompt an imitative response.

multi-element baseline design See alternating treatments design.

multiple baseline design A single-subject experimental design in which a treatment is replicated across (1) two or more students, (2) two or more behaviors, or (3) two or more settings. Functional relationships may be demonstrated as changes in the dependent variables that occur with the systematic and sequenced introduction of the independent variable.

multiple schedule design See alternating treatments design.

natural aversive stimulus See unconditioned aversive stimulus.

natural reinforcers See primary reinforcers.

negative practice Massed or exaggerated practice of an inappropriate behavior. Decreased occurrence results from fatigue or satiation.

negative reinforcement The contingent removal of an aversive stimulus immediately following a response. Negative reinforcement increases the future rate or probability of the response.

noncontingent reinforcement (NCR) The delivery of reinforcers at predetermined intervals regardless of student behavior.

nonseclusionary time-out A time-out procedure wherein the student is not removed from the instructional setting in which reinforcers are being dispensed. The teacher denies access to reinforcement and manipulates the environment to signal a period of time during which access is denied.

observational recording systems Methods of data collection used to record aspects of behavior while it actually occurs (event recording, interval recording, duration recording, and latency recording).

occasion An antecedent event is said to "occasion" a response when the response occurs reliably in its presence when reinforcement is no longer provided.
operant conditioning The arrangement of environmental variables to establish a functional relationship between a voluntary behavior and its consequences.
operational definition Providing concrete examples of a target behavior. This minimizes disagreements among observers as to the behavior's occurrence.
ordinate The vertical or *y* axis of a graph. The amount or level of the target behavior is represented along the ordinate.
outcome recording See permanent product recording.
overcorrection A procedure used to reduce the occurrence of an inappropriate behavior. The student is taught the appropriate behavior through an exaggeration of experience. There are two forms of overcorrection. In restitutional overcorrection, the student must restore or correct an environment he has disturbed to its condition before the disturbance. The student must then improve it beyond its original condition, thereby overcorrecting the environment. In positive-practice overcorrection, the student, having behaved inappropriately, is required to engage in exaggerated practice of appropriate behaviors.
pairing Simultaneous presentation of primary and secondary reinforcers to condition the secondary reinforcer. Once the association has been established, the secondary reinforcer takes over the reinforcing function, and the primary reinforcer is no longer necessary.
permanent product recording Recording tangible items or environmental effects that result from a behavior, for example, written academic work (also called outcome recording).
pinpointing Specifying in measurable, observable terms a behavior targeted for change.
PLACHECK A data recording system, similar to time sampling, in which several students are observed at the end of each interval.
positive-practice overcorrection See overcorrection.
positive reinforcement The contingent presentation of a stimulus immediately following a response, which increases the future rate or probability of the response. Written as S^{R+}.
positive reinforcer A stimulus that when presented immediately after a response increases the future rate or probability of that response.
Premack principle A principle stating that any high-probability activity may serve as a positive reinforcer for any low-probability activity (also called activity reinforcement).
prerequisites Skills that a student must already have in his repertoire before a given task can be taught successfully.
primary reinforcers Stimuli (such as food) that may have biological importance to an individual; such stimuli are innately motivating (also called natural, unlearned, unconditioned reinforcers).
prompt An added stimulus that increases the probability that the S^D will occasion the desired response (also known as supplementary antecedent stimulus).
punisher A consequent stimulus that decreases the future rate or probability of a behavior.
punishment The contingent presentation of a stimulus immediately following a response, which decreases the future rate or probability of the response.
rate The frequency of a behavior during a defined time period.
ratio graphs Graphs on which all data are plotted at rate per minute.
ratio schedules Schedules for the delivery of reinforcers contingent on the number of correct responses. In a fixed-ratio (FR) schedule, the number of appropriate responses required for reinforcement is held constant. For example, FR5 would reinforce every fifth appropriate response. In a variable-ratio (VR) schedule, the number of appropriate responses required for reinforcement varies. For example, VR5 would reinforce on the average of every fifth appropriate response.
ratio strain A disruption of response performance that follows when the schedule of reinforcement has been thinned so quickly that the ratio between correct responding and reinforcement is too great to maintain an appropriate rate of responding.
reinforcer A consequent stimulus (S^R) that increases or maintains the future rate or probability of occurrence of a behavior.
reinforcer sampling Allowing students to come in contact with potential reinforcers. Reinforcer sampling allows teachers to determine which reinforcers are likely to be effective with individual students. It also allows students to become familiar with previously unknown potential reinforcers.
reliability The consistency of data collection reports among independent observers. The coefficient of reliability is determined by the formula. Also known as interobserver agreement.
respondent conditioning The process of pairing stimuli so that an unconditioned stimulus elicits a response. Most such responses are reflexive; they are not under voluntary control.
response See behavior.
response-cost Reducing inappropriate behavior through withdrawal of specific amounts of reinforcer contingent upon the behavior's occurrence.
response-duration schedules Schedules for the delivery of reinforcers contingent on how long a student engages in a continuous behavior. In a fixed-response-duration (FRD) schedule, the duration of the behavior required for reinforcement is held constant. For example, FRD10 minutes would deliver reinforcement following each 10 minutes of appropriate behavior. In a variable-response-duration (VRD) schedule, the amount of time required for reinforcement varies. For example, VRD10 minutes would deliver reinforcement following an average of 10 minutes of appropriate behavior.
response generalization Unprogrammed changes in similar behaviors when a target behavior is modified. See generalization.
response prompts Teaching procedures in which a student is assisted to respond until the response is under stimulus control.
restitutional overcorrection See overcorrection.
return to baseline See reversal design.
reversal design A single-subject experimental design that removes a treatment condition after intervention in order to verify the existence of a functional relationship. This design has four phases: baseline, imposition of treatment, removal of treatment (also known as return to baseline), and reimposition of treatment (also called ABAB design).

S^D See stimulus control.
S-delta (S^Δ) See stimulus control.
satiation A condition that occurs when there no longer is a state of deprivation.
scatter plot assessment A form of information gathering for functional assessment through direct observation of behavior.
schedules of reinforcement The patterns of timing for delivery of reinforcers (see intermittent schedules, interval schedules, ratio schedules, and response-duration schedules).
seclusionary time-out A time-out procedure that removes the student from the instructional setting as the means of denying access to reinforcement.
secondary reinforcers Stimuli that are initially neutral but acquire reinforcing qualities through pairing with a primary reinforcer (also called conditioned reinforcers).
self-evaluation See self-recording.
self-instruction The process by which a student provides verbal prompts to himself or herself in order to direct or maintain a particular behavior.
self-monitoring See self-recording.
self-observation See self-recording.
self-punishment Self-administration of punishing consequences contingent on behavior.
self-recording Data collection on one's own behavior (also called self-observation, self-evaluation, or self-monitoring).
self-reinforcement (self-punishment) Administering consequences to oneself. Students may be taught to select reinforcers (or punishers), determine criteria for their delivery, and deliver the consequences to themselves.
setting events Circumstances in an individual's life, ranging from cultural influences to an uncomfortable environment, that temporarily alter the power of reinforcers.
shaping Teaching new behaviors through differential reinforcement of successive approximations to a specified target behavior.
single-subject designs Experimental investigations in which each individual serves as his own control. (See AB design, alternating treatments design, changing conditions design, changing criterion design, multiple baseline design, and reversal design.)
social reinforcers A category of secondary reinforcers that includes facial expressions, proximity, contact, privileges, words, and phrases.
social validity The importance of behaviors changed to the community; the acceptability of procedures to consumers.
stimulus class See concept.
stimulus control The relationship in which an antecedent causes behavior or serves as a cue for the behavior to occur. Repeated occurrences of the behavior depend on its being reinforced. An antecedent that serves as an appropriate cue for occasioning a response and therefore results in reinforcement is known as a discriminative stimulus (S^D). An antecedent that does not serve as an appropriate cue for occasioning a response and therefore does not result in reinforcement is known as an S-delta (S^Δ).
stimulus generalization See generalization.
stimulus overselectivity A tendency to attend to only one or a few aspects of a stimulus rather than the stimulus as a whole.
stimulus prompt An alteration of a stimulus to increase the probability of correct responding, often used in errorless learning procedures.
stimulus satiation A condition that exists when an object or event that previously occasioned some response has been presented so frequently that the response no longer occurs in its presence.
supplementary antecedent stimulus See prompt.
task analysis The process of breaking down a complex behavior into its component parts.
terminal behavior The ultimate goal of an intervention (used with shaping).
thinning Making reinforcement gradually available less often or contingent on greater amounts of appropriate behavior.
time-out Reducing inappropriate behavior by denying the student access, for a fixed period of time, to the opportunity to receive reinforcement.
time sampling An observational recording system in which an observation period is divided into equal intervals; the target behavior is observed at the end of each interval.
topography The physical form or description of a motor behavior.
trend A description of data represented on a graph. An ascending or descending trend is defined as three data points in a single direction.
trial A discrete opportunity for occurrence of a behavior. A trial is operationally defined by its three behavioral components: an antecedent stimulus, a response, and a consequating stimulus. The delivery of the antecedent stimulus marks the beginning of the trial, and the delivery of the consequating stimulus signifies the termination of the trial.
unconditioned aversive stimulus A stimulus that results in physical pain or discomfort to an individual (also called universal, natural, or unlearned aversive stimulus).
unconditioned reinforcers See primary reinforcers.
universal aversive stimulus See unconditioned aversive stimulus.
unlearned aversive stimulus See unconditioned aversive stimulus.
unlearned reinforcers See primary reinforcers.
variable Attributes unique to the individual involved in the study or to conditions associated with the environment of the study.
variable-interval (VI) schedule See interval schedules.
variable-ratio (VR) schedule See ratio schedules.
variable-response-duration (VRD) schedule See response-duration schedules.
voluntary consent Consent that is obtained without recourse to threats or rewards.

References

Achenbach, T. H., & Lewis, M. 1971. A proposed model for clinical research and its application to encopresis and enuresis. *Journal of American Academy of Child Psychiatry, 10,* 535–554.

Adair, J., & Schneider, J. 1993. Banking on learning: An incentive system for adolescents in the resource room. *Teaching Exceptional Children, 25* (2), 30–34.

Adams, C., & Kelley, M. 1992. Managing sibling aggression: Overcorrection as an alternative to time-out. *Behavior Therapy, 23,* 707–717.

Adams, N., Martin, R., & Popelka, G. 1971. The influence of time-out on stutterers and their dysfluency. *Behavior Therapy, 2,* 334–339.

Adkins, V., & Matthews, R. 1997. Prompted voiding to reduce incontinence in community-dwelling older adults. *Journal of Applied Behavior Analysis, 30,* 153–156.

Agran, M., Fodor-Davis, J., & Moore, S. 1992. The effects of peer-delivered self-instructional training on a lunch-making work task for students with severe handicaps. *Education and Training in Mental Retardation, 27,* 230–240.

Aiken, J., & Salzberg, C. 1984. The effects of a sensory extinction procedure on stereotypic sounds of two autistic children. *Journal of Autism and Developmental Disorders, 14,* 291–299.

Alberto, P., Heflin, J., & Andrews, D. 2002. Use of the time-out ribbon procedure during community-based instruction. *Journal of Autism and Developmental Disorders, 26,* 297–311.

Alberto, P. A., Sharpton, W. R., Briggs, A., & Stright, M. H. 1986. Facilitating task acquisition through the use of a self-operated auditory prompting system. *Journal of the Association for Persons with Severe Handicaps, 11,* 85–91.

Alberto, P. A., Sharpton, W., & Goldstein, D. 1979. *Project Bridge: Integration of severely retarded students on regular education campuses.* Atlanta: Georgia State University.

Alberto, P., Troutman, A., & Briggs, T. 1983. The use of negative reinforcement to condition a response in a deaf-blind student. *Education of the Visually Handicapped, 15,* 43–50.

Altman, K., & Haavik, S. 1978. Punishment of self-injurious behavior in natural settings using contingent aromatic ammonia. *Behavior Research and Therapy, 16,* 85–96.

Anderson, N., Hawkins, J., Hamilton, R., & Hampton, J. 1999. Effects of transdisciplinary teaming for students with motor disabilities. *Education and Training in Mental Retardation and Developmental Disabilities, 34* (3), 330–341.

Anderson-Inman, L., Walker, H. M., & Purcell, J. 1984. Promoting the transfer of skills across settings: Trans-environmental programming for handicapped students in the mainstream. In W. Heward, T. E. Heron, D. S. Hill, & J. Trap-Porter (Eds.), *Focus on behavior analysis in education.* Columbus, OH: Merrill.

Apolito, P., & Sulzer-Azaroff, B. 1981. Lemon-juice therapy: The control of chronic vomiting in a twelve-year-old profoundly retarded female. *Education and Treatment of Children, 4,* 339–347.

Ardoin, S., Martens, B., & Wolfe, L. 1999. Using high-probability instruction sequences with fading to increase student compliance during transitions. *Journal of Applied Behavior Analysis, 32,* 339–351.

Arndorfer, R., Miltenberger, R., Woster, S., Rortvedt, A., & Gaffaney, T. 1994. Home-based descriptive and experimental analysis of problem behaviors in children. *Topics in Early Childhood Special Education, 14* (1), 64–87.

Arntzen, E., Halstadtro, A., & Halstadtro, M. 2003. Training play behavior in a 5-year-old boy with developmental disabilities. *Journal of Applied Behavior Analysis, 36,* 367–370.

Atthowe, J. M. 1973. Token economies come of age. *Behavior Therapy, 4,* 646–654.

Axelrod, S. 1987. Functional and structural analyses of behavior: Approaches leading to reduced use of punishment procedures? *Research in Developmental Disabilities, 8,* 165–178.

Axelrod, S. 1996. What's wrong with behavior analysis? *Journal of Behavioral Education, 6,* 247–256.

Axelrod, S., Moyer, L., & Berry, B. 1990. Why teachers do not use behavior modification procedures. *Journal of Educational and Psychological Consultation, 1* (4), 310–320.

Ayllon, T. 1963. Intensive treatment of psychotic behavior by stimulus satiation and food reinforcement. *Behavior Research and Therapy, 1,* 53–61.

Ayllon, T. 1977. *Personal communication.*

Ayllon, T., & Azrin, N. 1968. *The token economy: A motivational system for therapy and rehabilitation*. New York: Appleton-Century-Crofts.

Ayllon, T., & Kelly, K. 1974. Reinstating verbal behavior in a functionally mute retardate. *Professional Psychology, 5,* 385–393.

Ayllon, T., & Milan, M. 1979. *Correctional rehabilitation and management: A psychological approach*. New York: Wiley.

Ayllon, T., & Roberts, M. D. 1974. Eliminating discipline problems by strengthening academic performance. *Journal of Applied Behavior Analysis, 7,* 71–76.

Ayllon, T., Layman, D., & Kandel, H. J. 1975. A behavioral-educational alternative to drug control of hyperactive children. *Journal of Applied Behavior Analysis, 8,* 137–146.

Ayllon, T. A., & Michael, J. 1959. The psychiatric nurse as a behavior engineer. *Journal of the Experimental Analysis of Behavior, 2,* 323–334.

Azrin, N. H. 1960. Effects of punishment intensity during variable-interval reinforcement. *Journal of the Experimental Analysis of Behavior, 3,* 128–142.

Azrin, N. H., & Foxx, R. M. 1971. A rapid method of toilet training the institutionalized retarded. *Journal of Applied Behavior Analysis, 4,* 89–99.

Azrin, N. H., & Holz, W. C. 1966. Punishment. In W. A. Honig (Ed.). *Operant behavior: Areas of research and application*. New York: Appleton-Century-Crofts.

Azrin, N. H., & Powers, M. 1975. Eliminating classroom disturbances of emotionally disturbed children by positive practice procedures. *Behavior Therapy, 6,* 525–534.

Azrin, N. H., & Wesolowski, M. D. 1974. Theft reversal: An overcorrection procedure for eliminating stealing by retarded persons. *Journal of Applied Behavior Analysis, 7,* 577–581.

Azrin, N. H., & Wesolowski, M. D. 1975. The use of positive practice to eliminate persistent floor sprawling by profoundly retarded persons. *Behavior Therapy, 6,* 627–631.

Azrin, N. H., Hake, D. G., Holz, W. C., & Hutchinson, R. R. 1965. Motivational aspects of escape from punishment. *Journal of the Experimental Analysis of Behavior, 8,* 31–44.

Azrin, N. H., Holz, W. C., & Hake, D. F. 1963. Fixed-ratio punishment. *Journal of the Experimental Analysis of Behavior, 6,* 141–148.

Azrin, N. H., Hutchinson, R. R., & Hake, D. J. 1966. Extinction-induced aggression. *Journal of the Experimental Analysis of Behavior, 9,* 191–204.

Azrin, N. H., Kaplan, S. J., & Foxx, R. M. 1973. Autism reversal: Eliminating stereotyped self-stimulation of retarded individuals. *American Journal on Mental Deficiency, 78,* 241–248.

Azrin, N. H., Sneed, T. J., & Foxx, R. M. 1973. Drybed: A rapid method of eliminating bedwetting (enuresis) of the retarded. *Behavior Research and Therapy, 11,* 427–434.

Azrin, V., Azrin, N. H., & Armstrong, P. 1977. The student-oriented classroom: A method of improving student conduct and satisfaction. *Behavior Therapy, 8,* 193–204.

Baer, A. M., Rowbury, T., & Baer, D. M. 1973. The development of instructional control over classroom activities of deviant preschool children. *Journal of Applied Behavior Analysis, 6,* 289–298.

Baer, D. 1977. Just because it's reliable doesn't mean that you can use it. *Journal of Applied Behavior Analysis, 10,* 117–119.

Baer, D. M. 1971. Behavior modification: You shouldn't. In E. A. Ramp and B. L. Hopkins (Eds.), *A new direction for education: Behavior analysis* (Vol. 1). Lawrence, KS: University of Kansas Support and Development Center for Follow Through.

Baer, D. M. 1984. Does research on self-control need more control? *Analysis and Intervention in Developmental Disabilities, 4,* 211–284.

Baer, D. M. 1999. *How to plan for generalization*. Austin, TX, Pro-Ed.

Baer, D. M., & Wolf, M. M. 1968. The reinforcement contingency in preschool and remedial education. In R. D. Hess & R. M. Bear (Eds.), *Early education: Current theory, research, and action*. Chicago: Aldine.

Baer, D. M., & Wolf, M. M. 1970. The entry into natural communities of reinforcement. In R. Ulrich, T. Stachnik, & J. Mabry (Eds.), *Control of human behavior* (Vol. 2). Glenview, IL: Scott, Foresman.

Baer, D. M., Wolf, M. M., & Risley, T. R. 1968. Some current dimensions of applied behavior analysis. *Journal of Applied Behavior Analysis, 1,* 91–97.

Baer, D. M., Wolf, M. M., & Risley, T. R. 1987. Some still-current dimensions of applied behavior analysis. *Journal of Applied Behavior Analysis, 20,* 313–327.

Baer, R., Blount, R., Detrich, R., & Stokes, T. 1987. Using intermittent reinforcement to program maintenance of verbal/nonverbal correspondence. *Journal of Applied Behavior Analysis, 20,* 179–184.

Bailey, D. 1984. Effects of lines of progress and semilogarithmic charts on ratings of charted data. *Journal of Applied Behavior Analysis, 17,* 359–365.

Bailey, D. B., Wolery, M., & Sugai, G. M. 1988. *Effective teaching: Principles and procedures of applied behavior analysis with exceptional children*. Boston: Allyn & Bacon.

Bailey, J., & Meyerson, L. 1969. Vibration as a reinforcer with a profoundly retarded child. *Journal of Applied Behavior Analysis, 2,* 135–137.

Bailey, S., Pokrzywinski, J., & Bryant, L. 1983. Using water mist to reduce self-injurious and stereotypic behavior. *Applied Research in Mental Retardation, 4,* 229–241.

Bainbridge, N., & Myles, B. S. 1999. The use of priming to introduce toilet training to a child with autism. *Focus on Autism and Other Developmental Disabilities, 14 (2),* 106–109.

Baker, L. 1982. An evaluation of the role of metacognitive deficits in learning disabilities. *Topics in Learning and Learning Disabilities, 2* (1), 27–35.

Balsam, P. D., & Bondy, A. S. 1983. The negative side effects of reward. *Journal of Applied Behavior Analysis, 16,* 283–296.

Balson, P. M. 1973. Case study: Encopresis: A case with symptom substitution. *Behavior Therapy, 4,* 134–136.

Bandura, A. 1965. Influence of models' reinforcement contingencies on the acquisition of imitative responses. *Journal of Personality and Social Psychology, 1,* 589–595.

Bandura, A. 1969. *Principles of behavior modification*. New York: Holt, Rinehart & Winston.

Bandura, A. 1975. The ethics and social purposes of behavior modification. In C. M. Franks and G. T. Wilson (Eds.), *Annual review of behavior therapy, theory & practice* (Vol. 3, pp. 13–20). New York: Brunner/Mazel.

Barbetta, P. 1990. GOALS: A group-oriented adapted levels systems for children with behavior disorders. *Academic Therapy, 25,* 645–656.

Barkley, R., Copeland, A., & Sivage, C. 1980. A self-control classroom for hyperactive children. *Journal of Autism and Developmental Disorders, 10,* 75–89.

Barlow, D., & Hayes, S. 1979. Alternating treatments design: One strategy for comparing the effects of two treatments in a single subject. *Journal of Applied Behavior Analysis, 12,* 199–210.

Barlow, D., & Hersen, M. 1984. *Single case experimental designs: Strategies for studying behavior change.* New York: Pergamon Press.

Baron, A., Kaufman, A., & Rakavskas, I. 1967. Ineffectiveness of "time-out" punishment in suppressing human operant behavior. *Psychonomic Science, 8,* 329–330.

Barrish, H. H., Saunders, M., & Wolf, M. M. 1969. Good behavior game: Effects of individual contingencies for group consequences on disruptive behavior in a classroom. *Journal of Applied Behavior Analysis, 2,* 119–124.

Barry, L. M., & Messer, J. J. 2003. A practical application of self-management for students diagnosed with attention deficit/hyperactivity disorder. *Journal of Positive Behavioral Interventions, 5,* 238–248.

Barry, L., & Burlew, S. 2004. Using social stories to teach choice and play skills to children with autism. *Focus on Autism and Other Developmental Disabilities, 19,* 45–51.

Barton, E. J., & Ascione, F. R. 1979. Sharing in preschool children: Facilitation, stimulus generalization, response generalization, and maintenance. *Journal of Applied Behavior Analysis, 12,* 417–430.

Barton, L., Brulle, A., & Repp, A. C. 1987. Effects of differential scheduling of time-out to reduce maladaptive responding. *Exceptional Children, 53,* 351–356.

Barton-Arwood, S., Wehby, J., Gunter, P., & Lane, K. 2003. Functional behavior assessment rating scales: Intrarater reliability with students with emotional or behavioral disorders. *Behavioral Disorders, 28,* 386–400.

Bateman, B., & Linden, M. A. 1998. *Better IEPs* (3rd ed.). Longmont, CO: Sopris West.

Batshaw, M. L., & Conlon, C. J. 1997. Substance abuse: a preventable threat to development. In M. L. Batshaw (Ed.), *Children with disabilities* (pp. 143–162). Baltimore: Brookes.

Bauer, A., Shea, T., & Keppler, R. 1986. Levels systems: A framework for the individualization of behavior management. *Behavioral Disorders, 12,* 28–35.

Baumann, B., & Vitali, D. 1982. Facial screening to eliminate trichotillomania in developmentally disabled persons. *Behavior Therapy, 13,* 735–742.

Baumeister, A., & Baumeister, A. 1978. Suppression of repetitive self-injurious behavior by contingent inhalation of aromatic ammonia. *Journal of Autism and Childhood Schizophrenia, 8,* 71–77.

Bayley, N. 1993. *Bayley scales of infant development* (Revised). New York: The Psychological Corporation.

Beare, P., Severson, S., Brandt, P. 2004. The use of a positive procedure to increase engagement on task and decrease challenging behavior. *Behavior Modification, 28,* 28–44.

Becker, J., Turner, S., & Sajwaj, T. 1978. Multiple behavioral effects of the use of lemon juice with a ruminating toddler-age child. *Behavior Modification, 2,* 267–278.

Becker, W. C., & Engelmann, S. E. 1978. Systems for basic instruction: Theory and applications. In A. Catania & T. Brigham (Eds.), *Handbook of applied behavior analysis: Social and instructional processes* (pp. 57–92). Chicago: Science Research Associates.

Becker, W. C., Engelmann, S., & Thomas, D. R. 1975a. *Teaching 1: Classroom management.* Chicago: Science Research Associates.

Becker, W. C., Engelmann, S., & Thomas, D. R. 1975b. *Teaching 2: Cognitive learning and instruction.* Chicago: Science Research Associates.

Belfiore, P., Lee, D., Vargas, A., & Skinner, C. 1997. Effects of high-preference single-digit mathematics problem completion on multiple-digit mathematics problem performance. *Journal of Applied Behavior Analysis, 30,* 327–330.

Bellamy, G. T., Horner, R. & Inman, D. 1979. *Vocational habilitation of severely retarded adults: A direct technology.* Baltimore: University Park Press.

Bennett, K., & Cavanaugh, R. A. 1998. Effects of immediate self-correction, delayed self-correction, and no correction on the acquisition and maintenance of multiplication facts by a fourth-grade student with learning disabilities. *Journal of Applied Behavior Analysis, 31,* 303–306.

Benoit, R. B., & Mayer, G. R. 1974. Extinction: Guidelines for its selection and use. *The Personnel and Guidance Journal, 52,* 290–295.

Berg, W. K., & Wacker, D. P. 1989. Evaluation of tactile prompts with a student who is deaf, blind, and mentally retarded. *Journal of Applied Behavior Analysis, 22,* 93–99.

Berry, H. K. 1969. Phenylketonuria: Diagnosis, treatment and long-term management. In G. Farrell (Ed.), *Congenital mental retardation.* Austin: University of Texas Press.

Bierman, K., Miller, C., & Stabb, S. 1987. Improving the social behavior and peer acceptance of rejected boys: Effects of social skill training with instruction and prohibitions. *Journal of Consulting and Clinical Psychology, 55,* 194–200.

Bijou, S. W., Peterson, R. F., & Ault, M. H. 1968. A method to integrate descriptive and experimental field studies at the level of data and empirical concepts. *Journal of Applied Behavior Analysis, 1,* 175–191.

Bijou, S., Peterson, R., Harris, F., Allen, K., & Johnston, M. 1969. Methodology for experimental studies of young children in natural settings. *Psychological Record, 19,* 177–210.

Billings, D. C., & Wasik, B. H. 1985. Self-instructional training with preschoolers: An attempt to replicate. *Journal of Applied Behavior Analysis, 18,* 61–67.

Billingsley, F. F. 1987. Where are the generalized outcomes? (An examination of instructional objectives.) *Journal of the Association for Persons with Severe Handicaps, 11,* 176–181.

Billingsley, F. F., & Romer, L. T. 1983. Response prompting and the transfer of stimulus control: Methods, research, and a conceptual framework. *Journal of the Association for Persons with Severe Handicaps, 8,* 3–12.

Binder, L., Dixon, M., & Ghezzi, P. 2000. A procedure to teach self-control to children with attention deficit hyperactivity disorder. *Journal of Applied Behavior Analysis, 33,* 233–237.

Birnbrauer, J. S., Bijou, S. W., Wolf, M. M., & Kidder, J. D. 1965. Programmed instruction in the classroom. In L. P. Ullmann & L. Krasner (Eds.), *Case studies in behavior modification.* New York: Holt, Rinehart & Winston.

Birnbrauer, J. S., Wolf, M. M., Kidder, J. D., & Tague, C. E. 1965. Classroom behavior of retarded pupils with token reinforcement. *Journal of Experimental Child Psychology, 2,* 219–235.

Birnie-Selwyn, B., & Guerin, B. 1997. Teaching children to spell. *Journal of Applied Behavior Analysis, 30,* 69–91.

Bloom, B. S. (Ed.). 1956. *Taxonomy of educational objectives handbook I: Cognitive domain.* New York: David McKay.

Blum, N., Mauk, J., McComas, J., & Mace, C. 1996. Separate and combined effects of methylphenidate and a behavioral intervention on disruptive behavior in children with mental retardation. *Journal of Applied Behavior Analysis, 29,* 305–320.

Bogart, L., Piersel, W., & Gross, E. 1995. The long-term treatment of life-threatening pica: A case study of a woman with profound mental retardation living in an applied setting. *Journal of Developmental and Physical Disabilities, 7,* 39–49.

Boring, E. G. 1950. *A history of experimental psychology.* New York: Appleton-Century-Crofts.

Borkowski, J. G. 1992. Metacognitive theory: A framework for teaching literacy, writing, and math skills. *Journal of Learning Disabilities, 25* (4), 253–257.

Bornstein, P. H. 1985. Self-instructional training: A commentary and state-of-the-art. *Journal of Applied Behavior Analysis, 18,* 69–72.

Bornstein, P. H., & Quevillon, R. P. 1976. The effects of a self-instructional package on overactive preschool boys. *Journal of Applied Behavior Analysis, 9,* 179–188.

Bornstein, P., Hamilton, S., & Quevillon, R. 1977. Behavior modification by long distance: Demonstration of functional control over disruptive behavior in a rural classroom setting. *Behavior Modification, 1,* 369–380.

Borrero, J., Vollmer, T., & Wright, C. 2002. An evaluation of contingency strength and response suppression. *Journal of Applied Behavior Analysis, 35,* 337–347.

Boullin, D. J., Coleman, M., O'Brien, R. A., & Rimland, B. 1971. Laboratory predictions of infantile autism based on 5-hydroxytryptamine efflux from blood platelets and their correlation with the Rimland E-2 score. *Journal of Autism and Childhood Schizophrenia, 1,* 63–71.

Bourbeau, P. E., Sowers, J., & Close, D. E. 1986. An experimental analysis of generalization of banking skills from classroom to bank settings in the community. *Education and Training of the Mentally Retarded, 21,* 98–107.

Boyle, J., & Hughes, C. 1994. Effects of self-monitoring and subsequent fading of external prompts on the on-task behavior and task productivity of elementary students with moderate mental retardation. *Journal of Behavioral Education, 4,* 439–457.

Bradley-Johnson, S., Johnson, C., & Sunderman, P. 1983. Comparison of delayed prompting and fading for teaching preschoolers easily confused letters and numbers. *Journal of School Psychology, 21,* 327–335.

Branham, R., Collins, B., Schuster, J., & Kleinert, H. 1999. Teaching community skills to students with moderate disabilities: Comparing combined techniques of classroom simulation, videotape modeling, and community-based instruction. *Education and Training in Mental Retardation and Developmental Disabilities, 34* (2), 170–181.

Brigance, A. 1999. *Brigance diagnostic inventory of basic skills* (Revised). Billerica, MA: Curriculum Associates.

Briggs, A., Alberto, P. A., Berlin, K., McKinley, C., Sharpton, W. R., & Ritts, C. 1990. Generalized use of a self-operated audio prompt system. *Education and Training in Mental Retardation, 25,* 381–389.

Britton, L., Carr, J., Kellum, K., Dozier, C., & Weil, T. 2000. A variation of noncontingent reinforcement in the treatment of aberrant behavior. *Research in Developmental Disabilities, 21,* 425–435.

Brooks, A., Todd, A., Tofflemoyer, S., & Horner, R. 2003. Use of functional assessment and a self-management system to increase academic engagement and work completion. *Journal of Positive Behavior Interventions, 5,* 144–152.

Brooks, J. G. 1990. Teachers and students: Constructivists forging new connections. *Educational Leadership, 47* (5), 68–71.

Brophy, J. 1981. Teacher praise: A functional analysis. *Review of Educational Research, 51,* 5–32.

Broussard, C., & Northrup, J. 1995. An approach to functional assessment and analysis of disruptive behavior in regular education classrooms. *School Psychology Quarterly, 10,* 151–164.

Broussard, C., & Northup, J. 1997. The use of functional analysis to develop peer interventions for disruptive classroom behavior. *School Psychology Quarterly, 12,* 65–76.

Browder, D. M., & Shapiro, E. S. 1985. Applications of self-management to individuals with severe handicaps: A review. *Journal of the Association for Persons with Severe Handicaps, 10,* 200–208.

Browder, D., & Minarovic, T. 2000. Utilizing sight words in self-instruction training for employees with moderate mental retardation in competitive jobs. *Education and Training in Mental Retardation and Developmental Disabilities, 35* (1), 78–89.

Brown, K., Wacker, D., Derby, K. M., Peck, S. Richman, D., Sasso, G., et al. 2000. Evaluating the effects of functional communication training in the presence and absence of establishing operations. *Journal of Applied Behavior Analysis, 33,* 53–71.

Brown, L., Nietupski, J., & Hamre-Nietupski, S. 1976. The criterion of ultimate functioning. In M. A. Thomas (Ed.), *Hey, don't forget about me!* (pp. 2–15). Reston, VA: CEC Information Center.

Brownell, K. D., Coletti, G., Ersner-Hershfield, R., Hershfield, S. M., & Wilson, G. T. 1977. Self-control in school children: Stringency and leniency in self-determined and externally imposed performance standards. *Behavior Therapy, 8,* 442–455.

Browning, E. R. 1983. A memory pacer for improving stimulus generalization. *Journal of Autism and Developmental Disorders, 13,* 427–432.

Browning, R. M. 1980. *Teaching the severely handicapped child: Basic skills for the developmentally disabled.* Boston: Allyn & Bacon.

Bruner, J. S. 1960. *The process of education.* Cambridge, MA: Harvard University Press.

Bryan, L., & Gast, D. 2000. Teaching on-task and on-schedule behaviors to high-functioning children with autism via picture activity schedules. *Journal of Autism and Developmental Disorders, 30* (6), 553–564.

Bryan, T., & Bryan, J. 1978. *Understanding learning disabilities.* Sherman Oaks. CA: Alfred.

Bryant, L. E., & Budd, K. S. 1982. Self-instructional training to increase independent work performance in preschoolers. *Journal of Applied Behavior Analysis, 15,* 259–271.

Buchard, J. D., & Harig, P. T. 1976. Behavior modification and juvenile delinquency. In H. Leitenberg (Ed.), *Handbook of behavior modification and behavior therapy.* Upper Saddle River, NJ: Prentice Hall.

Buggey, T. 1999. Look! I'm on TV: Using videotaped self-modeling to change behavior. *Teaching Exceptional Children, 31,* 27–30.

Buisson, G., Murdock, J., Reynolds, K., & Cronin, M. 1995. Effects of tokens on response latency of students with hearing impairments in a resource room. *Education and Treatment of Children, 18* (4), 408–421.

Burchard, J. D., & Barrera, F. 1972. An analysis of time-out and response cost in a programmed environment. *Journal of Applied Behavior Analysis, 5,* 271–282.

Burgio, L. D., Whitman, T. L., & Johnson, M. R. 1980. A self-instructional package for increasing attending behavior in educable mentally retarded children. *Journal of Applied Behavior Analysis, 13,* 443–459.

Burron, D., & Bucher, B. 1978. Self-instructions as discriminative cues for rule-breaking of rule-following. *Journal of Experimental Child Psychology, 26,* 46–57.

Byrne, G. 1989. We have met the enemy and it is us! *Science, 243,* 32.

Cade, T., & Gunter, P. 2002. Teaching students with severe emotional or behavioral disorders to use a musical mnemonic technique to solve basic division calculations. *Behavioral Disorders, 27,* 208–214.

Callahan, K., & Rademacher, J. 1999. Using self-management strategies to increase the on-task behavior of a student with autism. *Journal of Positive Behavior Interventions, 1* (2), 117–122.

Callicott, K. J., & Park, H. 2003. Effects of self-talk on academic engagement and academic responding. *Behavioral Disorders, 29,* 48–64.

Cameron, J., & Pierce, W. D. 1994. Reinforcement, reward, and intrinsic motivation: A meta-analysis. *Review of Educational Research, 64,* 363–423.

Cameron, J., Banko, K. M. & Pierce, W. D. 2001. Pervasive negative effects of rewards on intrinsic motivation: The myth continues. *The Behavior Analyst, 24,* 1–44.

Cameron, M., Luiselli, J., Littleton, R., & Ferrelli, L. 1996. Component analysis and stimulus control assessment of a behavior deceleration treatment package. *Research in Developmental Disabilities, 17* (3), 203–215.

Campbell, C. R., & Stremel-Campbell, K. 1982. Programming "loose training" as a strategy to facilitate language generalization. *Journal of Applied Behavior Analysis, 15,* 295–305.

Capshew, J. H. 1993. Engineering behavior: Project Pigeon, World War II, and the conditioning of B. F. Skinner. *Technology & Culture,* Fall, 835–857.

Carey, R., & Bucher, B. 1983. Positive practice overcorrection: The effects of duration of positive practice on acquisition and response duration. *Journal of Applied Behavior Analysis, 16,* 101–109.

Carey, R., & Bucher, B. 1986. Positive practice overcorrection: Effects of reinforcing correct performance. *Behavior Modification, 10,* 73–92.

Carpenter, L. B. 2001. Utilizing travel cards to increase productive student behavior, teacher collaboration, and parent-school communication. *Education and Training in Mental Retardation and Developmental Disabilities, 36,* 318–322.

Carpenter, S., & McKee-Higgins, E. 1996. Behavior management in inclusive classrooms. *Remedial and Special Education, 17,* 196–203.

Carr, E. G. 1977. The motivation of self-injurious behavior. A review of some hypotheses. *Psychological Bulletin, 84,* 800–816.

Carr, E. G. 1996. The transfiguration of behavior analysis: Strategies for survival. *Journal of Behavioral Education, 6,* 263–270.

Carr, E. G., & Kologinsky, E. 1983. Acquisition of sign language by autistic children: II. Spontaneity and generalization effects. *Journal of Applied Behavior Analysis, 16,* 297–314.

Carr, E. G., Binkoff, J. A., Kologinsky, E., & Eddy, M. 1978. Acquisition of sign language by autistic children. I: Expressive labeling. *Journal of Applied Behavior Analysis, 11,* 489–501.

Carr, E. G., Smith C. E., Giacin, T. A., Whelan, B. M., & Pancari, J. 2003. Menstrual discomfort as a biological setting event for severe problem behavior: Assessment and intervention. *American Journal on Mental Retardation, 108,* 117–133.

Carr, E., & Durand, M. 1985. Reducing behavior problems through functional communication training. *Journal of Applied Behavior Analysis, 18,* 111–126.

Carr, E., & Newsom, C. 1985. Demand-related tantrums: Conceptualization and treatment. *Behavior Modification, 9,* 403–426.

Carr, E., Levin, L., McConnachie, G., Carlson, J., Kemp, D., & Smith, C. 1994. *Communication-based intervention for problem behavior: A user's guide for producing positive change.* Baltimore: Paul Brookes.

Carr, E., Robinson, S., & Palumbo, L. 1990. The wrong issue: Aversive versus nonaversive treatment. The right issue: Functional versus nonfunctional treatment. In A. Repp & N. Singh (Eds.), *Perspectives on the use of nonaversive and aversive interventions for persons with developmental disabilities.* Sycamore, IL: Sycamore Publishing.

Carr, J., & Britton, L., 1999. Idiosyncratic effects of noncontingent reinforcement on problematic speech. *Behavioral Interventions, 14,* 37–43.

Carr, J., Coriaty, S., Wilder, D., Gaunt, B., Dozier, C., Britton, L., et al. 2000. A review of "noncontingent" reinforcement as treatment for the aberrant behavior of individuals with developmental disabilities. *Research in Developmental Disabilities, 21,* 377–391.

Carr, J., Dozier, C., Patel, M. Adams, A., & Martin, N. 2002. Treatment of automatically reinforced object mouthing with noncontingent reinforcement and response blocking: experimental analysis and social validation. *Research in Developmental Disabilities, 23,* 37–44.

Carr, J., Nicolson, A., & Higbee, T. 2000. Evaluation of a brief multiple-stimulus preference assessment in a naturalistic context. *Journal of Applied Behavior Analysis, 33,* 353–357.

Carton, J., & Schweitzer, J. 1996. Use of a token economy to increase compliance during hemodialysis. *Journal of Applied Behavior Analysis, 29,* 111–113.

Case, L. P., Harris, K. R., & Graham, S. 1992. Improving the mathematical problem-solving skills of students with learning disabilities. *Journal of Special Education, 26* (1), 1–19.

Cashwell, T., Skinner, C., & Smith, E. 2001. Increasing second-grade students' reports of peers' prosocial behaviors via direct instruction, group reinforcement, and progress feedback: A replication and extension. *Education and Treatment of Children, 24,* 161–175.

Cassel, J., & Reid, R. 1996. Use of a self-regulated strategy intervention to improve word problem-solving skills of students with mild disabilities. *Journal of Behavioral Education, 6,* 153–172.

Cautela, J. R. 1971. Covert conditioning. In A. Jacobs & L. B. Sacs (Eds.), *The psychology of private events: Perspective on covert response systems*. Academic Press.

Cavalier, A., Ferretti, R., & Hodges, A. 1997. Self-management within a classroom token economy for students with learning disabilities. *Research in Developmental Disabilities, 18* (3), 167–178.

Cavanaugh, R., Heward, W., & Donelson, F. 1996. Effects of response cards during lesson closure on the academic performance of secondary students in an earth science course. *Journal of Applied Behavior Analysis, 29,* 403–406.

Chadwick, B. A., & Day, R. C. 1971. Systematic reinforcement: Academic performance of underachieving students. *Journal of Applied Behavior Analysis, 4,* 311–319.

Chance, P. 1992. The rewards of learning. *Phi Delta Kappan,* November, 200–207.

Charlop-Christy, M., & Haymes, L. 1998. Using objects of obsession as token reinforcers for children with autism. *Journal of Autism and Developmental Disorders, 28* (3), 189–198.

Cheney, T., & Stein, N. 1974. Fading procedures and oddity learning in kindergarten children. *Journal of Experimental Child Psychology, 17,* 313–321.

Chin, H., & Bernard-Opitz, V. 2000. Teaching conversational skills to children with autism. *Journal of Autism and Developmental Disorders, 30* (6), 569–582.

Cicero, F., & Pfadt, A. 2002. Investigation of a reinforcement-based toilet training procedure for children with autism. *Research in Developmental Disabilities, 23,* 319–331.

Cihak, D., & Alaimo, D. 2003. Using personal digital assistants (PDA) for collecting observational data in the classroom. (Bureau for Students with Multiple and Severe Disabilities Monograph). Atlanta, GA: Georgia State University, Department of Educational Psychology and Special Education.

Cihak, D., Alberto, P., Kessler, K., & Taber, T. 2004. An investigation of instructional scheduling arrangements for community-based instruction. *Research in Developmental Disabilities, 25,* 1–22.

Cihak, D., Alberto, P., Troutman, A., & Flores, M. in press. *Creating graphs for the classroom and publication* [Webtext]. Columbus, OH: Prentice Hall.

Cipani, E. 1995. Be aware of negative reinforcement. *Teaching Exceptional Children, 27* (4), 36–40.

Clinton, L., & Boyce, K. 1975. Acquisition of simple motor imitative behavior in mentally retarded and near mentally retarded children. *American Journal of Mental Deficiency, 79,* 695–700.

Cohen-Almeida, D., Graff, R., & Ahearn, W. 2000. A comparison of verbal and tangible stimulus preference assessments. *Journal of Applied Behavior Analysis, 33,* 329–334.

Cole v. Greenfield-Central Community Schools, 667 F. Supp. 56 (S.D.Ind. 1986).

Cole, G., Montgomery, R., Wilson, K., & Milan, M. 2000. Parametric analysis of overcorrection duration effects. *Behavior Modification, 24,* 359–378.

Coleman, C., & Holmes, P. 1998. The use of noncontingent escape to reduce disruptive behaviors in children with speech delays. *Journal of Applied Behavior Analysis, 31,* 687–690.

Collins, B., & Griffen, A. 1996. Teaching students with moderate disabilities to make safe responses to product warning labels. *Education and Treatment of Children, 19* (1), 30–45.

Cone, J. D. 1973. Assessing the effectiveness of programmed generalization. *Journal of Applied Behavior Analysis, 6,* 713–718.

Conley, O., & Wolery, M. 1980. Treatment by overcorrection of self-injurious eye gouging in preschool blind children. *Journal of Behavior Therapy and Experimental Psychiatry, 11,* 121–125.

Connell, J., & Witt, J. 2004. Applications of computer-based instruction: Using specialized software to aid letter-name and letter-sound recognition. *Journal of Applied Behavior Analysis, 37,* 67–71.

Connolly, A. 1998. *Key math diagnostic arithmetic test* (Revised). Circle Pines, MN: American Guidance Service.

Conroy, M., Asmus, J., Ladwig, C., Sellers, J., & Valcante, G. 2004. The effects of proximity on the classroom behaviors of students with autism in general education settings. *Behavioral Disorders, 29,* 119–129.

Conroy, M., Fox, J., Bucklin, A., & Good, W. 1996. An analysis of the reliability and stability of the Motivation Assessment Scale in assessing the challenging behaviors of persons with developmental disabilities. *Education and Training in Mental Retardation and Developmental Disabilities, 31,* 243–250.

Conroy, M., Fox, J., Crain, L., Jenkins, A., & Belcher, K. 1996. Evaluating the social and ecological validity of analog assessment procedures for challenging behaviors in young children. *Education and Treatment of Children, 19* (3), 233–256.

Cooper, J. 1981. *Measurement and analysis of behavioral techniques.* Upper Saddle River, NJ: Merrill/Prentice Hall.

Cooper, J. 1981. *Measuring behavior* (2nd ed.). Columbus, OH: Merrill.

Cooper, J., Heron, T., & Heward, W. 1987. *Applied behavior analysis.* Columbus, OH: Merrill.

Cooper, L., Wacker, D., Thursby, D., Plagmann, L., Harding, J., Millard, T., et al. 1992. Analysis of the effects of task preferences, task demands, and adult attention on child behavior in outpatient and classroom settings. *Journal of Applied Behavior Analysis, 25,* 823–840.

Copeland, S. R., & Hughes, C. 2000. Acquisition of a picture prompt strategy to increase independent performance. *Education and Training in Mental Retardation and Developmental Disabilities, 35,* 294–305.

Corte, H. E., Wolf, M. M., & Locke, B. J. 1971. A comparison of procedures for eliminating self-injurious behavior of retarded adolescents. *Journal of Applied Behavior Analysis, 4,* 201–213.

Costenbader, V., & Reading-Brown, M. 1995. Isolation timeout used with students with emotional disturbance. *Exceptional Children, 61* (4), 353–363.

Cowdery, G., Iwata, B., & Pace, G. 1990. Effects and side effects of DRO as treatment of self-injurious behavior. *Journal of Applied Behavior Analysis, 23,* 497–506.

Craft, M. A., Alber, S. R., & Heward, W. L. 1998. Teaching elementary students with developmental disabilities to recruit teacher attention in a general education classroom: Effects on teacher praise and academic productivity. *Journal of Applied Behavior Analysis, 31,* 399–415.

Craighead, W. E., Kazdin, A. E., & Mahoney, M. J. 1976. *Behavior modification: Principles, issues, and applications.* Boston: Houghton Mifflin.

Cravioto, J., & Delicardie, E. 1975. Environmental and nutritional deprivation in children with learning disabilities. In W. M. Cruickshank and D. P. Hallahan (Eds.), *Psychoeducational practices: Perceptual and learning disabilities in children* (Vol. 1). Syracuse, NY: Syracuse University Press.

Crawford, J., Brockel, B., Schauss, S., & Miltenberger, R. 1992. A comparison of methods for the functional assessment of stereotypic behavior. *Journal of the Association for Persons with Severe Handicaps, 17,* 77–86.

Cronin, K. A., & Cuvo, A. J. 1979. Teaching mending skills to mentally retarded adolescents. *Journal of Applied Behavior Analysis, 12,* 401–406.

Crossman, E. 1975. Communication. *Journal of Applied Behavior Analysis, 8,* 348.

Cruz, L., & Cullinan, D. 2001. Awarding points, using levels to help children improve behavior. *Teaching Exceptional Children, 33,* 16–23.

Csapo, M. 1981. Comparison of two prompting procedures to increase response fluency among severely handicapped learners. *Journal of the Association for the Severely Handicapped, 6,* 39–47.

Cunningham, E., & O'Neill, R. 2000. Comparison of results of functional assessment and analysis methods with young children with autism. *Education and Training in Mental Retardation and Developmental Disabilities, 35,* 406–414.

Dahlquist, L., & Gil, K. 1986. Using parents to maintain improved dental flossing skills in children. *Journal of Applied Behavior Analysis, 19,* 255–260.

Dalton, T., Martella, R., Marchand-Martella, N. 1999. The effects of a self-management program in reducing off-task behavior. *Journal of Behavioral Education, 9,* 157–176.

Daly, M., Jacob, S., King, D., & Cheramie, G. 1984. The accuracy of teacher predictions of student reward preferences. *Psychology in the Schools, 21,* 520–524.

Darden, S. & Horner, R. H. 1993. Manipulating setting events to decrease problem behaviors. *Teaching Exceptional Children, 24,* 53–55.

Dattilo, J., & Camarata, S. 1991. Facilitating conversation through self-initiated augmentative communication treatment. *Journal of Applied Behavior Analysis, 24* (2), 369–378.

Davis, C. A., Brady, M. P., Williams, R. E., & Burta, M. 1992. The effects of self-operated auditory prompting tapes on the performance fluency of persons with severe mental retardation. *Education and Training in Mental Retardation, 27,* 39–49.

Davis, W. E., & McCaul, E. J. 1991. The emerging crisis: Current and projected status of children in the United States [Monograph]. Orono, ME: Institute for the Study of At-Risk Students.

Davison, G. C., & Stuart, R. B. 1975. Behavior therapy and civil liberties. *American Psychologist, 30* (7), 755–763.

Day, R., Rea, J., Schussler, N., Larsen, S., & Johnson, W. 1988. A functionally based approach to the treatment of self-injurious behavior. *Behavior Modification, 12,* 565–589.

De La Paz, S. 1999. Self-regulated strategy instruction in regular education settings: Improving outcomes for students with and without learning disabilities. *Learning Disabilities Research & Practice, 14* (2), 92–106.

De Lahunt, J., & Curran, J. P. 1976. Effectiveness of negative practice and self-control techniques in the reduction of smoking behavior. *Journal of Consulting and Clinical Psychology, 44,* 1002–1007.

DeCatanzaro, D., & Baldwin, G. 1978. Effective treatment of self-injurious behavior through a forced arm exercise. *Journal of Applied Behavior Analysis, 11,* 433–439.

Dehaven, E. D., Corley, M. J., Hofeling, D. V., & Garcia, E. 1982. Developing generative vocational behaviors in a business setting. *Analysis and Intervention in Developmental Disabilities, 2,* 345–356.

Deitz, D. E. D., & Repp, A. C. 1983. Reducing behavior through reinforcement. *Exceptional Education Quarterly, 3,* 34–46.

Deitz, S. M., & Repp, A. C. 1973. Decreasing classroom misbehavior through the use of DRL schedules of reinforcement. *Journal of Applied Behavior Analysis, 6,* 457–463.

Deitz, S. M., & Repp, A. C. 1974. Differentially reinforcing low rates of misbehavior with normal elementary school children. *Journal of Applied Behavior Analysis, 7,* 622.

Delbert, A. N., & Harmon, A. S. 1972. *New tools for changing behavior.* Champaign, IL: Research Press.

DeLeon, I. G., Iwata, B. A., Conners, J., & Wallace, M. D. 1999. Examination of ambiguous stimulus preferences with duration-based measures. *Journal of Applied Behavior Analysis, 32,* 111–114.

DeLeon, I., & Iwata, B. 1996. Evaluation of a multiple-stimulus presentation format for assessing reinforcer preferences. *Journal of Applied Behavior Analysis, 29,* 519–533.

DeLeon, I., Anders, B., Rodriguez-Catter, V., & Neidert, P. 2000. The effects of noncontingent access to single- versus multiple-stimulus sets on self-injurious behavior. *Journal of Applied Behavior Analysis, 33,* 623–626.

DeLeon, I., Fisher, W., Herman, K., & Crosland, K. 2000. Assessment of a response bias for aggression over functionally equivalent appropriate behavior. *Journal of Applied Behavior Analysis, 33,* 73–77.

Dember, W., & Jenkins, J. 1970. *General psychology: Modeling behavior and experience.* Upper Saddle River, NJ: Prentice Hall.

Denny, M. 1980. Reducing self-stimulatory behavior of mentally retarded persons by alternative positive practice. *American Journal of Mental Deficiency, 84,* 610–615.

Denny, P., & Test, D. 1995. Using the one-more-than technique to teach money counting to individuals with moderate mental retardation: A systematic replication. *Education and Treatment of Children, 18* (4), 422–432.

Deno, S., & Jenkins, J. 1967. *Evaluating preplanning curriculum objectives.* Philadelphia: Research for Better Schools.

Derby, K. M., Wacker, D., Sasso, G., Steege, M., Northup, J., Cigrand, K., et al. 1992. Brief functional assessment techniques to evaluate aberrant behavior in an outpatient setting: A summary of 79 cases. *Journal of Applied Behavior Analysis, 25,* 713–721.

Desrochers, M., Hile, M., & Williams-Mosely, T. 1997. Survey of functional assessment procedures used with individuals who display mental retardation and severe problem behaviors. *American Journal on Mental Retardation, 101,* 535–546.

Dewey, J. 1939. *Experience and education.* New York: Macmillan.

DeWitt, M., Aman, M., & Rojahn, J. 1997. Effects of reinforcement contingencies on performance of children with mental retardation and attention problems. *Journal of Developmental and Physical Disabilities, 9* (2), 101–115.

Dewson, M., & Whiteley, J. 1987. Sensory reinforcement of head turning with nonambulatory, profoundly mentally retarded persons. *Research in Developmental Disabilities, 8,* 413–426.

Diamond, G. W., & Cohen, H. J. 1987. AIDS and developmental disabilities. *Prevention Update,* National Coalition on Prevention of Mental Retardation.

Dickens v. Johnson Country Board of Education, 661 F. Supp. 155 (E. D. Tenn. 1987).

Didden, R., Prinsen, H., & Sigafoos, J. 2000. The blocking effect of pictorial prompts on sight-word reading. *Journal of Applied Behavior Analysis, 33* (3), 317–320.

Digangi, S. A., Maag, J. W., & Rutherford, R. B. 1991. Self-graphing of on-task behavior: Enhancing the reactive effects of self-monitoring on on-task behavior and academic performance. *Learning Disability Quarterly, 14* (3), 221–230.

Dixon, M. R., Hayes, L. J., Binder, L. M., Manthey, S., Sigman, C., & Zdanowski, D. M. 1998. Using a self-control training procedure to increase appropriate behavior. *Journal of Applied Behavior Analysis, 31,* 203–210.

Doke, L. A., & Risley, T. R. 1972. The organization of day-care environments: Required vs. optional activities. *Journal of Applied Behavior Analysis, 5,* 405–420.

Doke, L., & Epstein, L. 1975. Oral overcorrection: Side effects and extended applications. *Journal of Experimental Child Psychology, 20,* 496–511.

Doke, L., Wolery, M., & Sumberg, C. 1983. Treating chronic aggression. *Behavior Modification, 7,* 531–556.

Dollard, N., Christensen, L., Colucci, K., & Epanchin, B. 1996. Constructive classroom management. *Focus on Exceptional Children, 29* (2), 1–12.

Donnelly, D., & Olczak, P. 1990. The effect of differential reinforcement of incompatible behaviors (DRI) on pica for cigarettes in persons with intellectual disability. *Behavior Modification, 14,* 81–96.

Dorsey, M. F., Iwata, B. A., Ong, P., & McSween, T. E. 1980. Treatment of self-injurious behavior using a water mist: Initial response suppression and generalization. *Journal of Applied Behavior Analysis, 13,* 343–353.

Dougherty, S., Fowler, S., & Paine, S. 1985. The use of peer monitors to reduce negative interaction during recess. *Journal of Applied Behavior Analysis, 18,* 141–153.

Dowrick, P. W. 1999. A review of self-modeling and related interventions. *Applied and Preventive Psychology, 8,* 23–29.

Drabman, R. S., Spitalnik, R., & O'Leary, K. D. 1973. Teaching self-control to disruptive children. *Journal of Abnormal Psychology, 82,* 10–16.

Drasgow, E., Halle, J. W., & Ostrosky, M. M. 1998. Effects of differential reinforcement on the generalization of a replacement mand in three children with severe language delays. *Journal of Applied Behavior Analysis, 31,* 357–374.

Drash, P., Ray, R. L., & Tudor, R. 1989. An inexpensive event recorder. *Journal of Applied Behavior Analysis, 22,* 453.

Ducharme, D. E., & Holborn, S. W. 1997. Programming generalization of social skills in preschool children with hearing impairments. *Journal of Applied Behavior Analysis, 30,* 639–651.

Ducharme, J., & Van Houten, R. 1994. Operant extinction in the treatment of severe maladaptive behavior. *Behavior Modification, 18* (2), 139–170.

Duker, P., & Jutten, W. 1997. Establishing gestural yes-no responding with individuals with profound mental retardation. *Education and Training in Mental Retardation, 32* (1), 59–67.

Duker, P., & van Lent, C. 1991. Inducing variablity in communicative gestures used by severely retarded individuals. *Journal of Applied Behavior Analysis, 24,* 379–386.

Duker, P., Hensgens, Y., & Venderbosch, S. 1995. Effectiveness of delayed feedback on the accuracy of teaching communicative gestures to individuals with severe mental retardation. *Research in Developmental Disabilities, 16,* 479–488.

Dunlap, G., & Fox, L. 1999. A demonstration of behavioral support for young children with autism. *Journal of Positive Behavior Interventions, 1* (2), 77–87.

Dunlap, G., & Kern, L. 1996. Modifying instructional activities to promote desirable behavior: A conceptual and practical framework. *School Psychology Quarterly, 11,* 297–312.

Dunlap, G., Koegel, R., Johnson, J., & O'Neill, R. 1987. Maintaining performance of autistic clients in community settings with delayed contingencies. *Journal of Applied Behavior Analysis, 20,* 185–191.

Dunlap, K. 1928. A revision of the fundamental law of habit formation. *Science, 67,* 360–362.

Dunlap, K. 1930. Repetition in breaking of habits. *The Scientific Monthly, 30,* 66–70.

Dunlap, K. 1932. *Habits, their making and unmaking.* New York: Liverright.

DuPaul, G., Guevremont, D., & Barkley, R. 1992. Behavioral treatment of attention-deficit hyperactivity disorder in the classroom. *Behavior Modification, 16,* 204–225.

Durand, V. M. 1990. *Severe behavior problems: A functional communication training approach.* New York: Guilford Press.

Durand, V. M. 1999. Functional communication training using assistive devices: Recruiting natural communities of reinforcement. *Journal of Applied Behavior Analysis, 32,* 247–267.

Durand, V. M., & Carr, E. 1987. Social influences on "self-stimulatory" behavior. *Journal of Applied Behavior Analysis, 20,* 119–132.

Durand, V. M., & Carr, E. 1991. Functional communication training to reduce challenging behavior: Maintenance and application in new settings. *Journal of Applied Behavior Analysis, 24,* 251–264.

Durand, V. M., & Carr, E. 1992. An analysis of maintenance following functional communication training. *Journal of Applied Behavior Analysis, 25,* 777–794.

Durand, V. M., & Crimmins, D. 1988. Identifying the variables maintaining self-injurious behavior. *Journal of Autism and Developmental Disorders, 18,* 99–117.

Durand, V. M., & Crimmins, D. 1992. *The Motivation Assessment Scale (MAS).* Topeka, KS: Monaco & Associates Inc.

Durand, V. M., Berotti, D., & Weiner, J. 1993. Functional communication training: Factors affecting effectiveness, generalization, and maintenance. In J. Reichle & D. Wacker (Eds.), *Communicative alternatives to challenging behavior: Integrating functional assessment and intervention strategies* (pp. 317–340). Baltimore: Paul Brookes.

Dyer, K., Schwartz, I., & Luce, S. 1984. A supervision program for increasing functional activities for severely handicapped students in a residential setting. *Journal of Applied Behavior Analysis, 17* (2), 249–259.

Eckert, T., Ardoin, S., Daly, E., & Martens, B. 2002. Improving oral reading fluency: A brief experimental analysis of combining an antecedent intervention with consequences. *Journal of Applied Behavior Analysis, 35,* 271–281.

Ellingson, S., Miltenberger, R., Stricker, J., Galensky, T., & Garlinghouse, M. 2000. Functional assessment and intervention for challenging behaviors in the classroom by general classroom teachers. *Journal of Positive Behavior Interventions, 2,* 85–97.

Ellingson, S., Miltenberger, R., Stricker, J., Garlinghouse, M., Roberts, J., Galensky, T., & Rapp, J. 2000. Analysis and treatment of finger sucking. *Journal of Applied Behavior Analysis, 33* (1), 41–52.

Ellis, D., Cress, P., & Spellman, C. 1992. Using timers and lap counters to promote self-management of independent exercise in adolescents with mental retardation. *Education and Training in Mental Retardation, 27,* 51–59.

Ellis, J., & Magee, S. 1999. Determination of environmental correlates of disruptive classroom behavior: Integration of functional analysis into public school assessment process. *Education and Treatment of Children, 22,* 291–316.

Embregts, P. J. C. M. 2000. Effectiveness of video feedback and self-management on appropriate social behavior of youth with mild mental retardation. *Research in Developmental Disabilities, 21,* 409–423.

Emshoff, J. G., Redd, W. H., & Davidson, W. S. 1976. Generalization training and the transfer of treatment effects with delinquent adolescents. *Journal of Behavior Therapy and Experimental Psychiatry, 7,* 141–144.

Engelmann, S., & Carnine, D. 1982. *Theory of instruction: Principles and applications.* New York: Irvington.

Engelmann, S., & Colvin, G. 1983. *Generalized compliance training: A direct-instruction program for managing severe behavior problems.* Austin, TX: Pro-Ed.

Engelmann, S., Meyers, L., Carnine, L., Becker, W., Eisele, J., & Johnson, G. 1988. *Corrective reading: Decoding strategies.* Chicago: Science Research Associates.

Epstein, L. H., Doke, L. A., Sajwaj, T. E., Sorrell, S., & Rimmer, B. 1974. Generality and side effects of overcorrection. *Journal of Applied Behavior Analysis, 7,* 385–390.

Epstein, R. 1997. Skinner as self-manager. *Journal of Applied Behavior Analysis, 30,* 545–568.

Etzel, B. C., & LeBlanc, J. M. 1979. The simplest treatment alternative: The law of parsimony applied to choosing appropriate instructional control and errorless-learning procedures for the difficult-to-teach child. *Journal of Autism and Developmental Disorders, 9,* 361–382.

Evans, I., & Meyer, L. 1985. *An educative approach to problem behaviors: A practical decision model for interventions with severely handicapped learners.* Baltimore: Paul H. Brookes.

Fabry, B., Mayhew, G., & Hanson, A. 1984. Incidental teaching of mentally retarded students within a token system. *American Journal of Mental Deficiency, 89,* 29–36.

Fad, K., Patton, J., & Polloway, E. 2000. *Behavioral Intervention Planning.* Austin, TX: Pro-Ed.

Falcomata, T., Roane, H., Hovanetz, A., Kettering, T., & Keeney, K. 2004. An evaluation of response cost in the treatment of inappropriate vocalizations maintained by automatic reinforcement. *Journal of Applied Behavior Analysis, 37,* 83–87.

Falk, G., Dunlap, G., & Kern, L. 1996. An analysis of self-evaluation and videotape feedback for improving the peer interactions of students with externalizing and internalizing behavior problems. *Behavioral Disorders, 21,* 261–276.

Farlow, L., & Snell, M. 1994. *Making the most of student performance data.* Washington, DC: American Association on Mental Retardation.

Favell, J. 1973. Reduction of stereotypes by reinforcement of toy play. *Mental Retardation, 11,* 21–23.

Favell, J. E., McGimsey, J. F., & Jones, M. L. 1978. The use of physical restraint in the treatment of self-injury and as positive reinforcement. *Journal of Applied Behavior Analysis, 11,* 225–241.

Favell, J. E., McGimsey, J. F., Jones, M. L., & Cannon, P. 1981. Physical restraint as positive reinforcement. *American Journal of Mental Deficiency, 85,* 425–432.

Fee, V., Matson, J., & Manikam, R. 1990. A control group outcome study of a nonexclusionary time-out package to improve social skills with preschoolers. *Exceptionality, 1,* 107–121.

Fehr, A., & Beckwith, B. 1989. Water misting: Treating self-injurious behavior in a multiply handicapped, visually impaired child. *Journal of Visual Impairment & Blindness, 83,* 245–248.

Feingold, B. F. 1975. *Why your child is hyperactive.* New York: Random House.

Felixbrod, J. J., & O'Leary, K. D. 1974. Self-determination of academic standards by children: Toward freedom from external control. *Journal of Educational Psychology, 66,* 845–850.

Ferguson, E., & Houghton, S. 1992. The effects of contingent teacher praise, as specified by Canter's assertive discipline programme, on children's on-task behaviour. *Educational Studies, 18,* 83–93.

Ferritor, D. E., Buckholdt, D., Hamblin, R. L., & Smith, L. 1972. The noneffects of contingent reinforcement for attending behavior on work accomplished. *Journal of Applied Behavior Analysis, 5,* 7–17.

Ferster, C. B., & Skinner, B. F. 1957. *Schedules of reinforcement.* New York: Appleton-Century-Crofts.

Ferster, C. B., Culbertson, S., & Boren, M. C. P. 1975. *Behavior principles* (2nd ed.). Upper Saddle River, NJ: Prentice Hall.

Ferster, C., & Culbertson, S. 1982. *Behavior principles* (3rd ed.). Englewood Cliffs, NJ: Prentice Hall.

Ferster, C., Culbertson, S., & Boren, M. 1974. *Behavior principles* (2nd ed.). Englewood Cliffs, NJ: Prentice Hall.

Ficus, R., Schuster, J., Morse, T., & Collins, B. 2002. Teaching elementary students with cognitive disabilities food preparation skills while embedding instructive feedback in the prompt and consequent event. *Education and Training in Mental Retardation and Developmental Disabilities, 37,* 55–69.

Fine, S. 1973. Family therapy and a behavioral approach to childhood obsessive-compulsive neurosis. *Archives of General Psychiatry, 28,* 695–697.

Finkel, A., Derby, K. M., Weber, K., McLaughlin, T. F. 2003. Use of choice to identify behavioral function following an inconclusive brief functional analysis. *Journal of Positive Behavior Interventions, 5,* 112–121.

Firman, K., Beare, P., & Loyd, R. 2002. Enhancing self-management in students with mental retardation: Extrinsic versus intrinsic procedures. *Education and Training in Mental Retardation and Developmental Disabilities, 37,* 163–171.

Fisher, W., & Iwata, B. 1996. On the function of self-restraint and its relationship to self-injury. *Journal of Applied Behavior Analysis, 29,* 93–98.

Fisher, W., Grace, N., & Murphy, C. 1996. Further analysis of the relationship between self-injury and self-restraint. *Journal of Applied Behavior Analysis, 29,* 103–106.

Fisher, W., O'Connor, J., Kurtz, P., DeLeon, I., & Gotjen, D. 2000. The effects of noncontingent delivery of high and low preference stimuli on attention maintained destructive behavior. *Journal of Applied Behavior Analysis, 33,* 79–83.

Fisher, W., Piazza, C., Bowman, L., & Amari, A. 1996. Integrating caregiver report with a systematic choice assessment to enhance reinforcer identification. *American Journal on Mental Retardation, 101,* 15–25.

Fisher, W., Piazza, C., Bowman, L., Hagopian, L., Owens, J., & Slevin, I. 1992. A comparison of two approaches for identifying reinforcers for persons with severe and profound disabilities. *Journal of Applied Behavior Analysis, 25,* 491–498.

Fisher, W., Piazza, C., Bowman, L., Hanley, G., & Adelinis, J. 1997. Direct and collateral effects of restraints and restraint fading. *Journal of Applied Behavior Analysis, 30,* 105–120.

Fisher, W., Thompson, R., Piazza, C., Crosland, K., & Gotjen, D. 1997. On the relative reinforcing effects of choice and differential consequences. *Journal of Applied Behavior Analysis, 30,* 423–438.

Flood, W., & Wilder, D. 2002. Antecedent assessment and assessment-based treatment of off-task behavior in a child diagnosed with attention deficit-hyperactivity disorder. *Education and Treatment of Children, 25,* 331–338.

Flood, W., Wilder, D., Flood, A., & Masuda, A. 2002. Peer-mediated reinforcement plus prompting as treatment for off-task behavior in children with attention deficit hyperactivity disorder. *Journal of Applied Behavior Analysis, 35,* 199–204.

Fosnot, C. 1996. Constructivism: A psychological theory of learning. In C. Fosnot (Ed.), *Constructivism: Theory, perspectives, and practice,* (pp. 8–33). New York: Teachers College Press.

Fovel, J., Lash, P., Barron, D., & Roberts, M. S. 1989. A survey of self-restraint, self-injury, and other maladaptive behaviors in an institutionalized retarded population. *Research in Developmental Disabilities, 10* (4), 377–382.

Fowler, S. A., & Baer, D. M. 1981. "Do I have to be good all day?": The timing of delayed reinforcement as a factor in generalization. *Journal of Applied Behavior Analysis, 14,* 13–24.

Foxx, R. 1990. "Harry": A ten-year follow-up of the successful treatment of a self-injurious man. *Research in Developmental Disabilities, 10,* 377–382.

Foxx, R. M. 1976. Increasing a mildly retarded woman's attendance at self-help classes by overcorrection and instruction. *Behavior Therapy, 7,* 390–396.

Foxx, R. M., & Azrin, N. H. 1972. Restitution: A method of eliminating aggressive-disruptive behavior of retarded and brain-damaged patients. *Behavior Research and Therapy, 10,* 15–27.

Foxx, R. M., & Azrin, N. H. 1973. The elimination of autistic self-stimulatory behavior by overcorrection. *Journal of Applied Behavior Analysis, 6,* 1–14.

Foxx, R. M., & Azrin, N. H. 1973. *Toilet training the retarded: A rapid program for day and nighttime independent toileting.* Champaign, IL: Research Press.

Foxx, R. M., & Shapiro, S. T. 1978. The time-out ribbon: A nonseclusionary timeout procedure. *Journal of Applied Behavior Analysis, 11,* 125–136.

Foxx, R. M., McMorrow, M. J., & Mennemeier, M. 1984. Teaching social/vocational skills to retarded adults with a modified table game: An analysis of generalization. *Journal of Applied Behavior Analysis, 17,* 343–352.

Foxx, R., & Bechtel, D. 1982. Overcorrection. In M. Hersen, R. Eisler, & P. Miller (Eds.), *Progress in behavior modification* (Vol. 13, pp. 227–288). New York: Academic.

Foxx, R., & Shapiro, S. 1978. The timeout ribbon: A nonexclusionary timeout procedure. *Journal of Applied Behavior Analysis, 11,* 125–136.

Fradenburg, L., Harrison, R., & Baer, D. 1995. The effect of some environmental factors on inter-observer agreement. *Research in Developmental Disabilities, 16* (6), 425–437.

France, K., & Hudson, S. 1990. Behavior management of infant sleep disturbance. *Journal of Applied Behavior Analysis, 23,* 91–98.

Frank, A. R., Wacker, D. P., Berg, W. K., & McMahon, C. M. 1985. Teaching selected microcomputer skills to retarded students using picture prompts. *Journal of Applied Behavior Analysis, 18,* 179–185.

Franklin, R., Allison, D., & Gorman, B. 1996. *Design and analysis of single-case research.* Mahwah, NJ: Erlbaum Publishing.

Franks, C. M., & Wilson, G. T. (Eds.). 1976. *Annual review of behavior therapy, theory & practice.* New York: Brunner/Mazel.

Fredericksen, L. W., & Fredericksen, C. B. 1975. Teacher determined and self-determined token reinforcement in a special education classroom. *Behavior Therapy, 6,* 310–314.

Freeland, J., & Noell, G. 1999. Maintaining accurate math responses in elementary school students: The effects of delayed intermittent reinforcement and programming common stimuli. *Journal of Applied Behavior Analysis, 32* (2), 211–215.

Freeman, B., Graham, V., & Ritvo, E. 1975. Reduction of self-destructive behavior by overcorrection. *Psychological Reports, 37,* 446.

Freeman, K. A., & Dexter-Mazza, E. T. 2004. Using self-monitoring with an adolescent with disruptive classroom behavior. *Behavior Modification, 28,* 402–419.

Friman, P. 1990. Nonaversive treatment of high-rate disruption: Child and provider effects. *Exceptional Children, 57,* 64–69.

Friman, P. 2000. "Transitional objects" as establishing operations for thumb sucking. *Journal of Applied Behavior Analysis, 33* (4), 507–509.

Friman, P., & Poling, A. 1995. Making life easier with effort: Basic findings and applied research on response effort. *Journal of Applied Behavior Analysis, 28,* 583–590.

Fuchs, L., & Fuchs, D. 1986. Effects of systematic formative evaluation: A meta-analysis. *Exceptional Children, 53,* 199–208.

Fuchs, L., Fuchs, D., & Deno, S. 1988. Importance of goal ambitiousness and goal mastery to student achievement. *Exceptional Children, 52,* 63–71.

Fueyo, V., & Bushell, D. 1998. Using number line procedures and peer tutoring to improve the mathematics computation of low-performing first graders. *Journal of Applied Behavior Analysis, 31,* 417–430.

Gable, R. 1999. Functional assessment in school settings. *Behavioral Disorders, 24,* 246–248.

Gagne, R. 1985. *The conditions of learning & theory of instruction* (4th ed.). Fort Worth, TX: Holt, Rinehart & Winston, Inc.

Garcia, E. 1974. The training and generalization of a conversational speech form in nonverbal retardates. *Journal of Applied Behavior Analysis, 7,* 137–149.

Garcia, E., Baer, D. M., & Firestone, I. 1971. The development of generalized imitation within topographically determined boundaries. *Journal of Applied Behavior Analysis, 4,* 101–112.

Garcia, E., Guess, D., & Byrnes, J. 1973. Development of syntax in a retarded girl using procedures of imitation, reinforcement, and modelling. *Journal of Applied Behavior Analysis, 6,* 299–310.

Gast, D., & Nelson, C. M. 1977a. Legal and ethical considerations for the use of timeout in special education settings. *The Journal of Special Education, 11,* 457–467.

Gast, D., & Nelson, C. M. 1977b. Time-out in the classroom: Implications for special education. *Exceptional Children, 43,* 461–464.

Gast, D., & Wolery, M. 1987. Severe maladaptive behaviors. In M. E. Snell (Ed.), *Systematic instruction of people with severe handicaps* (3rd ed.). Columbus, OH: Merrill.

Gay, G. 2002. Culturally responsive teaching in special education for ethnically diverse students; setting the stage. *Qualitative Studies in Education, 15,* 613–629.

Gaylord-Ross, R. J., & Holvoet, J. 1985. *Strategies for educating students with severe handicaps.* Boston: Little, Brown.

Gelfand, D. L., & Hartmann, D. P. 1975. *Child behavior analysis and therapy.* New York: Pergamon Press.

Gelfand, D. M., Jenson, W. R., & Drew, C. J. 1988. *Understanding children's behavior disorders.* New York: Holt, Rinehart & Winston.

Gesell, A., & Ilg, F. L. 1943. *Infant and child in the culture of today.* New York: Harper.

Gibbs, J., & Luyben, P. 1985. Treatment of self-injurious behavior: Contingent versus noncontingent positive practice overcorrection. *Behavior Modification, 9,* 3–21.

Gilbert, G. 1975. Extinction procedures: Proceed with caution. *Mental Retardation, 13,* 25–29.

Gilberts, G., Agran, M., Hughes, C., & Wehmeyer, M. 2001. The effects of peer delivered self-monitoring strategies on the participation of students with severe disabilities in general education classrooms. *JASH, 26,* 25–36.

Goldiamond, I. 1975. Toward a constructional approach to social problems: Ethical and constitutional issues raised by applied behavior analysis. In C. M. Franks & G. T. Wilson (Eds.), *Annual review of behavior therapy, theory & practice* (Vol. 3, pp. 21–63). New York: Brunner/Mazel.

Goldstein, K. 1939. *The organism.* New York: American Book.

Golonka, Z., Wacker, D., Berg, W., Derby, K., Harding, J., & Peck, S. 2000. Effects of escape to alone versus escape to enriched environments on adaptive and aberrant behavior. *Journal of Applied Behavior Analysis, 33,* 243–246.

Grace, N., Thompson, R., & Fisher, W. 1996. The treatment of covert self-injury through contingencies on response products. *Journal of Applied Behavior Analysis, 29,* 239–242.

Graff, R., & Libby, M. 1999. A comparison of presession and within-session reinforcement choice. *Journal of Applied Behavior Analysis, 32,* 161–173.

Green, C., Gardner, S., Canipe, V., & Reid, D. 1994. Analyzing alertness among people with profound multiple disabilities. *Journal of Applied Behavior Analysis, 27,* 519–531.

Green, C., Reid, D., White, L., Halford, R., Brittain, D., & Gardner, S. 1988. Identifying reinforcers for persons with profound handicaps: Staff opinion vs. systematic assessment of preferences. *Journal of Applied Behavior Analysis, 21,* 31–43.

Greenwood, C. R., Sloane, N. H., Jr., & Baskin, A. 1974. Training elementary aged peer-behavior managers to control small group programmed mathematics. *Journal of Applied Behavior Analysis, 7,* 103–114.

Gronlund, N. 1985. *Stating objectives for classroom instruction.* New York: Macmillan.

Gross, A., Berler, E., & Drabman, R. 1982. Reduction of aggressive behavior in a retarded boy using a water squirt. *Journal of Behavior Therapy and Experimental Psychiatry, 13,* 95–98.

Grossi, T., & Heward, W. 1998. Using self-evaluation to improve the work productivity of trainees in community-based restaurant training program. *Education and Training in Mental Retardation and Developmental Disabilities, 33* (3), 248–263.

Grskovic, J., & Belfiore, P. 1996. Improving the spelling performance of students with disabilities. *Journal of Behavioral Education, 6,* 343–354.

Guess, D., Sailor, W., Rutherford, G., & Baer, D. M. 1968. An experimental analysis of linguistic development: The productive use of the plural morpheme. *Journal of Applied Behavior Analysis, 1,* 297–306.

Gumpel, T., & Shlomit, D. 2000. Exploring the efficacy of self-regulatory training as a possible alternative to social skills training. *Behavioral Disorders, 25,* 131–141.

Gutowski, S. 1996. Response acquisition for music or beverages in adults with profound multiple handicaps. *Journal of Developmental and Physical Disabilities, 8* (3), 221–231.

Haberman, M. 1995. *Star teachers of children in poverty.* West Lafayette, IN: Kappa Delta Pi.

Hagopian, L., Farrell, D., & Amari, A. 1996. Treating total liquid refusal with backward chaining and fading. *Journal of Applied Behavior Analysis, 29,* 573–575.

Hagopian, L., Wilson, D., & Wilder, D. 2001. Assessment and treatment of problem behavior maintained by escape from attention and access to tangible items. *Journal of Applied Behavior Analysis, 34,* 229–232.

Haisten, C. C. 1996. The role of verbalization in correspondence training procedures employed with students with severe emotional/behavioral disorders. Unpublished doctoral dissertation, Georgia State University.

Hall, C. S. 1954. A primer of Freudian Psychology. Cleveland: World Publishing.

Hall, C., Sheldon-Wildgen, J., & Sherman, J. A. 1980. Teaching job interview skills to retarded clients. *Journal of Applied Behavior Analysis, 13,* 433–442.

Hall, R. B., & Hall, M. 1980. *How to use time-out.* Lawrence, KS: H&H Enterprises.

Hall, R. V., & Fox, R. G. 1977. Changing-criterion designs: An applied behavior analysis procedure. In B. C. Etzel, J. M. LeBlanc, & D. M. Baer (Eds.), *New developments in behavioral research: Theory, method and application.* Hillsdale, NJ: Lawrence Erlbaum Associates, Inc., Publishers (In honor of Sidney W. Bijou).

Hall, R. V., & Hall, M. C. 1980. *How to select reinforcers.* Lawrence, KS: H&H Enterprises.

Hall, R. V., Fox, R., Willard, D., Goldsmith, L., Emerson, M., Owen, M., et al. 1971. The teacher as observer and experimenter in the modification of disputing and talking-out behaviors. *Journal of Applied Behavior Analysis, 4,* 141–149.

Hall, R. V., Lund, D., & Jackson, D. 1968. Effects of teacher attention on study behavior. *Journal of Applied Behavior Analysis, 1,* 1–12.

Hallahan, D. P., Kneedler, R. D., & Lloyd, J. W. 1983. Cognitive behavior modification techniques for learning disabled children: Self-instruction and self-monitoring. In J. D.

McKinney and L. Feagans (Eds.), *Current topics in learning disabilities* (Vol. 1). Norwood, NJ: Ablex.

Halle, J. W. 1989. Identifying stimuli in the natural environment that control verbal responses. *Journal of Speech and Hearing Disorders, 54,* 500–504.

Halle, J. W., & Holt, B. 1991. Assessing stimulus control in natural settings: An analysis of stimuli that acquire control during training. *Journal of Applied Behavior Analysis, 24,* 579–589.

Hamad, C., Isley, E., & Lowry, M. 1983. The use of mechanical restraint and response incompatibility to modify self-injurious behavior: A case study. *Mental Retardation, 21,* 213–217.

Handen, B., Parrish, J., McClung, T., Kerwin, M., & Evans, L. 1992. Using guided compliance versus time out to promote child compliance: A preliminary comparative analysis in an analogue context. *Research in Development Disabilities, 13,* 157–170.

Hanley, G., Piazza, C., & Fisher, W. 1997. Noncontingent presentation of attention and alternative stimuli in the treatment of attention-maintained destructive behavior. *Journal of Applied Behavior Analysis, 30* (2), 229–237.

Hanley, G., Piazza, C., Fisher, W., & Eidolons, J. 1997. Stimulus control and resistance to extinction in attention-maintained SIB. *Research in Developmental Disabilities, 18,* 251–260.

Hanley, G., Piazza, C., Keeney, K., Blackeley-Smith, A., & Worsdell, A. 1998. Effects of wrist weights on self-injurious and adaptive behaviors. *Journal of Applied Behavior Analysis, 31,* 307–310.

Harding, J., Wacker, D., Berg, W., Barretto, A., Winborn, L., & Gardner, A. 2001. Analysis of response class hierarchies with attention-maintained problem behaviors. *Journal of Applied Behavior Analysis, 34,* 61–64.

Harding, J., Wacker, D., Berg, W., Cooper, L., Asmus, J., Mlela, K., et al. 1999. An analysis of choice making in the assessment of young children with severe behavior problems. *Journal of Applied Behavior Analysis, 32,* 63–82.

Haring, N. G. 1988. *Investigating the problem of skill generalization: Literature review III.* Seattle, WA: Washington Research Organization.

Haring, N. G., & Liberty, K. A. 1990. Matching strategies with performance in facilitating generalization. *Focus on Exceptional Children, 22* (8), 1–16.

Haring, T. G., Breen, C. G., Weiner, J., Kennedy, C. H., & Bednersh, F. 1995. Using videotape modeling to facilitate generalized purchasing skills. *Journal of Behavioral Education, 5,* 29–53.

Haring, T., & Kennedy, C. 1990. Contextual control of problem behavior in students with severe disabilities. *Journal of Applied Behavior Analysis, 23,* 235–243.

Haring, T., Roger, B., Lee, M., Breen, C., & Gaylord-Ross, R. 1986. Teaching social language to moderately handicapped students. *Journal of Applied Behavior Analysis, 19,* 159–171.

Harris, F. R., Johnston, M. K., Kelley, C. S., & Wolf, M. M. 1964. Effects of social reinforcement on repressed crawling of a nursery school child. *Journal of Educational Psychology, 55,* 34–41.

Harris, J. 1996. Physical restraint procedures for managing challenging behaviours presented by mentally retarded adults and children. *Research in Developmental Disabilities, 17* (2), 99–134.

Harris, K. R., Graham, S., Reid, R., McElroy, K., & Hamby, R. S. 1994. Self-monitoring of attention versus self-monitoring of performance; Replication and cross-task comparison studies. *Learning Disabilities Quarterly, 17,* 121–139.

Harris, V. W., & Herman, J. A. 1973. Use and analysis of the "Good Behavior Game" to reduce disruptive classroom behavior. *Journal of Applied Behavior Analysis, 6,* 405–417.

Harrison, J., Gunter, P., Reed, T., & Lee, J. 1996. Teacher instructional language and negative reinforcement: A conceptual framework for working with students with emotional and behavioral disorders. *Education and Treatment of Children, 19* (2), 183–196.

Hartmann, D. P., & Atkinson, D. 1973. Having your cake and eating it too: A note on some apparent contradictions between therapeutic achievements and design requirements in N-1/21 studies. *Behavior Therapy, 4,* 589–591.

Hartmann, D. P., & Hall, R. V. 1976. The changing criterion design. *Journal of Applied Behavior Analysis, 9,* 527–532.

Haughton, E., & Ayllon, T. 1965. Production and elimination of symptomatic behavior. In L. P. Ullmann & L. Krasner (Eds.), *Case studies in behavior modification* (pp. 94–98). New York: Holt, Rinehart & Winston.

Haupt, E. J., Van Kirk, M. J., & Terraciano, T. 1975. An inexpensive fading procedure to decrease errors and increase retention of number facts. In E. Ramp & G. Semb (Eds.), *Behavior analysis: Areas of research and application.* Upper Saddle River, NJ: Prentice Hall.

Hawkins, R. P., & Dotson, V. S. 1975. Reliability scores that delude: An Alice in Wonderland trip through the misleading characteristics of inter-observer agreement scores in interval recording. In E. Ramp & G. Semb (Eds.), *Behavior analysis: Areas of research and application* (pp. 359–376). Englewood Cliffs, NJ: Prentice-Hall.

Hay, D., Murray, P., Cecire, S., & Nash, A. 1985. Social learning and social behavior in early life. *Child Development, 56,* 43–57.

Hay, L., Nelson, R., & Hay, W. 1977. Some methodological problems in the use of teachers as observers. *Journal of Applied Behavior Analysis, 10,* 345–348.

Hay, L., Nelson, R., & Hay, W. 1980. Methodological problems in the use of participant observers. *Journal of Applied Behavior Analysis, 13,* 501–504.

Hayes v. Unified School District No. 377, 877 F. 2d 809 (10th Cir. 1989).

Hayes, S. C., & Nelson, R. O. 1983. Similar reactivity produced by external cues and self-monitoring. *Behavior Modification, 7,* 183–196.

Hayes, S. C., Rosenfarb, I., Wulfert, E., Munt, E. D., Korn, Z., & Zettle, R. D. 1985. Self-reinforcement effects: An artifact of social standard setting? *Journal of Applied Behavior Analysis, 18,* 201–214.

Hegel, M., & Ferguson, R. 2000. Differential reinforcement of other behavior (DRO) to reduce aggressive behavior following traumatic brain injury. *Behavior Modification, 24,* 94–101.

Heller, M., & White, M. 1975. Rates of teacher approval and disapproval to higher and lower ability classes. *Journal of Educational Psychology, 67,* 796–800.

Herrnstein, B. J., & Loveland, D. H. 1964. Complex visual concept in the pigeon. *Science, 146,* 549–550.

Hersen, M., & Barlow, D. H. 1976. *Single-case experimental designs: Strategies for studying behavior change.* New York: Pergamon Press.

Hersen, M., & Bellack, A. S. 1977. Assessment of social skills. In A. R. Ciminero, K. S. Calhoun, & H. E. Adams (Eds.), *Handbook for behavioral assessment*. New York: Wiley.

Hetherington, E. M., & Parke, R. D. 1986. *Child psychology: A contemporary viewpoint* (3rd ed.). New York: McGraw-Hill.

Heward, W. L. 2003. Ten faulty notions about teaching and learning that hinder the effectiveness of special education. *The Journal of Special Education, 36,* pp. 186–205.

Heward, W. L., & Eachus, H. T. 1979. Acquisition of adjectives and adverbs in sentences written by hearing impaired and aphasic children. *Journal of Applied Behavior Analysis, 12,* 391–400.

Higa, W. R., Tharpe, R. G., & Calkins, R. P. 1978. Developmental verbal control of behavior: Implications for self-instructional training. *Journal of Experimental Child Psychology, 26,* 489–497.

Higbee, T., Carr, J., & Harrison, C. 1999. The effects of pictorial versus tangible stimuli in stimulus-preference assessments. *Research in Developmental Disabilities, 20,* 63–72.

Higgins, J., Williams, R., & McLaughlin, T. F. 2001. The effects of a token economy employing instructional consequences for a third-grade student with learning disabilities: A data-based case study. *Education and Treatment of Children, 24,* 99–106.

Hill, W. F. 1963. *Learning: A survey of psychological interpretations*. San Francisco: Chandler.

Hill, W. F. 1970. *Psychology: Principles and problems*. Philadelphia: Lippincott.

Hinerman, P., Jenson, W., Walker, G., & Peterson, P. 1982. Positive practice overcorrection combined with additional procedures to teach signed words to an autistic child. *Journal of Autism and Developmental Disorders, 12,* 253–263.

Hinton, L. M., & Kern, L. 1999. Increasing homework completion by incorporating student interests. *Journal of Positive Behavior Interventions, 1* (4), 231–234.

Holden, C. 1973. Psychosurgery: Legitimate therapy or laundered lobotomy? *Science, 173,* 1104–1112.

Holland, J. G., & Skinner, B. F. 1961. *The analysis of behavior.* New York: McGraw-Hill.

Holman, J. 1977. The moral risk and high cost of ecological concern in applied behavior analysis. *Journal of Teacher Education, 37,* 27–34.

Holmes, G., Cautela, J., Simpson, M., Motes, P., & Gold, J. 1998. Factor structure of the school reinforcement survey schedule: School is more than grades. *Journal of Behavioral Education, 8,* 131–140.

Homme, L., Csanyi, A., Gonzales, M., & Rechs, J. 1970. *How to use Contingency contracting in the classroom*. Champaign, IL: Research Press.

Honig v. Doe, 56 S. Ct. 27 1988.

Horcones, 1992. Natural reinforcements: A way to improve education. *Journal of Applied Behavior Analysis, 25,* 71–75.

Horner, R. D., & Baer, D. M. 1978. Multiple-probe technique: A variation on the multiple baseline. *Journal of Applied Behavior Analysis, 11,* 189–196.

Horner, R. H., & Budd, C. M. 1985. Acquisition of manual sign use: Collateral reduction of maladaptive behavior, and factors limiting generalization. *Education and Training of the Mentally Retarded, 20,* 39–47.

Horner, R. H., Eberhard, J. M., & Sheehan, M. R. 1986. Teaching generalized table bussing: The importance of negative teaching examples. *Behavior Modification, 10,* 457–471.

Horner, R. H., Jones, D., & Williams, J. A. 1985. A functional approach to teaching generalized street crossing. *Journal of the Association for Persons with Severe Handicaps, 13,* 71–78.

Horner, R. H., McDonnell, J. J., & Bellamy, G. T. Undated. Teaching generalized skills: General case instruction in simulation and community settings (Contract No. 300-82-0362). Unpublished manuscript, University of Oregon.

Horner, R. H., Williams, J. A., & Stevely, J. D. 1984. Acquisition of generalized telephone use by students with severe mental retardation. Unpublished manuscript.

Horner, R. T., & Harvey, M. T. 2000. Review of antecedent control: Innovative approaches to behavioral support. *Journal of Applied Behavior Analysis, 33,* 643–651.

Horner, R., & Day, H. 1991. The effects or response efficiency on functionally equivalent competing behaviors. *Journal of Applied Behavior Analysis, 24,* 719–732.

Horner, R., Sprague, J., O'Brien, M., & Heathfield, L. 1990. The role of response efficiency in the reduction of problem behaviors through functional equivalence training: A case study. *Journal of the Association for Persons with Severe Handicaps, 15,* 91–97.

Horner, R., Vaughn, B., Day, H., & Ard, W. 1996. The relationship between setting events and problem behavior: Expanding our understanding of behavioral support. In L. Koegel, R. L. Koegel, & G. Dunlap (Eds:), *Positive behavioral support: Including people with difficult behaviors in the community.* Baltimore, MD: Paul H. Brookes.

Horton, S. 1987. Reduction of disruptive mealtime behavior by facial screening. *Behavior Modification, 11,* 53–64.

Hughes, C. & Hendrickson, J. M. 1987. Self-monitoring with at-risk students in the regular class setting. *Education and Treatment of Children, 10,* 225–236.

Hughes, C., & Agran, M. 1993. Teaching persons with severe disabilities to use self-instruction in community settings: An analysis of applications. *Journal for the Association of Severe Handicaps, 18,* 261–274.

Hughes, C., Korinek, L., & Gorman, J. 1991. Self-management for students with mental retardation in public school settings: A research review. *Education and Training in Mental Retardation, 26,* 271–291.

Hughes, C., & Lloyd, J. W. 1993. An analysis of self-management. *Journal of Behavioral Education, 3,* 405–425.

Hughes, C., Ruhl, K. L., & Misra, A. 1989. Self-management with behaviorally disordered students in school settings. A promise unfulfilled. *Behavioral Disorders, 14,* 250–262.

Hughes, C., Rung, L. L., Wehmeyer, M. L., Agran, M., Copeland, S. R., & Hwang, B. 2000. Self-prompted communication book use to increase social interaction among high school students. *Journal of the Association for Persons with Severe Handicaps, 25,* 153–166.

Hughes, C. A., & Boyle, J. R. 1991. Effects of self-monitoring for on-task behavior and task productivity on elementary students with moderate mental retardation. *Education and Treatment of Children, 14,* 96–111.

Huguenin, N. 1993. Reducing chronic noncompliance in an individual with severe mental retardation to facilitate community integration. *Mental Retardation, 31,* 332–339.

Huguenin, N., & Mulick, J. 1981. Nonexclusionary timeout: Maintenance of appropriate behavior across settings. *Applied Research in Mental Retardation, 2,* 55–67.

Humphrey, L. L., Karoly, P., & Kirschenbaum, D. S. 1978. Self-management in the classroom: Self-imposed response-cost versus self-reward. *Behavior Therapy, 9,* 592–601.

Hunter, M. 1984. Knowing, teaching, and supervising. In P. Hosford (Ed.), *Using what we know about teaching.* Alexandria, VA: Association for Supervision and Curriculum Development.

Hupp, S. C. 1986. Effects of stimulus mode on the acquisition, transfer, and generalization of categories by severely mentally retarded children and adolescents. *American Journal of Mental Deficiency, 90,* 579–587.

Hutchinson, S. W., Murdock, S. Y., Williamson R. D., & Cronin, M. E. (2000). Self-Recording PLUS encouragement equals improved behavior. Teaching Exceptional Children, 32, 54–58.

Hyman, P., Oliver, C., & Hall, S. 2002. Self-injurious behavior, self-restraint, and compulsive behaviors in Cornelia de Lange syndrome. *American Journal on Mental Retardation, 107,* 146–154.

Inglesfield, E., & Crisp, A. 1985. Teaching dressing skills to the severely mentally handicapped: A comparison of intensive and non-intensive strategies. *British Journal of Mental Subnormality, 31,* 46–53.

Irvin, D., Realon, R., Hartley, J., Phillips, J., Bradley, F., & Daly, M. 1996. The treatment of self-injurious hand mouthing by using a multi-component intervention with individuals positioned in a small group. *Journal of Developmental and Physical Disabilities, 8* (1), 43–59.

Irvin, D., Thompson, T., Turner, W., & Williams, D. 1998. Utilizing increased response effort to reduce chronic hand mouthing. *Journal of Applied Behavior Analysis, 31,* 375–385.

Isley, E., Kartsonis, C., McCurley, C., Weisz, K., & Roberts, M. S. 1991. Self-restraint: A review of etiology and applications in mentally retarded adults with self-injury. *Research in Developmental Disabilities, 12* (1), 87–95.

Iwata, B. 1987. Negative reinforcement in applied behavior analysis: An emerging technology. *Journal of Applied Behavior Analysis, 20,* 361–378.

Iwata, B. A., & Bailey, J. S. 1974. Reward versus cost token systems: An analysis of the effects on students and teacher. *Journal of Applied Behavior Analysis, 7,* 567–576.

Iwata, B., & DeLeon, I. 1996. *The functional analysis screening tool.* The Florida Center on Self-Injury. Gainesville, FL: The University of Florida.

Iwata, B., Dorsey, M., Slifer, K., Bauman, K., & Richman, G. 1994. Toward a functional analysis of self-injury. *Journal of Applied Behavior Analysis, 27,* 197–209. (Reprint of original article published in *Analysis and Intervention in Developmental Disabilities, 2,* 3–20.)

Iwata, B., Pace, G., Dorsey, M., Zarcone, J., Vollmer, T., Smith, R., et al. 1994. The functions of self-injurious behavior: An experimental epidemiological analysis. *Journal of Applied Behavior Analysis, 27,* 215–240.

Iwata, B., Pace, G., Kalsher, M., Cowdery, G., & Cataldo, M. 1990. Experimental analysis and extinction of self-injurious escape behavior. *Journal of Applied Behavior Analysis, 23,* 11–27.

Jackson, D. A., & Wallace, R. F. 1974. The modification and generalization of voice loudness in a fifteen-year-old retarded girl. *Journal of Applied Behavior Analysis, 7,* 461–471.

Jahr, E. 2001. Teaching children with autism to answer novel wh-questions by utilizing a multiple exemplar strategy. *Research in Developmental Disabilities, 22,* 407–423.

Jens, K. G., & Shores, R. E. 1969. Behavioral graphs as reinforcers for work behavior of mentally retarded adolescents. *Education and Training of the Mentally Retarded, 4,* 21–28.

Johnson, L. A., & Graham, S. 1990. Goal setting and its application with exceptional learners. *Preventing School Failure, 34,* 4–8.

Johnson, P., Schuster, J., & Bell, R. 1996. Comparison of simultaneous prompting with and without error correction in teaching science vocabulary words to high school students with mild disabilities. *Journal of Behavioral Education, 6,* 437–458.

Johnston, J. M. 1979. On the relation between generalization and generality. *The Behavior Analyst, 2,* 1–6.

Johnston, J. M. 1996. Distinguishing between applied research and practice. *The Behavior Analyst, 19,* 35–47.

Johnston, J. M., & Johnston, G. T. 1972. Modification of consonant speech-sound articulation in young children. *Journal of Applied Behavior Analysis, 5,* 233–246.

Johnston, J., & Pennypacker, H. 1993. *Strategies and tactics of behavioral research* (2nd ed.). Hillsdale, NJ: Erlbaum.

Jolivette, K., Wehby,J., Canale, J., & Massey, N. 2001. Effects of choice-making opportunities on the behavior of students with emotional and behavioral disorders. *Behavioral Disorders, 26,* 131–145.

Jones, K., Drew, H., & Weber, N. 2000. Noncontingent peer attention as treatment for disruptive classroom behavior. *Journal of Applied Behavior Analysis, 33,* 343–346.

Jones, K., Drew, H., & Weber, N. 2000. Noncontingent peer attention as treatment for disruptive classroom behavior. *Journal of Applied Behavior Analysis, 33,* 343–346.

Jones, M. C. 1924. A laboratory study of fear: The case of Peter. *The Pedagogical Seminary and Journal of Genetic Psychology, 31,* 308–315.

Journal of Applied Behavior Analysis. 2000. 33 (3), 399.

Journal of Teacher Education, 37. Thousand Oaks, CA: SAGE.

Kaestle, C. F. (Ed.). 1973. *Joseph Lancaster and the monitorial school movement: A documentary history.* New York: Teachers College Press.

Kagel, J. H., & Winkler, R. C. 1972. Behavioral economics: Areas of cooperative research between economics and applied behavior analysis. *Journal of Applied Behavior Analysis, 5,* 335–342.

Kahng, S. W., & Iwata, B. 1998. Computerized systems for collecting real-time observational data. *Journal of Applied Behavior Analysis, 31* (2), 253–261.

Kahng, S. W., & Iwata, B. 1999. Correspondence between outcomes of brief and extended functional analysis. *Journal of Applied Behavior Analysis, 32,* 149–159.

Kahng, S. W., Abt, K., & Schonbachler, H. 2001. Assessment and treatment of low-rate high-intensity problem behavior. *Journal of Applied Behavior Analysis, 34,* 225–228.

Kahng, S. W., Iwata, B., Fischer, S., Page, T., Treadwell, K., Williams, D., et al. 1998. Temporal distributions of problem behavior based on scatter plot analysis. *Journal of Applied Behavior Analysis, 31,* 593–604.

Kahng, S., Boscoe, J., & Byrne, S. 2003. The use of an escape contingency and a token economy to increase food acceptance. *Journal of Applied Behavior Analysis, 36,* 349–353.

Kallman, W. H., Hersen, M., & O'Toole, D. H. 1975. The use of social reinforcement in a case of conversion reaction. *Behavior Therapy, 6,* 411–413.

Kamps, D., Dugan, E., Potucek, J., & Collins, A. 1999. Effects of cross-age peer tutoring networks among students with autism and general education students. *Journal of Behavioral Education, 9* (2), 97–115.

Kamps, D., Kravits, T., Stolze, J., & Swaggart, B. 1999. Prevention strategies for at-risk students and students with EBD in urban elementary schools. *Journal of Emotional and Behavioral Disorders, 7,* 178–188.

Kanfer, F. 1975. Self-management methods. In F. Kanfer & A. Goldstein (Eds.), *Helping people change: A textbook of methods.* New York: Pergamon Press.

Kaplan, P., Kohfeldt, J., & Sturla, K. 1974. *It's positively fun: Techniques for managing learning environments.* Denver: Love Publishing.

Karen, R. L. 1974. *An introduction to behavior theory and its applications.* New York: Harper & Row.

Karsh, K., Repp, A., Dahlquist, C., & Munk, D. 1995. In vivo functional assessment and multi-element interventions for problem behaviors of students with disabilities in classroom settings. *Journal of Behavioral Education, 5* (2), 189–210.

Kasper-Ferguson, S., & Moxley, R. A. 2002. Developing a writing package with student graphing of fluency. *Education and Treatment of Children, 25,* 249–267.

Kauchak, D. P., & Eggen, P. D. 1998. *Learning and teaching.* Boston: Allyn & Bacon.

Kaufman, K. F., & O'Leary, K. D. 1972. Reward, cost, and self-evaluation procedures for disruptive adolescents in a psychiatric hospital school. *Journal of Applied Behavior Analysis, 5,* 293–309.

Kayser, J. E., Billingsley, F. F., & Neel, R. S. 1986. A comparison of in context and traditional instructional approaches: Total task single trial vs. backward chaining multiple trial. *Journal of the Association for Persons with Severe Handicaps, 11,* 28–38.

Kazdin, A. 1977. Artifact, bias, and complexity of assessment: The ABCs of reliability. *Journal of Applied Behavior Analysis, 10,* 141–150.

Kazdin, A. 1994. *Behavior modification in applied settings.* Pacific Grove, CA: Brooks/Cole Publishing Co.

Kazdin, A. 2000. *Behavior modification in applied settings.* Belmont, CA: Wadsworth.

Kazdin, A. 2001. *Behavior modification in applied settings* (6th ed.). Belmont, CA: Wadsworth.

Kazdin, A. E. 1972. Response cost: The removal of conditioned reinforcers for therapeutic change. *Behavior Therapy, 3,* 533–546.

Kazdin, A. E. 1973. Methodological and assessment considerations in evaluating reinforcement programs in applied settings. *Journal of Applied Behavior Analysis, 6,* 517–531.

Kazdin, A. E. 1976. Statistical analyses for single-case experimental designs. In M. Hersen & D. Barlow (Eds.), *Single-case experimental designs: Strategies for studying behavior change* (pp. 265–316). New York: Pergamon Press.

Kazdin, A. E. 1977. Assessing the clinical or applied importance of behavior change through social validation. *Behavior Modification, 1,* 427–451.

Kazdin, A. E. 1977. *The token economy: A review and evaluation.* New York: Plenum Press.

Kazdin, A. E. 1982. *Single-case research designs.* New York: Oxford University Press.

Kazdin, A. E. 1998. *Research design in clinical psychology* (3rd. ed.). Boston: Allyn & Bacon.

Kazdin, A. E. 2001. *Behavior modification in applied settings* (6th ed.). Belmont, CA: Wadsworth.

Kazdin, A. E., & Bootzin, R. R. 1972. The token economy: An evaluative review. *Journal of Applied Behavior Analysis, 5,* 343–372.

Kazdin, A. E., & Polster, R. 1973. Intermittent token reinforcement and response maintenance in extinction. *Behavior Therapy, 4,* 386–391.

Kee, M., Hill, S., & Weist, M. 1999. School-based behavior management of cursing, hitting, and spitting in a girl with profound retardation. *Education and Treatment of Children, 22,* 171–178.

Kelley, M. L., & McCain, A. 1995. Promoting academic performance in inattentive children. *Behavior Modification, 19* (3), 357–375.

Kennedy, C. H., & Meyer, K. A. 1998. Establishing operations and the motivation of challenging behavior. In J. K. Luiselli & M. J. Cameron (Eds.), *Antecedent control: Innovative approaches to behavioral support.* Baltimore: Paul H. Brooks.

Kennedy, C., & Haring, T. 1993. Teaching choice making during social interactions to students with profound multiple disabilities. *Journal of Applied Behavior Analysis, 26,* 63–76.

Kennedy, C., & Souza, G. 1995. Functional analysis and treatment of eye poking. *Journal of Applied Behavior Analysis, 28,* 27–37.

Kennedy, C., Meyer, K., Knowles, T., & Shukla, S. 2000. Analyzing the multiple functions of stereotypical behavior for students with autism. *Journal of Applied Behavior Analysis, 33* (4), 559–571.

Kern, L., Dunlap, G., Clarke, S., & Childs, K. 1994. Student-assisted functional assessment interview. *Diagnostique, 19,* 29–39.

Kern, L., Koegel, R., & Dunlap, G. 1984. The influence of vigorous versus mild exercise on autistic stereotyped behaviors. *Journal of Autism and Developmental Disorders, 14,* 57–67.

Kern, L., Koegel, R., Dyer, K., Blew, P., & Fenton, L. 1982. The effects of physical exercise on self-stimulation and appropriate responding in autistic children. *Journal of Autism and Developmental Disorders, 12,* 399–419.

Kern, L., Mantegna, M., Vorndran, C., Bailin, D., & Hilt, A. 2001. Choice of task sequence to reduce problem behaviors. *Journal of Positive Behavior Interventions, 3,* 3–10.

Kern, L., Wacker, D. P., Mace, F. C., Falk, G. D., Dunlap, G., & Kromrey, J. D. 1995. Improving the peer interactions of students with emotional and behavioral disorders through self-evaluation procedures: A component analysis and group application. *Journal of Applied Behavior Analysis, 28,* 47–59.

Kern-Dunlap, L., Dunlap, G., Clarke, S., Childs, K. E., White, R. L., & Stewart, M. P. 1992. Effects of a video tape feedback package on the peer interactions of children with serious behavioral and emotional challenges. *Journal of Applied Behavior Analysis, 25,* 355–364.

Kessler, J. W. 1966. *Psychopathology of childhood.* Upper Saddle River, NJ: Prentice Hall.

Kifer, R. E., Lewis, M. A., Green, D. R., & Phillips, E. L. 1974. Training predelinquent youths and their parents to negotiate conflict situations. *Journal of Applied Behavior Analysis, 7,* 357–364.

Kimball, J. W., Kinney, E. M., Taylor, B. A., & Stromer, R. 2003. Lights, camera, action: Using engaging computer-cued activity schedules. *Teaching Exceptional Children, 36,* 40–45.

Kincaid, M., & Weisberg, P. 1978. Alphabet letters as tokens: Training preschool children in letter recognition and labeling during a token exchange period. *Journal of Applied Behavior Analysis, 11,* 199.

Kinch, C., Lewis-Palmer, T., Hagan-Burke, S., & Sugai, G. 2001. A comparison of teacher and student functional behavior assessment interview information from low-risk and high-risk classrooms. *Education and Treatment of Children, 24,* 480–494.

King-Sears, M. E. 1999. Teacher and researcher co-design self-management content for an inclusive setting: Research training, intervention, and generalization effects on student performance. *Education and Training in Mental Retardation and Developmental Disabilities, 34,* 134–156.

Kirby, F. D., & Shields, F. 1972. Modification of arithmetic response rate and attending behavior in a seventh-grade student. *Journal of Applied Behavior Analysis, 5,* 79–84.

Kirby, K. C., & Bickel, W. K. 1988. Toward an explicit analysis of generalization: A stimulus control interpretation. *The Behavior Analyst, 11,* 115–129.

Kitchener, R. F. 1980. Ethical relativism and behavior therapy. *Journal of Consulting and Clinical Psychology, 48,* 1–7.

Klein, R. G, & Last, C. G. 1989. *Anxiety disorders in children.* Newbury Park, CA: Sage.

Kleinert, H. L., & Gast, D. L. 1982. Teaching a multihandicapped adult manual signs using a constant time delay procedure. *Journal of the Association of the Severely Handicapped, 6* (4), 25–32.

Knight, M., Ross, D., Taylor, R., & Ramasamy, R. 2003. Constant time delay and intersperal of known items to teach sight words to students with mental retardation and learning disabilities. *Education and Training in Mental Retardation and Developmental Disabilities, 38,* 179–191.

Kodak, T., Grow, L., & Northup, J. 2004. Functional analysis and treatment of elopement for a child with attention deficit hyperactivity disorder. *Journal of Applied Behavior Analysis, 37,* 229–232.

Koegel, L., Koegel, R., Frea, W., & Fredeen, R. 2001. Identifying early intervention targets for children with autism in inclusive school settings. *Behavior Modification, 25,* 745–761.

Koegel, R. L., & Rincover, A. 1974. Treatment of psychotic children in a classroom environment: I. Learning in a large group. *Journal of Applied Behavior Analysis, 7,* 45–59.

Koegel, R. L., & Rincover, A. 1977. Research on the difference between generalization and maintenance in extra-therapy responding. *Journal of Applied Behavior Analysis, 10,* 1–12.

Koegel, R. L., Harrower, J. K., & Koegel, L. K. 1999. Support for children with developmental disabilities in full inclusion classrooms through self-management. *Journal of Positive Behavior Interventions, 1,* 26–34.

Koegel, R. L., O'Dell, M. C., Koegel, L. K. 1987. A natural language teaching paradigm for nonverbal autistic children. *Journal of Autism and Developmental Disorders, 17,* 187–200.

Koffka, K. 1935. *Principles of Gestalt psychology.* New York: Harcourt, Brace & World.

Kohler, F., Strain, P., Hoyson, M., & Jamieson, B. 1997. Merging naturalistic teaching and peer-based strategies to address the IEP objectives of preschoolers with autism: An examination of structural and child behavior outcomes. *Focus on Autism and Other Developmental Disabilities, 12,* 196–206.

Kohler, F., Strain, P., Hoyson, M., Davis, L., Donina, W., & Rapp, N. 1995. Using a group-oriented contingency to increase social interactions between children with autism and their peers. *Behavior Modification, 19* (1), 10–32.

Kohn, A. 1993. *Punished by rewards.* Boston: Houghton Mifflin.

Krantz, P. J. & McClannahan, L. E. 1998. Social interaction skills for children with autism: A script-fading procedure for beginning readers. *Journal of Applied Behavior Analysis, 31,* 191–202.

Krantz, P. J., & McClannahan, L. E. 1993. Teaching children with autism to initiate to peers: Effects of a script-fading procedure. *Journal of Applied Behavior Analysis, 26,* 121–132.

Krasner, L. 1976. Behavioral modification: Ethical issues and future trends. In H. Leitenberg (Ed.), *Handbook of behavior modification and behavior therapy* (pp. 627–649). Englewood Cliffs, NJ: Prentice-Hall.

Krathwohl, D. 1998. *Methods of educational & social science research: An integrated approach.* New York City: Addison Wesley Longman.

Krumboltz, J. D., & Krumboltz, H. D. 1972. *Changing children's behavior.* Upper Saddle River, NJ: Prentice Hall.

Kuhn, D., DeLeon, I., Fisher, W., & Wilke, A. 1999. Clarifying an ambiguous functional analysis with matched and mismatched extinction procedures. *Journal of Applied Behavior Analysis, 32,* 99–102.

Lagomarcino, T. R., Hughes, C., & Rusch, F. R. 1989. Utilizing self-management to teach independence on the job. *Education and Training of the Mentally Retarded, 24* (2), 139–148.

Lahey, B. B., McNees, M. P., & McNees, M. C. 1973. Control of an obscene "verbal tic" through timeout in an elementary school classroom. *Journal of Applied Behavior Analysis, 6,* 101–104.

Lalli, J., Casey, S., & Kates, K. 1995. Reducing escape behavior and increasing task completion with functional communication training, extinction, and response chaining. *Journal of Applied Behavior Analysis, 28,* 261–268.

Lalli, J., Casey, S., & Kates, K. 1997. Noncontingent reinforcement as treatment for severe problem behavior: Some procedural variations. *Journal of Applied Behavior Analysis, 30,* 127–137.

Lalli, J., Kates, K., & Casey, S. 1999. Response covariation: The relationship between correct academic responding and problem behavior. *Behavior Modification, 23* (3), 339–357.

Lalli, J., Livezey, K., & Kates, K. 1996. Functional analysis and treatment of eye poking with response blocking. *Journal of Applied Behavior Analysis, 29,* 129–132.

Lalli, J., Zanolli, K., & Wohn, T. 1994. Using extinction to promote response variability in toy play. *Journal of Applied Behavior Analysis, 27,* 735–736.

Lambert, N., Nihira, K., & Leland, H. 1993. *AAMR adaptive behavior scales: School edition* (2nd ed.). Austin, TX: ProEd.

Lancioni, G. E., & O'Reilly, M. F. 2001. Self-management of instruction cues for occupation: Review of studies with people with severe and profound developmental disabilities. *Research in Developmental Disabilities, 22,* 41–65.

Lancioni, G., Brouwer, J., & Coninx, F. 1992. Automatic cueing strategies to reduce drooling in people with mental handicap. *International Journal of Rehabilitation Research, 15,* 341–344.

Lancioni, G., O'Reilly, M., & Emerson, E. 1996. A review of choice research with people with severe and profound developmental disabilities. *Research in Developmental Disabilities, 17* (5), 391–411.

Lane, K., Wehby, J., Menzies, H., Doukas, G., Munton, S., & Gregg, R. 2003. Social skills instruction for students at risk for antisocial behavior: The effects of small-group instruction. *Behavioral Disorders, 28,* 229–248.

Lannie, A., & Martens, B. 2004. Effects of task difficulty and type of contingency on students' allocation of responding to math worksheets. *Journal of Applied Behavior Analysis, 37,* 53–65.

Laski, F. J. 1991. Achieving integration during the second revolution. In H. L. Meyer, C. A. Peck, & L. Brown (Eds.), *Critical issues in the lives of people with severe disabilities* (pp. 409–421). Baltimore, MD: Paul H. Brooks.

Lassman, K., Jolivette, K., & Wehby, J. 1999. Using collaborative behavioral contracting. *Teaching Exceptional Children, 31,* 12–18.

Lattal, K., & Neef, N. 1996. Recent reinforcement-schedule research and applied behavior analysis. *Journal of Applied Behavior Analysis, 29,* 213–230.

Laushey, K., & Heflin, L. J. 2000. Enhancing social skills of kindergarten children with autism through the training of multiple peers as tutors. *Journal of Autism and Developmental Disorders, 30* (3), 183–193.

Le Grice, B., & Blampied, N. M. 1997. Learning to use video recorders and personal computers with increasing assistance prompting. *Journal of Developmental and Physical Disabilities, 9,* 17–29.

Leatherby, J., Gast, D., Wolery, M., & Collins, B. 1992. Assessment of reinforcer preference in multi-handicapped students. *Journal of Developmental and Physical Disabilities, 4* (1), 15–36.

LeBlanc, L., & Matson, J. 1995. A social skills training program for preschoolers with developmental delays. *Behavior Modification, 19* (2), 234–246.

Lee, C., & Tindal, G. A. 1994. Self-recording and goal setting: Effects on on-task and math productivity of low-achieving Korean elementary school students. *Journal of Behavioral Education, 4,* 459–479.

Lee, D., & Belfiore, P. 1997. Enhancing classroom performance: A review of reinforcement schedules. *Journal of Behavioral Education, 7* (2), 205–217.

Lennox, D., Miltenberger, R., & Donnelly, D. 1987. Response interruption and DRL for the reduction of rapid eating. *Journal of Applied Behavior Analysis, 20,* 279–284.

Lennox, O. B. & Miltenberger, R. 1989. Conducting a functional assessment of problem behavior in applied settings. *Journal of the Association for Persons with Severe Handicaps, 14,* 304–311.

Lenz, M., Singh, N., & Hewett, A. 1991. Overcorrection as an academic remediation procedure. *Behavior Modification, 15,* 64X–73.

Leon, J. A., & Pepe, H. J. 1983. Self-instructional training: Cognitive behavior modification for remediating arithmetic deficits. *Exceptional Children, 50,* 54–60.

Lerman, D., & Iwata, B. 1996. A methodology for distinguishing between extinction and punishment effects associated with response blocking. *Journal of Applied Behavior Analysis, 29,* 231–233.

Lerman, D., & Iwata, B. 1996. Developing a technology for the use of operant extinction in clinical settings: An examination of basic and applied research. *Journal of Applied Behavior Analysis, 29,* 345–382.

Lerman, D., Iwata, B., & Wallace, M. 1999. Side effects of extinction: Prevalence of bursting and aggression during the treatment of self-injurious behavior. *Journal of Applied Behavior Analysis, 32,* 1–8.

Lerman, D., Iwata, B., Rainville, B., Adelinis, J., Crosland, K., & Kogan, J. 1997. Effects of reinforcement choice on task responding in individuals with developmental disabilities. *Journal of Applied Behavior Analysis, 30,* 411–422.

Lerman, D., Iwata, B., Shore, B., & Kahng, S. 1996. Responding maintained by intermittent reinforcement: Implications for the use of extinction with problem behavior in clinical settings. *Journal of Applied Behavior Analysis, 29,* 153–171.

Lerman, D., Kelley, M., Van Camp, C., & Roane, H. 1999. Effects of reinforcement magnitude on spontaneous recovery. *Journal of Applied Behavior Analysis, 32,* 197–200.

Lerman, D., Vorndran, C., Addison, L., & Kuhn, S. 2004. A rapid assessment of skills in young children with autism. *Journal of Applied Behavior Analysis, 37,* 11–26.

Levendoski, L. S., & Cartledge, G. 2000. Self-monitoring for elementary school children with serious emotional disturbances: Classroom applications for increased academic responding. *Behavioral Disorders, 25,* 211–224.

Lewin, K. 1951. *Field theory in social science.* New York: Harper & Row.

Lewis, T., & Sugai, G. 1996. Descriptive and experimental analysis of teacher and peer attention and the use of assessment-based intervention to improve pro-social behavior. *Journal of Behavioral Education, 6,* 7–24.

Lewis, T., Scott, T., & Sugai, G. 1994. The problem behavior questionnaire: A teacher-based instrument to develop functional hypotheses of problem behavior in general education classrooms. *Diagnostique, 19* (2–3), 103–115.

Liberman, R. P., Teigen, J., Patterson, R., & Baker, V. 1973. Reducing delusional speech in chronic, paranoid schizophrenics. *Journal of Applied Behavior Analysis, 6,* 57–64.

Lim L., Browder, D., & Sigafoos, J. 1998. The role of response effort and motion study in functionally equivalent task designs and alternatives. *Journal of Behavioral Education, 8,* 81–102.

Lindberg, J., Iwata, B., Kahng, S. W., & DeLeon, I. 1999. DRO contingencies: An analysis of variable-momentary schedules. *Journal of Applied Behavior Analysis, 32,* 123–136.

Linton, J., & Singh, N. 1984. Acquisition of sign language using positive practice overcorrection. *Behavior Modification, 8,* 553–566.

Litow, L., & Pumroy, D. K. 1975. A brief review of classroom group-oriented contingencies. *Journal of Applied Behavior Analysis, 8,* 341–347.

Litt, M., & Schreibman, L. 1981. Stimulus-specific reinforcement in the acquisition of receptive labels by autistic children. *Analysis and Intervention in Developmental Disabilities, 1,* 171–186.

Livi, J., & Ford, A. 1985. Skill transfer from a domestic training site to the actual homes of three moderately handicapped students. *Education and Training of the Mentally Retarded, 20,* 69–82.

Lloyd, J. W., & Hughes, C. 1993. Introduction to the self-management series. *Journal of Behavioral Education, 3,* 403–404.

Lloyd, J., Bateman, D., Landrum, T., & Hallahan, D. 1989. Self-recording of attention versus productivity. *Journal of Applied Behavior Analysis, 22,* 315–323.

Lloyd, J., Eberhardt, M., & Drake, G. 1996. Group versus individual reinforcement contingencies within the context of group study conditions. *Journal of Applied Behavior Analysis, 29,* 189–200.

Lohrmann-O'Rourke, S. & Zirkel, P. A. 1998. The case law on aversive interventions for students with disabilities. *Exceptional Children, 65,* pp. 101–123.

Long, E., Miltenberger, R., Ellingson, S., & Ott, S. 1999. Augmenting simplified habit reversal in the treatment of oral-digital habits exhibited by individuals with mental retardation. *Journal of Applied Behavior Analysis, 32,* 353–365.

Lovaas, O. I., & Simmons, J. Q. 1969. Manipulation of self-destruction in three retarded children. *Journal of Applied Behavior Analysis, 2,* 143–157.

Lovaas, O. I., Koegel, R., Simmons, J. Q., & Long, J. S. 1973. Some generalization and follow-up measures on autistic children in behavior therapy. *Journal of Applied Behavior Analysis, 6,* 131–166.

Lovaas, O. I., Schreibman, L., Koegel, R. L., & Rhen, R. 1971. Selective responding by autistic children to multiple sensory input. *Journal of Abnormal Psychology, 77,* 211–222.

Lovitt, T. C. 1973. Self-management projects with children with behavioral disabilities. *Journal of Learning Disabilities, 6,* 138–154.

Lovitt, T. C., & Curtiss, K. A. 1969. Academic response rate as a function of teacher- and self-imposed contingencies. *Journal of Applied Behavior Analysis, 2,* 49–53.

Luciano, M. C. 1986. Acquisition, maintenance, and generalization of productive intraverbal behavior through transfer of stimulus control procedures. *Applied Research in Mental Retardation, 7,* 1–20.

Luiselli, J. 1980. Controlling disruptive behaviors of an autistic child: Parent-mediated contingency management in the home setting. *Education and Treatment of Children, 3,* 195–203.

Luiselli, J. 1986. Modification of self-injurious behavior: An analysis of the use of contingently applied protective equipment. *Behavior Modification, 10,* 191–203.

Luiselli, J., 1994. Effects of noncontingent sensory reinforcement on stereotypic behaviors in a child with posttraumatic neurological impairment. *Journal of Behavior Therapy and Experimental Psychiatry, 25,* 325–330.

Luiselli, J. 1996. Multicomponent intervention for challenging behaviors of a child with pervasive developmental disorder in a public school setting. *Journal of Developmental and Physical Disabilities, 8* (3), 211–219.

Luiselli, J. K., & Cameron, M. J. 1998. *Antecedent control: Innovative approaches to behavioral support.* Baltimore: Paul H. Brooks.

Luiselli, J., & Rice, D. 1983. Brief positive practice with a handicapped child: An assessment of suppressive and re-educative effects. *Education and treatment of Children, 6,* 241–250.

Lyon, C., & Lagarde, R. 1997. Tokens for success: Using the graduated reinforcement system. *Teaching Exceptional Children, 29* (6), 52–57.

Maag, J. W., Reid, R., & DiGangi, S. A. 1993. Differential effects of self-monitoring attention, accuracy, and productivity. *Journal of Applied Behavior Analysis, 26,* 329–344.

Mabee, W. 1988. The effects of academic positive practice on cursive letter writing. *Education and Treatment of Children, 11,* 143–148.

MacDuff, G. S., Krantz, P. J., & MacClannahan, L. E. 1993. Teaching children with autism to use photographic activity schedules: Maintenance and generalization of complex response chains. *Journal of Applied Behavior Analysis, 26,* 89–97.

Mace, A., Shapiro, E., & Mace, F. 1998. Effects of warning stimuli for reinforcer withdrawal and task onset on self-injury. *Journal of Applied Behavior Analysis, 31,* 679–682.

Mace, F., Lalli, J., & Lalli, E. 1991. Functional analysis and treatment of aberrant behavior. *Research in Developmental Disabilities, 12,* 155–180.

Mace, F., Page, T., Ivancic, M., & O'Brien, S. 1986. Effectiveness of brief time-out with and without contingent delay: A comparative analysis. *Journal of Applied Behavior Analysis, 19,* 79–86.

Mace, F C., Page, T. J., Ivancic, M. T., & O'Brien, S. 1986. Analysis of environmental determinants of aggression and disruption in mentally retarded children. *Applied Research in Mental Retardation, 7,* 203–221.

MacPherson, E. M., Candee, B. L., & Hohman, R. J. 1974. A comparison of three methods for eliminating disruptive lunchroom behavior. *Journal of Applied Behavior Analysis, 7,* 287–297.

Magee, S., & Ellis, J. 2000. Extinction effects during the assessment of multiple problem behaviors. *Journal of Applied Behavior Analysis, 33* (3), 313–316.

Mager, R. 1997. *Preparing instructional objectives* (3rd ed). Atlanta, GA: The Center for Effective Performance, Inc.

Maher, G. 1989. Punch out: A behavior management technique. *Teaching Exceptional Children, 21,* 74.

Mahoney, M. J. 1974. *Cognition and behavior modification.* Cambridge, MA: Ballinger.

Mahoney, M. J., Kazdin, A. E., & Lesswing, N. J. 1974. Behavior modification: Delusion or deliverance? In C. M. Franks & G. T. Wilson (Eds.), *Annual review of behavior therapy, theory & practice* (Vol. 2, pp. 11–40). New York: Brunner/Mazel.

Malott, R. W., Whaley, D. C., & Malott, M. E. 1997. *Elementary principles of behavior.* Upper Saddle River, NJ: Prentice Hall.

Mancina, C., Tankersley, M., Kamps, D., Kravitz, T., & Parrett, J. 2000. Brief report: Reduction of inappropriate vocalization for a child with autism using a self-management treatment program. *Journal of Autism and Developmental Disorders, 30,* 599–606.

Marchand-Martella, N., Martella, R., Bettis, D., & Blakely, M. in press. Project PALS: A description of a high school-based tutorial program using Corrective Reading and peer-delivered instruction. *Reading and Writing Quarterly.*

Marchetti, A. G., McCartney, J. R., Drain, S., Hooper, M., & Dix, J. 1983. Pedestrian skills training for mentally retarded adults: Comparison of training in two settings. *Mental Retardation, 21,* 107–110.

Marcus, B., & Vollmer, T. 1996. Combining noncontingent reinforcement and differential reinforcement schedules as treatment for aberrant behavior. *Journal of Applied Behavior Analysis, 29,* 43–51.

Marholin, D., II, & Gray, D. 1976. Effects of group response-cost procedures on cash shortages in a small business. *Journal of Applied Behavior Analysis, 9,* 25–30.

Marshall, H. 1965. The effect of punishment on children. A review of the literature and a suggested hypothesis. *Journal of Genetic Psychology, 106,* 23–33.

Marshall, K. J., Lloyd, J. W., & Hallahan, D. P. 1993. Effects of training to increase self-monitoring accuracy. *Journal of Behavioral Education, 3,* 445–459.

Martens, B., Muir, K., & Meller, P. 1988. Rewards common to the classroom setting: A comparison of regular and self-contained room student ratings. *Behavior Disorders, 13,* 169–174.

Martin, J., Rusch, F., James, V., Decker, P., & Trtol, K. 1974. The use of picture cues to establish self-control in the preparation of complex meals by mentally retarded adults. *Applied Research in Mental Retardation, 3,* 105–119.

Martin, R. 1975. *Legal challenges to behavior modification: Trends in schools, corrections, and mental health*. Champaign, IL: Research Press.

Mason, B. 1974. Brain surgery to control behavior. *Ebony, 28* (4), 46.

Mason, S., McGee, G., Farmer-Dougan, V., & Risley, T. 1989. A practical strategy for ongoing reinforcer assessment. *Journal of Applied Behavior Analysis, 22,* 171–179.

Massey, N. G., & Wheeler, J. 2000. Acquisition and generalization of activity schedules and their effects on task engagement in a young child with autism in an inclusive pre-school classroom. *Education and Training in Mental Retardation and Developmental Disabilities, 35* (3), 326–335.

Mastropieri, M. A., & Scruggs, T. E. 1984. Generalization: Five effective strategies. *Academic Therapy, 19,* 427–431.

Mastropieri, M., Jenne, T., & Scruggs, T. 1988. A level system for managing problem behaviors in a high school resource program. *Behavioral Disorders, 13,* 202–208.

Matson, J., & Keyes, J. 1988. Contingent reinforcement and contingent restraint to treat severe aggression and self-injury in mentally retarded and autistic adults. *Journal of the Multihandicapped Person, 1,* 141–148.

Matson, J., & Stephens, R. 1977. Overcorrection of aggressive behavior in a chronic psychiatric patient. *Behavior Modification, 1,* 559–564.

Matson, J., & Vollmer, T. 1995. *User's guide: Questions about behavior function (QABF)*. Baton Rouge, LA: Scientific Publishers.

Matson, J., Esveldt-Dawson, K., & Kazdin, A. E. 1982. Treatment of spelling deficits in mentally retarded children. *Mental Retardation, 20,* 76–81.

Matson, J., Sevin, J., Fridley, D., & Love, S. 1990. Increasing spontaneous language in three autistic children. *Journal of Applied Behavior Analysis, 23,* 227–233.

May, J., Mcallister, J., Risley, T. Twardosz, S., & Cox, C. 1974. *Florida guidelines for the use of behavioral procedures in state programs for the retarded*. Tallahassee: Florida Division of Retardation.

Mayhew, G., & Harris, F. 1979. Decreasing self-injurious behavior: Punishment with citric acid and reinforcement of alternative behaviors. *Behavior Modification, 3,* 322–336.

Mazaleski, J., Iwata, B., Rodgers, T., Vollmer, T., & Zarcone, J. 1994. Protective equipment as treatment for stereotypic hand mouthing: Sensory extinction or punishment effects? *Journal of Applied Behavior Analysis, 27,* 345–355.

McCarl, J. J., Svobodny, L., & Beare, P. L. 1991. Self-recording in a classroom for students with mild to moderate mental handicaps: Effects on productivity and on-task behavior. *Education and Training in Mental Retardation, 26,* 79–88.

McCarty, T., Griffin, S., Apolloni, T., & Shores, R. 1977. Increased peer-teaching with group-oriented contingencies for arithmetic performance in behavior-disordered adolescents. *Journal of Applied Behavior Analysis, 10,* 313.

McComas, J. J. Lalli, J. S. & Benavides, C. 1999. Increasing accuracy and decreasing latency during clean intermittent self-catheterization procedures with young children. *Journal of Applied Behavior Analysis, 32,* (2), 217–220.

McComas, J., Hoch, H., Paone, D., & El-Roy, D. 2000. Escape behavior during academic tasks: A preliminary analysis of idiosyncratic establishing operations. *Journal of Applied Behavior Analysis, 33,* 479–493.

McConnell, J. V. 1970. Stimulus/response: Criminals can be brainwashed now. *Psychology Today, 3,* 14–18, 74.

McDonnell, A., & Sturmey, P. 2000. The social validation of three physical restraint procedures: a comparison of young people and professional groups. *Research in Developmental Disabilities, 21,* 85–92.

McDonnell, J., Johnson, J., Polychronis, S., & Risen, T. 2002. Effects of embedded instruction on students with moderate disabilities enrolled in general education classes. *Education and Training in Mental Retardation and Developmental Disabilities, 37,* 363–377.

McDougal, D. & Brady, M. P. 1998. Initiating and fading self-management interventions to increase math fluency in general education classes. *Exceptional Children, 64,* 151–166.

McDowell, C., & Keenan, M. 2001. Developing fluency and endurance in a child diagnosed with attention deficit hyperactivity disorder. *Journal of Applied Behavior Analysis, 34,* 345–348.

McGee, G. G., Krantz, P. J., & McClannahan, L. E. 1986. An extension of incidental teaching procedures to reading instruction for autistic children. *Journal of Applied Behavior Analysis, 19,* 147–157.

McGee, G. G., Krantz, P. J., Mason, D., & McClannahan, L. E. 1983. A modified incidental-teaching procedure for autistic youth: Acquisition and generalization of receptive object labels. *Journal of Applied Behavior Analysis, 16,* 329–338.

McGinnis, J. C., Friman, P., & Carlyon, W. 1999. The effect of token rewards on "intrinsic" motivation for doing math. *Journal of Applied Behavior Analysis, 32,* 375–379.

McGonigle, J., & Rojahn, J. 1989. An experimental analysis of visual screening and DRO for stereotyped behavior in young children with developmental disabilities. *Journal of the Multihandicapped Person, 2,* 251–270.

McGonigle, J., Duncan, D., Cordisco, L., & Barrett, R. 1982. Visual screening: An alternative method for reducing stereotypic behaviors. *Journal of Applied Behavior Analysis, 15,* 461–467.

McKeegan, G., Estill, K., & Campbell, B. 1984. Use of nonseclusionary time-out for the elimination of stereotypic behavior. *Journal of Behavior Therapy and Experimental Psychiatry, 15,* 261–264.

McLaughlin, T. F. 1976. Self-control in the classroom. *Review of Educational Research, 46,* 631–663.

McNaughton, D., Hughes, C., & Ofiesh, N. 1997. Proofreading for students with learning disabilities: Integrating computer and strategy use. *Learning Disabilities Research and Practice, 12* (1), 16–28.

McSweeny, A. J. 1978. Effects of response cost on the behavior of a million persons: Charging for directory assistance in Cincinnati. *Journal of Applied Behavior Analysis, 11,* 47–51.

Medland, M. B., & Stachnik, T. J. 1972. Good-behavior game: A replication and systematic analysis. *Journal of Applied Behavior Analysis, 5,* 45–51.

Meichenbaum, D. H. 1977. *Cognitive-behavior modification: An integrative approach*. New York: Plenum Press.

Meichenbaum, D. H., & Goodman, J. 1971. Training impulsive children to talk to themselves: A means of developing self-control. *Journal of Abnormal Psychology, 77,* 115–126.

Meyer, K. 1999. Functional analysis and treatment of problem behavior exhibited by elementary school children. *Journal of Applied Behavior Analysis, 32,* 229–232.

Michael, J. 1982. Distinguishing between discriminative and motivational functions of stimulus. *Journal of the Experimental Analysis of Behavior, 37,* 149–155.

Miller, U., & Test, D. 1989. A comparison of constant time delay and most-to-least prompting in teaching laundry skills to students with moderate retardation. *Education and Training in Mental Retardation, 24,* 363–370.

Miltenberger, R., Rapp, J., & Long, E. 1999. A low-tech method for conducting real-time recording. *Journal of Applied Behavior Analysis, 32* (1), 119–120.

Miltonberger, R. G., Roberts, J. A., Ellingson, S., Galensky, T., Rapp, J. T., Long, E. S., et al. 1999. Training and generalization of sexual abuse prevention skills for women with retardation. *Journal of Applied Behavior Analysis, 32,* 385–388.

Miner, D. 1991. Using nonaversive techniques to reduce self-stimulatory hand-mouthing in a visually impaired and severely retarded student. *RE:view, 22* (4), 185–193.

Mishel, W., & Patterson, C. J. 1976. Substantive and structural elements of effective plans for self-control. *Journal of Personality and Social Psychology, 34,* 942–950.

Mitchell, R. J., Schuster, J. W., Collins, B. C., & Gassaway, L. J. 2000. Teaching vocational skills with a faded auditory prompting system. *Education and Training in Mental Retardation and Developmental Disabilities, 35,* 415–427.

Mitchem, K. J., Young, K. R., West, R. P., & Benyo, J. 2001. CWPASM: A classwide peer-assisted self-management program for general education classrooms. *Education and Treatment of Children, 24,* 111–140.

Mogel, S., & Schiff, W. 1967. Extinction of a head-bumping symptom of eight years' duration in two minutes: A case report. *Behavior Research and Therapy, 5,* 131–132.

Molgaard, K. 2001. *Count It* V 2.7 Manual. Retrieved August 18, 2002, from http://palmguy.surfhere.net.

Moore, J., & Edwards, R. 2003. An analysis of aversive stimuli in classroom demand contexts 2003. *Journal of Applied Behavior Analysis, 36,* 339–348.

Moore, J., Edwards, R., Wilczynski, S., & Olmi, D. 2001. Using antecedent manipulations to distinguish between task and social variables associated with problem behaviors exhibited by children of typical development. *Behavior Modification, 25,* 287–304.

Moore, J., Mueller, M., Dubard, M., Roberts, D., & Sterling-Turner, H. 2002. The influence of therapist attention on self-injury during a tangible condition. *Journal of Applied Behavior Analysis, 35,* 283–286.

Morales v. Turman, 383 F. Supp. 53 (E.D. TX. 1974).

Morin, V., & Miller, S. 1998. Teaching multiplication to middle school students with mental retardation. *Education and Treatment of Children, 21,* 22–36.

Morris, R. 1976. *Behavior modification with children.* Cambridge, MA: Winthrop Publications.

Morrow, W. R., & Gochros, H. L. 1970. Misconceptions regarding behavior modification. *The Social Service Review, 44,* 293–307.

Morse, T. E., & Schuster, J. W. 2000. Teaching elementary students with moderate disabilities how to shop for groceries. *Exceptional Children, 66,* 273–288.

Morton, W. L., Heward, W. L., & Alber, S. R. 1998. When to self-correct: A comparison of two procedures on spelling performance. *Journal of Behavioral Education, 8,* 321–335.

Mosk, M. D., & Bucher, B. 1984. Prompting and stimulus shaping procedures for teaching visual-motor skills to retarded children. *Journal of Applied Behavior Analysis, 17,* 23–34.

Mowrer, D., & Conley, D. 1987. Effect of peer administered consequences upon articulatory responses of speech defective children. *Journal of Communication Disorders, 20,* 319–326.

Moyer, J. R., & Dardig, J. C. 1978. Practical task analysis for educators. *Teaching Exceptional Children, 11,* 16–18.

Mueller, M., Edwards, R., & Trahant, D. 2003. Translating multiple assessment techniques into an intervention selection model for classrooms. *Journal of Applied Behavior Analysis, 36,* 563–573.

Mueller, M., Moore, J., Doggett, R. A., & Tingstrom, D. 2000. The effectiveness of contingency-specific and contingency-nonspecific prompts in controlling bathroom graffiti. *Journal of Applied Behavior Analysis, 33* (1), 89–92.

Mueller, M., Wilczynski, S., Moore, J., Fusilier, I., & Trahant, D. 2001. Antecedent manipulations in a tangible condition: Effects of stimulus preference on aggression. *Journal of Applied Behavior Analysis, 34,* 237–240.

Munk, D. D., & Repp, A. C. 1994. The relationship between instructional variables and problem behavior: A review. *Exceptional Children, 60,* 390–401.

Neef, N., Nelles, D., Iwata, B., & Page, T. 2003. Analysis of precurrent skills in solving mathematics story problems. *Journal of Applied Behavior Analysis, 36,* 21–33.

Neef, N., Walters, J., & Egal, A. 1984. Establishing generative yes/no responses in developmentally disabled children. *Journal of Applied Behavior Analysis, 17,* 453–460.

Neisworth, J., Hunt, F., Gallop, H., & Nadle, R. 1985. Reinforcer displacement: A preliminary study of the clinical application of CRF/EXT effect. *Behavior Modification, 9,* 103–115.

Nelson, J. R., Roberts, M., Mathur, S., & Rutherford, R. 1999. Has public policy exceeded our knowledge base? A review of the functional behavioral assessment literature. *Behavioral Disorders, 24,* 169–179.

Newman, B., Buffington, D., & Hemmes, N. 1996. Self-reinforcement used to increase the appropriate conversation of autistic teenagers. *Education and Training in Mental Retardation and Developmental Disabilities, 31* (4), 304–309.

Newman, B., Buffington, D. M., O'Grady, M. A., McDonald, M. E., Poulson, C. L., & Hemmes, N. S. 1995. Self-management of schedule-following in three teenagers with autism. *Behavioral Disorders, 20,* 191–196.

Newman, B., Reinecke, D. R., & Kurtz, A. L. 1996. Why be moral: Humanist and behavioral perspectives. *The Behavior Analyst, 19,* 273–280.

Nichols, P. 1992. The curriculum of control: Twelve reasons for it, some arguments against it. *Beyond Behavior, 3,* 5–11.

Ninness, H. A. C., Ellis, J., & Ninness, S. K. 1999. Self-assessment as a learned reinforcer during computer interactive math performance: An experimental analysis. *Behavior Modification, 23,* 403–418.

Northup, J. 2000. Further evaluation of the accuracy of reinforcer surveys: A systematic replication. *Journal of Applied Behavior Analysis, 33,* 335–338.

Northup, J., George, T., Jones, K., Broussard, C., & Vollmer, T. 1996. A comparison of reinforcer assessment methods: The utility of verbal and pictorial choice procedures. *Journal of Applied Behavior Analysis, 29,* 201–212.

Northup, J., Wacker, D., Berg, W., Kelly, L., Sasso, G., & DeRaad, A. 1994. The treatment of severe behavior problems in school settings using a technical assistance model. *Journal of Applied Behavior Analysis, 27,* 33–47.

Northup, J., Wacker, D., Sasso, G., Steege, M., Cigrand, K., Cook, J., et al. 1991. A brief functional analysis of aggressive and alternative behavior in an outclinic setting. *Journal of Applied Behavior Analysis, 24,* 509–522.

O'Brien, S., Ross, L., & Christophersen, E. 1986. Primary encopresis: Evaluation and treatment. *Journal of Applied Behavior Analysis, 19,* 137–145.

O'Brien, T. P., Riner, L. S., & Budd, K. S. 1983. The effects of a child's self-evaluation program on compliance with parental instructions in the home. *Journal of Applied Behavior Analysis, 16,* 69–79.

O'Leary, K. D. 1968. The effects of self-instruction on immoral behavior. *Journal of Experimental Child Psychology, 6,* 297–301.

O'Leary, K. D. 1972. The assessment of psychopathology in children. In H. C. Quay & J. S. Werry (Eds.), *Psychopathological disorders of childhood* (pp. 234–272). New York: Wiley.

O'Leary, K. D., & Becker, W. C. 1967. Behavior modification of an adjustment class. *Exceptional Children, 33,* 637–642.

O'Leary, K. D., & O'Leary, S. G. (Eds.). 1977. *Classroom management: The successful use of behavior modification* (2nd ed.). New York: Pergamon Press.

O'Leary, K. D., Becker, W. C., Evans, M. B., & Saudargas, R. A. 1969. A token reinforcement program in a public school: A replication and systematic analysis. *Journal of Applied Behavior Analysis, 2,* 3–13.

O'Leary, K. D., Poulos, R. W., & Devine, V. T. 1972. Tangible reinforcers: Bonuses or bribes? *Journal of Consulting and Clinical Psychology, 38,* 1–8.

O'Neill, R., Horner, R., Albin, R., Sprague, J., Storey, K., & Newton, J. S. 1997. *Functional assessment and program development for problem behavior* (2nd ed.). Pacific Grove, CA: Brooks/Cole Publishing Co.

O'Neill, R., Horner, R., Albin, R., Storey, K., & Sprague, J. 1990. *Functional analysis of problem behavior.* Sycamore, IL: Sycamore Press.

O'Reilly, M. F., Lancioni, G. E., & Kierans, I. 2000. Teaching leisure social skills to adults with moderate mental retardation: An analysis of acquisition, generalization, and maintenance. *Education and Training in Mental Retardation and Developmental Disabilities. 35* (3), 250–258.

O'Reilly, M., Lancioni, G., & Taylor, I. 1999. An empirical analysis of two forms of extinction to treat aggression. *Research in Developmental Disabilities, 20,* 315–325.

O'Reilly, M., Lancioni, G., King, L., Lally, G., & Dhomhnaill, O. 2000. Using brief assessments to evaluate aberrant behavior maintained by attention. *Journal of Applied Behavior Analysis, 33,* 109–112.

Odom, S., & Strain, P. 1986. A comparison of peer-initiation and teacher-antecedent interventions for promoting reciprocal social interaction of autistic preschoolers. *Journal of Applied Behavior Analysis, 19,* 59–71.

Oliver, C., Hall, S., Hales, J., Murphy, G., & Watts, D. 1998. The treatment of severe self-injurious behavior by the systematic fading of restraints: Effects on self-injury, self-restraint, adaptive behavior, and behavior correlates of affect. *Research in Developmental Disabilities, 19,* 143–165.

Oliver, C., Murphy, G., Hall, S., Arron, K., & Leggett, J. 2003. Phenomenology of self-restraint. *American Journal on Mental Retardation, 108,* 71–81.

Oliver, C., Oxener, G., Hearn, M., & Hall, S. 2001. Effects of social proximity on multiple aggressive behaviors. *Journal of Applied Behavior Analysis, 34* (1), 85–88.

Ollendick, T., & Matson, J. 1976. An initial investigation into the parameters of overcorrection. *Psychological Reports, 39,* 1139–1142.

Ollendick, T., Matson, J., Esveldt-Dawson, K., & Shapiro, E. 1980. Increasing spelling achievement: An analysis of treatment procedures utilizing an alternating treatments design. *Journal of Applied Behavior Analysis, 13,* 645–654.

Olson, R., Wise, B., Conners, F., Rack, J., & Fulker, D. 1989. Specific deficits in component reading and language skills: Genetic and environmental influences. *Journal of Learning Disabilities, 22* (6), 339–348.

Olympia, D. E., Sheridan, S. M., & Andrews, D. 1994. Using student-managed interventions to increase homework completion and accuracy. *Journal of Applied Behavior Analysis, 27,* 85–99.

Orsborn, E., Patrick, H., Dixon, R., & Moore, D. 1995. The effects of reducing teacher questions and increasing pauses on child talk during morning news. *Journal of Behavioral Education, 5* (3), 347–357.

Ottenbacher, K. 1993. Interrater agreement of visual analysis in single-subject decisions: Quantitative review and analysis. *American Journal on Mental Retardation, 98,* 135–142.

Ottenbacher, K., & Cusick, A. 1991. An empirical investigation of interrater agreement for single-subject data using graphs with and without trend lines. *Journal of the Association for Persons with Severe Handicaps, 16,* 48–55.

Pace, G. M., & Toyer, E. A. 2000. The effects of a vitamin supplement on the pica of a child with severe mental retardation. *Journal of Applied Behavior Analysis, 33,* 619–622.

Pace, G., Ivancic, M., Edwards, G., Iwata, B., & Page, T. 1985. Assessment of stimulus preference and reinforcer value with profoundly retarded individuals. *Journal of Applied Behavior Analysis, 18,* 249–255.

Pace, G., Iwata, B., Edwards, G., & McCosh, K. 1986. Stimulus fading and transfer in the treatment of self-restraint and self-injurious behavior. *Journal of Applied Behavior Analysis, 19,* 381–389.

Paclawskyj, T., Matson, J., Rush, K., Smalls, Y., & Vollmer, T. 2000. Questions about behavioral function (QABF): A behavioral checklist for functional assessment of aberrant behavior. *Research in Developmental Disabilities, 21,* 223–229.

Palkes, H., Stewart, M., & Kahana, K. 1968. Porteus maze performance of hyperactive boys after training in self-directed verbal commands. *Child Development, 39,* 817–826.

Pancsofar, E. L., & Bates, P. 1985. The impact of the acquisition of successive training exemplars on generalization. *Journal of the Association for Persons with Severe Handicaps, 10,* 95–104.

Panyan, M. C., & Hall, R. V. 1978. Effects of serial versus concurrent task sequencing on acquisition, maintenance, and generalization. *Journal of Applied Behavior Analysis, 11,* 67–74.

Panyan, M. P. 1980. *How to use shaping.* Lawrence, KS: H & H Enterprises.

Parrish, J., Cataldo, M., Kolko, D., Neef, N., & Engel, A. 1986. Experimental analysis of response covariation among compliant and inappropriate behavior. *Journal of Applied Behavior Analysis, 19,* 241–254.

Parsons, M., Reid, D., Green, C. 2001. Situational assessment of task preferences among adults with multiple severe disabilities in supported work. *JASH, 26,* 50–55.

Partington, J., Sundberg, M., Newhouse, L., & Spengler, S. 1994. Overcoming an autistic child's failure to acquire a tact repertoire. *Journal of Applied Behavior Analysis, 27* (4), 733–734.

Patel, M., Carr, J., Kim, C., Robles, A., & Eastridge, D. 2000. Functional analysis of aberrant behavior maintained by automatic reinforcement: Assessments of specific sensory reinforcers. *Research in Developmental Disabilities, 21,* 393–407.

Patterson, E. T., Panyon, M. C., Wyatt, S., & Morales, E. September 1974. Forward vs. backward chaining in the teaching of vocational skills to the mentally retarded: An empirical analysis. *Paper presented at the 82nd Annual Meeting of the American Psychological Association,* New Orleans.

Patterson, G. R. 1965. An application of conditioning techniques to the control of a hyperactive child. In L. P. Ullmann & L. Krasner (Eds.), *Case studies in behavior modification* (pp. 370–375). New York: Holt, Rinehart & Winston.

Patton, J. R., Payne, J. S., & Beirne-Smith, M. 1990. *Mental retardation* (3rd ed.). Upper Saddle River, NJ: Merrill/ Prentice Hall.

Pelios, L., Morren, J., Tesch, D., & Axelrod, S. 1999. The impact of functional analysis methodology on treatment choice for self-injurious and aggressive behavior. *Journal of Applied Behavior Analysis, 32,* 185–195.

Peters, R., & Davies, K. 1981. Effects of self-instructional training on cognitive impulsivity of mentally retarded adolescents. *American Journal of Mental Deficiency, 85,* 377–382.

Peterson, N. 1982. Feedback is not a new principle of behavior. *Behavior Analyst, 5,* 101–102.

Phillips, D. C., & Kelly, M. E. 1975. Hierarchical theories of development in education and psychology. *Harvard Educational Review, 45,* 351–375.

Phillips, E. L., Phillips, E. A., Fixsen, D. L., & Wolf, M. M. 1971. Achievement place: Modification of the behaviors of predelinquent boys within a token economy. *Journal of Applied Behavior Analysis, 4,* 45–59.

Piaget, J., & Inhelder, B. 1969. *The psychology of the child.* New York: Basic Books.

Piazza, C., Adelinis, J., Hanley, G., Goh, H., & Delia, M. 2000. An evaluation of the effects of matched stimuli on behaviors maintained by automatic reinforcement. *Journal of Applied Behavior Analysis, 33,* 13–27.

Piazza, C., Fisher, W., Hanley, G., LeBlanc, L., Worsdell, A., Lindauer, S., et al. 1998. Treatment of pica through multiple analyses of its reinforcing functions. *Journal of Applied Behavior Analysis, 31,* 165–189.

Piazza, C., Hanley, G., & Fisher, W. 1996. Functional analysis and treatment of cigarette pica. *Journal of Applied Behavior Analysis, 29,* 437–450.

Piazza, C., Moes, D., & Fisher, W. 1996. Differential reinforcement of alternative behavior and demand fading in the treatment of escape-maintained destructive behavior. *Journal of Applied Behavior Analysis, 29,* 569–572.

Piazza, C., Patel, M., Gulotta, C., Seven, B., & Layer, S. 2003. On the relative contributions of positive reinforcement and escape extinction in the treatment of food refusal. *Journal of Applied Behavior Analysis, 36,* 309–324.

Pierce, K. I., & Schreibman, L. 1994. Teaching daily living skills to children with autism in unsupervised settings through pictorial self-management. *Journal of Applied Behavior Analysis, 27,* 471–481.

Pierce, W. D., & Cheney, C. 2004. *Behavior analysis and learning* (3rd ed.). Mahwah, NJ: Lawrence Erlbaum.

Pierce, W. D., & Eppling, W. F. 1999. *Behavior analysis and learning.* Upper Saddle River, NJ: Prentice Hall.

Pigott, H. E., Fantuzzo, J., & Clement, P. 1986. The effects of reciprocal peer tutoring and group contingencies on the academic performance of elementary school children. *Journal of Applied Behavior Analysis, 19,* 93–98.

Pinkston, E. M., Reese, N. M., LeBlanc, J. M., & Baer, D. M. 1973. Independent control of a preschool child's aggression and peer interaction by contingent teacher attention. *Journal of Applied Behavior Analysis, 6,* 115–124.

Poling, A., & Byrne, T. 1996. Reactions to Reese: Lord, let us laud and lament. *The Behavior Analyst, 19,* 79–82.

Poling, A., & Normand, M. 1999. Noncontingent reinforcement: An inappropriate description of time-based schedules that reduce behavior. *Journal of Applied Behavior Analysis, 32,* 237–238.

Poling, A., Methot, L., & LeSage, M. 1994. *Fundamentals of behavior analytic research.* New York: Plenum Press.

Polirstok, S. R., & Greer, R. D. 1977. Remediation of mutually aversive interactions between a problem student and four teachers by training the student in reinforcement techniques. *Journal of Applied Behavior Analysis, 10,* 707–716.

Polloway, E., & Polloway, C. 1979. Auctions: Vitalizing the token economy. *Journal for Special Educators, 15,* 121–123.

Prater, M. A., Joy, R., Chilman, B., Temple, J., & Miller, S. R. 1991. Self-monitoring of on-task behavior by adolescents with learning disabilities. *Learning Disability Quarterly, 14* (3), 164–177.

Premack, D. 1959. Toward empirical behavior laws: I. Positive reinforcement. *Psychological Review, 66,* 219–233.

Proctor, M., & Morgan, D. 1991. Effectiveness of a response cost raffle procedure on the disruptive classroom behavior of adolescents with behavior problems. *School Psychology Review, 20,* 97–109.

Pugach, M. C., & Warger, C. L. 1996. *Curriculum trends, special education, and reform: Refocusing the conversation.* New York: Teacher's College Press.

Pyles, D., & Bailey, J. 1990. Diagnosing severe behavior problems. In A. Repp & N. Singh (Eds.), *Perspectives on the use of nonaversive and aversive interventions for persons with developmental disabilities* (pp. 381–401). Sycamore, IL: Sycamore Press.

Rachlin, H. 1974. Self-control. *Behaviorism, 2,* 94–107.

Rachman, S. 1963. Spontaneous remission and latent learning. *Behavior Research and Therapy, 1,* 3–15.

Rapport, M., Murphy, A., & Bailey, J. 1982. Ritalin vs. response cost in the control of hyperactive children: A within-subject comparison. *Journal of Applied Behavior Analysis, 15,* 205–216.

Raschke, D. 1981. Designing reinforcement surveys: Let the student choose the reward. *Teaching Exceptional Children, 14,* 92–96.

Reed, H., Thomas, E., Sprague, J., & Horner, R. 1997. The student guided functional assessment interview: An analysis of student and teacher agreement. *Journal of Behavioral Education, 7* (1), 33–45.

Reese, R. M., Sherman, J., & Sheldon, J. 1998. Reducing disruptive behavior of a group-home resident with autism and mental retardation. *Journal of Autism and Developmental Disorders, 28,* 159–165.

Reid, J., Tombaugh, T., & Van den Heuvel, K. 1981. Application of contingent physical restraint to suppress stereotyped body rocking of profoundly retarded persons. *American Journal of Mental Deficiency, 86,* 78–85.

Reinecke, D. R., Newman, B., & Meinberg, D. L. 1999. Self-management of sharing in three pre-schoolers with autism. *Education and Training in Mental Retardation and Developmental Disabilities, 34,* 312–317.

Reitman, D., & Drabman, R. 1999. Multifaceted uses of a simple time-out record in the treatment of a noncompliant 8-year-old boy. *Education and Treatment of Children, 22,* 136–145.

Remington, B. 1991. *The challenge of severe mental handicap: A behavior analytic approach.* New York: Wiley & Sons.

Repp, A. 1983. *Teaching the mentally retarded.* Englewood Cliffs, NJ: Prentice Hall.

Repp, A. C., & Deitz, D. E. D. 1979. Reinforcement-based reductive procedures: Training and monitoring performance of institutional staff. *Mental Retardation, 17,* 221–226.

Repp, A. C., Barton, L., & Brulle, A. 1983. A comparison of two procedures for programming the differential reinforcement of other behavior. *Journal of Applied Behavior Analysis, 16,* 435–445.

Repp, A. C., Nieminen, G., Olinger, E., & Brusca, R. 1988. Direct observation: Factors affecting the accuracy of observers. *Exceptional Children, 55,* 29–36.

Repp, A. C., Roberts, D. M., Slack, D. J., Repp, C. F., & Berkler, M. S. 1976. A comparison of frequency, interval, and time-sampling methods of data collection. *Journal of Applied Behavior Analysis, 9,* 501–508.

Repp, A., & Karsh, K. 1994. Hypothesis-based interventions for tantrum behaviors in persons with developmental disabilities in school settings. *Journal of Applied Behavior Analysis, 27,* 21–31.

Repp, A., Deitz, S., & Deitz, D. 1976. Reducing inappropriate behaviors in classrooms and in individual sessions through DRO schedules of reinforcement. *Mental Retardation, 14,* 11–15.

Repp, A., Felce, D., & Barton, L. 1988. Basing the treatment of stereotypic and self-injurious behavior on hypotheses of their causes. *Journal of Applied Behavior Analysis, 21,* 281–290.

Repp, A., Felce, D., & Barton, L. 1991. The effects of initial interval size on the efficacy of DRO schedules of reinforcement. *Exceptional Children, 58,* 417–425.

Reynolds, G. S. 1961. Behavioral contrast. *Journal of the Experimental Analysis of Behavior, 4,* 57–71.

Reynolds, L., & Kelley, M. L. 1997. The efficacy of a response cost-based treatment package for managing aggressive behavior in preschoolers. *Behavior Modification, 21* (2), 216–230.

Rhode, G., Morgan, D. P., & Young, K. R. 1983. Generalization and maintenance of treatment gains of behaviorally handicapped students from resources rooms to regular classrooms using self-evaluation procedures. *Journal of Applied Behavior Analysis, 16,* 171–188.

Richards, S., Taylor, R., Ramasamy, R., & Richards, R. 1999. *Single subject research: Applications in educational and clinical settings.* San Diego: Singular Publishing Inc.

Richman, D., Berg, W., Wacker, D., Stephens, T., Rankin, B., & Kilroy, J. 1997. Using pretreatment and posttreatment assessments to enhance and evaluate existing treatment packages. *Journal of Applied Behavior Analysis, 30,* 709–712.

Richman, D., Wacker, D., & Winborn, L. 2000. Response efficiency during functional communication training: Effects of effort on response allocation. *Journal of Applied Behavior Analysis, 34,* 73–76.

Richman, D., Wacker, D., Asmus, J., Casey, S., & Andelman, M. 1999. Further analysis of problem behavior in response class hierarchies. *Journal of Applied Behavior Analysis, 32,* 269–283.

Richman, G. S., Reiss, M. L., Bauman, K. E., & Bailey, J. S. 1984. Teaching menstrual care to mentally retarded women: Acquisition, generalization, and maintenance. *Journal of Applied Behavior Analysis, 17,* 441–451.

Rimm, D. C., & Masters, J. C. 1979. *Behavior therapy: Techniques and empirical findings.* New York: Academic Press.

Rincover, A. 1981. *How to use sensory extinction.* Lawrence, KS: H&H Enterprises.

Rincover, A., & Devany, J. 1982. The application of sensory extinction procedures to self-injury. *Analysis and Intervention in Developmental Disabilities, 2,* 67–81.

Rincover, A., & Koegel, R. L. 1975. Setting generality and stimulus control in autistic children. *Journal of Applied Behavior Analysis, 8,* 235–246.

Ringdahl, J., Vollmer, T., Marcus, B., & Roane, H. 1997. An analogue evaluation of environmental enrichment: The role of stimulus preference. *Journal of Applied Behavior Analysis, 30,* 203–216.

Risley, T. R. 1975. Certify procedures not people. In W. S. Wood (Ed.), *Issues in evaluating behavior modification* (pp. 159–181). Champaign, IL: Research Press.

Ritschl, C., Mongrella. J., & Presbie, R. 1972. Group time-out from rock and roll music and out-of-seat behavior of handicapped children while riding a school bus. *Psychological Reports, 31,* 967–973.

Rivera, M. O., Koorland, M. A., & Fueyo, V. 2002. Pupil-made pictorial prompts and fading for teaching sight words to a student with learning disabilities. *Education and Treatment of Children, 25,* 197–207.

Roane, H., Fisher, W., & McDonough, E. 2003. Progressing from programmatic to discovery research. A case example with the overjustification effect. *Journal of Applied Behavior Analysis, 36,* 35–46.

Roberts, M. 1988. Enforcing chair timeouts with room time-outs. *Behavior Modification, 12,* 353–370.

Roberts, R. N., Nelson, R. O., & Olson, T. W. 1987. Self-instruction: An analysis of the differential effects of instruction and reinforcement. *Journal of Applied Behavior Analysis, 20,* 235–242.

Roberts-Gwinn, M., Luiten, L., Derby, K., Johnson, T., & Weber, K. 2001. Identification of competing reinforcers for behavior maintained by automatic reinforcement. *Journal of Positive Behavior Interventions, 3,* 83–87.

Robin, A. L., Armel, S., & O'Leary, K. D. 1975. The effects of self-instruction on writing deficiencies. *Behavior Therapy, 6,* 178–187.

Rodewald, H. K. 1979. *Stimulus control of behavior.* Baltimore: University Park Press.

Rodi, M. S., & Hughes, C. 2000. Teaching communication book use to a high school student using a milieu approach. *Journal of the Association for Persons with Severe Handicaps, 25,* 175–179.

Rogers, C. R., & Skinner, B. F. 1956. Some issues concerning the control of human behavior: A symposium. *Science, 124,* 1057–1066.

Rojahn, J., McGonigle, J., Curcio, C., & Dixon, J. 1987. Suppression of pica by water mist and aromatic ammonia. *Behavior Modification, 11,* 65–74.

Rolider, A., & Van Houten, R. 1985. Movement suppression in time-out for undesirable behavior in psychotic and severely developmentally delayed children. *Journal of Applied Behavior Analysis, 18,* 275–288.

Rolider, A., Williams, L., Cummings, A., & Van Houten, R. 1991. The use of brief movement restriction procedure to eliminate severe inappropriate behavior. *Journal of Behaviour Therapy and Experimental Psychiatry, 22* (1), 23–30.

Rollings, J., Baumeister, A., & Baumeister, A. 1977. The use of overcorrection procedures to eliminate the stereotyped behaviors of retarded individuals: An analysis of collateral behaviors and generalization of suppressive effects. *Behavior Modification, 1,* 29–46.

Romaniuk, C., Miltenberger, R., Conyers, C., Jenner, N. H., Jurgens, M., & Ringenberg, C. 2002. The influence of activity choice on problem behaviors maintained by escape versus attention. *Journal of Applied Behavior Analysis, 35,* 349–362.

Rortvedt, A., & Miltenberger, R. 1994. Analysis of a high-probability instructional sequence and time-out in the treatment of child noncompliance. *Journal of Applied Behavior Analysis, 27,* 327–330.

Rosenbaum, M. S., & Drabman, R. S. 1979. Self-control training in the classroom: A review and critique. *Journal of Applied Behavior Analysis, 12,* 467–485.

Ross, D. 2002. Replacing faulty conversational exchanges for children with autism by establishing a functionally equivalent alternative response. *Education and Training in Mental Retardation and Developmental Disabilities, 37,* 343–362.

Ross, D., & Greer, R. 2003. Generalized imitation and the mand: Inducing first instances of speech in young children with autism. *Research in Developmental Disabilities, 24,* 58–74.

Rotholz, O., & Luce, S. 1983. Alternative reinforcement strategies for the reduction of self-stimulatory behavior in autistic youth. *Education and Treatment of Children, 6,* 363–377.

Rothstein, L. F. 1990. *Special education law.* New York: Longman.

Rowling, J. K. 1998. *Harry Potter and the chamber of secrets.* New York: Scholastic Press.

Rusch, F., & Close, D. 1976. Overcorrection: A procedural evaluation. *AAESPH Review, 1,* 32–45.

Rusch, F., Connis, R., & Sowers, J. 1978. The modification and maintenance of time spent attending to task using social reinforcement, token reinforcement and response cost in an applied restaurant setting. *Journal of Special Education Technology, 2,* 18–26.

Rutherford, B. 1940. The use of negative practice in speech therapy with children handicapped by cerebral palsy, athetoid type. *Journal of Speech Disorders, 5,* 259–264.

Ryan, J., & Peterson, R. 2004. Physical restraint in school. *Behavioral Disorders, 29,* 154–168.

Saigh, P., & Umar, A. 1983. The effects of a good behavior game on the disruptive behavior of Sudanese elementary school students. *Journal of Applied Behavior Analysis, 16,* 339–344.

Sainato, D., Maheady, L., & Shook, G. 1986. The effects of a classroom manager role on the social interaction patterns and social status of withdrawn kindergarten students. *Journal of Applied Behavior Analysis, 19,* 187–195.

Sajwaj, T., Libet, J., & Agras, S. 1974. Lemon-juice therapy: The control of life-threatening rumination in a six-month-old infant. *Journal of Applied Behavior Analysis, 7,* 557–563.

Salend, S. 1988. Effects of a student-managed response cost system on the behavior of two mainstreamed students. *Elementary School Journal, 89,* 89–97.

Salend, S., & Gordon, B. 1987. A group-oriented time-out ribbon procedure. *Behavioral Disorders, 12,* 131–137.

Salend, S., & Kovalich, B. 1981. A group response cost system mediated by free tokens. *American Journal of Mental Deficiency, 86,* 184–187.

Salend, S., & Lamb, E. 1986. Effectiveness of a group-managed interdependent contingency system. *Learning Disability Quarterly, 9,* 268–273.

Salend, S., & Maragulia, D. 1983. The time-out ribbon: A procedure for the least restrictive environment. *Journal for Special Educators, 20,* 9–15.

Salend, S., & Meddaugh, D. 1985. Using a peer-mediated extinction procedure to decrease obscene language. *The Pointer, 30,* 8–11.

Sasso, G., Conroy, M., Stichter, J., & Fox, J. 2001. Slowing down the bandwagon: The misapplication of functional assessment for students with emotional or behavioral disorders. *Behavioral Disorders, 26,* 282–296.

Sasso, G., Reimers, T., Cooper, L., Wacker, D., Berg, W., Steege, M., et al. 1992. Use of descriptive and experimental analyses to identify the functional properties of aberrant behavior in school settings. *Journal of Applied Behavior Analysis, 25,* 809–821.

Saudargas, R., & Zanolli, K. 1990. Momentary time sampling as an estimate of percentage time: A field validation. *Journal of Applied Behavior Analysis, 23,* 533–537.

Saunders, R., & Koplik, K. 1975. A multi-purpose data sheet for recording and graphing in the classroom. *AAESPH Review, 1,* 1.

Schepis, M., Reid, D., & Behrman, M. 1996. Acquisition and functional use of voice output communication by persons with profound multiple disabilities. *Behavior Modification, 20* (4), 451–468.

Schloss, P., & Smith, M. 1987. Guidelines for ethical use of manual restraint in public school settings for behaviorally disordered students. *Behavioral Disorders, 12,* 207–213.

Schloss, P., Kobza, S., & Alper, S. 1997. The use of peer tutoring for the acquisition of functional math skills among students with moderate mental retardation. *Education and Treatment of Children, 20* (2), 189–208.

Schlosser, R., Blischak, D., Belfiore, P., Bartley, C., & Barnett, N. 1998. Effect of synthetic speech output and orthographic feedback on spelling in a student with autism. *Journal of Autism and Developmental Disorders, 28* (4), 309–317.

Schmit, J., Alper, S., Raschke, D., & Ryndak, D. 2000. Effects of using a photographic cueing package during routine school transitions with a child who has autism. *Mental Retardation, 38,* 131–137.

Schnaitter, R. 1999. Some criticisms of behaviorism. In B. A. Thyer (Ed.), *The philosophical legacy of behaviorism.* Dordrecht, The Netherlands: Kluwer Academic Publishers.

Schopler, E., Reichler, R., & Renner, B. 1986. *The childhood autism rating scale.* New York: Irvington, Inc.

Schreibman, L. 1975. Effects of within-stimulus and extra-stimulus prompting on discrimination learning in autistic children. *Journal of Applied Behavior Analysis, 8,* 91–112.

Schreibman, L., & Charlop, M. H. 1981. S^D versus S^Δ fading in prompting procedures with autistic children. *Journal of Experimental Child Psychology, 34,* 508–520.

Schroeder, G. L., & Baer, D. M. 1972. Effects of concurrent and serial training on generalized vocal imitation in retarded children. *Development Psychology, 6,* 293–301.

Schroeder, S. R., & MacLean, W. 1987. If it isn't one thing, it's another: Experimental analysis of covariation in behavior management data of severely disturbed retarded persons. In S. Landesman & P. Vietze (Eds.), *Living environments and mental retardation* (pp. 315–338). Washington, D.C.: AAMD Monograph.

Schroeder, S. R., Oldenquist, A., & Rohahn, J. 1990. A conceptual framework for judging the humaneness and effectiveness of behavioral treatment. In A. C. Repp & N. N. Singh (Eds.), *Perspectives on the use of nonaversive and aversive interventions for persons with developmental disabilities.* New York: Sycamore.

Schultz, D. P. 1969. *A history of modern psychology.* New York: Academy Press.

Schumaker, J. B., Hovell, M. F., & Sherman, J. A. 1977. An analysis of daily report cards and parent-managed privileges in the improvement of adolescents' classroom performance. *Journal of Applied Behavior Analysis, 10,* 449–464.

Schumaker, J., & Sherman, J. A. 1970. Training generative verb usage by imitation and reinforcement procedures. *Journal of Applied Behavior Analysis, 3,* 273–287.

Schussler, N. G., & Spradlin, J. E. 1991. Assessment of stimuli controlling the requests of students with severe mental retardation during a snack routine. *Journal of Applied Behavior Analysis, 24,* 791–797.

Schuster, J., & Griffen, A. 1993. Teaching a chained task with a simultaneous prompting procedure. *Journal of Behavioral Education, 3* (3), 299–315.

Schuster, J., Morse, T., Griffen, A., & Wolery, T. 1996. Teaching peer reinforcement and grocery words: An investigation of observational learning and instructional feedback. *Journal of Behavioral Education, 6,* 511–533.

Schwarz, M. L., & Hawkins, R. P. 1970. Application of delayed reinforcement procedures to the behavior of an elementary school child. *Journal of Applied Behavior Analysis, 3,* 85–96.

Scott, T., & Nelson, C. M. 1999. Using functional behavioral assessment to develop effective intervention plans: Practical classroom applications. *Journal of Positive Behavior Interventions, 1,* 242–251.

Secan, K., Egel, A., & Tilley, C. 1989. Acquisition, generalization, and maintenance of question-answering skills in autistic children. *Journal of Applied Behavior Analysis, 22* (2), 181–196.

Sedlak, R. A., Doyle, M., & Schloss, P. 1982. Video games: A training and generalization demonstration with severely retarded adolescents. *Education and Training for the Mentally Retarded, 17,* 332–336.

Sewell, T., Collins, B., Hemmeter, L., & Schuster, J. 1998. Using simultaneous prompting within an activity-based format to teach dressing skills to preschoolers with developmental delays. *Journal of Early Intervention, 21* (2), 132–145.

Seymour, F. W., & Stokes, T. F. 1976. Self-recording in training girls to increase work and evoke staff praise in an institution for offenders. *Journal of Applied Behavior Analysis, 9,* 41–54.

Shabani, D. B., Katz, R. C., Wilder, D. A., Beauchamp, K., Taylor, C. R., & Fischer, K. J. 2002. Increasing social initiations in children with autism: Effects of a tactile prompt. *Journal of Applied Behavior Analysis, 35,* 79–83.

Shafer, M. S., Inge, K. J., & Hill, J. 1986. Acquisition, generalization, and maintenance of automated banking skills. *Education and Training of the Mentally Retarded, 21,* 265–272.

Shimbukuro, S. M., Prater, M. A., Jenkins, A., & Edelen-Smith, P. 1999. The effects of self-monitoring of academic performance on students with learning disabilities and AAA/ADHD. *Education and Treatment of Children, 22,* 397–414.

Shore, B., Iwata, B., DeLeon, I., Kahng, S., & Smith, R. 1997. An analysis of reinforcer substitutability using object manipulation and self-injury as competing responses. *Journal of Applied Behavior Analysis, 30,* 21–41.

Short, E. J., & Weissberg-Benchell, J. 1989. The triple alliance for learning: Cognition, metacognition, and motivation. In C. B. McCormick, G. E. Miller, and M. Pressley (Eds.), *Cognitive strategy research: From basic research to educational applications* (pp. 33–63). New York: Springer-Verlag.

Shriver, M. D., & Allen, K. D. 1997. Defining child noncompliance. An examination of temporal parameters. *Journal of Applied Behavior Analysis, 30,* 173–176.

Shriver, M., & Piersal, W. 1994. The long-term effects of intrauterine drug exposure: Review of recent research and implications for early childhood special education. *Topics in Early Childhood Special Education, 14,* 161–183.

Shukla, S., Kennedy, C., & Cushing, L. S. 1999. Intermediate school students with severe disabilities: Supporting their social participation in general education classrooms. *Journal of Positive Behavior Interventions, 1* (3), 130–140.

Sidman, M. 1960. *Tactics of scientific research: Evaluating experimental data in psychology.* Boston: Authors Cooperative.

Siegel, G. M., Lenske, J., & Broen, P. 1969. Suppression of normal speech disfluencies through response cost. *Journal of Applied Behavior Analysis, 2,* 265–276.

Sigafoos, J., Couzens, D., Roberts, D., Phillips, C., & Goodison, K. 1996. Teaching requests for food and drink to children with multiple disabilities in a graphic communication mode. *Journal of Developmental and Physical Disabilities, 8* (3), 247–262.

Sigafoos, J., Penned, D., & Versluis, J. 1996. Naturalistic assessment leading to effective treatment of self-injury in a young boy with multiple disabilities. *Education and Treatment of Children, 19* (2), 101–123.

Sigueland, E. 1968. Reinforcement patterns and extinction in human newborns. *Journal of Experimental Child Psychology, 6,* 431–442.

Silverman, K., Watanabe, K., Marshall, A., & Baer, D. 1984. Reducing self-injury and corresponding self-restraint through the strategic use of protective clothing. *Journal of Applied Behavior Analysis, 17,* 545–552.

Simmons, D., Fuchs, D., Fuchs, L., Hodges, J., Mathes, P. 1994. Importance of instructional complexity and role reciprocity to classwide peer tutoring. *Learning Disabilities Research & Practice, 9,* 203–212.

Simpson, R. G., & Eaves, R. C. 1985. Do we need more qualitative research or more good research? A reaction to Stainback and Stainback. *Exceptional Children, 51,* 325–329.

Singh, N. 1979. Aversive control of breath-holding. *Journal of Behavior Therapy and Experimental Psychiatry, 10,* 147–149.

Singh, N. 1980. The effects of facial screening on infant self-injury. *Journal of Behavior Therapy and Experimental Psychiatry, 11,* 131–134.

Singh, N. 1987. Overcorrection of oral reading errors. *Behavior Modification, 11,* 165–181.

Singh, N. 1990. Effects of two error-correction procedures on oral reading errors. *Behavior Modification, 14,* 188–199.

Singh, N., & Bakker, L. 1984. Suppression of pica by overcorrection and physical restraint: A comparative analysis. *Journal of Autism and Developmental Disorders, 14,* 331–340.

Singh, N., & Singh, J. 1986. Increasing oral reading proficiency: A comparative analysis of drill and positive practice overcorrection procedures. *Behavior Modification, 10,* 115–130.

Singh, N., & Singh, J. 1988. Increasing oral reading proficiency through overcorrection and phonic analysis. *American Journal of Mental Retardation, 93,* 312–319.

Singh, N., & Winton, A. 1984. Effects of a screening procedure on pica and collateral behaviors. *Journal of Behavior Therapy and Experimental Psychiatry, 15,* 59–65.

Singh, N., Beale, I., & Dawson, M. 1981. Duration of facial screening and suppression of self-injurious behavior: Analysis using an alternative treatments design. *Behavioral Assessment, 3,* 411–420.

Singh, N., Dawson, M., & Manning, P. 1981. Effects of spaced responding DRL on the stereotyped behavior of profoundly retarded persons. *Journal of Applied Behavior Analysis, 14,* 521–526.

Singh, N., Landrum, T., Ellis, C., & Donatelli, L. 1993. Effects of thioridazine and visual screening on stereotypy and social behavior in individuals with mental retardation. *Research in Developmental Disabilities, 14,* 163–177.

Singh, N., Singh, J., & Winton, A. 1984. Positive practice overcorrection of oral reading errors. *Behavior Modification, 8,* 23–37.

Singh, N., Watson, J., & Winton, A. 1986. Treating self-injury: Water mist spray versus facial screeing or forced arm exercise. *Journal of Applied Behavior Analysis, 19,* 403–410.

Skinner, B. F. 1953. *Science and human behavior.* New York: Macmillan.

Skinner, B. F. 1957. *Verbal behavior.* New York: Appleton-Century-Crofts.

Skinner, B. F. 1963. Operant behavior. *American Psychologist, 18,* 503–515.

Skinner, B. F. 1968. *The technology of teaching.* New York: Appleton-Century-Crofts.

Skinner, B. F. 1969. Communication. *Journal of Applied Behavior Analysis, 2,* 247.

Skinner, B. F. 1971. *Beyond freedom and dignity.* New York: Knopf.

Skinner, B. F., & Vaughan, M. E. 1983. *Enjoy old age: A program of self-management.* New York: Warner Books.

Skinner, C., Cooper, L., & Cole, C. 1997. The effects of oral presentation previewing rates on reading performance. *Journal of Applied Behavior Analysis, 30,* 331–333.

Slavin, R. E. 1991. Group rewards make groupwork work: A response to Kohn. *Educational Leadership,* February, 89–91.

Smith, A., Piersel, W., Filbeck, R., & Gross, E. 1983. The elimination of mealtime food stealing and scavenging behavior in an institutionalized severely mentally retarded adult. *Mental Retardation, 21,* 255–259.

Smith, B., Sugai, G., & Brown, D. 2000. A self-management functional assessment-based behavior support plan for a middle school student with EBD. *Journal of Positive Behavior Interventions, 2,* 208–218.

Smith, D. 1979. The improvement of children's oral reading through the use of teacher modeling. *Journal of Learning Disabilities, 12,* 172–175.

Smith, L. D. 1992. On prediction and control: B. F. Skinner and the technological ideal of science. *American Psychologist, 47,* 216–223.

Smith, M., & Heflin, L. J. 2001. Supporting positive behavior in public schools: An intervention program in Georgia. *Journal of Positive Behavior Interventions, 3,* 39–47.

Smith, R. G., & Iwata, B. A. 1997. Antecedent influences on behavior disorders. *Journal of Applied Behavior Analysis, 30,* 343–375.

Smith, R. L., Collins, B. C., Schuster, J. W., & Kleinert, H. 1999. Teaching table cleaning skills to secondary students with moderate/severe disabilities: Facilitating observational learning during instructional downtime. *Education and Training in Mental Retardation and Developmental Disabilities, 34,* 342–353.

Smith, R., & Churchill, R. 2002. Identification of environmental determinants of behavior disorders through functional analysis of precursor behaviors. *Journal of Applied Behavior Analysis, 35,* 125–136.

Smith, R., Iwata, B., & Shore, B. 1995. Effects of subject versus experimenter-selected reinforcers on the behavior of individuals with profound developmental disabilities. *Journal of Applied Behavior Analysis, 28,* 61–71.

Smith, R., Iwata, B., Goh, H., & Shore, B. 1995. Analysis of establishing operations for self-injury maintained by escape. *Journal of Applied Behavior Analysis, 28,* 515–535.

Smith, R., Lerman, D., & Iwata, B. 1996. Self-restraint as positive reinforcement for self-injurious behavior. *Journal of Applied Behavior Analysis, 29,* 99–102.

Smith, R., Russo, L., & Le, D. 1999. Distinguishing between extinction and punishment effects of response blocking: A replication. *Journal of Applied Behavior Analysis, 32,* (3) 367–370.

Smith, S., & Farrell, D. 1993. Level system use in special education: Classroom intervention with prima facie appeal. *Behavioral Disorders, 18* (4), 251–264.

Snell, M., & Loyd, B. 1991. A study of effects of trend, variability, frequency, and form of data on teachers' judgments about progress and their decisions about program change. *Research in Developmental Disabilities, 12,* 41–62.

Sobsey, D. 1990. Modifying the behavior of behavior modifiers. In A. Repp & N. Singh (Eds.), *Perspectives on the use of nonaversive and aversive interventions for persons with developmental disabilities* (pp. 421–433). Sycamore, IL: Sycamore Publishing.

Solomon, R. W., & Wahler, R. G. 1973. Peer reinforcement control of classroom problem behavior. *Journal of Applied Behavior Analysis, 6,* 49–56.

Sparrow, S. S., Balla, D. A., & Ciccetti, O. V. 1998. *Vineland adaptive behavior scales, classroom edition.* Circle Pines, MN: American Guidance Service.

Spitz, D., & Spitz, W. 1990. Killer pop machines. *Journal of Forensic Science, 35,* 490–492.

Spooner, F. 1981. An operant analysis of the effects of backward chaining and total task presentation. *Dissertation Abstracts International, 41,* 3992A [University Microfilms No. 8105615].

Spooner, F., & Spooner, D. 1983. Variability: An aid in the assessment of training procedures. *Journal of Precision Teaching, 4* (1), 5–13.

Spooner, F., & Spooner, D. 1984. A review of chaining techniques: Implications for future research and practice. *Education and Training of the Mentally Retarded, 19,* 114–124.

Sprague, J. R., & Horner, R. H. 1984. The effects of single instance, multiple instance, and general case training on generalized vending machine use by moderately and severely handicapped students. *Journal of Applied Behavior Analysis, 17,* 273–278.

Sprague, J., Holland, K., & Thomas, K. 1997. The effect of noncontingent sensory reinforcement, contingent sensory reinforcement, and response interruption on stereotypical and self-injurious behavior. *Research in Developmental Disabilities, 18,* 61–77.

Staats, A. W., & Staats, C. K. 1963. *Complex human behavior.* New York: Holt, Rinehart & Winston.

Stafford, A., Alberto, P., Fredrick, L., Heflin, J., & Heller, K. 2002. Preference variability and the instruction of choice making with students with severe intellectual disabilities. *Education and Training in Mental Retardation and Developmental Disabilities, 37,* 70–88.

Stahmer, A. C., & Schreibman, L. 1992. Teaching children with autism appropriate play in unsupervised environments using a self-management treatment package. *Journal of Applied Behavior Analysis, 25,* 447–459.

Stainback, S., & Stainback, W. 1992. Schools as inclusive communities. In W. Stainback & S. Stainback (Eds.), *Controversial issues confronting special education: Divergent perspectives* (pp. 29–43). Boston: Allyn & Bacon.

Stainback, S., & Stainback, W. 1984. Broadening the research perspective in special education. *Exceptional Children, 50,* 400–408.

Stainback, W., Payne, J., Stainback, S., & Payne, R. 1973. *Establishing a token economy in the classroom.* Columbus, OH: Merrill.

Stainback, W., Stainback, S., & Strathe, M. 1983. Generalization of positive social behavior by severely handicapped students: A review and analysis of research. *Education and Training of the Mentally Retarded, 18,* 293–299.

Steed, S. E., & Lutzker, J. R. 1997. Using picture prompts to teach an adult with developmental disabilities to independently complete vocational tasks. *Journal of Developmental and Physical Disabilities, 9,* 117–133.

Steed, S. E., & Lutzker, J. R. 1999. Recorded auditory prompts: A strategy to increase independent prevocational task completion in individuals with dual diagnosis. *Behavior Modification, 23*(1) 152–168.

Steege, M., & Northup, J. 1998. Functional analysis of problem behavior: A practical approach for school psychologists. *Proven Practice, 1,* 4–12.

Steege, M., Wacker, D., Cigrand, K., Berg, W., Novak, C., Reimers, T., et al. 1990. Use of negative reinforcement in the treatment of self-injurious behavior. *Journal of Applied Behavior Analysis, 23,* 459–467.

Stella, M. E., & Etzel, B. C. 1978. Procedural variables in errorless discrimination learning: Order of S^D and S^Δ manipulation. Toronto, Canada: American Psychological Association.

Stephens, T. M. 1976. *Directive teaching of children with learning and behavioral handicaps.* Columbus, OH: Merrill.

Stern, G., Fowlers, S., & Kohler, F. 1988. A comparison of two intervention roles: Peer monitor and point-earner. *Journal of Applied Behavior Analysis, 21,* 103–109.

Steuart, W. 1993. Effectiveness of arousal and arousal plus overcorrection to reduce nocturnal bruxism. *Journal of Behavior Therapy & Experimental Psychiatry, 24,* 181–185.

Stevens, K. B., & Schuster, J. W. 1987. Effects of a constant time delay procedure on the written spelling performance of a learning disabled student. *Learning Disability Quarterly, 10,* 9–16.

Stevenson, H., & Odom, R. 1964. Visual reinforcement with children. *Journal of Experimental Child Psychology, 1,* 248–255.

Stevenson, J., & Clayton, F. 1970. A response duration schedule: Effects of training, extinction, and deprivation. *Journal of the Experimental Analysis of Behavior, 13,* 359–367.

Stewart, C., & Singh, N. 1986. Overcorrection of spelling deficits in mentally retarded persons. *Behavior Modification, 10,* 355–365.

Stewart, M., & Bengier, D. 2001. An analysis of volleyball coaches' coaching behavior in a summer volleyball team camp. *Physical Educator, 58,* 86–103.

Stokes, T. F., & Baer, D. M. 1976. Preschool peers as mutual generalization-facilitating agents. *Behavior Therapy, 7,* 549–556.

Stokes, T. F., & Baer, D. M. 1977. An implicit technology of generalization. *Journal of Applied Behavior Analysis, 10,* 349–367.

Stokes, T. F., Baer, D. M., & Jackson, R. L. 1974. Programming the generalization of a greeting response in four retarded children. *Journal of Applied Behavior Analysis, 7,* 599–610.

Stolz, S. B. 1977. Why no guidelines for behavior modification? *Journal of Applied Behavior Analysis, 10,* 541–547.

Strauss, A. A., & Lehtinen, L. E. 1947. *Psychopathology and education of the brain-injured child.* New York: Grune & Stratton.

Strauss, A. A., & Werner, H. 1942. Disorders of conceptual thinking in the brain-injured child. *Journal of Nervous and Mental Disease, 96,* 153–172.

Streifel, S., & Wetherby, B., 1973. Instruction-following behavior of a retarded child and its controlling stimuli. *Journal of Applied Behavior Analysis, 6,* 663–670.

Stricker, J., Miltenberger, R., Garlinghouse, M., Deaver, C., & Anderson, C. 2001. Evaluation of an awareness enhancement device for the treatment of thumb sucking in children. *Journal of Applied Behavior Analysis, 34* (1), 77–80.

Stromer, R., MacKay, H., McVay, A., & Fowler, T. 1998. Written lists as mediating stimuli in the matching-to-sample performances of individuals with mental retardation. *Journal of Applied Behavior Analysis, 31* (1), 1–19.

Sturmey, P. 1994. Assessing the functions of aberrant behaviors: A review of psychometric instruments. *Journal of Autism and Developmental Disorders, 24,* 293–304.

Sturmey, P. 1995. Analog baselines: A critical review of the methodology. *Research in Developmental Disabilities, 16* (4), 269–284.

Sulzer-Azaroff, B., & Mayer, G. R. 1977. *Applying behavior-analysis procedures with children and youth.* New York: Holt, Rinehart & Winston.

Sulzer-Azaroff, B., & Mayer, G. R. 1986. *Achieving educational excellence.* New York: Holt, Rinehart & Winston.

Sulzer-Azaroff, B., Thaw, J., & Thomas, C. 1975. Behavioral competencies for the evaluation of behavior modifiers. In W. S. Wood (Ed.), *Issues in evaluating behavior modification* (pp. 47–98). Champaign, IL: Research Press.

Summers, J., Rincover, A., & Feldman, M. 1993. Comparison of extra- and within-stimulus prompting to teach prepositional discriminations to preschool children with developmental disabilities. *Journal of Behavioral Education, 3* (3),287–298.

Sumner, J., Meuser, S., Hsu, L., & Morales, R. 1974. Overcorrection treatment of radical reduction of aggressive-disruptive behavior in institutionalized mental patients. *Psychological Reports, 35,* 655–662.

Sutherland, K., Wehby, J., & Copeland, S. 2000. Effect of varying rates of behavior-specific praise on the on-task behavior of students with EBD. *Journal of Emotional and Behavioral Disorders, 8,* 2–8.

Sweeney, W. J., Salva, E., Cooper, J. O., & Talbert-Johnson, C. 1993. Using self-evaluation to improve difficult-to-read handwriting of secondary students. *Journal of Behavioral Education, 3,* 427–443.

Symons, F., McDonald, L., & Wehby, J. 1998. Functional assessment and teacher collected data. *Education and Treatment of Children, 21,* 135–159.

Taber, T. A., Alberto, P. A., & Fredrick, L. D. 1998. Use of self-operated auditory prompts by workers with moderate mental retardation to transition independently through vocational tasks. *Research in Developmental Disabilities, 19,* 127–145.

Tang, J., Patterson, T., & Kennedy, C. 2003. Identifying specific sensory modalities maintaining the stereotypy of students with multiple profound disabilities. *Research in Developmental Disabilities, 24,* 433–451.

Tanner, B. A., & Zeiler, M. 1975. Punishment of self-injurious behavior using aromatic ammonia as the aversive stimulus. *Journal of Applied Behavior Analysis, 8,* 53–57.

Tarpley, H., & Schroeder, S. 1979. Comparison of DRO and DRI on rate of suppression of self-injurious behavior. *American Journal of Mental Deficiency, 84,* 188–194.

Tawney, J., & Gast, D. 1984. *Single subject research in special education.* Columbus, OH: Merrill.

Taylor, B. R. & Levin, L. 1998. Teaching a student with autism to make verbal initiations: Effects of a tactile prompt. *Journal of Applied Behavior Analysis, 31,* 651–654.

Taylor, B., & Harris, S. 1995. Teaching children with autism to seek information: Acquisition of novel information and generalization of responding. *Journal of Applied Behavior Analysis, 28* (1), 3–14.

Terrace, H. S. 1966. Stimulus control. In W. K. Honig (Ed.), *Operant behavior: Areas of research and application.* New York: Appleton-Century-Crofts.

Test, D. W., & Spooner, F. 1996. *Community-based instructional support.* Washington, D.C.: American Association on Mental Retardation.

Test, D. W., Spooner, F., Keul, P. K., & Grossi, T. 1990. Teaching adolescents with severe disabilities to use the public telephone. *Behavior Modification, 14,* 157–171.

Thomas, A., & Birch, R. 1984. Genesis and evolution of behavior disorders: From infancy to early adult life. *American Journal of Psychiatry, 141,* 1–9.

Thomas, A., & Chess, S. 1977. *Temperament and development.* New York: Brunner/Mazel.

Thomas, J. D., Presland, I. E., Grant, M. D., & Glynn, T. L. 1978. Natural rates of teacher approval and disapproval in grade-7 classrooms. *Journal of Applied Behavior Analysis, 11,* 91–94.

Thompson, R., Fisher, W., & Contrucci, S. 1998. Evaluating the reinforcing effects of choice in comparison to reinforcement rate. *Research in Developmental Disabilities, 19,* 181–187.

Thompson, R., Fisher, W., Piazza, C., & Kuhn, D. 1998. The evaluation and treatment of aggression maintained by attention and automatic reinforcement. *Journal of Applied Behavior Analysis, 31,* 103–116.

Thorndike, E. L. 1905. *The elements of psychology.* New York: Seiler.

Thorndike, E. L. 1931. *Human learning.* New York: Appleton-Century-Crofts.

Tincani, M., Castrogiavanni, A., & Axelrod, S. 1999. A comparison of the effectiveness of brief versus traditional functional analyses. *Research in Developmental Disabilities, 20,* 327–338.

Todd, A., Horner, R., & Sugai, G. 1999. Self-monitoring and self-recruited praise: Effects on problem behavior, academic engagement, and work completion in a typical classroom. *Journal of Positive Behavior Interventions, 1* (2), 66–76.

Tolman, E. C. 1932. *Purposive behavior in animals and men.* New York: Appleton-Century-Crofts.

Touchette, P. E., & Howard, J. S. 1984. Errorless learning: Reinforcement contingencies and stimulus control transfer in delayed prompting. *Journal of Applied Behavior Analysis, 17,* 175–188.

Touchette, P., MacDonald, R., & Langer, S. 1985. A scatter plot for identifying stimulus control of problem behavior. *Journal of Applied Behavior Analysis, 18,* 343–351.

Trant, L. 1977. Pictorial token card (communication). *Journal of Applied Behavior Analysis, 10,* 548.

Trap, J. J., Milner-Davis, P., Joseph, S., & Cooper, J. O. 1978. The effects of feedback and consequences on transitional cursive letter formation. *Journal of Applied Behavior Analysis, 11,* 381–393.

Trask-Tyler, S. A., Grossi, T. A., & Heward, W. L. 1994. Teaching young adults with developmental disabilities and visual impairments to use tape-recorded recipes: Acquisition, generalization, and maintenance of cooking skills. *Journal of Behavioral Education, 4,* 283–311.

Trice, A., & Parker, F. 1983. Decreasing adolescent swearing in an instructional setting. *Education and Treatment of Children, 6,* 29–35.

Troutman, A. C. 1977. Stimulus control: A procedure to facilitate generalization from resource rooms to regular classrooms. Unpublished doctoral dissertation, Georgia State University.

Trovato, J., & Bucher, B. 1980. Peer tutoring with or without home-based reinforcement, for reading remediation. *Journal of Applied Behavior Analysis, 13,* 129–141.

Tucker, M., Sigafoos, J., & Bushnell, H. 1998. Use of noncontingent reinforcement in the treatment of challenging behavior: A review and clinical guide. *Behavior Modification, 22,* 529–547.

Turkewitz, H., O'Leary, K. D., & Ironsmith, M. 1975. Generalization and maintenance of appropriate behavior through self-control. *Journal of Consulting and Clinical Psychology, 43,* 577–583.

Turnbull, H. R., Wilcox, B., Stowe, M., & Turnbull, A. 2001. IDEA requirments for use of PBS. *Journal of Positive Behavior Interventions 3,* 11–18.

Twardosz, S., & Sajway, T. 1972. Multiple effects of a procedure to increase sitting in a hyperactive, retarded boy. *Journal of Applied Behavior Analysis, 5,* 73–78.

Twyman, J., Johnson, H., Buie, J., & Nelson, C. M. 1994. The use of a warning procedure to signal a more intrusive timeout contingency. *Behavioral Disorders, 19* (4), 243–253.

Ulman, J. D., & Sulzer-Azaroff, B. 1975. Multi-element baseline design in educational research. In E. Ramp & G. Semb (Eds.), *Behavior analysis: Areas of research and application* (pp. 377–391). Upper Saddle River, NJ: Prentice Hall.

Umbreit, J. 1995. Functional assessment and intervention in a regular classroom setting for the disruptive behavior of a student with attention deficit hyperactivity disorder. *Behavior Disorders, 20,* 267–278.

Umbreit, J., Lane, K., & Dejud, C. 2004. Improving classroom behavior by modifying task difficulty: Effects of increasing the difficulty of too-easy tasks. *Journal of Positive Behavior Interventions, 6,* 13–20.

Van Camp, C., Lerman, D., Kelley, M., Contrucci, S., & Vorndran, C. 2000. Variable-time reinforcement schedules in the treatment of socially maintained problem behavior. *Journal of Applied Behavior Analysis, 33,* 545–557.

Van Camp, C., Lerman, D., Kelley, M., Roane, H., Contrucci, S., & Vordran, C. 2000. Further analysis of idiosyncratic antecedent influences during the assessment and treatment of problem behavior. *Journal of Applied Behavior Analysis, 33* (2), 207–221.

van den Pol, R. A., Iwata, B. A., Ivancic, M. T., Page, T. J., Need, N. A., & Whitely, F. P. 1981. Teaching the handicapped to eat in public places: Acquisition, generalization and maintenance of restaurant skills. *Journal of Applied Behavior Analysis, 14,* 61–69.

Van Houten, R. 1993. The use of wrist weights to reduce self-injury maintained by sensory reinforcement. *Journal of Applied Behavior Analysis, 26,* 197–203.

Van Houten, R., Axelrod, S., Bailey, J. S., Favell, J. E., Foxx, R. M., Iwata, B. A., et al. 1988. The right to effective behavioral treatment. *The Behavior Analyst, 11,* 111–114.

Van Houten, R., Nau, P., Mackenzie-Keating, S., Sameoto, D., & Colavecchia, B. 1982. An analysis of some variables influencing the effectiveness of reprimands. *Journal of Applied Behavior Analysis, 15,* 65–83.

Vasta, R., & Wortman, H. 1988. Nocturnal bruxism treated by massed negative practice. *Behavior Modification, 12,* 618–626.

Vaughn, S., Bos, C., & Schumm, J. 2000. *Teaching exceptional, diverse, and at-risk students in the general education classroom.* Boston: Allyn and Bacon.

Vollmer, T. 1999. Noncontingent reinforcement: Some additional comments. *Journal of Applied Behavior Analysis, 32,* 239–240.

Vollmer, T., & Bourret, J. 2000. An application of the matching law to evaluate the allocation of two- and three-point shots by college basketball players. *Journal of Applied Behavior Analysis, 33* (2), 137–150.

Vollmer, T., & Iwata, B. 1991. Establishing operations and reinforcement effects. *Journal of Applied Behavior Analysis, 24,* 279–291.

Vollmer, T., & Iwata, B. 1992. Differential reinforcement as treatment for behavior disorder: Procedural and functional variations. *Research in Developmental Disabilities, 13,* 393–417.

Vollmer, T., Borrero, J., Lalli, J., & Daniel, D. 1999. Evaluating self-control and impulsivity in children with severe behavior disorders. *Journal of Applied Behavior Analysis, 32* (4), 451–466.

Vollmer, T., Iwata, B., Zarcone, J., Smith, R., & Mazaleski, J. 1993. The role of attention in the treatment of attention-maintained self-injurious behavior: Noncontingent reinforcement and differential reinforcement of other behavior. *Journal of Applied Behavior Analysis, 26,* 9–21.

Vollmer, T., Marcus, B., & Ringdahl, J. 1995. Noncontingent escape as treatment for self-injurious behavior maintained by negative reinforcement. *Journal of Applied Behavior Analysis, 28,* 15–26.

Vollmer, T., Ringdahl, J., Roane, H., & Marcus, B. 1997. Negative side effects of noncontingent reinforcement. *Journal of Applied Behavior Analysis, 30,* 161–164.

Vollmer, T., Roane, H., Ringdahl, J., & Marcus, B. 1999. Evaluating treatment challenges with differential reinforcement of alternative behavior. *Journal of Applied Behavior Analysis, 32,* 9–23.

Voltz, D. L. 1999. Empowering diverse learners at the middle level. *Middle School Journal, 30,* 29–36.

Voltz, D. L. 2003. Personalized contextual instruction. *Preventing School Failure, 47,* 138–143.

Wacker, D. P., & Berg, W. K. 1983. Effects of picture prompts on the acquisition of complex vocational tasks by mentally retarded adolescents. *Journal of Applied Behavior Analysis, 16,* 417–433.

Wacker, D., Berg, W., McMahon, C., Templeman, M., McKinney, J., Swarts, V., Visser, M., & Marquardt, P. 1988. An evaluation of labeling-then-doing with moderately handicapped persons. *Journal of Applied Behavior Analysis, 21,* 369–380.

Wacker, D., Berg, W., Wiggins, B., Muldoon, M., & Cavanaugh, J. 1985. Evaluation of reinforcer preferences for profoundly handicapped students. *Journal of Applied Behavior Analysis, 18,* 173–178.

Wacker, D., Harding, J., Cooper, L., Derby, K., Peck, S., Asmus, J., Berg, W., & Brown, K. 1996. The effects of meal schedule and quantity on problematic behavior. *Journal of Applied Behavior Analysis, 29,* 79–87.

Wacker, D., Steege, M., Northup, J., Sasso, G., Berg, W., Reimers, T., et al. 1990. A component analysis of functional communication training across three topographies of severe behavior problems. *Journal of Applied Behavior Analysis, 23,* 417–429.

Walker, H. M., & Buckley, N. K. 1972. Programming generalization and maintenance of treatment effects across time and across settings. *Journal of Applied Behavior Analysis, 5,* 209–224.

Walker, H. M., Mattsen, R. H., & Buckley, N. K. 1971. The functional analysis of behavior within an experimental class setting. In W. C. Becker (Ed.), *An empirical basis for change in education.* Chicago: Science Research Associates.

Wallace, I. 1977. Self-control techniques of famous novelists. (Introduction by J. J. Pear.) *Journal of Applied Behavior Analysis, 10,* 515–525.

Wallace, M., & Iwata, B. 1999. Effects of session duration on functional analysis outcomes. *Journal of Applied Behavior Analysis, 32,* 175–183.

Wallace, M., & Knight, D. 2003. An evaluation of a brief functional analysis format within a vocational setting. *Journal of Applied Behavior Analysis, 36,* 125–128.

Walls, R. T., Zane, T., & Ellis, W. D. 1981. Forward chaining, backward chaining, and whole task methods for training assembly tasks. *Behavior Modification, 5,* 61–74.

Walton, D. 1961. Experimental psychology and the treatment of a tiqueur. *Journal of Child Psychology and Psychiatry, 2,* 148–155.

Watkins, L., Sprafkin, J., & Krolokowski, D. 1990. Effects of video-based training on spoken and signed language acquisition by students with mental retardation. *Research in Developmental Disabilities, 11,* 273–288.

Watras, J. 1986. Will teaching applied ethics improve schools of education? *Journal of Teacher Education, 37,* 13–16.

Watson, J. B. 1914. *Behavior: An introduction to comparative psychology.* New York: Holt, Rinehart & Winston.

Watson, J. B. 1919. *Psychology from the standpoint of a behaviorist.* Philadelphia: Lippincott.

Watson, J. B. 1925. *Behaviorism.* New York: Norton.

Watson, J. B., & Raynor, R. 1920. Conditioned emotional reactions. *Journal of Experimental Psychology, 3,* 1–4.

Watson, J., Singh, N., & Winton, A. 1986. Suppressive effects of visual and facial screening on self-injurious finger-sucking. *American Journal of Mental Deficiency, 90,* 526–534.

Watson, L. S. 1967. Application of operant conditioning techniques to institutionalized severely and profoundly retarded children. *Mental Retardation Abstracts, 4,* 1–18.

Webber, J., Scheuermann, B., McCall, C., & Coleman, M. 1993. Research on self-monitoring as a behavior management technique in special education classrooms: A descriptive review. *Remedial and Special Education, 14,* 38–56.

Webster's third new international dictionary. 1986. Springfield, MA: Merriam-Webster.

Wechsler, D. 2003. *The Wechsler intelligence scale for children-IV.* San Antonio, TX: The Psychological Corporation.

Wehby, J. H., & Hollahan, M. S. 2000. Effects of high-probability requests on the latency to initiate academic tasks. *Journal of Applied Behavior Analysis, 33,* 259–262.

Welch, M. W., & Gist, J. W. 1974. *The open token economy system: A handbook for a behavioral approach to rehabilitation.* Springfield, IL: Charles C. Thomas.

Werner, H., & Strauss, A. A. 1940. Causal factors in low performance. *American Journal of Mental Deficiency, 45,* 213–218.

Werry, J. S. 1986. Organic factors in childhood psychopathology. In H. G. Quay & J. S. Werry (Eds.), *Psychopathological disorders of childhood* (3rd ed.). New York: Wiley.

Werts, M. G., Caldwell, N. K., & Wolery, M. 1996. Peer modeling of response chains: Observational learning by students with disabilities. *Journal of Applied Behavior Analysis, 29,* 53–66.

Werts, M., Caldwell, N., & Wolery, M. 1996. Peer modeling of response chains: Observational learning by students with disabilities. *Journal of Applied Behavior Analysis, 29,* 53–66.

Werts, M., Zigmond, N., & Leeper, D. 2001. Paraprofessional proximity and academic engagement: Students with disabilities in primary aged classrooms. *Education and Training in Mental Retardation and Developmental Disabilities, 36,* 424–440.

Wesolowski, M., & Zawlocki, R. 1982. The differential effects of procedures to eliminate an injurious self-stimulatory behavior (digito-ocular sign) in blind retarded twins. *Behavior Therapy, 13,* 334–345.

White, A., & Bailey, J. 1990. Reducing disruptive behaviors of elementary physical education students with sit and watch. *Journal of Applied Behavior Analysis, 23,* 353–359.

White, M. A. 1975. Natural rates of teacher approval and disapproval in the classroom. *Journal of Applied Behavior Analysis, 8,* 367–372.

White, O. R. 1977. Behaviorism in special education: An arena for debate. In R. D. Kneedler & S. G. Tarber (Eds.), *Changing perspectives in special education.* Columbus, OH: Merrill.

White, O. R., & Haring, N. G. 1980. *Exceptional teaching* (2nd ed.). Columbus, OH: Merrill.

White, O., & Liberty, K. 1976. Evaluation and measurement. In N. G. Haring & R. L. Schielfelbusch (Eds.), *Teaching special children.* New York: McGraw-Hill.

Whitman, T. L. 1987. Self-instruction, individual differences, and mental retardation. *American Journal of Mental Deficiency, 92,* 213–223.

Whitman, T. L. 1990. Self-regulation and mental retardation. *American Journal on Mental Retardation, 94* (4), 347–362.

Wicker, T. 1974, February 8. A bad idea persists. *The New York Times,* p. 31.

Wilcox, B., & Bellamy, G. T. 1982. *Design of high school programs for severely handicapped students.* Baltimore: Paul H. Brookes.

Wilder, D., Draper, R., Williams, W., & Higbee, T. 1997. A comparison of noncontingent reinforcement, other competing stimulation, and liquid rescheduling for the treatment of rumination. *Behavioral Interventions, 12,* 55–64.

Wilder, D., Masuda, A., O'Connor, C., & Baham, M. 2001. Brief functional analysis and treatment of bizarre vocalizations in an adult with schizophrenia. *Journal of Applied Behavior Analysis, 34* (1), 65–68.

Wilkinson, G. S. 1993. *Wide range achievement test—Revision 3.* Wilmington, DE: Wide Range, Inc.

Williams, G., Donley, C., & Keller, J. 2000. Teaching children with autism to ask questions about hidden objects. *Journal of Applied Behavior Analysis, 33* (4), 627–630.

Williams, J., Koegel, R., & Egel, A. 1981. Response-reinforcement relationships and improved learning in autistic children. *Journal of Applied Behavior Analysis, 14,* 53–60.

Wilson, P. G., Schepis, M. M., Mason-Main, M. 1987. In vivo use of picture prompt training to increase independent work at a restaurant. *Journal of the Association for Persons with Severe Handicaps, 12,* 145–150.

Wilson, R., Majsterek, D., & Simmons, D. 1996. The effects of computer-assisted versus teacher-directed instruction on the multiplication performance of elementary students with learning disabilities. *Journal of Learning Disabilities, 29* (4), 382–390.

Windsor, J., Piche, L., & Locke, P. 1994. Preference testing: A comparison of two presentation methods. *Research in Developmental Disabilities, 15,* 439–455.

Winett, R. A., & Winkler, R. C. 1972. Current behavior modification in the classroom: Be still, be quiet, be docile. *Journal of Applied Behavior Analysis, 5,* 499–504.

Winton, A., & Singh, N. 1983. Suppression of pica using brief-duration physical restraint. *Journal of Mental Deficiency Research, 27,* 93–103.

Winton, A., Singh, N., & Dawson, M. 1984. Effects of facial screening and blindfold on self-injurious behavior. *Applied Research in Mental Retardation, 5,* 29–42.

Wolery, M. & Gast, D. L. 1984. Effective and efficient procedures for the transfer of stimulus control. *Topics in Early Childhood Special Education, 4,* 52–77.

Wolf, M. 1978. Social validity: The case for subjective measurement or how applied behavior analysis is finding its heart. *Journal of Applied Behavior Analysis, 11,* 203–214.

Wolfe, L. H., Heron, T. E., & Goddard, Y. L. 2000. Effects of self-monitoring on the on-task behavior and written language performance of elementary students with learning disabilities. *Journal of Behavior Education, 10,* 49–73.

Wood, D., Frank, A., & Wacker, D. 1998. Teaching multiplication facts to students with learning disabilities. *Journal of Applied Behavior Analysis, 31* (3), 323–338.

Wood, R., & Flynn, J. M. 1978. A self-evaluation token system versus an external evaluation token system alone in a residential setting with predelinquent youth. *Journal of Applied Behavior Analysis, 11,* 503–512.

Wood, S., Murdock, J., Cronin, M., Dawson, N., & Kirby, P. 1998. Effects of self-monitoring on on-task behaviors of at-risk middle school students. *Journal of Behavioral Education, 8* (2), 263–279.

Wood, S. J., Murdock, J. Y., & Cronin, M. E. 2002. Self-monitoring and at-risk middle school students. *Behavior Modification, 26,* 605–626.

Wood, S. J., Murdock, J. Y., Cronin, M. E., Dawson, N. M., & Kirby, P. C. 1998. Effects of self-monitoring on on-task behaviors of at-risk middle school students. *Journal of Behavioral Education, 8,* 263–279.

Woodcock, R. 1998. *Woodcock reading mastery tests—revised.* Circle Pines, MN: American Guidance Service.

Woods, T. S. 1984. Generality in the verbal tacting of autistic children as a function of "naturalness" in antecedent control. *Journal of Behavior Therapy and Experimental Psychiatry, 15,* 27–32.

Woods, T. S. 1987. Programming common antecedents: A practical strategy for enhancing the generality of learning. *Behavioural Psychotherapy, 15,* 158–180.

Woolcock, W. W., & Lengel, M. B. 1987. Use of general case instruction with visually impaired, multiply handicapped adults in the sorting of national zip codes. *Journal of Visual Impairment and Blindness, 81,* 110–114.

Worsdell, A., Iwata, B., & Wallace, M. 2002. Duration-based measures of preference for vocational tasks. *Journal of Applied Behavior Analysis, 35,* 287–290.

Wright, C. W., & Schuster, J. W. 1994. Accepting specific versus functional student responses when training chained tasks. *Education and Training in Mental Retardation and Developmental Disabilities, 30,* 43–56.

Wright, C., & Vollmer, T. 2002. Evaluation of a treatment package to reduce rapid eating. *Journal of Applied Behavior Analysis, 35,* 89–93.

Wright, H. 1960. Observational study. In P. H. Mussen (Ed.), *Handbook of research methods in child development.* New York: Wiley.

Wunderlich, R. C. 1977. The hyperactivity complex. *Journal of Optometric Vision Development, 8* (1), 8–45.

Wyatt v. Stickney, 344 F. Supp. 373, 344 F. Supp. 387 (M. D. Ala. 1972) affirmed sub nom. Wyatt v. Aderholt, 503 F. 2nd 1305 (5th Cir. 1972).

Wylie, A., & Grossman, J. 1988. Response reduction through superimposition of continuous reinforcement: A systematic replication. *Journal of Applied Behavior Analysis, 21,* 201–206.

Yarbrough, S., & Carr, E. 2000. Some relationships between informant assessment and functional analysis of problem behavior. *American Journal on Mental Retardation, 105,* 130–151.

Yates, A. J. 1958. Symptoms and symptom substitution. *Psychological Review, 65,* 371–374.

Yates, A. J. 1970. *Behavior therapy.* New York: Wiley.

Yell, M. 1994. Time-out and students with behavior disorders: A legal analysis. *Education and Treatment of Children, 17* (3), 293–301.

Zabel, M. 1986. Time-out use with behaviorally disordered students. *Behavioral Disorders, 11,* 15–20.

Zanolli, K., Daggett, J., Ortiz, K., & Mullins, J. 1999. Using rapidly alternating multiple schedules to assess and treat aberrant behavior in natural settings. *Behavior Modification, 23,* 358–379.

Zarcone, J., Crosland, K., Fisher, W., Worsdell, A., & Herman, K. 1999. A brief method for conducting negative-reinforcement assessment. *Research in Developmental Disabilities, 20,* 107–124.

Zarcone, J., Fisher, W., & Piazza, C. 1996. Analysis of free-time contingencies as positive versus negative reinforcement. *Journal of Applied Behavior Analysis, 29,* 247–250.

Zarcone, J., Iwata, B., Mazaleski, J., & Smith, R. 1994. Momentum and extinction effects on self-injurious escape behavior and noncompliance. *Journal of Applied Behavior Analysis, 27,* 649–658.

Zarcone, J., Iwata, B., Vollmer, T., Jagtiani, S., Smith, R., & Mazaleski, J. 1993. Extinction of self-injurious escape behavior with and without instructional fading. *Journal of Applied Behavior Analysis, 26,* 353–360.

Zarcone, J., Rodgers, T., Iwata, B., Rourke, D., & Dorsey, M. 1991. Reliability analysis of the motivational assessment scale: A failure to replicate. *Research in Developmental Disabilities, 12,* 349–360.

Zegiob, L., Alford, G. L., & House, A. 1978. Response suppressive and generalization effects of facial screening on multiple self-injurious behavior in a retarded boy. *Behavior Therapy, 9,* 688.

Zegiob, L., Jenkins, J., Becker, J., & Bristow, A. 1976. Facial screening: Effects on appropriate and inappropriate behaviors. *Journal of Behavior Therapy and Experimental Psychiatry, 7,* 355–357.

Zhang, J., Gast, D., Horvat, M., & Dattilo, J. 2000. Effect of constant time delay procedure on motor skill completion durations. *Education and Training in Mental Retardation and Developmental Disabilities, 35,* 317–325.

Zhou, L., Goff, G., & Iwata, B. 2000. Effects of increased response effort on self-injury and object manipulation as competing responses. *Journal of Applied Behavior Analysis, 33,* 29–40.

Ziegler, S. 1994. The effects of attentional shift training on the execution of soccer skills. *Journal of Applied Behavior Analysis, 27* (3), 545–552.

Zimmerman, E. H., & Zimmerman, J. 1962. The alteration of behavior in a special classroom situation. *Journal of the Experimental Analysis of Behavior, 5,* 59–60.

Zirpoli, T. J., & Melloy, K. J. 1993. *Behavior management: Applications for teachers and parents.* New York: Macmillan.

Name Index

Page references followed by "t" indicate tables.

Subject Index

Page references followed by "f" indicate figures; "t," tables.